CANADIAN CITIES IN TRANSITION

Fifth Edition

CANADIAN CITIES IN TRANSITION
Perspectives for an Urban Age

Edited by Pierre Filion • Markus Moos
Tara Vinodrai • Ryan Walker

OXFORD
UNIVERSITY PRESS

OXFORD
UNIVERSITY PRESS

Oxford University Press is a department of the University of Oxford.
It furthers the University's objective of excellence in research, scholarship,
and education by publishing worldwide. Oxford is a registered trade mark of
Oxford University Press in the UK and in certain other countries.

Published in Canada by Oxford University Press
8 Sampson Mews, Suite 204,
Don Mills, Ontario M3C 0H5 Canada

www.oupcanada.com

First Edition published in 1991
Second Edition published in 2000
Third edition published in 2006
Fourth edition published in 2010

Library and Archives Canada Cataloguing in Publication
Canadian cities in transition : perspectives for an urban age / edited by
Pierre Filion, Markus Moos, Tara Vinodrai, Ryan Walker.—Fifth edition.

Includes bibliographical references and index.
ISBN 978-0-19-900818-6 (pbk.)

1. Cities and towns—Canada—Textbooks.   2. Urbanization—Canada—Textbooks.
I. Filion, Pierre, 1952-, author, editor   II. Moos, Markus, 1980-, author, editor
III. Vinodrai, Tara, 1974-, author, editor   IV. Walker, Ryan Christopher, 1975-, author, editor

HT127.C32 2015   307.760971   C2014-907921-4

Cover image: © Julius Grill

Oxford University Press is committed to our environment.
This book is printed on Forest Stewardship Council® certified paper
and comes from responsible sources.

MIX
Paper from
responsible sources
FSC® C103567

Printed and bound in Canada

1 2 3 4 — 18 17 16 15

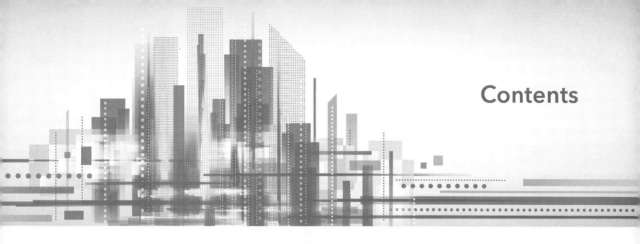

Contents

Part III   Planning, Policy, and Challenges in an Urban Age

Publisher's Preface

Introducing *Canadian Cities in Transition*

Oxford University Press is proud to introduce the fifth edition of *Canadian Cities in Transition: Perspectives for an Urban Age*, edited by Pierre Filion, Markus Moos, Tara Vinodrai, and Ryan Walker.

The new edition retains its unique Canadian focus in urban geography and urban planning while providing a relevant and comprehensive survey of urbanization from both modern and traditional perspectives. From founding principles to the current trends shaping the discipline today, *Canadian Cities in Transition* explores the recent and ongoing transformational change to our urban environment while building on the strength of previous editions and their authoritative contributions.

Highlights of the New Edition

- **New voices.** A blend of new and seasoned scholars brings a lively mix of perspectives in the field of urban geography and planning to the text, and ensures balance in the interpretation of trends, both past and present, that are shaping Canadian cities in the twenty-first century.

- **New chapter on gender and sexuality in urban areas.** Created in response to cutting-edge research and new directions in teaching, this new chapter on gender, sexuality, and the city explores how these factors shape experiences of urban areas.

- **New and expanded topical coverage.** Coverage of issues including accessibility, gentrification, and creative class theory draw students into the current and relevant social and physical factors that have an impact on the nation's urban environments.

- **Canadian perspective.** *Canadian Cities in Transition* remains the only book in urban geography and urban planning to focus on Canadian urban areas and the uniquely Canadian forces that shape our cities.

- **Updated data and visuals.** The most recent statistics and new additions to the art program help to contextualize key issues and locales.

This fifth edition of *Canadian Cities in Transition: Perspectives for an Urban Age* is designed to serve a number of purposes. It is an introduction for university students to the Canadian urban phenomenon, presenting different facets of the city: its historical evolution, economic dynamics, environmental impacts, dependence on natural systems, urban lifestyles, cultural makeup, social structure, infrastructures, governance, planning, and design. The volume also aims to assist the next generation of citizens, consumers, experts, business people, and politicians in their efforts to solve the urban problems—traffic congestion, different forms of environmental damage, crime, social segregation, inequality, housing affordability, governance—that they are inheriting. Canadian cities are not simply a collection of problems to be solved, however, and this book helps to articulate the promise of Canada's urban age, where people and public space are re-centred for economic, environmental, and social reasons, and where "quality" instead of simply "growth" becomes a unifying hallmark of urbanism. The book offers the most current knowledge and perspectives on the Canadian city. The contributors review the recent literature and research on different aspects of the city, and provide their expert opinion on how to focus our examination of contemporary urban issues. Finally, the volume provides an update on urban Canada by identifying the main characteristics of the contemporary Canadian urban phenomenon, its problems, achievements, and opportunities. In this regard, the text will help students and other citizens make sense of the vast flow of information on cities circulated by the media. Because quality information is a condition for judicious decisions, knowledge of the city is vital to effective planning, private and public development, and consumer choice.

The text is situated at the confluence of different disciplines with an urban dimension: mainly geography and urban planning, but also economics, political science, sociology, ecology, and history. It focuses on different urban themes and draws on all the disciplines relevant to their exploration. It also considers cities belonging to all size categories as well as to different Canadian regions. Contributors who represent all parts of the country are able to highlight cross-country differences as well as similarities by drawing on examples from their own regions.

The 25 chapters of this edition are organized into three parts. The two chapters in Part I, written by Pierre Filion and Trudi Bunting, serve an introductory role by setting the context for the inquiries that occupy the following chapters. In Chapter 1, they lay out seven universal properties common to all cities. These properties explain the existence of the urban phenomenon as well as its different manifestations over time. The next chapter provides historical background by exploring the themes of transition and transformation that are at the centre of the book. It describes three different epochs of urban development in Canada: the pre-World-War-II city, the rise of suburbanization in the postwar period, and the urban development patterns—both new and inherited—that have prevailed since the post-industrial structural shifts of the 1970s. The chapter closes the first section with an exploration of possible future trajectories of urban development.

The 10 chapters in Part II, "The Structuring Parameters of Cities in an Urban Age," look at the fundamental aspects of cities that determine their form, dynamics, and evolution. This second part also examines how cities adapt to changing societal and global contexts. In Chapter 3, Peter V. Hall demonstrates how global trends—economic, demographic, political, and cultural—reverberate on Canadian cities. He argues that Canadian cities are increasingly integrated into global networks, a source of prosperity for some and decline for others. Chapter 4, by William E. Rees, is about the environmental impact of cities. It pictures them as an important contributor to global environmental damage. The chapter also explores the vulnerability of cities to environmental deterioration and the need for them to deploy long-term sustainability strategies. With Chapter 5, by Tara Vinodrai, the book begins an examination of urban economics, which will be the subject of a number of subsequent chapters. Vinodrai focuses on how cities are affected by present and recent economic trends and how they have responded to these trends. She acknowledges the shift away from the industrial to the post-industrial city and the rising importance of innovative and knowledge sectors of the economy. She sees this trend as having both positive and negative impacts on cities. Chapter 6 also focuses on the economy of cities. Here, Tom Hutton and Tara Vinodrai concentrate on the locational dynamics of employment. They show how job location within cities is a consequence of both broad economic trends and the specificities of metropolitan regions, which explains why different urban areas present different employment distribution patterns. Chapter 7, by Ivan Townshend and Ryan Walker, is about social changes affecting cities: demography, life course, and lifestyles. Among other things, the chapter highlights the effects of aging, the extension of youth, and the coexistence of numerous lifestyles, as well as the impact of these trends on the built environment and on community dynamics within our cities. In Chapter 8, Audrey Kobayashi and Valerie Preston focus on immigration and the resulting social diversity. They chart the geography of immigration in Canada—the urban areas that especially attract immigrants and where immigrants concentrate in these cities. They also describe new urban phenomena associated with immigration, such as the emergence of "ethnoburbs," and the broader policy frameworks through which immigration is managed. The subject of Chapter 9 is social

polarization. Alan Walks identifies a range of factors accounting for growing income polarization among households over the last decades. He also paints a picture of the urban consequences of polarization—an urban social geography that is increasingly characterized by unevenness—and the policy responses that could address social inequality. In Chapter 10, Ahmed El-Geneidy, Zachary Patterson, and Evelyne St-Louis use the lens of accessibility to examine the relationship between transportation and land use. Following a history of urban transport, congestion levels, and the distribution of transport mode share between private automobiles, active transport, and public transit in Canadian cities are compared with urban areas internationally. The authors discuss how the modelling of travel demand is changing in pursuit of a multi-modal sustainable approach that blends transport options with land-use decisions. Chapter 11, by Zack Taylor and Neil Bradford, examines how urban governance has been reshaped in the context of shifting federal and provincial policy landscapes, resulting in the need for an approach they refer to as the "New Localism." The last contribution of this part of the book, Chapter 12 by Andrejs Skaburskis and Markus Moos, examines the economics of urban land use. The chapter introduces the structuring parameters of urban land use and describes the origin and operation of urban land markets as well as their outcomes. Skaburskis and Moos end by introducing the dimensions of timing and strategy to help explain development decisions that challenge our conventional views of when, where, and how intensively land is capitalized.

Part III is about responses to contemporary trends and challenges affecting our cities, as well as specific policy approaches seeking to enhance Canadian urbanism. In Chapter 13, Maged Senbel and Alexandra Lesnikowski explore the challenges and opportunities inherent in various approaches to sustainable urban design intended to create low-carbon, resilient, and healthy neighbourhoods. Chapter 14, by Alison Bain, deals with emerging places in Canada's inner or central cities: gentrified neighbourhoods, high-rise condominiums, and the like. It relates the conditions that have led to their development and the impact of these places on the social structure and the functioning of cities. If Chapter 9 described polarization *within* urban areas, Chapter 15, by Betsy Donald and Heather M. Hall, zeroes in on polarization *among* urban areas. It describes the multiple challenges that declining urban areas face and policy responses that could mitigate the consequences of decline. This issue is increasingly relevant given the present concentration of demographic and economic growth in a few large metropolitan regions and their surroundings. Donald and Hall convey the opportunities missed by urban decision-makers too narrowly focused on growth rather than on qualitative development. Chapter 16, by Amy Siciliano, Deborah Cowen, and Neil Smith, deals with fear and insecurity in the city. It demonstrates how fear is constructed and leads to calls for security measures that often result in infringements of freedom. The chapter shows how behaviour and politics in the city respond to fear and insecurity. In Chapter 17, Jill L. Grant and Pierre Filion pursue the planning transition theme introduced in Chapter 2 through an exploration of the newer urban forms emerging in the Canadian city. Chapter 17 is about the loud call within the planning profession for a change in urban development trends. It describes and evaluates attempts at intensifying the urban environment while acknowledging the counter-effect of many new automobile-dependent urban forms, such as power malls. Ryan Walker and Jill Gunn examine the movement, market, and meeting functions of public space in Chapter 18, focusing on streets and squares in our city centres. Topics range from the conceptual to measurement and metrics, and to lessons learned over multiple generations of scholarship and observation to enhance the design and programming of public spaces. The connections between activity and urban form are discussed. The authors give examples of how public life is being re-ignited in the shared spaces of our cities by place-specific public art and performance, by re-calibrating transportation infrastructure to induce more of the movement we want in our urban age, and by decades- or centuries-old lessons

for good physical design of streets and squares. Chapter 19, by Richard Harris, is devoted to housing, the single largest user of space in Canadian cities. The chapter reviews the socio-economic and geographic landscape of housing in Canada and the policy environment in which housing is managed, and ends with a discussion of some of the pressing issues facing the Canadian housing system as a whole.

Subsequent chapters in Part III are attuned to pressing or newly emergent urban issues. In Chapter 20, Markus Moos considers the age and generational dimensions of urban restructuring. He tracks the changing age compositions of our cities and the changing location patterns of young adults and seniors. Moos points to growing segregation of young adults in central areas of our cities and discusses the deteriorating economic prospects of those just entering labour markets. He describes current policies aimed at planning for an aging population and explores exclusion and inequalities arising from ageism. Chapter 21, by Evelyn J. Peters, examines Aboriginal peoples in Canadian cities. The chapter documents their concentration in certain cities and the emergence of an urban culture among Canadian Aboriginal peoples—a phenomenon likely to accelerate in the future given the differential rate of natural increase among First Nations and Métis populations in comparison with other native-born Canadians and newcomers. The chapter also considers how cities and urban services are adapting in response to the rising strength of urban Aboriginal cultures. Damaris Rose explores the nature of gender and sexuality in the city in Chapter 22. She adopts a perspective that underscores the freedoms and constraints confronting gender differences and the expression of sexual preferences in cities. The chapter discusses the impact of values and of the spatial organization of cities on the lives of women. It also looks at how LGBT people (lesbian, gay, bisexual, and transgender) negotiate the city. Chapter 23, by Alison Blay-Palmer and Karen Landman, looks at the new-found interest in the geography of food, as evidenced in movements such as the 100-mile diet. This chapter is about how food is procured and distributed within Canadian cities. Issues include accessibility to different forms of food outlets and the problem of food deserts, efforts to increase reliance on food grown nearby, and food production within cities themselves. Reflective of the increasingly suburban nature of urban life in Canada, Chapter 24, by Jean-Paul D. Addie, Robert S. Fiedler, and Roger Keil, is an exploration of how understandings of the Canadian urban form are broadening to include the conceptual study of suburbanisms, the "cities on the edge." Chapter 25, a conclusion by Markus Moos and Tara Vinodrai, offers final thoughts on the need to search for new urban models to understand our urban age, arguing that we should consider the dynamics of Canadian cities through at least three overarching themes: structure, state, and sustainability.

Contributors

Jean-Paul D. Addie
Department of Science, Technology, Engineering, and Public Policy
University College London

Alison Bain
Department of Geography
York University

Alison Blay-Palmer
Department of Geography and Environmental Studies
Wilfrid Laurier University

Neil Bradford
Department of Political Science
Huron University College, Western University

Trudi Bunting
Department of Geography and Environmental Management
University of Waterloo

Deborah Cowen
Department of Geography and Program in Planning
University of Toronto

Betsy Donald
Department of Geography
Queen's University

Ahmed El-Geneidy
School of Urban Planning
McGill University

Robert S. Fiedler
Department of Geography
York University

Pierre Filion
School of Planning
University of Waterloo

Jill L. Grant
School of Planning
Dalhousie University

Jill Gunn
Department of Geography and Planning
University of Saskatchewan

Heather M. Hall
International Centre for Northern Governance and Development
University of Saskatchewan

Peter V. Hall
Urban Studies Program
Simon Fraser University

Richard Harris
School of Geography and Earth Science
McMaster University

Tom Hutton
School of Community and Regional Planning
University of British Columbia

Roger Keil
Faculty of Environmental Studies
York University

Audrey Kobayashi
Department of Geography
Queen's University

Karen Landman
School of Environmental Design and Rural
Development
University of Guelph

Alexandra Lesnikowski
School of Community and Regional Planning
University of British Columbia

Markus Moos
School of Planning
University of Waterloo

Zachary Patterson
Department of Geography, Planning and
Environment
Concordia University

Evelyn J. Peters
Urban and Inner City Studies
University of Winnipeg

Valerie Preston
Department of Geography
York University

William E. Rees
School of Community and Regional Planning
University of British Columbia

Damaris Rose
Centre urbanisation culture société
Institut national de la recherche scientifique (INRS)

Maged Senbel
School of Community and Regional Planning
University of British Columbia

Amy Siciliano
Department of Geography
St. Mary's University

Andrejs Skaburskis
School of Urban and Regional Planning
Queen's University

Neil Smith (1954–2012)
Department of Anthropology, Earth and
Environmental Sciences
City University of New York

Evelyne St-Louis
School of Urban Planning
McGill University

Zack Taylor
Department of Human Geography
University of Toronto, Scarborough

Ivan Townshend
Department of Geography
University of Lethbridge

Tara Vinodrai
Department of Geography and Environmental
Management & School of Environment, Enterprise
and Development
University of Waterloo

Ryan Walker
Department of Geography and Planning
University of Saskatchewan

Alan Walks
Department of Geography and Program
in Planning
University of Toronto

PART I

Changing Parameters of Urban Form, Structure, and Policy

This book is premised on the view that we are undergoing societal changes of epochal magnitude, changes that reverberate within our cities: deindustrialization and the turn to a service-based economy, social polarization, increasing levels of immigration, aging, rising environmental awareness associated with a sense of urgency regarding the need to deal with the mitigation of urban environmental impacts, and so on. These changes are fuelling accelerated urban growth in some metropolitan regions while being responsible for stagnation or even decline in other urban centres. Another expression of the contrasting urban effects of such changes is their stimulation of outward development while concomitantly fostering the intensification and gentrification of the central areas of large metropolitan regions. The main theme of the four prior editions has been that cities are all about change, that "transition" is part of the nature of urbanity. However, it may well be the case that urban change is accelerating and that the transition theme is even more relevant now than it was in the four previous editions of the book. This fifth edition is an update on what we have learned about urban change since the publication of the last volume; it includes new chapters on emerging urban issues and trends. Most of the chapters in this volume (particularly those in Parts II and III) are oriented toward elucidating the character of what might become a twenty-first-century urban entity that evolves away from twentieth-century trajectories.

Since the fifth edition of *Canadian Cities in Transition* is an exploration of the current state of knowledge on the overarching issues shaping cities today, it is imperative that this introductory part (Part I) deal with what we know theoretically about urban form and structure thus far. We do this from an historic perspective that moves us from ancient times, when cities first appeared (*circa* 3000 BC), to the end of the twentieth century. Setting out this historic approach is important for three reasons:

1. It demonstrates the existence, from both a theoretical and an empirical perspective, of universal urban properties present throughout history.
2. It provides important context for understanding current styles of urban development and the marked ways in which the "new" city departs from the old.
3. In cities it is especially true that "the past is always with us" (see in particular the capitalization property of cities in Chapter 1) and that past development styles continue as a living legacy within the urban landscape.

The preoccupation of the two chapters in Part I with the shape of the city is echoed throughout the volume. Several chapters advance new knowledge on emerging urban forms; and the concluding chapter returns specifically to questions of urban form by asking whether current interpretive models are suited to an understanding of new development patterns and social and functional distributions.

All contributions to the volume acknowledge difficulties in urban policy-making due to the inherent complexity, uncertainty, and contradictions of cities. As this first part is devoted to a historical and theoretical discussion, it largely concentrates on complexity and contradictions. Each subsequent chapter addresses in its own way the uncertainty (along with the complexity and contradictions) associated with the urban reality.

Chapter 1 introduces the seven principles or properties that we believe comprise the essence of the city. These characteristics pertain to cities of the past, present, and—as far as we are able to foresee—the future. Likewise, these properties apply to urban settlements globally. Six of these principles—production, proximity, reproduction, capitalization, place, and governance—relate to the human dimensions of the urban phenomenon. The seventh property, environment, by which we mean the "biophysical" environment, refers to the physical and natural features of cities. The point is that all urban places have distinctive environments that explain their location, site, or situation and that contribute to making them "good" places to live and do business. The additional insight that we bring to our understanding of urban environments is that the process of urbanization itself has a huge negative impact on the biophysical environment. The call for the development of new sustainable forms of urban development and the retrofitting of urban environments to reduce ecological "footprints" and render them more "environment-friendly" is a late twentieth-century and early twenty-first-century awakening that speaks to growing uncertainty. This recent awakening, on the part of scholars, planners, politicians, and the residents of urban environments, also helps to explain the huge nature of the change being called for (and witnessed) at present in the relationship between cities and the biophysical environment.

Chapter 2 discusses Canada's past urban evolutionary development. The attention is on change in the urban structure of cities, which is the combined outcome of several tendencies, including demographic and economic change, emerging values, and the spread of new technologies, particularly those having to do with transportation. The chapter introduces three successive urban structures, which are increasingly complex. The first, which expressed reliance on walking and public transit, was compact and highly centralized. It was followed in the post-World-War-II decades by accelerated decentralization in an urban setting that was rapidly adapting to escalating automobile use. Finally, we are now witnessing in the larger metropolitan regions what will perhaps emerge as a hybrid urban form, which combines automobile-induced decentralization with growing centralization in the core and in networks of suburban nodes.

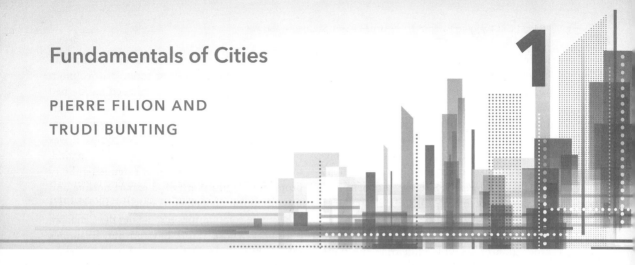

Fundamentals of Cities

PIERRE FILION AND
TRUDI BUNTING

Introduction

This volume is about understanding and dealing with change and transition in twenty-first-century cities. At the outset, however, we need sound knowledge of how cities operate and how they relate to broader societal trends in order to address contemporary urban issues. More often than not, past mistakes can be seen in hindsight to be the result of deficient understanding of urban dynamics. Yet cities resist understanding because they are such complex systems. We can argue that, along with language, the large city is the most intricate of human creations. In both cases, complexity stems from the presence of a relatively stable structure upon which interchangeable elements can be affixed in different fashions. In the case of language the structure is syntax, which supports nearly unlimited combinations of words; cities, on the other hand, owe their structure to major infrastructure networks, which provide connections between different assemblages of buildings and other land uses. The degree of complexity further increases when we consider economic and value systems behind the creation of the urban built environment, the multiple ways people use this environment, and the perceptions and interpretations of this environment and of the activities that take place therein.

The present chapter introduces universal properties that define the city and represent universal features of the urban phenomenon. While Canadian cities have their own distinctiveness—a central theme in this book—they share many similarities with their counterparts developed at different times in different parts of the globe. This chapter, then, establishes some basic principles inherent to urban areas from the very beginning of urban settlement.

Seven properties are fundamental to understanding the urban phenomenon, regardless of time or place: *production, proximity, reproduction, capitalization, place, governance,* and *environment* (Table 1.1). These properties account for the existence of cities, their diverse configurations, and the way they operate, along with the need for specialized knowledge and interventions to deal with urban issues, and have been inherent in the city from its beginnings some 4000 years ago in China and Mesopotamia. As expected, their manifestations vary across periods. The seven properties that we set out here provide a framework to discuss problems confronting the contemporary Canadian city and possible solutions.

Production

Throughout history the foremost raison d'être for urban settlement has been accommodation of the need for specialized production activities that could not survive in isolation in rural settings—e.g., markets, production of fine crafts, centralized governance. Indeed, if asked why they live in a city, most people will respond to the effect that "I work there or a member of my family does." Economic production creates jobs and brings people into the city and is thus the main reason for urban growth. Economic production, too, is the property most often associated with transformative change in **urban form** and structure. Thus, for example, Canada's first mercantile settlements were established to export "staple" products, such as fish, furs, and timber, to European colonial "mother" countries.

A further impetus for urban growth was the administration of resource industries and transportation systems required for their export. These conditions were conducive to the growth of only a small number of cities, however. But with agricultural development, centres grew to service rural areas, and then with wide-scale industrialization urban growth took off in Canada as it did in other developed countries (Innis, 1995a [1931], 1995b [1938]).

Many economic activities, of course, are aimed at the consumption needs of a city's own residents (Watkins, 1980). What most sets urban settlements apart from traditional self-reliant rural economies, however, is the city's historic inability to satisfy all its consumption requirements. As a result, it becomes imperative that cities export so as to generate the revenues needed to acquire products that can only be obtained outside their territory. Inside the urban envelope, for example, the need for specialized activities to be close to one another and to their workers (the proximity property discussed below) rules out any possibility of devoting large surfaces to agriculture as would be needed to feed a large resident population (at least this has been the case until recent attempts at urban-based agriculture) (Christensen, 2007; Lawson, 2005). A city also must reach beyond its territory to secure other products and resources essential for sustaining its population and economic activity, including different forms of staples and energy and, often, water. Research shows that cities depend for their natural resources on a territory (or **ecological footprint**; see Rees, Chapter 4) that far exceeds the urbanized perimeter.

For a city to exist, it must be in a position to export sufficient goods and services to counterbalance its imports. But exports need not be tied to products. Capital cities, for example, export decisions and derive their monetary returns from tax revenues; likewise, in medieval times, it was not unusual for cities to draw taxes, often in kind, from a hinterland to which they extended military protection. Cities that fail to export decline and may disappear altogether, as illustrated by the fate of resource communities throughout the Canadian periphery whose staple has run out. Examples include Elliot Lake, Ontario; Schefferville, Quebec; and Canso, Nova Scotia (Gill and Reed, 1997; Lorch, Johnston, and Challen, 2004; see Donald and Hall, Chapter 15).

Over recent decades, goods and resources (including labour) that cities draw from outside their territory have increasingly originated from foreign countries and continents. Canadian producers have also moved toward new international markets. This change in the reach of economic exchange is loosely referred to as **globalization** (see Hall, Chapter 3). In the global period, the interdependence that existed in the past between the city and a well-defined **hinterland** has lost much of its importance (Derudder and Witlox, 2004; Friedman, 2005; Taylor, 2001). The tendency today is for cities to transform and consume goods from around the world and sell their products on international markets. Yet, there are signs that present and future change, driven by environmental awareness and escalating energy costs, may bring about a renewed emphasis on nearness in economic exchanges (Rubin, 2009). Could economic globalization survive an eventual $200 barrel of oil? Thus, Chapter 23 discusses responses to the new emphasis on "local" procurement of goods and services, particularly foodstuffs (e.g., the **100-mile diet**—see Harris, 2009; *Time*, 2006), that accompanies attempts to decrease the urban "footprint" and so make Canadian cities more environmentally sustainable (see Blay-Palmer and Landman, Chapter 23). But it remains the case that cities have to trade with areas outside their territory, either near or afar.

Though the nature of export-based specialized economic production has changed dramatically in the last hundred years in Canadian cities, economic production still is imperative for urban growth and development. With the decline of routine production, developed countries such as Canada must rely on innovation and knowledge-intensive activities in order to compete on the world stage (the new economy is sometimes spoken about as a "knowledge" economy) (see Vinodrai, Chapter 5). This explains the emphasis Florida (2002, 2005) places on measures cities can take to attract the creative class that he sees as key to the knowledge economy. Above all, the growing importance of the service sector relative to the manufacturing sector has characterized the last decades (Daniels and Bryson, 2002). This trend was acutely felt in both Canada and the US when the economic crisis of 2008–9 threatened to wipe out General Motors and Chrysler, and thus a large share of the North American car industry. The transition is highly visible, moreover, in the urban landscape. On the one hand, we see abandoned industrial premises (or their twenty-first-century "makeover" as lofts), and, on the other, we are confronted with an explosion of restaurants and personal services, and places of entertainment and cultural activities (Jones, Comfort, and Hillier, 2005) (see Bain, Chapter 14). The shift toward the service economy is also felt, albeit with less intensity, within cities' export sphere. Among services Canadian cities export are financial services, engineering and development expertise, and culture.

If deindustrialization persists, Canadian cities may become focused on services and resources, with major centres being responsible for the production, administration, and export of services and resources, and smaller ones for the extraction and early-stage transformation of commodities. A renewed emphasis on staples would bring us back to early phases of Canadian economic development, even if urban distribution and forms have clearly evolved over the centuries (see Chapter 2). While their common resource orientation ties eighteenth-century fur-trading depots along the St Lawrence or eighteenth- and nineteenth-century fishing communities along Canada's Atlantic coast with fast-growing Alberta oil-patch communities, their configuration obviously differs sharply.

It is important, finally, to point out that production impacts all aspects of urban life, which is particularly notable in periods of transformative change such as the present. Thus, for example, Chapter 9 speaks to increasing socio-economic polarization in the Canadian city in the twenty-first century. The chapter attributes this change primarily to a shift in the prevailing economic regime, to deindustrialization and the rise of the hourglass income distribution characteristic of the growing service sector.

Proximity

Individuals and activities have always congregated in cities to facilitate communication and minimize the cost (in terms of time, effort, and money) of interaction. If we probed reasons why people live in cities, most would place the need to be close to work at or near the top of their list of answers. Other explanations would include proximity to educational establishments, to shopping opportunities, to cultural activities, to entertainment and recreation, to family and friends, and to medical facilities. People opt for urban living because of their need for frequent interaction outside the home. Likewise, businesses and institutions locate in cities so they can be close to their market, labour force, and the establishments with which they maintain linkages (in other words, to enjoy agglomerative economies). By concentrating activities and people and thus creating proximity, the city makes frequent interactions affordable in terms of cost and time. In a rural setting, in contrast, many recurring contacts that are routine in the city would involve prohibitive transportation times and/or costs due to long distances. A by-product of interaction is innovation (Hall, 1999); ease of interaction is why cities have been catalysts for change in the social, economic, technological, and cultural realms. The renewed attraction of central-city living that so distinguishes cities of the twenty-first century from the previous era is closely related to widespread recognition that the urban environment, unlike the suburbs, promotes and welcomes all kinds of low-cost and/or spontaneous interactions.

The city can be perceived as comprising numerous overlapping markets of frequently repeated exchanges. The fact that cities are fundamentally places of economic enterprise makes daily commuting between residences and workplaces of unparalleled importance in explaining urban structure. Also important from an economic perspective are linkage networks between enterprises, which benefit from proximity, especially in the case of just-in-time delivery. Other frequent exchanges that affect the size and spatial organization of cities include the connections of retail facilities to their market and of public services to their clients. In addition, markets connect cultural and recreational activities to their public—the archetypical attraction of the city's "bright lights."

Proximity is a relative condition, largely determined by prevailing transportation systems and activity distribution patterns (see El-Geneidy, Patterson, St-Louis, Chapter 10). In the 1960s the urban planner Richard Meier (1962) pointed out how innovation in both communication and transportation could trigger new transformative eras of urban development. Urbanist Lewis Mumford in *The City in History* (1961) provides details that lend credence to Meier's hypothesis. Mumford points out that in the pre-industrial city, which depended on non-mechanized forms of transportation (primarily walking and horse-powered transportation), the principle of proximity dictated that important activities be centralized; likewise, the principle of proximity meant that the outer expanse of the built-up, urbanized perimeter was largely dictated by the prevailing mode of transportation.

The car- and truck-dominated contemporary city, on the other hand, takes on a highly decentralized form. In the decentralized or dispersed metropolis, adequate accessibility levels can be maintained over large territories so that residents and activities can consume far more land than in the past (Bottles, 1987). As rush-hour gridlock across an extensive section of Highway 401 attests, effective early twenty-first-century boundaries of the Greater Toronto Area run from Kitchener–Waterloo–Cambridge in the west to beyond Clarington in the east (a distance of 165 km). Similarly, heavy commuter traffic extends from the City of Toronto to points south toward Niagara Falls and north toward Orillia (a distance of 180 km). This extended Toronto region is referred to as the Greater Golden Horseshoe in recent planning documents (Ontario, 2006). But the proximity principle remains influential even in these more dispersed circumstances, as evidenced by the enduring existence of higher densities in cities than in the countryside, and at accessibility peaks within the city itself (at rail transit stations and junctions of major arterials and/or expressways). Chapter 2 in this volume can be read as a testimonial to the changing role that accessibility has played since the early twentieth century in promoting, first, centralization and high-density styles of urban development; second, dispersion and low density; and recently, a return to high residential density, at least in central parts of the metropolitan envelope.

Today, debate is ongoing as to whether our ability to substitute telecommunications for actual movement holds the potential for an even more dispersed urban form. But forecasts predicting the death of the city as we know it have proven to be wrong because they did not anticipate the impact of a changing mode of production on urban form. The "new" urban economy, with its focus on services, entertainment, and culture, has witnessed a renewed centralization of activities and has considerably elevated the importance of face-to-face contact and spontaneous connecting. In large metropolitan regions this is reflected in the increase in inner-city living, where access to all kinds of people and activities is within a short walk.

Reproduction

As properties of the urban phenomenon, production and reproduction are intimately tied to each other. Reproduction, as understood in the Marxian sense, centres on the conditions essential to the continued provision of an ample labour force, i.e., the literal re-production of workers. These requisites include birth and child-rearing but also other conditions that relate most directly to the well-being of family/household units within the city: health care, education, social services, family and community support facilities, immigration policies, etc. (Castells, 1977; Jessop, 2002: 47, 77).

Before disease control, engineered infrastructure, public health, food security, and general welfare improved rapidly after the Industrial Revolution, living conditions were unhealthy in cities. Afflicted by successive epidemics, for long periods cities were unable to maintain their populations without a constant inflow from the country (Howard, 1968; Russel, 1972). Only after the introduction of water treatment and sewer systems and the advent of immunization did city living cease to be a worse threat to health than living in rural areas. Indeed, historians have traced the origins of urban planning to early efforts at alleviating adverse health effects associated with the crowding and pollution of the early industrial city (Hodge, 1998). Still, we should avoid being smug about the improved health conditions of contemporary cities. The SARS epidemic, possible deadly flu epidemics, adverse health effects associated with poor air quality and other sources of pollution, and increasing obesity due to insufficient exercise in an auto-centric culture all point to health problems associated with the contemporary city (Ali and Keil, 2006; Frumkin, Frank, and Jackson, 2004).

At the most fundamental level, Canada's low birth rate—and consequent inability to reproduce its own population—is the fundamental reason why rates of foreign immigration have soared over recent decades. Immigration policies are thus central to the city's reproduction property, especially since, in Canada, large cities are the destination of virtually all immigrants (Hou and Bourne, 2006; Knowles, 2007; see Kobayashi and Preston, Chapter 8).

Beyond demographic growth, examples of reproduction-related urban sites include homes,

schools, hospitals, and water treatment and distribution systems, as well as parks and other recreational facilities that promote health and reduce stress. A smooth operation of the reproduction system allows employers to find an abundant workforce that is healthy, qualified, and possesses a work ethic compatible with types of employment present in a given city. Reproductive activities are usually centred on the home but are increasingly supplemented with services provided by outside agencies in the public and private sectors. Today, in fact, reproduction-related consumption of both services (e.g., fast food, child care) and goods (e.g., dishwashers, microwave ovens, health and hygiene and home maintenance products) represents an important outlet for the production sector. In reality, virtually all household consumption can be seen as having a reproductive aspect. Meanwhile, resources needed for reproduction-related goods and services are derived from the production sector in the form of household expenditure and tax revenues.

A clear feminist dimension to our present understanding of reproduction concerns movement away from the traditional role of women. In the past, and still to a large degree, women have assumed the major burden of reproductive work without any payment. While "equal pay for equal work" has yet to be achieved in most sectors of the economy, the majority of Canadian women (ages 15–64) now participate in the labour force (Beaudry and Lemieux, 2000). Women's roles in both the productive and reproductive spheres have considerable impact on the way we live (see Townshend and Walker, Chapter 7) and on how essential services, such as health, education, and child care, are delivered. Increased participation of women in productive sectors of the economy, for example, appears to be an important driver of our consumerist lifestyles as well as of demographic stagnation. Had it not been for the massive entry of women into the job market over the past 50 years, household incomes and standards of living would have declined considerably. Labour force participation of all adult household members, however, also can be a source of tension, as in the case of more health care being off-loaded to the home at a time when there is unlikely to be a stay-at-home caregiver to assist with ill family members (Allan and Crow, 1989; Wakabayshi and Donata, 2005).

Today, we witness growing public-sector difficulties in providing essential conditions for reproduction. From the Great Depression until roughly the early 1980s, governments expanded the welfare state and thereby their role in the reproduction sphere. In recent decades, however, the opening of international markets has allowed producers to seek low-tax and low-wage jurisdictions offshore, thus cutting corporate-based fiscal revenues; at the same time, public resentment about high tax levels has made increasing income tax a politically unrealistic option (Campeau, 2005; Finkel, 2006; Graham, Swift, and Delaney, 2009). As a result, governments have faced reduced spending capacity (see Hall, Chapter 3). Paradoxically, the subsequent cutbacks in public-sector reproduction services have coincided with rising expectations and demand for such services. At the very time when near-total engagement of working-age adults in the labour force makes it difficult for them to attend to the reproduction needs of society (having and rearing children) and of their dependants (old parents and sick or disabled family members), government support in these matters is either stagnant or declining.

In this same vein, the knowledge-intensive economy places a growing burden on the post-secondary education system. The response has been a gradual shift from public to private funding, evidenced by inflating community college and university fees. Yet, the persistent shift toward private funding is a major source of social inequality (see Walks, Chapter 9). Under-funding of reproduction-related public infrastructures and services can cause tragedies whose costs, in terms of suffering and monetary expense, far exceed initial savings. Two examples come to mind. In Ontario, attempts to economize on water quality inspection have been associated with the 2000 Walkerton *E. coli* outbreak, causing seven deaths and making 2000 residents ill (O'Connor, 2002). And in 2005, insufficient maintenance of New Orleans' water retention systems resulted in billions of dollars in damages

(as well as numerous casualties) in the wake of Hurricane Katrina (Brunsma, Overfelt, and Picou, 2007; Horne, 2006). The same logic pertains, in a less dramatic fashion, to the consequences of reduced services in sectors such as social services, education, and health care. For example, deferred treatment of health problems can bring about enormous suffering and productivity losses, often with cumulative costs far beyond that of the treatment.

Capitalization

The capitalization property of cities derives from their compact spatial form. Because urban land is scarce, it becomes the object of substantial capital investment so its use can be maximized. *Capitalization* refers to the vast resources invested to accommodate agglomerations of residents, businesses, and services. The nature of capitalization and, hence, the form cities take are largely influenced by the engineering possibilities of the time. Over the centuries, improving technologies have promoted larger city size and, until the relatively recent predilection for suburban forms, higher densities.

Once built-up urban environments are capitalized and populated, they become highly durable and thus contribute a considerable degree of continuity to the urban landscape. As a result, they become a factor in path dependence (favouring the perpetuation of existing patterns at the expense of innovation) (Pierson, 2000; see Filion and Bunting, Chapter 2). However, as technology and lifestyles tend to change faster than urban form, capitalization of urban land also engenders obsolescence. Change, especially concerning modes of production or transportation technologies, demands adjustments of the built environment to new conditions. But a city is not easily retrofitted. Typically, costs of redevelopment on brownfield or greyfield sites are higher than those on undeveloped land, often called greenfield sites, at the urban edge. While financial constraints can play a critical role, they are not the only impediment to altering the urban environment. One obstacle to urban environment adaptability is the symbiosis that binds patterns of behaviour to built environments. For example, high-capacity road systems encourage reliance on the automobile and the truck, and high rates of car and truck use generate a continued demand for improved and expanded roads (Noland, 2000; Parthasarathi, Levinson, and Karamalaputi, 2003). Another obstacle to changing the way the built environment is capitalized comes in the form of citizen resistance that occurs when proposals for redevelopment of previously built-up areas clash with residents' strong emotional attachment to their homes and neighbourhoods. An important challenge facing planners and politicians today, then, is how to reconcile citizens' attachment to their home "places," where they desire to maintain the status quo (NIMBY [not in my back yard]), with the need for change—particularly in the face of looming environmental crisis (Inhaber, 1998).

Capitalization trends over the past decades have promoted two very different urban forms. First, across Canada most urban development still occurs in suburban-like settings. Large investments are targeted, therefore, at the conditions required for suburban growth: for example, peripheral expressways, arterials, local road systems, water and sewer systems, and public services, such as schools and hospitals. At the same time, a sizable private industry is dedicated to suburban residential and commercial development, which caters to an enduring strong demand for suburban living. Interest groups that presently oppose measures to contain peripheral urban development mostly stem from these industries. Meanwhile, following a downtown office boom that began in the 1960s and lasted until the late 1980s, inner cities of large metropolitan regions are experiencing residential intensification, largely in the form of high-rise condominiums (Filion, 2000).

We cannot underestimate the importance on the economy of investments, both from the private and the public sectors, targeted at the urban environment. The home is indeed the main asset for a majority of households. The presence of a speculative dimension to urban-related investments,

which mirrors the dynamics of the stock market, is thus not surprising. This is especially the case since space is limited within metropolitan regions and the development process can take years. Such conditions can result in an imbalance between vigorous demand and lagging supply, which translates into escalating property prices. Recent events demonstrate the adverse impacts on the economy of the bursting of a speculative property bubble. As property values inflated, many households used their rising equity as collateral for growing consumer debt, which left them exposed when house values tumbled in 2008 and 2009. The situation has been worse in the US than in Canada, where measures to encourage home ownership, and thus fuel property values, have been less aggressive (Immergluck, 2009; Zandi, 2009).

Place

Sense of place is the least tangible among urban properties discussed in this chapter. This does not mean, however, that sense of place is any less important. Indeed, a renewed sensitivity to place most distinguishes current styles of urban development from earlier, modern growth (see Fordism). Enhanced interest in place is consistent with a shift in economic priority from the city as a centre of industrial production to the city as primarily an agglomeration of services, including culture and entertainment. Urbanites always attach meaning to space, whether it conforms to developers' intent or not. Recently, however, developers have been paying more attention to the messages conveyed by place, either in an effort to reap financial benefits or simply to enhance users' well-being (see Walker and Gunn, Chapter 18).

The noted geographer Yi-Fu Tuan (1974) coined the term topophilia to denote the personal identity with, and love of, a place. Thus, whereas "space" relations in cities are mostly about objective attributes of proximity and access, "place" is all about subjective attachment. Design-oriented professionals—such as Jane Jacobs (1961), Jon Lang (1994), planner Kevin Lynch (1964, 1984), and architect Christopher Alexander (1979; Alexander, Ishikawa, and Silverstein, 1977)—believe that fundamental "place" principles can provide guidelines to good urban form. They argue that, applied to urban development, such principles will lead to higher quality of life (the topophilia factor) as well as to more efficient use of urban space. Scholars such as Relph (1976, 1987) use the term "sense of place" in a related fashion to speak about subjective and emotional feelings associated with different parts of the urban environment. Relph argues that in modern times the perpetuation of monotonous landscapes in the suburbs and the lack of concern about imaging and good urban design left a vacuum in the urban entity. Others have been concerned that most people who live in car-oriented cities are missing out by virtue of being "detached" from their surroundings, and that the quality of individual and collective life, as well as the quality of the physical environment, has deteriorated as a result (e.g., Kunstler, 1993, 1996).

The diminishment of topophilic places as intrinsic urban attributes is considered characteristic of the industrial city. Meanwhile the elevation, indeed celebration, of positive features of strong places is one of the foremost differences distinguishing the postmodern city from the modern, industrial city (Ellin, 1999; Lance, Dixon, and Gillham, 2008; see Walker and Gunn, Chapter 18). Nonetheless, even in the largest of Canadian cities, detachment from landscape remains largely characteristic of the suburban environments, where most current residents of Canadian cities spend much of their time. In suburban settings, place attachment is mostly associated with the home and the neighbourhood. Other places are considered to be, at best, highly standardized (such as shopping malls and power centres) or, at worst, "junkscapes" (as in the case of haphazard car-oriented retail strips).

Place, then, is the attribute of urbanity that engenders strong connections, positive or negative, between urban dwellers and the locales that surround them. Specific characteristics of place that are favoured will vary in terms of the particular style or symbolic meaning conveyed through urban developments at any point in time. Radical or transformative change, as occurred during the Industrial Revolution, can cause a shift in the extent to which topophilia is elevated as an urban property. Sense of place is thus highly fluid. Former industrial areas provide a good example of this fluidity—these were avoided by most urbanites until their rebirth as loft developments toward the end of the twentieth century (Zukin, 1982). If the industrial transformation led to a relative demise of principles of good urban design, we seem to stand today at another crossroads of transformative shift in urban development wherein the "selling" or marketing of place has increasingly become an intended goal of municipal land-use policies. Aspects of cities that are highlighted for publicity purposes, such as economic development or tourism, reflect the evolution in the types of places that people value. If smokestacks were considered to be iconic of progressive cities at the turn of the last century, in the 1960s city promotions featured sleek modernist office towers, thus reflecting a shift in the economy from a predominance of blue- to white-collar employment. The emphasis is now on cultural and festival places, heritage buildings and neighbourhoods, and well-designed public spaces.

In sum, place is the intangible that makes some locales feel good while others do not and that invites or repels visitors. Place interfaces with all the other properties discussed here. Under conditions of the "new" economy, the manipulation of place properties has become a marketing device used to attract global interest and bring in outside investment (see Zukin, 1991). Thus, place features can be seen as a lure for the creative class, and are associated with the benefits of economic development believed to derive from this class (Florida, 2002, 2005; see Vinodrai, Chapter 5).

Governance

As understood here, governance consists of administrative structures and political processes aimed at generating policies suited to the specific circumstances confronting cities.[1] The proximity and capitalization properties central to urban as compared to non-urban settlements require distinct management measures for the urban community (e.g., Booth and Jouve, 2005; Lightbody, 2006). Proximity requires collective control and co-operation between nearby neighbours over communal space. The smooth functioning of cities relies on shared infrastructures (e.g., transportation, communication, electricity, water mains, and sewers) and services (e.g., policing and garbage collection) and on a battery of legal measures (e.g., property rights, payment for shared facilities, bylaws) intended to assure the orderly cohabitation of a wide variety of land uses. Haphazard development decisions can plunge a city into a state of chaos. For example, without planning controls noisy and polluting industries and high-traffic generators could locate in residential areas. Likewise, new developments could proceed without heeding infrastructural capacity, thus provoking all sorts of bottlenecks. A pure laissez-faire approach is clearly not suited to the city.

Various types of administrative arrangements have developed to provide urban infrastructures, services, and controls. These administrations have been local or regional or have been lodged in senior governments, as is the case with provincial ministries of municipal affairs or federal housing programs. Issues of governance generally belong to the public sector, but some urban management responsibilities can be vested in community-based or private-sector organizations. Over time, as cities grew, as buildings became bigger and required more infrastructure (roads, water, sewage), as reliance on mechanized forms of transportation (particularly the automobile) increased, and as the public demanded more and better services, administrations responded by becoming larger and more complex.

The need for interventions specific to the urban context has spawned disciplines and university programs that generate and impart the knowledge essential to these interventions. Relevant disciplines include urban planning, urban geography, urban sociology, urban economics, and subfields within civil engineering.

Today, coincident with the growing realization of the importance of local governance in matters such as environmental protection, economic development, the equitable provision of services, and the promotion of health and quality of life, we face the harsh reality that municipal administrations are confronting severe financial restrictions (Donald, 2002; Lightman and Irving, 1991). Even more than higher levels of government, local municipalities have been dealt huge budget cuts. In the absence of a reliable funding stream from these higher levels, municipalities presently rely primarily on limited tax revenues. Yet, at the same time, municipalities have incurred increased costs associated with the added responsibilities they have assumed. This has led to the launching of a movement of local administrations calling for a "new deal for cities." Reacting to demands from cities, the federal government has allocated a substantial share of its economic stimulus program to municipal infrastructure projects, both to repair existing infrastructures and to build new ones, including new roads and public transit services (Canada, 2009: 142–6).

Environment

To survive in the long term, cities must respect their natural environment. In recent years, human life everywhere has been threatened by an environment where soil, air, and water quality is severely degraded. As a consequence, increased dangers to health arise from by-products of our industrial and consumption processes. In the past, cities were generally situated at favourable locales; the immediate environment would usually be chosen for reasons of "site" (e.g., Quebec City's easily defendable position or Halifax's deep and sheltered harbour) or "situation" (good connectivity by water in the case of Montreal or by rail in the case of western Canadian cities—Winnipeg is a prime example). Usually, however, the regional environment had not been thought of in active terms.

As demonstrated in Chapter 4, even today cities tend to ignore to a large extent the environmental damage they inflict by exporting their pollution. Thus, for example, by sending its garbage to a Michigan landfill, Toronto does not have to deal directly with the consequences of its consumption. In a similar vein, the Montreal sewer system discharges its partially treated effluents downstream from Montreal Island in the St Lawrence River, and

Victoria still pumps raw sewage in the Strait of Juan de Fuca. The core argument of Chapter 4 is that cities have an environmental footprint that exceeds, manifold, their built area (Rees, 2008; Wackernagel and Rees, 1996).With time, environmental awareness has extended its scope from the very local to the global (Carr, 2005; Krooth, 2009). Prior to the twentieth century, the well-off classes would leave cities during times when disease spread most quickly; the urban residences of the wealthy would also command sites that were deemed to be most attractive and relatively "risk-free" according to the dictates of the time. In the 1950s the nascent environmental movement targeted local consequences of pollution, e.g., high bacteria counts preventing swimming and air pollution caused by specific close-by industries (Crenson, 1971). Later, as air pollution worsened due mostly to rising automobile use, environmental awareness became metropolitan in scale. Residents of metropolitan regions soon became conscious of the fact that retreating to distant leafy suburbs offered little relief from many forms of air pollution. Today, environmental awareness is decidedly global. There is increasing realization that with a world population exceeding seven billion, much of which is moving toward a consumerist lifestyle, the effects of human behaviour on the entire biosphere are inevitable (Friedman, 2008). Recognition of global environmental impacts was prompted by the depletion of the ozone layer, which led to the signing of the Montreal Protocol in 1987 to control the emission of chlorofluorocarbons—ozone-damaging compounds found in aerosol containers and refrigeration equipment. But above all, global environmental awareness is driven by concern over climate change. And as hubs of industrial production and consumption containing over 50 per cent of the world population, cities are major contributors to global warming. It is thus inevitable that any attempt to control greenhouse gas emissions will have major urban repercussions.

In his book *Collapse: How Societies Choose to Fail or Succeed*, Jared Diamond has documented the disappearance of civilizations over the ages due to circumstances affecting their immediate natural environment (Diamond, 2005; see also Whyte, 2008). In some instances, climate change (then mostly the outcome of natural circumstances) caused droughts; in other cases, communities and entire civilizations carelessly depleted the natural resources on which they depended. The lesson from Diamond's book is that the survival of any human group, and of humanity itself, depends on its ability to achieve sustainable forms of development in harmony with the natural environment. Otherwise, that group is doomed. The same goes for cities, except for the fact that they have long been successful in exporting, and thus overlooking, their environmental harm. But with the increasingly global impact of human activity, it is becoming difficult for cities to ignore their environmental effects. The environmentally related collapse of individual civilizations can now be transposed to a worldwide scale. It is now the fate of human civilization in its entirety (and thus the global urban system) that is at stake. Scenarios of doom in a warmer planet proliferate, with stark implications for cities: the flooding of low-lying coastal urban areas; unprecedented heat waves that will take a heavy toll on vulnerable urban populations; and violent conflicts over remaining water sources and fertile areas as deserts expand (Dyer, 2008; Schwartz and Randall, 2003; Smil, 2008). To be sure, cities have engaged in initiatives to alleviate their environmental impact (Register, 2006; Satterthwaite, 1999). Yet, while these measures have had positive results at local and regional levels (cleaner air and water, soil decontamination, preservation of natural areas), it remains to be seen if their scope will be sufficient to abate global trends such as climate change (Marcotullio and McGranahan, 2007).

Conclusion

In an effort to conceptualize the urban phenomenon, this chapter has considered its essentials. Seven properties—production, proximity, reproduction, capitalization, place, governance, and environment—are present in all cities across history (for a summary, see Table 1.1). These

Table 1.1	Urban Properties and Their Effects on the Contemporary City	
Properties	**Definition**	**Manifestation in the Contemporary City**
Production	Need for cities to produce goods and services for their own residents and to be exported beyond their territories to ensure the purchase of the goods and services that cannot be procured within their territories. Production attracts people to cities.	Links between cities and their hinterlands are replaced by economic interconnections between cities across the world. Transition from an industrialized to a service economy along with a renewed emphasis on resources.
Proximity	Cities are made of numerous overlapping markets of frequently repeated exchanges, with a predominant structuring role taken by the labour market. Proximity makes these exchanges possible; otherwise they would be ruled out by excessive travel time and cost.	Reliance on the car has greatly extended spatial range whereby repeated exchanges can be carried out. However, decentralization tendencies are in part countered by the stress placed on culture, entertainment, and, generally, face-to-face contacts by new economic tendencies.
Reproduction	Reproduction refers to the different conditions needed for the availability of a labour force that is well suited to the needs of the production sector of an urban area. A narrow definition of reproduction relates to the replacement of generations and the presence of conditions needed to maintain health. A broader definition includes education and much of household consumption, including even entertainment.	With the vast majority of working-age adults in the labour force, Canada faces below-reproduction birth rates, and households have difficulties in providing reproduction-related services to their members. The problem is that increasing demand for state reproduction-related services happens at a time when public-sector willingness and capacity to intervene is limited by insufficient resources.
Capitalization	Refers to all investments in the built environment of cities, as well as to this built environment itself. The capitalization property of cities derives from its dense urban environment. Capitalization is a factor of stability and durability for cities, and can be an obstacle to implementing innovations.	Over recent decades capitalization in cities has taken two forms: suburban development and inner-city intensification. Urban capitalization is conducive to speculation as demonstrated in the recent property bubble and associated adverse economic consequences.
Place	Place is about feelings, either positive or negative, associated with different locales in the urban environment. It refers to subjective reactions to these aspects of the city. Efforts are made by different professions involved in urban development to associate positive meaning with their projects. The types of urban places that are most valued vary over time.	Renewed attention given to place characteristics coincides with the growing importance of services and leisure in the post-industrial city. Quality places are seen as a way of attracting the creative class, which has the potential to propel an urban area's economy. Meanwhile, standard and poor-quality places are still being produced, especially in the suburban retailing sector.
Governance	Cities require interventions that are suited to their reality and, thus, specialized forms of administrations to formulate and deliver these interventions. They also rely on the knowledge that is essential to these interventions. Cities need to deal with issues related to concentration of activities and urban infrastructures.	Expansion of administrations with responsibility for urban interventions in response to growing demand for such interventions. This expansion is followed by cutbacks in tight budgetary circumstances. Under pressure from the municipal lobby, the federal government has directed an important share of its economic stimulus budget to urban infrastructures.

(continued)

Table 1.1	*(continued)*	
Properties	**Definition**	**Manifestation in the Contemporary City**
Environment	Historically, to survive, cities had to respect their environment. Cities that did not do so were unable to draw natural resources essential to their survival and vanished over time.	Cities are able to draw resources from ever-longer distances. They are thus less dependent on their immediate environment. At the same time, environmental awareness becomes global, and concern about different planetary impacts of cities (especially on global warming) is on the rise.

properties help to explain the reasons for the existence of cities and identify the main principles that drive their functioning. While this chapter has been about shared features of cities, the remainder of the book is about ramifications of the urban phenomenon. The book investigates diverse facets of cities and differences in how these facets manifest themselves according to their place within a metropolitan region and the position of a city in Canada's urban system. It also looks at how different aspects of society are mirrored in cities. Chapter 1 has been about common characteristics of urban areas; the remainder of the book is about their multiple dimensions.

Review Questions

1. In your opinion, do the seven properties described in the chapter cover all aspects of the urban phenomenon? If not, which would you add?
2. Which properties, in your estimation, are the most important in the present context? How is this different from previous periods?

Note

1. For a fuller discussion of municipal governance, see Andrew Sancton, "City Politics: Municipalities and Multi-Level Governance," Chapter 17 in Bunting and Filion (2006), at: www.oupcanada.com/filion.

References

Alexander, C. 1979. *The Timeless Way of Building*. New York: Oxford University Press.

——, S. Ishikawa, and M. Silverstein. 1977. *A Pattern Language: Towns, Buildings, Construction*. New York: Oxford University Press.

Allan, G., and G. Crow, eds. 1989. *Home and Family: Creating the Domestic Sphere*. Basingstoke: Macmillan.

Ali, S.H., and R. Keil. 2006. "Global cities and the spread of infectious disease: The case of severe acute respiratory syndrome (SARS) in Toronto, Canada," *Urban Studies* 43: 491–509.

Beaudry, P., and T. Lemieux. 2000. *Evolution of the Female Labour Force Participation Rate in Canada, 1976–1994: A Cohort Analysis*. Hull, QC: Human Resources Development Canada, Applied Research Branch.

Booth, P., and B. Jouve, eds. 2005. *Metropolitan Democracies: Transformations of the State and Urban Policy in Canada, France and Great Britain*. Aldershot, Hants: Ashgate.

Bottles, S. 1987. *Los Angeles and the Automobile: The Making of a Modern City*. Berkeley: University of California Press.

Brunsma, D.L., D. Overfelt, and J.S. Picou. 2007. *The Sociology of Katrina: Perspective on a Modern Catastrophe*. Lanham, MD: Rowman & Littlefield.

Campeau, G. 2005. *From UI to EI: Waging War Again on the Welfare State*. Vancouver: University of British Columbia Press.

Canada. 2009. *Canada's Economic Action Plan: Budget 2009*. Ottawa: Department of Finance Canada. At: www.budget.gv.ca/2009/pdf/budget-planbudgetaire-eng.pdf

Carr, M. 2005. *Bioregionalism and Civil Society: Democratic Challenges to Corporate Globalism*. Vancouver: University of British Columbia Press.

Castells, M. 1977. *The Urban Question: A Marxist Approach*. London: Edward Arnold.

Christensen, R. 2007. "SPIN-Farming: Advancing urban agriculture from pipe dream to populist movement," *Sustainability: Science, Practice and Policy* 3, 2: 57–60.

Crenson, M.A. 1971. *The Un-politics of Air Pollution: A Study of Non-decision-making in the Cities.* Baltimore: Johns Hopkins University Press.

Daniels, P.N., and J.R. Bryson. 2002. "Manufacturing services and servicing manufacturing: Knowledge-based cities and changing forms of production," *Urban Studies* 39: 977–91.

Derudder, B, and F. Witlox. 2004. "Assessing central places in a global age: On the networked localization strategies of advanced producer services," *Journal of Retailing and Consumer Services* 11: 171–80.

Diamond, J. 2005. *Collapse: How Societies Choose to Fail or Succeed.* New York: Viking.

Donald, B. 2002. "Spinning Toronto's golden age: The making of a 'city that worked,'" *Environment and Planning A* 34: 2127–54.

Dyer, G. 2008. *Climate Wars.* Toronto: Random House Canada.

Ellin, N. 1999. *Postmodern Urbanism*, rev. edn. Princeton, NJ: Princeton University Press.

Filion, P. 2000. "Balancing concentration and dispersion? Public policy and urban structure in Toronto," *Environment and Planning C, Government and Policy* 18: 163–89.

Finkel, A. 2006. *Social Policy and Practice in Canada: A History.* Waterloo, ON: Wilfrid Laurier University Press.

Florida, R.I. 2002. *The Rise of the Creative Class: And How It's Transforming Work, Leisure, Community and Everyday Life.* New York: Basic Books.

——. 2005. *Cities and the Creative Class.* New York: Routledge.

Friedman, T.L. 2005. *The World Is Flat: A Brief History of the Twenty-First Century.* New York: Farrar, Straus and Giroux.

——. 2008. *Hot, Flat, and Crowded: Why the World Needs a Green Revolution, and How We Can Renew Our Global Future.* London: Allen Lane.

Frumkin, H., L.D. Frank, and R. Jackson. 2004. *The Public Health Impacts of Sprawl.* Washington: Island Press.

Gill, A.M., and M.G. Reed. 1997. "The reimaging of a Canadian resource town: Postproductivism in a North American context," *Applied Geographic Studies* 1: 129–47.

Graham, J.R., K. Swift, and R. Delaney. 2009. *Canadian Social Policy: An Introduction.* Toronto: Pearson Prentice-Hall.

Hall, P. 1999. *Cities in Civilization: Culture, Innovation, and Urban Order.* London: Phoenix.

Harris, E. 2009. "Neoliberal subjectivities or a politics of the possible? Reading for difference in alternative food networks," *Area* 41: 55–63.

Hodge, G. 1998. *Planning Canadian Communities: An Introduction to the Principles, Practice, and Participants.* Toronto: ITP Nelson.

Horne, J. 2006. *Breach of Faith: Hurricane Katrina and the Near Death of a Great American City.* New York: Random House.

Hou, F., and L.S. Bourne. 2006. "The migration–immigration link in Canada's gateway cities: A comparative study of Toronto, Montreal, and Vancouver," *Environment and Planning A* 38: 1505–25.

Howard, S. 1968. *Medieval Cities.* New York: Braziller.

Immergluck, D. 2009. *Foreclosed: High-Risk Lending, Deregulation, and the Undermining of America's Mortgage Market.* Ithaca, NY: Cornell University Press.

Inhaber, H. 1998. *Slaying the NIMBY Dragon.* New Brunswick, NJ: Transaction.

Innis, H.A. 1995a [1931]. "Transportation as a factor in Canadian economic history," in D. Drache, ed., *Staples, Markets and Cultural Change: Selected Essays, Harold A. Innis.* Montreal and Kingston: McGill-Queen's University Press.

——. 1995b [1938]. "The penetrative process of the price system on new world states," in D. Drache, ed., *Staples, Markets and Cultural Change: Selected Essays, Harold A. Innis.* Montreal and Kingston: McGill-Queen's University Press.

Jacobs, J. 1961. *The Death and Life of Great American Cities.* New York: Random House.

Jessop, B. 2002. *The Future of the Capitalist State.* Cambridge: Polity Press.

Jones, P., D. Comfort, and D. Hillier. 2005. "Regeneration through culture," *Geography Review* 18, 4: 21–3.

Knowles, V. 2007. *Strangers at Our Gates: Canadian Immigration and Immigration Policy, 1540–2007.* Toronto: Dundurn.

Krooth, R. 2009. *Gaia and the Fate of Midas: Wrenching Planet Earth.* Lanham, Md: University Press of America.

Kunstler, J.H. 1993. *The Geography of Nowhere: The Rise and Decline of America's Man-Made Landscape.* New York: Simon & Shuster.

——. 1996. *Home from Nowhere: Remaking Our Everyday World for the Twenty-First Century.* New York: Simon & Shuster.

Lance, J.B., D. Dixon, and O. Graham. 2008. *Urban Design for an Urban Century: Placemaking for People.* New York: Wiley.

Lang, J. 1994. *Urban Design: The American Experience.* New York: Van Nostrand Reinhold.

Lawson, L.J. 2005. *City Bountiful: A Century of Community Gardening in America.* Berkeley: University of California Press.

Lightbody, J.M.A. 2006. *City Politics, Canada.* Peterborough, ON: Broadview Press.

Lightman, E., and A. Irving. 1991. "Restructuring Canada's welfare state," *Journal of Social Policy* 20: 65–86.

Lorch, B., M. Johnson, and D. Challen. 2004. "Views of community sustainability after a mine closure: A case study of Manitouwadge, Ontario," *Environments* 32: 15–29.

Lynch, K. 1964. *The Image of the City*. Cambridge, MA: MIT Press.

———. 1984. *Good City Form*. Cambridge, MA: MIT Press.

Marcotullio, P., and G. McGranahan, eds. 2007. *Scaling Urban Environmental Challenges From Local to Global and Back*. London: Earthscan.

Meier, R.L. 1962. *A Communications Theory of Urban Growth*. Cambridge, MA: MIT Press.

Mumford, L. 1961. *The City in History: Its Origins, Its Transformations, Its Prospects*. New York: Harcourt, Brace and World.

Noland, R.B. 2000. "Relationship between highway capacity and induced vehicle travel," *Transportation Research Part A, Policy and Practice* 35: 47–72.

O'Connor, D.R. 2002. *Report on the Walkerton Inquiry: The Event of May 2000 and Related Issues*. Toronto: Queen's Printer for Ontario (Parts 1 and 2). At: www.attorney general.jus.gov.on.ca/english/about/pubs/walkerton/part1/

Ontario. 2006. *Growth Plan for the Greater Golden Horseshoe*. Toronto: Government of Ontario, Ministry of Public Infrastructure.

Parthasarathi, P., D.M. Levinson, and R. Karamalaputi. 2003. "Induced demand: A microscopic perspective," *Urban Studies* 40: 1335–51.

Pierson, P. 2000. "Increasing returns, path dependence, and the study of politics," *American Political Science Review* 94: 251–67.

Rees, W.E. 2008. "Human nature, eco-footprints and environmental injustice," *Local Environment: The International Journal of Justice and Sustainability* 13: 685–701.

Register, R. 2006. *EcoCities: Rebuilding Cities in Balance with Nature*, rev. edn. Gabriola Island, BC: New Society Publishers.

Relph, E. 1976. *Place and Placelessness*. London: Pion.

———. 1987. *The Modern Urban Landscape*. Baltimore: Johns Hopkins University Press.

Rubin, J. 2009. *Why Your World Is About to Get a Whole Lot Smaller: Oil and the End of Globalization*. New York: Random House.

Russel, J.C. 1972. *Medieval Regions and Their Cities*. Newton Abbot: David and Charles Press.

Sancton, A. 2006. "City politics: Municipalities and multi-level governance, in T. Bunting and P. Filion, eds., *Canadian Cities in Transition*. Don Mills, ON: Oxford University Press.

Satterthwaite, D., ed. 1999. *Sustainable Cities*. London: Earthscan.

Schwartz, P., and D. Randall. 2003. *An Abrupt Climate Change Scenario and Its Implications for United States National Security*. A report commissioned by the US Defense Department. Washington.

Smil, V. 2008. *Global Catastrophes and Trends: The Next 50 Years*. Cambridge, MA: MIT Press.

Taylor, P.J. 2001. "Urban hinterworlds: Geographies of corporate service provision under conditions of contemporary globalization," *Geography* 86: 51–60.

Time. 2006. "The lure of the 100-mile diet," 11 June. At: www.time.com/time/magazine/article/0,9171,1200783,00.html

Tuan, Y. 1974. "Space and place: A humanistic perspective," *Progress in Geography* 6: 233–46.

Wackernagel, M., and W.E. Rees. 1996. *Our Ecological Footprint: Reducing Human Impact on the Earth*. Gabriola Island, BC: New Society Publishers.

Wakabayshi, C., and K.M. Donata. 2005. "The consequences of caregiving: Effects on women's employment and earnings," *Population Research and Policy Review* 24: 467–88.

Watkins, A.J. 1980. *The Practice of Urban Economics*. Beverly Hills, CA: Sage.

Whyte, I. 2008. *World without End? Environmental Disaster and the Collapse of Empires*. London: I.B. Tauris.

Zandi, M. 2009. *Financial Shock: A 360° Look at the Subprime Mortgage Implosion, and How to Avoid the Next Financial Crisis*. Upper Saddle River, NJ: FT Press.

Zukin, S. 1982. *Loft Living: Culture and Capital in Urban Change*. Baltimore: Johns Hopkins University Press.

———. 1991. *Landscapes of Power: From Detroit to Disney World*. Berkeley: University of California Press.

Urban Transitions: The History and Future of Canadian Urban Development

PIERRE FILION AND
TRUDI BUNTING

2

Introduction

The present chapter discusses the evolution of cities, how they change over time. The chapter concentrates on the factors that bring about urban transitions. What form do these factors take? What circumstances favour their emergence? And in what conditions are they most apt to alter urban development trajectories and thus launch new urban patterns? Our attempts at answering these questions will examine tensions between urban inertia and forces of change. The urban phenomenon entails major sources of inertia, the most obvious being the inherent durability of the built environment. At the same time, however, it is under pressure to adapt to society-wide changes. Clearly, those trends that result in profound and lasting transformations of society will have more impact than those that are more fleeting and superficial. But in all instances, factors inducing urban change will need to overcome urban inertia.

The chapter first considers the tension between urban inertia and change; it then goes on to describe factors of urban transformation. The remainder of the chapter is given to a description of three periods of urban development in Canada: the pre-1945 city; the 1945–1975 period when suburbanization prevailed; and post-1975 development patterns, characterized by a critique of, as well as ongoing prevalence of, forms inherited from the previous period. The chapter closes with an exploration of possible future urban transitions.

Inertia and Change

If you happen to look at pictures taken over time of a given urban location, you will note a discrepancy between changes affecting their foreground and background. You will observe in the foreground variations in the modes of transportation: an early predominance of streetcars, which were gradually replaced by automobiles with their changing size and design. People, too, will change. You will see either more or fewer pedestrians, according to fluctuations in the appeal of the area, changes in their clothing and hairstyles, shifts in the prevalence of age groups in response to variations in the nature of close-by activities and, in the Canadian context, increasing racial diversity over time. In addition, the signs in front of the stores, the appearance of their facades, and, above all, the content of shop windows will undergo repeated transformations. In comparison, the background of these pictures, comprising the buildings themselves, will appear to be much more static. It is not that transformations affecting the built environment do not take place but, rather, that such changes happen much more slowly. It is as though the photos of the foreground and background were taken by two different time-lapse cameras: one showing transformations at a rapid pace; and the other presenting changes that unfold much more slowly.

You would experience this phenomenon more directly were you to return to the neighbourhood of your childhood after a 15-year absence. You could not escape feeling the contrast between how much you have changed in 15 years and how closely the neighbourhood conforms to your memories, provided it was not the object of major development or redevelopment as happens at the edge of urban areas and in certain central sectors. True, some things will be different. Neighbours will have been replaced and some homes will have been painted different colours. Here and there new additions will have been built. But, overall, the neighbourhood will have changed very little. Meanwhile, 15 years in a young person's life bring many important transformations.

Cities do not offer a clean canvas. They always come with an inheritance—the weight of the past—limiting possible transformations. There is naturally the persistence of the built environment. The large sums required in construction deter a systematic replacement of old by new **urban forms**. The redevelopment of a site involves assembling the land, possibly at a cost exceeding market value due to the presence of owners who are not necessarily motivated to sell. Redevelopment also entails acquiring the site's structures and then incurring the cost of demolishing them—hence the predilection for greenfield development over re-urbanization. However, when the value of the land (determined largely by its accessibility and the prestige of its location) substantially exceeds that of the buildings occupying it, a site is ripe for redevelopment (see Skaburskis and Moos, Chapter 12). Such a tendency is seen in the succession of buildings in downtowns of growing cities. Indeed, it is not unusual for three generations of buildings or more to have occupied given downtown sites in Toronto or Montreal (Gad, 1991).

The endurance of the built environment is not, however, the sole source of urban inertia. The urban phenomenon provides fertile ground for spawning powerful **path dependencies** (Atkinson and Oleson, 1996; Pierson, 2000). A city's form (land use patterns) and dynamics (people's behaviour, including their transportation choices) are kept in place by interactions between different components of the urban reality. Transforming these interactions, and thus urban form and dynamics, is made difficult by the fact that doing so must involve all interconnected aspects of the city, engaged in any given interaction.

The most fundamental and influential of the **urban dynamics** that give rise to path dependencies are those that evolve around the mutual relationship between transportation and land use. Different modes of transportation foster different accessibility patterns, which in turn influence the nature of the built environment (e.g., compact vs. sprawling) (Boarnet and Crane, 2001; Frank, Kavage, and Appleyard, 2007; Millward and Xue, 2007; van de Coevering and Schwanen, 2006) (see El-Geneidy, Patterson, and St-Louis, Chapter 10). At the same time, urban forms shaped by a given mode of transportation result in additional demand for this mode. Once such a relationship is embedded, it becomes difficult to modify modes of transportation without simultaneously transforming land use, and vice versa.

In addition, there are other powerful urban path dependencies at work. One example is the mutual expectation that prevails between developers and their clients. As in the case of the transportation–land use relationship, a profound transformation of the city requires a concurrent modification of the expectations of both developers and clients. There is also the dependence of municipal administrations on property tax, which causes them to stick to conventional development in order to avoid financial risks that come with innovation. A final example of a path dependency is attachment on the part of residents to existing urban settings and their suspicion of any change to their living .environment. These sentiments explain the prevalence of NIMBY (not in my back yard) reactions (Curic and Bunting, 2006; Schively, 2007). But urban path dependencies are not immutable, as visible transformations of cities over time attest.

Factors of Change

We now consider seven interrelated factors of change. While most factors unfold at the scale of a society as a whole, and beyond in the case of global trends, some emanate at the local level. The factors discussed are the economy, demography, technology, **governance**, values, urban models, and the consequences of urban growth and decline. While we consider the impact of these factors on cities, we must remember that cities themselves also shape these factors.

The Economy

Economic trends affect the city in different ways. Most obviously, as economic prosperity fuels urban growth, development models popular in periods of economic expansion come to dominate the urban environment (Frenken and Boschma, 2007; Glaeser, 2000). In this sense, prosperity acts as a catalyst for urban development models. Which is not to say, however, that periods of economic growth necessarily bring changes in urban development. Economic expansion may simply lead to a further extension of established urban forms into new areas.

Economic changes also lead to adaptive efforts to ensure that urban environments can accommodate these transformations. Governance (discussed below) generally plays a key role in this matter. Reliant on the economic performance of their jurisdiction for their fiscal entries and the satisfaction of their electorate, governments indeed show deep interest in the economic competitiveness of the urban areas under their mandate (Harvey, 1990). It follows that a foremost motivation for policies targeting urban areas is to ensure their compatibility with the requirements of economic development, as interpreted by public sector agencies.

Spaces of consumption bear the mark of economic tendencies: economic performance and shifts in the importance of different economic sectors have an impact on the type and amount of housing that is built, as well as on the quantity and format of retailing and services. The same goes for spaces of production. Moreover, the consequences of the distribution of resources within society, which varies with the evolution of the economy, are visible in the urban environment: homelessness, overcrowding, and poor-quality housing contrast with opulent high-rise condo towers and large single-family-home subdivisions.

Demography

Demography is a measure of urban growth or decline, as cities are generally ranked according to their population. In Canada, a country where the labour force is mobile and reliance on immigration is high, the demographic growth of cities tends to be closely tied to their economic performance (Bourne and Rose, 2001). People are attracted to urban areas that offer well-paying jobs and leave those parts of the country where the economy is depressed (see Donald and Hall, Chapter 15).

The impact of demography on cities takes different forms. For example, variations in the size of different age **cohorts** leave their imprint on cities. The presence of children, moreover, is associated with outdoor space, hence the predilection of families for ground-related housing (single-family and semi-detached homes as well as townhouses). Meanwhile, young and old adults are more likely to opt for high-density living (see Harris, Chapter 19; Moos, Chapter 20). From a demographic point of view, the Canadian urban history of the past 60 years has largely been shaped by the life cycle of the baby boom generation, although immigration is gradually overtaking its influence (Foot with Stoffman, 1996; Trovato, 2009).

Technology

Technology is at the heart of the urban phenomenon. In the past, construction techniques were a prerequisite for permanent human settlement, as were the technologies required to carry essential resources to cities: baskets, jugs, bottles, carts, and, eventually, mechanical means of transportation. Perhaps most remarkable was the expertise the Roman Empire developed to bring clean water to major cities. Some of its aqueducts still stand. Not only did technologies enable the creation of cities, they also provided the conditions for their growth. Before the advent of public-health measures (largely reliant on technologies), cities were victims of repeated epidemics, to the extent that it was difficult for them to maintain their population level; life was often short in cities. Then, from the second half of the nineteenth century onwards, knowledge of the conditions required for healthy urban living led to a number of innovations: water treatment, vaccination, and antibiotics (Rosen, 1993 [1958]). Just as basic construction techniques were conditions for the launching of the urban phenomenon, health-related "technologies" were essential to public health in urban areas.

Successive transportation technologies—trains, streetcars, subways, and automobiles—have most transformed the urban form over the past two centuries. Different types of rail transportation shaped a distinctive urban form, which contrasts with the previous pattern fashioned by walking and animal traction. In a similar fashion, the automobile fostered an urban morphology that superseded the one inherited from the railway era (Graham and Marvin, 2001; Muller, 2004). The most recent technological innovations concern information technology: personal computers, the Internet, smart phones, and tablets. While these devices have a profound impact on our lives, their effect on the city is not as clear (Audirac, 2005; Sohn, Tschangho, and Hewings, 2005). As yet, there is no evidence of significant reduction in commuting or a change in urban form resulting from the widespread adoption of these communication technologies (see El-Geneidy, Patterson, and St-Louis, Chapter 10).

Governance

The organizational structure of public agencies has a determining effect on the priorities they adopt and their capacity to carry them out. Across Canada, municipal administrations have undergone considerable organizational change over the last decades. These include annexations, amalgamations, and the creation of regional administrations. The purpose of these reorganizations is to design governments appropriate to the size of the geographic areas they cover, and to more effectively govern metropolitan areas that have grown beyond political boundaries (Collin, Léveillée, and Poitras, 2002; LeBlanc, 2006; Meligrana, 2004; Vojnovic, 2000). The organizational architecture of public institutions also determines which groups of interests are best able to influence their decision-making. Some institutional structures make ample room for public participation while others are responsive primarily to dominant economic interests. In addition, changes in the priorities of the different levels of government reverberate on cities by causing fluctuations in the funding earmarked for infrastructures and shifts in the types of projects that will benefit from public sector resources (see Taylor and Bradford, Chapter 11).

Values

Beliefs or values that are widely held in a society can have multiple repercussions on cities. They affect consumer choice and, thus, the type of housing that is built, along with the forms that retailing takes and the nature of available services. A society's values also have an effect on the political process and thereby influence policy-making, including policies targeting urban issues. Values can have a unifying or divisive effect. At times, there may be near consensus regarding dominant values, which then contribute to the zeitgeist (the spirit of the times) of a given society. In other instances, disagreement over values may be a source of social divisions (Harvey, 1990; Hutcheon, 2002). As they change over time, values are a factor in social and urban transformation (see Bain, Chapter 14).

Urban Planning Models

Since the end of World War II, urban planning has had a major influence on the form urban development takes. Over the 70 years since the war, urban planning has mostly been concerned with the specialization of land use, relying on zoning to prevent the co-existence of incompatible activities. For example, land uses that can depress quality of life and property values are kept away from residential areas. Planning has also strived, not always successfully, to balance land use and the capacity of infrastructures in order to prevent bottlenecks, for instance by expanding road capacity in growing metropolitan areas. In its effort to organize cities, planning draws inspiration from models proposing different patterns of urban development. The last 100 years or so have witnessed the influence of the Garden City (new, fully planned, and self-contained low-density communities with plentiful green space), Tower-in-the-Park housing (high-rise buildings erected in a park-like setting), transit-oriented development (medium- and high-density development located adjacent to public transit stations), and New Urbanism models (attempts at replicating pedestrian-oriented forms as they existed before World War II). Some of these—in particular the Garden City and the Tower in the Park—have captured the imagination of planners, developers, and the public and have contributed to shaping the urban environment (Fishman, 1977; Howard, 2003 [1902]; Le Corbusier, 1973 [1933]). The impact of the other models has been more modest (at least until now). Note that planning models are rarely implemented in a pure fashion but are, rather, the object of compromises and adjustments as they confront the realities of the policy-making and development process. Still, they can inspire those who look for alternatives to prevailing urban forms.

Changes in the Size of Urban Regions

One of the factors that account for differences in how urban areas function and are organized is their size. Small urban areas offer a more limited range of options (employment, retailing, public and private services, modes of transportation, and types of neighbourhoods) than large metropolitan regions. In Canada, large metropolitan regions (Toronto, Montreal, and Vancouver) have strong downtowns and extensive public transit systems,

and they register heavy traffic congestion and long commutes. In contrast, small urban areas are often decentralized and automobile oriented. Access by car in these metropolitan regions is made easy by their modest size and relative absence of congestion.

These size-related differences suggest that as urban areas grow (or shrink) they experience transformations in their structure and dynamics (Bessey, 2002). Calgary illustrates changes associated with the growing size of an urban area. When the Calgary metropolitan region reached a population of 593,000 in 1981, it inaugurated a light-rail transit system (the CTrain). Before this, it was a near fully automobile-dependent and largely decentralized metropolitan region. Over the following years, Calgary's downtown area grew considerably, while the CTrain system was extended on an ongoing basis. Today, as the population of metropolitan Calgary reaches 1,215,000 (2011 census), it boasts a light-rail network that extends 56 kilometres; a strong downtown, especially in terms of employment; and a growing core population as traffic congestion is on the rise and the advantages of core area living become more apparent.

Factors of urban change are interconnected. For example, economic growth provides a fertile terrain for the spread of innovations, whose accommodation in the urban environment requires government interventions that involve, in certain cases, setting up new infrastructure networks. Fiscal rewards generated by periods of prosperity provide the means for governments to engage in such interventions. Public support for the idea of a major urban transition is also helpful, as is a planning model that portrays and justifies the proposed transformations.

As indicated, factors of change must overcome deeply rooted path dependencies. It follows that large-scale urban transitions will occur only when path dependencies are weakened and factors of change are both aligned and powerful. These circumstances explain the periodic toppling of long periods of stability by transformative epochs when conditions are conducive to urban transitions. We now turn to the history of Canadian cities in order to identify the major transitions that have marked their evolution.

Canadian Urban Transformations

The focus of this chapter is on relatively recent urban transformations, that is, those that have unfolded since 1945. However, we begin by briefly looking at the pre-1945 Canadian urban history and describing the urban form this period bequeathed to the post–World War II city. While the characteristics of cities vary in any period, some generalities may be observed in each time period.

From Urban Origins to 1945: The Development of the Railroad

Until the second half of the nineteenth century, walking was the main mode of transportation in Canadian cities. Their relatively small size made it possible to access most destinations on foot. However, major transformations unfolded in the latter part of that century that had considerable effects on transportation within Canadian urban areas, as well as on their structure and size. From the 1860s, for example, horse-drawn streetcars serviced the largest Canadian cities. In 1866, the first electric streetcar began operation in Windsor, Ontario. Quickly thereafter, systems spread across the country, so much so that by World War I streetcars were present in 48 Canadian urban areas.

Unlike prior animal traction, electric streetcars were able to provide relatively cheap mass transportation. The presence of streetcars allowed cities to expand rapidly at a time of accelerated population growth, primarily the result of industrialization. The streetcars propelled the first generation of suburbs. These suburbs were generally constituted of a commercial street along the streetcar line, with stores on the ground floor and apartments above (Jacobs, 1961). The remainder of the neighbourhood was residential, often with an industrial presence, and within walking distance of streetcar stops. From the late nineteenth century, in Montreal and Toronto railway companies operated commuter services on their main lines. These train services shaped peripheral urban development, which took the form of commuter suburbs centred on railway stations (Hoyt, 1939; Warner, 1962). In their original configuration, these commuter suburbs were still within walking distance from train stations even though the built form was generally low density.

Together, streetcar and commuter rail systems made it possible to focus much office, retail, and service development on a central point—the downtown. It was the capacity of these systems to draw passengers from the entire metropolitan region and deliver them downtown that propelled the growth of this sector and the appearance of its early twentieth-century hallmarks, the department store and the office skyscraper (Colby, 1933).

Another profound urban transformation that took place from the late nineteenth century to 1945 was the proliferation of large industrial areas along railway lines, which stimulated urban development. Industrialization came later in Canada than in the United Kingdom and the United States. The rapid urban development that industrialization triggered in these two countries in the early- (in the UK) and mid- (in the US) nineteenth century reached Canada only in the latter part of that century (Naylor, 2006; Smucker, 1980).

The late nineteenth century, then, marked the passage from small walking cities to much larger rail-oriented cities. The influence of rail on urban development resulted in the rapid construction of streetcar lines, the introduction of commuter rail, the resulting commuter suburbs, as well as the development of large industrial districts along railway lines. (See Figure 2.1 for a depiction of some of the key features of the pre-1945 city.)

From 1945 to 1975: "Urban Dispersion" in the Fordist City

The 15 years or so that followed the end of World War II, often called the Fordist period (see

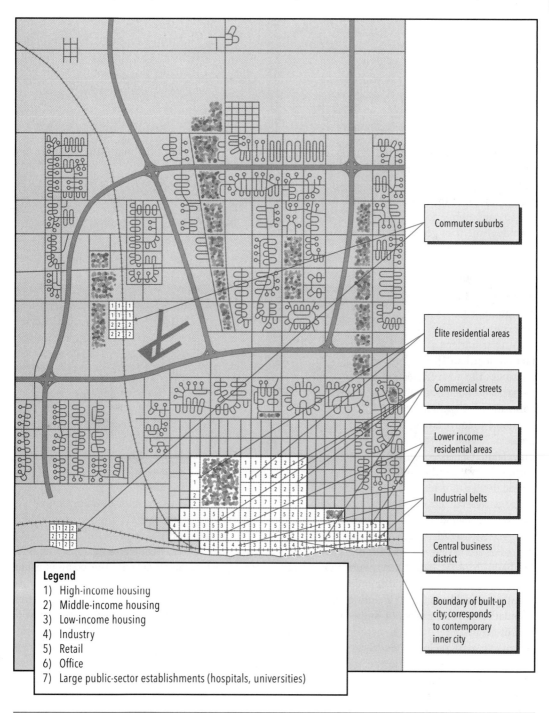

Commuter suburbs

Élite residential areas

Commercial streets

Lower income residential areas

Industrial belts

Central business district

Boundary of built-up city; corresponds to contemporary inner city

Legend
1) High-income housing
2) Middle-income housing
3) Low-income housing
4) Industry
5) Retail
6) Office
7) Large public-sector establishments (hospitals, universities)

Figure 2.1   **Urban Structure before 1945**

Fordism), witnessed the formulation and implementation of a new model of urban development, which involved an all-out adaptation of the city to the automobile (Hardwick, 2004; Sewell, 2009). We label this model "urban dispersion" to highlight, along with its land use specialization, the dependence on the automobile and the city's low density, as well as its radical departure from multi-functional centralization (Filion, Bunting, and Warriner, 1999). In dispersed urban environments, employment, retailing, services, and institutions are mostly scattered along numerous axes of automobile accessibility. Once in place, the path dependencies generated by urban dispersion ensured this model's entrenchment and a strengthening of the relationship between generalized automobile reliance and land use. The postwar urban transition may well represent the deepest change cities have ever experienced in a relatively short period.

A near-perfect alignment of the identified factors of urban change made such a transition possible. (The next sub-section, which explores the obstacles to a large-scale transition in the present context, will highlight the exceptional nature of the transformative circumstances that materialized between 55 and 70 years ago.) A prosperous economy fanned mass consumption of automobiles. Although cars had been around by this time for nearly 50 years, it was the postwar economy that made a generalized reliance on this technology possible as a ballooning middle class acquired vehicles. The two decades following World War II were characterized by rapid population growth driven by the birth of the baby boom generation and, to a lesser extent, the arrival of immigrants. With so many households engaged in rearing children, the popularity over these years of single-family homes and of neighbourhoods with plentiful green space is not surprising. Governments were, moreover, enablers of this postwar urban transformation. Healthy public finances, buttressed by prosperity, allowed governments to build infrastructure, especially highways, required for the accommodation of transformative trends.

Dominant values of the time also promoted urban change. Wide-scale adherence to modernism and the attendant rejection of traditions, for example, explains the popularity of new car-dominated suburban-type environments at the expense of older inner-city areas (Sewell, 1993). What is more, after nearly two decades of privation due to the Great Depression and wartime restrictions, there was a pent-up aspiration for a middle-class consumerist lifestyle. New suburban subdivisions, with their abundant private interior and exterior space, were ideally suited to the accumulation of consumer goods (Hamel, 1993; Hayden, 2003; Miron, 1988; Spurr, 1976). Over the 1930s and the early part of the 1940s, while urban development was at a virtual standstill, visionaries came up with models of automobile-reliant forms of urbanization. Representations of these models were mainstays of the world's fairs of the time (Leinberger, 2008; Rydell and Schiavo, 2010). The planning profession drew on two models from prior decades for inspiration: the Garden City for low-density suburban areas and the Tower-in-the-Park perspective for some suburban development, but mostly for inner-city urban renewal projects. Finally, the rapid urban growth of the time meant that urban areas were moving beyond population and economic activity thresholds where existing infrastructure systems and demands were in equilibrium—hence the need for new infrastructure.

One cannot exclude the role of serendipity in such an apparently flawless alignment of factors of change. But at the same time, there is clear evidence of intentional strategies to transform cities into agents of consumption. The postwar urban transformation happened at a time when several mechanisms contributed to swell consumption and thereby ensure that demand kept up with rising industrial productivity. These mechanisms included government transfer payments and trade unions, both of which were instrumental in creating a blue- and white-collar middle class (Aglietta, 1979; Jessop and Sum, 2006). There were also Keynesian policies, government subsidies common during Fordism, meant to stimulate demand

(Frazer, 1994; Jones, 2008). Some of these took the form of infrastructure development and others of guaranteed mortgages for single-family home purchasers (Dennis and Fish, 1972). Policy-makers of the time were aware of the sizable economic spinoffs the construction and sale of a new home generate: building materials, construction workforce, new appliances, and furniture (Harris, 2004; see Harris, Chapter 19). In addition, by encouraging the purchase and use of automobiles, the building of urban highways had similar effects.

Over this period, while Canada took part in the continental trend toward urban dispersion, it did so with more moderation than the US. In Canada, unlike in many US metropolitan regions where inner-city blight was common, inner-city neighbourhoods remained for the most part vibrant. Moreover, while in most US urban areas urban transportation policies were entirely focused on the car, large Canadian cities adopted a more balanced approach. Toronto inaugurated its first subway line in 1954, and the Montreal metro began operation in 1966.

In the present age of repeated recessions, deindustrialization, and social polarization, it is easy to look back longingly at this period as an economic utopia. We must, however, avoid glorifying this time. If it was true that the middle class was expanding in a climate of job security and rising standards of living, it was also true that a large segment of the population was excluded from the rewards of this economic system. White men dominated the workplace; the prevailing conformity made it difficult for people with alternative lifestyles. As well, by today's standards, goods were expensive; they also lacked the diversity the present global economy provides. Indeed, despite all its downsides, globalization can be credited for the fact that—despite stagnating incomes—more of us can afford a wide range of goods, including electronics products. Finally, as cities at that time became cauldrons of consumption in a car-oriented environment, they contributed to a narrowing of transportation options and urban ways of life (public transit services are a poor alternative to the automobile in dispersed urban settings and virtually all journeys exceed walkable distances), depleted quality of life due to time spent in traffic, and a deterioration in air quality (Miller and Shalaby, 2003).

Figure 2.2 identifies some of the more salient properties of suburban areas developed in the postwar period, such as the separation of unlike activities (e.g., housing and industry) (see also Addie, Fiedler, and Keil, Chapter 24). With rising car use and the presence of expressways and arterials, land values and density gradients became flatter, creating numerous points of equivalent importance. Major expressway interchanges and arterial intersections became sites for regional malls or power malls (Jones, 2006; Jones and Simmons, 1990). Other locations offering good accessibility along, off, or close to high-capacity roads attracted industrial and business parks, small retail malls, and self-standing retail and service establishments (e.g., fast-food outlets, car dealerships, gas stations, and so on). Land-hungry activities such as university campuses also opted for suburban locations. Suburbs distinguished themselves from the inner city by adopting an inwardly focused system of curvilinear streets within super blocks.

Meanwhile, quality of life in inner-city neighbourhoods suffered considerably from the construction of highways intended to improve suburban commuters' accessibility to the downtown (Nowlan and Nowlan, 1970). A perceived decline of the older housing stock was a major incentive for urban renewal schemes that demolished existing structures to make way for public housing. More frequently, though, "slum clearance" was the outcome of private development (Birch, 1971; Bourne, 1967; Hoover and Vernon, 1962; Miron, 1993; Smith, 1964). While everywhere the share of metropolitan jobs and retailing found in the central business district (CBD) declined, in large metropolitan regions these districts enjoyed considerable absolute office and retailing growth. The situation was different in smaller urban areas where the CBD shrunk in both relative and absolute terms (Filion and Hammond, 2009).

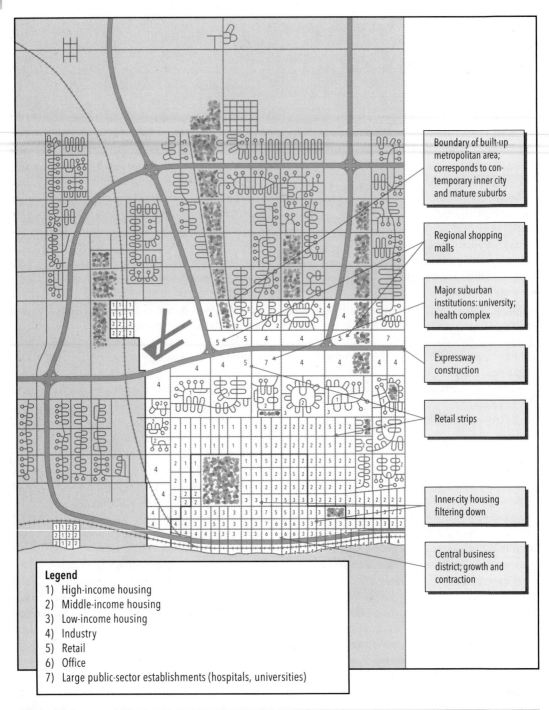

Boundary of built-up metropolitan area; corresponds to contemporary inner city and mature suburbs

Regional shopping malls

Major suburban institutions: university; health complex

Expressway construction

Retail strips

Inner-city housing filtering down

Central business district; growth and contraction

Legend
1) High-income housing
2) Middle-income housing
3) Low-income housing
4) Industry
5) Retail
6) Office
7) Large public-sector establishments (hospitals, universities)

Figure 2.2   **Urban Structure, 1945–1975**

Post 1975: Dissatisfaction with Modern Urban Expansion

From the early 1970s, attitudes toward prevailing patterns of urban development became progressively less supportive. Residents were becoming more aware and less tolerant of the downsides of existing urban patterns, giving rise to two types of reactions. Some took the form of (1) political responses, congealing into (2) citizen protest movements, whose reverberations were felt within city councils. These reactions had a profound impact on the form that city growth took thereafter. The most important issues such protest movements tackled were the halting of both public sector sponsored urban renewal and the construction of urban expressways. Indeed, everywhere in Canada (with the exception of the Ville-Marie Expressway in Montreal) these movements were successful in ending the construction of urban expressways. In contrast, suburban expressways, whose right of way had generally been safeguarded from the time individual suburbs were originally planned and therefore did not require expropriations and demolitions, went ahead. This change in attitude toward dispersed patterns also caused some middle-class households, who would have previously routinely opted for suburban living, to choose inner-city locations (Lees, Slater, and Wyly, 2008; Ley, 1996). These were the households that fuelled inner city redevelopment processes, which have been gathering momentum ever since (see Bain, Chapter 14).

Other circumstances caused dispersed urbanization to lose some of its gloss. Economic growth had slowed, with recessions becoming deeper and more frequent. A sputtering economy made it difficult for depleted government budgets to bankroll the heavy infrastructure expenses of dispersed urbanization, especially their transportation networks. As expected, one outcome was a deterioration of traffic conditions. It is not irrelevant, given the energy-hungry nature of dispersed urbanization, that global oil supply disruptions often played a role in triggering recessions. As environmental concerns gathered momentum, the dispersed model was cast in an increasingly negative light because of its automobile reliance. It was first blamed for worsening air pollution and more recently for high emissions of greenhouse gases (see Rees, Chapter 4). All of this was taking place as income stagnation and polarization was impairing the housing consumption potential of the middle class.

In the face of rising critiques of urban dispersion and increasing discordance between this model and society-wide economic conditions, one might expect that we would be at the cusp of another profound urban transition. Urban reality suggests otherwise. The dispersed model appears to be deeply entrenched and, if anything, the object of an ever-advancing mutual adaptation between driving and land use. For example, recent retail and entertainment formats, such as new-generation super-markets, power malls, big-box stores, and multi-screen cinemas, draw from large catchment areas of motorists.

Meanwhile, the factors of urban change that propelled the postwar urban transformation are not likely to be as effective in the present context. We have already seen that economic growth has slowed considerably since the 1945–1975 period, as has demographic expansion. With a birth rate below replacement since the early 1970s, Canada relies on immigration to maintain a slow overall population growth (see Kobayashi and Preston, Chapter 8). These economic and demographic conditions account for the fact that across the country the proportion of the urban built environment that is added annually is modest compared to the situation that prevailed over the previous period. From a technological perspective, the extraordinary wave of information technology innovation has had, to date, limited impact on **urban form** and dynamics. For example, although information technology makes it possible for many people to work from home, workplace regulations, peer pressure, and a desire to fully fit in with co-workers account for the fact that these innovations have had negligible effects on commuting and residential location patterns (Janelle, 2004; Moos and Skaburskis, 2007). Add to this an absence of new modes of urban transportation and we have an explanation for the limited effects of emerging technologies on the way cities operate, in sharp contrast with the impact of the widespread acquisition of cars in the 1950s and 1960s. Leaner economic times make it difficult for governments to invest the large sums needed to create extensive and efficient public transit systems, which could spawn alternative forms of urban development.

Any transformative initiative on the part of governments must also confront the present currency of the neoliberal ideology, which gives precedence to market trends over government intervention (Brenner and Theodore, 2002; Hackworth, 2006; Harvey, 2005). Fragmentation of values also impedes governments' urban transformation capacity by ruling out consensus around an alternative urban model. The vanishing common ground is not unrelated to the economic polarization of society as the size of the middle-class is reduced due to deindustrialization and a bifurcation of the economy between low- and high-wage service-sector jobs. Whereas in the postwar period the dispersed model of urbanization garnered widespread public support, there is no comparable adherence to a dominant model at the present time. Alternative urban forms, such as those represented by New Urbanism and transit-oriented development, have failed to capture the public's imagination to an extent comparable to the postwar enthusiasm for dispersed patterns (Duany, Plater-Zyberk, and Speck, 2000; Grant and Bohdanow, 2008; Talen, 2000). Meanwhile, attachment to prevailing suburban forms remains strong. Rob Ford won the 2010 Toronto mayoral election handily on a platform upholding suburban values and lifestyles, especially reliance on the automobile, against assaults from so-called "downtown elites." He was particularly vocal in his opposition to surface rail transit schemes, which would interfere with driving conditions. Finally, with demographic growth concentrated in a few metropolitan regions, these regions must adjust their transportation and urban form to their expanding size. Such pressures are absent from other, slow- or no-growth, urban areas.

There is thus much doubt about the capacity of achieving a major urban transition at the present

time (Table 2.1). Factors of urban transformation, and concentration, currently muster insufficient power relative to the entrenchment of urban dispersion. It is difficult to see how cities can overcome 70 years of massive public- and private-sector investment in urban dispersion, along with the path dependencies such urban development generates (White, 2003). There has been no replication of the alignment of factors of urban change that triggered the previous great urban transformation. All of this leaves cities in a predicament. Changes of attitudes on the part of many and discordance between urban dispersion and present trends affecting society do not translate into different ways of building cities. To be sure, such transformations do happen in certain urban sectors, for example, the high-rise condominium boom in downtown Toronto and Vancouver, but despite some examples of urban and suburban infill much current urban growth still conforms to the dispersed model (Berelowitz, 2005; Punter, 2003).

Figure 2.3 confirms that while the post-1975 period has not ushered in a profound urban transition, it has resulted in a number of innovations (also see Table 2.1). With the decentralization of offices from downtowns, the period has witnessed the creation of suburban business (or office) parks, and, more recently, the emergence of so-called suburban downtowns that combine office, retail, and high-rise residential concentrations with civic centres (Cervero, 1986; Filion, 2007; Garreau, 1991) (see Grant and Filion, Chapter 17). On the retail scene, the appearance of big-box stores and power centres has disrupted retail distributions inherited from previous periods (Jones and Doucet, 2000; Jones and Simmons, 1990). Meanwhile, although the density of suburban employment and retail space has either remained steady or declined, that of residential areas is on the rise. Homes are generally larger than they were in the previous period, but occupy comparatively smaller lots. Nonetheless, auto-based configurations of residential developments continue. One major difference between the two generations of suburban residential areas concerns the nature of green space. Whereas suburban green areas in the

Table 2.1   Conditions for Urban Transitions: The Post–World War II Period and the Present Time

Conditions for Post–World War II Urban Transitions	Insufficient Conditions for Urban Transitions at the Present Time
The Economy Prolonged period of prosperity; expansion of the middle class; consumerist lifestyle	Faltering economy; decline of the middle class; income polarization; globalization
Demography Rapid population growth, baby boom; many families with children; popularity of single-family homes and suburbs with abundant green space	Slow demographic growth; fewer households with children
Technology The automobile had been around for many decades; economic conditions were present over the period for the generalization of its use	Explosion of information technology innovations but they have limited impact on urban form and transportation; no new transportation technology
Governance Governments are enablers of post-WWII urban transformations; healthy public sector budgets and adoption of measures to sustain the economy: suburban-type development as well as expressways and arterials	Depleted government coffers prevent major public sector investments in new infrastructure; impedes large-scale public transit schemes
Values Conformity, modernist values; rejection of traditions; broad-scale support for the suburban model; pent-up demand for a consumerist lifestyle	Fragmentation of values in parallel with income polarization; absence of consensus around any urban model
Planning Models Pre-WWII visions of car-oriented cities; draws from Garden City and Tower-in-the-Park models	Recentralization model dominates in planning documents but its popularity is mostly confined to planning circles
Changes in the Size of Urban Regions With urban growth there is a need to redefine urban infrastructures	Fast growth in some large metropolitan regions, where there is a need to adapt infrastructures; much slower growth or decline in other cases

previous period came mostly in the form of large private lots and public playgrounds, more space is now allocated to the preservation of natural features, such as woods, creeks and their riparian zones, and marshes and ponds (Hough, 2004; Manuel, 2003).

Another suburban innovation over the post-1975 period has been the introduction of the New Urbanism model of development. However, this urban formula has not caught on as much as originally anticipated. In large metropolitan regions, the previous period was a time of downtown and inner-city large-scale commercial and residential redevelopment (mostly high-rise rental apartments); the focus during the present epoch has been on **gentrification** and residential **intensification**, mostly in the form of high-rise condominiums. The inner city and the core have become a highly appealing place to live for a large segment of the population sensitive to their urban

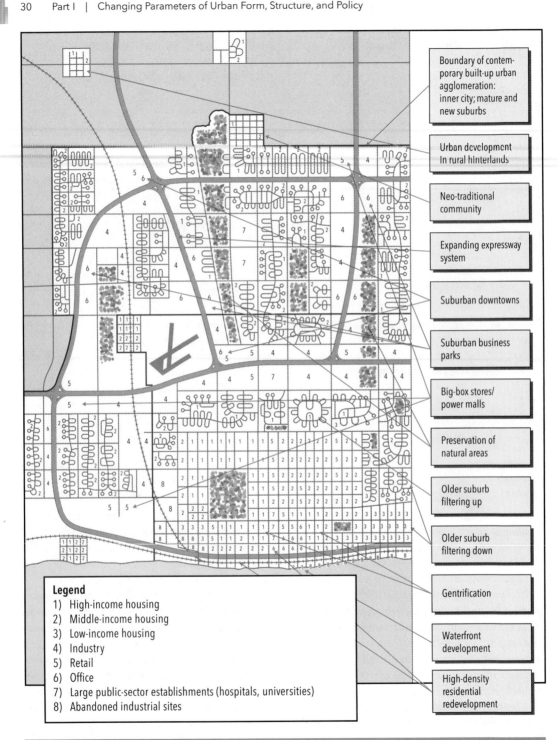

Boundary of contemporary built-up urban agglomeration: inner city; mature and new suburbs

Urban development in rural hinterlands

Neo-traditional community

Expanding expressway system

Suburban downtowns

Suburban business parks

Big-box stores/ power malls

Preservation of natural areas

Older suburb filtering up

Older suburb filtering down

Gentrification

Waterfront development

High-density residential redevelopment

Legend
1) High-income housing
2) Middle-income housing
3) Low-income housing
4) Industry
5) Retail
6) Office
7) Large public-sector establishments (hospitals, universities)
8) Abandoned industrial sites

Figure 2.3   **Urban Structure, 1975 to Present**

amenities: entertainment, culture, proximity to workplaces, and walking-hospitable environments.

Conclusion: Possible Future Transitions

With the emergence of suburban office and employment nodes—areas of high employment concentrations—and the resurgence of the down-town, some have speculated that we may be moving toward a new urban form characterized by several nodes (not just one downtown), which are connected by higher-density transportation corridors, and surrounded by low-density expanses of residential or commercial development (Moos and Mendez, 2013). In fact, a survey of North American planning documents with a metropolitan-wide focus indicates a near consensus among planning agencies around an alternative pattern of urban development involving the further development of downtowns, the creation of new secondary urban centres in the suburbs, and the interconnection of these different centres by public transit (either rail transit or bus rapid transit) (Filion and Kramer, 2012). The recentralization model purports to abate land consumption, car reliance, and the need for additional highway infrastructures associated with urban growth. It is thus in accord with environmental values, economic concerns, and the quest by many residents for locations with handy urban amenities. If implemented on a grand scale, we anticipate that this model will have a profound transformative effect on urban form and transportation. But we can also expect barriers to implementing this strategy. First, there is no large-scale public mobilization around the recentralization concept. It is still mostly the domain of planners. Second, even if the land-use dimensions of recentralization can be achieved largely through planning regulations, and thus avoid straining already tight public sector budgets, major funding will still be required for the public transit investments essential to the achievement of this type of urbanization (Filion and Kramer, 2011). It is a challenge for governments to fund new transit projects in a time of fiscal conservatism, although some funding is also increasingly obtained from the private sector for such projects.

A recentralization strategy may, however, cause serious shifts in the social geography of urban areas. In a fashion that mirrors the supersession of social by environmental issues in the urban planning discourse of the last two decades, plans emphasize the environmental benefits of recentralization but give scant attention to its possible impact on different social groups (Gunder, 2006). In its ideal version, this strategy would bring centrality and accessibility to everyone by saturating a metropolitan region with centres and different types of rapid transit. A more realistic but also more problematic outcome would be the creation of a limited number of centres and new rapid-transit lines. These centres themselves, along with the areas surrounding them and the bordering rapid-transit lines, would be perceived as attractive residential locations. And because areas offering such urban amenities and accessibility potential would be limited, they would likely be objects of gentrification resulting from competition for location in these sectors. Over time, and under pressure from higher-income groups, incumbent residents would move out and therefore be deprived of the new advantages offered by these areas—this has been referred to as eco-gentrification (Quastel, Moos and Lynch, 2012).

We cannot exclude the possibility of technical innovations having a transformative impact on cities. But such innovations would have to fulfill a number of conditions to be widely adopted and to contribute to a transformation of the urban environment. In the present economic climate, it is difficult to foresee the setting up of expensive new infrastructures. In consequence, to be successful new technologies would have to rely on cheaper infrastructures than prior technologies, as in the case of cellular phones in comparison to landlines, or accommodate themselves of existing infrastructures. Perhaps the most probable urban transportation innovation on the horizon is the driver-less, and perhaps eventually fully electric, Google car. A key advantage of this innovation would be its suitability to existing transportation infrastructures. In fact, allowing cars to travel safely faster and closer to each other would raise the efficiency of highway networks. But as this technology would accentuate the urban impacts of the car, without however its adverse safety, energy, and pollution consequences, it would be more likely to reinforce, rather than cause a departure from, the dispersed model.

Review Questions

1. What were the main factors influencing the structure of Canadian cities during different periods of urban development?
2. How do you think the structure of Canadian cities will change in the next 20 to 30 years? Explain what factors you think would bring about these changes.
3. Considering the city you grew up in, what factors were important in shaping the physical urban structure? How so?

References

Aglietta, M. 1979. *A Theory of Capitalist Regulation: The U.S. Experience*. London: New Left Books.

Atkinson, G., and T. Oleson. 1996. "Urban sprawl as a path dependent process," *Journal of Economic Issues* 30: 609–15.

Audirac, I. 2005. "Information technology and urban form: Challenges to smart growth," *International Regional Science Review* 28: 119–45.

Berelowitz, L. 2005. *Dream City: Vancouver and the Global Imagination*. Vancouver: Douglas & McIntyre.

Bessey, K.M. 2002. "Structure and dynamics in an urban landscape: Toward a multiscale view," *Ecosystems* 5: 360–75.

Birch, D. 1971. "Toward a stage model of urban growth," *Journal of the American Institute of Planners* 37: 78–87.

Boarnet, M.G., and R. Crane. 2001. *Travel by Design: The Influence of Urban Form on Travel*. Oxford: Oxford University Press.

Bourne, L.S. 1967. *Private Redevelopment of the Central City*. Chicago: University of Chicago, Department of Geography Research Paper No. 112.

———, and D. Rose. 2001. "The changing face of Canada: The uneven geographies of population and social change," *The Canadian Geographer* 45: 105–19.

Brenner, N., and N. Theodore, eds. 2002. *Spaces of Neoliberalism: Urban Restructuring in North America and Western Europe*. Malden, MA: Blackwell.

Cevero, R. 1986. "Urban transit in Canada: Integration and innovation at its best," *Transportation Quarterly* 40: 293–316.

Colby, C. 1933. "Centripetal and centrifugal forces in urban geography," *Annals, Association of American Geographers* 23: 1–20.

Collin, J-P., J. Léveillée, and C. Poitras. 2002. "New challenges and old solutions: Metropolitan reorganization in Canadian and US city regions," *Journal of Urban Affairs* 24: 317–32.

Curic, T., and T. Bunting. 2006. "Does compatible mean same as? Lessons learned from the residential intensification of surplus hydro lands in four older suburban neighbourhoods in the City of Toronto," *Canadian Journal of Urban Research* 15: 202–24.

Dennis, M., and S. Fish. 1972. *Programs in Search of a Policy*. Toronto: Hakkert.

Duany, A., E. Plater-Zyberk, and J. Speck. 2000. *Suburban Nation: The Rise of Sprawl and the Decline of the American Dream*. New York: North Point Press.

Filion, P. 2007. *The Urban Growth Centre Strategy in the Greater Golden Horseshoe: Lessons from Downtowns, Nodes and Corridors*. Toronto: Neptis Foundation.

———, T. Bunting, and K. Warriner. 1999. "The entrenchment of urban dispersion: Residential preferences and location patterns in the dispersed city," *Urban Studies* 36: 1317–47.

———, and K. Hammond. 2009. "When planning fails: Downtown malls in mid-size cities," *Canadian Journal of Urban Research* 17, 2: 1–27.

———, and A. Kramer. 2011. "Metropolitan-scale planning in neo-liberal times: Financial and political obstacles to urban form transition," *Space and Polity* 15: 197–212.

———, ———. 2012. "Transformative metropolitan development models in large Canadian urban areas: The predominance of nodes," *Urban Studies* 49: 2237–64.

Fishman, R. 1977. *Urban Utopias in the Twentieth Century: Ebenezer Howard, Frank Lloyd Wright, and Le Corbusier*. New York: Basic Books.

Foot, D.K., with D. Stoffman. 1996. *Boom, Bust and Echo: Profiting from the Demographic Shift in the New Millennium*. Toronto: Macfarlane Walter and Ross.

Frank, L.D., S. Kavage, and S. Appleyard. 2007. "The urban form and climate change gamble," *Planning* 73: 18–23.

Frazer, W.J. 1994. *The Legacy of Keynes and Friedman: Economic Analysis, Money, and Ideology*. Westport, CT: Praeger.

Frenken, K., and R.A. Boschma. 2007. "A theoretical framework for evolutionary economic geography: Industrial dynamics and urban growth as a branching process," *Journal of Economic Geography* 7: 635–49.

Gad, G. 1991. "Toronto's financial district." *The Canadian Geographer* 35: 203–7.

Garreau, J. 1991. *Edge City: Life on New Frontier*. New York: Doubleday.

Glaeser, E.L. 2000. "The new economics of urban and regional growth," in G.L. Clark, M.P. Feldman, and M.S. Gertler, eds., *The Oxford Handbook of Economic Geography*. Oxford: Oxford University Press.

Graham, S., and S. Marvin. 2001. *Splintering Urbanism: Networked Infrastructures, Technological Mobilities and the Urban Condition*. New York: Routledge.

Grant, J.L., and S. Bohdanow. 2008. "New urbanism developments in Canada: A survey," *Journal of Urbanism* 1: 109–27.

Gunder, M. 2006. "Sustainability: Planning's saving grace on road to perdition?" *Journal of Planning Education and Research* 26: 208–21.

Hackworth, J. 2006. *The Neoliberal City: Governance, Ideology, and Development in American Urbanism*. Ithaca, NY: Cornell University Press.

Hamel, P. 1993. "Modernity and postmodernity: The crisis of urban planning," *Canadian Journal of Urban Research* 2: 16–29.

Hardwick, M.J. 2004. *Mall Maker: Victor Gruen, Architect of an American Dream*. Philadelphia, PA: University of Pennsylvania Press.

Harris, R. 2004. *Creeping Conformity: How Canada Became Suburban, 1900–1960*. Toronto: University of Toronto Press.

Harvey, D. 1990. *The Conditions of Postmodernity: An Enquiry into the Origins of Cultural Change*. Oxford: Blackwell.

Harvey, D. 2005. *A Brief History of Neoliberalism*. Oxford: Oxford University Press.

Hayden, D. 2003. *Building Suburbia: Green Fields and Urban Growth, 1820–2000*. New York: Pantheon Books.

Hoover, E.M., and R. Vernon. 1962. *Anatomy of a Metropolis*. New York: Doubleday Anchor.

Hough, M. 2004. *Cities and Natural Processes: A Basis for Sustainability*. London: Routledge.

Howard, E. 2003 [1902]. *To-morrow: A Peaceful Path to Real Reform*. London: Routledge.

Hutcheon, L. 2002. *The Politics of Postmodernism*, 2nd edn. London: Routledge.

Hoyt, H. 1939. *The Structure and Growth of Residential Neighborhoods in American Cities*. Washington: Federal Housing Administration.

Jacobs, J. 1961. *The Death and Life of Great American Cities*. New York: Random House.

Janelle, D.G. 2004. "Impact of information technologies," in S. Hanson and G. Giuliano, eds., *The Geography of Urban Transportation*. New York: Guilford.

Jessop, B., and N.-L. Sum. 2006. *Beyond the Regulation Approach: Putting Capitalist Economies in their Place*. Cheltenham: Edward Elgar.

Jones, J.P. 2008. *Keynes's Vision: Why the Great Depression Did Not Return*. London: Routledge.

Jones, K. 2006. "The urban retail landscape," in T. Bunting and P. Filion, eds., *Canadian Cities in Transition: Local through Global Perspectives*, 3rd edn. Toronto: Oxford University Press.

——, and M. Doucet. 2000. "Big-box retailing and the urban retail structure: The case of the Toronto area," *Journal of Retailing and Consumer Services* 7: 233–47.

——, and J. Simmons. 1990. *The Retail Environment*. London: Routledge.

LeBlanc, M-F. 2006. "Two tales of municipal reorganization: Toronto's and Montreal's diverging paths towards regional governance and social sustainability," *Canadian Journal of Political Science* 39: 571–90.

Le Corbusier. 1973 [1933]. *The Athens Charter*. New York: Grossman.

Lees, L., T. Slater, and E.K. Wyly. 2008. *Gentrification*. New York: Routledge.

Leinberger, C.B. 2008. *The Option of Urbanism: Investing in a New American Dream*. Washington: Island Press.

Ley, D. 1996. *The New Middle Class and the Remaking of the Central City*. Oxford: Oxford University Press.

Manuel, P.M. 2003. "Cultural perceptions of small urban wetlands: Cases from the Halifax Regional Municipality, Nova Scotia, Canada," *Wetlands* 23: 921–40.

Meligrana, J. ed. 2004. *Redrawing Local Government Boundaries: An International Study of Politics, Procedures, and Decisions*. Vancouver, BC: UBC Press.

Miller, E.J., and A. Shalaby. 2003. "Evolution of personal travel in the Toronto area and policy implication," *Journal of Urban Planning and Development* 129: 1–26.

Millward, H., and G. Xue. 2007. "Local urban form measures related to land-use and development period: A case study for Halifax, Nova Scotia," *Canadian Journal of Urban Research* 16: 53–72.

Miron, J. 1988. *Housing in Postwar Canada: Demographic Change, Household Formation and Housing Markets*. Montreal and Kingston: McGill-Queen's University Press.

——, ed. 1993. *House, Homes, and Community: Progress in Housing Canadians, 1945–1986*. Montreal and Kingston: McGill-Queen's University Press.

Moos, M., and P. Mendez. 2013. "Suburbanization and the remaking of metropolitan Canada," in R. Keil, ed., *Suburban Constellations: Governance, Land and Infrastructure in the 21st Century*. Berlin: Jovis Publishers.

——, and A. Skaburskis. 2007. "The characteristics and location of home workers in Montreal, Toronto and Vancouver," *Urban Studies* 44: 1781–1808.

Muller, P.O. 2004. "Transportation and urban form: Stages in the spatial evolution of the American metropolis," in S. Hanson and G. Guiliano, eds., *The Geography of Urban Transportation*. New York: Guilford.

Naylor, R.T. 2006. *The History of Canadian Business, 1867–1914.* Montreal and Kingston: McGill-Queen's University Press.

Nowlan, D., and N. Nowlan. 1970. *The Bad Trip: The Untold Story of Spadina Highway*. Toronto: Anansi Press.

Pierson, P. 2000. "Increasing returns, path dependence, and the study of politics," *American Political Science Review* 94: 251–67.

Punter, J. 2003. *The Vancouver Achievement: Urban Planning and Design*. Vancouver: University of British Columbia Press.

Quastel, N., M. Moos and N. Lynch, N. 2012. "Sustainability as density and the return of the social: The case of Vancouver, British Columbia," *Urban Geography* 33: 1055–84.

Rosen, G. 1993 [1958]. *A History of Public Health*. Baltimore, MD: The Johns Hopkins University Press.

Rydell, R.W., and L.B. Schiavo, ed. 2010. *Designing Tomorrow: America's World's Fairs of the 1930s*. New Haven, CT: Yale University Press.

Schively, C. 2007. "Understanding the NIMBY and LULU phenomena: Reassessing our knowledge base and informing future research," *Journal of Planning Literature* 21: 255–66.

Sewell, J. 1993. *The Shape of the City: Toronto Struggles with Modern Planning*. Toronto: University of Toronto Press.

——. 2009. *The Shape of the Suburbs: Understanding Toronto's Sprawl*. Toronto: University of Toronto Press.

Smith, W. 1964. *Filtering and Neighborhood Change*. Berkeley: University of California, Center for Real State and Urban Economics, Report No. 24.

Smucker, J. 1980. *Industrialization in Canada*. Scarborough, ON: Prentice-Hall.

Sohn, J., J.K. Tschangho, and G.J.D. Hewings. 2005. "Information technology and urban spatial structure: A comparative analysis of the Chicago and Seoul regions," in H.W. Richardson and C-H. C. Bae, eds., *Globalization and Urban Development*. Berlin: Springer.

Spurr, P. 1976. *Land and Urban Development: A Preliminary Study*. Toronto: James Lorimer.

Talen, E. 2000. "New urbanism and the culture of criticism," *Urban Geography* 21: 318–41.

Trovato, F. 2009. *Canada's Population in a Global Context: An Introduction to Social Demography*. Toronto: Oxford University Press.

van de Coevering, P., and T. Schwanen. 2006. "Re-evaluating the impact of urban form on travel patterns in Europe and North America," *Transport Policy* 13: 229–39.

Vojnovic, I. 2000. "The transitional impacts of municipal consolidations," *Journal of Urban Affairs* 22: 385–417.

Warner, B.J. 1962. *Streetcar Suburbs: The Process of Growth in Boston*. Cambridge, MA: Harvard University Press.

White, R. 2003. *Urban Infrastructure and Urban Growth in the Toronto Region: 1950s to the 1990s*. Toronto: Neptis Foundation.

PART II

The Structuring Parameters of Cities in an Urban Age

In this section we attempt to capture what we suspect may prove to be the structuring parameters of cities in an increasingly urban age. Undoubtedly, there will be factors we have overlooked or have yet to recognize as significant to the moulding of contemporary cities. Likewise, there may be features included that have only a secondary impact on current and future urban development trends. Either way, the following chapters consider how general forces of change have resonated within the built environment over recent decades.

Many of the structuring parameters identified throughout the book are new and, we would argue, pertain to the postmodern—as distinct from the modern—city. Forty or fifty years ago, features of globalism, environmental sustainability, and the new service economy were not recognized as relevant to city structure. Though widely recognized and even talked about by the average person on the street today, globalism in its many guises—international trade, outsourcing, immigration, heightened international political and institutional collaboration, imported consumer goods and services, etc.—was a less significant force on the urban landscape before 1975. Likewise, neither recognized nor understood in our grandparents' days were the many negative impacts that city building and day-to-day routines (e.g., the impact of auto and truck travel on fossil fuel depletion and global climate change) exert on the urban biophysical environment. As recently as 30 years ago, terms like "ecological footprint" or "urban metabolism" would probably not have made much sense within either scholarly or policy-oriented circles.

Fifty years ago, our modern cities and city systems were understood to be propelled by the forces of industrialism. In the 1990s, at least one scholar who wrote about impending deindustrialization foresaw "the end of work" as forces of automation and economic globalization devalued manual and routine labour in developed countries (Rifkin, 1995). As it turned out, technological, cultural, and economic changes did not so much bring an end to work as they profoundly transformed it. For example, virtually costless telecommunications have renewed the importance of face-to-face contacts for creative enterprises. A generation or more ago, art and culture were interpreted as singularly high-order services found to be localized in one or more entertainment districts near the centre of the city. At that time, scholars and policy-makers could hardly be blamed for viewing arts and culture as something of an urban "frill." Only with hindsight can we understand that it would be most unrealistic for "modern" urban thinkers to have anticipated that, by the twenty-first century, the creative sector would be seen as a driving force of economic growth and an essential tool in the kitbag of local economic developers everywhere.

As we move through Part II, we begin to examine parameters that have long been identified as important structuring features for cities and that have been clearly articulated in previous eras of urban development. Distinctive features of these long-recognized parameters have shifted markedly, however, in the twenty-first-century city and so today have a significantly different impact on city structure than in the past. Taking employment as an example, we witness the demise of not just inner-city but also much suburban industry. Likewise, the high-order producer services sector has expanded significantly, especially for business in the FIRE (finance, insurance, real estate) sector, a distinctive marker of the new economy in the core of our largest metropolitan areas. Those who understand historic patterns of urban form will quickly grasp that location of employment has a significant effect on where different classes of residents/workers choose to live and subsequently on how they travel to work. Less obvious perhaps is the role that interaction between any one urban parameter, such as employment location, and other urban parameters might play—e.g., the effect that the new creative economy has had on the overall regeneration of the central city.

Yet another major parameter of urban structure has long been identified in terms of social status. Geographers in the past have most often thought about patterns of urban social division in terms of a general integrative model that has been widely researched under the rubric of the "factorial" or "social ecology" of cities.[1] In the modern city, important differentiation of urban social space was found to be associated with three interrelated dimensions: socio-economic status, stage in the life cycle, and ethnicity. Today these same dimensions continue to give rise to important distinctions in both social space and activities or lifestyle, but urban social space has become much more complicated. Thus, for example, rather than a life-cycle continuum, as was characteristic of the "modern" city, where most households were of the nuclear family type, we now find entirely new arrangements, such as "blended families," alternative household types, and the growing predominance of single-person households. In our urban age, each of the three dimensions of intra-urban social space—life cycle and demography, economic status, and ethno-cultural diversity—has taken on sufficient differentiation to act as a somewhat independent dimension. Where once one model of social space could suffice, today's city requires much more multi-faceted analyses.

Another structuring feature of urban form is witnessed in the apparent inseparable dependence of urban form on prevailing modes of transportation. Thus, whether speaking of cities of the present or ancient past, it seems axiomatic to state that land-use patterns, along with other important parameters such as land value, will be a function of movement patterns and, conversely, that movement and transportation also become a function of land use and urban form. Chapter 2 described how the newer suburban parts of the modern Fordist city (see **Fordism**) have evolved through an intrinsic relationship between low-density suburban form and automotive dependency. Likewise, most of the territory of current cities—i.e., the area that includes the inner and outer suburbs—perpetuates the low-density auto-dependent dynamic, thereby explaining our inability to accommodate apparently inexhaustible demands for more expressway lanes.

The unprecedented level of uncertainty about the urban future that we now face is in large part a product of this dysfunctional but entrenched relationship between urban form and auto dependency. Thus, the call today across many disciplines and professions is for retrofitting of Canada's cities, redesigning them to support primarily transit, cycling, and pedestrian movement. Most certainly it is clear that current, restructured styles of neo-liberal governance will be hard-pressed, if even willing, to provide the resources needed to bring about reversal of this land-use transportation dynamic, involving, as it must, policy that will find disfavour with large segments of the urban population.

At the end of Part 2, we come to urban land values. As the final parameter introduced here, land values provide a good example of the complex interrelationships that exist within and between structuring forces in urban areas. We see, for example, that urban land values are both an expression of the other critical forces, such as demography and globalization and, at the same time, a shaper of urban structure in their own right, determining what type of activities can afford which locations.

Note

1. For spatial analysis of Canadian cities and Canada's urban social mosaic, see Robert A. Murdie and Carlos Teixeira, "Urban Social Space," Chapter 9 in Bunting and Filion (2006), at: www.oupcanada.com/filion.

Reference

Rifkin, J. 1995. *The End of Work: The Decline of the Global Labor Force and the Dawn of the Post-Market Era.* New York: G.P. Putnam's Sons.

Murdie, R., and C. Teixeira. 2006. "Urban Social Space," In T. Bunting and P. Filion, eds., *Canadian Cities in Transition,* 3rd edn. Don Mills, ON: Oxford University Press.

Global Flows: Making the City, Made in the City

3

PETER V. HALL

Introduction

From New Westminster, once the capital of British Columbia but now a suburb of Greater Vancouver, one can watch log booms containing trees felled elsewhere in the province being towed up the Fraser River. After being processed at one of the dwindling number of urban riverfront mills, they return downriver in vast open barges as woodchips, ready for processing into chipboard, pulp, and paper at both remote and local sites. Other wood products are placed on specialized railcars or in shipping containers for export. On the surface these flows appear timeless and unchanging; they are the tangible manifestations of the imprint of the Canadian staples export economy on the city.

We know, however, that this imprint has changed, and continues to change. In other parts of Greater Vancouver, most notably in the False Creek area adjacent to the downtown, industrial land uses related to the staples economy have given way to condos and live/work spaces. Here, flows of wood products have been replaced by flows of real-estate investment, immigrants, and digitally delivered services, resulting in a dramatically new form of urban (re)development (Hutton, 2008; Olds, 2001). Even the flow of material goods has changed dramatically in the past decades. Today, fewer milled products and more wood pellets and raw logs (Parfitt, 2007) are going east to China

and other emerging economies, as well as south to the United States and other traditional trading partners.

Across the Fraser River from New Westminster, in the edge cities of Surrey and Delta, the infrastructure of a new system of flows is taking shape. Most tangible is the South Fraser Perimeter Road: opened in 2013, the 40-kilometre route is intended to expedite the transport of ocean shipping containers between Deltaport and the CN rail yard in north Surrey, and from there to distribution centres across North America. Funded by both provincial and federal governments, the Perimeter Road is a centrepiece in the Asia-Pacific Gateway and Corridor Initiative designed to "contribute significantly to Canada's competitiveness in the rapidly changing world of global commerce" (Transport Canada, 2007).

At the core of the globalization perspective is the idea that the global flows that connect cities to other places around the world play an important role in shaping those urban places. These flows include products, goods and services, people, finance and investment, ideas, and policies—even diseases and illegal drugs. Global flows are not a new thing. Every city in Canada was formed in relation to some other far-flung location. And flows alone do not have the power to re-shape cities; globalization also involves new sets of social, political, and economic practices, relations, and discourses. Thus, the increasingly global origin and destination of the increased flows, plus their complex network organization, scale and diversity, and the ways people in their cities and regions have both shaped and responded to them, give the globalization perspective its analytical edge.

This chapter endeavours to capture the core of the globalization perspective while also reflecting on some of the debates that have swirled about it. In what follows we will outline some of the dimensions of the heightened global flows and the ways that scholars have theorized about their impact on the city. The globalization perspective is not a single, unified approach to understanding contemporary cities, nor is it without its critics, who assert that local dynamics are of equal if not greater importance. These critics declare that despite all the increased flow, indeed partly because of it, local, city-regional dynamics have gained heightened importance. This is one of the ironies of globalization: when many things are more mobile, some immobile people and places might be bypassed and ignored. However, other immobile practices and assets may become more valuable precisely because they cannot be easily replaced.

Globalization operates unevenly across space; cities do have, and will continue to have, very different experiences. The accelerated flows are structured at various scales, and most do not operate at a truly global scale. Instead, there are important continental (e.g., North American), regional (e.g., Cascadian or Midwestern), metropolitan (e.g., Greater Golden Horseshoe), and trans-oceanic (e.g., Pacific Rim) dimensions to globalization. It makes a difference that Windsor interacts more with Detroit, while Vancouver interacts more with Hong Kong. As cities in India, Brazil, and other emerging economies rise, some will become more closely associated with Canadian cities than others. Even within a given city-region, the effects of global flow are spatially uneven: the core areas of greater Vancouver are more susceptible to flows of people and property investment, while some suburbs are more heavily influenced by the flow of goods.

Today, it is also important to pay attention to the limitations of the globalization perspective. This chapter was written as the global economy emerged hesitantly from the "great recession." In 2009, the volume of merchandise exports declined by 12 per cent and production declined by 5 per cent, although both bounced back in 2010 (WTO, 2011). Trade flows grew more rapidly than the economy overall for most of the post–World War II period, but it remains to be seen whether the current recovery will continue and whether the practices and discourses of globalization will be transformed in the process.

Cities and Flows

You can see patterns of flow similar to those on the Fraser River and the new perimeter road in and around all Canadian cities. Indeed, the roads and highways leading from Toronto, Montreal, Calgary, and Vancouver each follow a familiar transect. Departing from the central city one passes suburbs, agricultural lands, and market towns before reaching such places as Sarnia, Trois-Rivières, Drumheller, and Hope, all once known for the natural resources they contained or to which they gave access. The landscape transitions that you can observe from your vehicle tell one kind of story about the forces shaping our urban agglomerations. It is an unequal—if co-dependent—landscape, knit together by flows of people, money, food, water, energy, and—particularly in the Canadian context—flows of natural resources (cf. Jacobs, 1985; McCann and Gunn, 1998). Some flows can easily be seen on the highway: passenger vehicles, school buses, delivery vans, and logging trucks. Evidence of flow can also be found in connective infrastructure: the highway itself as well as the canalized rivers, railroads, and power lines that run alongside it, and in nodes such as office parks, gas stations, and shopping malls. Some of the flows are not easily observed: natural gas pipelines are buried in underground infrastructure, while exchanges of knowledge, finance, and sharing are subsumed in banking, family, community, and professional social networks.

We can understand quite a lot about the social and economic functioning of our cities by examining these city–metropolitan and regional–hinterland flows, both the daily movements within and around a given city or contiguous metropolitan area, and the less frequent ones between the city and its regional hinterland. Flows are evidence of interaction, of valued relationships between people who are not in constant close proximity. For example, commuting patterns speak volumes about how we organize and separate our work and home lives, just as the log booms that arrive in one place and then leave as wood chips tell us something about the structure of the forestry industry. Very little about these flows is random; often, they are quite stable and durable. An individual commuter might follow the same well-trodden path to work for years. No one builds a pulp mill without first ensuring a continuous availability of feedstock. So flows can help us understand what is happening at the places where they originate and end, and about places in between. Supporting all of these flows are massive investments in infrastructure that, once sunk into the ground, shape and direct future interactions and relationships (Harvey, 1982). Indeed, flows are not passive; they exert an influence by virtue of their constant repetition.

It is thus a remarkable and important thing when flows change; it suggests that something profound has shifted at their origin or their destination, in the nature of their interactions, in the infrastructure and networks that connect them, or in some combination of these. Back on the highway leading from any Canadian city, it is clear that some flows, and some of the infrastructure that supports them, are not exclusively or even primarily related to the daily functioning of the city, the metropolitan area, or its regional hinterland. Instead, we see evidence of global flows that cross one or more international boundaries. Sometimes these global flows rely on the same infrastructure that organizes the more local flows, but they may also have their own new and more specialized network infrastructure (Graham and Marvin, 2001). For example, commuters will share the South

Fraser Perimeter Road with trucks moving ocean shipping containers for a small but vitally important portion of their long journey between remote locations of production in Asia and consumption in central Canada, Chicago, and beyond.

Likewise, airports have expanded to handle more and larger airplanes flying longer distances, but once passengers leave the terminal, they often share the same roads and transit systems as local residents. A distinctive social and economic landscape has emerged that reflects the flows through the airport—more immigrants live in the suburbs and more national distribution headquarters of global firms are located in the industrial parks near major airports. The core areas of the major cities also reflect a new set of flows of people, finance, and urban planning ideas; Canadian downtowns increasingly display less of a national character, becoming more like the cities elsewhere that they both model and inform.

More Flow, Differently Organized

Observations such as these lie at the heart of what we might call the "globalization perspective" that associates globalization with the "accelerated circulation of people, commodities, capital, money, identities and image through global space" (Brenner, 1999: 431). At the core of the globalization perspective in urban studies is the idea that connections and flows between places make a difference to the places they connect (Hall and Hesse, 2013). At least four characteristics of contemporary flows differentiate them from more conventional city–metropolitan and regional–hinterland flows. First, flows have changed qualitatively in regard to novelty and diversity in what is carried and in their more complex, network-based organization. Second, flows have increased quantitatively: more goods, people, and money are moving through our cities. Third, the origins and destinations have changed: it is not that national, provincial, and regional flows have ceased; rather, international flows have become relatively more important. And, those international connections are increasingly with emerging Asian (e.g., Mississauga-based Electrovaya's clean-technology partnerships in India) and South American (e.g., Vancouver-based Teck's mining operations in Chile) economies, supplementing longer-standing connections with Europe and the United States. Fourth, responses to flows—reactive and proactive, resistant and embracing—have become more intense and influential in shaping cities.

Consumer Products and Services

While consumer products with global cachet have been around for centuries, some of globalization's most iconic images are provided by products that are now consciously marketed to global consumers. Of course, McDonald's, Coca-Cola, Canada Dry, Toyota, Microsoft, and any number of consumer electronics companies spring to mind. Yet global consumer products are not only for the mass market; truly global brands are marketed in the luxury automobile, watch and jewellery, clothing, and bottled water markets. Even some consumer services have gone transnational and global, including H&R Block, Manulife, and Marriott, as well as Internet- and call centre-mediated services provided by such firms as Expedia, Amazon, and Visa. Despite their global brand-image, when we scratch the surface we find often that many of these products and services are not truly global: rather, they are heavily customized to meet local and regional cultural and market preferences. Either way, global consumer products and services exert a powerful set of images that reshape local consumption patterns.

Intermediate Goods and Producer Services

Behind all these consumer brands are complex flows of intermediate goods and producer services. Intermediate goods include the raw and bulk materials, parts, and components that are assembled to create consumer products. These components increasingly are organized in supply-chain systems or production networks (Dicken, 2003). The implications of this reorganization for

places in central Canada that are integrated into North American manufacturing industries have been profound. Woudsma (2013) identifies a series of policy responses and infrastructure investments addressed to the challenges of moving goods to, through, and around the Greater Toronto Area. Pressure is constant for improvements in road and border crossing infrastructure to speed the movement of goods within this regional, cross-border production network. These networks are exceedingly complex, and apparently are constantly changing. For example, as automobile assemblers have merged to become dominated by a smaller number of large, global players (e.g., Toyota, GM, VW) and have created common platforms, the tiers of suppliers have also become more hierarchical. First-tier auto component suppliers (e.g., Magna, DENSO, Bosch) are now as big as some of the assemblers they supply. Beneath the assemblers and first-tier suppliers are hundreds of small-component suppliers.

These production networks represent new and more complex organizational forms, and they entail new ways of organizing goods shipment, most notably in the intermodal ocean shipping container (see Levinson, 2006). The word "intermodal" refers to the way that the standard container can be moved from one transport mode to another with unprecedented speed and efficiency. The implications for urban development of this transport revolution, and related changes in freight and logistics, have been enormous (Hall and Hesse, 2013). Some ports have become much larger, serving more extensive hinterlands, and new forms of urban development have appeared, such as the intermodal yard and the suburban warehouse estate (Hesse, 2008; McCalla, Slack, and Comtois, 2001). In other former port locations, vacant waterfront industrial land blights the surrounding neighbourhoods until redevelopment dollars are attracted (Desfor et al., 2010).

Producer services also have been restructured on a global basis: accounting firms such as PricewaterhouseCoopers, advertising firms like Ogilvie & Mather, and banks such as HSBC and Citibank. These firms mobilize flows of finance, information, and highly skilled workers along the networks established by advanced telecommunications and airlines, and are concentrated in just a handful of global cities, primarily London, New York, Hong Kong, Tokyo, and Paris (Taylor, 2005).

People

The flow of people across international borders has always been a central feature of urban development in Canada, but the shift in the 1960s to an immigration policy that favoured human capital (rather than national origin), and subsequent increases in the annual targets, profoundly changed the impact of immigrants on Canadian cities. According to the 2011 National Household Survey (NHS), one in five people living in Canada were immigrants or non-permanent residents. As a result, the nature

and destination of these international movements of people have huge consequences for the geography of the Canadian economy. Immigrants settle overwhelmingly in the gateway cities of Montreal, Toronto, and Vancouver (Hiebert, 2000) (see Kobayashi and Preston, Chapter 8). Although there were some indications in the 2006 census and 2011 NHS of a shift in the settlement of immigrants from the Big Three cities to other metropolitan areas, immigration remains an overwhelmingly large-city phenomenon in Canada.

Table 3.1 shows the percentage of immigrants or non-permanent residents in each province and in the largest city (census metropolitan area or census agglomeration) in each province. Note that the largest city in each province has a higher percentage of immigrants than the province as a whole. Almost half (47.6 per cent) of those living

Table 3.1   Immigrants Concentrate in the Largest Cities

Province/Largest City (CMA/CA)	2011 Population	Per Cent Immigrants and Non-Permanent Residents
Newfoundland and Labrador	507,270	2.1
St John's, NL	193,830	3.7
Nova Scotia	906,175	6.1
Halifax, NS	384,540	9.4
Prince Edward Island	137,375	5.8
Charlottetown, PEI	63,015	8.9
New Brunswick	735,835	4.3
Moncton, NB	135,515	4.7
Quebec	7,732,525	13.5
Montreal, QC	3,752,475	24.1
Ontario	12,651,790	29.6
Toronto, ON	5,521,235	47.6
Manitoba	1,174,345	16.4
Winnipeg, MB	714,635	21.5
Saskatchewan	1,008,760	7.6
Saskatoon, SK	256,435	12.1
Alberta	3,567,980	19.7
Calgary, AB	1,199,125	28.1
British Columbia	4,324,455	29.1
Vancouver, BC	2,280,700	42.3
Canada	**32,852,325**	**21.7**

Source: Author's analysis of the 2011 National Household Survey, Statistics Canada.

in Toronto and two-fifths (42.3 per cent) of those living in Vancouver are immigrants. Meanwhile, we have seen increasing efforts by provincial- and municipal-level governments to develop their own immigration policies (e.g., provincial nominees) and immigrant settlement programs (e.g., the Toronto Regional Immigrant Employment Council; see Lo, 2008).

Immigrants are important not only because of their numbers and selective location but also because of how they profoundly transform places where they settle. Scholars examining cities and regions in the United States have noted that immigrants play an important role in transnational business networks that (re)shape development trajectories at both "ends" of the network (see Lo and Wang, 2007; Saxenian, 2006). Immigrants to Canada once clustered in inner-city **ethnic enclaves** but today settle across metropolitan areas in a more dispersed way (see Hiebert, 2000; Luk, 2007; Ooka, 2007), resulting in urban development patterns that Li (1998) has termed **ethnoburbs**. But movements of people under globalization are not only one-way permanent immigration moves. Canada is a stopping place for **transnational** migrants who may move on to new countries or return to their point of origin (see Kobayashi and Preston, Chapter 8).

Finance

Financial deregulation has come to be regarded as one of the key factors underpinning economic globalization (Dicken, 2003). Changes in banking and foreign exchange regulations made it easier to move money across national borders, much of which has found its way into investments in property developments that have transformed cities around the world. Flows of finance and investment are not blind to the particularities of place: patterns of property investment are highly selective and uneven. When real estate investors enter a new city, it takes time for them to learn about the local market, assemble land, and secure planning permissions; often, they rely on existing social relationships and local partners. Edgington (1996), for example, shows that between 1985 and 1993 Japanese-based real estate investors focused on tourism facilities in Vancouver and surrounding areas frequented by Japanese tourists. Over a similar time span, Olds (2001) traced investment by Hong Kong–based investors in Vancouver's residential real estate. He argues that even vast and fungible financial flows do not simply land in the city to transform its built environment. Rather, these flows are mediated and reshaped by the complex interaction between local and external actors.

Information and Ideas

Much attention has been paid to the role of computing and telecommunications technologies, which allow the rapid transfer of information across the globe (see Castells, 1996). The rapid movement of some—but not all—kinds of information from one place to another certainly has facilitated the emergence of global production alongside, in some cases, actual service networks, and the withdrawal of some production activities from cities in the developed world. Information technologies arguably contribute to relatively more service, cultural, and multi-media production in cities. More rapid and cheaper flows of digital information support other flows of goods, via order and shipment tracking; of people, via electronic messaging and cheaper phone calls home; and of money, via electronic transfers.

Beyond the transfer of information in the form of digital data, globalization is also associated with more rapid flows of ideas. Sometimes, these ideas are directly relevant to urban development, involving linkages between cities through city twinning, exchanges, networking, and even global associations of local governments (see Borja and Castells, 1997). Scholars have begun to pay more attention to the messy process of transferring policies from one jurisdiction to another. For example, Peck and Theodore (2001) have written about the transfer of welfare-to-work policies, while Ward (2006) explored the dispersion of **business improvement areas**. In his study of Vancouver's drug policy, McCann (2008: 2) uses the term "urban policy mobilities" to describe the way "in which policy knowledge and policy models move from city to city." Rejecting any implication that local actors are passive recipients of global ideas, he argues that the how of policy-making in global relational context entails a range of locally based actors, from politicians to policy professionals to activists and drug users, developing connections with experts from elsewhere and with related flows of knowledge in order to operationalize a new strategy to fight drug related harm. (McCann, 2008: 15)

"Nasty" Flows

It comes as no surprise that some undesirable flows—such as pathogens, illicit drugs, weapons, organized crime, human trafficking, and pollutants—are transported via the networks discussed above. These flows also disrespect national borders while favouring urban locations, perhaps in surprising ways. For example, since 2003 the City of Toronto has been exporting its solid waste to dumps in Michigan, allowing more consumption in Toronto but evoking strong opposition from US-based communities. In another example, in their edited volume on the SARS outbreak in cities such as Toronto, Hong Kong, and Singapore, Ali and Keil (2008: 12) point out the following:

[T]he SARS virus represented another flow type that connected global cities. The spread of SARS in this manner therefore underscores the fact that today infectious diseases cannot simply be considered a public health issue that is exclusively confined to the developing world or pegged to a particular spatial scale (whether it be the local, regional, or national).

And in a final example, terrorists have sometimes sought out global cities precisely because they are well-connected places from which media images resound.

The Effects of Flow: Theorizing the Global City

Thinking about globalization's impacts on the city via a list of flows is only a starting point. Having defined globalization as increased flow, we are immediately confronted by more complex questions: Which flows, if any, are more important than others? How do the various flows combine in particular places? Do they influence all cities in similar ways, or is their impact mediated by local forces? What are the actors and forces that underlie the flows? And, most importantly, what are the effects, both positive and negative, of increased flow? While there is no one comprehensive explanation, a number of theorists have attempted to understand the combined effects on the city of these global flows.

The concept of the world city or global city focuses on the role of cities in the organization of international economic activity. In their original statement of the "world city hypothesis," Friedmann and Wolff (1982: 309) argued that cities are nodal points in all those flows described above. Furthermore, some cities occupy a more dominant position than others:

At the apex of this hierarchy are found a small number of massive urban regions that we shall call world cities. Tightly interconnected with each other through decision-making and finance, they constitute a worldwide system of control over production and market expansion.

In the cities that are at the top of this global hierarchy, we expect to find concentrations of command-and-control functions, and advanced financial and other business services.

In giving prominence to the interconnections between dominant places, Friedmann and Wolff were influenced by established theories that emphasized the importance of flows between places tracing back to Sir Peter Hall's observations about a class of world cities, rising out of their respective national urban hierarchies and containing the headquarters or centres of international political, cultural, and economic power (Hall, 1966). Another line of influence was world systems theory (see Wallerstein, 1984), which analyzed the global dimensions of resource flows, dividing nations into an industrialized and democratic core, and a resource-exporting and underdeveloped periphery. Also, Friedmann and Wolff were influenced by the notion of the "new international division of labour," which emphasizes how international corporations separate their functions geographically, placing routine functions in low-cost locations, while keeping more specialized decision-making and control functions in core metropolitan areas (see Massey, 1984).

Friedmann's (1986) follow-up article identified a world city hierarchy, based on large cities' relative concentration of functions such as high finance, transnational corporate headquarters, and international institutions alongside rapid growth of population and of locally based business services, and manufacturing and transport facilities. Toronto is the only Canadian city mentioned by Friedmann; he identifies it as a secondary core city, alongside such cities as Miami, San Francisco, Madrid, and Sydney, but behind such primary cities as London, Paris, New York, Chicago, and Tokyo. This pattern is replicated in much of the subsequent research on "world city rankings"; for example, in Taylor's (2005) taxonomy of leading cities in globalization, Toronto is identified as an "incipient global city," alongside Boston, Chicago, and Madrid, but behind London and New York (the "leading duo") and Tokyo, Los Angeles, Paris, and San Francisco.

More important than the rankings are Friedmann's seven "theses" about how cities are affected by their place in, and relationship to, the world city hierarchy. A recurring theme is that world cities are characterized by a great degree of internal polarization (see Walks, Chapter 9). While "(w)orld cities are major sites for the concentration and accumulation of international capital" (1986: 73), they are

> characterized by a dichotomized labour force: on the one hand, a high percentage of professionals specialized in control functions and, on the other, a vast army of low-skilled workers engaged in manufacturing, personal services and the hotel, tourist

and entertainment industries that cater to the privileged classes for whose sake the world city primarily exists. (1986: 73)

Furthermore, "(w)orld cities are points of destination for large numbers of both domestic and/or international migrants" (1986: 75). These immigrants have unmet social needs, so "[w]orld city growth generates social costs at rates that tend to exceed the fiscal capacity of the state" (1986: 77).

Other researchers, most notably Sassen (1991), have picked up these themes, chronicling the rising inequality in most global cities. One challenge in interpreting these arguments in Canada is that Toronto is the only Canadian city with a claim to global status. However, other theories that look beyond the iconic global cities also predict rising polarization in the most globally connected places. Castells (1996), for example, has argued that the global economy is organized through a series of information networks. The fortunes of places are increasingly determined by their connections to these networks and while all places potentially connect to these networks, many may be bypassed. A central element of Castells's ideas about the impact of global flows is unevenness, in both spatial and social domains. In the social domain, Castells supports much of what Friedmann and Sassen argue, especially their contention that the global economy is associated with highly unequal labour markets. He also argues that the spatial organization of cities is likely to be highly uneven because, while some parts connect to global networks, other parts of the city are actively excluded from them (see Borja and Castells, 1997). More recent scholarship has moved away from the idea that some parts of the city are globally connected and others are not, instead emphasizing that while all cities are globally connected, not all connections are equally beneficial. For example, the congestion, pollution, and other negative externalities associated with the physical flows of goods are often unevenly distributed across metropolitan areas (De Lara, 2013).

The argument that polarization is most severe in the largest and most globally connected places resonates in the Canadian urban system. Among the major Canadian cities, a general increase in income inequality is evident. Recent studies by Hulchanski (2010) in Toronto and by Ley and Lynch (2012) in Vancouver have used the metaphor of the "three cities" to trace how rising income inequality since 1970 is contributing to polarization between wealthier neighbourhoods, typically near the urban core, and disadvantaged neighbourhoods, often located on the metropolitan periphery. A key factor driving this inequality is the fact that, since the 1980s, immigrant labour market incomes have lagged behind those of non-immigrants. Hall and Khan (2008) show that the immigrant earnings penalty is greatest in the largest Canadian cities where there are the most immigrants.

In Canada, too, increasing income inequalities are exacerbated by rapidly rising rents and/or house prices in the largest cities, which means increasing housing-affordability challenges (Bunting, Walks, and Filion, 2004; Moore and Skaburskis, 2004). In 2008, at the height of the boom in the oil patch, the president and CEO of the Calgary Chamber of Commerce commented that "(t)he current price of housing relative to incomes poses a significant challenge to Calgary businesses seeking to attract and retain employees—the number one issue confronting Chamber members" (Calgary Chamber of Commerce, 2008). Overall, there are indications that the trends in social inequality and housing unaffordability are combining to create some especially deprived neighbourhoods in the most global of Canadian cities. Walks and Bourne (2006) examine whether **ghettos**, neighbourhoods that combine racial or ethnic segregation with concentrated poverty, are emerging in Canadian cities. While they find some evidence of emerging ghettos in Toronto, they show that increased income inequality has not (yet?) led to the formation of ghettos in Canadian cities. Instead, they conclude that "the confluence of increasing income inequality and the particular geography of housing in each given place, including that of tenure, form and price, are more important in determining overall patterns of segregation" (Walks and Bourne, 2006: 295) (see Walks, Chapter 9).

This last observation highlights one of the key challenges facing the "world city hypothesis," namely, how to relate outcomes in specific places to the general increase in global flow. What are we to make of observations that flows of immigrants and rising labour market inequality do not necessarily lead to the predicted outcomes? One way of dealing with this challenge is to recognize the increasing complexity and fragmentation of the numerous flows that combine in unpredictable and often temporary ways under globalization. Appadurai (1996), for example, writes of the "disjunctive order" of the new global cultural economy (1996: 32). Instead of trying to relate globalization to a small number of potential outcomes, he developed an overlapping typology of different "-scapes" that are created by global flows. These are (1) ethnoscapes, involving the movement of people; (2) mediascapes, involving the creation and circulation of images; (3) technoscapes, involving mobile technology and information; (4) financescapes, involving global financial capital; and (5) ideoscapes, involving political ideals and ideologies. Appadurai further argues that understanding the impact of global flows on a given city requires understanding the ways in which diverse flows come together in different combinations and interact uniquely with particular localities. Likewise, Norcliffe (2001: 27) also argues that "there is not one narrative but many regional and local narratives that describe Canada's global connections, all of which are interrelated, with each one having greatest resonance for certain groups, in specific regions, at particular times." The implication is that comprehending the complexity of globalization means thinking locally as well as globally.

Reasserting the Local

The insistence on the importance of local dynamics despite increased global flows echoes older debates about the relative importance of those factors that make a place or region distinctive, and those factors or processes that connect places or regions. One such debate involved two famous

American economists, Douglas North and Charles Tiebout, in discussion about the origins of regional economic growth and development. Drawing on the ideas of, among others, Canadian Harold Innis (1930) about the society-shaping role of export staples, North (1955) argued that regional economies in the new world all developed in relation to some far-flung place. After initially exporting only a small number of resource-based products, economies would then diversify and urbanize. Tiebout's (1956) response was to insist that there is nothing automatic in the relationship between exports and regional growth; local conditions influence the success of the exporting enterprise, and only some places are able to capture and reinvest the value created by those exports. So regional development depends on exports; but exports are themselves dependent on regional qualities. This "chicken and egg" debate about how cities both make flows and are made by them continues in a variety of forums, with most scholars accepting the perspective that both local and global dimensions are important (see Lipietz, 1993).

A further complication in this debate is that what we call "local" (or, more precisely, "not global") today may have altered by tomorrow. Cox (1997) and others point out that spatial scales are not static and that under globalization various groups may try to redefine them in order to advance their agenda. Returning to Vancouver and the new perimeter road, a local-centred perspective would respond to the globalization perspective by observing that the flow of containerized goods by itself did not create the Asia-Pacific Gateway and its constituent warehouses, terminals, and new highways. Rather, these physical investments in the built environment are the result of a lot of hard work—both to assemble the finance and overcome community opposition—by those whose interests are served by more goods movement (Hall and Clark, 2010). For example, the Greater Vancouver Gateway Council, a coalition of port-related industries, lobbied for several years to attract government support for the infrastructure now under construction. These interests themselves were strengthened by changes in trade regulations and

the rise of global production systems that stimulated more trade-supporting infrastructure. They were also strengthened by alliances with regional public-sector agencies and provincial governments across western Canada. In the process, Vancouver-based actors engaged others outside of the Lower Mainland, thus creating new scales of activity.

How much weight, then, should we place on local versus global dynamics? It surely makes a difference which flows we are analyzing and against which specific urban developments. For example, in trying to explain why dynamic economic growth has remained concentrated in just a few regional clusters, scholars have focused on the factors that promote learning, innovation, and risk-taking—conditions not easily replicated that are the outcomes of distinctive local social relationships (see Storper, 1997). Although clusters are all different, each has developed through a combination of external sources of knowledge alongside local mechanisms of knowledge sharing and deployment. Canadian scholars have drawn on these ideas to understand clusters ranging from aerospace in Montreal to wireless telecommunications in Waterloo (Wolfe and Gertler, 2004).

However, this kind of theory is not as good at providing an account of whole cities and the multiplicity of flows and local dynamics that shape them. One type of argument made against the idea that there is something distinctive about "the global city" is the "ordinary cities" perspective (see Amin and Graham, 1997; Robinson, 2006). Developing out of criticisms of globalization perspectives that tend to focus on one or two attributes that make cities more or less competitive with other cities as sites for innovation or investment, Amin and Graham argue against concentrating

> exclusively on one element of urban life and city development 'culture,' social polarization, housing, industrial districts, politics, transport, governance, property development, planning and so on. Thus the very essence of the city—the concentration of diverse relational intersections between and within such activities and

elements—tends to be lost. Oscillations between dire predictions of urban doom and optimistic portrayals of an urban renaissance serve further to confuse. (Amin and Graham, 1997: 411)

Similarly, Robinson (2006), whose work is informed by cities in both developed and developing countries, insists that actual cities are diverse and heterogeneous. Rather than cities reflecting the impact of just a handful of global forces, what actually happens in a particular place is the result of the "unique" assembly of local and global social, institutional, cultural, and economic webs.

Echoes of this perspective can be found in recent writing about Canadian cities. Examining the case of Hong Kong immigrants in Vancouver, Mitchell argues that "certain kinds of flows . . . are central to neoliberal state formations but also are deeply disruptive to the national liberal, social, and political narratives as they have developed and become embedded through time in the crusty layers of urban social life" (2004: 3). The implication of this line of argument is that globalization impacts the city, not only through a process by which new, extra-local, and de-territorialized flows displace existing social relations. Global flows, such as those embodied in new immigrants with their own ideas, investments, and practices, also re-constitute spatial arrangements by working through existing and newly emerging social practices and politics.

Global and Local: Caveat and Conclusion

While Mitchell's case study points to the disturbing reactions of some Vancouverites to new immigrants, her conclusion is hopeful in the sense that it leaves the outcome of globalization open-ended. Thus, from cities in the Prairie provinces of Canada, so often portrayed in pessimistic terms, comes Silver's (2008) optimistic analysis of inner-city development in Winnipeg and Saskatoon. Silver relates the problems of concentrated

poverty, especially among Aboriginal residents, to wider global and regional economic restructuring processes, but argues that a distinctive form of development is emerging in response:

It is a unique form of development that has emerged largely spontaneously from the harsh realities of urban poverty in inner-city neighbourhoods, and that has been driven for the most part by inner-city residents themselves. Out of this process there has been created in Winnipeg's inner city, and is emerging in Saskatoon's core neighbourhoods, an "infrastructure" of community-based organizations with a particular way of working, guided by a distinctive and commonly-held philosophy. This infrastructure holds considerable promise for resolving the complex and now deeply entrenched problems arising from spatially concentrated racialized poverty, if it can continue to be patiently nurtured, and if it can be linked to an expanded and revised role for the state. (Silver, 2008: 1)

In conclusion, it seems sensible to accept the fundamental assertion of the globalization perspective, namely that the flows that connect cities to other places around the world play an important role in shaping those urban places. At the same time, local dynamics—both the unique constellation of flows in particular places and the way actors in those localities shape, understand, and respond to those flows—are vital to understanding actual patterns of urban development. And understanding the processes of global–local interaction is essential to good analysis and policy-making.

We also need to be aware that globalization, or at least some of the most significant global flows, has its limits in a time of economic recession, climate change, and questioning of the carbon-based economy. Canadian philosopher John Ralston Saul's 2005 book, *The Collapse of Globalism: And the Reinvention of the World*, seems especially prescient. Saul noted an emerging locally and nationally based countermovement to economic globalization and the neo-liberal spending policies, deregulation, and trade liberalization that have accompanied it. The potential demise of this set of economic policies and practices will surely change the relationship between cities and the global economy; but it will not change the fact that all Canadian cities have been, and will continue to be, shaped through their interaction with other, more- or less-remote places.

Review Questions

1. Identify major forces of globalization that have influenced Canadian cities.
2. How do forces of globalism interact with more regional or local forces?
3. Give an example of a global force that has impacted most Canadian cities; show how the impact is different in different places.

References

Ali, S.H., and R. Keil. eds. 2008. *Networked Disease: Emerging Infections in the Global City*. Malden, MA: Blackwell.

Amin, A. and S. Graham. 1997. "The ordinary city," *Transactions of the Institute of British Geographers* 22: 411–29.

Appadurai, A. 1996. *Modernity at Large: Cultural Dimensions of Globalization*. Minneapolis, MN: University of Minnesota Press.

Borja, J., and M. Castells. 1997. *Local and Global: Management of Cities in the Information Age*. London: Earthscan.

Brenner, N. 1999. "Globalization as re-territorialization: The re-scaling of urban governance in the European Union," *Urban Studies* 36: 431–51.

Bunting, T., A.R. Walks, and P. Filion. 2004. "The uneven geography of housing affordability stress in Canadian metropolitan areas," *Housing Studies* 19: 361–93.

Calgary Chamber of Commerce. 2008. "Chamber research report recommends solutions to Calgary's long-term housing affordability challenge," news release, 1 May. At: www.calgarychamber.com/resources/docs/May 1-Chamber Releases Major Calgary Housing Market Study.pdf

Castells, M. 1996. *The Rise of the Network Society*. Cambridge, MA: Blackwell.

Cox, K.R. ed. 1997. *Spaces of Globalization: Reasserting the Power of the Local*. New York: Guildford.

De Lara, J.D. 2013. "Goods movement and metropolitan inequality: Global restructuring, commodity flows and metropolitan development," in Hall and Hesse (2013).

Desfor, G., J. Laidley, D. Schubert, and Q. Stevens, eds. 2010. *Transforming Urban Waterfronts: Fixity and Flow*. Abingdon: Routledge.

Dicken, P. 2003. *Global Shift: Reshaping the Global Economic Map in the 21st Century*, 4th edn. New York: Guildford.

Edgington, D.W. 1996. "Japanese real estate investment in Canadian cities and regions, 1985–1993," *Canadian Geographer* 40: 292–305.

Fong, E., and C. Luk, eds. 2007. *Chinese Ethnic Businesses: Global and Local Perspectives*. London and New York: Routledge.

Friedmann, J. 1986. "The world city hypothesis," *Development and Change* 17: 69–84.

——, and G. Wolff. 1982. "World city formation: An agenda for research and action," *International Journal of Urban and Regional Research* 6: 309–44.

Graham, S., and S. Marvin. 2001. *Splintering Urbanism: Networked Infrastructures, Technological Mobilities and the Urban Condition*. New York: Routledge.

Hall, P.G. 1966. *The World Cities*. New York: McGraw-Hill.

Hall, P.V., and A. Clark. 2010. "Maritime ports and the politics of reconnection," in Desfor et al. (2010).

Hall, P.V., and A. Khan. 2008. "Differences in hi-tech and native-born immigrant wages and earnings across Canadian cities," *Canadian Geographer* 52: 271–90.

Hall, P.V., and M. Hesse, eds. 2013. *Cities, Regions and Flows*. Abingdon: Routledge.

Harvey, D. 1982. *The Limits to Capital*. New York: Oxford University Press.

Heisz, A. 2006. *Canada's Global Cities: Socio-economic Conditions in Montreal, Toronto and Vancouver*. Ottawa: Statistics Canada.

Hesse, M. 2008. *The City as Terminal: The Urban Context of Logistics and Freight Transport*. Aldershot: Ashgate.

Hiebert, D. 2000. *The Social Geography of Immigration and Urbanization in Canada: A Review and Interpretation*. Vancouver, BC: Vancouver Centre of Excellence on Immigration and Integration, Research on Immigration and Integration in the Metropolis, Working Paper #00–12.

Hulchanski, D. 2010. *The Three Cities Within Toronto: Income Polarization among Toronto's Neighbourhoods, 1970–2005*. Toronto: Cities Centre, University of Toronto.

Hutton, T. 2008. *The New Economy of the Inner City: Restructuring, Regeneration, and Dislocation in the 21st Century Metropolis*. New York: Routledge.

Innis, H. 1930. *The Fur Trade in Canada*. Toronto: University of Toronto Press.

Jacobs, J. 1985. *Cities and the Wealth of Nations*. New York: Vintage Books.

Levinson, M. 2006. *The Box: How the Shipping Container Made the World Smaller and the World Economy Bigger*. Princeton, NJ: Princeton University Press.

Ley, D., and N. Lynch. 2012. *Divisions and Disparities in Lotus-Land: Socio-Spatial Income Polarization in Greater Vancouver, 1970–2005*. Toronto: Cities Centre, University of Toronto.

Li, W. 1998. "Los Angeles's Chinese ethnoburb: From ethnic service center to global economy outpost," *Urban Geography* 19: 502–17.

Lipietz, A. 1993. "The local and the global: Regional individuality or inter-regionalism?" *Transactions of the Institute of British Geographers* 18: 8–18.

Lo, L. 2008. "DiverCity Toronto: Canada's premier gateway city," in M. Price and L. Benton-Short, eds., *Migrants to the Metropolis: The Rise of Immigrant Gateway Cities*. Syracuse, NY: Syracuse University Press.

——, and S. Wang. 2007. "The new Chinese business sector in Toronto: A spatial and structural anatomy of medium-sized and large firms," in Fong and Luk (2007).

Luk, C. 2007. "The global–local nexus and ethnic business location," in Fong and Luk (2007).

Massey, D. 1984. *Spatial Division of Labour: Social Structures and the Geography of Production*. London: Methuen.

McCalla R.J., B. Slack, and C. Comtois. 2001. "Intermodal freight terminals: Locality and industrial linkages," *Canadian Geographer* 45, 3: 404–14.

McCann, E.J. 2008. "Expertise, truth, and urban policy mobilities: Global circuits of knowledge in the development of Vancouver, Canada's "four pillar" drug strategy, *Environment and Planning A* 40: 885–904.

McCann, L.D., and A.M. Gunn. 1998. *Heartland and Hinterland: A Regional Geography of Canada*. Scarborough, ON: Prentice-Hall Canada.

Mitchell, K. 2004. *Crossing the Neoliberal Line: Pacific Rim Migration and the Metropolis*. Philadelphia, PA: Temple University Press.

Moore, E., and A. Skaburskis. 2004. "Canada's increasing housing affordability burdens," *Housing Studies* 19: 395–413.

Norcliffe, G. 2001. "Canada in a global economy," *Canadian Geographer* 45: 14–30.

North, D. 1955. "Location theory and regional economic growth," *Journal of Political Economy* 63: 243–58.

Olds, K. 2001. *Globalization and Urban Change: Capital, Culture and Pacific Rim Mega-projects*. Oxford: Oxford University Press.

Ooka, E. 2007. "Going to malls, being Chinese? Ethnic identity among Chinese youths in Toronto's ethnic economy," in Fong and Luk (2007).

Parfitt, B. 2007. *Wood Waste and Log Exports on the BC Coast*. Vancouver, BC: Canadian Centre for Policy Alternatives—BC Office.

Peck, J., and N. Theodore. 2001. "Exporting workfare/importing welfare-to-work: Exploring the politics of Third Way policy transfer," *Political Geography* 20, 427–60.

Robinson, J. 2006. *Ordinary Cities: Between Modernity and Development*. New York: Routledge.

Saul, J.R. 2005. *The Collapse of Globalism: And the Reinvention of the World*. Toronto: Viking Canada.

Sassen, S. 1991. *The Global City: New York, London, Tokyo*. Princeton, NJ: Princeton University Press.

Saxenian, A. 2006. *The New Argonauts: Regional Advantage in a Global Economy*. Cambridge, MA: Harvard University Press.

Silver, J. 2008. *The Inner Cities of Saskatoon and Winnipeg: A New and Distinctive Form of Development*. Ottawa: Canadian Centre for Policy Alternatives. At: www.policyalternatives.ca/documents/Manitoba_Pubs/2008/Inner_Cities_of_Saskatoon_and_Winnipeg.pdf

Storper, M. 1997. *The Regional World: Territorial Development in a Global Economy*. New York: Guildford.

Taylor, P. 2005. "Leading world cities: Empirical evaluations of urban nodes in multiple networks," *Urban Studies* 42: 1593–1608.

Tiebout, C. 1956. "Exports and regional economic growth," *Journal of Political Economy* 64: 160–4.

Transport Canada. 2007. "Canada's new government announces projects for the Asia-Pacific Gateway and Corridor Initiative," press release. Ottawa: Government of Canada. At: www.tc.gc.ca/mediaroom/releases/nat/2007/07-gc016e.htm#bg

Walks, R.A., and L.S. Bourne. 2006. "Ghettos in Canada's cities? Racial segregation, ethnic enclaves and poverty concentration in Canadian urban areas," *Canadian Geographer* 50: 273–97.

Wallerstein, I. 1984. *The Politics of the World Economy*. Cambridge: Cambridge University Press.

Ward, K. 2006. "'Policies in motion,' urban management and state restructuring: The trans-local expansion of Business Improvement Districts," *International Journal of Urban and Regional Research* 30: 54–75.

Wolfe, D., and M. Gertler. 2004. "Clusters from the inside and out: Local dynamics and global linkages," *Urban Studies* 41: 1071–93.

Woudsma, C. 2013. "Freight, land and local economic development," in Hall and Hesse (2013).

World Trade Organization (WTO). 2011. International trade statistics 2011, author's analysis of Appendix Table A1a. At: www.wto.org/english/res_e/statis_e/its2012_e/its12_appendix_e.htm

Getting Serious about Urban Sustainability: Eco-Footprints and the Vulnerability of Twenty-First-Century Cities

4

WILLIAM E. REES

At the heart of this assessment is a stark warning. Human activity is putting such a strain on the natural functions of the Earth that the ability of the planet's ecosystems to sustain future generations can no longer be taken for granted. (MEA, 2005: 5)

Introduction: Framing the Analysis

This chapter is concerned with the long-term sustainability of cities and urban civilization. My starting premise is that because of accelerating global ecological change, cities everywhere are facing unprecedented challenges to their functional integrity, even survival. Unprecedented challenges require unprecedented solutions. In keeping with this reality, I depart from most urban scholarship, which assumes a humanities and social-science perspective. Instead, I approach "the urban question" from a mainly biophysical point of view. Accelerating global change makes clear that society will not be able to ensure the sustainability of cities without a much fuller understanding of cities as ecological entities subject to biophysical laws.

With this in mind, the chapter begins with a brief consideration of the organic origins of cities and their subsequent evolution. Permanent settlements became possible as a result of technology-induced changes in the ecological "niche" of humans 10 millennia ago. However, the subsequent alienation of urban techno-industrial society from nature has produced modern cities that are not only incomplete as human ecosystems but that exist in essentially hostile relationship to the natural ecosystems that sustain them.

The next section uses ecological footprint analysis to illustrate the ecological "load" that inhabitants of modern cities impose on the natural world. The key question is this: How much of the surface of the earth do we occupy *ecologically* to sustain our material lifestyles? Pay attention, urban planners (also see Moos et al., 2006)! The eco-footprints of typical cities are hundreds of times larger than their political or built-up areas. In any functionally meaningful sense, does not this "hinterland" area constitute urban land as much as a parking lot does within the city limits?

I then consider the increasing vulnerability of modern cities to global ecological change. Urbanization represents the greatest mass migration of people ever. More people will be added to the world's cities in the first three or four decades of the twenty-first century, mostly through immigration, than had accumulated on the entire planet by the mid-twentieth century. But this trend implicitly assumes climate stability, adequate resources, and geopolitical calm. Just how secure will the world's six billion urbanites be if cities are besieged by climate change, rising sea levels, energy and food shortages, and violent conflict by mid- to late-century?

The final section examines the ecological leverage that cities can exercise in society's general quest for sustainability. What can cities do to decrease their eco-footprints and enhance their own prospects? How might rethinking the "city-as-ecosystem" help humanity to live sustainably within the carrying capacity of the earth?

Setting the Ecological Stage

While few people think of them as such, cities are biophysical entities. The fundamentally *organic* nature of cities is underscored by the fact that permanent settlements are actually a product of a change in human ecological circumstances. "The city" is an emergent phenomenon made possible by people's adoption of agriculture 10 millennia ago. Humanity's slowly developing ability to produce regular food surpluses triggered a truly "autocatalytic process—one that catalyses itself in a positive feedback cycle, going faster and faster once it has started" (Diamond, 1997). More food made higher population densities possible, enabled large permanent settlements with the specialized skills and inventiveness this implies, and shortened the time-spacing between children. This, in turn, enabled the higher populations to produce still more people, which increased both the demand for food and the technical and organizational capacity to produce it.

The first small, more-or-less permanent human settlements appeared barely 9000 years ago and another 3500 years passed before the first definable cities, with socially stratified societies and marked division of labour, emerged in southwest Asia (today's Middle East) around 5500 BC. In short, while we tend today to take the existence of cities for granted, they actually have a remarkably short history. They have been part of human reality for merely three per cent of the time since "modern" humans—*Homo sapiens*—stumbled onto the world stage about 250,000 years ago.

But there is more to this story than "surplus food leads to urban civilization." The shift from the nomadic hunter-gatherer lifestyle to a more agriculture-based, settlement-centred way of life represents a major transformation of human ecological reality and may well constitute the most critical branch-point to date in the evolution of *Homo sapiens*. First, consider that with large-scale agriculture, people switched from merely taking what wild nature had to offer to manipulating entire landscapes in order to redirect as much as possible of nature's productivity to strictly human ends. In this way, humans became the most significant "patch-disturbance" species on earth (Rees, 2000). Indeed, agriculture and agriculture-induced urbanization constitute a great leap forward in an accelerating process that has gradually seen humans become the most important geological force changing the face of the planet.

Second—and, regrettably, given the enormous ecological impacts of industrial cities—the very process of urbanization insulates city-dwellers from the negative consequences of their own ecological dysfunction. The migration of people to cities distances them physically from the ecosystems that support them and, even more important, from the direct negative consequences of subsequent landscape degradation. In short, the separation of people's lives and livelihoods *from* the land diminishes urbanites' sense of felt connectedness *to* the land—humanity's apparent abandonment of the countryside critically reshapes people's spatial relationships and psychological sensitivities to nature. Thus doubly blinded, many urbanites, particularly in high-income developed countries, are blissfully unaware that they remain ecological actors and fail to see the growing threat their consumer lifestyles pose to the distant ecosystems on which they remain dependent.

Modern humans' failure to appreciate themselves as ecological beings actually reflects a deep cognitive bias. Our evolving techno-scientific paradigm has erected such a powerful perceptual barrier between humanity and the rest of the natural world that human "exceptualism" has become a defining characteristic of industrial society. Certainly, modern urbanites do not generally think of "the city" in biological terms. Even urban scholars have only recently acknowledged and begun to study the human ecological dimensions of urbanization and cities. Most discussions of urbanization still view the process mainly as a demographic or economic phenomenon made possible by the intensification of agriculture, increased resource productivity, and improvements in communications and transportation technology. Cities are perceived as concentrations of people; as areas dominated by the built environment; as places of intense social interaction; as the seats of government; as hotbeds of political conflict; as the nexus of national transportation and communication systems; and as the engines of national economic growth—but rarely as biological phenomena. Some observers actually—and falsely—interpret urbanization as evidence that humanity is *transcending* nature, that the human enterprise is "decoupling" from "the environment."

This chapter is intended to address this perceptual gap. A major purpose is to show that, while urbanization represents a dramatic shift in urbanites' spatial/psychological relationships to the land, *there is no corresponding change in eco-functional relationships*. Indeed, far from reducing people's dependence on productive ecosystems, urbanization generally implies an increase in our per capita ecological footprints. From this perspective, urbanization and the modern city remain bio-ecological phenomena fully explicable only in light of human evolutionary history and fundamental biophysical laws. Failure to understand ourselves and our cities as ecological entities will doom our quest for global sustainability and expose an increasingly vulnerable global urban civilization to the spectre of collapse.

Cities and the Human Ecosystem

By now almost everyone interested in cities is familiar with the term urban ecosystem. Prominent urban analysts have long recognized that the city could be conceived as an ecosystem (e.g., Douglas, 1981), and today there is even a scientific journal called *Urban Ecosystems*. Nevertheless, the concept itself remains ambiguous. For example, a majority of the papers in *Urban Ecosystems* focus on the impacts of urbanization on plants and animals or on remnant "natural" ecosystems within the city. This shows that most natural scientists who study urban ecosystems cast the city as a somewhat unnatural habitat for *other* species.[1] To ecologists, the urban ecosystem consists of the assemblage of non-human species in the city, and the purpose of their inquiries is to determine how these species have adapted to the structural and chemical characteristics of the "built environment" (Rees, 2003). Remarkably, humans are excluded from the analysis except as their actions affect these other species. This conception of urban ecosystems is a clear reflection of Cartesian dualism or human exceptualism, which means people are viewed as separate from nature in the human mind.

On the other hand, those who do acknowledge humans as the major ecological actors in the city err if they see "the city" per se as the modern human ecosystem. To qualify as a complete human ecosystem, a city would have to contain a sufficient complement of producer organisms (green plants), macro-consumers (animals, including humans), micro-consumers (bacteria and fungi), and abiotic factors to support its human population indefinitely. Any complete ecosystem consists of a self-organizing, self-sustaining assemblage of living species existing in complementary relationships with each other and the physical environment. Ecosystems are energized by the unidirectional cascade of solar energy and maintained in perpetuity by the continuous recycling of chemical nutrients.

Clearly, from this perspective no modern city qualifies as a functionally complete human ecosystem. Some essential defining parts are missing altogether (e.g., virtually the entire relevant producer complex), and others (micro-consumers) are insufficiently abundant for functional integrity. Just as significantly, the spatial separation of people from the rest of their supportive ecosystems (e.g., agricultural and forest lands) inhibits the on-site application of organic matter and the recycling of phosphorus, nitrogen, and other nutrients contained in human wastes. In effect, urbanization transforms local, integrated, cyclical ecological production systems into global, horizontally disintegrated, unidirectional, throughput systems (Rees, 1997). Ironically, the resultant continuous "leakage" of nutrients from farmland in shipments of food to cities (and ultimately the sea) threatens to undermine organic agriculture even as it gains ground in the urban marketplace.

In a crude but useful metaphor, the city might be described as a human feedlot (Rees, 2003). Like cities, feedlots are densely populated almost entirely by a single macro-consumer species—for example, cattle (or pigs, or chickens, which today are raised using even more constrained industrial methods). However, the grain fields that produce the feed for feedlot animals may be located hundreds of kilometres from the feedlot itself. Also missing are adequate populations of micro-consuming decomposers. Having separated the functionally inseparable, industrial feedlots short-circuit even the possibility of within-system decomposition and nutrient recycling. As a result, vast quantities of manure containing vital nutrients are rarely re-deposited on range- or cropland for nutrient recycling but, rather, are disposed of inappropriately, contaminating soils and surface and subsurface waters at a distance and over large areas.[2]

Of course, cities are more ecologically complex than feedlots but, in structural terms, cities are to their human inhabitants what feedlots are to cattle. The largest and functionally most important components of urbanites' ecosystems—the assemblage of producer organisms that feed city-dwellers and provide them with oxygen, most of the micro-consumers that complete their nutrient cycles, and the various sub-systems that perform myriad other vital life-support functions—all are found in rural "environments" increasingly scattered all over the planet. Also, like feedlots, cities generate enormous quantities of waste that cannot be assimilated within those cities, making them the major source of pollution of the global commons. In short, cities are nodes of intense resource consumption and waste generation entirely dependent for their survival on the productive and assimilative capacities of ecosystems increasingly located at great distances from

the cities themselves. In both ecological and spatial terms, "the city" constitutes only a small fraction of the total urban-centred human ecosystem.

The Human Ecological Footprint

The next questions are these: Just how extensive is the human ecosystem? How much of the productive capacity of the ecosphere do humans need to sustain urban industrial society? One way to approach these questions is through ecological footprint analysis (Rees, 1992; 2013; Wackernagel and Rees, 1996). A variant and extension of energy and material flows assessment (Haberl et al., 2004), eco-footprint analysis starts from a comprehensive inventory of the annualized energy and material flows required to support any specified population—an individual, a city, a nation, or the entire world. We also quantify the flow of waste carbon dioxide generated in this production/consumption process (carbon dioxide is the greatest waste by weight of industrial countries, hence the "carbon footprint"). Eco-footprinting is further based on the fact that many of these material and energy flows can be converted into a corresponding area of productive land and water ecosystems. Thus, we formally define the ecological footprint of a specified population as follows:

> The area of land and water ecosystems required, on a continuous basis, to produce the resources that the population consumes and to assimilate its (carbon-dioxide) wastes, wherever on Earth the relevant land/water is located (see Rees 2013; 2006).[3]

The area of a population's theoretical eco-footprint (EF) depends on four factors: the population size; the average material standard of living; the productivity of the land/water base (whether local or "imported" in trade goods); and the efficiency of resource harvesting, processing, and use. Regardless of the relative importance of these factors and how they interact, every population has an ecological footprint. In addition, the productive land and water area captured by eco-footprint analysis represents much of the "natural capital" (the productive ecosystems or *biocapacity*) required to meet the study population's consumptive and assimilative demand.[4] One can also interpret the eco-footprint in thermodynamic terms as the area of natural "solar collector" needed to regenerate the biomass and chemical energy equivalents of the useful resources and fossil energy consumed and dissipated by the study population.

Significantly, population EFs constitute mutually exclusive appropriations of nature. The biocapacity used by one population is not available for use by another. True, the grain grown in a particular region may wind up in export shipments to several countries, but the total area of cropland involved is the sum of the areas required by the individual populations. In the final analysis, *all human populations are competing for the productive capacity (biocapacity) of the earth.*

Table 4.1 shows the equivalence-adjusted[5] per capita EFs and domestic biocapacities for a selection of countries from among the richest to among the poorest using 2008 data from the *Living Planet Report 2012* (WWF, 2012). Note the considerably larger load imposed on the ecosphere by wealthy, mainly urban consumers compared to that imposed by mainly rural peasants. The citizens of

Table 4.1 The Eco-Footprints and Biocapacities of Selected Nations

Country	Per Capita Eco-Footprint (global ha)	Per Capita Domestic Biocapacity (gha)	Overshoot Factor
World	**2.7**	**1.8**	**1.5**
United States	7.2	3.9	1.8
Australia	6.7	14.6	0.5
Canada	6.4	15.0	0.4
Netherlands	6.3	1.0	6.3
Greece	4.9	1.6	3.1
France	4.9	3.0	1.6
United Kingdom	4.7	1.5	3.1
Germany	4.6	1.9	2.4
Japan	4.2	0.6	7.0
Malaysia	3.9	2.4	1.6
Hungary	3.5	2.8	1.3
Mexico	3.3	1.5	2.2
Brazil	2.9	9.6	0.3
Thailand	2.5	1.1	2.3
China	2.1	0.9	2.3
Peru	2.0	3.9	0.5
Nigeria	1.4	0.9	1.6
Ethiopia	1.1	0.7	1.6
Indonesia	1.1	1.4	0.8
India	0.9	0.4	2.3
Bangladesh	0.7	0.3	2.3
Afghanistan	0.5	0.4	1.3

Source: Data extracted from WWF (2012).

wasteful, high-income countries like Canada and the US have average EFs of six to ten global hectares (gha), or up to 20 times larger than the EFs of the citizens of the world's poorest countries, such as Bangladesh and Afghanistan. European countries and Japan typically have per capita EFs in the four to six gha range. China is fairly representative of the emerging economies, which show rapidly growing EFs of 1.5 to 3 gha. These data also reflect the global income gap: the richest 20 per cent of the human family spend more than 70 per cent of world income; the poorest 20 per cent subsist on less than 2 per cent (Ortiz and Cummins, 2011).

The final column of Table 4.1 shows each country's "overshoot factor." This is a simple ratio of the national average eco-footprint compared to per capita domestic biocapacity. Countries with overshoot factors larger than one impose a greater burden on the ecosphere than could be supported by their domestic ecosystems. These countries are at least partially dependent on trade and on exploitation of the global commons to maintain their current lifestyles (i.e., their average per capita consumption levels). The Netherlands, for example, uses six times as much productive land/ water outside its borders as is found within the country. Japan's demand for biocapacity is seven times its domestic supply. Both the US and China are also significantly in overshoot. All such countries are running "ecological deficits" with the rest of the world.

A few countries with overshoot ratios less than one are living within their "natural incomes" and thus seem to have ecological surpluses. They only *seem* to have surpluses, however, because the extra biocapacity in most cases is being traded away to cover the ecological deficits of other countries. The agricultural, forestry, and fisheries surpluses of Canada, for example, serve a large export market. Trade, therefore, contributes proportionately to the ongoing degradation of the nation's soils, forests, and fish stocks (Kissinger and Rees, 2009).

Ominously, the world as a whole is in a state of overshoot (first line of Table 4.1). Human demand exceeds the earth's regenerative/assimilative capacity by about 50 per cent. We are living, in part, by depleting and dissipating as waste the fossil carbon fuels and even the "renewable" natural capital (fish, forests, soils, etc.) that have accumulated in ecosystems over millions of years.

The Global Reach of Cities

Cities, of course, are virtually all in an ecological deficit. Urban populations are almost totally dependent on rural people, ecosystems, and life-support processes that are increasingly scattered all over the planet (Girardet, 2004; Newman and Jennings, 2008; Rees, 1992; 2003). In some respects, this relationship is a two-way, mutualistic one—rural areas benefit from urban markets, from the products of urban factories, from urban-based services, from technology transfers from urban areas, etc. However, while rural populations have survived historically without cities, the ecological dependence of urbanites on "the hinterland" is almost absolute. (For example, even urban agriculture, one ecological function that is becoming more common, cannot provide for all of the city's food needs.) *There can be no urban sustainability without rural sustainability* even if the "rural" for any particular city is scattered all over the planet. Understanding the nature of rural–urban interdependence is essential to understanding the total human ecosystem and to understanding urban sustainability.

In theory, estimating a city's eco-footprint is no different from estimating that of an entire country. In practice, however, matters are more complicated, hindered by a lack of local data: no statistical or planning agencies monitor the flow of biophysically significant goods and services across municipal boundaries. While some urban EF studies do attempt to compile local data (Moore and Rees, 2013), others use "quick and dirty" extrapolation from national eco-footprint estimates, sometimes with adjustments for local conditions, income differences, etc. (e.g., FCM, 2005). The latter method produces more accurate city footprint numbers for highly urbanized, high-income countries than for less-urbanized, poorer countries.

So, just how great is a typical modern city's debt to the global countryside? Despite methodological and data-quality differences, urban eco-footprint studies invariably show that the EFs of typical modern high-income cities exceed their geographic or political areas by two to three orders of magnitude. Following are examples:

- Based on locally adjusted per capita EF estimates, the people of Toronto and Vancouver "occupy" an ecosystem area outside their municipal boundaries 292 and 390 times larger, respectively, than the cities themselves (FCM, 2005). Even the lower-density metropolitan areas of these cities have EFs 57 times bigger than the respective urban regions (Table 4.2). The citizens of Toronto and Vancouver might want to contemplate the implications of this growing extra-territorial dependence as they sprawl out over Canada's most productive farmland in an era of global change. Where will they turn when they can no longer import essential foods from distant elsewheres?

- Under varying management assumptions of cities' ability to cope with regional waste-management issues, Folke et al. (1997) estimated that the 29 largest cities of the Baltic region require, for resources and certain categories of waste assimilation, an area of forest, agricultural, marine, and wetland ecosystems 565–1130 times larger than the area of the cities themselves.

- With a population of 33 million and a per capita EF of about 4.2 gha, metropolitan Tokyo's total eco-footprint is 138,600,000 gha. However, the entire domestic biocapacity of Japan is only about 76,200,000 gha. In short, Tokyo, with only 26 per cent of Japan's population, lives on an area of productive ecosystems 1.8 times larger than the nation's entire terrestrial biocapacity.[6] Clearly, if Japan were required by changing global circumstances to subsist on its domestic biocapacity, the country would have difficulty supporting even the population of its capital city.

- Warren-Rhodes and Koenig (2001) estimated that Hong Kong, with almost seven million people, has a total eco-footprint of 332,150 km² to 478,300 km² (5.0–7.2 ha per capita) (the range reflects two estimates of carbon sink land requirements). Hong Kong's eco-footprint is at least 303 times the total land area of the Hong Kong Special Administrative Region (1097 km²) and 3020 times the built-up area of the city (110 km²).

These data show clearly that, in material terms, "sustainable city" is an oxymoron (Rees, 1997). Modern cities are urban black holes sweeping up the productivity of a vastly larger and increasingly global resource hinterland and spewing an equivalent quantity of waste back into it. They are compact nodes of consumption living parasitically on the productivity and assimilative capacity of a vastly larger "undeveloped" area, portions of which

City or Region	Population (2006)	Per Capita Eco-Footprint (gha)	Area (hectares)	Total Eco-Footprint (gha)	Ratio of EF to Actual Area
Vancouver	578,041	7.71	11,400	4,456,696	390
Metro Vancouver	2,116,580	7.71	278,736	16,318,832	57
Toronto	2,503,281	7.36	63,000	18,424,148	292
Greater Toronto	5,555,912	7.36	712,500	40,891,512	57

Table 4.2   The Eco-Footprints of Toronto and Vancouver (EF data from FCM 2005)

may be thousands of kilometres from the built-up area at the centre.

While some have interpreted the consumptive and polluting power of cities as an anti-urban argument, it is nothing of the sort. Cities do have enormous ecological footprints; however, as we shall see, cities actually offer several advantages over more dispersed settlement patterns in the quest for sustainability (also see Senbel and Lesnikowski, Chapter 13). Eco-footprinting also suggests several other paradoxes about current perceptions of cities. For example, why is the lifeless asphalt of the mall parking lot considered to be urban land, while cropland vital to the survival of the city is not? What does it mean for urban planning if 99.5 per cent of the de facto urban (eco)system lies outside the municipal boundaries, out of sight and beyond the control of those it supports? Perhaps we should redefine what we mean by urban (eco)system.

Finally, eco-footprinting underscores a material reality that is all but ignored in the sustainability literature—no individual, no city, and no country can achieve sustainability if the system of which it is a part is unsustainable. Vancouver, Toronto, or Montreal might become exemplars of sustainable urban design and lifestyles (Vancouver is trying with its "Greenest City" initiative), but if the global system of which they are a part remains on an unsustainable path, then even our model cities would be taken down by, for example, severe climate change, depleted resources, and resultant geopolitical instability. Given such interdependence, the best any sub-global system can attain independently is a state of quasi-sustainability. "Quasi-sustainable" describes that level of economic activity and energy/material consumption per capita that, if extended to the entire system, would result in global sustainability (Rees, 2009). In 2013, quasi-sustainability implies a per capita eco-footprint of less than 1.8 gha (1.8 gha was the equitable per capita share of global biocapacity in 2008 [WWF, 2012]). Since Canadians' average eco-footprint is 6.4 gha per capita, we would have to reduce consumption by 72 per cent to meet the quasi-sustainability standard!

The Vulnerability of Modern Cities

Increasing global interdependence obviously has enormous implications for the security of urban populations in an era of global change. (For globalization processes, see Hall, Chapter 3.) Cities have grown so large and have such enormous eco-footprints, not because size necessarily confers great advantage, but simply because they could—historically, globalization and trade have ensured the abundant supplies and uninterrupted flows of the energy and other material resources required to grow the modern metropolis. But this raises an increasingly awkward question in an era of global change: just how secure is any city of millions, or even a relative "town" of 100,000, if resource scarcity, shifting climate, or geopolitical unrest threatens to cut it off from vital sources of supply? There are several interrelated reasons to believe this is not an idle question:

1. Reliable food supplies should be of increasing concern to urbanizing populations (Kissinger and Rees, 2009). Just to keep pace with UN medium population growth projections, agricultural output will have to increase by over 50 per cent by 2050; however, to improve the diets of malnourished people, output will have to increase by 100 per cent.[7] Achieving increases of this magnitude may be difficult. Indeed, global grain production is levelling off. By 1990, 562 million hectares (38 per cent) of the world's roughly 1.5 billion hectares of cropland had become significantly eroded or otherwise degraded; 300 million hectares (21 per cent) of cultivated land—enough to feed almost all of Europe—has been lost to production, and we are losing five to seven million hectares annually (FAO, 2000; SDIS, 2004). Depending on the climate and agricultural practices, moreover, topsoil is being "dissipated" 16 to 300 times as fast as it is regenerated. So far, the impact has been masked because we have managed to substitute fossil fuel for depleted soils and landscape degradation, but that may be about to change.

2. Modern cities are dependent on abundant, cheap fossil fuel. No other resource has changed the structure of economies, the nature of technologies, the balance of geopolitics, and the quality of human life as much as petroleum (Duncan and Youngquist, 1999). Fossil fuels, especially oil, still supply about 85 per cent of humanity's total energy demand and are essential for transportation, space and water heating, and electricity generation. Oil is also a major factor in the so-called green revolution. Mechanization, diesel-powered irrigation, the capacity to double-crop, and agro-chemicals (fertilizers and pesticides) made from oil and natural gas account for 79–96 per cent of the increased yields of wheat, rice, and maize production since 1967 (Cassman, 1999; Conforti and Giampietro, 1997). For these reasons, the peaking of global petroleum extraction may represent a singular event in modern history, posing a unique challenge to geopolitical stability and urban security (Campbell, 1999; Duncan and Youngquist, 1999; Laherrere, 2003). "Peak oil" could have an enormous impact on the price and availability of food and on urban transportation, urban form, and the future size of cities.[8]

3. Other analysts suggest that climate change is the greatest threat to urban civilization and could even bring the world to the edge of anarchy (e.g., CSIS, 2007; Schwartz and Randall, 2003). Even modest shifts in weather patterns could disrupt historic water availability, thus undermining both agricultural production and urban water supplies. In *The Age of Consequences*, Washington's Center for Strategic and International Studies suggests that human-induced warming could end peaceful global integration as various nations contract inwardly to conserve what they need—or expand outwardly to *take* what they need—for survival. In the event of "severe climate change," corresponding to an average increase in global temperature of 2.6°C by 2040 (now deemed to be increasingly likely), non-linear changes in biophysical systems will give rise to non-linear socio-political events. People will abandon regions where food and water are scarce and flee areas devastated by increasingly frequent severe storms, droughts, rising seas, and floods. Combined with food, energy, and water shortages, cross-border migration will impose great pressure on the cohesion of nations. War is likely and nuclear war is possible (CSIS, 2007).

Such dismal scenarios seem increasingly likely in light of findings of recent climate studies (e.g., Anderson and Bows, 2008; Hansen et al., 2008; World Bank, 2012). Current loose "targets" for controlling climate change include stabilizing carbon dioxide at 350 parts per million by volume (but it actually reached 400 ppmv for the first time in 2013) and maintaining temperature increases below 2°C. However, according to Anderson and Bows (2008), "an optimistic interpretation of the current framing of climate change implies that stabilization [of greenhouse gases (GHG)] much below 650 ppmv CO_2e [carbon dioxide equivalents] is improbable." This is partly because, in order to stabilize at 650 ppmv CO_2e, the majority of OECD nations will soon have to begin decarbonizing at rates in excess of six per cent per year, which would likely require a planned economic recession (Anderson and Bows, 2008). We should note that atmospheric GHG concentrations of 650 ppmv CO_2e imply a catastrophic 4°C increase in mean global temperature, compared to the "mere" 2.6°C increase assumed in CSIS's already horrific "severe climate change" scenario.[9] Models suggest that 4°C warming would be sufficient to convert much of the US, Southern Europe, China, India, Africa, and South America into uninhabitable wastelands (see Vince, 2009), displacing billions of people and jeopardizing prospects for maintaining any form of global civilization.

The good news in all this is that determined action to address climate change could ameliorate the peak oil problem and vice versa. If the world were to reduce CO_2 emissions by six per cent per year to avoid the worst of climate change, the drop in demand for oil might keep pace with declining "production."

Toward the "One Planet" City

Industrialized world reductions in material consumption, energy use, and environmental degradation of over 90 per cent will be required by 2040 to meet the needs of a growing world population fairly within the planet's ecological means. (BCSD, 1993)

This is a world in overshoot—we have exceeded long-term global carrying capacity—yet both population and per capita consumption are increasing and material expectations are rising all over the world. This is a fundamentally unsustainable situation—to raise just the present world population sustainably to North American material standards would require the biocapacity of three additional earth-like planets (Rees, 2013). The *really* inconvenient truth is that, to achieve sustainability, global energy and material throughput must decrease, not grow.

Techno-industrial society is a self-proclaimed, science-based society but we are not acting consistently with our best science. The risks associated with anticipated global change certainly demand major restructuring and may well require a planned economic contraction. For sustainability with greater equity, wealthy countries will have to free up the ecological space necessary for needed growth in the developing world (Rees, 2008). High-income nations should therefore work to limit the energy and material throughput required to sustain urban life (Lenzen, Dey, and Barney, 2004; Newman and Jennings, 2008; Rees, 2009). For example, to achieve one-planet living, Canadians should be taking steps *now* to reduce their eco-footprints by the necessary 72 per cent from 6.4 gha to their "equitable earth-share" of 1.8 gha per capita (Table 4.1).

Clearly, achieving such targets will require a dramatic shift in prevailing economic beliefs, values, and consumer lifestyles—as much as 60–70 per cent of the material flows through cities are attributable to personal consumption. Although much of the technology needed to make the transition relatively painless is already available (von Weizsäcker et al., 2009), and "managing without growth" is both economically possible and could *improve* quality of life (Victor, 2008), there is scant evidence that the necessary cultural shift is underway. Certainly no national government, the United Nations, or any other official international organization has begun to articulate in public the social, regulatory, trade, tax, and related economic policies required to induce the needed reductions in energy and material throughput. Despite repeated warnings that staying our present course spells catastrophe for billions of people (MEA, 2005; UCS, 1992), the modern world remains mired in a swamp of cognitive dissonance and collective denial (Rees, 2009).

Mainstream responses to date not only fail to address the problem of ecological overshoot, but seem designed, instead, to reproduce the status quo by other means. Such "innovations" as hybrid cars, green buildings, smart growth, the New Urbanism, green consumerism, and even much of the eco-cities movement generally assume that we can achieve sustainability through technological innovation and greater material and economic efficiency alone. This is a conceptual error—historically, efficiency has actually *increased* consumption by, for example, raising incomes and lowering prices. With more money chasing cheaper goods and services, throughput rises. In effect, improved efficiency simply makes industrial growth–bound society more efficiently unsustainable. By contrast, some eco-villages are inspired by social goals, such as sharing and community co-operation, that can result in reductions in the ecological footprint (Moos et al., 2006).

The Urban Sustainability Multiplier

The climate crisis won't be solved by changing light bulbs and inflating your tires more, planting a tree and driving a little less. It's going to require a truly fundamental shift in how we build our cities and live in them. (Register, 2009)

Getting serious about urban sustainability obviously requires more determined action than society has yet been willing to contemplate. Fortunately, the very factors that make wealthy cities weigh so heavily on the ecosphere—the concentration of people and the localized intensity of energy/material consumption and waste generation—also give them considerable economic and technical leverage in shrinking their eco-footprints.

To enable cities to take full advantage of this leverage, provincial and municipal governments must create the land-use legislation and zoning bylaws that urban planners need to eliminate sprawl and consolidate and densify existing built-up areas. Compact cities have the potential to be vastly less energy- and material-intensive than today's sprawling suburban cities.[10] The economies of scale and the agglomeration economies associated with high-density settlements confer a substantial "urban sustainability multiplier" on cities (Rees, 1999). Benefits of densification are as follows:

- Lower biophysical and economic costs per capita of providing piped treated water, sewer systems, waste collection, and most other forms of infrastructure and public amenities
- A greater range of options for material recycling, reuse, and remanufacturing, as well as a concentration of the specialized skills and enterprises needed to make these things happen
- Reduced per capita demand for occupied land
- Greater possibilities for electricity co-generation, district heating/cooling, and the use of waste-process heat from industry or power plants to reduce the per capita use of fossil fuel for water and space heating
- Increased opportunities for co-housing, car-sharing, tool libraries, and other co-operative relationships that have lower capital requirements (consumption) per household and individual
- More ways to greatly reduce the (mostly fossil) energy consumption by motor vehicles through walking, cycling, and public transit

- More "social contagion," i.e., facilitating the spread of nearly sustainable lifestyle choices (e.g., "voluntary simplicity")
- The potential to implement the principles of low throughput "industrial ecology" (i.e., the ideal of closed-circuit industrial parks in which the waste energy or materials of some firms are essential feed-stocks for others)

Walker and Rees (1997) show that the increased density and consequent energy and material savings associated with condos and high-rise apartments, compared to single-family houses, can reduce that part of the per capita urban ecological footprint associated with housing type and related transportation needs by about 40 per cent.

As noted, however, efficiency gains alone will not enable society to achieve "one-planet living" (Moore and Rees, 2013). Sustainability and security demand that cities everywhere become less consumption-driven and more materially self-reliant. Indeed, cities may be forced down this unfamiliar path by either or both the rising cost of oil-based transportation or the rapid phase-out of fossil fuels needed to avoid severe climate change (target: 80 per cent decarbonization by 2050). Certainly, there is no place for the fossil-fueled automobile—or any cars at all—in the eco-cities of the future (Register, 2009). For these reasons, urban designers must begin now to rethink cities so they function as complete ecosystems. This is the ultimate form of bio-mimicry.

Bio-mimicry at the city level requires re-localizing many ecological and economic functions. The least vulnerable and most resilient urban eco-system might be a new form of regional eco-city state (or bioregion) in which a densely built-up core is surrounded by its essential ecosystems (see Grant and Filion, Chapter 17, and Blay-Palmer and Landman, Chapter 23).[11] The central idea is to consolidate as much as possible of the city's productive hinterland in close proximity to its consumptive centre. In effect, without preventing *essential* trade, this would internalize the widely scattered external eco-footprints of our present cities into more compact and manageable city-centred regions that could function as complete human ecosystems. Such a transformed home place, "rather than being merely the site of consumption, [would], through its very design, produce some of its own food and energy, as well as become the locus of work for its residents" (Van der Ryn and Calthorpe, 1986). Eco-city states would be less a burden on, and more a contributor to, the life-support functions of the ecosphere than contemporary cities.

Most importantly, the bioregionalized city would reconnect urban populations both physically and psychologically to "the land." Because inhabitants would be, and would see themselves to be, more directly dependent on local ecosystems, they would have a powerful incentive—currently negated by imports—to manage their land and water resources sustainably in the face of global change. (Ideally, political control over the productive land and resource base of the consolidated region would pass from the provinces to new eco-city state governments.) Less reliant on imports, their populations would be partially insulated from at least external climate vagaries, resource shortages, and distant violent conflicts. Note, too, that if the entire world were organized into a system of self-reliant bioregions, each managed in a way to conserve adequate per capita stocks of natural capital, the aggregate effect would be global sustainability.

Canada is one of the few countries with sufficient space and resources for many of its cities to be readily reorganized along bioregional lines. Regrettably, this is no longer an option for many large consumer cities in small countries. Remember Tokyo with its eco-footprint spanning two Japans? The best such mega-cities can do in the face of global change is to reduce their material demands as much as possible and hope their national governments can negotiate reliable supplies of vital resources from areas that still have surplus capacity. Some cities may have to disperse. Certainly, not all urban regions will be able to be self-sustaining, but in a crowded world every urban agglomeration has an obligation to contribute to global sustainability by taking appropriate action within its own jurisdiction (McGranahan and Satterthwaite, 2003).

Of course, "appropriate action" will vary greatly among cities. This discussion has focused mainly on the sustainability implications of global change for wealthy cities. But many millions of people live under deplorable conditions in the barrios, slums, and squatter settlements of Third World cities. The greatest environmental problems facing these people are poor diets and the lack of potable water and sanitary sewage. Unlike the already wealthy, the world's urban poor would benefit from *increased* incomes and greater consumption. The global community should assist them to *grow* their eco-footprints. In this light, an appropriate strategy for rich and poor cities alike would be to manage gross consumption so that average per capita eco-footprints converge from above and below toward 1.8 gha, each person's equitable share of global biocapacity.[12]

Conclusion

Historically, environmental concerns about cities were confined to the local public-health effects of air, water, and land pollution that preoccupy impoverished cities today. However, the fourfold rise in human numbers and the order of magnitude increase in economic activity during the twentieth century undermined basic life-support systems and raised ecological concerns to the global scale.

Despite increasing costs and risks, the world community remains addicted to material growth. Many studies of urban metabolism (e.g., Brunner, 2007) seem concerned mainly with alternative technologies and better resource management that would enable cities to maintain their growth trajectories. Kennedy, Cuddihy, and Engel-Yan (2007) acknowledge that energy, material, and water throughput is increasing with modernization, even on a per capita basis; therefore, we should expect greater loss of ecosystem function and biodiversity. And, *if necessary*, urban policy-makers might consider strategies to slow exploitation. However, the authors convey no particular sense of urgency. Similarly, Decker et al. (2000) recognize the accelerating degradation of earth systems, but imply a fairly smooth succession to the point where "modern megacities will . . . begin to climax when global fossil fuel reserves are exhausted and global water and food resources are maximally utilized." Few academic studies acknowledge the possibility of implosion or urge the kind of dramatic response to prevent it that now seems justified by global change science.

This chapter attempts to fill the gap. I argue that we are witnessing the dissipative destruction of globally essential ecosystems and vital life-support functions and that the process is accelerating with population growth and rising material expectations. Given the increasing probability of severe climate change, resource shortages, large-scale population displacements, and resultant geo-political chaos, the world should be focused on corrective action *now*. The transition to sustainability will be anything but smooth and predictable if there is further delay.

Environmental scientists are sometimes dismissed as purveyors of gloom and doom. However, if global change science is correct, it is defenders of the growth-based status quo that are leading us toward the abyss. We can still turn "spaceship Earth" around. Humans are an intelligent species uniquely capable of rational analysis, extensive co-operation, and planning ahead to shape a desirable future. As a first step, society must acknowledge that (un)sustainability represents the greatest problem the world community has ever faced. Indeed, for perhaps the first time in history, individual and national self-interests arguably now coincide with humanity's *collective* interests. No person, city, or nation can be sustainable on its own. We are all part of the same ecosystemic hierarchy in which human sub-systems (e.g., cities and nation-states) are utterly dependent on maintaining the operational integrity of the whole (the ecosphere itself).

In these circumstances, government intervention in the economy for the common good is fully justified—after all, human-induced global change is indicative of gross market failure. Indeed, achieving global sustainability will require a concerted *inter*governmental program of global

sustainability planning that incorporates population reduction, articulation of less material-intense but more satisfying lifestyles, and reshaping our cities in the image of natural ecosystems.

Business as usual is not a viable option. Rich countries will have to abandon the idea of continuous economic growth and learn to share more equitably the economic and ecological output of the planet. The immediate material objective of the great restructuring should be to reduce gross consumption and waste production to match the regenerative capacity of the ecosphere. The ultimate goal is to create a positive future for all, characterized by ecological stability, greater social equity, and enhanced economic security.

Transition toward an ecologically sustainable urban society is a 100-year project, and there is no excuse not to begin immediately. Certainly, the problems of both developed and developing world cities are well documented, and many partial solutions have been proposed (e.g., Marcotullio and McGranahan, 2007; Martine et al., 2008; Satterthwaite, 1999). Some of the best and most accessible handbooks for urban sustainability are explicitly based on treating cities as true ecosystems (Newman and Jennings, 2008; Register, 2006). The only question is whether our growth-addicted global culture is capable of acknowledging and responding effectively to the challenge. Our species is facing its greatest test: whether high-intelligence, reasoned analysis, and common interests can trump base emotions, instinctive intransigence, and myopic self-interest. Humanity can theoretically continue to thrive but only if urban civilization is able to adapt purposefully to living within the earth's carrying capacity.

Review Questions

1. Why are cities not functioning as true eco-systems?
2. What are the implications of the ecological-footprint perspective in terms of the global environmental impacts of cities, and in terms of cities' environmental vulnerability?

3. What can be done to reduce cities' ecological footprint?

4. What are the main environmental threats on the horizon for cities?

Notes

1. One paper in the March 2009 issue of the journal even struggles with the question of whether "the ecosystem concept [is] relevant when humans are part of the system" (Pickett and Grove, 2009). The remaining eight articles focus on other aspects of non-human ecology.

2. Since livestock feedlots are a sub-system of the human urban industrial system, it is not surprising that they are similar to cities in eco-structure.

3. For fuller details of the method, including inclusions, exceptions, and limitations, see Rees (2006; 2013), WWF (2008), and various links at www.footprintnetwork.org/en/index.php/GFN/.

4. Eco-footprint analysis obviously does not capture all human impacts on earth, only those that can readily be converted into corresponding, mutually exclusive ecosystem areas (e.g., food and fibre production, carbon sequestration, built-up areas). We therefore cannot include pollutants such as ozone-depleting chemicals or the toxic residues accumulating in our food chain.

5. To enable fair comparisons among countries, the national EF and biocapacity data in Table 4.1 are presented in terms of standardized or "global" hectares (gha), i.e., the equivalent area of ecosystems of global average productivity.

6. The area of Japan is only about 37,770,000 ha, but Japan's terrestrial ecosystems are considerably more productive than the world average, which increases the country's biocapacity to over 76,000,000 gha.

7. This situation is complicated by the diversion of grain, especially maize, to biofuel production.

8. Conventional crude extraction peaked in 2006, and it is doubtful whether the output of tar sands, shale oil, and other forms of unconventional petroleum will keep pace with the accelerating depletion of conventional oil fields (see Hughes, 2013). Renewable alternatives are not yet major contributors to the energy budget and are often poor substitutes for fossil fuels.

9. Even the generally conservative World Bank (2012) agrees that the world is on track for 4°C warming and that this "must be avoided."

10. Many North Americans fear density, but the City of Vancouver illustrates that excellent urban design can actually draw families from the suburbs to live in high-density urban communities. In 2008, the city actually had to restrict further residential high-rise construction in its high-amenity downtown core because it was displacing office development.

11. For a history and philosophy of the bioregional movement, see Carr (2005).

12. Note that as the human population increases and productive ecosystems are degraded, this "equitable earth-share" declines.

References

Anderson, K., and A. Bows. 2008. "Reframing the climate change challenge in light of post-2000 emission trends," *Philosophical Transactions of the Royal Society A* 266: 3863–82. At: http://rsta.royalsocietypublishing.org/content/366/1882/3863.abstract

Association for the Study of Peak Oil and Gas (ASPO). 2008. *Newsletter* No. 91.

Brunner, P.H. 2007. "Reshaping urban metabolism," *Journal of Industrial Ecology* 11(2): 11–13.

Business Council for Sustainable Development (BCSD). 1993. *Getting Eco-Efficient* (Report of the BCSD First Antwerp Eco-Efficiency Workshop, Nov. 1993). Geneva: BCSD.

Campbell, C.C. 1999. *The Imminent Peak of World Oil Production.* At: www.hubbertpeak.com/campbell/commons.htm

Carr, M. 2005. *Bioregionalism and Civil Society: Democratic Challenges to Corporate Globalism.* Vancouver, BC: University of British Columbia Press.

Cassman, K.G. 1999. "Ecological intensification of cereal production systems: Yield potential, soil quality, and precision agriculture," *Proceedings of the National Academy of Science* 96: 5952–9.

Center for Strategic and International Studies (CSIS). 2007. *The Age of Consequences: The Foreign Policy and National Security Implications of Climate Change.* Washington, DC: CSIS. At: www.csis.org/media/csis/pubs/071105_ageof consequences.pdf

Conforti, P., and M. Giampietro. 1997. "Fossil energy use in agriculture: An international comparison," *Agriculture, Ecosystems and Environment* 65: 231–43.

Decker, E.H., S. Elliott, F.A. Smith, D.R. Blake, and F.S. Rowland. 2000. "Energy and material flow through the urban ecosystem," *Annual Review, Energy and Environment* 25: 685–740.

Diamond, J. 1997. *Guns, Germs, and Steel: The Fates of Human Societies.* New York: Norton.

Douglas, I. 1981. "The city as an ecosystem," *Progress in Physical Geography* 5: 315–67.

Duncan, R.C., and W. Youngquist. 1999. "Encircling the peak of world oil production," *Natural Resources Research* 8: 219–32.

Federation of Canadian Municipalities (FCM). 2005. *Ecological Footprints of Canadian Municipalities and Regions*. Edmonton, Alberta: Report for the Federation of Canadian Municipalities prepared by Anielski Management. At: www.anielski.com/Documents/EFA%20Report%20FINAL%20Feb%202.pdf

Folke, C., A. Jansson, J. Larsson, and R. Costanza. 1997. "Ecosystem appropriation by cities," *Ambio* 26: 167–72.

Food and Agriculture Organization (FAO). 2000. *Land Resource Potential and Constraints at Regional and Country Levels*. Rome: Land and Water Development Division, Food and Agriculture Organization of the United Nations.

Girardet, H. 2004. "The metabolism of cities," in S. Wheeler and T. Beatley, eds., *Sustainable Urban Development Reader*. London: Routledge.

Haberl, H., M. Fischer-Kowalski, J. Krausmann, H. Weisz, and V. Winiwarter. 2004. "Progress toward sustainability? What the conceptual framework of material and energy flow accounting (MEFA) can offer," *Land Use Policy* 21: 199–213.

Hansen, J., M. Sato, P. Kharecha, D. Beerling, R. Berner, V. Masson-Delmotte, M. Pagani, M. Raymo, D.L. Royer, and J.C. Zachos. 2008. "Target atmospheric CO_2: Where should humanity aim?" *The Open Atmospheric Science Journal* 2: 217–31.

Hughes, J.D. 2013. *Drill Baby, Drill—Can Unconventional Fuels Usher in a New Era of Energy Abundance?* Santa Rosa, CA: Post Carbon Institute.

Kennedy, C., J. Cuddihy, and J. Engel-Yan. 2007. "The changing metabolism of cities," *Journal of Industrial Ecology* 11 (2): 43–59.

Kissinger, M., and W.E. Rees. 2009. "Footprints on the prairies: Degradation and sustainability of Canadian agricultural land in a globalizing world," *Ecological Economics* 68: 2309–15.

Laherrere J. 2003. "Forecast of Oil and Gas Supply to 2050," paper presented to Petrotech 2003, New Delhi. At: www.hubbertpeak.com/laherrere/Petrotech 090103.pdf

Lenzen, M., C. Dey, and F. Barney. 2004. "Energy requirements of Sydney households," *Ecological Economics* 49: 375–99.

McGranahan, G., and D. Satterthwaite. 2003 "Urban centres: An assessment of urban sustainability," *Annual Review of Environmental Resources* 28: 243–74.

Marcotullio, P., and G. McGranahan, eds. 2007. *Scaling Urban Environmental Challenges—From Local to Global and Back*. London: Earthscan.

Martine, G., G. McGranahan, M. Montgomery, and R. Fernández-Castilla, eds. 2008. *The New Global Frontier—Urbanization, Poverty and Environment in the 21st Century*. London: Earthscan.

Millennium Ecosystem Assessment (MEA). 2005. "Living beyond our means: Natural assets and human well-being (Statement from the Board)," *Millennium Ecosystem Assessment*. At: www.millenniumassessment.org/documents/document.429.aspx.pdf

Moore, J., and W.E. Rees. 2013. "Getting to one planet living," in *State of the World—Is Sustainability Still Possible?* Washington, DC: Island Press.

Moos, M., J. Whitfield, L. Johnson, and J. Andrey. 2006. "Does design matter? The ecological footprint as a planning tool at the local level," *Journal of Urban Design* 11: 195–224.

Newman, P., and I. Jennings. 2008. *Cities as Sustainable Ecosystems*. Washington, DC: Island Press.

Ortiz, I., and M. Cummins. 2011. *Global Inequality: Beyond the Bottom Billion*. UNICEF Social and Economic Policy Working Paper. New York: United Nations Children's Fund (UNICEF).

Pickett, S.T.A., and J.M. Grove. 2009. "Urban ecosystems: What would Tansley do?" *Urban Ecosystems* 12: 1–8.

Rees, W.E. 1992. "Ecological footprints and appropriated carrying capacity: What urban economics leaves out," *Environment and Urbanization* 4: 120–30.

——. 1997. "Is 'sustainable city' an oxymoron?" *Local Environment* 2: 303–10.

——. 1999. "The built environment and the ecosphere: A global perspective," *Building Research and Information* 27: 206–20.

——. 2000. "Patch disturbance, eco-footprints, and biological integrity: Revisiting the Limits to Growth," in D. Pimentel, L. Westra, and R. Noss, eds., *Ecological Integrity: Integrating Environment, Conservation and Health*. Washington, DC: Island Press.

——. 2003. "Understanding urban ecosystems: An ecological economics perspective," in A. Berkowitz et al., eds., *Understanding Urban Ecosystems*. New York: Springer-Verlag.

——. 2006. "Ecological footprints and biocapacity: Essential elements in sustainability assessment," in J. Dewulf and H. Van Langenhove, eds., *Renewables-Based Technology: Sustainability Assessment*. Chichester: John Wiley and Sons.

——. 2008. "Human nature, eco-footprints and environmental injustice," *Local Environment: The International Journal of Justice and Sustainability* 13: 685–701.

——. 2009. "The ecological crisis and self-delusion: Implications for the building sector," *Building Research and Information* 37: 300–11.

——. 2013. "Ecological footprint, concept of," in: S.A. Levin, ed., *Encylopedia of Biodiversity* (2nd Edition, Volume 2). Waltham, MA: Academic Press.

Register, R. 2006. *EcoCities: Rebuilding Cities in Balance with Nature*, rev. edn. Gabriola Island, BC: New Society. See also: "An interview with Richard Register, author of *Ecocities: Building Cities in Balance with Nature.*" At: www.sustainablecityblog.com/2009/03/richard-register-interview/

———. 2009. "Cities can save the earth," *Foreign Policy in Focus*, 12 May. At: www.fpif.org/fpiftxt/6113

Satterthwaite, D., ed. 1999. *Sustainable Cities.* London: Earthscan.

Schwartz, P., and D. Randall. 2003. *An Abrupt Climate Change Scenario and Its Implications for United States National Security.* Washington, DC: A report commissioned by the US Defense Department.

Sustainable Development Information Service (SDIS). 2004. *Disappearing Land: Soil Degradation.* Washington, DC: SDIS, Global Trends, World Resources Institute.

Union of Concerned Scientists (UCS). 1992. *World Scientists' Warning to Humanity.* At: www.ucsusa.org/about/1992-world-scientists.html

Van der Ryn, S., and P. Calthorpe. 1986. *Sustainable Communities: A New Synthesis for Cities and Towns.* San Francisco, CA: Sierra Club Books.

Victor, P. 2008. *Managing without Growth: Slower by Design, Not Disaster.* Cheltenham: Edward Elgar.

Vince, G. 2009. "Surviving in a warmer world," *New Scientist* 201, 2697: 29–33.

von Weizsäcker, E., K. Hargroves, M. Smith, C. Desha, and P. Stasinopoulos. 2009. *Factor 5: Transforming the Global Economy through 80% Increase in Resource Productivity.* London and Droemer, Germany: Earthscan,

Wackernagel, M., and W.E. Rees. 1996. *Our Ecological Footprint: Reducing Human Impact on the Earth.* Gabriola Island, BC: New Society.

Walker, L., and W.E. Rees. 1997. "Urban density and ecological footprints: An analysis of Canadian households," in M. Roseland, ed., *Ecocity Dimensions.* Gabriola Island, BC: New Society.

Warren-Rhodes, K., and A. Koenig. 2001. "Ecosystem appropriation by Hong Kong and its implications for sustainable development," *Ecological Economics* 39: 347–59.

World Bank. 2012. *Turn Down the Heat: Why a 4°C Warmer World Must Be Avoided.* Washington DC: World Bank. At: http://documents.worldbank.org/curated/en/2012/11/17097815/turn-down-heat-4%C2%B0c-warmer-world-must-avoided

World Wildlife Fund (WWF). 2008. *Living Planet Report 2008.* Gland, Switzerland: World Wide Fund for Nature.

———. 2012. *Living Planet Report 2012.* Gland, Switzerland: World Wide Fund for Nature.

Economic Change in Canadian Cities: Innovation, Creativity, and the Knowledge-Based Economy

5

TARA VINODRAI

Introduction

Cities—despite their enduring materiality—are dynamic and ever-changing, responding to and being shaped by economic, social, political, and cultural forces. While there is no question that cities are important social, cultural, and political spaces, it is their key role as *economic spaces* that is the focus of this chapter. While cities have always been important economic spaces, the precise nature of their economic roles and activities has evolved over time. In the past four decades, cities in advanced capitalist societies have undergone significant deindustrialization and economic restructuring marked by the growth of the service sector, the increasing importance of a highly educated—and sometimes highly mobile—workforce valued for its embodied knowledge and capacity to innovate, as well as a decline in "blue collar" jobs. These economic changes have often been accompanied by labour market disorganization, characterized by declining private-sector unionization and the transformation of employment relations, including an increase in flexible, part-time, temporary, and precarious work. Scholars, policy-makers, and the popular and business press refer to the new economy, the knowledge-based economy, or—more controversially—the creative economy; these terms become shorthand to describe the contemporary economy. In this chapter, I examine how these economic changes have been experienced in Canadian cities.

I begin by briefly exploring the context in which the economic landscapes of Canadian cities have changed over the past four decades. The chapter proceeds to document some key socio-economic transformations in the Canadian economy since the 1970s. The third section more closely examines three key dynamics that characterize the economic transitions in Canadian cities: the changing landscape of manufacturing; the transformation of urban economies towards more innovation-based and knowledge-intensive forms of economic activity; and the ascendance of creative and cultural activities. However, these changes have not affected all Canadian cities in the same way. While the broader shift from a natural resource-based or manufacturing-based economy to one based on tertiary and quaternary-order service activities generally holds true across Canadian cities, the contours of this change are path-dependent (that is, shaped by past history and events) and vary from city to city based on their unique local histories, institutions, politics, economic development strategies, and regional contexts. Paying attention to how different Canadian cities have developed and adapted over time is therefore important. Statistical data[1] and other forms of evidence are used throughout the chapter to illustrate these issues.

Beyond Fordism:
Towards a Post-Industrial,
Knowledge-Based Economy

Before looking at the specific changes that have occurred in Canadian cities, it is important to understand how advanced capitalist societies have evolved over the past several decades. There is general agreement that the nature of production and its associated labour market structures, employment relations, and forms of governance have evolved from those dominating the post–World War II period, characterized as Fordism (Amin, 1994; Bryson and Henry, 2005; Storper and Scott, 1992). In the narrowest sense, Fordism is associated with a set of production practices pioneered by Henry Ford and applied to the automotive manufacturing industry in the early twentieth century. These practices included a detailed division of labour resulting in simplified, deskilled tasks requiring minimal job training; a high degree of labour control; highly standardized and routinized manufacturing; and dedicated machinery organized in an assembly line model allowing for mass production. The ascendance and widespread adoption of this organizational form rested not only on the production practices themselves but on an accompanying set of institutional and organizational practices that enabled their success. Fordism is therefore understood more broadly by social scientists as an economy-wide set of institutional architectures that sustained production and promoted economic growth in North America and Europe from the end of World War II until the early 1970s. What the French Regulation School refers to as the "regime of accumulation" (in this case, Fordist mass production) requires a complementary "mode of regulation" (Amin, 1994; Boyer, 2005; Jenson, 1990). In this case, most advanced, capitalist countries found an appropriate regulatory apparatus in the form of the Keynesian (see Keynesianism) welfare state articulated through strong national state intervention, regulation and control, and social welfare provision. The contours of this model, however, varied across

nation states (Boyer, 2005; Tickell and Peck, 1992). Jenson (1990) has argued that Canada's particular form of Fordism, what she refers to as "permeable Fordism," was produced through a set of historical processes and negotiated between government, business, and the organized labour movement beginning in the interwar period; it was designed to deliver higher wages, full employment, minimal labour unrest, as well as a set of social programs to support social reproduction. Alongside a leading role for a redistributive welfare state during the postwar period, other institutional forms supported the reproduction and sustainability of the broader economic system. However, in the early 1970s, it became apparent that these particular institutional arrangements were increasingly strained across advanced, capitalist economies as profit levels declined, global competition intensified, and broader economic restructuring resulting from rising oil prices placed the system in crisis (Harvey, 1990).

In seeking to characterize the subsequent developments of the capitalist system, scholars have referred to the coming of a post-industrial (Bell, 1973) or risk society (Beck, 2000), post-Fordism or after-Fordism (see Amin, 1994), an era of flexible specialization (Piore and Sabel, 1984) or flexible accumulation (Harvey, 1990), and—most recently—an emerging form of cognitive-cultural capitalism (Scott, 2007).[2] Despite differences among social scientists in terms of the language and theoretical apparatus used to describe the nature of contemporary capitalism, there is widespread agreement that the economy has changed in both quantitative and qualitative terms over the past decades, particularly in the types of industries leading growth, the forms of work associated with this paradigm, and their associated geographies. The most striking shift has been the tremendous growth of service-based industries, which can be attributed to the introduction of new technologies allowing for significant automation; the outsourcing and relocation of production-oriented activities to offshore locations; and changing patterns of consumption, including demand for improved and differentiated services as well as differentiated goods that require more creative and service-based inputs in their production and distribution. Scott (2007: 1466) notes that

> much of productive activity today involves digital technologies and flexible organization sustaining the expansion of sectors that thrive on innovation, product diversity and the provision of personalized services . . . Labor processes have come to depend more and more on intellectual and affective human assets (at both high and low levels of remuneration), and are increasingly less focused on bluntly routinized mental or manual forms of work.

He identifies technology-intensive manufacturing; services; fashion-oriented, neo-artisanal production; and cultural-products industries as the key drivers of growth and innovation in the contemporary economy.

The question remains this: what role do cities play in this new economy? Observers identify two competing trends that raise questions about the continued vitality of cities in an age of **globalization**. On the one hand, transportation and communication technologies have allowed for shifts in terms of the locational choices of firms, industries, and—increasingly—workers (Moos and Skaburskis, 2007). In this view, economic activities are no longer tied to particular locations; capital and labour are increasingly footloose—able to relocate to any location. This has led to pronouncements of the "death of distance," the "end of geography," and the emergence of a "flat world" (Cairncross, 1997; Friedman, 2005). On the other hand, scholars have argued that place—especially the city—has become even more important in the contemporary economy (Morgan, 2004). Despite technological advances in transportation and communications that reduce the costs and barriers to interaction over space and time, many of the industries critical to producing the content, tools, and infrastructure of this new economy are agglomerated in particular *urban* locations. In other words, economic activity—particularly the

forms associated with the new economy—remains spatially concentrated in cities.

It is this spatial agglomeration—what Porter (1998) calls "clustering"—that enables firms involved in similar activities to draw on shared local resources and collective infrastructure, to reduce transaction costs, and to gain other efficiencies. Firms benefit from local access to deep pools of specialized, skilled labour; from proximity to suppliers, service providers, and other related and supporting industries; and from closeness to sophisticated customers who provide demand-side impetus for developing and improving products and services, although this latter characteristic remains contested (Wolfe and Gertler, 2004). In addition to these traditional agglomeration economies or externalities, firms benefit from knowledge spillovers, the ability to monitor their competition, and access to local institutional supports. In other words, agglomeration enables learning, knowledge flows, co-operation, and competition (Maskell and Malmberg, 1999; Wolfe and Gertler, 2004). Of course, firms are connected to other places through complex divisions of labour, and through supply and commodity chains. As well, markets and firms access knowledge through both local and non-local partners and networks (Bathelt, Malmberg, and Maskell, 2004; Gertler, 2008). However, there are compelling reasons why firms often remain agglomerated in particular cities. Most fundamental among these—from an economic perspective—is the growing importance of knowledge and learning to innovation, and the creation of economic value in the contemporary era.

Cities provide many of the necessary conditions to support the innovation, learning, and knowledge generation and circulation processes integral to the development of dynamic clusters or specialized agglomerations of activity. Moreover, scholars increasingly recognize that learning and innovation—critical for firms' competitiveness—are inherently *social* processes that rely on interaction between different economic actors, such as firms, industry and professional associations, universities, government, public and private research and development laboratories, technology transfer offices, unions, venture capitalists, and other organizations (Gertler, 2001; Wolfe and Bramwell, 2008). While these interactions can be in person (e.g., meetings, conferences, trade shows, other events) or electronically mediated (e.g., email, videoconferencing, social media, virtual environments), there is agreement that the primarily *tacit* nature of a lot of knowledge demands that some of the most important interactions occur face-to-face in order for understanding, learning, and the sharing of ideas to take place (Gertler, 2003, 2008; Storper and Venables, 2004). Cities, because of the density of activity, provide an ideal environment where such interactions are easily made possible and are more likely to occur since norms and values are shared.

Human capital, particularly highly skilled labour—referred to as knowledge workers, talent, the creative class (Florida, 2002), the new class (Gouldner, 1979), or the new middle class (Ley, 1996)—should not be overlooked as an important embodied input into the innovation process. These workers often provide specialized skills, creativity, ideas, and know-how to knowledge-intensive production and the innovation process. Cities have been increasingly described as the preferred location for these workers. Richard Florida's (2002) bestselling and controversial book, *The Rise of the Creative Class*, is often associated with this view. Florida suggests that creativity is the key driver of the contemporary economy and that a particular (and growing) group of workers (the creative class) are driving economic growth. Place is central to his argument. Echoing Jane Jacobs and other urban theorists, Florida suggests that cities are ideal environments to foster and support creativity. The creative class is attracted to cities, but not just any cities; those cities that have high-quality social environments and low barriers to entry into labour markets and networks, and that are diverse and open to differences will be particularly attractive. To capture this dynamic, Florida invokes the 3Ts (technology, talent, and tolerance) to suggest that cities that achieve high scores on these variables will be the winners in today's economy. And while Florida's broad observations about the transformation of the labour market and its geography are

not entirely original (cf. Gouldner, 1979; Ley, 1996; Scott, 2001), the creative class label (or brand) has resonated with policy-makers, practitioners, and the general public. (How many urban scholars are ever mentioned in *Vanity Fair*?) Moreover, urban policy-makers in Canada, the US, and further afield have very quickly (and often uncritically) adopted a "creative class policy script" that shifts focus away from creating a favourable business climate toward one favourable to attracting the urban elite (see Peck, 2005).

As indicated in several other chapters, the creative class thesis has been highly influential and highly controversial (cf. Hutton and Vinodrai, Chapter 6; Bain, Chapter 14). While some critique has focused on Florida's own role in promoting his perspective (for example, through his consultancy work and speaking tours), others raise issues related to theory, methods, empirical evidence, and policy translation (Peck, 2005). Scholars have raised fundamental questions related to the direction of causality and choice of variables in the model (Shearmur, 2007; Storper and Scott, 2009), as well as the troubling dark side of catering to the creative class thereby contributing to growing inequality (McCann, 2007; Peck, 2005). Issues have been raised concerning the mobility patterns of creative workers (Deslisle and Shearmur, 2010), the absence of differentiation amongst creative workers (Markusen, 2006), the applicability to smaller cities and rural regions (Lewis and Donald, 2010; McGranahan and Wojan, 2007), and the lack of attention paid to outcomes in different institutional contexts (Vinodrai, 2013).

The creative class thesis has spurred empirical inquiry that both confirms and disrupts the creative class thesis, and Canadian scholars have been actively involved in this debate. Gertler et al.'s (2002) study was the first to explore whether or not the correlations and relationships observed in Florida's work on the 3Ts were similar outside the US context. They found similar relationships between these key variables in Canadian cities, although there were important national differences between Canada and the US related to educational attainment and immigration. Lewis and Donald

(2010) argue that smaller cities are marginalized by creative class theory and policy. They advocate for a perspective that emphasizes sustainability and livability, along with quality of place offered by smaller Canadian cities, such as Kingston. A collaborative national research project involving Canadian geographers, planners, and other social scientists studied the dynamics of talent attraction and retention across 15 Canadian cities. Overwhelmingly, the evidence suggests that talent attraction and retention dynamics are nuanced and complex, dependent on both individual characteristics (e.g., occupation, ethnic identity) and place-specific context (e.g., location, city size, local institutions and culture) (see Grant, 2014).

In subsequent work, Florida and his colleagues have addressed many of the critiques raised above—although undoubtedly not to the satisfaction of some of his critics, who question the emphasis on those who are often most privileged in economy and society. Nonetheless, academics will likely continue to engage in this debate, refining, refuting, or rejecting its theoretical foundations and critically examining evidence and outcomes from cities in Canada and abroad.

Related to these discussions of creativity is the growing importance of intangible inputs (such as symbolic, design, and aesthetic content) rather than tangible assets in the production of goods and services (Lash and Urry, 1994; Scott, 2001). One group of industries is assuming a more prominent role: cultural products industries, which include film and television production, music recording, book publishing, video game production, live theatre, and other entertainment. Studies consistently demonstrate that these industries have high levels of creative content, are engaged in a constant search for novelty, and are often susceptible to rapid shifts in consumer demands, necessitating higher rates of innovation and easy access to information about changing tastes and styles (Power and Scott, 2004; Vinodrai and Keddy, forthcoming). As a result, the agglomeration economies described above are of paramount importance; moreover, these creative and cultural activities tend to agglomerate in *major urban centres* for a number of reasons (Scott,

2001, 2004). First, firms need constant access to cutting-edge knowledge and pools of highly skilled labour. Second, workers benefit from being able to develop their careers while living in "cool," diverse urban environments and neighbourhoods, although this can lead to polarizing, gentrification dynamics (Ley, 1996; Zukin, 1982; see Walks, Chapter 9; Bain, Chapter 14). Third, these urban environments are said to provide inspiration; in turn, elements of place become embedded in outputs (Lloyd , 2006; Molotch, 2002). Fourth, this type of work often involves flexible organizational forms, such as project-based work, that expose workers (despite their professional status) to high levels of individual risk through self-employment, contract-based work, and freelancing (Ekinsmyth, 2002; Grabher, 2002; Vinodrai, 2006, 2013). The nature of the industries and of work itself requires well-developed (local) social and knowledge networks to access key information about jobs, projects, styles, and leading-edge developments—all of which are most readily available in large, diverse cities.

The above discussion foregrounds how broader economic changes (re)shape urban economies and labour markets and highlights how cities have become even more important sites of economic activity in the contemporary era. The remainder of this chapter documents how Canada's urban economies have changed since the crisis of Fordism and the rise of a knowledge-based economy, marked by the dominance of new forms of work, industrial activity, and technologies.

The Rise of Canada's Post-Industrial Economy?

To put an empirical face to this discussion, in this section I examine how Canada's economic landscape has changed since the early 1970s. Specifically, I focus on the significant shifts in the relative importance of different industries, as well as changes in the characteristics of the Canadian labour force. To emphasize the shift in the types of industries that have gained prominence, I distinguish between goods- and services-producing industries. Goods-producing industries include agriculture, forestry, fishing, mining, oil and gas, utilities, construction, and manufacturing. Services-producing industries include retail, business, personal care, health care, education, and public administration. As is evident from this list, the services sector is incredibly diverse, entailing many types of work and activities (Bryson and Daniels, 2007). Moreover, the cultural products industries identified earlier cannot be easily classified as either goods or services in the traditional sense (Scott, 2001, 2007). Figure 5.1 shows the relative contributions of the goods- and services-producing sectors to Canadian employment between 1976 and 2013. It demonstrates that the growth of the Canadian economy

has rested on the services-producing industries. In 1976, goods-producing industries accounted for 34.5 per cent of Canadian employment. By 2013, this had declined to 21.9 per cent. Employment in goods-producing industries did not decline in absolute terms, however, suggesting that this remains an important sector. Table 5.1 examines this dynamic more closely by comparing employment gains and losses across 16 sectors of the Canadian economy between 1976 and 2013. The overwhelming majority of the employment gains were in the services-producing sector and the highest annual growth rates were in professional, scientific, and technical services (4.6 per cent) and business, building, and other support services (4.1 per cent); followed by health care and social assistance (2.7 per cent); information, culture, and

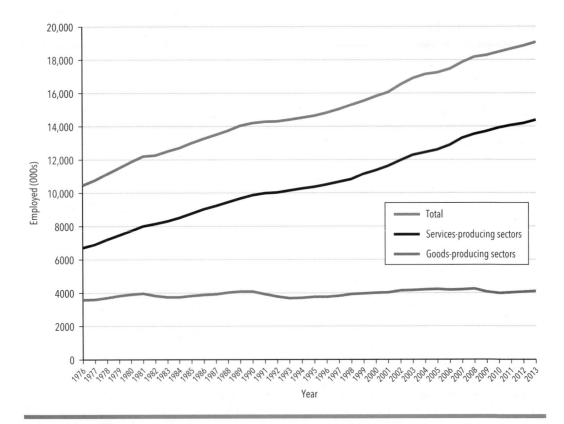

Figure 5.1   Employment (000s) by Industrial Sector in Canada, 1976–2013

Source: Statistics Canada, *Labour Force Survey Historical Review, 1976–2013* (author's calculations).

| Table 5.1 | Employment (000s) by Industry in Canada, 1976–2013 |

	1976	2013	Change	% Change	Annual Growth Rate (%)
Goods-producing sector	*3,628*	*4,140*	*512*	*14.1*	*0.4*
Agriculture	479	330	(149)	(31.1)	(1.0)
Forestry, fishing, mining, quarrying, oil and gas	278	398	121	43.5	1.0
Utilities	113	146	33	28.8	0.7
Construction	768	1,436	669	87.1	1.7
Manufacturing	1,990	1,829	(161)	(8.1)	(0.2)
Services-producing sector	*6,723*	*14,432*	*7,709*	*114.7*	*2.1*
Trade	1,664	2,834	1,169	70.3	1.4
Transportation and warehousing	594	900	307	51.7	1.1
Finance, insurance, real estate, and leasing	544	1,149	605	111.2	2.0
Professional, scientific, and technical services	265	1,396	1,131	427.6	4.6
Business, building, and other support services	176	778	602	341.9	4.1
Educational services	701	1,339	638	91.1	1.8
Health care and social assistance	826	2,221	1,395	168.8	2.7
Accommodation and food services	368	832	464	126.3	2.2
Information, culture, and recreation	459	1,213	754	164.1	2.7
Other services	452	801	350	77.4	1.6
Public administration	675	968	293	43.4	1.0
Total, all industries	**10,491**	**18,876**	**8,385**	**79.9**	**1.6**

Source: Statistics Canada, *Labour Force Survey Historical Review, 1976–2013* (author's calculations).

recreation industries (2.7 per cent); and accommodation and food services (2.2 per cent). Agriculture and manufacturing both experienced an overall decline in employment. These broad shifts in industrial structure have not been felt evenly across the Canadian urban system, however, as discussed later in this chapter (see also Hutton and Vinodrai, Chapter 6).

Alongside shifts in the industrial structure of the Canadian economy have been parallel changes in the characteristics of the workforce. Levels of human capital (as measured by formal education levels) in Canada have increased steadily since the mid-1970s. Between 1976 and 2013, the proportion of the Canadian population age 15 or older with at least a bachelor's degree has more than tripled from 7.2 per cent to 22.7 per cent. During this same period, the gap in labour force participation rates

between men and women has narrowed considerably. In 1976, there was a 32 per cent difference between the participation rates of men (77.7 per cent) and women (45.7 per cent). By 2013, there was only a nine per cent difference in the participation rates of men (71.1 per cent) and women (62.1 per cent), marking a convergence in the participation rates of men and women and a significant feminization of the workforce in the post-industrial era. Job tenure (the average length of time that a worker holds a particular job) is often used as an indicator of labour market stability. Job tenure in Canada has fluctuated over the past several decades. While easy interpretation is confounded by factors such as the aging of the workforce and the arrival of new entrants into the workforce (i.e., increased participation by women, new immigrants), some of this variability can be controlled for by examining a specific age **cohort** (see Moos, Chapter 20). From the 1970s to the mid-1990s, job tenure among 25- to 44-year-olds (individuals normally in the early and mid-stages of their careers) increased steadily, meaning that individuals in this age cohort were generally staying in the same job for long periods of time (Figure 5.2). However, the flattening of average job tenure in this cohort in the late-1980s and early-1990s reflects the economic recession that resulted in many workers being laid off and losing their jobs. The steady decrease in job tenure beginning in the mid-1990s reflects changes in the nature of the labour market. In emerging industries and occupations, work is generally more flexible and precarious. In existing industries, there has been an erosion of the prevalence of full-time, stable work leading to a greater prevalence

of temporary, contract, and part-time work, as well as higher levels of self-employment (Benner, 2002; Christopherson, 2002; Vosko, 2006).

Finally, Table 5.2 shows how Canada's occupational structure has changed between 1971 and 2011. While the overall labour force grew at a rate of 1.8 per cent annually over this period, there is variation among occupational groups. Growth rates were higher than the national average in management (4.2 per cent), professional (4.1 per cent), medicine and health (3.1 per cent), business and finance (1.9 per cent), and sales and services (2.1 per cent) occupations. Barring the latter category, these occupational groups are the building blocks of the **creative class** and provide empirical confirmation of the increasing professionalization of the workforce over the past several decades. It is worth noting that sales

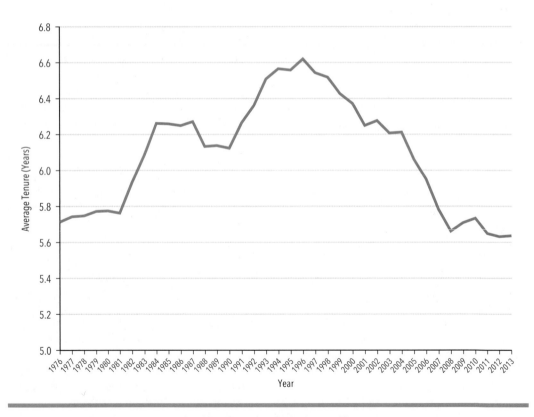

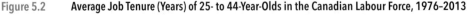

Figure 5.2   Average Job Tenure (Years) of 25- to 44-Year-Olds in the Canadian Labour Force, 1976–2013

Source: Statistics Canada, *Labour Force Survey Historical Review, 1976–2007* (author's calculations).

Table 5.2	Employment (000s) by Occupation in Canada, 1971–2011				
	1971	**2011**	**Change**	**% Change**	**Annual Growth Rate (%)**
Managerial occupations	372	1,964	1,592	427.8	4.2
Professional occupations	767	3,806	3,039	396.2	4.1
Medicine and health-related occupations	327	1,107	780	238.6	3.1
Business, finance, and clerical occupations	1,374	2,902	1,528	111.2	1.9
Sales and service occupations	1,786	4,068	2,282	127.8	2.1
Primary occupations	666	398	(268)	(40.3)	(1.3)
Processing and machining occupations	1,210	805	(405)	(33.5)	(1.0)
Construction, trades, transport-equipment operating occupations	2,127	2,538	411	19.3	0.4
Total, all occupations	**8,627**	**17,588**	**8,961**	**103.9**	**1.8**

Source: Statistics Canada, *Census of Population, 1971;* Statistics Canada, *National Household Survey, 2011* (author's calculations).

and services occupations had the second-highest gain in absolute terms and accounted for just under one-quarter of the employment gains between 1971 and 2011. Work in these areas, while essential to the (re)production of cities, typically offers lower wages, is highly feminized, requires fewer credentials, and exposes workers to higher levels of job insecurity (Cervenan, 2009; Vosko, 2006). This is a worrying trend that reveals the paradox that the very economic activities associated with the knowledge-based or creative economy may also lead to rising inequality and social exclusion (Gertler, 2001; Scott, 2007; Storper and Scott, 2009; Walks, Chapter 9). The occupation groups that experienced decline, as expressed by their annual growth rates, were primary (−1.3 per cent) and processing and machining (−1 per cent) occupations. These statistics reconfirm the trend toward deindustrialization.

Toward a Knowledge-Based Economy? The Economic Transformation of Canadian Cities

Economic change in Canadian cities must be understood in the context of these broader shifts

in the Canadian economy. In this section, I examine how **deindustrialization** and the growth of the knowledge-based economy have occurred unevenly across Canada's urban system (on resulting urban decline in some cases, see Donald and Hall, Chapter 15). I focus on three significant changes that epitomize this economic transition. First, given the wrenching deindustrialization experienced by many Canadian cities, I examine the evolving manufacturing landscape, placing emphasis on Ontario's cities where these changes have been most acute. Second, given the increasing emphasis on the importance of innovation and knowledge to the growth of cities, I explore the economic development paths taken by different Canadian cities in responding to these changes. Finally, given the increased attention being paid to culture and creativity in cities, I examine the cultural industries, paying special attention to Canada's three largest urban centres where these activities are more prominent and well developed compared to other Canadian cities.

Evolving Manufacturing Landscapes

While the above discussion highlighted the decline in the relative importance of manufacturing to the Canadian economy, this has not affected all Canadian cities in the same way. Table 5.3 shows that, in 1971, manufacturing accounted for more than one-third of employment in Brantford (40 per cent), Kitchener (39.1 per cent), Oshawa (39.2 per cent), Hamilton (34.5 per cent), Windsor (33 per cent), and St. Catharines–Niagara (33 per cent). By 2011, these percentages had dropped to 16.7 per cent in Brantford, 18.8 per cent in Kitchener, 9.9 per cent in Oshawa, 11.8 per cent in Hamilton, 18.8 per cent in Windsor, and 9.9 per cent in St. Catharines–Niagara. These dramatic changes in

Table 5.3	Manufacturing Industry Employment in Canadian Cities, 1971–2011					
	1971		2011		1971–2011	
	Local Employment	% Local	Local Employment	% Local	Local Employment	% Local
Toronto	315,570	25.4	293,790	10.0	(21,780)	(15.4)
Montreal	276,770	25.6	213,660	10.7	(63,110)	(14.9)
Vancouver	78,750	16.6	81,645	6.6	2,895	(10.0)
Kitchener	41,360	39.1	49,225	18.8	7,865	(20.2)
Edmonton	24,965	11.4	44,620	6.6	19,655	(4.8)
Hamilton	73,255	34.5	43,475	11.8	(29,780)	(22.7)
Calgary	19,830	11.2	41,835	5.8	22,005	(5.3)
Winnipeg	44,425	18.2	36,340	9.1	(8,085)	(9.1)
Quebec City	21,910	12.3	30,935	7.3	9,025	(5.0)
London	28,670	22.1	28,620	11.6	(50)	(10.5)
Windsor	34,820	33.0	27,820	18.8	(7,000)	(14.2)
Ottawa-Gatineau	20,670	7.9	24,135	3.5	3,465	(4.4)
St Catharines–Niagara	41,355	33.0	19,245	9.9	(22,110)	(23.1)
Oshawa	19,375	39.2	18,615	9.9	(760)	(29.3)
Guelph	8,245	29.6	15,220	19.4	6,975	(10.3)
Sherbrooke	6,890	21.4	13,005	12.8	6,115	(8.6)
Brantford	14,245	40.0	11,540	16.7	(2,705)	(23.3)
Halifax	7,885	8.3	10,285	4.6	2,400	(3.6)
Saskatoon	5,230	9.8	9,875	6.6	4,645	(3.2)
Trois-Rivières	9,680	28.0	9,095	12.2	(585)	(15.8)
Victoria	7,135	8.8	6,065	3.2	(1,070)	(5.6)
Regina	5,815	9.4	6,055	5.0	240	(4.5)
Saint John	6,935	16.3	5,305	8.0	(1,630)	(8.3)
Sarnia	9,465	29.0	5,190	12.2	(4,275)	(16.8)
Peterborough	8,285	30.7	5,140	8.8	(3,145)	(21.9)
Sault Ste Marie	11,235	34.4	4,565	11.7	(6,670)	(22.7)
St John's	3,335	6.9	4,380	4.1	1,045	(2.9)
Kingston	4,490	12.0	4,000	4.8	(490)	(7.2)
Sudbury	8,030	12.9	3,295	4.0	(4,735)	(8.9)
Thunder Bay	7,430	15.9	2,970	4.8	(4,460)	(11.1)
Canada	1,593,595	19.6	1,619,290	9.2	25,695	(10.4)

Source: Statistics Canada, *Census of Population, 1971*; Statistics Canada, *National Household Survey, 2011* (author's calculations).

the relative importance of manufacturing reflect large employment losses primarily experienced in southern Ontario and Quebec, the historical manufacturing centres of Canada.

A similar portrait of the dramatic reconstitution emerges when examining the occupations most closely associated with the production side of manufacturing: processing and machining occupations (considered the core of blue-collar work). Table 5.4 shows that, between 1971 and 2011, processing and machining occupations declined in their relative importance across Canadian cities,

Table 5.4	Employment in Processing and Machining Occupations in Canadian Cities, 1971–2011					
	1971		2011		1971–2011	
	Local Employment	% Local	Local Employment	% Local	Local Employment	% Local
Toronto	182,255	14.6	149,040	5.1	(33,215)	(9.6)
Montreal	169,310	15.7	85,440	4.3	(83,870)	(11.4)
Vancouver	59,000	12.4	38,365	3.1	(20,635)	(9.4)
Kitchener	27,565	26.0	22,260	8.5	(5,305)	(17.5)
Edmonton	22,150	10.1	18,725	2.8	(3,425)	(7.4)
Hamilton	42,335	19.9	18,475	5.0	(23,860)	(14.9)
Winnipeg	32,670	13.4	18,055	4.5	(14,615)	(8.9)
Calgary	15,505	8.7	16,790	2.3	1,285	(6.4)
London	17,780	13.7	14,650	6.0	(3,130)	(7.8)
Windsor	23,920	22.7	13,810	9.3	(10,110)	(13.4)
Quebec City	17,105	9.6	12,440	2.9	(4,665)	(6.7)
Oshawa	11,870	24.0	9,875	5.2	(1,995)	(18.8)
St Catharines–Niagara	27,620	22.0	8,840	4.5	(18,780)	(17.5)
Ottawa–Gatineau	16,580	6.4	8,280	1.2	(8,300)	(5.2)
Guelph	5,515	19.8	8,255	10.5	2,740	(9.3)
Brantford	8,980	25.2	6,330	9.1	(2,650)	(16.1)
Sherbrooke	4,865	15.1	5,885	5.8	1,020	(9.3)
Saskatoon	4,560	8.6	4,805	3.2	245	(5.4)
Trois-Rivières	6,850	19.8	4,185	5.6	(2,665)	(14.2)
Halifax	6,705	7.0	3,885	1.8	(2,820)	(5.3)
Regina	4,655	7.6	2,725	2.2	(1,930)	(5.3)
Peterborough	4,775	17.7	2,695	4.6	(2,080)	(13.1)
Victoria	6,875	8.5	2,630	1.4	(4,245)	(7.1)
St John's	3,585	7.5	2,460	2.3	(1,125)	(5.2)
Sarnia	4,860	14.9	2,290	5.4	(2,570)	(9.5)
Saint John	4,875	11.4	2,275	3.4	(2,600)	(8.0)
Sault Ste Marie	6,540	20.0	1,800	4.6	(4,740)	(15.4)
Sudbury	7,845	12.6	1,630	2.0	(6,215)	(10.6)
Kingston	3,545	9.5	1,600	1.9	(1,945)	(7.6)
Thunder Bay	6,440	13.8	1,505	2.5	(4,935)	(11.4)
Canada	1,210,025	14.0	805,040	4.6	(404,985)	(9.4)

Source: Statistics Canada, *Census of Population, 1971*; Statistics Canada, *National Household Survey, 2011* (author's calculations).

yet these shifts were felt unevenly across Canadian cities. Large absolute losses were experienced in Canada's largest cities. In Toronto, the absolute number of processing and machining jobs declined (33,215) and by 2011, workers in these occupations accounted for a smaller proportion of employment, declining from 14.6 per cent to 5.1 per cent. Montreal experienced a sharp absolute decline in this type of employment (83,870), leading to a decline from 15.7 per cent to 4.3 per cent in the proportion of the labour force accounted for by processing and machining occupations. Many of Ontario's small and mid-sized cities saw both the number and share of employment decrease in processing and machining occupations. For example, St. Catharines–Niagara and Hamilton saw employment in processing and machining occupations decrease by 18,780 (a 17.5 per cent decrease in share of employment) and 23,860 (a 14.9 per cent decrease in share of employment), respectively. This can be attributed to significant restructuring in the dominant industries in these cities: automotive and steel (Warrian and Mulhern, 2009).

Manufacturing remains important in several Canadian cities, however, and—in some cases—deindustrialization has not been an important dynamic of local economic change. For example, western Canadian cities like Vancouver and Calgary were never major manufacturing sites and their economies are more connected to extractive and natural resource–based industries (Hutton, 2010; see also Hutton and Vinodrai, Chapter 6). Even though cities like Toronto and Montreal have witnessed significant changes in their manufacturing base, manufacturing industries still account for a similar proportion of employment in each city (10 per cent and 10.7 per cent, respectively), including manufacturing in areas such as biotechnology, pharmaceuticals, medical equipment and assistive technologies (MAT), and other life sciences. The life sciences provide an interesting case of the evolution of manufacturing, including the strong links between advanced manufacturing and related services. Toronto and Montreal both have firms engaged in a range of life science activities. Montreal is more specialized in pharmaceuticals,

whereas Toronto has a more diverse mix of activities. In each city, the life sciences industries are embedded in a broader regional and national innovation system and benefit from an array of institutional supports (Gertler and Vinodrai, 2009; Lowe and Gertler, 2005, 2009). National strategies and policies, such as the 1983 National Biotechnology Strategy, tax incentives to stimulate R&D expenditures (particularly the Scientific Research and Economic Development tax credits), and in Montreal the creation of National Research Council (NRC) laboratories focused on biotechnology, were critical to the industry's development.

Different provincial policies related to public health care also contribute to each city's development trajectory. Quebec's provincial drug plan provided a 15-year exclusive approval guarantee for brand-name drugs, even if generic alternatives were available. Since the 1970s, however, Ontario has required patients to purchase cheaper, generic versions of drugs when available. Consequently, Montreal has a high proportion of brand-name drug producers, whereas generic producers are more prominent in Toronto.

At the local level, publicly funded research occurring in the universities and teaching hospitals has created opportunities for entrepreneurship and innovation. Toronto has a long history of medical research and innovation at the University of Toronto and elsewhere in the city, including the founding of Dow Pharmaceuticals in the 1880s, the establishment of the Connaught Laboratories at the University of Toronto in 1914, the discovery of insulin in the early twentieth century, as well as other medical breakthroughs. Moreover, Lowe and Gertler (2005: 26) suggest that Toronto's economic diversity, including "a wide range of sophisticated service industries, including finance and professional/producer services, [and] a strong manufacturing base in industries such as automotive, food products, electronics, specialized machinery and aerospace," has provided opportunities for cross-sectoral knowledge exchange and convergence between different types of technologies leading to the diversity of highly innovative life science activities.

Manufacturing is also still important in a number of smaller and mid-sized cities in Ontario, in part because the automotive industry (including automotive parts suppliers and car assembly plants) has historically been one of Ontario's strongest economic sectors (Rutherford and Holmes, 2008a, 2008b). While the automotive industry has faced a series of challenges related to the economic downturn, it remains an important employer in metropolitan regions such as Kitchener and Windsor, the respective locations of Toyota and Ford plants. In 2011, in fact, manufacturing still accounted for almost one-fifth of employment in Kitchener (18.8 per cent) and Windsor (18.8 per cent). However, Kitchener's manufacturing base is more diverse than just automotive manufacturing. While large companies such as BlackBerry (formerly Research In Motion [RIM]) and Maple Leaf Foods no longer have manufacturing facilities in the city-region, there remains a base of large-scale manufacturing employers, including Dare Foods Limited, Krug (furniture), and Rimowa (luxury luggage). In addition to these larger industrial employers, a wide range of smaller companies engaged in information and communications technology (ICT), machinery, furniture, and other manufacturing continue to operate. With the understanding that Canadian manufacturing faces challenges, business and civic leaders, universities, and government in Waterloo Region have made an effort to sustain local manufacturing activity by establishing the Manufacturing Innovation Network (MIN) (Nelles, forthcoming). The MIN is a regional initiative intended to encourage manufacturers to adopt new business practices and technologies, become more innovative, and solve common problems through sharing information and expertise with the end goal of helping local manufacturers remain competitive in the global economy.

Overall, the transformation and restructuring of the manufacturing industries is clearly far more complex than first meets the eye. There has been a significant decline in the relative importance of the manufacturing industries and an even more acute decline in the proportion of the labour force in production-oriented occupations. Yet there remain pockets of high-technology and traditional manufacturing. This raises two related points regarding deindustrialization and the nature of manufacturing activity itself. First, even though employment in the manufacturing sector declined in general, the workers most affected are those in production-oriented jobs. Deindustrialization involves both the transformation of work and sectoral shifts in employment. Second, manufacturing comprises a diverse range of sub-sectors, including automotive and automotive parts, steel, office furniture, machinery, food, and other goods, which are affected by different dynamics related to innovation, technological change, levels of unionization, and market demand. Some forms of manufacturing remain prominent in the Canadian landscape and some Canadian cities still have a relatively large manufacturing presence.

Innovation and the Knowledge-Based Economy

The previous section highlighted the substantial decline in manufacturing and its associated forms of work, as well as the place-specific evolution of this transition given the specific histories and geographies of particular Canadian cities. Likewise, the emergence of the knowledge-based economy has been experienced differently across Canadian cities. As noted earlier, there has been a widespread professionalization of the workforce, leading to the growth of occupations that require higher levels of formal education and specialized knowledge, such as scientists, engineers, lawyers, planners, architects, writers, designers, and other artistic, cultural, social science, and technical occupations; these are the occupations associated with the creative class. Table 5.5 shows the growth of this occupational group across 30 Canadian cities between 1971 and 2011. Professionals accounted for 8.9 per cent of the labour force in 1971 but more than doubled in their relative importance by 2011, accounting for 21.6 per cent of the workforce. In stark contrast to the fate of processing and machining jobs (above), which declined in relative terms in all 30 Canadian cities, professional occupations grew in both absolute and relative terms across all of these cities. Again, this did not occur evenly and there is a

| Table 5.5 | Employment in Professional Occupations in Canadian Cities, 1971–2011 |

	1971		2011		1971–2011	
	Local Employment	*% Local*	*Local Employment*	*% Local*	*Local Employment*	*% Local*
Toronto	122,055	9.8	701,915	23.8	579,860	14.0
Montreal	106,520	9.9	473,405	23.7	366,885	13.9
Vancouver	41,600	8.8	289,900	23.3	248,300	14.5
Ottawa–Gatineau	36,905	14.2	207,395	30.2	170,490	16.0
Calgary	20,035	11.3	173,005	24.2	152,970	12.9
Edmonton	22,650	10.4	142,825	21.2	120,175	10.8
Quebec City	19,480	10.9	106,445	25.2	86,965	14.3
Winnipeg	22,700	9.3	88,640	22.2	65,940	12.9
Hamilton	18,645	8.8	79,540	21.5	60,895	12.8
Kitchener	9,105	8.6	57,830	22.1	48,725	13.5
Halifax	9,945	10.4	55,250	25.0	45,305	14.6
London	12,320	9.5	51,760	21.0	39,440	11.5
Victoria	7,450	9.2	48,240	25.7	40,790	16.5
Oshawa	3,950	8.0	40,080	21.3	36,130	13.3
St Catharines–Niagara	10,140	8.1	34,455	17.7	24,315	9.6
Saskatoon	6,125	11.5	31,740	21.2	25,615	9.7
Windsor	8,255	7.8	29,095	19.7	20,840	11.8
St John's	4,540	9.4	26,780	24.9	22,240	15.5
Regina	6,080	9.9	25,660	21.0	19,580	11.1
Sherbrooke	4,000	12.4	23,065	22.7	19,065	10.3
Kingston	4,990	13.4	22,705	27.3	17,715	14.0
Guelph	3,315	11.9	17,980	22.9	14,665	11.0
Sudbury	5,390	8.7	16,740	20.4	11,350	11.7
Trois-Rivières	3,330	9.6	16,150	21.7	12,820	12.0
Thunder Bay	3,850	8.3	14,055	22.9	10,205	14.7
Saint John	3,215	7.5	13,470	20.3	10,255	12.8
Peterborough	2,980	11.0	13,190	22.6	10,210	11.6
Brantford	2,475	6.9	12,110	17.5	9,635	10.5
Sault Ste Marie	2,895	8.9	7,970	20.4	5,075	11.5
Sarnia	3,735	11.4	7,520	17.6	3,785	6.2
Canada	**766,550**	**8.9**	**3,805,855**	**21.6**	**3,039,305**	**12.8**

Source: Statistics Canada, *Census of Population, 1971*; Statistics Canada, *National Household Survey, 2011* (author's calculations).

relationship to city size (see Beckstead and Brown, 2006). Indeed, Canada's largest cities (Toronto, Montreal, Vancouver, Ottawa) experienced some of the largest increases in the proportion of the labour force accounted for by professionals, as did several smaller regional centres, such as St John's,

Halifax, Victoria, and Quebec City. Beckstead and Vinodrai (2003) have shown that growth in these occupations has been experienced across almost all industrial sectors, including typically "low-tech" sectors, such as mining and other natural resource-based sectors. Further work by Beckstead and Gellatly (2006) confirms that mining and oil and gas extraction industries, as well as the manufacturing industries, rank highly in terms of employing scientists and engineers. In other words, even traditional industries are increasingly relying on knowledge-based inputs.

Sudbury provides an interesting case of the shift toward **knowledge-intensive economic activity**. As a northern Ontario city dominated by the mining sector, including large multinational companies such as Inco (owned by the Brazilian company, Vale) and Falconbridge (owned by the Swiss company, Xstrata), the city has been strongly influenced by the restructuring of the mining industry. Between 1971 and 2011, the proportion of employment accounted for by Sudbury's primary industries (e.g., mining, forestry, and other extractive and natural resource-based activities) declined from 26.6 per cent to 8.7 per cent. This reflects the ongoing layoffs and outsourcing that occurred from the mid-1970s onward among local mining firms (Warrian and Mulhern, 2009). While such downsizing has unquestionably had negative effects on Sudbury and its surrounding communities, at the same time, a small but technology-intensive cluster of mining supply and service companies has emerged. The layoffs of highly skilled workers from the large mining companies in the city-region resulted in the emergence of a new set of firms that drew on the existing local skill base and provided services to the large mining companies. Moreover, Sudbury's high-technology mining services sector is increasingly supported by the emergence of several organizations, such as the Northern Centre for Advanced Technology (NORCAT), the Centre for Excellence in Mining Innovation (CEMI), and the Sudbury-and-area Mining Supply and Service Association (SAMSSA); these organizations actively promote the sector's development as a means of sparking broader economic development in the city and in the wider region. In addition, there is a growing role for Laurentian University as a key supplier of highly skilled labour and provider of leading-edge research (Warrian and Mulhern, 2009).

Parallel stories of how the pre-existing economic base of cities shape and condition their subsequent reinvention and transformation are evident in other urban areas. Turning to Hamilton, where the steel industry has left a heavy imprint on the city's economy, the city's transition to knowledge-intensive activities has been shaped by its existing industrial base and through the activities of the local, publicly funded university. One focus of Hamilton's shift towards a more diversified, service- and knowledge-based economy has related to health care and health sciences. While a significant part of Hamilton's growing reputation in health is due to McMaster University's School of Medicine, which offers a distinctive, experientially based form of medical education, one of the primary reasons for health services emerging in Hamilton can be attributed to the pre-existing automotive and steel industries. As Warrian (2009: 18) notes, "Hamilton citizens also tend to have generous medical benefits from unions and the government which means that specialized medical services—such as designed orthotics—are often paid for. Union health benefits have provided the financial base and market for these emergent health services firms." In other words, the presence of the Canadian Auto Workers (now part of Unifor) and United Steel Workers unions in Hamilton was critical in driving demand for and financing Hamilton's emerging health services sector, which has produced world-class innovations.

Elsewhere, the knowledge-based economies of Canadian cities have been built on long-term public investments. For example, the emergence of Ottawa's ICT cluster, specializing in photonics and telecommunications, is partly the result of a long-standing investment in publicly funded government laboratories, as well as a product of particular historical events and regulatory decisions. This includes the founding of a key firm, Bell Northern Research (BNR), which anchored the ICT industry in Ottawa beginning in the 1950s. As Lucas, Sands, and Wolfe (2009: 194) write,

[T]he original decision by Northern Electric in the late-1950s to establish a research facility in the region was made after a judicial decision in the US cut off its ready access to patents from the Western Electric

Co. Its purchase of a substantial tract of land on the outskirts of Ottawa as the future home of Bell Northern Research (BNR) was largely because the concentration of federal government laboratories in the nation's capital created a steady stream of industrial engineers, researchers, and managers moving into the region.

BNR and a subsequent failed subsidiary were the training grounds for several entrepreneurs who left the company to start their own businesses in Ottawa, leading to the development of a critical mass of firms and workers specialized in ICT and related activities. Moreover, several organizations, such as Invest Ottawa (formerly the Ottawa Centre

for Research and Innovation), have emerged that are dedicated to promoting networking among firms to encourage firm learning, knowledge sharing, and problem solving. This local associative activity, alongside support from local and provincial government programs, the presence of national research laboratories, and the research activity of local universities, encourages the ongoing development and growth of this high-tech industry within the city.

The Cultural Economies of Canadian Cities

As noted earlier, the creative and cultural industries are increasingly important to urban economies. Figure 5.3 shows the growth of employment

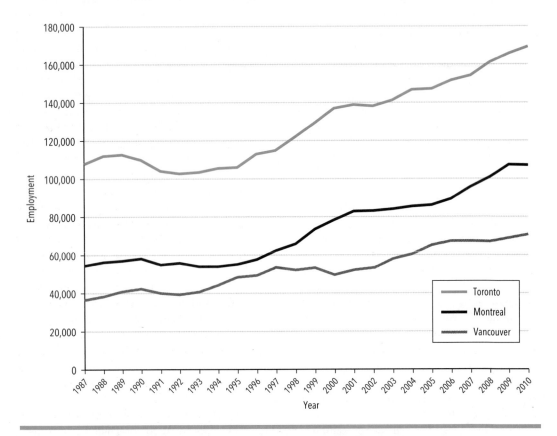

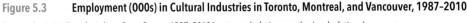

Figure 5.3   **Employment (000s) in Cultural Industries in Toronto, Montreal, and Vancouver, 1987–2010**

Source: Statistics Canada, *Labour Force Survey, 1987–2010* (custom tabulations; author's calculations).

in the cultural industries in Toronto, Montreal, and Vancouver between 1987 and 2010; these three cities account for just over half of Canadian employment in the cultural industries. Over this time period, the average annual growth rates of the cultural industries in Toronto (2.1 per cent), Montreal (3.3 per cent), and Vancouver (3.3 per cent) significantly outpaced the overall growth rates in each city. While these industries also experienced employment growth throughout this period, Figure 5.3 demonstrates accelerated growth beginning in the mid-1990s, which may be attributed to the increased adoption and widespread use of the Internet as a platform for new media applications (Britton, Tremblay, and Smith, 2009). The trajectories in each of these three cities have been shaped by their own local histories, institutions, and policies. In other words, although all three of Canada's largest urban centres have a large concentration of cultural industries, one should not simply assume their character or development paths will be identical, given different pre-existing conditions and institutions.

For example, Vancouver's development trajectory is unique compared to many Canadian and US cities. As Barnes and Hutton (2009: 1252) note,

> to use the Canadian economic historian Harold Innis's (1930) term, Vancouver first developed as a "local metropole" within British Columbia's staples economy and based on the extraction, processing and export of natural resources, most prominently in forestry, fishing and mining. Vancouver's role was primarily a control and distribution centre for staples goods, and only secondarily, a processing site.

Yet the new economy has taken hold in Vancouver, and the city is now viewed as an appealing location for firms and workers involved in a range of creativity- and culture-oriented endeavours (Hutton, 2010; Hutton and Vinodrai, Chapter 6). The quality-of-life factors identified by Florida (2002) related to lifestyle amenities certainly figure heavily in accounts of why workers

and firms are attracted to Vancouver (Britton, Tremblay, and Smith, 2009). However, this only partially explains the growth of Vancouver's creative and cultural industries. Vancouver has emerged recently as a growing hot bed for video game production and other new media applications, with companies like Electronic Arts—one of the largest video game developers in the world—and other gaming companies located there. But there is a longer history that explains Vancouver's new media industry development. First, the industry draws on resources that were already present in the local economy, including film and television, which provided the initial talent base for this emerging industry. Second, Vancouver's video game industry can be traced back to at least the early 1980s with the founding of Distinctive Software, which was acquired by Electronic Arts in the early 1990s. Similar to Vancouver's other cultural industries (such as film and television), entertainment-oriented new media firms in Vancouver generally are focused on international markets and are tied to other places through international capital flows (Barnes and Hutton, 2009; Britton, Tremblay, and Smith, 2009). Finally, several unique public and quasi-public institutions provide support to Vancouver's new media industry, such as the University of British Columbia's Media and Graphics Interdisciplinary Centre (MAGIC), which connects researchers with other local players to enable new product development; and DigiBC, a dedicated umbrella industry association that brings together various institutions, organizations, and other interested parties to promote and develop the mobile and wireless, video games, animation and special effects, social media, and online marketing industries.

In Toronto, the municipal government has identified the cultural sector as one of several key clusters that are critical to its economic development trajectory. A recent study found that employment in Toronto's cultural industries grew at a faster rate than did the cultural industries in several other major North American cities, including San Francisco, Los Angeles, and Chicago (Gertler et al., 2006; Vinodrai and Gertler, 2007).

Yet such growth rests on several important territorial assets and institutional supports. Toronto's cultural industries have been nurtured by public funding for the arts and culture at the local, provincial, and national levels. Moreover, a diverse set of public and private organizations support the development of these industries. For example, Toronto's film industry is supported by several city-level initiatives, including the following: (1) the Toronto Film, Television and Digital Media Office, which provides logistical and regulatory support; (2) a Film Board, made up of industry players and local councillors that creates strategies and policies to promote and support Toronto's film and television industry; and (3) Pinewood Toronto Studios (formerly Filmport), Canada's largest film and media production complex located along the city's waterfront.

In addition to these city-supported initiatives, Toronto's film industry has benefited from federal institutions, such as the National Film Board (NFB) and the Canadian Broadcasting Corporation (CBC), as well as provincial programs, including the Ontario Film and Television Tax Credit (Gertler et al., 2006). Toronto has also become a destination for film consumption, hosting the Toronto International Film Festival (TIFF), with its home at the TIFF Bell Lightbox in Toronto's entertainment district, as well as other events, such as the Canadian Film Centre's Worldwide Short Film Festival (WSFF). In addition to film and television, there is a critical mass of fashion, design, art, architecture, music, new media, and other cultural activities (Britton, Tremblay, and Smith, 2009; Leslie and Brail, 2008; Vinodrai, 2006, 2013; Vinodrai and Gertler, 2007). Publicly funded institutions of higher education, such as Sheridan College, Seneca College, the Ontario College of Art and Design, Ryerson University, and George Brown College, offer programs in animation, design, and other culture-related programs that develop the local talent so critical to the survival of these industries. For new media and advertising in particular, the presence of local demand generated by other sectors, especially financial and business services, has helped to buoy these industries.

Conclusion

This chapter has traced how the economic landscapes of Canadian cities have profoundly changed since the crisis and decline of Fordism and its associated production and employment relations, regulatory mechanisms, and other institutions. On the one hand, the occupational composition of Canadian cities reflects an increasing demand for knowledge, creativity, and formal qualifications. On the other hand, the sectoral composition of Canadian cities has slowly transformed to one where services-producing industries (including higher-order, knowledge-intensive services and lower-order services) have eclipsed goods-producing industries in terms of their relative importance to urban economies. Three key features of this economic transition were examined in detail. First, Canada's manufacturing base has declined and transformed over the past several decades. Second, there has been a shift toward knowledge-based and innovation-oriented activity. Third, creative and cultural economic activities have become increasingly important, particularly in large cities. However, as seen throughout the chapter, economic transitions unfold slowly and urban economies evolve over time—not divorced from either broader macroeconomic, political, social, and cultural conditions or their particular local contexts. The transition toward a post-industrial economy has been experienced differentially across Canadian cities, and their economic development trajectories are path-dependent. In other words, the specific industrial histories, individual characteristics, and territorial assets of city-regions matter to their economic development. Furthermore, public investments at the local, provincial, and national levels clearly have been important in shaping these outcomes.

On a final note, the emphasis on innovation, and on knowledge-based economic development and growth, points to some troubling questions about the nature of work and the fortunes of individuals, communities, and cities. Scholars have raised questions about the polarizing dynamics related to the emergence of a knowledge-based, creative economy, often associated with an increasingly deepening divide between professional, managerial, technical, and scientific workers (often referred to as the creative class) and workers occupying lower-wage, routinized service work jobs (Gertler, 2001; Scott, 2007; Storper and Scott, 2009). Moreover, some of these same tendencies exist within the industries associated with the emerging knowledge-based economy itself, with significant implications for the urban labour markets in which they are situated. These issues remain challenging questions for scholars and policy-makers to understand and address. As students and scholars interested in contemporary urban and economic change, it is our task to understand the ongoing economic transitions in Canadian cities and the implications for individuals, for communities, and for cities.

Acknowledgements

The author thanks Michael Seasons (School of Planning, University of Waterloo) for research assistance. This chapter has been greatly enhanced through the author's participation in the Innovation Systems Research Network (ISRN) directed by Meric Gertler and David Wolfe at the University of Toronto and its Social Sciences and Humanities Research Council (SSHRC)–funded studies of clusters, innovation and economic development in Canada, and the economic and creativity performance of Canadian cities.

Review Questions

1. What economic transitions are Canadian cities presently undergoing?
2. How can cities promote economic change? How can they be made to embrace economic performance?
3. What are the consequences of deindustrialization for Canadian cities?
4. How does the rise of the knowledge-based economy affect cities?

Notes

1. Throughout this chapter, Statistics Canada data are used, including the 1971 Census of Population and the 2011 National Household Survey (NHS). There are some issues in comparing NHS results to data from earlier census periods due to changes in how data are collected (see Appendix A). However, the focus on long-term trends at an aggregate level as well as the relatively low global non-response rates for the 2011 NHS variables used mitigate these issues to a degree. Nonetheless, data should be used with caution.
2. Debates continue about the particular expressions or "varieties" of capitalism that may exist across different nation-states and how this (re)produces different *neo-liberal* governance regimes at a variety of scales (Hall and Soskice, 2001; Peck and Theodore, 2007); a detailed discussion is beyond the scope of this chapter.

References

Amin, A., ed. 1994. *Post-Fordism: A Reader*. Cambridge, MA: Blackwell.

Barnes, T., and T. Hutton. 2009. "Situating the new economy: Contingencies of regeneration and dislocation in Vancouver's inner city," *Urban Studies* 46: 1247–69.

Bathelt, H., A. Malmberg, and A. Maskell. 2004. "Clusters and knowledge: Local buzz, global pipelines and the process of knowledge creation," *Progress in Human Geography* 28: 31–56.

Beck, U. 2000. *The Brave New World of Work*. Cambridge: Cambridge University Press.

Beckstead, D., and M.W. Brown. 2006. *Innovation Capabilities: Science and Engineering Employment in Canadian and US Cities*. Ottawa: Analytical Studies Branch, Statistics Canada, Canadian Economy in Transition Series. Catalogue no. 11–622–MIE2006012.

———, and G. Gellatly. 2006. *Innovation Capabilities: Science and Engineering Employment in Canada and the United States*. Ottawa: Analytical Studies Branch, Statistics Canada, Canadian Economy in Transition Series. Catalogue no. 11–622–MIE2006011.

———, and T. Vinodrai. 2003. *Dimensions of Occupational Change in Canada's Knowledge Economy, 1971–1996*. Ottawa: Analytical Studies Branch, Statistics Canada, Canadian Economy in Transition Series. Catalogue no. 11–622–MIE2003004.

Bell, D. 1973. *The Coming of Post-Industrial Society: A Venture in Social Forecasting*. New York: Basic Books.

Benner, C. 2002. *Work in the New Economy: Flexible Labor Markets in Silicon Valley*. Malden, MA: Blackwell.

Boyer, R. 2005. "How and why capitalisms differ," *Economy and Society* 34: 509–57.

Britton, J.N.H., D.-G. Tremblay, and R. Smith. 2009. "Contrasts in clustering: The example of Canadian new media," *European Planning Studies* 17: 281–301.

Bryson, J., and N. Henry. 2005. "The global production system: From Fordism to post-Fordism," in P. Daniels, M. Bradshaw, D. Shaw, and J. Sidaway, eds., *An Introduction to Human Geography: Issues for the 21st Century*. Harlow: Pearson.

Bryson, J.B., and P.W. Daniels, eds. 2007. *The Handbook of Service Industries*. Cheltenham, UK: Edward Elgar.

Cairncross, F. 1997. *The Death of Distance: How the Communications Revolution Is Changing Our Lives*. Cambridge, MA: Harvard Business Press.

Cervenan, A. 2009. *Service Class Prosperity in Ontario*. Toronto: University of Toronto, Martin Prosperity Institute (Ontario in the Creative Age Working Paper Series).

Christopherson, S. 2002. "Project work in context: Regulatory change and the new geography of media," *Environment and Planning A* 34: 2003–15.

Deslisle, F., and R. Shearmur. 2010. "Where does all the talent flow? Migration of young graduates and nongraduates, Canada 1996–2001," *The Canadian Geographer* 54: 305–23.

Ekinsmyth, C. 2002. "Project organization, embeddedness, and risk in magazine publishing," *Regional Studies* 36: 229–44.

Florida, R. 2002. *The Rise of the Creative Class*. New York: Basic Books.

Friedman, T. 2005. *The World Is Flat: A Brief History of the Twenty-First Century*. New York: Farrar, Straus, and Giroux.

Gertler, M.S. 2001. "Urban economy and society in Canada: Flows of people, capital and ideas," *ISUMA: The Canadian Journal of Policy Research* 2, 3: 119–30.

——. 2003. "Tacit knowledge and the economic geography of context, or the undefinable tacitness of being (there)," *Journal of Economic Geography* 3: 75–99.

——. 2008. "Buzz without being there? Communities of practice in context," in A. Amin and J. Roberts, eds., *Community, Economic Creativity and Organization*. Oxford: Oxford University Press.

—— et al. 2006. *Imagine a Toronto: Strategies for a Creative City*. Toronto: University of Toronto, Munk Centre for International Studies.

——, R. Florida, G. Gates, and T. Vinodrai. 2002. *Competing on Creativity: Placing Ontario's Cities in North American Context*. Toronto: Ontario Ministry of Enterprise, Opportunity and Innovation and the Institute for Competitiveness and Prosperity.

——, and T. Vinodrai. 2009. "Life sciences and regional innovation: One path or many?" *European Planning Studies* 17: 235–61.

Gouldner, A. 1979. *The Future of Intellectuals and the Rise of the New Class*. New York: Seabury.

Grabher, G. 2002. "The project ecology of advertising: Talents, tasks, and teams," *Regional Studies* 36: 245–62.

Grant, J.L, ed. 2014. *Seeking Talent for Creative Cities: The Social Dynamics of Innovation*. Toronto: University of Toronto Press.

Hall, P.A., and D. Soskice, eds. 2001. *Varieties of Capitalism: The Institutional Foundations of Comparative Advantage*. Oxford: Oxford University Press.

Harvey, D. 1990. *The Condition of Postmodernity*. Cambridge, MA: Blackwell.

Hutton, T.A. 2010. *The New Economy of the Inner City: Restructuring, Regeneration and Dislocation in the Twenty-First-Century Metropolis*. London and New York: Routledge.

Jenson, J. 1990. "Representations in crisis: The roots of Canada's permeable Fordism," *Canadian Journal of Political Science* 23: 653–83.

Lash, S., and J. Urry. 1994. *Economies of Signs and Spaces*. London: Sage.

Leslie, D., and S. Brail. 2008. "The role of quality of place in attracting and retaining fashion design talent," presented at the Joint ONRIS/MRI Workshop. Toronto, 6–7 Nov.

Lewis, N.M., and B. Donald. 2010. "A new rubric for creative city potential in Canada's smaller cities," *Urban Studies* 47: 29–54.

Ley, D. 1996. *The New Middle Class and the Remaking of the Central City*. Toronto: Oxford University Press.

Lloyd, R. 2006. *Neo-Bohemia: Art and Commerce in the Post-industrial City*. New York: Routledge.

Lowe, N., and M.S. Gertler. 2005. "Diversity and the evolution of a life-science innovation system: The Toronto region in comparative perspective," in D.A. Wolfe and M. Lucas, eds., *Global Networks and Local Linkages: The Paradox of Cluster Development in an Open Economy*. Montreal and Kingston: McGill-Queen's University Press.

——, and ——. 2009. "Building on diversity: Institutional foundations of hybrid strategies in Toronto's life sciences complex," *Regional Studies* 43: 589–603.

Lucas, M., A. Sands, and D.A. Wolfe. 2009. "Regional clusters in a global industry: ICT clusters in Canada," *European Planning Studies* 17: 189–209.

Markusen, A. 2006. "Urban development and the politics of a creative class: Evidence from the study of artists," *Environment and Planning A* 38: 1921–40.

Maskell, P., and A. Malmberg. 1999. "Localised learning and industrial competitiveness," *Cambridge Journal of Economics* 23: 167–85.

McCann, E. 2007. "Inequality and politics in the creative city-region: Questions of livability and state strategy," *International Journal of Urban and Regional Research* 31: 188–96.

McGranahan, D.A., and T.R. Wojan. 2007. "Recasting the creative class to examine growth processes in rural and urban counties," *Regional Studies* 41: 197–216.

Molotch, H. 2002. "Place in product," *International Journal of Urban and Regional Research* 26: 665–88.

Moos, M., and A. Skaburskis. 2007. "The characteristics and location of home workers in Montreal, Toronto and Vancouver," *Urban Studies* 44: 1781–1808.

Morgan, K. 2004. "The exaggerated death of geography: Learning, proximity and territorial innovation systems," *Journal of Economic Geography* 4: 3–22.

Nelles, J. forthcoming. "Myth making and the 'Waterloo Way': Exploring associative governance in Kitchener-Waterloo," in N. Bradford and A. Bramwell, eds., *Governing Urban Economies: Innovation and Inclusion in Canadian City-Regions*. Toronto: University of Toronto Press.

Peck, J. 2005. "Struggling with the creative class," *International Journal of Urban and Regional Research* 29: 740–70.

——, and N. Theodore. 2007. "Variegated capitalism," *Progress in Human Geography* 31: 731–72.

Piore, M.J., and C. Sabel. 1984. *The Second Industrial Divide: Possibilities for Prosperity*. New York: Basic Books.

Porter, M.E. 1998. "Clusters and the new economics of competition," *Harvard Business Review* (Nov.–Dec.): 77–90.

Power, D., and A.J. Scott, eds. 2004. *The Cultural Industries and the Production of Culture*. London: Routledge.

Rutherford, T., and J. Holmes. 2008a. "Engineering networks: University–industry networks in southern Ontario automotive industry clusters," *Cambridge Journal of Regions, Economy and Society* 1: 247–64.

——, and ——. 2008b. "The flea on the tail of the dog: Power in global production networks and the restructuring of Canadian automotive clusters," *Journal of Economic Geography* 8: 519–44.

Scott, A.J. 2001. *The Cultural Economy of Cities: Essays on the Geography of Image-producing Industries*. Oxford: Sage.

——. 2004. "Cultural-products industries and urban economic development: Prospects for growth and market contestation in global context," *Urban Affairs Review* 39: 461–90.

——. 2007. "Capitalism and urbanization in a new key? The cognitive-cultural dimension," *Social Forces* 85: 1466–82.

Shearmur, R. 2007. "The new knowledge aristocracy: The creative class, mobility and urban growth," *Work, Organization, Labour, and Globalization* 1: 31–47.

Storper, M., and A.J. Scott, eds. 1992. *Pathways to Industrialization and Regional Development*. London: Routledge.

——, and ——. 2009. "Rethinking human capital, creativity and urban growth," *Journal of Economic Geography* 9: 147–67.

——, and A.J. Venables. 2004. "Buzz: Face-to-face contact and the urban economy," *Journal of Economic Geography* 4: 351–70.

Tickell, A., and J. Peck. 1992. "Accumulation, regulation and the geographies of post-Fordism: Missing links in regulationist research," *Progress in Human Geography* 16: 190–218.

Vinodrai, T. 2006. "Reproducing Toronto's design ecology: Career paths, intermediaries, and local labor markets," *Economic Geography* 82: 237–63.

——. 2013. "Design in a downturn? Creative work, labour market dynamics and institutions in comparative perspective," *Cambridge Journal of Regions, Economy and Society* 6: 159–76.

——, and M.S. Gertler. 2007. *Measuring the Creative Economy: The Structure and Economic Performance of Ontario's Creative, Cultural and New Media Clusters*. Toronto: Government of Ontario, Ministry of Culture.

——, and S. Keddy. forthcoming. "Projects and project ecologies," in C. Jones, M. Lorenzen, and J. Sapsed, eds., *The Oxford Handbook of Creative and Cultural Industries*. Oxford: Oxford University Press.

Vosko, L., ed. 2006. *Precarious Employment: Understanding Labour Market Insecurity in Canada*. Montreal and Kingston: McGill-Queen's University Press.

Warrian, P. 2009. "Biotech in lunch buckets: The curious knowledge networks in Steeltown," paper presented at the 10th annual meeting of the Innovation Systems Research Network, Halifax, 30 Apr.

——, and C. Mulhern. 2009. "From metal bashing to materials science and services: Advanced manufacturing and mining clusters in transition," *European Planning Studies* 17: 281–301.

Wolfe, D.A., and A. Bramwell. 2008. "Innovation, creativity and governance: Social dynamics of economic performance in city-regions," *Innovation: Management, Policy and Practice* 10: 170–82.

——, and M.S. Gertler. 2004. "Clusters from the inside and out: Local dynamics and global linkages," *Urban Studies* 41: 1071–93.

Zukin, S. 1982. *Loft Living: Culture and Capital in Urban Change*. Baltimore: Johns Hopkins University Press.

Employment, Labour Markets, and Urban Change in Canada

6

TOM HUTTON AND
TARA VINODRAI

Introduction: Employment and Urban Transition in Canada

Over the past quarter-century, Canada has developed not simply as an *urban* society but, more emphatically, as a *metropolitan* society. More than two-thirds of the national population and jobs are situated in the nation's 33 metropolitan areas. Over time, ever-increasing shares of the national population, employment, services, and advanced industrial capacity concentrate in the higher echelons of the Canadian urban system. Greater Toronto, Montreal, Vancouver, Ottawa-Gatineau, Calgary, and Edmonton—with metropolitan populations ranging from just over 1 million to 5.5 million—are increasingly influential in configuring Canada's national economic systems, social agenda, and polity.

Canada's metropolitan cities also function as the nation's global gateways (see Kobayashi and Preston, Chapter 8), constitute the principal centres of higher education and research and development, and comprise the influential sites that underpin creativity and innovation. These same metropolitan regions attract a disproportionate share of international immigrants, who will in turn shape to a large extent the future growth of the labour force, as well as Canada's urban and regional economies, community morphologies, and

multicultural identities (see Filion and Bunting, Chapter 2; Hall, Chapter 3; Vinodrai, Chapter 5). At the same time, medium-size Canadian cities, such as Waterloo, Saskatoon, and Halifax, have found new vocations, notably in the knowledge economy. Overall, city-regions are the critical geospatial elements of the emerging Canadian economy (Moos and Skaburskis, 2009).

Employment represents one of the key measures of analysis for understanding processes of growth and change in cities. The quantity and quality of jobs generated, and labour force participation rates, are leading indicators of the robustness of national, regional, and metropolitan economies. As well, employment is directly linked to incomes and to socio-economic welfare and well-being. And it provides both a metric of economic change among Canadian city-regions and an entrée into larger experiences of metropolitan transformation.

Processes of employment growth and change in Canadian cities are perhaps best understood as *multiscalar flows*. At the Canadian urban system level, employment change reflects structural tendencies, such as the shift from manufacturing to service employment, as well as factors contingent to particular regions, such as urban scale, path dependencies, industrial structure, and policy factors. Change at the national level also reflects the forces of globalization, notably in the concentrations of specialized services (head offices, intermediate finance, and business services) within cities at the peak of the national urban hierarchy.

At the regional scale, employment is an important metric in assessing changes in the metropolitan *space-economy*: the geography of work within urban areas. The metropolis typically comprises agglomerations of linked industries and labour, including major *regional clusters and nodes*, such as the corporate complex of the central business district (CBD), as well as industrial estates, secondary commercial centres, airports and ports, and universities and science parks.

In this chapter we present a concise digest of labour force data for selected city-regions,[1] drawing out aspects of commonality as well as important contrasts. Next, we describe the forces shaping new patterns of enterprise and employment in Canadian city-regions, and outline new geography of employment, including the new economic spaces in the suburbs and the role of employment in the formation of the "new inner city." Synergies of social, market, and policy factors, we shall see, reproduce space and landscape. The conclusion is based on conjecture about future conditions of employment change in Canadian cities.

Industrial Structure and Employment in Canadian Cities

Certain structural elements are common to most Canadian cities and indeed to urban areas within the developed world generally, including, notably, the decline of basic manufacturing and the concomitant rise of service industries and occupations. The service sector is made up of an exceptionally diverse array of industries, including those catering to final demand (i.e., services used by households, such as education, retail, personal, and most public-sector services), as well as to intermediate demand (i.e., providers of inputs to other businesses and industries), for example commercial banking, and business services (Bryson and Daniels, 2007). Service industries also contain a large and growing cultural industry component. About 80 per cent of the labour force of the larger

Canadian cities is comprised of services, with the goods-producing industries (principally manufacturing and construction) accounting for the bulk of the remainder (see Vinodrai, Chapter 5). Most Canadian cities now encompass only very small primary sectors—the extractive industries, such as forestry, agriculture, and mining—essentially residuals of earlier periods of development. But there are important distinctions to acknowledge in the industrial structure of labour and employment among the Canadian cities, derived from scale and specialization, path dependency (legacies of historical development, embedded competitive advantages), and confluences of domestic and global forces.

The Ottawa-Gatineau city-region represents a striking example of path dependency specialization, with almost one-quarter of the regional labour force (24.4 per cent) in the public administration category: almost twice the proportion for Halifax (13.3 per cent), a provincial capital with high dependency on public sector employment, and more than five times the proportion of public administration workers in Toronto (4.5 per cent), a provincial capital city with significant cadres of federal and municipal workers.

Montreal was the first major Canadian city to experience industrialization, followed by Toronto, and these two cities (together with smaller industrial satellite communities in southern Ontario and along the St. Lawrence river) jointly comprised the industrial "core" of Harold Innis's (1933) classic core–periphery model of the Canadian economy. The Greater Toronto Area (GTA) encompasses the largest complex of manufacturing capacity in Canada, with a manufacturing labour force of 293,790, according to the 2011 National Household Survey (Table 6.1), while Montreal's labour force includes 213,660 workers in manufacturing (Table 6.2). For both city-regions, manufacturing accounted for approximately 10 per cent of total labour force in 2011. But manufacturing continues a long process of decline. Between 2001 and 2011, Toronto and Montreal each lost more than a quarter of its manufacturing workforce, shrinking by an average of 2.9 per cent and 3.4 per cent per year,

Table 6.1   Labour Force by Industry Group, Toronto, 2001–2011[1]

Industry	2001 #	2001 %	2006 #	2006 %	2011 #	2011 %	2001–11 Growth
All Industries	2,522,025	100.0	2,758,700	100.0	2,946,835	100.0	1.6
11 Agriculture, forestry, fishing, and hunting	9,430	0.4	9,720	0.4	9,950	0.3	0.5
21 Mining and oil and gas extraction	2,665	0.1	4,660	0.2	4,695	0.2	5.8
22 Utilities	15,770	0.6	16,030	0.6	18,340	0.6	1.5
23 Construction	124,395	4.9	148,895	5.4	162,085	5.5	2.7
31–33 Manufacturing	395,970	15.7	371,275	13.5	293,790	10.0	(2.9)
41 Wholesale trade	151,870	6.0	166,325	6.0	167,275	5.7	1.0
44–45 Retail trade	272,680	10.8	293,465	10.6	316,655	10.7	1.5
48–49 Transportation and warehousing	123,135	4.9	140,200	5.1	147,545	5.0	1.8
51 Information and cultural industries	100,755	4.0	101,850	3.7	110,435	3.7	0.9
52 Finance and insurance	177,210	7.0	193,760	7.0	230,180	7.8	2.6
53 Real estate and rental and leasing	56,890	2.3	66,115	2.4	71,745	2.4	2.3
54 Professional, scientific, and technical services	246,655	9.8	267,625	9.7	299,680	10.2	2.0
55 Mngmt. of companies and enterprises	4,835	0.2	5,570	0.2	4,180	0.1	(1.4)
56 Admin./support, waste mngmt.	121,490	4.8	143,270	5.2	148,380	5.0	2.0
61 Educational services	143,985	5.7	172,990	6.3	206,275	7.0	3.7
62 Health care and social assistance	189,450	7.5	222,140	8.1	260,540	8.8	3.2
71 Arts, entertainment, and recreation	47,875	1.9	55,300	2.0	58,820	2.0	2.1
72 Accommodation and food services	141,560	5.6	157,680	5.7	170,940	5.8	1.9
81 Other services (except public admin.)	110,745	4.4	127,635	4.6	132,990	4.5	1.8
91 Public administration	84,655	3.4	94,195	3.4	132,330	4.5	4.6

1. For this and other tables in this chapter, the reader should exercise caution in comparing data from the *2011 National Household Survey* and previous census periods due to changes in data collection procedures. However, the data illustrate important trends at an aggregate level and the NHS data have relatively low global non-response rates. See Appendix A.

Source: Statistics Canada, *Census of Population 2001*; Statistics Canada, *Census of Population 2006*; Statistics Canada, *2011 National Household Survey* [authors' calculations].

respectively. In contrast, Vancouver's manufacturing labour force is much smaller in both absolute and relative terms, accounting for only 6.6 per cent of the city-region total in 2011. Moreover, Vancouver's manufacturing sector declined at a slower rate (1.9 per cent per year) between 2001 and 2011 (Table 6.3). Vancouver never developed as a fully industrial city on the model of its larger (and older) central Canadian counterparts, but its mix of mostly small production industries (including food products, garment production, and niche-level advanced-technology industries) has proven relatively resilient compared to other Canadian cities.

Table 6.2   Labour Force by Industry Group, Montreal, 2001–2011

Industry	2001 #	2001 %	2006 #	2006 %	2011 #	2011 %	2001–11 Growth
All Industries	1,765,760	100.0	1,923,975	100.0	1,994,720	100.0	1.2
11 Agriculture, forestry, fishing, and hunting	7,210	0.4	9,215	0.5	8,900	0.4	2.1
21 Mining and oil and gas extraction	1,465	0.1	2,035	0.1	2,405	0.1	5.1
22 Utilities	12,425	0.7	16,115	0.8	16,510	0.8	2.9
23 Construction	70,870	4.0	88,790	4.6	99,550	5.0	3.5
31–33 Manufacturing	301,945	17.1	260,530	13.5	213,660	10.7	(3.4)
41 Wholesale trade	103,015	5.8	108,185	5.6	105,935	5.3	0.3
44–45 Retail trade	200,355	11.3	232,440	12.1	242,920	12.2	1.9
48–49 Transportation and warehousing	90,840	5.1	94,995	4.9	97,580	4.9	0.7
51 Information and cultural industries	69,230	3.9	70,170	3.6	70,025	3.5	0.1
52 Finance and insurance	78,555	4.4	89,190	4.6	94,380	4.7	1.9
53 Real estate and rental and leasing	29,760	1.7	35,015	1.8	36,625	1.8	2.1
54 Professional, scientific, and technical services	140,410	8.0	159,500	8.3	178,740	9.0	2.4
55 Mngmt. of companies and enterprises	2,075	0.1	2,750	0.1	2,280	0.1	0.9
56 Admin./support, waste mngmt.	70,980	4.0	81,545	4.2	86,545	4.3	2.0
61 Educational services	117,580	6.7	136,600	7.1	153,030	7.7	2.7
62 Health care and social assistance	173,340	9.8	206,855	10.8	232,195	11.6	3.0
71 Arts, entertainment, and recreation	33,310	1.9	41,590	2.2	42,120	2.1	2.4
72 Accommodation and food services	99,845	5.7	113,655	5.9	121,235	6.1	2.0
81 Other services (except public admin.)	81,985	4.6	89,380	4.6	87,875	4.4	0.7
91 Public administration	80,565	4.6	85,405	4.4	102,200	5.1	2.4

Source: Statistics Canada, *Census of Population 2001*; Statistics Canada, *Census of Population 2006*; Statistics Canada, *2011 National Household Survey* [authors' calculations].

While manufacturing remains important for some Canadian cities, manufacturing represents only a small proportion of the metropolitan labour force for many; therefore, the story for many Canadian cities concerns performance in the service sector. As in other leading Organisation for Economic Co-operation and Development (OECD) economies, the fortunes of Canadian cities are shaped by the dimensions, degree of specialization, and growth dynamics of advanced services.

While the GTA encompasses the largest industrial production sector in Canada, its primacy within the national economy, and its claims to **global city** status, rest on its platform of specialized service industries, firms, and labour. To illustrate, Toronto's professional, scientific, and technical services labour force—a key marker of socio-economic transformation, as defined in Daniel Bell's seminal work on *The Coming of Post-Industrial Society* (1973)—reached almost 300,000 workers in 2011,

Table 6.3   Labour Force by Industry Group, Vancouver, 2001–2011

Industry	2001		2006		2011		2001–11
	#	%	#	%	#	%	Growth
All Industries	1,049,910	100.0	1,150,490	100.0	1,245,760	100.0	1.7
11 Agriculture, forestry, fishing, and hunting	13,275	1.3	13,890	1.2	12,695	1.0	(0.4)
21 Mining and oil and gas extraction	2,250	0.2	4,380	0.4	5,065	0.4	8.5
22 Utilities	6,200	0.6	5,705	0.5	7,470	0.6	1.9
23 Construction	53,800	5.1	73,385	6.4	84,540	6.8	4.6
31–33 Manufacturing	99,055	9.4	97,805	8.5	81,645	6.6	(1.9)
41 Wholesale trade	56,020	5.3	61,655	5.4	60,430	4.9	0.8
44–45 Retail trade	116,520	11.1	124,960	10.9	135,255	10.9	1.5
48–49 Transportation and warehousing	65,700	6.3	65,600	5.7	68,600	5.5	0.4
51 Information and cultural industries	44,355	4.2	42,145	3.7	45,020	3.6	0.1
52 Finance and insurance	54,115	5.2	55,640	4.8	62,665	5.0	1.5
53 Real estate and rental and leasing	24,730	2.4	29,580	2.6	33,155	2.7	3.0
54 Professional, scientific, and technical services	91,720	8.7	107,490	9.3	120,590	9.7	2.8
55 Mngmt. of companies and enterprises	970	0.1	2,155	0.2	1,745	0.1	6.0
56 Admin./support, waste mngmt.	45,530	4.3	53,725	4.7	56,840	4.6	2.2
61 Educational services	74,480	7.1	83,200	7.2	93,600	7.5	2.3
62 Health care and social assistance	99,350	9.5	107,065	9.3	125,495	10.1	2.4
71 Arts, entertainment, and recreation	24,050	2.3	27,350	2.4	30,560	2.5	2.4
72 Accommodation and food services	81,555	7.8	91,585	8.0	97,010	7.8	1.8
81 Other services (except public admin.)	51,610	4.9	59,060	5.1	61,695	5.0	1.8
91 Public administration	44,630	4.3	44,115	3.8	61,680	5.0	3.3

Source: Statistics Canada, *Census of Population 2001*; Statistics Canada, *Census of Population 2006*; Statistics Canada, *2011 National Household Survey* [authors' calculations].

comprising 10.2 per cent of the GTA's total. The key financial, insurance, and real estate (FIRE) sector labour force, numbering just under 180,000 in 2001 (or 7 per cent of the regional total), increased to 230,180 (or 7.8 per cent of the regional total) between 2001 and 2011. In Montreal the professional, scientific, and technical labour force grew from about 140,000 to about 180,000 between 2001 and 2011, growing at an annual rate of 2.4 per cent per year (Tables 6.1 and 6.2).

Calgary, the growth leader among Canada's major cities, presents a storyline of spectacular expansion in its key industrial specialization, the mining and oil and gas sector, where the labour force expanded from 27,880 in 2001 to 45,265 by 2011, the annual growth rate of 5 per cent a year in this sector was well above the overall city's average growth rate of 2.4 per cent (Table 6.4). Buttressing this propulsive sector of the Calgary economy, the professional, scientific, and technical labour force also expanded by

Table 6.4   Labour Force by Industry Group, Calgary, 2001–2011

Industry	2001 #	2001 %	2006 #	2006 %	2011 #	2011 %	2001-11 Growth
All Industries	564,045	100.0	653,505	100.0	715,270	100.0	2.4
11 Agriculture, forestry, fishing, and hunting	4,090	0.7	3,755	0.6	4,015	0.6	(0.2)
21 Mining and oil and gas extraction	27,880	4.9	42,390	6.5	45,265	6.3	5.0
22 Utilities	4,880	0.9	6,630	1.0	8,295	1.2	5.4
23 Construction	40,435	7.2	53,670	8.2	62,105	8.7	4.4
31–33 Manufacturing	49,495	8.8	48,660	7.4	41,835	5.8	(1.7)
41 Wholesale trade	28,275	5.0	31,440	4.8	31,725	4.4	1.2
44–45 Retail trade	60,870	10.8	68,575	10.5	76,835	10.7	2.4
48–49 Transportation and warehousing	34,895	6.2	37,235	5.7	40,080	5.6	1.4
51 Information and cultural industries	18,930	3.4	17,355	2.7	16,270	2.3	(1.5)
52 Finance and insurance	23,230	4.1	25,035	3.8	27,095	3.8	1.6
53 Real estate and rental and leasing	12,600	2.2	14,665	2.2	15,810	2.2	2.3
54 Professional, scientific, and technical services	61,530	10.9	75,815	11.6	83,390	11.7	3.1
55 Mngmt. of companies and enterprises	1,080	0.2	1,375	0.2	1,210	0.2	1.1
56 Admin./support, waste mngmt.	24,230	4.3	27,135	4.2	28,730	4.0	1.7
61 Educational services	33,290	5.9	37,960	5.8	43,930	6.1	2.8
62 Health care and social assistance	45,795	8.1	55,860	8.5	66,740	9.3	3.8
71 Arts, entertainment, and recreation	12,185	2.2	14,460	2.2	15,960	2.2	2.7
72 Accommodation and food services	38,920	6.9	42,685	6.5	43,125	6.0	1.0
81 Other services (except public admin.)	25,250	4.5	29,485	4.5	31,875	4.5	2.4
91 Public administration	16,200	2.9	19,320	3.0	30,980	4.3	6.7

Source: Statistics Canada, *Census of Population 2001*; Statistics Canada, *Census of Population 2006*; Statistics Canada, *2011 National Household Survey* [authors' calculations].

3.1 per cent per year between 2001 and 2011, while financial and insurance labour grew by 1.6 per cent annually over the same period.

As crucial as these specialized services are to advanced economies, in terms of productivity gains, wealth generation, and salaries, our necessarily succinct profile acknowledges the high proportion of employment in the broader public sector. In the GTA, for example, the labour force in the educational services and health care and associated social services totalled almost 470,000 in 2011, up from just over 330,000 in 2001; over this time period, these industry groups experienced brisk annual growth rates of 3.7 per cent and 3.2 per cent, respectively. In the Ottawa case, these two industries reached almost 125,000 workers, with annual growth rates of 3.0 per cent and 2.9 per cent, respectively (Table 6.5). Public services tend to be more resistant to recession than employment in private-sector services, often acting

Table 6.5   Labour Force by Industry Group, Ottawa-Gatineau, 2001–2011

	2001		2006		2011		2001–11
Industry	#	%	#	%	#	%	Growth
All Industries	585,935	100.0	627,010	100.0	687,005	100.0	1.6
11 Agriculture, forestry, fishing, and hunting	4,010	0.7	3,690	0.6	3,395	0.5	(1.7)
21 Mining and oil and gas extraction	290	0.0	645	0.1	680	0.1	8.9
22 Utilities	1,915	0.3	2,410	0.4	2,600	0.4	3.1
23 Construction	26,970	4.6	30,890	4.9	36,555	5.3	3.1
31–33 Manufacturing	44,600	7.6	28,760	4.6	24,135	3.5	(6.0)
41 Wholesale trade	14,230	2.4	15,470	2.5	16,705	2.4	1.6
44–45 Retail trade	58,660	10.0	65,025	10.4	69,140	10.1	1.7
48–49 Transportation and warehousing	20,610	3.5	20,960	3.3	20,300	3.0	(0.2)
51 Information and cultural industries	21,685	3.7	18,870	3.0	17,460	2.5	(2.1)
52 Finance and insurance	19,015	3.2	19,115	3.0	21,695	3.2	1.3
53 Real estate and rental and leasing	9,635	1.6	10,635	1.7	11,005	1.6	1.3
54 Professional, scientific, and technical services	61,365	10.5	59,650	9.5	58,630	8.5	(0.5)
55 Mngmt. of companies and enterprises	295	0.1	310	0.0	335	0.0	1.3
56 Admin./support, waste mngmt.	25,830	4.4	29,705	4.7	27,075	3.9	0.5
61 Educational services	39,480	6.7	43,970	7.0	52,475	7.6	2.9
62 Health care and social assistance	53,325	9.1	61,905	9.9	71,490	10.4	3.0
71 Arts, entertainment, and recreation	11,620	2.0	13,640	2.2	13,815	2.0	1.7
72 Accommodation and food services	34,485	5.9	38,355	6.1	41,220	6.0	1.8
81 Other services (except public admin.)	26,175	4.5	29,790	4.8	30,695	4.5	1.6
91 Public administration	111,740	19.1	133,200	21.2	167,600	24.4	4.1

Source: Spencer and Vinodrai (2009); Statistics Canada (2013) *2011 National Household Survey*; [authors' calculations]

to buffer local economies during downturns. This is especially true for smaller and mid-size urban communities, which in many cases do not encompass the large, specialized business and financial sectors found in the major metropolitan cities.

Employment in the construction sector represents a useful bellwether of urban growth. Despite the recent downturn, the economic and physical growth of large Canadian cities has been facilitated by the expansion of the construction labour force.

Between 2001 and 2006, the GTA's construction labour force grew by almost one-fifth, from almost 125,000 to 150,000. While growth slowed between 2006 and 2011, construction maintained its share of the regional labour force (5.5 per cent), and employment increased by another 12,000 people. Montreal's construction labour force expanded by almost one-quarter from just over 70,000 to just under 90,000 between 2001 and 2006; by 2011, employment reached almost 100,000 in this sector. But the leading cities of Canada's "New West" experienced the most dramatic growth in construction. In Calgary, the construction sector expanded from 40,435 in 2001 to 62,105 in 2011, growing annually by 4.4 per cent (Table 6.4). Meanwhile metropolitan Vancouver, which experienced a housing boom and had large injections of capital in the local economy as part of the leadup to the 2010 Winter Olympics during this period, had an increase from 53,800 to 84,540 during the same period, growing at 4.6 per cent annually, compared to the overall growth rate of 1.7 per cent for the Vancouver labour force (Table 6.3).

While labour force and employment have experienced impressive growth within the Canadian urban system, successive phases of innovation and restructuring over the past two decades have caused some destabilization of employment and labour force. Moreover, the recent economic downturn will produce new structural contractions as well as more transient effects. Fluctuations in the metropolitan labour force are accompanied in many cases by shifts in the location of enterprise and associated patterns of land use and city structure, a theme we shall turn to below.

Changing Dynamics of Employment Location in the Canadian City

As in other advanced societies, the location of employment in Canadian cities exhibits both continuities and disjuncture. Within the urban production sector (services as well as goods) firms and labour still congregate within agglomerations and clusters, to reduce input costs, and to benefit from knowledge spillovers and other externalities. Firms in the consumption sector, such as retail, personal, and many public services (such as K–12 education), still tend to "follow the population" and are growing most rapidly in suburban areas with expanding residential communities. But a new mix of factors is reshaping the location of labour and, consequently, the geography of work, in Canadian cities.

Technological Innovation and the "New Economy" of the City

Among factors of change we can acknowledge advances in *telecommunications technologies* and the digital revolution. Information and communications technologies haven't meant the "death of distance." Rather, information technologies have in some ways augmented the traditional advantages of locational proximity and face-to-face contact (Wheeler, Aoyama, and Warf, 2000). But advanced telecom systems also open up new possibilities of conducting economic activity over extended space—for example, e-businesses, telecommuting, and use of the Internet for input sourcing, staff recruitment, and marketing. So, the effects of technological innovation in communications include both the *concentration* of activities in major centres, such as Toronto, that enjoy advantages of advanced telecommunications and other knowledge networks, as well as the *diffusion/dispersion* of work and employment, including teleworking and telecommuting.

Globalization and the New International Division of Labour

A second major bundle of change underpinning new employment patterns concerns *the international division of labour*. The "new international division of labour" (Fröbel, Heinrichs, and Kreye, 1980) was associated with the shift of industrial production from the developed West to the emergent economies of East Asia and Southeast Asia. More recently, a yet newer international division of labour entails larger, more diverse, and more complex movements of labour for short- or long-term periods across global space, shaped by bilateral trade agreements, sectoral treaties, corporate takeovers, strategic partnerships, and new approaches to supply chain management (see Hall, Chapter 3).

In Canadian cities, we see clear evidence of these trends, notably in the following:

1. A consolidation of the North American auto industry, forcing labour contractions and

continued plant closures in a number of southern Ontario cities

2. A reorganization of the pulp and paper sector, principally in Quebec and British Columbia, in response to global oversupply and market decline (e.g., in the newspaper business)

3. A takeover of Hamilton's steel mills by foreign multinationals, owing to a range of factors, including the intention of multinational steel corporations to capture critical expertise embedded in the Hamilton steel sector (Warrian, 2009)

4. The rise of film and video production in Toronto, Montreal, and Vancouver, attributed to a range of factors, including Hollywood's desire to achieve operational economies (seen in the growth of "runaway productions") and concentrations of local talent in each city.

International Immigration and the Reshaping of Urban Labour Markets

International immigration is well-established as a leading agent of transformation in urban-regional employment growth and change. For the largest cities, especially Toronto and Vancouver, immigration comprises a major growth component. The regional labour force has benefited greatly from inflows of workers, including large proportions of younger, working-age immigrants; significant numbers of entrepreneurial immigrants, with new energy and expertise; and investors who have expanded the pool of capital for business start-ups and development. New immigrants also contribute to the *global connectivity* of Canada's cities through communications and knowledge transfer operating between immigrants and co-ethnics abroad: a clear competitive advantage in the knowledge economy.

Market Interdependencies and the Location of Employment

Another set of influences is subsumed within the general category of markets, specifically *housing*, *property*, and *consumption markets*.

First, housing characteristics (price, supply, type) exert significant influences on employment location within urban-regional labour markets. In some of the larger cities, notably Toronto, Vancouver, and Calgary, inflationary housing markets have acted to reduce housing options for many, and to increase the spatial separation between place of work and place of residence.

Second, the property market acts as a filter on the location of economic activity and employment. To illustrate: the insistent revalorization of inner-city property markets, a quarter-century following the collapse of the urban core's manufacturing sector, has displaced low-income populations and low-margin firms, especially in Toronto, Vancouver, and Montreal. As a second example, relatively low land costs in suburban/exurban areas have tended to encourage the proliferation of low-density land use and employment formation, including business and industrial parks and retail strips. Clearly, a business case (including considerations of cost and convenience) exists for these low-density employment sites. But they are difficult to service by public transit and are, thus, highly auto-dependent, thereby contributing to increased carbon emissions.

Finally, trends in consumption influence certain kinds of activity and labour, e.g., the importance of consumption amenities for attracting cultural workers and the creative class. Whether or not we're inclined to accept the ebullient prognosis of "amenity as destiny" (Florida, 2002; for a counter-argument, see Storper and Scott, 2009), it seems clear that the distinctive amenity package of the urban core is important in attracting talent.

Policy Factors and the Location of Employment

Planning and policies directly, or indirectly, shape the metropolitan space-economy and labour force. At the regional level, these include not only plans for urban structure and land use, but also public investments in transportation (public transit as well as highway/road construction). At the local municipal level, public agencies exercise significant control over the location of enterprises and employment by means of zoning and land use policies and, less directly, through building and development guidelines, infrastructure provision, and fiscal policies. The past two decades have seen the emergence of more assertive economic development programs (including economic development strategies, sector programs, and talent attraction/retention policies) in Canada, in what David Harvey (1989) has referred to as a shift from "managerial" to "entrepreneurial" governance.

A spectrum of more localized programs influences metropolitan employment, including the following:

1. Local regeneration programs, which promote investment and start-ups in specific locations, notably in low-income communities with inadequate access to jobs
2. Business improvement area (BIA) initiatives, designed to improve the local environment (taxation, amenities, information networks, and services), and normally initiated by the local business community
3. Brownfield redevelopment or retrofitting, involving older inner suburban districts in need of new investments and employment opportunities
4. "Compact and complete" community programs designated for special zones of employment and residential concentration within urban-regional strategies
5. New Urbanism projects on the metropolitan periphery, which may include new employment formation in business, retail, and personal services, alongside residential tracts.

The Changing Space-Economy and Patterns of Employment

Owing in large part to the mix of factors described above, the last quarter-century has seen significant changes in the industrial structure (mix of industries and employment), space economy, and spatial divisions of labour in the Canadian metropolis. Canadian cities for the most part still present a profile that includes a relatively robust central

area, including specialized industries, firms, and labour; and reinvestments in the core driven by new housing and residential districts, consumption, and specialized production. Indeed, a variant of the "back to the city" movement has included the introduction of new social classes and cohorts in such cities as Vancouver, Toronto, Montreal, and Halifax, among others. This has been facilitated in some cases by city planning and policies, including rezoning, housing policies, and public realm improvements. That said, the urban core has been essentially stripped of its manufacturing capacity, and the high growth trajectory of the downtown office sector of the 1970s and 1980s has slowed appreciably, so there has been both a relative and an absolute shift of employment growth to the suburbs.

The Rise of Suburban Employment in Canadian City-Regions

While manufacturing has been in secular decline in most Canadian city-regions since the 1970s, what remains is highly concentrated in the suburbs and exurbs, especially on the fringes of the Greater Toronto Area (GTA). Suburban areas also encompass major concentrations of warehousing and distribution activity, taking advantage of the larger land parcels available on the periphery, as well as access to major regional transportation installations (ports, airports, rail systems, highways).

A second principal category of suburban employment within Canadian city-regions comprises the services catering to final demand that are linked to residential populations. These include local government and other public institutions; public education; large concentrations of retail services, including major shopping malls, retail strips, and more scattered retail outlets; and personal services, including professional services such as medical, dental, legal, and accounting services.

Over the past two decades or so suburban areas have attracted new industries, institutions, and associated labour, marking the continuing development and maturation of these areas. As well, these industries and institutions have been the subject of a major international research project, called "Global Suburbanisms" and directed by Roger Keil at York University, Toronto (see Addie, Fieldler, and Keil, Chapter 24). These industries and institutions include, for example, science parks and research and development (R&D) facilities; universities and other tertiary educational institutions; secondary business, financial, and commercial centres; film production and other cultural industries; and recreational and leisure development. As well, international airports have expanded significantly, generating new suburban employment, notably at Pearson International Airport (in Mississauga) and Vancouver International Airport (in Richmond, in Vancouver's inner suburbs), each of which constitutes a major regional growth pole.

Contrasts and Commonalities in Urban Structure and Employment Patterns

While **suburbanization** as described represents a spatial feature of urban growth and change, the experience of labour formation in Canadian cities presents contrasts in the basic geography of enterprise, economic development, and employment. In the Greater Toronto Area (GTA), Canada's largest metropolis, the **central business district** (CBD)'s corporate office complex of specialized financial, head office, and commercial activities underpins that city's global status and functions. Over the past two decades, an internationally significant cultural economy has developed within Toronto's metropolitan core, including high design performance and exhibition space, a thriving cultural production sector (including film production as well as new media, graphic design, and music), and complementary amenities—each of which has generated substantial creative industry employment. That said, the fastest growing areas are in the GTA's suburban communities, including Mississauga (about 700,000 people, and almost half a million jobs), Scarborough (older industrial suburb), and Markham. While we tend to associate **edge cities** (after Garreau, 1991) with the American urban experience, the GTA also encompasses representations of this particular phenomenon, with large

commercial centres, business parks, and industrial estates distributed on the outer margins of the city-region, to an extent not seen anywhere else in Canada (Bourne, Britton, and Leslie, 2011).

In contrast, Montreal's economic structure exhibits a characteristically "strong centre" profile, with employment (especially in terms of the most specialized industries and labour) still concentrated on the Island and in Laval. As is well known, Montreal lost its "western gateway" functions (including transportation [Coffey, 1994]), and, more decisively, its national primacy in banking and corporate control, to Toronto (Polèse and Shearmur, 2004) during the 1970s. But the metropolitan core has reconstituted itself over the past two decades as a zone of business services, tourism, and cultural industries and institutions, catering to regional and, selectively, to international markets. Indeed, as two specialists on Montreal's development have observed, the slow-growth trajectory of the 1970s and 1980s has meant that Montreal's downtown and central neighbourhoods are still relatively intact, preserving a built environment conducive to the arts, design, innovation, and convivial urbanism—all features of Montreal's renaissance since the 1990s (Shearmur and Rantisi, 2011). That said, Montreal's suburbs encompass significant manufacturing, including an important high-tech sector specializing in aerospace and transportation, following the decline of long-established inner-city districts such as Lachine in southwest Montreal, as well as port, warehousing, and distributional industries and employment.

The Ottawa-Gatineau metropolis presents still another city-region model of economic development and employment formation, shaped both by its national capital roles and by more recent developments. The metropolitan core of Ottawa is dominated by federal government institutions, agencies, and employment, with significant clusters of business services, retail, and consumption that cater to the large tourism sector as well as to local demand. The suburbs, meanwhile, encompass important high-tech clusters. The steep decline of Nortel, one of Canada's truly propulsive advanced-technology corporations in the 1990s, has attenuated the growth trajectory of the suburbs, but Kanata, in particular, boasts a nationally important cluster of biotech and telecommunications industries. Both federal government and socio-cultural influences are crucial to patterns of growth. In the words of leading scholars,

> the city exemplifies the strong intersections between politics, ethno-cultural diversity, gender and industry location dynamics in a highly suburbanized metropolitan development.... Ottawa–Gatineau's weak manufacturing sector and strong service-based employment makes it a compelling example of the complex geographies of work in post-industrial urban Canada. (Andrew, Ray, and Chiasson, 2008)

Much discussed in the media and elsewhere is a shift in national growth (population, employment, and investment) toward western Canada; aggregate data tend to support this thesis. But this growth is locationally selective, favouring Vancouver and Calgary, the leading urban centres of the "New West."

Vancouver offers a distinctive case study in sustained growth in the postwar period. Here, the 1980s was a decade of transformative change, marked by the decline of Vancouver's role as the centre of an expanding provincial resource economy and by the integration of Vancouver into the markets, capital flows, and migration patterns of the Asia-Pacific (Olds, 2001). The outcomes of these transformative processes of change are complex but include the comprehensive redevelopment of the urban core and the rapid growth of the suburbs. With regard to the first, global forces served to strip the city of much of its head-office and senior management functions. In 1991, the city's seminal *Central Area Plan* enabled a major reallocation of land resources in the core, consolidating the office complex within a smaller CBD, and privileging housing in most of the inner city though the central area still encompasses about 200,000 jobs (Vancouver, 2008). And the city still

has about one-third of the approximately 900,000 jobs in the regional labour force. But the Vancouver suburbs are leading growth as about three-quarters of the regional population of 2.2 million are located beyond the City of Vancouver. The older inner suburbs, such as Burnaby, Richmond, and North Vancouver, possess major employment centres, including designated regional town centres, universities and colleges (e.g., Simon Fraser University and British Columbia Institute of Technology in Burnaby), advanced-technology industries, and major gateway facilities (Vancouver International Airport in Richmond). These older inner suburbs also enjoy a favourable jobs-to-residents balance. But the newer, outer suburbs—notably Surrey but also Delta, Coquitlam, and Langley—are experiencing the highest growth rates: the population of Surrey approaches a half-million, and the municipality is experiencing significant job growth. On the whole, though, the outer suburbs are deficient in jobs, relative to the resident population, and much of the job growth is occurring in scattered, low-density developments, posing problems for regional and local planners.

Calgary represents the other leading urban growth pole in western Canada. At just over 1 million people, it has a little less than half of Vancouver's population. Aside from this scalar difference are other, perhaps more consequential, contrasts between these two largest western metropolitan cities. Vancouver, stripped of many of its leading corporations and embedded firmly in a "post-staples" development modality, exhibits a classic entrepreneurial SME (small- to medium-size enterprise) economy and labour force, with industrial diversification including high education, gateway functions, film production, and new media. Calgary, on the other hand, presents the classic image of an essentially "monocultural economy," driven by Alberta's oil and gas industry. Over the past decade or so, Calgary has supplanted Vancouver as the leading head-office centre west of Toronto. A physical consequence of this trajectory is the development of a major corporate head-office complex in Calgary's downtown, anchoring the regional economy and reinforcing the core as the region's centre of economic gravity. Moreover, the expansion of corporate head offices has generated ancillary expansion in the intermediate service sector, notably business and financial services, as well as in the consumption amenities that constitute derived demand features of the office economy, such as restaurants, fitness clubs, and the like. Beyond the urban core, Calgary presents a largely dispersed and diffused regional economy and labour force, albeit with Calgary International Airport and some substantial office and business parks constituting significant clusters.

The New Economy and the Remaking of the Central City

The 1970s and 1980s saw the dramatic rise of the CBD's corporate office complex, and an associated workforce of segmented office labour, as well as the collapse of Fordist manufacturing and blue-collar labour within the traditional industrial districts of the inner city (Bourne and Ley, 1993; Ley, 1996). More recently, successive phases of innovation and restructuring have transformed the economy and labour force of the metropolis, including a powerful cultural inflection (Scott, 1997), and have shaped change in the urban core's land use, social morphology, and housing markets (Hutton, 2008, 2009).

In many cities among advanced societies, including those in Canada, the initial groups to recolonize the inner city's post-industrial terrains of disinvestment and decline included artists and designers. In Toronto, Montreal, and Vancouver, new uses have included museums, galleries, studios, and exhibition spaces, presaging the full-blown cultural makeover of the core now seen as a marker of globalizing cities. Then, by the mid-1990s, the technology boom gave rise to a "new economy" construct in the inner city, comprising new media, digital art, and the ubiquitous dot.coms alongside more conventional cultural industries (Hutton, 2004; Pratt, 2000). The new economy phenomenon displaced both low-income residents and marginal creative workers, a trajectory only

attenuated by the collapse of the technology sector of 2000–1, in the wake of oversupply and the inflation of technology stocks.

The late twentieth-century new economy has been replaced by a "new cultural economy" of production and consumption in the city, a sector that has absorbed many of the innovations in production and communications technologies of the digital age, but taking in a far larger set of industries, institutions, and labour. The locational preferences of the new cultural economy are shaped in large part by *agglomeration*: the oft-replicated co-location of firms and labour that produces input and transactional cost savings, knowledge spillovers, and opportunities for co-operation and collaboration. So, important locational continuities span periods of development. Further, the cultural economy operates within the conventional economic parameters of markets, firms, production networks, and competition. But the attraction of the urban core—and more particularly the heritage landscapes of the post-industrial inner city—for cultural industries and creative labour involves a more diverse and complex array of factors, which these agencies and workers can draw on for creative production, as depicted schematically in Figure 6.1.

The foundational elements of "space and spatiality" include: (1) the distinctive localized micro-spaces of the core, which provide ideal territories for intensive interaction, facilitating the exchange and transfer of tacit knowledge and information so critical to the functioning of the knowledge economy; and (2) the unique built environment of the inner city, in the form of heritage industrial structures, older housing, and the new structures associated with the most recent phase of redevelopment in the city. The resonant landscapes of the inner city combine with the rich amenity package of the core to produce the well-known milieu effects conducive to creativity and innovation in the knowledge economy.

The urban core also possesses an important "talent advantage" for creativity (Figure 6.1), in the form of the mix of human, social, and cultural capital concentrated within the inner city. These include artists, designers, and "neo-artisanal" workers (Norcliffe and Eberts, 1999) who value the commingling of social and economic worlds characteristic of the core, the distinctive "social density" of core area neighbourhoods and communities, and the "neo-bohemian" creative producers and consumers widely acknowledged as drivers of the cultural economy. At the larger metropolitan level, the emergence of a "new cultural economy" concentrated within the urban core reflects the emerging regional divisions of industrial activity and labour, a process Allen Scott has described as the continuing "specialization of the internal spaces of the metropolis" (Scott, 1988).

The development of the city's cultural economy is supported by heritage preservation, supports for artists and designers, and land use and zoning programs that preserve land resources for cultural production amid the high-development terrains of the urban core. But over the past decade, cultural

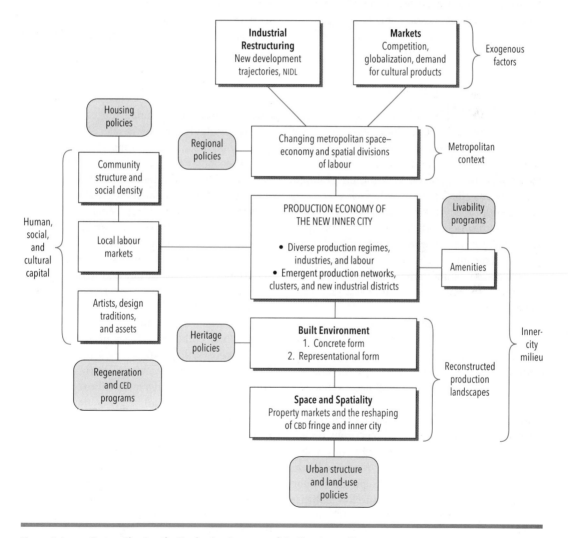

Figure 6.1   Factors Shaping the Production Economy of the New Inner City

Source: Hutton (2008). *The New Economy of the Inner City*, Routledge

planning and programming for the creative sector have entered the policy mainstream (Vinodrai, 2013), abetted by the energetic pitch of Richard Florida and his acolytes (Florida, 2008), who insist that cities' prosperity is inextricably linked to the creative impulse. Others caution a more measured stance on the potential for culture and creativity as forces of urban regeneration (see Evans, 2001, 2009) or, in some cases, a rejection of the more excessive claims of the cultural economy as just the latest in a sequence of neo-liberal siren songs (Peck, 2005). However, the overall message of culture as panacea for urban stagnation has proven seductive to more and more cities (Hutton, forthcoming).

The Cultural Economy in Canadian Cities: Reference Cases

Inner-city districts of Canadian cities have been recast as zones of creative innovation, production, and consumption. In medium-size cities such as Halifax, Quebec City, and Victoria, for example, the old inner city has been redeployed as a site of creative production (artists, graphic designers, architects, and the like), consumption, and spectacle, drawing on the unique heritage landscapes and legacies of those cities, complementing the important capital, administrative, and public-agency functions long-established in central urban precincts.

In the major Canadian metropolitan cities, the scale of the "new cultural economy" is larger and includes a greater range of specialized industries and labour. As noted earlier, the preservation of Montreal's core area urban fabric has provided an ideal environment for nurturing cultural industries in districts such as the Plateau and Mile End, complemented by the City's famously tolerant lifestyle orientation and vibrant consumption sector. Among Canadian cities generally, Montreal boasts perhaps the most generous state/public support for the creative sector, reflecting a well-established state commitment to fostering the city's unique cultural values, assets, and practices as well as sector-specific programs for film, fashion, and architecture (Klein and Tremblay, 2008).

The situation of the new cultural economy within the inner city's dense and diverse landscapes and communities generates a mixed palette of outcomes, including dislocation as well as revitalization/regeneration, vividly illustrated by experiences in Toronto and Vancouver. In the case of the former, Catungal, Leslie, and Hii (2009) have documented the development trajectory of Liberty Village, a 45-acre brownfield site on the western margins of the downtown, and proximate to the old industrial community of Parkdale. The district once included well-known manufacturing operations such as Inglis (electrical appliances) and Massey-Ferguson (agricultural equipment), an assortment of firms redolent of Toronto's heyday as a major Canadian industrial city. The formative years of Liberty Village's evolution as a cultural precinct included the classic experience of recolonization of obsolescent industrial space by artists, as early as the 1970s. The "new cultural economy" phase then began "in earnest" in the mid-1990s, "during the rise of the so-called dot-com industry, a technology-driven period of economic boom" (Catungal, Leslie, and Y. Hii, 2009: 1099). The district's development was facilitated by the government's abolition of monopolies over local telecommunications services, which led to developers offering advanced Internet services to attract new media firms; its development was also aided by the deregulation of municipal zoning laws, which served to facilitate the recycling of industrial buildings for new uses. On the face of it, Liberty Village stands as a major success story in cultural programming as the instrument of urban regeneration. But a more critical perspective suggests at least a partial failure of the project, in terms of addressing "attendant urban problems such as gentrification, inequality, working poverty, and racialised exclusion" (Catungal, Leslie, and Hii, 2009: 1111).

At a finer grain of resolution we can identify more specific employment profiles and regeneration/dislocation outcomes within the inner city. In Vancouver, for example, the last decade-and-a-half or so has seen the emergence of discrete, specialized production zones in the metropolitan core, differentiated by product sector, labour, and proximate impacts (Figure 6.3), producing a new geography of employment extending well beyond the CBD (Figure 6.4). At the top of the cultural production pyramid is Yaletown, a high-integrity heritage district between the Downtown South and Concord Pacific new residential communities. Yaletown enjoys the optimal location, richest amenity package, and most exclusive cachet of all the inner-city districts, reflected in its land prices and rents. Yaletown attracts many of the high-end, most successful, new-economy firms, including video game production, software designers, and Internet design and imaging concerns. The very high prices ensure a ruthless filtering process and continuous turnover of firms, but the scope of social dislocation is limited by the mostly upscale housing and consumption spaces in the area. On the other hand, Victory Square presents a grittier landscape "look and feel," and attracts a more

start-up and/or struggling firm profile relative to Yaletown, but nonetheless a significant upgrading experience, given its location proximate to the Downtown Eastside (Barnes and Hutton, 2009). The intimate juxtaposition of creative industry workers alongside the marginal communities of the Downtown Eastside presents a vivid example of the increasingly finer-grained geography of employment in the city.[1]

Conclusion: Emergent Morphologies of Urban Employment

Important continuities are to be seen in the location of employment in Canadian cities, notably (at the urban system level) in the primacy of the Greater Toronto Area (GTA); in the growing dominance of

Figure 6.2   Yaletown

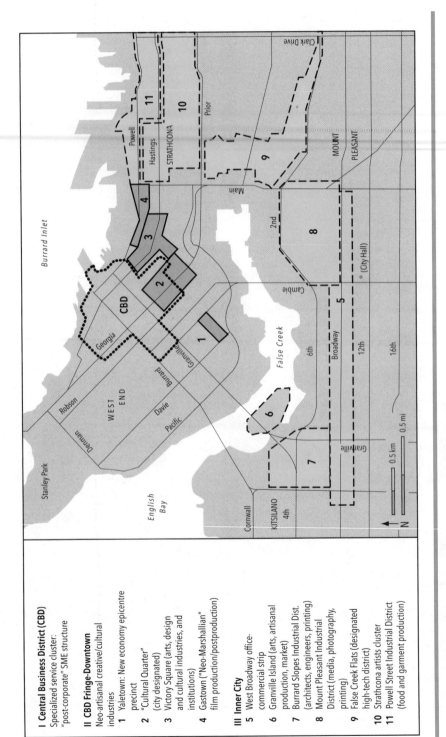

I Central Business District (CBD)
Specialized service cluster:
"post-corporate" SME structure

II CBD Fringe-Downtown
Neo-artisanal creative/cultural
industries
1 Yaletown: New economy epicentre
precinct
2 "Cultural Quarter"
(city designated)
3 Victory Square (arts, design
and cultural industries, and
institutions)
4 Gastown ("Neo-Marshallian"
film production/postproduction)

III Inner City
5 West Broadway office-
commercial strip
6 Granville Island (arts, artisanal
production, market)
7 Burrard Slopes Industrial Dist.
(architects, engineers, printing)
8 Mount Pleasant Industrial
District (media, photography,
printing)
9 False Creek Flats (designated
high-tech district)
10 Strathcona artists cluster
11 Powell Street Industrial District
(food and garment production)

Figure 6.3   **Vancouver: Central Business District, Downtown, and Inner City**

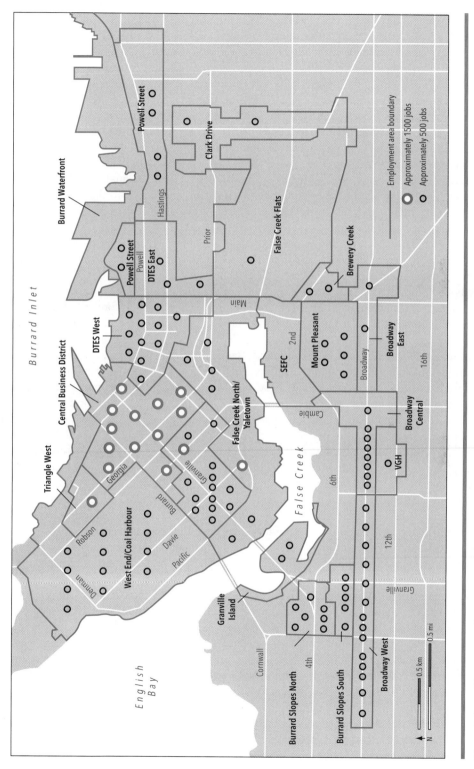

Figure 6.4   Vancouver: Job Density in CBD, Downtown, and Inner City

the largest city-regions; and (at the intra-metropolitan scale) in the persistence of agglomeration in the location of specialized industries and labour. That said, in many other respects *change* is the defining trend in the structure and spatiality of employment in Canadian city-regions, driven by globalization, accelerated industrial restructuring, insistent technological change, intensified market competition, and a series of economic shocks and stresses over the past two decades.

At the national urban system level, Canada has six city-regions with populations exceeding one million—the GTA, Montreal, Vancouver, Ottawa-Gatineau, Calgary, and Edmonton. Common to each is an ascendant service sector; concentrations of specialized, advanced service labour; and a powerful "professionalization" trajectory. But the development formula for each of these major city-regions presents important contrasts: Toronto and Montreal have large, but declining, manufacturing employment levels, while Vancouver has a small but relatively stable manufacturing sector. Within the dominant service economy, Toronto and Calgary have major head-office sectors, relative to the diminished corporate control presence in Montreal and the almost "post-corporate" character of Vancouver's economy.

Spatially, Toronto and Vancouver feature central-city, new industry formations in the cultural sector, combined with a residential trajectory driven both by new condominium development and the adaptive re-use of obsolescent industrial and commercial buildings. On the evidence of the past decade or so, however, volatility in the mix of industries, firms, and employment within these new economy sites suggests that the inner city has become a zone of experimentation and innovation rather than a domain of durable and deeply embedded production firms and labour. In each city-region, too, the growth of suburban employment is an important commonality, but there are major contrasts of scale and industrial mix: the GTA exhibits a suburban and edge/edgeless city formation almost on an American metropolitan scale because it includes Mississauga, which would rank among Canada's 10 largest cities if considered as an autonomous settlement.

Below the level of the "big six" Canadian city-regions, we can identity large but relatively slower-growing cities characterized by a balance of services, manufacturing, and distribution industries (Winnipeg, Regina, Hamilton, Saint John), as well as smaller cities that have capitalized on an industrial niche and employment specializations. These include, notably, cities with important higher education and R&D vocations (Waterloo, Saskatoon, Halifax), high-amenity cities with considerable in-migration "pull" (Kelowna, Niagara-on-the-Lake), and the "satellite" manufacturing cities on and just beyond the periphery of the GTA, including Oshawa, Windsor, and Oakville. The latter have functioned as sites of advanced production and skilled, highly paid manufacturing labour consequent to the Canada–US auto pact. But the current shakeout in the North American auto industry certainly imperils the viability of these crucial employment centres.

The past three decades have witnessed a sequence of innovation and restructuring phases in Canadian cities, including the structural decline of basic manufacturing common to most advanced societies that produced a major downturn in central Canada in the late 1980s and early 1990s, the crash of the technology boom of 2000, and, afterwards, the deep contractions associated with the 2008 economic downturn and its subsequent (at time of writing) halting recovery. Although the full effect of the downturn is still unknown, as in the previous episodes of restructuring and recession it has generated both transitory contractions as well as permanent losses of capacity and labour in key industries, such as banking and finance, the auto sector, and primary industries.

As we project the conditions for employment formation and location likely to develop over the next decade and beyond, it is difficult to imagine how a more stable labour force could emerge within Canada's urban landscapes. To the destabilizing effects of technological substitution for labour and market competition, we can add migration, demographic trends, and property market pressures, although most concede that these factors can produce positive effects (innovation, creativity, efficiency) as well as negative impacts (structural unemployment, dislocation and displacement, polarization, and marginalization). Walks (2011) offers a particularly incisive analysis of labour market change and "socio-spatial polarization" in Canadian cities (see also Walks, Chapter 9). Increasingly, "precarious" employment conditions (i.e., contingent, temporary, informal, and often poorly remunerated) are making inroads in previously secure forms of work in the Canadian city, including professions within legal services and the health-care sector. As well, these employment conditions are increasingly viewed as normal in industries such as video game production (Siemiatycki, 2013). Growing awareness and acceptance of climate change will force further changes to business practices, again producing in some cases significant job losses but also stimulating the formation of new environmental industries, firms, and labour: part and parcel of the cycles of transition and the ever-shifting geography of employment in Canadian cities.

Acknowledgements

The authors would like to acknowledge the cartographic contributions of Eric Leinberger (Department of Geography, University of British Columbia) in preparing and adapting the maps included in this chapter, as well as Michael Seasons (School of Planning, University of Waterloo) for assistance in updating the data tables. Tom Hutton acknowledges Routledge (Taylor & Francis) for granting permission to include Figure 6.1. We owe a debt of gratitude to a number of colleagues for statistical data and acute insights on employment structure and location in Canadian cities, notably Richard Shearmur (INRS-Montreal), Jim Simmons (University of Toronto and Ryerson), and Greg Spencer (University of Toronto). Larry Bourne read the previous version of this chapter and contributed useful ideas for revision.

Review Questions

1. What does change in the intra-urban location of employment imply about overall change in the structure of metropolitan areas across Canada?

2. Referring to a particular employment type, explain how its changing location can be seen to be brought about by multi-scalar flows.

Note

1. For data on inter- and intra-urban employment distribution, see also William J. Coffey and Richard G. Shearmur, "Employment in Canadian Cities," Chapter 14 in Bunting and Filion (2006) at: www.oupcanada.com/filion.

References

Andrew, C., B. Ray, and G. Chiasson. 2009. "Capital formation," paper prepared for "Trajectories of Change in Canadian Urban Regions" project. Ottawa: University of Ottawa.

Barnes, T.J., and T.A. Hutton. 2009. "Situating the new economy: Contingencies of regeneration and dislocation in Vancouver's inner city," *Urban Studies* 46: 1247–69.

Bell, D. 1973. *The Coming of Postindustrial Society: A Venture in Social Forecasting.* New York: Basic Books.

Bourne, L.S., J.N.H. Britton, and D. Leslie. 2011. "The Greater Toronto Region: The challenges of economic restructuring, social diversity and globalization," In Bourne et al., *Canadian Urban Regions: Trajectories of Growth and Change.* Toronto: Oxford University Pres.

——, T.A. Hutton, R. Shearmur, and J. Simmons. 2011. *Canadian Urban Regions: Trajectories of Growth and Change.* Toronto: Oxford University Press.

——, and D.F. Ley. 1993. *The Changing Social Geography of Canadian Cities.* Montreal and Kingston: McGill-Queen's University Press.

Bryson, J.B., and P.W. Daniels, eds. 2007. *The Handbook of Service Industries.* Cheltenham, UK: Edward Elgar.

Catungal, J.-P., D. Leslie, and Y. Hii. 2009. "Geographies of displacement in the creative city: The case of Liberty Village, Toronto," *Urban Studies* 46: 1095–114.

Coffey, W.J. 1994. *The Evolution of Canada's Metropolitan Economies.* Montreal: Institute for Research on Public Policy.

Evans, G. 2001. *Cultural Planning: An Urban Renaissance?* London and New York: Routledge.

——. 2009. "Creative cities, creative spaces and urban policy," *Urban Studies* 46: 1003–40.

Florida, R. 2002. *The Creative Class: And How It's Transforming Work, Leisure, Community and Everyday Life.* New York: Basic Books.

——. 2008. *Who's Your City? How the Creative Class Is Making Where to Live the Most Important Decision of Your Life.* New York: Basic Books.

Fröbel, F., J. Heinrichs, and O. Kreye. 1980. *The New International Division of Labour*. Cambridge: Cambridge University Press.

Garreau, J. 1991. *Edge City: Life on the New Frontier*. New York: Doubleday.

Harvey, D. 1989. "From managerialism to entrepreneurialism: Transformation in urban governance in late capitalism," *Geografiska Annaler SeriesB—Human Geography* 88B: 145–58.

Hutton, T.A. 2004. "The new economy of the inner city," *Cities* 21, 2: 89–108.

——. 2008. *The New Economy of the Inner City: Restructuring, Regeneration and Dislocation in the Twenty-First-Century Metropolis*. London and New York: Routledge.

——. 2009. "The inner city as site of cultural production *sui generis*: A review essay," *Geography Compass* 3: 600–29.

——. (forthcoming) *Cities and the Cultural Economy*. Abingdon: Routledge.

Innis, H. 1933. *Problems of Staple Production in Canada*. Toronto: Ryerson.

Klein, J.-L., and D.-G. Tremblay. 2008. "The actors of civil society and their role in metropolitan governance: Toward a more inclusive governance?" Paper presented at the annual meeting of the Innovation Systems Research Network, Montreal, 30 Apr.–2 May.

Ley, D.F. 1996. *The New Middle Class and the Remaking of the Central City*. Oxford: Oxford University Press.

Moos, M., and A. Skaburskis. 2009. "Workplace restructuring and urban form: The changing national settlement patterns of the Canadian workforce," *Journal of Urban Affairs* 32: 25–53.

Norcliffe, G., and D. Eberts. 1999. "The new artisan and metropolitan space: The computer animation industry in Toronto," in J.-M. Fontan, J.-L. Klein, and D.-G. Tremblay, eds., *Entre la métropolisation et le village global: Les scènes territoriales de la reconversion*. Quebec: Presses de l'Université du Québec.

Olds, K. 2001. *Globalization and Urban Change: Capital, Culture, and Pacific Rim Megaprojects*. Oxford: Oxford University Press.

Peck, J. 2005. "Struggling with the creative class," *International Journal of Urban and Regional Research* 29: 740–70.

Polèse, M., and R. Shearmur. 2004. "Culture, language and the location of high-order services functions: The case of Montréal and Toronto," *Economic Geography* 80: 329–50.

Pratt, A. 2000. "New media, the new economy, and new spaces," *Geoforum* 31: 425–36.

Scott, A.J. 1988. *Metropolis: From Division of Labor to Urban Form*. Berkeley: University of California Press.

——. 1997. "The cultural economy of cities," *International Journal of Urban and Regional Research* 21: 323–39.

Shearmur, R., and N. Rantisi. 2011. "Montreal: Rising again from the same ashes" In Bourne et al., *Canadian Urban Regions: Trajectories of Growth and Change*. Toronto: Oxford University Press.

Siemiatycki, E. 2013. *Consumption City: Precarious Labour and Capital in Vancouver, British Columbia*. Unpublished PhD thesis, Department of Geography, University of British Columbia.

Storper, P., and A.J. Scott. 2009. "Rethinking human capital, creativity and urban growth," *Journal of Economic Geography* 9: 147–67.

Vancouver, City of. 2008. *Metropolitan Core Jobs and Economy Land Use Plan*. Planning Department, Central Area Division.

Vinodrai, T. 2013. "Design in a downturn? Creative work, labour market dynamics and institutions in comparative context," *Cambridge Journal of Regions, Economy and Society* 6: 159–76.

Walks, A. 2011. "Economic Restructuring and Trajectories of Socio-Spatial Polarization in the Twenty-First-Century Canadian City," in Bourne et al., *Canadian Urban Regions: Trajectories of Growth and Change*. Toronto: Oxford University Press.

Warrian, P. 2009. "Biotech in lunch buckets: The curious knowledge networks in Steel Town," paper presented to annual meeting of the Innovation Systems Research Network, Halifax, 29 Apr.–1 May.

Wheeler, J.O., Y. Aoyama, and B. Warf, eds. 2000. *Cities in the Telecommunications Age: The Fracturing of Geographies*. New York: Routledge.

Life Course and Lifestyle Changes: Urban Change through the Lens of Demography

7

IVAN TOWNSHEND AND
RYAN WALKER

Introduction

Demographic change is an important driver of social, economic, political, and cultural change. It affects the evolution or emergence of lifestyles, consumption patterns, housing markets, intergenerational relations, types of social inclusion and exclusion, and diversity. In the urban environment we see manifestations of demographic change through time, and we see and experience the spatial outcomes of demography in our everyday lives.

Even a brief introduction suggests that urbanists are working in the dark if they do not have some appreciation for demographic, life course, and lifestyle changes affecting Canadian cities. Accordingly, in this chapter we outline a selection of demographic trends that are important structuring parameters of twenty-first-century urbanism in Canada. The first section examines some of the key features of Canadian demographic change. The second follows with a discussion of the life course transitions people typically experience and how these relate to lifestyle changes. The third section brings demographic, life course, and lifestyle changes together through a look at a selected series of effects on the built environment.

Key Forces of Social and Demographic Change in Canadian Cities

According to the 2011 Census of Population, Canada is home to 33.5 million people. By international standards we are a medium-sized country, ranked as only the thirty-eighth largest in population out of 240 countries (The World Fact Book, 2013–14). By comparison, the population of China is 39 times larger and the population of the United States is more than nine times that of Canada. Nevertheless, Canada has experienced tremendous population growth in recent decades and in recent years has been the fastest growing of all G8 countries. Indeed, the country's population has more than doubled since 1951. It is important to understand the sources of this growth. Demographers typically allocate population growth or change to three distinctive components: fertility (births), mortality (deaths), and migration (immigration).

Patterns of fertility in Canada have changed dramatically over the past few decades (Figure 7.1). If you are in your twenties now, think back to your great-grandparents' or grandparents' generations—those most likely born in the 1920s or 1930s. It was common for these people to be born into relatively large families, and, by the time the women born after World War I were in their peak child-bearing years in the late 1940s to early 1960s, as a group they were producing a greater number of children than at any other time in Canada's history. In the late 1950s, fertility rates peaked at almost four offspring per woman of child-bearing age (Statistics Canada, 2008b). Children of the post-World War II period are part of the biggest cohort of children ever born in this country, the so-called "baby boomers." The baby boomers are a notable feature of Canada's age structure and have had an impact on Canadian society at every stage of their progression through the life course, impacting everything from their need for schools, jobs, and housing, as well as their consumer preferences (Foot with Stoffman, 1996). Population pyramids, which depict the age-sex structure of a population, clearly show this large "bulge" of baby boomers, and as they have aged, this bulge has gradually moved through the age structure (Figure 7.2). One analogy used to describe this process is the "pig in

the python," a symbolic statement of how, through time, the baby boomers are detectable within the age structure of the population (Dytchwald, 1990).

Figure 7.1 shows that following the introduction of new birth control methods, such as the pill in 1961 (legalized for birth control in 1968), and the increased choices of women with respect to the termination of pregnancies, fertility rates began to plummet in the early 1960s and continued a systematic decline until the late 1980s. Despite a very modest increase in fertility during the late 1980s (the baby boom echo), fertility rates continued to decline until the present, reaching the lowest levels around 2001 at just over 1.5 children per woman (Statistics Canada, 2008a), but climbed modestly to 1.7 by 2008 before dropping to 1.6 by 2011 (Statistics Canada, 2013a). This pattern of change in fertility through time is common to most of the developed world and is a significant feature of what has been called the second demographic transition (Bourne and Rose, 2001; Lesthaeghe, 1995). There are a number of implications of such fertility trends. Quite simply, fewer babies being

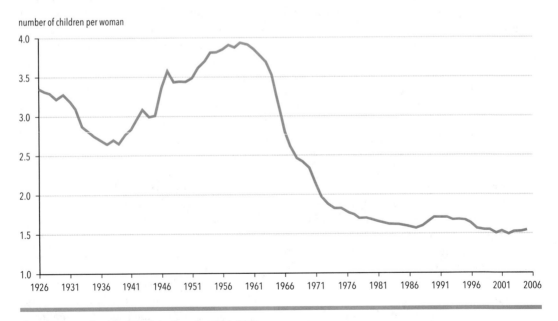

number of children per woman

Figure 7.1   **Total Fertility Rate, Canada, 1926–2006**

Source: Statistics Canada (2008b: 8).

born contributes to population aging, increasing the average (median) age, which has risen from 23.9 years in 1921 to 40.6 years in 2011. A second implication of low levels of fertility surrounds the issue of population replacement. Generally, after accounting for the chances of accidental death or infant mortality, the replacement rate is 2.1 children born to every woman. In other words, to maintain a stable population size, every woman needs to give birth to 2.1 children. Given that fertility rates have been below replacement levels since the late 1960s and are significantly below replacement at present, in the absence of immigration the Canadian population would decline as baby boomers pass away over this and subsequent decades. Immigration is a critical feature of stabilizing population levels as well as population growth in Canada.

The low aggregate figures for fertility rates across the Canadian population mask a demographic issue of great transformative potential in some cities, particularly in western Canada.

The fertility rate among Aboriginal women in 2006 was 2.6 children, considerably higher than among non-Aboriginal women (1.5 children) and above the replacement rate (2.1 children). In cities like Saskatoon, Regina, and Prince Albert, Saskatchewan, children and youth (i.e., aged 24 years and younger) made up just over half of the Aboriginal urban population in 2011 (Statistics Canada, 2013b). The Aboriginal population accounts for a significant part of the total urban population in each of these cities (approximately 9 per cent in Saskatoon, 10 per cent in Regina, 39 per cent in Prince Albert). According to population projections by Statistics Canada, by 2031 Aboriginal people could make up between 21 and 24 per cent of the population of Saskatchewan. The corresponding figure in Manitoba is between 18 and 21 per cent (Statistics Canada, 2011a).

The second component of population growth is death. Like most industrialized Western societies, Canada has seen profound increases in life

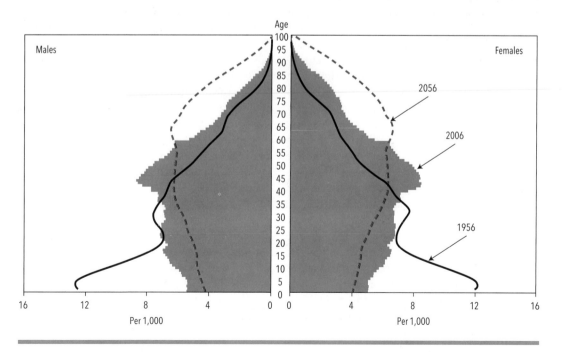

Figure 7.2   **Population Pyramids, 1956, 2006, and Projection for 2056**

Source: Statistics Canada (2008b: 25).

expectancy at birth during the nineteenth and twentieth centuries. The earliest estimates in Canada (for 1831) placed male life expectancy at only 38.3 years and female life expectancy at 39.8 years (Beaujot, 1991). A century later (1931), life expectancies at birth had increased dramatically to 60 years for men and 62.1 years for women—an increase of 57 and 56 per cent, respectively. For men, life expectancy at birth has risen from 60 in 1931 to 78.8 years in 2007, and for women from 62.1 in 1931 to 83.3 years in 2007 (Nagnur, 1986; Statistics Canada, 2008a, 2013c). Patterns of survival have changed dramatically, primarily as a result of advances in health care as well as improved nutrition and lifestyles. Two key features of survival have contributed to changes in the demographic structure of Canadians: (1) the decline and near elimination of infant mortality and (2) the increased life expectancy at almost all ages, and especially in old age. Together, these two features have led to an increasing "rectangularization" of the survival curve, whereby the tendency is toward an even distribution of the population between the different age groups (Fries, 1980; Kraus, 1988; Simmons-Tropea and Osborn, 1993).

In the early part of the twentieth century (1931), infant mortality accounted for a significant portion of death in Canada, with approximately 1 in 10 children not surviving to their first birthday (Statistics Canada, 2008a). By 2009, infant mortality had been virtually eradicated with fewer than 4.9 children per thousand dying before age one (Statistics Canada, 2013d). The second aspect of survival, the increase in longevity, can be seen at almost every age. In Canada, a man aged 65 in 2009 can expect to live another 18.5 years while a woman aged 65 can expect to live another 21.6 years (Statistics Canada, 2013e). The aggregate figures for the Canadian population do, however, mask a disparity between Aboriginal and non-Aboriginal peoples in life expectancy. In 2001, the life expectancy of Aboriginal men and women was about five years less than for non-Aboriginal Canadians (Statistics Canada, 2008e). Results from the 2011 census, moreover, indicate that the life expectancy of the Aboriginal population remains

shorter than the non-Aboriginal population (Statistics Canada, 2013f).

One notable issue is the disparity in life expectancies and survival patterns between men and women, with women surviving longer than men, although the gap has been closing in recent years. This situation is sometimes referred to as the "feminization of survival," meaning that old age in Canada is increasingly characterized by widowhood. This demographic has implications for the size and composition of elderly households and living arrangements. A second notable issue, when coupled with declining fertility rates, is that greater life expectancy contributes to population aging, reflecting the fact that death is being compressed into a relatively short period at the end of the scale of life expectancy. Changes in survival patterns have had important impacts on life course transitions and lifestyles, aspects of society that will be discussed later in the chapter.

Migratory increase is the third component of population growth. Canada has long been recognized as a country of immigrants, and distinctive waves of immigration to this country have been documented (Boyd and Vickers, 2000; Hiller, 2006; see Kobayashi and Preston, Chapter 8). Figure 7.3 shows the trends in the share of population growth attributable to natural increase and to migration. Between the early 1980s and 2010, the share of migratory increase has risen dramatically, and in 2010 migration was responsible for 65 per cent of population growth (Statistics Canada, 2008b; Chagnon and Milan, 2011). Demographic projections show that immigration is essential to the sustainability and growth of the Canadian population because, unless fertility rates begin to rise again, deaths in Canada will outnumber births (to be expected in an aging population) by about 2030, and the Canadian population could become entirely dependent on immigration for its growth. Immigration has helped reduce the rate of population aging that otherwise would have occurred. More than ever before, immigration has contributed to this country's rich social diversity. In 2011, 6.8 million people, or one in five persons (20.6 per cent), in Canada were immigrants, and 3.5 per cent

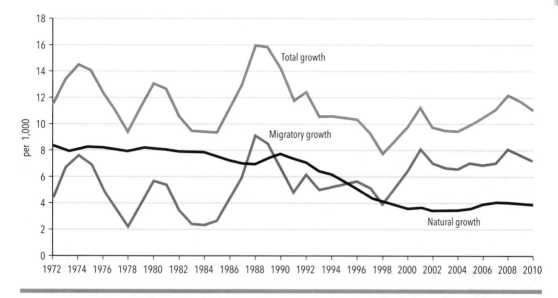

Figure 7.3   Total, Natural, and Migratory Population Growth Rates, Canada, 1972–2010

Source: Chagnon, Jonathan, and Anne Milan. (2011). *Population Growth: Canada, Provinces and Territories, 2010*. Statistics Canada cat. no. 91-209-X. Ottawa: Minister of Industry; page 1.

(1.2 million) of the population were recent immigrants, having arrived in the previous five years (Statistics Canada, 2013g).

Earlier immigrant streams to Canada had been mainly European in origin so social distance within different waves of immigrants or between immigrants and the host Canadian society were minimized. However, since the 1970s other originating regions, such as Africa, the Caribbean, Latin America, and especially Asia, have been favoured in Canadian immigration public policy. Nearly 80 per cent of Canada's new immigrants were from these regions by the 1990s (Bourne and Rose, 2001; Boyd and Vickers, 2000; Halli and Driedger, 1999) (see Kobayashi and Preston, Chapter 8). Increasingly, immigrant streams have been visible minorities with higher levels of social distance from earlier European immigrants, or from charter groups (British and French). As a result, between 1981 (the first time visible minorities were enumerated) and 2011 the share of visible minorities in the population increased from 3.2 million (11.2 per cent) to 6.3 million (19.1 per cent) people. In

short, social diversity on the basis of visible minority status and ethnicity is increasing the social mix in Canada with important implications for urban social life in this country. However, in 2011 three in ten visible minority persons were Canadian-born (Statistics Canada, 2008c; Statistics Canada, 2013g). In this regard, too, we should point out that the 1.4 million Aboriginal Canadians are not considered "visible minorities" in the accounting of Statistics Canada (see Peters, Chapter 21).

While Canada's population is aging overall, the migratory decisions made by both younger and older Canadians regarding their ultimate choice of destination creates interesting city-specific differences (Murdie and Teixeira, 2006). Examples include the movement to retirement centres like Kelowna and Victoria or to relatively younger communities with greater employment opportunities and lower cost of living, such as Calgary and Saskatoon (see Moos, Chapter 20). Domestic migration trends, presented at a provincial scale in Table 7.1, are an important source of population redistribution and a structuring parameter of

Canadian cities as well. Studies have shown that jobs in the mining, oil, and gas sectors and in public administration are key drivers of interprovincial migration (Statistics Canada, 2008a). Some provinces consistently gain from interprovincial migration, others consistently lose, and others such as Saskatchewan and Newfoundland may experience dramatic changes in gains or losses (Table 7.1). With low but relatively uniform fertility rates across the country (except for the North), population redistribution between Canadian cities is a significant source of urban change (Bourne and Rose, 2001). Bourne and Rose found, for example, that over a five-year period the number of interprovincial moves was roughly the same as the number of immigrants to Canada. They also found that Canada's 25 largest metropolitan areas have had a net domestic migrant loss over the past couple of decades (the result of "domestics" either moving to an alternative metropolitan area—e.g., from an eastern metropolitan area to Calgary or Vancouver—or to outer parts of their own extended metropolitan area—e.g., from the Toronto CMA to outer parts of the Greater Toronto Area [GTA], i.e.,

to high-growth places such as Guelph, Kitchener, and Oshawa). This shifting is dramatically different from international immigrant streams where a handful of the largest Canadian cities receive the majority share of newcomers (see Kobayashi and Preston, Chapter 8).

Changes in Life Course and Lifestyles

Fertility, mortality, and migration have introduced important changes in the ways the Canadian population has grown and will continue to grow. These factors point to a society that registers age or generational imbalances in cohort sizes, is aging rapidly, and—by necessity, if not by design—is becoming more ethno-culturally diverse. Structural changes in our economy and society have also laid a foundation, however, for remarkable changes in how individuals negotiate life course changes, how they form households and families, and the rich diversity of lifestyles comprising our contemporary society.

Table 7.1	Net Interprovincial Migration Rates								
Province	1966-71	1971-6	1976-81	1981-6	1986-91	1991-6	1996-2001	2001-6	2006-11
NF	−3.3	−1.4	−3.7	−3.1	−2.6	−4.3	−6.1	−1.3	1.0
PE	−1.0	2.3	0.0	1.4	−0.7	1.2	0.1	0.5	0.4
NS	−1.1	0.7	−1.1	0.8	−0.6	−0.8	−0.2	−0.9	−0.4
NB	−1.3	1.6	−1.3	−0.2	−0.9	−0.3	−1.2	−1.5	−0.1
QC	−1.3	−1.1	−2.4	−1.1	−0.4	−0.6	−0.9	−0.2	−0.3
ON	0.8	−0.7	−1.0	1.2	0.5	−0.5	0.5	−0.2	−0.4
MB	−3.4	−2.9	−4.6	−0.2	−3.5	−1.9	−1.8	−2.0	−1.0
SK	−7.6	−3.5	−0.7	−0.3	−6.4	−2.2	−2.7	−2.8	1.6
AB	1.7	4.0	11.3	−1.3	−1.1	0.1	4.7	3.1	0.8
BC	6.9	4.7	4.8	0.4	4.6	4.8	−0.7	0.6	0.9
YK	12.1	2.2	−2.6	−11.4	3.4	2.4	−9.4	−1.2	2.0
NWT	6.2	2.0	−5.0	−1.6	−3.4	−0.7	−8.6	−1.8	−4.0
NU	NA	NA	NA	NA	NA	NA	−1.4	−1.3	0.3

Source: Data for 1966-2006 compiled from Statistics Canada (2008a: 82). Data for 2006–11 computed by authors from Statistics Canada, *2011 National Household Survey*, Catalogue #99-103-X2011027. Rates expressed as percentage of base population for each period.

A useful starting point for this discussion is the idea of the life course. Individuals typically go through a number of life course transitions, and researchers have devised numerous schema to depict some of the significant transition events and life course stages (Clark, 2007; Hareven and Adams, 1982; Murphy, 1987). Life course perspectives emphasize the importance and uniqueness of individual biography in relation to social and historical time, but at the same time they recognize that at any given time there will be a certain degree of synchronicity of individual and collective biographies. For example, the transition from child or adolescent to adult is typically marked by a series of transition events, such as leaving school, leaving the parental home, gaining full-time employment, and entering a conjugal union (living with a partner as a spouse or common-law couple). Over the past century or so, the normative expectations around the timing and characteristics of such events has changed, as young people today generally spend a longer period of time in childhood and education prior to initiating the independent adulthood stage of life. Likewise, the institution of retirement, coupled with life expectancies in later

life, has radically transformed the lives of elderly people and afforded new opportunities for lifestyles of leisure outside of years in the labour force (Atchley, 1992; Markides and Cooper, 1987). A useful schema is to consider a broad life course conceptualization, originally devised as part of the Theory of the Third Age (Laslett, 1987; 1991). This schema recognizes four major stages or "ages" in life. Figure 7.4 is a simplification of some of the key features of these four ages.

The First Age is a time of dependence, socialization, immaturity, and education. Clearly, the First Age begins at birth and, at first, is characterized by babyhood, childhood, and initial instruction. It is a period of socialization and, for the most part, dependence on others. In general, this phase of the life course has been expanded through time as young people delay and elongate the timing of major transitions between the First Age and Second Age. Young people are staying in school longer, pursuing graduate education to a greater extent, delaying entry into the labour force, living in the parental home for a longer period, and postponing or foregoing conjugal unions and child-bearing. In the early 1970s, about three-quarters of Canadian

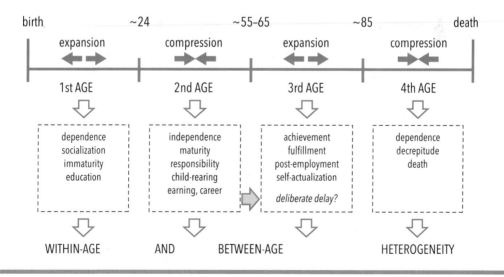

Figure 7.4   **Summary Conceptualization of the Third Age Divisions of the Life Course**

Source: Davies, W.K.D. and Townshend, I.J. (eds) (2002). *Monitoring Cities: International Perspectives*. International Geographical Union, Urban Commission.

young adults had left school by age 22, whereas by 2006 less than half had left by this age (Clark, 2007). While women often make these transitions younger than men, their delays in transition are often linked to post-secondary education. Over the past few decades, significant increases have occurred in Canadians', especially women's, educational attainment; indeed, since the early 1990s women have outnumbered men in Canadian universities (Statistics Canada, 2008d). The share of young adults aged 20–24 living in the parental home has also increased dramatically over the last 30 years, rising from 41.5 per cent in 1981 to 59.3 per cent in 2011. The propensity for those in their early twenties (ages 20–24) to live as couples has also decreased, from 36.4 per cent in 1981 to 16.1 per cent in 2011 (Statistics Canada, 2013h).

The Second Age, beginning around 24 years for many (although the transition is individualistic and as noted is increasingly delayed), is a period of independence, maturity, responsibility, and labour force activity. This typically is a period when most people start a career and a family, attain and maintain some degree of power and authority over others, and enjoy all the social and legal privileges of adulthood. For the population as a whole, this life course phase has become truncated (in relative terms) over the past century. Increases in survival, coupled with the individual ability to cease work at earlier ages—primarily as a result of the institutionalization of personal, corporate, and public retirement savings schemes, and the social sanction of early retirement—have accentuated the tendency toward earlier retirement (McDonald and Wanner, 1984, 1990; Roadburg, 1985). In recent years, however, we may be seeing a reversal of the trend to early retirement or, at least, episodic retirement, partial retirement, or various forms of bridge employment as people exit and re-enter the labour force (Hebert and Luong, 2008; Marshall and Ferraco, 2007; Singh and Verna, 2001; Stone, 2006). In general, however, the Second Age has become relatively compressed in time. Typically, it occupies a smaller fraction of an individual's life course.

The same processes that have resulted in the compression of the Second Age of the life course have caused the relative elongation of the Third Age. This phase generally describes active and healthy seniors in society but is marked by a movement out of the labour force, or at least partial retirement. For many, and particularly early retirees, nearly as much of their life will be spent in retirement as was spent in the Second Age. The Third Age is, demographically speaking, an unprecedented opportunity for a large share of society (and increasingly large in an aging society) to engage in many years of fulfillment outside of the labour force (Laslett, 1991). Considering advances in life expectancy at all ages, it is quite possible that someone who enters the labour force at 25 and retires at 55 will spend as many years in retirement as in the labour force. This concept has been marketed fervently by financial institutions (e.g., London Life's "Freedom 55") and developers, and was embraced and planned for by many. The outlook on seniors' lifestyles can be seen in many cities in North America, most notably in new forms of exclusive retirement villages and age-restricted developments. Although the vast majority of Canadians do not work past the age of 65, and the majority of retirees are early retirees, the 1980s and 1990s may have been overly optimistic about the potential for universal early retirement. While there has been a systematic decline in the average age of retirement since the 1970s, retirement ages seem to have levelled off in the late 1990s; recent evidence suggests that retirement is becoming increasingly complex, with multiple labour force exits and entries. In 2011, a record proportion of 60- to 64-year-olds were still in the labour force (46 per cent) while the average retirement age was 61.5 years.

The Fourth Age, marked for many people as the late seventies or early eighties, comprises the later years in life or, more generally, the time when people have been called the "old-old" (Neugarten, 1974). As of 1996, the disability-free life expectancy (for both sexes) of someone aged 65 in Canada was 11.7 years; not until the elderly are in their mid-eighties do we see a majority of seniors experiencing severe disabilities, a period akin to Shakespeare's seventh age of man, with increasing loss of mobility and independence, health concerns, senility, and decrepitude (Laslett, 1991; Norland, 1994). Either way, for most, this last phase of the life course has been pushed well past the normal (65-year-old) age of retirement, and compressed, from an historical point of view, largely as a function of advances in health care and nutrition.

Considerable heterogeneity prevails in the timing of transitions within each of the four ages, as in the social composition of people within each of these phases of the life course, when people may be differentiated by age, socio-economic status, family structures, ethnicity, "race," gender, and lifestyles. These differences no doubt create highly variable pathways through the life course, different opportunities and constraints, various inequalities, and different life experiences and biographies. As these generalized life course phases intersect with micro and macro differentiation in our society, they define the potential for myriad life paths and expressions of lifestyles.

One of the most important trends in Canadian society over the past quarter-century has been the revolutionary changes in the structure and composition of households and families. We have already seen how basic demographic changes, such as those of fertility and survival, have been influential in reshaping the age structure of the population, have led to fewer younger people, and have resulted in an aging population. These trends do not occur in isolation from broader forces of societal change, however; that is, changes in normative behaviours and life choices throughout the life course. The shifting choices that people make with respect to household and lifestyle fundamentally affect the urban experience.

Smaller Households

In 1901, the average household in Canada had five people. In 2011 the average had been cut in half and was 2.5 people. The size of Canadian households has been declining for more than a century (Rose and Villeneuve, 2006). This transformation in the size of households is largely attributable to the growth (both absolute and relative) in the number of small households and the decline of large households of four or more people. Figure 7.5 shows how dramatic these changes have been, with the number of single-person households rising from 1.68 million in 1981 to 3.67 million in 2011, an increase of 118 per cent over this time period. For the first time ever, the 2011 Census counted more one-person households than couple households with children. The number of two-person households has also risen dramatically from 2.40 million in 1981 to 4.54 million in 2011, an increase of 89 per cent over the past quarter-century. The number of three- or four-person households has also increased, but only marginally, while the number of households with five or more people has declined. By 2011, the majority (61.7 per cent) of Canadian households were small households of one or two people (Figure 7.6).

Within the smaller household group, the fastest-growing segment has been single-person households. Since the household is generally considered the basic unit of consumption as well as a means of achieving economies of scale in living expenses, there are some important implications for the rise in single-person households, especially in terms of housing affordability (as a result of increased consumption of/demand for smaller units) and income distributions (Miron, 1993). The rise of the single-person household is linked to what some have described as a major shift in the propensity to live alone, and is one of the most significant demographic trends observed in Canadian society, with rates rising from 2.6 per cent in 1951 to 12.3 per cent in 2001 (Clark, 2007; Rose and Villeneuve, 2006). Living alone used to be a principal feature of rural, non-farming areas but is now linked to urban lifestyles and the changing socio-cultural values surrounding the meaning of living alone. While living alone may have been a significant phase for people in the early stages of the Second Age (i.e., having just left the "nest") or for some in the later stages of the Third Age, it has become increasingly prevalent for people to live alone in mid-life as well as in later life (Laslett, 1991). Also, as noted earlier in the chapter, a feminization of survival in Canada means that old

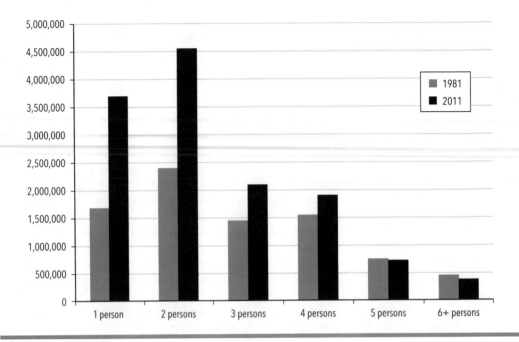

Figure 7.5   Number of Households by Household Size, 1981 and 2011

Source: Compiled from data in Statistics Canada, 1982 and 2011b.

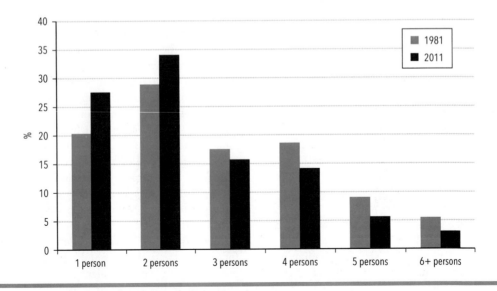

Figure 7.6   Percentage of Households by Size, 1981 and 2011

Source: Compiled from data in Statistics Canada, 1982, and 2011b.

age increasingly is characterized by widows living alone in single-person households.

A further reason for the rise in single-person households has been changes in the values and meanings surrounding marriage and family formation and delays in conjugal unions, both of which are linked to the later transition from the First to the Second Age. The age of first marriage for both men and women has been rising steadily since the 1960s, reaching approximately 30 years for men and 28 years for women by 2003 (Clark, 2007; Statistics Canada, 2008a). Considerably fewer young adults are entering marriage or other conjugal relationships at an early age. In 1971, for example, 65 per cent of men and 80 per cent of women were in or had been in a conjugal relationship by the age of 25. By 2001 these rates were almost halved, dropping to 34 and 49 per cent, respectively. Young adults, or those in the early stages of the Second Age, more often are choosing to live alone. Interestingly, among young people there is also an increasing tendency to live alone even when coupled—a phenomenon sometimes called "living apart together (LAT)" or "non-cohabiting couples" (Turcotte, 2013). There may be many reasons for this, including work circumstances, choice, or the desire to maintain independence even though coupled. In 2011, 31 per cent of people aged 20–24 and 17 per cent of those aged 25–29 were in a LAT relationship (Turcotte, 2013).

New Family Configurations and Fluid Conjugal Relationships

Just as there have been significant changes in the size and composition of households, so have there been major transformations in the meaning and composition of families in Canada. In 2011, the most prevalent family form was a married couple with children living at home (36.2 per cent of families), followed by married couples without children at home (30.8 per cent). Especially noteworthy about changing family configurations are the changes in the relative shares of different family forms (Figure 7.7). Married couples with children living at home are the only type of family to have experienced negative growth over the past quarter-century. This decline has been offset by the rise of alternate family forms, especially common-law families—either with or without children—and the dramatic

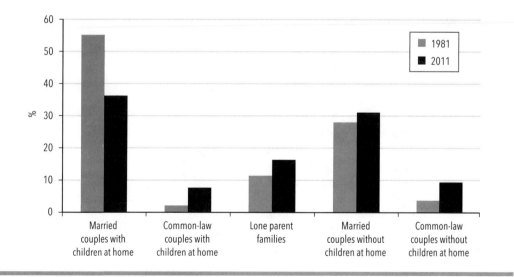

Figure 7.7   **Percentage of Census Families by Structure, 1981 and 2011**

Source: Compiled from data in Statistics Canada (1982, 2011b).

rise of single-parent families. It is estimated that by 2020 as many people will be living in common-law unions as in marriages (Milan, 2000). Together, the share of families without children at home has risen from 32 per cent in 1981 to 40 per cent in 2011, thereby contributing to declining household sizes.

The fluidity with which people move in and out of various types of families also has increased. In part due to separation and divorce but also because common-law unions are less stable than marriages, people more frequently move in and out of relationships throughout their life course, most notably during the Second and Third Age (Milan, 2000). Less than 10 per cent of marriages end in divorce within the first five years of marriage, whereas about half of common-law unions dissolve within that time frame (Milan, 2000; Statistics Canada, 2008a). Despite the fact that about four in ten marriages end in divorce, which also contributes to the formation of single-person households, approximately 75 per cent will remarry or recouple, creating an episodic pattern of marriage and remarriage. This pattern gives rise to a variety of configurations of blended and step-families, either married or common-law.

New forms of family and household formation can also be seen among same-sex couples. Recent years have seen a growing social acceptance and institutionalization of the rights of same-sex couples, including the legalization of same-sex marriages in 2005. Canadian same-sex couples were first enumerated with voluntary identification in 2001, and while undoubtedly under-reported, it was estimated that there were just over 34,000 same-sex couples in Canada, about 0.5 per cent of all couple families. By 2011 this count had risen to about 65,000, or about 0.8 per cent of all couples. These couples are not necessarily all small households or couples without children at home, although this is the case for the vast majority. Nine per cent of same-sex couples reported having children under the age of 24 living at home in 2011.

The Complexity of Lifestyles

Geographers and planners have long been interested in the ways that people use their time, how time is allocated to different functions in space, how space is segmented with different types of people or consumers, and how lifestyles are manifest in time–space interactions (Chapin, 1965). While a relative paucity of spatially oriented lifestyle studies took place in the 1980s and 1990s, in recent years a resurgence of interest in lifestyle has produced a number of studies, in particular about the ways in which people create lifestyle spaces or spatial lifestyles (Schnell and Benjamini, 2001; 2002; Townshend and Davies, 1999). Schnell and Benjamini (2002) remind us that lifestyles are an intersection of time, activity, and space patterns, and so lifestyles can differ on such things as the radius of daily activity; the importance of telecommunications; types and intimacy of social relations; extent of orientation to a home base; and differences in the value placed on family, social life, work, and leisure.

Lifestyles are often associated with or labelled in regard to population subgroups or in terms of market-based geo-demographic segments, so it makes little sense to try to define First Age, Second Age, and Third Age lifestyles. Within each of these phases of the life course, multiple lifestyles will manifest themselves. It is not uncommon, for example, for market researchers to develop complex segmentation models and typologies to define groups of people within distinctive generations (Statistics Canada, 2012b) based on their consumption preferences (Cahill, 2006). Many of these typologies attempt to link key lifestyle traits with behaviours, outlook on life, types of social relationships, and especially consumption preferences of particular generations. Foot (with Stoffman, 1996), for example, has shown how some of these lifestyle traits have changed through Canadian generations, impacting everything from people's preferences for different types of social relationships to demands for housing.

Others have focused specifically on selected generations, such as the "Millennials," which may also be referred to as the Net Generation, Screenagers, Digital Natives, Generation Y, or the Echo Boom generation (Alsop, 2008; Howe and Strauss, 2007; see canadianmillennials.ca). While there is no agreed-on range of birth dates for the millennial generation, they are loosely considered to be those born between the early 1980s and 2000, and so may be either in the First or Second Age. They are the children of the late baby boomers and early baby-bust generation (Statistics Canada, 2012b), and sometimes are called the "most wanted" generation in history. This generation of people is said to exhibit very different lifestyle orientations from previous generations (Howe and Strauss, 2007). They have few siblings, have always been considered special or important to their parents, are electronically savvy, value tight social networks, appreciate and value social and ethnic diversity, are group- or team-oriented rather than individualistic, and eschew preferential treatment. They also are high achievers and career-oriented. Some have claimed that these are "trophy kids," both as trophies to their parents (almost all are planned pregnancies) and because they have grown up in school and sports activities where everyone received a prize or trophy for participating. From a demographic and especially geographical perspective, these individuals, as a subset of those in their First Age, have a unique set of preferences, behaviours, form of social networking, consumption potential, and propensity to be involved in civic affairs. As they move through the various transitions and stages of the life course, they will leave their own generation and lifestyle impact. However, while such generalizations may have some validity, there is in fact considerable heterogeneity within the Millenials, leading market researchers to "segment" Millenials into a variety of sub-groups (see canadianmillennials.ca).

Lifestyles are highly differentiated in the Second Age. Indeed, researchers have studied the values and lifestyles of the hippie generation and the yuppies (young urban professionals), and have explored the activities and social relations of "swingles" (swinging singles) in large metropolitan areas, or are beginning to focus on the lifestyles of the non-cohabiting LAT couples (Turcotte, 2013). However, another example of the popularization of lifestyles as a demographic by-product can be seen in the book and film, *Bridget Jones's Diary* (*Economist*, 2001; Fielding, 1996; Partridge, 1973; Smith, 1987; Starr and Carns, 1972). While the film is a light-hearted romantic comedy, it also portrays a very serious side of the urban lifestyle (Maguire, 2001). Bridget Jones is a 30-something, single, highly educated professional working in the creative economy in a major metropolitan area (London). She lives alone in a small flat—a single-person household—and apart from juggling time at the gym and work, has plenty of time, money, and a passion for spending on things fashionable, frivolous, and fun. Her lifestyle is consumption-oriented—dining out, frequenting upscale wine bars, going on weekend holiday getaways, etc. She strives to enjoy her career, to find romance, and perhaps at some point to marry. Relatives and coupled friends constantly remind her that "the clock is ticking" and that her delay in marriage and child-bearing may become problematic. Bridget longs for acceptance outside her tightly knit group of friends, all of whom live similar lifestyles and are similarly fun- and consumption-oriented. True as the Bridget character is to life, it has been argued that many singles and other single-person households adopt their friendship network (which for Bridget is a heterogeneous group of professionals and artists, of diverse ethnic backgrounds and sexual orientation) as a surrogate family, in what some have suggested is a new form of "urban tribe" or "fictive kin" (*Economist*, 2001; Martin-Mathews, 2001; Rose and Villeneuve, 2006).

A similar example of lifestyles that underscores a related but important trend of single female lifestyles and consumption potential is illustrated by the characters in the American TV series *Sex and the City*. In this show, the single young female (SYF) life, or the "new girl order" is celebrated as the quintessential postmodern lifestyle and is indeed a global trend. As Hymowitz (2007) explains, the new girl order is a combination of trends of delayed marriage, expanded higher education and labour-force participation, and increasing urbanization. Together with global media it has produced an international lifestyle such as that portrayed by Carrie Bradshaw in *Sex and the City*.

Meanwhile, it has been noted that the "Bridget Jones Economy" or the Carrie Bradshaw lifestyle is an urban reality in many large cities. This demographic and the associated lifestyle have both a spatial and economic footprint (*Economist*, 2001; Hymowitz, 2007). They are clustered predominantly in central-city apartments, often in close proximity to urban nightlife and in areas with high densities of singles. They are key consumers of emerging goods and services in these areas, including functions such as dry cleaners, health food stores, specialty delicatessens, supermarkets specializing in small portions and prepared foods, Internet kiosks, dating services, travel agencies, wine bars, specialty clothing boutiques, and health professionals. Hymowitz (2007) suggests that the SYF phenomenon has even driven diamond merchants to re-think their markets, with one company introducing a "right-hand ring"—a diamond for women with no marital prospects but longing for a rock. In some places, like Tokyo, distinctive central city residential geographies of SYF are emerging, such as entire neighbourhoods and districts defined by condominiums for the SYF lifestyle (Kubo and Yui, 2012). In other words, the Bridget Jones or Carrie Bradshaw factor may be a lifestyle in the sense that it incorporates a particular constellation of identity, taste, consumption, style, and leisure. Most importantly, it is very much a spatial lifestyle. Such lifestyles and living arrangements are also triggers of change in the social complexity and social ecology of cities (Davies and Murdie, 1991; Kubo and Yui, 2012; see Walks, Chapter 9; Bain, Chapter 14; Moos, Chapter 20).

The Third Age also is marked by social and lifestyle diversity, and the concept of "seniors" as a homogeneous group with similar traits fails to capture this diversity. One lifestyle phenomenon that has garnered recent attention from younger hipsters and real estate professionals is the movement of a growing number of aging baby boomers into the central city, a cohort playfully referred to as the "Broken Hip-sters" (*Wall Street Journal*, 2013). The impact of the typically wealthy aging baby boomers on the real estate market of the city centre, and on the younger (and often less affluent) hipsters that have pioneered the urban *lifestyle* there, has yet to be fully understood economically and culturally.

As the large baby boomer cohort progresses through the stages of transition to retirement, or the Third Age, this group's diversity and consumption potential will be even more noticeable (Foot with Stoffman, 1996). In fact, the diversity of this population is fuel for market researchers and housing developers who try to isolate distinctive lifestyle segments and cater to variations in demand for goods, services, and housing. While websites are dedicated to the Third Age, successful aging, and advice on matters on everything from seniors' lifestyles and finance to relationships and sex (e.g., www.thirdage.com), market research professionals have also tried to isolate distinctive segments of third-agers. Acronyms such as SUPPIES (Senior Urban Professionals), WOOPIES (Well-Off Older People), OPALS (Older People with Active Lifestyles), RAPPIES (Retired Affluent Professionals), or DUMPIES (Destitute Unprepared Mature People) have been used to capture some of the market and lifestyle differences (Dytchwald, 1990; Karpel, 1995). Housing developers have recognized that the elderly are not a homogeneous group, and have employed labels such as the Go-Go segment (active healthy retirees), Slow-Go segment (not very active, failing health), and the No-Go segment (extremely frail, or Fourth Age) to identify sub-groups with respect to housing needs (Seiler, 1986). While all of these may be gross generalizations, they are based on recognizable differences in lifestyle, behaviour, and consumption.

Demography, Lifestyle, and the Built Environment

There is little doubt that age, life cycle stage, and lifestyle have become increasingly commodified, not just in geo-demographic marketing but in the built environment. Developers have responded to a variety of age, preference, and lifestyle niche markets, the result being increasing diversity in the residential landscape. Two of the biggest trends in this area are the growth in condominium ownership and the rise of residential niche communities.

Given the increase in small households without children at home, more housing options today offer a smaller, more convenient, and often maintenance-free lifestyle. Condominium ownership, a type of common interest development first adopted in Canada in the late 1960s, has seen a dramatic increase over the past few decades, with the share of households owning condominiums rising from 3.5 per cent in 1981 to 10.9 per cent in 2006 (Lo, 1996; McKenzie, 1994; 2003; Rea, McKay, and LeVaseur, 2008; Walker and Carter, 2010; see Harris, Chapter 19). Condominium living is considerably more prevalent in metropolitan areas, with rates as high as 31 per cent in Vancouver, 18.6 per cent in Toronto, and 13.3 per cent in Montreal. In some cities, such as Toronto, condominium developments now account for the majority of new housing starts.

A second trend in response to the rise in differentiated lifestyles and preferences among those in their Second or Third Age has been innovation in the way residential communities are designed and developed. Many of these changes are linked to new expressions of the privatization of space and communities. Whereas the typical planned community of the 1950s or 1960s may have followed neighbourhood unit design principles, entire subdivisions today are being developed in response to changes in demography and lifestyle preferences, taking on a variety of expressions of product differentiation, gating, and exclusivity (Hodge and Gordon, 2014; Perry, 1929). The rise of gated communities (a type of common interest development) in various countries, including Canada, has been studied in some detail, with many authors expressing concern about the consequences of such developments, especially the loss of the public realm to private space (see Grant and Filion, Chapter 17; Blakely and Snyder, 1997; Blandy et al., 2003; McKenzie, 1994; Punter, 1990; Townshend, 2006; Webster, Glaze, and Frantz, 2002). Blakely and Snyder's (1999) pioneering study of gated communities in the United States identified three main types: (1) lifestyle communities (including retirement communities, golf course communities, and new towns), (2) prestige communities, and (3) security zone communities. Others have attempted to define typologies of gated communities in Canada and internationally (Coy and Pohler, 2002;

Glaze, 2002; Grant, 2005; Grant and Mittelsteadt, 2004; Landman, 2006; Raposo, 2006). Despite difficulties in defining such typologies, the function of these designs clearly is to create landscapes of exclusivity and exclusion; as one author noted, these proprietary neighbourhoods are consumed as club goods within a kind of "shareholder democracy" (Glaze, 2002). The supply of and demand for private and gated residential communities doubtless will continue. Likely, also, is increased product differentiation as developers refine these commodities to appeal to more tightly defined lifestyles and market segments (Lang and Danielsen, 1997). This means that the geographical manifestation of private neighbourhoods in the city will become more complex and more differentiated.

Other forms of residential community privatization are evident in the built environment. Townshend (2006), for example, has discussed the trend toward the thematic development of subdivisions since the 1960s. Initial expressions of these, such as the development of golf course communities, were perhaps in direct response to lifestyle demands and the pursuit of leisure. Along similar lines, a number of developers experimented with "lake communities" in which a private lake, with controlled access, forms the community's recreational nexus. By the 1980s other types of niche communities on a smaller scale began to appear in Canadian cities in the form of retirement villages specifically designed for and marketed to the 55-and-over population (i.e., appealing to the Third Age). Many of these developments, such as "Horizon Villages" with age-restrictive covenants, actively advertised the concept of "Freedom 55" and offered a commodified form of community in which residents could enjoy condominium ownership, maintenance-free living, and a socially homogeneous set of neighbours. The popularity of these types of retirement communities, with particular appeal to elderly single persons, has grown rapidly. In Calgary, for example, almost all residential subdivisions contain at least one of these developments and almost all new subdivisions incorporate plans for at least one retirement community (Townshend, 2006).

A range of different thematic foci for new residential areas has become common. While developers have continued to build lake and golf course communities, at least four other types occur. One is the development of New Urbanist or neo-traditional communities. In response to problems of conventional suburban development patterns, these communities attempt to foster a more traditional urban lifestyle, despite being constructed in new suburban regions (see Grant and Filion, Chapter 17). Following the ideas of leading proponents of New Urbanism, such as Andrés Duany and Elizabeth Plater-Zyberk, features of these developments include the return to a smaller or more human scale of mixed housing development and mixed land uses, the return to a narrow grid and more pedestrian-friendly street network, and a reduction in vehicular traffic (Katz, 1994). Neo-traditional communities usually include provision of a town centre with commercial and local administrative facilities, and aim to promote increased social interaction through design features such as front porches on houses and the placement of garages at the rear of lots. McKenzie Towne in Calgary and Cornell in Markham, just outside the Toronto CMA, are excellent examples of early efforts to adopt New Urbanist principles in Canadian cities.

A second type of new community has explicitly focused on environment in its design. In these the developer retains some natural environmental features within the design scheme (e.g., wetlands, natural prairie grassland, forest, bird sanctuary). The share of open recreational space in these communities is considerably higher than in other neighbourhood districts. It also is typically more than what is legally required for subdivision approval, with some communities boasting as much as 40–50 per cent of the land area of the district retained as natural environment. Developers seem to have capitalized on the recent trend toward environmental stewardship, so that residents of these areas pay compulsory homeowner association fees to ensure appropriate maintenance and use of the natural features, and to ensure they

remain intact in perpetuity. In some cases, a private residents' clubhouse with meeting or sports facilities has been constructed as part of the overall plan.

A third type of thematic community development may be called wired or e-communities (Townshend, 2006). High technology is the primary selling feature of these areas, which are designed to deliver a well-connected community with well-connected "smart homes." All homes in the development contain in-home network wiring for data, audio, and video distribution, and for connection to smart appliances. These communities are wired for broadband Internet connection at fibre-optic speed; but a key feature of these places is the presence of a local community intranet or web portal that functions as an electronic town hall or community centre for area residents to post and share information about local events or to buy and sell from each other. These developments are perhaps a response to a technology-oriented lifestyle and locality orientation, geared toward residents or consumers who demand "fast spaces" and connectivity within the city (McGuirk, 2003). Again, it is not uncommon for such communities to require membership and payment to a homeowner association to maintain this infrastructure.

The fourth type of thematic community development may be called multiple foci communities, consisting of different combinations of recreational amenities, environmental focus, telecommunication infrastructure, and so on. Thus, some of these planned subdivisions include a lake or golf course in addition to being constructed as e-communities. Still others include some environmental focus but also provide other private amenities, such as a wading pool, splash pool, or skating park for children. Others have some elements of New Urbanism in addition to private recreational ponds or resident clubhouses. New communities are evolving in such a way that any combination of specialized recreational, environmental, historical, and architectural design features (New Urbanism), high technology (e-community), or other feature can form the basis for the common interest development.

Conclusion

This chapter has presented some of the key demographic features of change in Canadian cities and linked them to the malleable boundaries of significant life course transitions. The conceptualization of life course as four "ages" is a useful rubric for tying demographic and lifestyle trends together and for proposing how these might relate to the differentiation and marketing of the built environment. The future of Canadian cities is tied to a greatly diversifying population. Much of that diversity is now quite visible in the form of culture, ethnicity, and Indigeneity, with the importance of each varying regionally. In the Prairie provinces, for example, those cities that do not embrace the rich contemporary cultures of their growing young First Nations and Métis populations will be left behind culturally, socially, and economically in the twenty-first century (Walker, 2008; Walker and Belanger, 2013).

Other forms of diversity relate to household sizes, conjugal relationships, and the greater propensity to live alone than has been the case in past decades. How is the Bridget Jones economy likely to continue affecting our inner cities and suburban areas? Finally, an aging society means that no form of lifestyle diversity, whether based on culture, ethnicity, Indigeneity, or household preferences, can be understood without inserting the centrality of the age dimension and the rising opportunities being taken by those in their Third Age of life. How will our built environment continue to change to serve the pig in the python as it moves through its elongated Third Age? Will those in their Third Age continue to advance suburban development that they have become accustomed to throughout their lives, even if modified to suit new lifestyle preferences (see Grant and Filion, Chapter 17)? Will some in their middle or late Second Age begin to re-think the amenity and locational value of the inner suburbs, and begin to modify these environments through knockdown-rebuild development or a type of gen-X-trification that has been identified in Australian cities (Wiesel et al., 2011)? Will the millennial generation opt for newer urban forms that turn away from conventional development patterns and instead promote better environmental stewardship (see Rees, Chapter 4; Blay-Palmer and Landman, Chapter 23) and qualitatively "urban" places (see Bain, Chapter 14; Walker and Gunn, Chapter 18)? Most of the other chapters in this book contemplate the impacts of diversity on Canadian cities in more specific ways, such as immigration (Kobayashi and Preston, Chapter 8), social polarization (Walks, Chapter 9), age (Moos, Chapter 20), and Indigeneity (Peters, Chapter 21). Consider this chapter a primer on the demographic and lifestyle changes that run through all phenomena that constitute urban Canada.

Review Questions

1. Describe at least three of the key forces of social and demographic change affecting contemporary Canadian cities.
2. What are some of the impacts that changing lifestyles may have on how we plan and develop our built environment?

References

Alsop, R. 2008. *The Trophy Kids Grow Up: How the Millennial Generation Is Shaking Up the Workplace*. Toronto: Jossey-Bass.

Atchley, R.C. 1982. "Retirement as a social institution," *Annual Review of Sociology* 8: 263–87.

Beaujot, R. 1991. *Population Change in Canada: The Challenges of Policy Adaptation*. Toronto: McClelland & Stewart.

Blakely, E., and M. Snyder. 1997. *Fortress America: Gated Communities in the United States*. Washington, DC: Brookings Institution Press.

Blandy, S., D. Lister, R. Atkinson, and J. Flint. 2003. *Gated Communities: A Systematic Review of the Research Evidence*. Bristol: Economic and Social Research Council, Centre for Neighbourhood Research, CNR Paper 12.

Bourne, L.S., and D. Rose. 2001. "The changing face of Canada: The uneven geographies of population and social change," *Canadian Geographer* 45: 105–19.

Boyd, M., and M. Vickers. 2000. "One hundred years of immigration to Canada," *Canadian Social Trends* (Fall); reprinted in *100 Years of Canadian Society*, Teachers Kit.

Bunting, T., and P. Filion, eds. 2006. *Canadian Cities in Transition: Local through Global Perspectives* (3rd edn.). Toronto: Oxford University Press.

Cahill, D. 2006. *Lifestyle Market Segmentation*. Toronto: Routledge.

Chagnon, J., and M. Milan. 2011. *Population Growth: Canada, Provinces and Territories, 2010*. Ottawa, ON: Statistics Canada, Component of Statistics Canada Catalogue no. 91-209-X.

Chapin, F.S. 1965. *Urban Land Use Planning* (2nd edn.). Urbana, IL: University of Illinois Press.

Clark, W. 2000. "One hundred years of education," *Canadian Social Trends* (Winter); reprinted in *100 Years of Canadian Society*, Teachers Kit.

———. 2007. "Delayed transitions of young adults," *Canadian Social Trends* (Winter).

Coy, M., and M. Pohler. 2002. "Gated communities in Latin American megacities: Case studies in Brazil and Argentina," *Environment and Planning B: Planning and Design* 29: 355–70.

Davies, W.K.D., and R.A. Murdie. 1991. "Measuring the social ecology of Canadian cities," in D. Ley and L. Bourne, eds., *The Changing Social Geography of Canadian Cities*. Montreal and Kingston: McGill-Queen's University Press.

———, and I.J. Townshend, eds. 2002. *Monitoring Cities: International Perspectives*. Lethbridge: Graphcom Printers.

Dytchwald, K. 1990. *Age Wave*. Toronto: Bantam Books.

Economist, The. 2001. "The Bridget Jones economy," 361, 8253: 68–70.

Fielding, H. 1996. *Bridget Jones's Diary*. London: Picador.

Foot, D., with D. Stoffman. 1996. *Boom, Bust and Echo: How to Profit from the Coming Demographic Shift*. Toronto: Macfarlane Walter and Ross.

Fries, F. 1980. "Aging, natural death, and the compression of morbidity," *New England Journal of Medicine* 303: 130–5.

Glasze, G. 2002. "Gated housing estates in the Arab world: Case studies in Lebanon and Riyadh, Saudi Arabia," *Environment and Planning B: Planning and Design* 29: 321–36.

Grant, J. 2005. "Planning responses to gated communities in Canada," *Housing Studies* 20: 277–89.

———, and L. Mittelsteadt. 2004. "Types of gated communities," *Environment and Planning B: Planning and Design* 31: 913–30.

Halli, S., and L. Driedger, eds. 1999. *Immigrant Canada: Demographic, Economic, and Social Challenges*. Toronto: University of Toronto Press.

Hareven, T.K., and K.J. Adams, eds. 1982. *Aging and Life Course Transitions: An Interdisciplinary Perspective*. New York: Guilford Press.

Hebert, B.P., and M. Luong. 2008. "Bridge employment," *Perspectives on Labour and Income* 9, 11. Statistics Canada Catalogue no. 75–001–X.

Hiller, H. 2006. *Canadian Society: A Macro Analysis* (5th edn.). Toronto: Pearson Prentice-Hall.

Hodge, G., and D. Gordon. 2014. *Planning Canadian Communities* (6th edn.). Scarborough, ON: Nelson Education.

Howe, N., and W. Strauss. 2007. *Millennials Go to College* (2nd edn.). Ithaca, NY: Paramount Books.

Hymowitz, K.S. 2007. "The New Girl Order." *City Journal* Autumn 2007. At: www.city-journal.org/html/17_4_new_girl_order.html

Karpel, C. 1995. *The Retirement Myth*. New York: Harper Collins.

Katz, P. 1994. *The New Urbanism*. New York: McGraw Hill.

Kraus, A.S. 1988. "Is a compression of morbidity in late life occurring? Examination of death certificate evidence," *Canadian Journal on Aging* 7: 58–70.

Kubo, T., and Y. Yui. 2012. "Changes in the condominium market in Japan after the 1990s," in M. Mantinan and N. Moore, eds., *Changes in the City* (Young Scholars Book 2). Santiago de Compostela: IDEGA-University of Santiago de Compostela and IGU Urban Commission.

Landman, K. 2006. "Privatising public space in post-apartheid South African cities through neighbourhood enclosures," *GeoJournal* 66: 133–46.

Lang, R., and K. Danielsen. 1997. "Gated communities in America: Walling out the world?" *Housing Policy Debate* 8: 867–99.

Laslett, P. 1987. "The emergence of the third age," *Ageing and Society* 7: 133–60.

———. 1991. *A Fresh Map of Life: The Emergence of the Third Age*. London: Weidenfeld and Nicolson.

Lesthaeghe, R. 1995. "The second demographic transition in Western societies: An interpretation," in K.O. Mason and A.M. Jensen, eds., *Gender and Family Change in Industrialized Countries*. Toronto: Oxford University Press.

Lo, O. 1996. "Condominium living," *Canadian Social Trends* (Summer): 41.

McDonald, P.L., and R.A. Wanner. 1984. "Socioeconomic determinants of early retirement in Canada," *Canadian Journal on Aging* 3:105–16.

———, and ———. 1990. *Retirement in Canada*. Toronto: Butterworths.

McGuirk, P. 2003. "The future of the city: A geography of connection and disconnection," *Geodate* 16: 5–9.

McKenzie, E. 1994. *Privatopia: Homeowner Associations and the Rise of Residential Private Government*. New Haven, CT: Yale University Press.

———. 2003. "Common-interest housing in the communities of tomorrow," *Housing Policy Debate* 14(1): 203–34.

Maguire, S., dir. 2001. *Bridget Jones's Diary*. Miramax Films.

Markides, K.S., and C.L. Cooper, eds. 1987. *Retirement in Industrialized Societies*. Toronto: John Wiley and Sons.

Marshall, K., and V. Ferraco. 2007. "Participation of older workers," *Perspectives on Labour and Income*, Statistics Canada Catalogue no. 75–001–XIE.

Milan, A. 2000. "One hundred years of families," *Canadian Social Trends* (Spring 2000), reprinted in *100 Years of Canadian Society*, Teachers Kit.

Miron, J.R. 1993. "Demography, living arrangement, and residential geography," in L.S. Bourne and D. Ley, eds., *The Changing Social Geography of Canadian Cities*. Montreal and Kingston: McGill-Queen's University Press.

Murdie, R., and C. Teixeira. 2006. "Urban social space," in Bunting and Filion (2006).

Murphy, M. 1987. "Measuring the family life cycle: Concepts, data and methods," in A. Bryman, B. Bytheway, P. Allatt, and T. Keil, eds., *Rethinking the Life Cycle*. London: Macmillan.

Nagnur, D. 1986. "Longevity and historical life tables: 1921–81 (abridged)," *Canada and the Provinces*. Ottawa, ON: Statistics Canada.

Neugarten, B. 1974. "Age groups in American society and the rise of the young-old," *Annals of the American Academy of Political and Social Science* 415 (1): 187–98.

Norland, J.A. 1994. *Profile of Canada's Seniors*. Ottawa, ON: Statistics Canada, Focus on Canada Series, Catalogue no. 96–312E.

Partridge, W. 1973. *The Hippie Ghetto: The Natural History of a Subculture*. New York: Holt, Rinehart and Winston.

Perry, C. 1929. "The neighborhood unit," in *Regional Survey of New York and Its Environs, Regional Survey*, vol. 7. New York: Neighborhood and Community Planning.

Punter, J.V. 1990. "The privatisation of the public realm," *Planning Practice and Research* 5: 9–18.

Raposo, R. 2006. "Gated communities, commodification and aestheticization: The case of the Lisbon metropolitan area," *GeoJournal* 66: 43–56.

Rea, W., D. McKay, and S. LeVaseur. 2008. *Changing Patterns in Canadian Homeownership and Shelter Costs*. Ottawa, ON: Statistics Canada Catalogue no. 97–554–X.

Roadburg, A. 1985. *Aging: Retirement, Leisure and Work in Canada*. Toronto: Methuen.

Rose, D., and P. Villeneuve. 2006. "Life stages, living arrangements, and lifestyles," in Bunting and Filion (2006).

Schnell, I., and Y. Benjamini. 2001. "The socio-spatial isolation of agents in everyday life spaces as an aspect of segregation," *Annals, Association of American Geographers* 91: 622–36.

——, and ——. 2002. "Measuring spatial lifestyles in Israel: A Tel-Aviv–Jaffa case study," in W.K.D. Davies and I. Townshend, eds., *Monitoring Cities: International Perspectives*. Calgary and Berlin: International Geographical Union, Urban Commission.

Seiler, S.R. 1986. "How to develop retirement communities for profit," *Real Estate Review* 16: 70–5.

Simmons-Tropea, D., and R. Osborn. 1993. "Disease, survival and death: The health status of Canada's elderly," in V.W. Marshall, ed., *Aging in Canada: Social Perspectives*. Markham, ON: Fitzhenry & Whiteside.

Singh, G., and A. Verma. 2001. "Is there life after career employment? Labour-market experience of early 'retirees,'" in V.W. Marshall, W.R. Heinz, H. Kruger, and A. Verma, eds., *Restructuring Work and the Life Course*. Toronto: University of Toronto Press.

Smith, N. 1987. "Of yuppies and housing: Gentrification, social restructuring, and the urban dream," *Environment and Planning D: Society and Space* 5: 151–72.

Starr, J., and D. Carns. 1972. "Singles in the city," *Society* 9: 43–8.

Statistics Canada. 1982. *1981 Census of Population, Private Households by Number of Persons, for Canada and Provinces, Urban Size Groups, Rural Non Farm and Rural Farm, 1981*. Catalogue 92-904, Table 3. At: https://archive.org/stream/1981929041982engfra#page/n19/mode/2up

——. 2007. *Immigration in Canada: A Portrait of the Foreign-born Population*. Catalogue no. 97–557–XIE.

——. 2008a. *Report on the Demographic Situation in Canada 2005 and 2006*. Catalogue no. 91–209–X.

——. 2008b. *Canadian Demographics at a Glance*. Catalogue no. 91–003–XIE.

——. 2008c. *Canada's Ethnocultural Mosaic*. Catalogue no. 97–562–X.

——. 2008d. *Educational Portrait of Canada*. Catalogue no. 97–560–X.

——. 2008e. *Aboriginal Peoples in Canada in 2006: Inuit, Métis and First Nations*. Catalogue no. 97–558–XIE.

——. 2010a. *Population Projections for Canada, Provinces and Territories: 2009 to 2036*. Catalogue no. 91-520-X

——. 2010b. *Projections of the Diversity of the Canadian Population: 2006 to 2031*. Catalogue no. 91-551-X

——. 2011a. *Population Projections by Aboriginal Identity in Canada, 2006 to 2031*. Catalogue no. 91-552-X

——. 2011b Census of Population. *Household Type (17), Household Size (9) and Structural Type of Dwelling (10) for Private Households of Canada, Provinces, Territories, Census Metropolitan Areas and Census Agglomerations, 2011 Census*. Catalogue Number 98-313-XCB2011022.

——. 2012a. *Fifty Years of Families in Canada: 1961 to 2011*. Catalogue no. 98-312-X2011003.

——. 2012b. *Generations in Canada*. Catalogue no. 98-311-X2011003

——. 2013a. Table 102-4505. Crude birth rate, age-specific and total fertility rates (live births), Canada, provinces and territories, annual (rate), CANSIM (database).

——. 2013b. NHS Focus on Geography Series. Catalogue no. 99-010-X2011005.

——. 2013c. *Aboriginal Peoples in Canada: First Nations People, Metis and Inuit.* Catalogue no. 99-011-X2011001

——. 2013d. Table 102-0512. Life expectancy, at birth and at age 65, by sex, Canada, provinces and territories, annual (years), CANSIM (database).

——. 2013e. Table 102-0502. Deaths, by month, Canada, provinces and territories, annual, CANSIM (database).

——. 2013f. Table 102-0504. Deaths and mortality rates, by age group and sex, Canada, provinces and territories, annual, CANSIM (database).

——. 2013g. *Immigration and Ethnocultural Diversity in Canada.* Catalogue no. 99-010-X2011001.

——. 2013h. *Living Arrangements of Young Adults Aged 20–29.* Catalogue no. 98-312-X2011003.

Stone, L. 2006. *New Frontiers of Research on Retirement.* Ottawa, Ont.: Statistics Canada Catalogue no. 75–511–XIE.

The World Factbook, 2013–14. 2013. Washington, DC: Central Intelligence Agency, 2013. At: www.cia.gov/library/publications/the-world-factbook/index.html

Townshend, I.J. 1997. *An Urban Geography of the Third Age.* Calgary, AB: University of Calgary, Ph.D. Thesis.

——. 2002. "Age segregated and retirement communities in the third age: The differential contribution of place-community to self-actualization," *Environment and Planning B: Planning and Design* 29: 371–96.

——. 2006. "From public neighbourhoods to multi-tier private neighbourhoods: The evolving ecology of neighbourhood privatization in Calgary," *GeoJournal* 66: 103–20.

——, and W.K.D. Davies. 1999. "The derivation of shopper typologies in business revitalization zones," *Papers and Proceedings of the Applied Geography Conferences* 22: 132–45.

Turcotte, M. 2013. *Living apart together.* Insights on Canadian Society, Statistics Canada Catalogue no. 75-006-X.

Trovato, F. 1987. "A longitudinal analysis of divorce and suicide in Canada," *Journal of Marriage and Family* 49: 193–203.

Walker, R.C. 2008. "Improving the interface between urban municipalities and Aboriginal communities," *Canadian Journal of Urban Research* 17 (suppl.): 20–36.

——, and Y. Belanger. 2013. "Aboriginality and planning in Canada's large Prairie cities," in R.C. Walker, T. Jojola, and D. Natcher, eds., *Reclaiming Indigenous Planning.* Montreal and Kingston: McGill-Queen's University Press.

——, and T. Carter. 2010. "At home in the city: Housing and neighbourhood transformation," in T. Bunting, P. Filion, and R. Walker, eds., *Canadian Cities in Transition: New Directions in the Twenty-first Century,* 4th edn. Toronto: Oxford University Press.

Wall Street Journal (Online). 2013. "Hip, urban, middle-aged; baby-boomers are moving into trendy urban neighbourhoods, but young residents aren't always thrilled," 8 August: n.p.

Webster, C., G. Glasze, and K. Frantz. 2002. "Guest editorial: The global spread of gated communities," *Environment and Planning B: Planning and Design* 29: 315–20.

Wiesel, I., R. Freestone, S. Pinnegar, and B. Randolph. 2011. "Gen-X-Trification? Generation shifts and the renewal of low-density housing in Sydney's suburbs," in *State of Australian Cities Conference* (pp. 26–29).

International Migration and Immigration: Remaking the Multicultural Canadian City

8

AUDREY KOBAYASHI AND VALERIE PRESTON

Introduction

Canadian cities have been profoundly influenced by international migration, one of the most dynamic processes of social change, both historically and at the present time. Migrants, temporary and permanent, from all over the world join the labour force, choose places to live, send their children to schools, participate in cultural activities, alter consumer choices, and become a part of civic life. They remake the urban landscape, often dramatically, but many aspects of their lives remain invisible, marked by inequality and injustice. Their stories are part of the dynamic set of social relations that constitute Canadian urban life.

This chapter addresses the wide range of ways in which international migration—the movement of people across national borders for economic opportunity, refuge, and family unification (Stalker, 2008)—has shaped Canadian cities. We consider the varied social, political, and economic contexts that have defined the settlement of immigrants, the roles of family and communities in initiating and supporting newcomers, and the spatial patterns of settlement across different cities and within cities. We also discuss the development and ongoing transformation of immigration policy, which regulates the flow of immigrants and affects their ability to adjust to and integrate within Canadian society.

Understanding contemporary immigration is impossible without thinking about the historical trends that preceded it. During the past decade, Canada has received nearly 2,400,000 permanent residents and another 3,300,000 temporary migrants (Citizenship and Immigration Canada, 2012). That number of temporary migrants, people entitled to live in Canada for fixed time periods specified by their visas, is one of the largest in the postwar period. Immigrants have also increased in cities and towns outside the traditional destinations of Montreal, Toronto, and Vancouver, shifting the map of immigrant settlement. Public policies that regulate immigration have both shaped and responded to the composition of the twenty-first-century migrant population.

Immigration as a Demographic Process

Since Canada's inception as a colonial nation, our cities have been populated by immigrants and generations of their descendants. Montreal, for example, was built by French and British settlers, including fur traders and merchants, military and administrative officers, and workers who laboured in the factories, on the docks, and in the transportation system that linked Eastern cities to the rest of Canada. In Toronto, the early population included British merchants and administrators, American Loyalists, and workers from many countries, their numbers growing and shifting over time. By 1881, about 88 per cent of Canadians were of British or French ancestry; about 6 per cent, German; and about 3 per cent, Aboriginal. No other group exceeded 1 percent of the total (Applied History Research Group, 1997). The major source of urban growth during the nineteenth and early twentieth centuries was not immigration, however, but a combination of the natural increase of the long settled population and rural-to-urban migration of the Canadian-born (Buckley, 1960). By 1891, immigrants comprised just 13 per cent of Canada's total population. Nearly half of the total population lived in Ontario and the largest city of Toronto, and nearly a third lived in Quebec and its largest city of Montreal. The balance of the country was much more sparsely populated, and cities such as Vancouver and Winnipeg were small. About 80 per cent of the urban population at that time was Canadian-born, and the largest number born outside Canada had come from Britain (Applied History Research Group, 1997).

During the late nineteenth and early twentieth centuries, successive groups, mainly European immigrants, made their ways to Toronto and Montreal. Both cities received large numbers of Irish immigrants during the famine years that started in the 1840s. Later came Italian, German, and Jewish immigrants, many of whom joined the construction and garment industries. In Vancouver, built as a western terminus for the railway that arrived in 1885, sawmills shipped lumber produced with immigrant labour to growing Eastern Canadian cities.

Over the next two decades, immigration added significantly to the Canadian population, altering its distribution permanently and unevenly. Many of the nearly two million British immigrants who arrived between 1901 and 1921 found their way to the cities. Young English men were recruited for farming and factory work, and English women for domestic help, but the Canadian government set its priorities on peopling the west (Hawkins, 1988). Between 1896 and 1905, Minister of the Interior Clifford Sifton was responsible for recruiting as many farmers as possible, targeting American and British immigrants as well as thousands of Eastern Europeans, whom he deemed inappropriate for

urban life but well suited to the harsh conditions of Prairie farming (Knowles, 2006; Simmons, 2010). By the early twentieth century, Winnipeg became the country's most ethnically diverse city, as trainloads of Eastern European newcomers were encouraged to settle the West.

Racialized minorities, however, were excluded. Chinese immigrants, who had settled in Vancouver after being recruited to build the railway, were required to pay a fee to enter the country. The so-called head tax severely curtailed the entry of Chinese immigrants after 1885. Thousands of Japanese workers hired by Vancouver sawmills established a significant community until their entry, too, was curtailed by a "Gentlemen's Agreement" in 1908. In that year, the government also passed the "Continuous Passage" regulation that prohibited passengers on any ship that had made a stop before arriving in Canada from settling in Canada. The regulation was invoked in 1914 to prevent passengers from India who had arrived on the *Komagata Maru* from disembarking in Vancouver (Knowles, 2006).

By the beginning of World War I, following the influx of over 500,000 newcomers in 1913 alone, people born outside Canada represented about 22 per cent of the national population (Kalbach and McVey, 1971), but their ethnic composition had not altered much. The largest groups were still English (30 per cent), French (28 per cent), Scottish (13 per cent), and Irish (13 per cent), followed distantly by German (3 per cent).

Demographic change due to immigration has not been haphazard. As we have noted, the Canadian government did a significant amount of steering, especially to the Prairie provinces. Immigrants are naturally attracted to areas where they find livelihood opportunities, often through "chain migration," the successive sponsorship of relatives and co-nationals by earlier arrivals. Thus, the largest immigrant populations became established in the largest cities: Montreal, Toronto, and later Vancouver (MTV), although the distribution, timing, and numbers of immigrants vary considerably among these cities (Simmons, 2010).

The MTV phenomenon has continued, although the numbers of immigrants settling in each city and their countries of origin have shifted. Immigration levels dropped during the Great Depression of the 1930s but rose sharply after World War II, fuelled by migrants fleeing economic and political struggles in Europe. For example, Jewish populations and the numbers of displaced persons from the Baltic states and Central Europe rose, especially in Toronto and Montreal. Then, after the 1956 Soviet invasion, large numbers of Hungarians came to Canada, particularly to Toronto. Later, fleeing the Vietnam War, many refugees from Vietnam, Laos, and Cambodia settled in French-speaking Montreal (Germain and Rose, 2000). That war also saw a less visible demographic shift as tens of thousands of American war resisters headed for Canada and settled in cities and small towns (Hardwick and Mansfield, 2009). During the late 1960s, changes to the Immigration Act and its associated regulations removed privileged status for European immigrants. Earthquakes in Portugal encouraged thousands of emigrants to leave, joining compatriots already settled in Montreal and Toronto. Similarly, when drought struck the Horn of Africa in the 1980s, Canadian planes were sent to collect famine-ravished refugees, and our cities began to receive large numbers of newcomers from Ethiopia, Somalia, and Eritrea. When Idi Amin rose to power in Uganda in 1971,

many fleeing that country, especially those of South Asian background, took up residence in Canadian cities. Thousands of Iranians left in the wake of the Ayatollah Khomeini's ascendency in 1979, many settling in the suburbs of North York and Richmond Hill in Toronto and in North Vancouver. By 1989, the largest refugee group was from Poland, which was undergoing political and economic upheaval. That year saw the largest movement of immigrants to date, from Hong Kong, to Vancouver and Toronto. A decade later when that phenomenon slowed, the number of Hong Kong born Canadians had reached 241,000.

By the 1990s, another demographic shift had taken place as the majority of immigrants became racialized minorities, particularly from East Asia but increasingly also from South Asia, Africa, and Latin America. Immigration from the Philippines increased dramatically, notably attracting large numbers of domestic and health-care workers, who settled in smaller cities such as Winnipeg and Calgary as well as MTV. In 2011, Filipinos were the largest group of recent immigrants, followed closely by those from the Republic of China, who have made up the largest overall number of immigrants over the past decade and a half (Table 8.1).

There has also been a spatial shift (Table 8.2). The vast majority of newcomers, more than 90 per

Table 8.1	Top 10 Countries of Birth for Recent Immigrants, 1981-2011

2011 National Household Survey[4]	1981 Census	1991 Census	2001 Census	2006 Census
Philippines	United Kingdom	Hong Kong	PRC	PRC
People's Republic of China (PRC)	Viet Nam	Poland	India	India
India	United States	PRC	Philippines	Philippines
United States	India	India	Pakistan	Pakistan
Pakistan	Philippines	Philippines	Hong Kong	United States
United Kingdom	Jamaica	United Kingdom	Iran	South Korea
Iran	Hong Kong	Viet Nam	Taiwan	Romania
South Korea	Portugal	United States	United States	Iran
Colombia	Taiwan	Lebanon	South Korea	United Kingdom
Mexico	PRC	Portugal	Sri Lanka	Colombia

Source: Statistics Canada (2013: 8); Chiu, Tran, and Maheux (2007: 10).

Table 8.2   Distribution of Immigrants Between MTV and Other Canadian Locations, 1986–2011

	Per cent of Immigrant Population				
Location	1986	1996	2001	2006	2011
Toronto CMA	31.6	35.7	37.3	37.5	37.4
Montreal CMA	11.8	11.8	11.4	12	12.5
Vancouver CMA	10	12.7	13.6	13.4	13.5
MTV	53.4	60.2	62.3	62.9	63.4
Outside MTV	46.6	39.8	37.7	37.1	36.6

Sources: Statistics Canada (2013: 12); Chiu, Tran, and Maheux (2007; 12); and Citizenship and Immigration Canada (2005).

cent in 2011, still settle in metropolitan areas and Toronto is still the destination for about one-third, or 32.8 per cent, of recent immigrants; however, increasing numbers are locating outside MTV. Calgary, Edmonton, and Winnipeg attracted larger shares of recent immigrants in 2011 than they did in 2006. And since 2000, small metropolitan areas such as Windsor and London have also received more newcomers. The regionalization of settlement reflects recent changes in immigration policy that we will take up later.

Growing numbers of temporary migrants—international students, temporary foreign workers, caregivers, and refugee claimants—also live in Canada's cities. They are a vulnerable population with limited rights to residency, political participation, and services. Since 1987, their numbers have more than tripled from 186,252 to an estimated 705,231 people in 2011 (Citizenship and Immigration Canada, 2012). Almost two-thirds (63.4 per cent) of temporary residents plan to live in metropolitan areas; however, they are more dispersed than immigrants who settle permanently. Sponsored by individual employers in large and small cities and towns and studying in post-secondary institutions and high schools across the country, less than half of temporary residents who entered the country in 2011, only 43.7 per cent, lived in MTV.

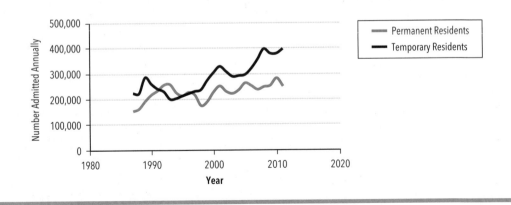

Figure 8.1   **Permanent and Temporary Residents, 1987–2011**

Source: Citizenship and Immigration Canada (2012: 4, 52).

Immigration as a Dynamic Social Process

International migration is best understood as an event, or series of events, in the life course. A life course approach shows that migration decisions are not random but socially structured (Kobayashi and Preston, 2007). Notwithstanding the complex economic and political contexts that certainly influence migration, decisions to leave one's country take into account numerous factors (Stalker, 2008). Hopes and dreams are tied to people's aspirations for and the availability of work, children's education, lifestyle, and the well-being of an entire—sometimes extended—family. People therefore make decisions around the needs of families, not just individuals, and decisions occur at certain times in the life course: upon entering the labour force, when adopting a life partner or having children, at key points in children's education, and sometimes on retirement. Most people plan their journeys, often waiting for protracted periods to receive authorization from Canadian embassies and consulates abroad. In choosing a destination, migrants also consider their social contacts at the destination, particularly the presence of relatives or an established ethnocultural community.

Many practices of everyday life, from finding a job to participating in cultural events and worship, are organized through social networks of immigrants and their Canadian-born descendants. A comparative study of Ethiopian and Somali immigrants demonstrated that immigrants who are well established and have dense social networks tend to fare better economically (Danso, 2002). Scholars increasingly interpret migration as the transfer of human capital, including education, job skills, and enabling social networks, from one part of the world to another. Accumulated capital eases the transition to new homes and adds to the destination city as a whole (Massey, 2012; Stalker, 2008).

Approximately 11 per cent of newcomers are convention refugees[1] (Citizenship and Immigration, 2012). The conditions that create refugees may be abrupt and extreme—a natural disaster, a civil war, or other violence—although in many cases refugees have languished in temporary camps, sometimes for years at a time. All of the stresses of the refugee process are added to the other challenges of migration so that settlement and integration may be extremely difficult.

A century ago international migration was usually a one-way trip. Today it is increasingly transnational, meaning that migrants maintain a "transnational field" of social, economic, and political linkages with their countries of origin. They may move back and forth between origin and destination so that migration is circular rather than one-way, and they often use modern modes of communication, such as Skype and instant messaging, to stay in close touch with family, friends, and popular culture. Some men become "astronauts," working abroad to support families in Canada. Other transnationals send young children to be cared for by grandparents. Still others encourage grown children to move to the parents' country of origin for economic opportunities. While many immigrants maintain transnational ties to assuage longing for familiar people and culture, others are motivated by discriminatory experiences in Canada that restrict their employment prospects, or by the desire to take advantage of their Canadian credentials and experience in places enjoying rapid economic growth (Ley, 2013; Preston, Kobayashi and Man, 2006).

Relations between ethnocultural groups and with the larger society are a crucial aspect of the urban social context for immigrants. The process of immigration has always been socially normative. Newcomers are expected to adapt to, and even assimilate, the norms of the dominant groups. This expectation makes two problematic assumptions, however: (1) that there *is* a norm, based mainly on British and to some degree on French cultural heritages, that provides the social and cultural terms to which newcomers *should* adapt and assimilate; and (2) that members of the dominant groups will indeed welcome newcomers on an equal basis (Hall, 2000; Kymlicka, 2007). Both assumptions belie the concept of multiculturalism, to which we return shortly.

Immigration is thus a dynamic social process that can be understood along a number of social dimensions, including relationships within the family, with friends and ethnocultural or faith-based communities, and with the larger society, which is diverse in its attitudes to immigration and in its willingness to change as Canadian social dynamics shift. The social conditions faced by immigrants in different Canadian cities are, therefore, mixed and often contradictory. Many newcomers enjoy the benefits of immigration, especially in circumstances where they are preceded by family members and others from the same origin. Destination cities welcome their human capital, including their contributions to a rich and varied cultural landscape. At the same time, newcomers face challenging barriers, not only in overcoming the difficulties of transition to a new place but also due to discriminatory practices and hostile attitudes.

Immigration and Canadian Urban Landscapes

Immigration has its most visible imprint on the residential and commercial landscapes of Canadian cities. Early immigrant communities that grew up around clusters of boarding houses provided both shelter and the basic commercial services that immigrants required, including employment services, translation, and banking. Today, residential and commercial landscapes are layered and varied across and between cities. They can be richly textured landscapes of cultural expression, or they can be segregated and marginalized landscapes of exclusion and poverty. For some newcomers, such as German immigrants in Winnipeg, the visible landscape now contains almost no clues as to their arrival and passage. Others, such as Chinese immigrants in the suburbs of Toronto and Vancouver, have transformed the landscape.

The Commercial Landscape

Commercial streetscapes have developed to cater to the specific needs of migrant groups, often one of the few places where newcomers can participate in the urban economy. Initially, such areas served cultural and practical needs and provided services not available in the larger community. For example, Pender Street in Vancouver developed on the margins of the city as a place populated by Chinese immigrants but shunned by the dominantly white citizens (Anderson, 1995). From these beginnings Pender Street grew to become a colourful landscape dominated by small stores and cafes that came to be known outside the neighbourhood as "Chinatown." Similar neighbourhoods, some consisting of only a few buildings, others of several blocks, developed in most Canadian cities. By the 1970s, they had become symbolic of the multicultural city and were targets of redevelopment projects that marketed them as tourist destinations, as much for the dominant population as for the immigrant community (Lai, 2011).

A few blocks from Pender Street, Vancouver's Powell Street became a commercial strip for Japanese immigrants in the early twentieth century as white residents moved to newer parts of the city, away from the mills and other noxious industries. The transformation of the landscape reflected the needs of recent arrivals: small, single family homes were adapted to contain businesses providing basic necessities, such as groceries, employment services, translation, and informal banking services. The buildings were also extended backwards from the street as boarding houses for the thousands of single Japanese men who moved to Vancouver to find work (Jackson and Kobayashi, 1994) (Figure 8.2). This once thriving area, however, was completely dismantled when Japanese Canadians were forcibly removed during the 1940s.

In Montreal, "The Main" was a strip of businesses on Boulevard St-Laurent that catered to many different European immigrants (Germain and Rose, 2000). Dominated by Jewish immigrants in the 1920s and 1930s, this landscape later captured the popular imagination through novels such as *St Urbain's Horseman* by Mordecai Richler, which describes the life of Jake Hersh, a successful movie director who can never entirely leave behind the Montreal neighbourhood where he

Figure 8.2   Powell Street in Vancouver in 1928, showing commercial development by Japanese immigrants.

Source: Dominion Photo Company, Vancouver Public Library 21773.

grew up. Indeed, Richler once commented that he was still so rooted in the neighbourhood that "This is my time, my place and I have elected myself to get it right" (Richler, 1972: 19). Transformed since Quebec's Quiet Revolution, "The Main" is now home to upscale boutiques, restaurants, and bars; only a few of the original businesses remain.

In Toronto, the Ward—officially St John's Ward, the area covering and surrounding what is now City Hall and Nathan Phillips Square—was the commercial and residential landscape for many immigrants, including those of Irish, Jewish, Chinese, and Italian backgrounds. These new-comers endured unsafe and unhealthy living and working conditions (Bateman, 2012). The Ward has now completely disappeared, expropriated during the first decade of the twentieth century to make way first for City Hall then for a number

of hospitals—amid much controversy over how to maintain a "clean" city both morally and physically. It represents perhaps the first example of the displacement of minority groups to make way for new versions of public space. The Jewish population relocated along Spadina Avenue, where factories offered employment for men and women (Hiebert, 1993). As long as restrictive covenants made it difficult for Jews to buy property in many Toronto neighbourhoods, Jewish merchants concentrated in Kensington Market. They were replaced slowly as Portuguese immigrants moved into the neighbourhood after World War II. Along Spadina Avenue, Chinese businesses also took over the premises of many Jewish merchants, creating a thriving tourist attraction, identified as "Chinatown" by the City of Toronto.

Wei Li coined and defined the term **ethnoburbs** (Li, 2009) to capture emerging landscapes in suburban areas where the newest immigrants are settling. An ethnoburb is a suburban cluster of residential areas and business districts that is home to a concentration of at least one ethnic minority. Unlike traditional ports of entry, the population is heterogeneous, including multiple ethnocultural groups. Unlike earlier concentrations of businesses that often developed to serve the consumer needs of a local immigrant group, ethnoburbs result from the interactions among global, national, and local forces. Over the past two decades, as the Canadian government promoted immigration from Chinese-speaking countries—starting first with Hong Kong and then China and Taiwan—large sections of cities, especially in Vancouver and Toronto, have been transformed. Although such areas are still the destination of the dominant population seeking popular Asian-style food, their main purpose is to serve the consumer needs of growing Chinese ethnocultural communities (Lo, 2006). Malls covered in Chinese characters where many shopkeepers and their employees speak first in Cantonese or Mandarin are increasingly common in the suburbs of MTV. Some malls have been met with opposition on the grounds that they exclude long-settled residents who do not speak either Chinese language (Preston and Lo, 2000;

Zhuang, 2008). In one notorious example in suburban Toronto, the deputy mayor of Markham, commented that the growing Asian population was driving out "the backbone of Markham" (Verma, 2005). The municipal government responded by reiterating its support for diversity and establishing a race relations committee charged with promoting tolerance for diversity and equal treatment for all residents. The incident remains as testimony to the discrimination and racism that still mark contemporary Canadian cities.

The Residential Landscape

According to Carter and Vitiello (2012: 92), the "diversity of newcomers and of housing markets across North America results in such varied patterns that there is no such thing as a 'typical' immigrant housing experience." Yet finding adequate and affordable housing is a major concern for virtually all newcomers. Rising housing costs, shortages of rental housing, low incomes, discrimination by landlords and real estate agents, and cultural preferences for specific housing attributes combine to create different scenarios between cities and between newcomer groups within cities.

Recent scholarship has expanded our understanding of immigrant housing issues, showing that immigration status, income, ethnic and racial background, and household size and composition affect the security and quality of immigrants' housing.[2] Immigrants who are sponsored by family members already established in Canada do best initially in the housing market. They often live in multigenerational households that are sometimes crowded but usually safe and affordable (Hiebert, 2011). Immigrants selected to contribute to the Canadian economy on the basis of their qualifications and work experience often struggle with high housing costs. Largely because of their low incomes, refugees, even those sponsored by the Canadian government, encounter enormous barriers to obtaining adequate, suitable, and affordable housing. While waiting to learn whether they will be recognized as bona fide refugees, they live in the least desirable housing, often paying

more than half their income for a dark room in a dank basement with shared kitchen and bathroom.

Over time, however, many immigrants find better-paid jobs and move into affordable, suitable, and well-maintained accommodation (Hiebert, 2009). Indeed, some immigrants, particularly those from Italy, Portugal, and Hong Kong, attain higher home ownership rates than the population as a whole (Murdie and Teixeira, 2003); however, pathways to home ownership differ. Many Hong Kong immigrants had substantial financial assets that allowed them to purchase housing upon arrival (Ley, 2010a; Moos and Skaburskis, 2010). Italian and Portuguese immigrants, on the other hand, often scrimped and saved to own housing (Teixeira, 2007), capitalizing upon connections in the construction industry to ease the strain wherever possible. Recent research (Hiebert, 2011) distinguishes immigrants who attain success in their housing careers from those who are stuck in unaffordable, unsatisfactory, overcrowded housing and at risk of homelessness, sometimes even after 10 years' residence in Canada. Affordability is a challenge facing immigrants in all Canadian cities because low-cost rental housing is in short supply (Hulchanski and Shapcott, 2004). In the 1990s, rental units in Montreal were more affordable than in either Toronto or Vancouver (Hiebert, 2009; Hiebert et al., 2006); however, average rents in all three metropolitan areas are converging.

Discrimination also places immigrants at a disadvantage (Murdie, 2008a). Although many feel that skin colour, ethnic background, and religion are major reasons for discrimination in Vancouver and Montreal, in Toronto immigrants are more likely to mention that landlords discourage tenants who have large families and many children, or those who are single mothers and dependent on welfare (Preston et al., 2011). It may be that in the Toronto metropolitan area, where almost half the population belongs to a racialized minority (Statistics Canada, 2013), many immigrants are renting from landlords who are from the same ethnocultural background, reducing the salience of skin colour as a marker of discrimination. Such is certainly not the case in Vancouver or in Montreal

(Francis and Hiebert, 2011; Hiebert et al., 2006, Rose and Charette, 2011).

Geographers who study the evolution of the modern city have observed that many immigrants settled initially near the city centre, where low-cost housing in old, crowded apartments was available adjacent to industrial plants that hired many newcomers. They moved outward to better quality and more spacious housing as their financial circumstances permitted (Park and Burgess, 1925; Wirth, 1928). While such patterns still fit some immigrant communities in Canadian cities, settlement patterns are now diverse (Figures 8.3, 8.4, and 8.5). Concentrations of racialized minorities, such as Chinese and South Asians, have increased in size and number at the same time that the **suburbanization** of immigrants has continued apace (Murdie,

2008b). In Toronto, some immigrants are locating directly in the postwar inner suburbs, where rental housing is available, while others follow the paths of earlier Jewish, Italian, and Portuguese immigrants who moved to newly developed suburbs as their economic circumstances improved (Teixeira, 2007). Still others, particularly Chinese, South Asian, Russian, and Persian immigrants, are locating directly in outer suburbs (Murdie, 2008b; Qadeer, Agrawal and Lovell, 2010). As Ray, Halseth, and Johnson (1997) found in Vancouver, some newcomers are typical suburbanites attracted by the characteristic spacious housing and large lots. Suburbanization is well established in Vancouver, where Chinese immigrants from China, Hong Kong, and Taiwan, and South Asians from India and Pakistan are transforming suburban

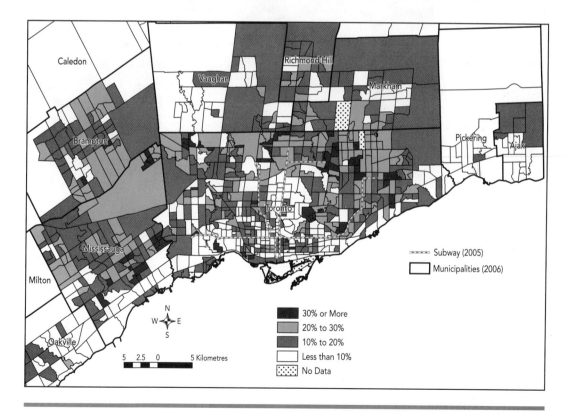

Figure 8.3   Recent Immigrant (2001–2006) Percentage of the Population by Census Tract, Toronto CMA, 2006

Source: Statistics Canada, Census 2006.

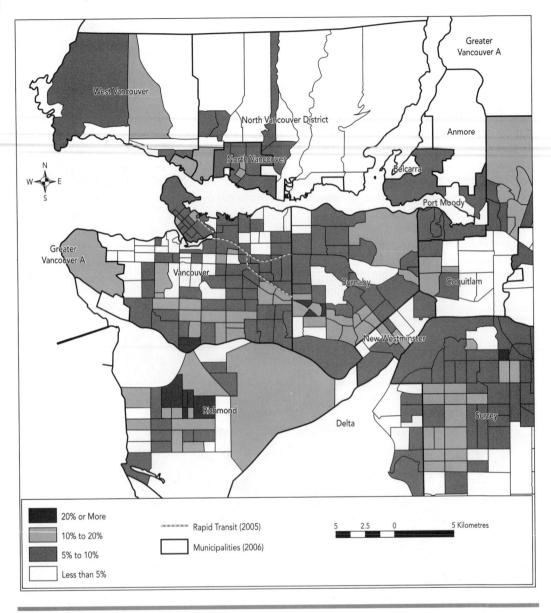

Figure 8.4   **Recent Immigrant (2001–2006) Percentage of the Population by Census Tracts, Vancouver CMA, 2006**

Source: Statistics Canada (2006).

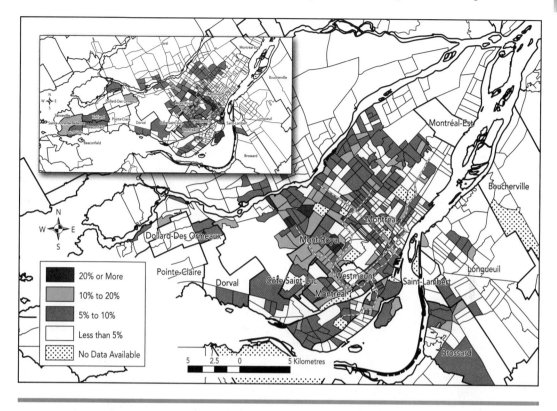

Figure 8.5 **Immigrants Who Arrived 2001–2006 as a Percentage of the Total Population, Montreal CMA, 2006**

Source: Statistics Canada (2006).

municipalities, such as Richmond and Surrey. In Montreal, newcomers are moving beyond the boundaries of the City of Montreal but they remain concentrated on the island, rather than in the newly developed suburbs to the north (Murdie, 2008b; Rose and Charette, 2011).

The persistent concentrations of immigrants and their children in Canadian cities are often appraised pejoratively as potential **ghettos**, with connotations of poverty, social disorder, and exclusion (Wacquant, 2004; Wirth, 1928).[3] Despite claims that immigrants who live in concentrations fail to integrate into Canadian society, there is no evidence of ghettos in Canadian cities (Murdie, 2008b; Walks and Bourne, 2006). Chinese and South Asian concentrations have increased in size and number, but the most recent analyses continue

to show that few minorities live in neighbourhoods where they are the majority, and residential concentration is not associated with poverty.[4] There is an expert consensus that many immigrants and their descendants in Canadian cities live in **ethnic enclaves**, spatial concentrations formed by residents' preference to live near others from the same ethnocultural group, rather than by the processes of exclusion as is the case in so-called ghettos (Murdie, 2008b; Qadeer, Agrawal, and Lovell, 2010).

This relatively benign view of minority concentrations reflects the low levels of segregation of racial and ethnic minorities in Canadian cities compared with those in American cities as well as the low correlations between levels of segregation and poverty. For example, many Italian immigrants and their descendants in Toronto live in an Italian enclave despite marked improvements in their average income, education, and occupational status (Murdie, 2008b). Concentrations of South Asian immigrants and their children are also readily apparent in the suburban landscapes of Toronto and Vancouver, where developers build large houses to accommodate multigenerational families (Agrawal, 2006). Other scholars, however, have found conflicting evidence (Darden, 2004; Darden and Fong, 2012; Teixeira, 2008), emphasizing how racism has shaped residential concentrations for some minorities in Canada.

Although many newcomers rely on their own initiatives and help from friends and family to settle, integration is often enhanced by services that are distributed unevenly across metropolitan areas (Smith and Ley, 2009). Historically, settlement and other social services were concentrated in central locations near the ports of entry where immigrants settled (Truelove, 2000). In the suburbs, there are often fewer services and infrequent and slow public transit. Ironically, newcomers who settle in private rental housing in the suburbs are often at a disadvantage compared to those who live in poor neighbourhoods where there is subsidized housing. Many of the services that locate nearby to assist the low-income populations in subsidized housing also serve immigrants (Smith and Ley, 2009). Those who move to the outer suburbs, where the population has grown faster than all types of social infrastructure, often travel long distances to find help or rely on their own resources and social contacts (Lo et al., 2010).

Recently, migrants' transnational activities have begun to alter the residential landscapes that immigrants construct in Canadian cities. While most immigrants move near friends and family, others are recruited by transnational networks of compatriots, and still others settle with an eye to maintaining economic and social ties to their homelands. Growing numbers of Filipinas, for example, recruit friends and families to work as live-in caregivers in the cities where the recruiters are settled (D'Addario, 2012). For Hong Kongers who wanted to operate businesses in their homeland, proximity to Asia was one of the main attractions of Vancouver (Ley, 2003; 2010a). Family ties and the desire to stay in touch with Hong Kong culture and politics also shape the identities of Hong Kong immigrants who have formed enclaves in suburban Vancouver and Toronto (Kobayashi, Preston, and Murnaghan, 2011; Ley, 2010a). Eager for a suburban family life, they patronize Chinese cultural activities and businesses that help their children retain knowledge of Chinese languages and culture, ensuring that after university graduation the Canadian-born children of immigrants can take advantage of economic opportunities in Asia. The ease with which financial assets can be transferred internationally allows some immigrants to purchase housing as soon as they arrive in Canada, which was the case for many Hong Kong migrants (Ley, 2010a; Preston, Kobayashi, and Siemiatycki, 2006). The housing decisions of other transnationals, however, are constrained by their social ties and social relationships at their places of origin. For example, Ghanaian women often rent cheap accommodation so that they can send as much money as possible to support children left in Ghana, a strategy shared by Filipinas (Pratt, 2004; Wong, 2000). Others forgo home ownership in Canada in order to build houses in their homelands (Firang, 2011; Owusu, 1998; Wong, 2000).

Transnational ties shape many immigrants' sense of belonging in Canada. Tibetan refugees living near downtown Toronto are typical. For them, home encompasses the altars where daily offerings remind them of religious observances in India and Tibet, the kitchens where Tibetan foods are prepared, and the computers that link them to friends and family (Logan, 2010).

Landscapes of Inequality

Despite the common perception of being universally accepting, Canadians have been intolerant of "Others."[5] Race, ethnicity, and class have always formed the basis of inequality in Canadian cities, and from the earliest days inequality was associated with immigration. By the 1890s, European immigrants lived in appalling conditions in the poorest areas of Montreal and Toronto. Cities were publicly viewed as places of privilege; and "foreigners"—of Jewish, Italian, Ruthenian, or Macedonian background—as unwanted, unsanitary, and immoral. Around the turn of the century, urban reform movements arose to "to purge urban centres of some of their worst ills, including prostitution, crime, and disease. In time, the philosophy that urban life was 'bad' and resulted in immoral, unhealthy, and un-British lifestyles affected the focus of future immigration campaigns" (Applied History Research Group, 1997). Eastern Europeans were shunted to the Prairies and, during World War I, many were interned as "enemy aliens."

Anti-"foreign" campaigns have also led to violence in Canadian cities. In February 1887, the night before Vancouver's first civic election, hundreds of white men attacked a camp of Chinese immigrant workers in an attempt to run them out of town (Donaldson, 2013). The "Chinatown" that, as mentioned, subsequently developed along Vancouver's Pender Street has been described by Kay Anderson (1995) as the product of racist public discourse and policy that created marginal populations in marginalized parts of the city. Among many instances of violence against Asian immigrants perhaps the most infamous is the September 1907 race riot that destroyed property on Pender Street and in the neighbouring Japanese immigrant district along Powell Street. When Asian workers, who provided many of the housekeeping and laundry services for the white population of Vancouver, staged a work stoppage to encourage an investigation (Gilmore, 2012; Sugimoto, 1973), the subsequent Royal Commission (Canada, 1908) led to the ironic "Gentlemen's Agreement" by which immigration from Japan was curbed.[6] This incident illustrates the collaboration between government and dominant group citizens to contain what they viewed as "foreign" populations, and one of the first attempts by a racialized minority to protest their treatment and to advocate for their place in the city. Japanese Canadians, moreover, both immigrants and the Canadian-born, were uprooted, dispossessed, and interned during the 1940s (Knowles, 2006). In addition, under the slogan "None is too many," European Jews were denied entry to Canada and returned to Europe, where they faced death camps during World War II (Abella and Troper, 1983). And most racialized minorities—again, whether immigrants or Canadian-born—did not receive the right to vote until the Citizenship Act was passed in 1947.

Study after study (Anderson, 1995; Darden, 2004; Darden and Fong, 2012; Francis, 2009; Francis and Hiebert, 2011; Isin and Siemiatycki, 2002; Lai and Huffey, 2009; Li, 2003; Murdie, 2002; Novac et al., 2004; Ray and Preston, 2009; Rose and Charette, 2011; Simmons, 2010; Teixeira, 2008) show that newcomers have faced prejudice, discrimination, unequal or unfair treatment, and racism throughout Canadian history. Islamophobia—discrimination against Muslim groups who are among the newest arrivals in Canada—is one of the most recent examples. Although the issue came to the fore after the events of 11 September 2001, Arab and Muslim populations have been subject to discrimination for much longer (Abu-Laban and Alladin, 1991; Arat-Koc, 2006; Kashmeri, 1991). Islamaphobia is highly visible in controversies over the siting of mosques and the right to wear religious dress in urban public places (Abu-Laban and Abu-Laban, 2007; Isin and Siemiatycki, 2002; Leroux, 2010).[7]

Racial profiling is not always visible but it is a powerful means of othering. In September 2002, Maher Arar, a telecommunications engineer with dual Canadian and Syrian citizenship, was detained by US authorities while changing planes at Kennedy International Airport, en route home to Canada. He was deported to Syria, where he was tortured and held for a year. After his return to Canada, a commission of inquiry found that he had no links to any terrorist organization, and he received an official apology and a compensatory settlement (Mazigh, 2008; Pither, 2008). Young black men also experience racial profiling, particularly in low-income neighbourhoods of major cities where the police regularly stop them. Resistance to the intimidating and questionable police requests for identification is met with suspicion and the potential threat of arrest (Wortley and

Owusu-Bempah, 2011). These cases highlight the uneven and unsafe landscapes of justice in Canada for Arabs, Muslims, and blacks.

In another example, after the small Quebec town of Hérouxville adopted a code of conduct for immigrants that specified actions unacceptable in Quebec society, Premier Jean Charest appointed a two-person commission of inquiry. Their report (Bouchard and Taylor, 2008) found that there are limits to reasonable accommodation, thus confirming a long established notion of a dominant Quebec culture based on the legacy of the original settlers. Opinions presented in town hall meetings across the province revealed that experiences of Otherness varied across Quebec, in part because minorities and recent immigrants are concentrated in Montreal. The diversity in Montreal is double-edged. On the one hand, it allows for mundane, daily encounters that inform people about their differences, combating the stereotypes at the root of Otherness; at the same time, tensions over cultural difference erupt where different ethnic and racialized groups live in close proximity (Bouchard and Taylor, 2008).

Although there have been many other instances of violence against immigrants, most of the inequality that is etched upon the urban landscape is neither so violent nor so fleeting. As we have shown above, residential segregation represents the most ubiquitous expression of inequality and inequity in the urban landscape. Nativist opposition to the cultural expression of both residential and commercial landscapes represents a form of cultural violence that strengthens anti-immigrant normativity. Places of worship constitute one of the most visible examples. Freedom of religion is a fundamental right guaranteed in the *Charter of Rights and Freedoms*. Religion is also one of the most significant markers of identity, for many surpassing any other form of citizenship belonging. In the days following 9/11, however, there were numerous acts of violence, including racist graffiti, personal attacks, and firebombing of mosques and temples, across Canada. The increasing number of non-Christian places of worship—including Hindu, Sikh, Islamic, or Buddhist temples, or

mosques—mark the growth and coming of age of immigrant communities (Isin and Siemiatycki, 2002; Mensah, 2005; 2008), yet as mentioned the locations of their places of worship are often contested (Germain, 2006; Germain and Gagnon, 2003; Hoernig, 2006; Qadeer and Chaudhry, 2000). As Hoernig's extensive research shows, religious communities often adapt to place-based opposition by locating in industrial areas rather than residential areas, as well as by reaching out to their neighbours in an effort to increase understanding (Hoernig and Zhuang, 2010).

Inequality for immigrants in the urban landscape is most acutely felt in the economic realm. Between 2001 and 2006, the percentage of immigrant households with low incomes increased at the same time as the share of Canadian-born households with low incomes declined (Picot, 2004). It is taking longer for immigrants to achieve the same earnings as their equally qualified and experienced Canadian-born counterparts. Seeking affordable housing, many recent immigrants are concentrating in urban neighbourhoods where low-cost rental housing is available. In Toronto, priority neighbourhoods, where the population is disproportionately low-income, are home to large, racialized immigrant populations (Hulchanski, 2007). With poor transit connections, residents are often isolated from a growing number of suburban jobs and the services that might facilitate their economic integration (Smith and Ley, 2009).

Immigration Policy as a Systemic Process

As we have already shown, the Canadian government has always played a dominant role in directing immigration trends, from outright attempts to exclude racialized minorities while encouraging European immigrant groups on the Prairies, to decisions over which groups to exclude during World War II and how to define refugee groups during the 1960s and 1970s. Even the acceptance of American war resisters during the Vietnam War was a contentious policy decision on the part of Prime Minister

Pierre Elliott Trudeau. Over time, immigration policies and procedures have had far-reaching consequences for Canadian cities.

A major shift occurred during the 1960s when Canada introduced a "points" system, which evaluated each applicant's educational and professional qualifications, work experience, and language abilities. This system, which limited the power of officials to make arbitrary decisions and removed racial background as a criterion for admission was used to recruit skilled workers and their families. To accelerate economic development, business class immigration was also introduced to attract experienced entrepreneurs and investors (Ley, 2003). Canadian policies also encouraged family reunification by allowing permanent residents and citizens with sufficient financial resources to sponsor their relatives. As a signatory to the 1951 UN Convention on Refugees, Canada also admitted immigrants who met the United Nations definition of a refugee, including government-assisted (GAR) and privately sponsored (PSR) refugees who were selected by consular officials abroad and refugee claimants who were recognized as bona fide refugees after their arrival in Canada.

The effect of the new legislation was swift. The number of source countries increased dramatically, and Asian countries quickly replaced European countries as the largest sources of immigrants (see Table 8.1 earlier in this chapter). People who self-identified as non-Aboriginal or non-white visible minorities accounted for 78 per cent of the immigrants who arrived between 2006 and 2011 (Statistics Canada, 2013). Attracted to Canada's metropolitan areas, the newcomers now constitute large racialized minorities in Montreal, Toronto, and Vancouver. In the Toronto metropolitan area, home to the largest visible minority population in Canada, almost one in two residents, or 47 per cent, identifies as a visible minority. The numbers of racialized minorities are smaller in Vancouver and Montreal, 45.2 per cent and 20.3 per cent, respectively. Five other metropolitan areas—Calgary, Edmonton, Ottawa-Gatineau, Winnipeg, and Hamilton—are home to more than 100,000 people who identify as racialized minorities

(Statistics Canada, 2013). This change in the backgrounds of urban residents has drawn attention to discrimination in urban housing and labour markets, the challenge of living with difference for all Canadians, and the success with which some Canadian municipalities are meeting the challenges of multicultural planning, while others are not (Qadeer, 1997).

During the 1990s, the government also reversed longstanding policies that reduced immigrant admissions during periods of economic recession (see Figure 8.1 earlier in this chapter). In response to growing concerns about Canada's declining birth rate and aging population, the government set an annual target for the total number of immigrants, approximately 1 per cent of the population, to be maintained regardless of the state of the Canadian economy. Each year since, the government has admitted between 200,000 and 300,000 immigrants; however, the proportion from each immigrant class—skilled worker and business class, family class, and refugee—has varied. Annual admissions of economic immigrants increased to approximately two-thirds of all permanent residents in 2011, and the percentages for refugees and family class immigrants have fallen to approximately 11 per cent and less than 30 per cent of annual admissions, respectively (Citizenship and Immigration, 2012). Recognized internationally as an immigrant-receiving country that actively recruits permanent residents, Canada has also become a major destination for temporary residents. Responding to employers' assertions of labour shortages, the number of people admitted on a temporary basis for specific jobs has increased from 294,525 in 1991 to 705,231 in 2011. Temporary residents are more dispersed than permanent residents; less than half lived in MTV. In municipalities of all sizes across the country, local governments are concerned by the rise in temporary residents since many are not eligible for publicly funded health and other essential services.

The growth of temporary migration occurred at the same time that some responsibility for immigrant selection and settlement devolved to the provinces. Immigration is a joint responsibility of the federal and provincial governments, but provincial interest in immigration was minimal until late in the twentieth century (Alboim and Cohl, 2012; Leitner and Preston, 2012). The initial and most substantial devolution occurred in 1991 when the Quebec–Canada Accord gave the provincial government of Quebec responsibility for selecting and settling immigrants in that province. In other provinces and territories, the federal government introduced the Provincial Nominee Program, allowing each provincial government to select a specified number of immigrants according to its own criteria as long as the immigrants were also admissible under federal health and security criteria.

The regionalization of immigration has been accompanied by growing diversity in settlement experiences among Canadian cities. Permanent residents are eligible to use government-funded services providing job and language training and information about Canadian society. Settlement services are available mainly through non-governmental organizations (NGOs) that work on contracts with the federal and provincial governments. The decentralized settlement service system is designed to respond to local needs in a cost-effective manner while ensuring universal access to services; however, the uneven geography of settlement services threatens access. Services remain concentrated in major metropolitan areas. As immigrants settle in growing numbers outside MTV, many find services are in short supply, particularly in small urban areas. There are local exceptions, however. For example, settlement agencies, some of them religiously organized, that developed in Winnipeg in the first two decades of the twentieth century have been revitalized. In Calgary, immigrant-serving agencies have evolved from volunteer organizations that sprang up initially to sponsor refugees. As provinces gained more power over settlement services in the first decade of the millennium, eligibility rules and service delivery also began to vary. In Quebec, eligibility for language training extends beyond the acquisition of citizenship, while newcomers who become citizens in other provinces and territories no longer qualify for these courses.

Settlement services play an immediate role in immigrant integration (Schellenberg and Maheux, 2007), but a multitude of government policies affect the welfare of newcomers. For example, the federal government's recent decision to provide medical services only to refugee claimants who pose a risk to public health or a public safety concern jeopardizes their chances to integrate (Alboim and Cohl, 2012). The housing challenges facing many newcomers also reflect the failure to develop a national strategy for affordable housing (Preston et al., 2009). Human rights and employment equity policies also play a crucial role in combating the discrimination that marginalizes and excludes many immigrants, particularly racialized minorities (Lai and Huffey, 2009; Novac et al., 2004; Preston and Ray, 2009).

Immigration and Multiculturalism: Policy or Way of Life?

No policy or practice has been more confused than Canada's official multiculturalism policy. The made-in-Canada policy has become a source of national pride since its inception in the early 1970s, but there is a vast range of understandings concerning what it is, where it came from, or for whom it was intended. At its very best the policy has been controversial and subject to ideological conflict, but the confusion goes beyond ideological camps as Canadians have struggled to reach a consensus about the meaning of multiculturalism.

Senator Paul Yuzyk, born in Canada of Ukrainian immigrant parents, introduced the term *multiculturalism* and became a tireless crusader to diversify the political and social power structure. Prime Minister Trudeau publicized it with a 1971 speech asserting that "Canada has two official languages, but no official culture" (Trudeau, 1971). At that time, the country was demographically multicultural, meaning that there was a plurality of ethnocultural groups residing in communities across the country. Trudeau's words introduced a period of symbolic multiculturalism as the federal government began to recognize "cultural" practices, including folk culture, food, religion, and heritage languages, which individual Canadians—whether born in Canada or in another country—should have a choice about maintaining (hence "no official culture"). After the repatriation of the Canadian Constitution and adoption of the *Charter of Rights and Freedoms* in the early 1980s, multiculturalism became increasingly structural, as questions of ethnocultural identity and equality rights were enshrined in policy and legislation (Kobayashi, 1993).

Popular understanding of *multiculturalism* has always been at odds with its designation as an official policy. Minorities—especially racialized minorities—have contended that the term has no meaning outside recognizing the right to full equality for all citizens, which would require addressing questions of racialization and discrimination (Kobayashi 2013; Ley 2010b). The more popular image, however, is of multiculturalism as a basis for "celebrating diversity" as a result of welcoming the Other into the Canadian family. In this popular image, there still exists a dominant, normative Canadian culture (about which Canadians might argue but many would agree exists), so multiculturalism is only for Others. But Others bring a range of consumer choices, such as "ethnic" restaurants, or cultural products, such as cinema and dance. According to Abu-Laban and Gabriel (2002), multiculturalism has become a commodity for sale, marketed within a "celebrating diversity" frame advocated by city governments, purveyors of consumer culture, and ethnocultural groups themselves. The City of Toronto, for example, festooned the city streets with banners stating "Diversity—our strength." This brand of multiculturalism is promoted through commercial sites, such as Kensington Market, where successive groups of newcomers bought and sold products that originated in different parts of the world, and in multicultural festivals, such as Caribana. Nearly all Canadian cities now include multicultural festivals as part of their summer activities. The question is whether these events divert an understanding of multiculturalism as a basis for human rights to one of increasing consumer choices for the dominant groups (Abu-Laban and Gabriel

2002; Kobayashi 1993; Ley 2010b). Such events also raise questions about for whom multiculturalism is intended. In a multicultural society in which there is no official culture, argue critics, the Other would not be created as an exotic commodification threatened by the rolling back of government policies that address equality rights.

One result of the multiculturalism-is-for-Others trope is that in recent years controversies have arisen over the "limits" to multiculturalism, that is, over whether it is possible to go "too far" in accommodating Others who are considered too far from the Canadian norm. Some claim that multiculturalism actually prevents newcomers from becoming full Canadians because it encourages them to stick with their own and to maintain cultural practices that are non-Canadian (Jedwab, 2005). Those who oppose or want to limit multiculturalism adopt a range of attitudes from outright hatred and xenophobia, to "multiculturalism within limits," to "multiculturalism for some but not for others," all of which are normative positions that posit Others against a vision of the ordinary—or assimilated—Canadian. These controversies are revealed in Canadian cities: landscaping changes are contested in Vancouver's most prestigious neighbourhoods (Ley, 1995); requests from Muslims and Orthodox Jews for zoning changes to accommodate their religious establishments are disputed in Montreal (Germain and Gagnon, 2003); and everywhere, immigrants complain that landlords object to their cooking and other cultural practices (Francis and Hiebert, 2011; Murdie, 2008a; Rose and Charette, 2011). These examples illustrate the need to understand multiculturalism within a larger context that includes practices of discrimination and racialization, as well as the range of cultural expression through which contemporary Canadian cities come to be (Ley, 2010b).

Conclusion

International migration is an ongoing geographic process with historical, demographic, social, and public policy dimensions. The urban landscape exhibits the cumulative effects of this dynamic process in a variety of ways, including commercial and residential clustering and exclusions, cultural artifacts, and, in some cases, marginalization and invisibility. Immigration is a normative process, regulated by state policies but also subject to the efforts of migrants to find places in their new society. Many of the stories that define their experiences have long-established roots, but many also represent recent changes. Migration occurs in a transnational field that involves the source and the destination countries, the immigrants themselves, and the entire population, including the long settled, who live in cities that are the more vibrant, complex, and fascinating for the changes that international migration continues to bring.

Review Questions

1. How has Canadian immigration policy influenced the ethnocultural makeup of Canadian cities?
2. Some people claim that Canadian cities have largely avoided the racial exclusion that occurs in many American cities. Do you think this is true? Be sure to explain the reasons for your opinion.
3. How have various ethnocultural groups transformed urban landscapes in Canadian cities?

Notes

1. A convention refugee is a person outside his or her country of nationality who is unable or unwilling to return to his or her country of nationality because of a well-founded fear of persecution on the grounds of religion, nationality, membership of a particular social group, or political opinion (United Nations, 1967).
2. See Murdie and Logan (2011) for a comprehensive bibliography about recent immigration and housing research in Canada.
3. *Ghetto* referred originally to the forced concentration of Jews in European cities, but it now describes any forced residential concentration of a minority (Wacquant, 2004).
4. Although information from the National Household Survey has been released, questions concerning the

quality of these data at the level of census tracts were not resolved at the time of writing, so it was impossible to create 2011 maps of ethnocultural groups.
5. *Othering* is a process of differentiation and demarcation by which the dominant group establishes and maintains social distance between itself and groups viewed as subordinate and inferior, henceforth labelled "Other" (Lister, 2004).
6. Chinese immigration had already been curtailed by the "head tax."
7. Although our discussion concentrates on mosques, the religious establishments and practices of non-Christian groups have been the subject of heated public debates (see Germain and Gagnon, 2003, for an example).

References

Abella, I.M., and H. Troper. 1983. *None Is Too Many: Canada and the Jews of Europe, 1933–1948*. Toronto: University of Toronto Press.

Abu-Laban, B., and M. I. Alladin. 1991. *Beyond the Gulf War: Muslims, Arabs and the West*. Edmonton: MRF Publishers.

Abu-Laban, Y., and B. Abu-Laban. 2007. "Reasonable accommodation in a global village," *Policy Options-Montreal* 28, 8: 28.

——, and C. Gabriel. 2002. *Selling Diversity: Immigration, Multiculturalism, Employment Equity and Globalization*. Peterborough: Broadview Press.

Agrawal, S.K. 2006. "Housing adaptations: A study of Asian Indian immigrant homes in Toronto," *Canadian Ethnic Studies* 38: 117–30.

Alboim, N., and K. Cohl. 2012. *Shaping the Future: Canada's Rapidly Changing Immigration Policies*. Toronto: Maytree Foundation.

Anderson, K. 1995. *Vancouver's Chinatown, Racial Discourse in Canada, 1875–1980* (2nd edn.). Kingston and Montreal: McGill-Queen's University Press.

Applied History Research Group, University of Calgary. 1997. *The Peopling of Canada: 1891–1921*. At: www.ucalgary.ca/applied_history/tutor/canada1891/index.html

Arat-Koc, S. 2006. "Whose transnationalism? Canada, 'clash of civilizations' discourse, and Arab and Muslim Canadians," in V. Satzewich and L. Wong, eds., *Transnational Identities and Practices in Canada*. Vancouver, BC: University of British Columbia Press.

Bateman, C. 2012. "A brief history of The Ward, Toronto's notorious slum." At: www.blogto.com/city/2012/06/a_brief_history_of_the_ward_torontos_notorious_slum/

Bouchard, G., and C. Taylor. 2008. *Building the Future: A Time for Reconciliation: Abridged Report*. Commission de consultation sur les pratiques d'accomodement reliées aux différences culturelles. At: www.accommodements. qc.ca

Buckley, K. 1960. "Historical estimates of internal migration in Canada," in E.F. Beach and J.C. Weldon, eds., *Canadian Political Science Association, Conference on Statistics 1960, Papers*. Toronto: University of Toronto Press.

Canada (Government of). 1908. *Report of W.L. Mackenzie King, C.M.G., Commissioner Appointed to Enquire into the Methods by Which Oriental Labourers Have Been Induced to Come to Canada*. Ottawa: King's Printer.

Carter, T., and D. Vitiello. 2012. "Immigrants, refugees, and housing," in C. Teixeira, W. Li, and A. Kobayashi, eds., *Immigrant Geographies of North American Cities*. Toronto: Oxford University Press.

Chui, T., Tran, K., and Maheux, H. 2007. *Immigration in Canada: A Portrait of the Foreign-Born Population, 2006 Census*. Ottawa: Statistics Canada. At: www12.statcan. ca/census-recensement/2006/as-sa/97-557/pdf/97-557-XIE2006001.pdf

Citizenship and Immigration Canada. 2005. *Recent Immigrants in Metropolitan Areas*. Ottawa: Statistics Canada. At: www.cic.gc.ca/english/pdf/research-stats/2001-canada.pdf

———. 2012. *Facts and Figures, Immigration Overview Permanent and Temporary Residents, 2011*. At: www.cic. gc.ca/english/resources/statistics/menu-fact.asp

D'Addario, S. 2012. *Finding Home: Geographical Links between Paid and Unpaid Work for Transnational Care Workers in Toronto's Suburbs*. Toronto: York University, PhD thesis.

Danso, R. 2002. *Ethnic Community Networks, Public Policy, and the Resettlement of Ethiopian and Somali Refugees in Toronto*. Kingston, ON: Queen's University, PhD thesis.

Darden, J. 2004. *The Significance of White Supremacy in the Canadian Metropolis of Toronto*. Lewiston: Edwin Mellen Press.

Darden, J., and E. Fong. 2012. "The spatial segregation and socio-economic inequality of immigrant groups," in C. Teixeira, W. Li, and A. Kobayashi, eds., *Immigrant Geographies of North American Cities*. Don Mills, ON: Oxford University Press.

Donaldson, J. 2013. "Remembering Vancouver's first race riot," *The Tyee*, 1 March. At: http://thetyee.ca/Life/2013/03/01/Vancouver-Race-Riot/

Firang, D.Y. 2011. *Transnational Activities and Their Impact on Achieving a Successful Housing Career in Canada: The Case of Ghanaian Immigrants in Toronto*. Toronto: University of Toronto, PhD thesis.

Francis, J. 2009. *"You Cannot Settle Like This": The Housing Situation of African Refugees in Metro Vancouver*. Vancouver, BC: Metropolis British Columbia (Working Paper 09-02).

———, and D. Hiebert. 2011. *Shaky Foundations: Precarious Housing and Hidden Homelessness among Refugees, Asylum Seekers, and Immigrants in Metro Vancouver*. Vancouver, BC: Metropolis British Columbia (Working Paper 11–18).

Germain, A. 2006. "Le municipal à l'épreuve de la multiethnicité: Aménagement des lieux de culte dites 'ethniques' et crise du zonage à Montréal," in A. Bourdin, M.-P. Lefeuvre, and P. Melé, *Les Règles du Jeu Urbain*. Paris: Descartes et Cie.

———, and J.E. Gagnon. 2003. "Minority places of worship and zoning dilemmas in Montreal," *Planning Theory and Practice* 4: 295–318.

———, and D. Rose. 2000. *Montreal: The Quest for a Metropolis*. New York: Wiley.

Gilmore, J. 2012. "Interpreting social disorder: The case of the 1907 Vancouver riots," *International Journal*, Spring: 485–95.

Hall, S. 2000. "The multi-cultural question," in B. Hesse, ed., *Unsettled Multiculturalisms, Diasporas, Entanglements, Disruptions*. London: Zed Books.

Hardwick, S.W., and G. Mansfield. 2009. "Discourse, identity, and 'Homeland as Other' at the Borderlands," *Annals of the Association of American Geographers* 99: 383–405.

Hawkins, F. 1988. *Canada and Immigration*. Kingston and Montreal: McGill-Queen's University Press.

Hiebert, D. 1993. "Jewish immigrants and the garment industry of Toronto: A study of ethnic and class relations," *Annals of the Association of American Geographers* 83: 243–71.

———. 2009. "Newcomers in the Canadian housing market: A longitudinal study, 2001–2005," *The Canadian Geographer* 53: 268–87.

———. 2011. *Precarious Housing and Hidden Homelessness among Refugees, Asylum Seekers, and Immigrants in Montréal, Toronto, and Vancouver: Introduction and Synthetic Executive Summary*. June. At: http://mbc. metropolis.net/assets/uploads/files/precarious_housing _NATL%20SUMMARY.pdf

———, ed. 2011. *Our Diverse Cities: British Columbia*. Number 8. Metropolis. At: www.metropolis.net/pdfs/odc_bc_2011_e.pdf

———, A. Germain, R. Murdie, V. Preston, J. Renaud, D. Rose, E. Wyly, V. Ferreira, P. Mendez, and A.M. Murnaghan. 2006. *The Housing Situation and Needs of Recent Immigrants in the Montreal, Toronto, and Vancouver CMAs: An Overview*. Ottawa: Canada Mortgage and Housing Corporation.

Hoernig, H.J. 2006. *Worship in the Suburbs: The Development Experience of Recent Immigrant Religious Communities*. Waterloo, ON: University of Waterloo, Ph.D. Thesis. At: http://etd.uwaterloo.ca/etd/hjhoerni2006.pdf

———, and Z. Zhuang. 2010. "New diversity: Social change as immigration," in T. Bunting and P. Filion, eds., *Canadian Cities in Transition: Local through Global Perspectives*. Toronto: Oxford University Press.

Hulchanski, D. 2007. "The three cities within Toronto: Income polarization among Toronto's neighbourhoods, 1970–2000." Toronto: Centre for Urban and Community Research, Research Bulletin 41. At: www.urbancentre.utoronto.ca/pdfs/researchbulletins/CUCS RB41_Hulchanski_Three_Cities_Toronto.pdf

——, and M. Shapcott. 2004. "Introduction: Finding room in Canada's housing system for all Canadians," in D. Hulchanski and M. Shapcott, eds., *Finding Room: Policy Options for a Canadian Rental Housing Strategy*. Toronto: CUCS Press, Centre for Urban and Community Studies.

Isin, E., and M. Siemiatycki. 2002. "Making space for mosques: Struggles for urban citizenship in diasporic Toronto," in S.H. Razack, ed., *Race, Space, and the Law: Unmapping a White Settler Society*. Toronto: Between the Lines.

Jackson, P., and A. Kobayashi. 1994. "Japanese Canadians and the racialization of labour in the British Columbia sawmill industry," *BC Studies: The British Columbian Quarterly* 103: 33–58.

Jedwab, J. 2005. "Neither finding nor losing our way: The debate over Canadian multiculturalism," *Canadian Diversity*, 4(1): 95.

Kalbach, W.E., and W.W. McVey. 1971. *The Demographic Basis of Canadian Society* (2nd edn.). Toronto: McGraw-Hill Ryerson.

Kashmeri, Z. 1991. *The Gulf Within: Canadian Arabs, Racism, and the Gulf War*. Toronto: J. Lorimer Publishers.

Knowles, V. 2006. *Strangers at Our Gates: Canadian Immigration and Immigration Policy*. Hamilton, ON: Dundurn Press.

Kobayashi, A. 1993. "Multiculturalism: Representing a Canadian institution," in J. Duncan and D. Ley, eds., *Place/Culture/Representation*. London: Routledge.

——. 2013. "Critical 'race' approaches," in N. Johnson, R. Schein, and J. Winders, *The Wiley-Blackwell Companion to Cultural Geography*. New York: Wiley.

——, and V. Preston. 2007. "Transnationalism through the life course: Hong Kong immigrants in Canada," *Asia Pacific Viewpoint*, 48, 2: 151–67.

——, V. Preston, and A.M. Murnaghan. 2011. "Place, affect, and transnationalism through the voices of Hong Kong immigrants to Canada," *Social & Cultural Geography*, 12: 871–88.

Kymlicka, W. 2007. *Multicultural Odysseys, Navigating the New International Politics of Diversity*. New York: Oxford University Press.

Lai, D.C. 2011. *Chinatowns: Towns within Cities in Canada*. Vancouver, BC: UBC Press.

——, and N. Huffey. 2009. "Experience of discrimination by visible minorities in small communities," *Our Diverse Cities* 6, Spring: 124–9.

Leitner, H., and V. Preston. 2012. "Going local: Canadian and American immigration policy in the new century," in C. Teixeira, W. Li, and A. Kobayashi, eds., *Immigrant Geographies of North American Cities*. Toronto: Oxford University Press.

Leroux, D. 2010. "Québec nationalism and the production of difference: The Bouchard-Taylor Commission, the Hérouxville code of conduct, and Québec's immigrant integration policy," *Quebec Studies* 49, Spring/Summer: 107–26.

Ley. 1995. "Between Europe and Asia: The case of the missing sequoias," *Cultural Geographies* 2: 185–210.

——. 2003. "Seeking *homo economicus*: The strange story of Canada's Business Immigration Program," *Annals, Association of American Geographers* 93: 426–41.

——. 2010a. *Millionaire Migrants: Trans-Pacific Life Lines*. West Sussex, UK: Wiley-Blackwell.

——. 2010b. "Multiculturalism: A Canadian defence," in S. Vertovec and S. Wessendorf, eds., *The Multiculturalism Backlash: European Discourses, Policies and Practices*. London: Routledge.

——. "Does transnationalism trump immigrant integration? Evidence from Canada's links with East Asia," *Journal of Ethnic and Migration Studies* 39, forthcoming.

Li, P.S. 2003. *Destination Canada: Immigration Debates and Issues*. Toronto: Oxford University Press.

Li, W. 2009. *Ethnoburb: The New Ethnic Community in Urban America*. Honolulu, HI: University of Hawaii Press.

Lister, R. 2004. *Poverty*. London: Polity Press.

Lo. L. 2006. "Suburban housing and indoor shopping: The production of the contemporary Chinese landscape in Toronto," in W. Li, ed., *From Urban Enclave to Ethnic Suburb: New Asian Communities in Pacific Rim Countries*. Honolulu, HI: University of Hawaii Press.

——, S. Wang, P. Anisef, V. Preston, and R. Basu. 2010. *Recent Immigrants' Awareness of, Access to, Use of, and Satisfaction with Settlement Services in York Region*. Toronto: CERIS—The Ontario Metropolis Centre (Working Paper No. 79).

Logan, J. 2010. "There's No Place Like Home": A Snapshot of the Settlement Experiences of Newcomer Tibetan Women in Parkdale Toronto. Toronto: York University, MA Thesis.

Massey, D.S. 2012. *Worlds in Motion: Understanding International Migration at the End of the Millennium*. New York: Oxford University Press.

Mazigh, M. 2008. *Hope and Despair: My Struggle to Free My Husband, Maher Arar*. Toronto: McClelland & Stewart.

Mensah, J. 2005. "On the ethno-cultural heterogeneity of Blacks in our 'ethnicities,'" *Canadian Issues*, Spring: 72–7.

——. 2008. "Religious transnationalism among Ghanaian immigrants in Toronto: A binary logistic regression analysis," *The Canadian Geographer* 52: 309–30.

Moos, M., and A. Skaburskis. 2010. "The globalization of urban housing markets: Immigration and changing housing demand in Vancouver," *Urban Geography*, 31: 724–49.

Murdie, R.A. 2002. "The housing careers of Polish and Somali newcomers in Toronto's rental market," *Housing Studies* 17: 423–43.

———. 2008a. "Pathways to housing: The experiences of sponsored refugees and refugee claimants in accessing permanent housing in Toronto," *International Migration & Integration* 9: 81–101.

———. 2008b. *Diversity and Concentration in Canadian Immigration: Trends in Toronto, Montreal and Vancouver, 1971–2006.* Toronto: Centre for Urban and Community Studies, University of Toronto, Research Bulletin 42.

———, and J. Logan. 2011. *Precarious Housing & Hidden Homelessness among Refugees, Asylum Seekers, and Immigrants: Bibliography and Review of Canadian Literature from 2005 to 2010.* CERIS Working Paper No. 84. Toronto, ON: CERIS—The Ontario Metropolis Centre. At: www.ceris.metropolis.net/wp-content/uploads/pdf/research_publication/working_papers/wp84.pdf

———, and C. Teixeira. 2003. "Towards a comfortable neighbourhood and appropriate housing: Immigrant experiences in Toronto," in P. Anisef and M. Lanphier, eds., *The World in a City.* Toronto: University of Toronto Press.

Novac, S., J. Darden, D. Hulchanski, and A. Seguin. 2004. "Housing discrimination in Canada: Stakeholder views and research gaps," in D. Hulchanski and M. Shapcott, eds., *Finding Room: Policy Options for a Canadian Rental Housing Strategy.* Toronto: CUCS Press, Centre for Urban and Community Studies.

Owusu, T.Y. 1998. "'To buy or not to buy': Determinants of home ownership among Ghanaian immigrants in Toronto," *The Canadian Geographer* 42: 40–52.

Park, R.E., and E.W. Burgess. 1925. *The City: Suggestions for Investigation of Human Behavior in the Urban Environment.* Chicago: University of Chicago Press.

Picot, G. 2004. "The deteriorating economic welfare of Canadian immigrants," *Canadian Journal of Urban Research* 13: 25–45.

Pither, K. 2008. *Dark Days: The Story of Four Canadians Tortured in the Name of Fighting Terror.* Toronto: Penguin.

Pratt, G. 2004. *Working Feminism.* Philadelphia: Temple University Press.

Preston, V., and L. Lo. 2000. "Asian theme malls in suburban Toronto: Land use conflict in Richmond Hill," *Canadian Geographer* 44: 86–94.

———, A. Kobayashi, and M. Siemiatycki. 2006. "Transnational urbanism: Toronto at a crossroads," in V. Satzewich and L. Wong, eds., *Transnational Identities and Practices in Canada.* Vancouver, BC: UBC Press.

———, A. Kobayashi, and G. Man. 2006. "Transnationalism, gender, and civic participation: Canadian case studies of Hong Kong immigrants," *Environment and Planning A* 38: 1633–51.

———, R.A. Murdie, S. D'Addario, P. Sibanda, and A.M. Murnaghan. 2011. *Precarious Housing and Hidden Homelessness among Refugees, Asylum Seekers, and Immigrants in the Toronto CMA.* CERIS Working Paper No. 87. Toronto: CERIS—The Ontario Metropolis Centre. At: http://mbc.metropolis.net/assets/uploads/files/Precarious_Housing_Toronto_study.pdf

———, R.A. Murdie, J. Wedlock, S. Agrawal, U. Anucha, S. D'Addario, M. Kwak, J. Logan, and A. M. Murnaghan. 2009. "Immigrants and homelessness—At risk in Canada's outer suburbs," *Canadian Geographer* 53: 288–304.

———, and B. Ray. 2009. "Geographies of discrimination: Variations in perceived discomfort and discrimination in Canada's gateway cities," *Journal of Immigrant and Refugee Studies* 7: 228–49.

Qadeer, M. 1997. "Pluralistic planning for multicultural cities: The Canadian practice," *Journal of the American Planning Association,* 63: 481–94.

———, S. Agrawal, and A. Lowell. 2010. "Evolution of ethnic enclaves in the Toronto Metropolitan Area, 2001–2006," *Journal of International Migration and Integration* 11: 315–39.

———, and M. Chaudhry. 2000. "The planning system and the development of mosques in the Greater Toronto area," *Plan Canada* 40: 17–21.

Ray, B.K., G. Halseth, and B. Johnson. 1997. "The changing 'face' of the suburbs: Issues of ethnicity and residential change in suburban Vancouver," *International Journal of Urban and Regional Research,* 21: 75–99.

———, and V. Preston. 2009. "Geographies of discrimination: Inter-urban variations in Canada," *Journal of Immigrant & Refugee Studies* 7: 228–49.

Richler, M. 1972. "Why I Write," *Shovelling Trouble.* Toronto: McClelland & Stewart.

Rose, D., and A. Charette. 2011. *Pierre angulaire ou maillon faible? Le logement des réfugiés, demandeurs d'asile et immigrants à Montréal.* Publication CMQ-IM-n° 45. Montreal: INRS-CUS. At: http://mbc.metropolis.net/assets/uploads/files/Montreal_Study_FR.pdf

Schellenberg, G., and H. Maheux. 2007. "Immigrants' perspectives on their first four years in Canada: Highlights from three waves of the Longitudinal Survey of Immigrants to Canada," *Canadian Social Trends* April: 2–17.

Simmons, A. 2010. *Immigration and Canada: Global and Transnational Perspectives.* Toronto: Canadian Scholars Press.

Smith, H. and D. Ley. 2009. "Even in Canada? The multiscalar construction and experience of concentrated immigrant poverty in gateway cities," *Annals of the Association of American Geographers* 98: 686–713.

Stalker, P. 2008. *The No-Nonsense Guide to International Migration.* Toronto: New Internationalist Press and Between the Lines.

Statistics Canada. 2013. *National Household Survey*. Ottawa: Statistics Canada. At: www12.statcan.gc.ca/nhs-enm/2011/as-sa/index-eng.cfm

Sugimoto, H. 1973. "The Vancouver Riot and its international significance," *The Pacific Northwest Quarterly* 64: 163–74.

Teixeira, C. 2007. "Residential experiences and the culture of suburbanization: A case study of Portuguese home-buyers in Mississauga," *Housing Studies* 22: 495–521.

——. 2008. "Barriers and outcomes in the housing searches of new immigrants and refugees: A case study of 'Black' Africans in Toronto's rental market," *Journal of Housing and the Built Environment* 23: 253–176.

Trudeau, P. 1971, October 8. "Federal Government's Response to Book IV of the Report of the Royal Commission on Bilingualism and Biculturalism," Parliament of Canada White Paper 283-4/101B. At: www.parl.gc.ca/Parlinfo/Compilations/FederalGovernment/PaperDetail.aspx?Paper=c6a4db8e-e464-430b-bbfe-ca77532e9ccb&Document=7540aaab-817f-4731-b9f4-86a578e4e261&Language=E

Truelove, M. 2000. "Services for immigrant women: an evaluation of locations," *The Canadian Geographer* 44: 135–151.

United Nations. 1967. *Protocol Relating to the Status of Refugees*, 31 January. United Nations, Treaty Series, vol. 606, p. 267. At: www.refworld.org/docid/3ae6b3ae4.html

United Nations High Commission for Refugees. 2010. *Asylum Levels and Trends in Industrial Countries 2009*. At: www.unhcr.org/4ba7341a9.html

Verma, S. 2005. "Multicultural Markham, 10 years on, immigrants' role divided town in 1995, now, Chinese-Canadians right at home," *Toronto Star*, 2 July.

Wacquant, L. 2004. "What is a ghetto? Constructing a sociological concept," in N.J. Smelser and P.B. Baltes, eds., *International Encyclopedia of the Social and Behavioral Sciences*. London: Pergamon.

Walks, R., and L.S. Bourne. 2006. "Ghettos in Canada's cities? Racial segregation, ethnic enclaves and poverty concentration in Canadian urban areas," *The Canadian Geographer* 50: 273–97.

Wirth, L. 1928. *The Ghetto*. Chicago: University of Chicago Press.

Wong, M. 2000. "Ghanaian women in Toronto's labour market: Negotiating gendered roles and transnational household strategies," *Canadian Ethnic Studies* 32, 2: 45–74.

Wortley, S., and A. Owusu-Bempah. 2011. "Crime and justice: The experiences of black Canadians," in B. Perry, ed., *Diversity, Crime, and Justice in Canada*. Toronto: Oxford University Press.

Zhuang, X.C. 2008. *Ethnic Retailing and the Role of Municipal Planning: Four Case Studies in the Greater Toronto Area*. Waterloo, Ont.: Dissertation, Department of Planning, University of Waterloo.

Growing Divisions: Inequality, Neighbourhood Poverty, and Homelessness in the Canadian City

9

ALAN WALKS

Introduction

How well a society ensures equality and equity among its citizens is a key measure of its health. Unfortunately, Canada and its cities have been growing more unequal, and increasingly segregated, over time. The Organisation for Economic Co-operation and Development (OECD) found that, between the mid-1990s and the mid-2000s, income inequality grew faster in Canada than in any other developed countries except Finland (OECD, 2008). Income inequality is growing at multiple spatial scales from the national level to the provincial and metropolitan scales, and on down to the level of neighbourhoods. It is foremost in Canada's cities where the factors driving social polarization are salient.

This chapter questions the forms that inequality and polarization take in Canadian urban areas. It begins by detailing the extent of shifts in income inequality and poverty between and within Canadian metropolitan areas. It examines the processes that have been producing and reproducing inequality, both those articulated structurally among households and individuals and spatially between neighbourhoods. The relationship between the spatial concentration of poverty, racialization processes, and immigrant settlement are also explored. The chapter then examines problems and forms of homelessness and the factors driving housing affordability stress,

homelessness, and shelter poverty. The chapter ends with a discussion of the implications of the trends outlined and the potential policy responses that might address growing social inequality.

"Growing Unequal": Trajectories of Inequality

Comparing trends from the mid-1970s onward, Canada's overall level of income inequality began rising in earnest in the early-to-mid 1990s (Heisz, 2007; see also Figure 1 in Walks, 2013a). Importantly, all the national growth in inequality is due to rising inequality among adults of working age, as the level of inequality among those aged 65 and over continued to decline. Over time, the Canadian political economy has done a good job at reducing inequality among seniors but a poor job at preventing rising inequality among everyone else.

National shifts in income inequality are reflected in rising inequality among households, and individuals, within Canada's metropolitan areas (Figure 9.1). While the most recent (2005) micro-data are obtainable only for a handful of CMAs, trends reveal a clear incline toward increasing social inequality, particularly in Canada's most globally connected cities (Toronto and Vancouver and, more recently, Calgary). Inequality has grown due to both increasing poverty and to higher incomes for the wealthy. Although not strictly a poverty line, Statistics Canada's low-income cut-offs (LICO) are often used as such. While the rate of low income has waxed and waned according to the economic fortunes of each metropolitan area, the general trend for many CMAs is slow growth upwards since the mid-1980s (see Figure 6.2a in Walks, 2011). Some CMAs, including Toronto and Vancouver, have seen increases in poverty during the 2000s, despite a booming economy that tended to reduce poverty elsewhere. A similar picture is painted by shifts in the proportion of households with incomes below $20,000 (Figure 9.2a).

However, it is the growth of high incomes that is even more responsible for household inequality (Figure 9.2b). Since 1970, the proportion of

households that reported annual incomes surpassing $100,000 (in constant 2000 dollars) has more than quadrupled, from only 3 per cent to 16 per cent. Every single CMA in Canada witnessed an increase in the proportion of households with high incomes, and this occurred despite declining household sizes (see Townshend and Walker, Chapter 7, and Moos, Chapter 20). Large cities, particularly Toronto, generally contain more high-income earners, while cities in Ontario and in the prairies (particularly Alberta) have seen the most rapid increases in high-income shares. Such trends reflect a more general phenomenon in which the wealthy have seen their incomes continually rise since the early 1990s (Saez and Veall, 2005). Across Canada, between 1990 and

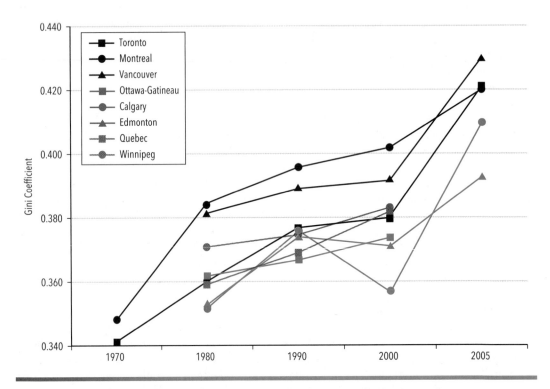

Figure 9.1   Level of Income Inequality (Gini) among Households, Eight Largest CMAs, 1970–2005

Notes: Units of analysis are households. Coefficients are Gini concentration ratios. The only CMAs in the 1970 PUMF are Toronto and Montreal. The 2005 data derive from the 2006 hierarchical Public Use Microdata File (PUMF), which only contained data for Toronto, Montreal, Vancouver, Calgary, and Edmonton. Note that the hierarchical PUMF sample for 2005 is structured differently from previous PUMF files. It is unclear how this affects the comparability of the results.

Source: Calculated by the author with the help of Richard Maaranan, from the Census of Canada, Public Use Microsample Files (PUMF), various years.

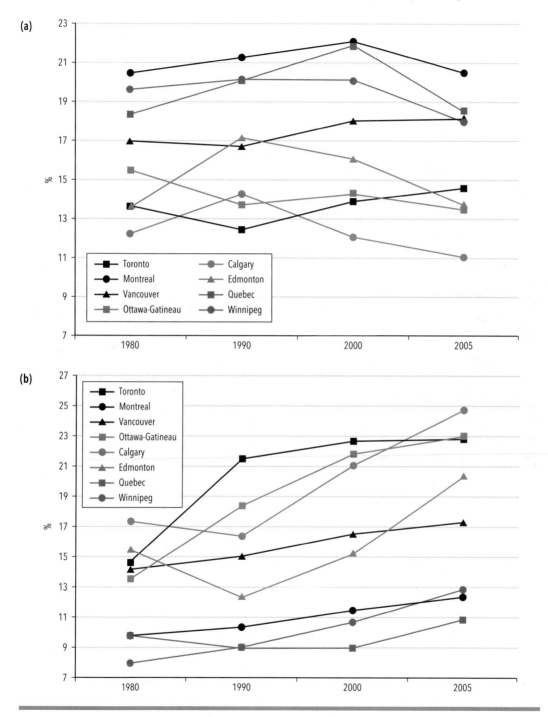

(a)

(b)

Figure 9.2   **Proportion (%) of Households with (a) Low and (b) High Incomes in 2000 Constant Dollars, Eight Largest CMAs, 1980–2005**

Source: Calculated from Census of Canada, 1981–2006, Custom Tabulations E1171, E982.

2000, the income share of the top 5 per cent of earners grew from 24 per cent to 29 per cent, while the wealthiest 0.1 per cent of earners saw their incomes double. Such trends mirror those in the United States (Ibid: 835–6). In turn, the proportion of households with "middle incomes" (between $20,000 and $100,000 in 2000 constant dollars) has consistently declined among CMAs—one indicator of increasing income polarization. Only in Montreal and Quebec did the trend toward a declining middle change course (slightly) over the early 2000s (see Table 6 in Walks, 2013a).

Factors Propelling Urban Social Inequality

Perhaps most important for fuelling the growth of income inequality and polarization in Canada's cities are the effects of globalization and deindustrialization. Some large Canadian metropolitan regions, including Toronto, Vancouver and Montreal, represent second-tier "global" or "world" cities specializing in producer services with strong connections to networks of global financial, information, and migration flows. But many smaller cities that specialized in what are now declining industrial sectors (or functioned as transportation depots for agricultural products) have seen their economies grow weaker under the onslaught of globalization and deindustrialization. Absolute forms of deindustrialization involve absolute reductions in the number of those employed in manufacturing, whereas relative forms involve declining proportions but still-growing numbers of workers. While driving new flows of investment and providing local employment booms, continental integration introduces a level of vulnerability for local workers who face the threat of plant relocation and restructuring of the production complexes and the shift of production to the US. The loss of manufacturing jobs is one of the single largest factors explaining the rise in income inequality among workers at the CMA level (Bolton and Breau, 2012).

Globalization is expected to lead to increasing labour force bifurcation and polarization (Sassen, 2001). Those with jobs linked to international finance and producer services experience rising earnings, while those working in most personal services, retail, and manufacturing experience falling wages. The efforts of those in what is termed the creative class to attain an increasing proportion of the total pie for themselves within the context of a globalizing economy is one key trend driving labour-market polarization (see Vinodrai, Chapter 5). A culture of compensation paid in yearly bonuses within the financial services industry and some other sectors has produced a sense of entitlement among a new managerial elite that is increasingly detached from the realities of most workers, and which increasingly resembles the parasitic Leisure Class examined by Veblen a century ago (2007 [1899]). The practice of paying even mid-level management with shares, bonuses, and stock options turns them into quasi-entrepreneurs in whose economic interest it is to further exploit the labour of those working under them (Sennett, 1998). When the data for different occupational sectors are disaggregated at the CMA level, the only jobs that have seen their relative incomes increase in any significant way since 1980 are managerial, administrative, and business occupations, particularly in Calgary and Toronto. Meanwhile, the incomes of most professionals (lawyers, engineers, doctors, teachers) have largely remained flat, and those employed in manufacturing, sales, and services have all tended to suffer from declining relative earnings (see Figure 6.4 in Walks, 2011).

Immigration

As Chapter 8 by Kobayashi and Preston makes clear, a number of Canadian cities have become quite racially and ethnically diverse, due to persistently high rates of immigration from East and South Asia, the Middle East, Africa, and Latin America. The geography of immigration flows overwhelmingly favour the largest "global" cities, particularly Toronto and Vancouver, while other cities, including Quebec City and many smaller cities, receive very few immigrants. Unfortunately, there is a clear pattern in which the incomes of recent immigrants have declined since 1980, relative to native-born Canadians (Figure 9.3a). In

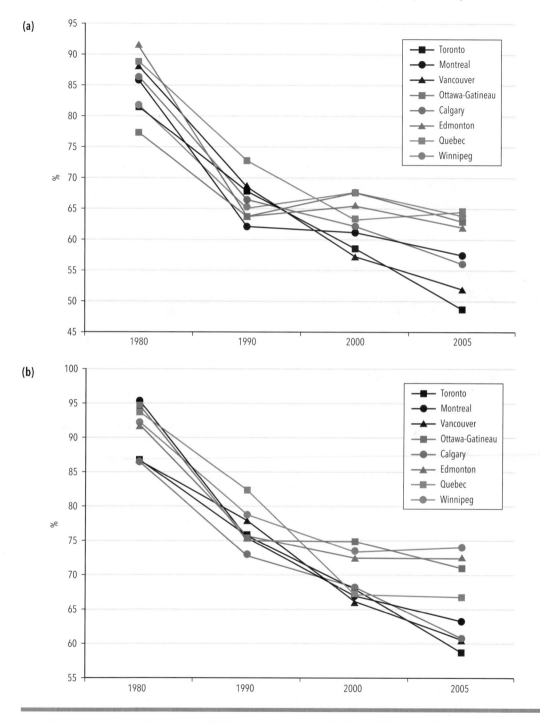

(a)

(b)

Figure 9.3   **Average Relative Incomes of (a) Recent Immigrants and (b) Visible Minorities, Eight Largest CMAs, 1980–2005**

Source: Calculated by the author with the help of Richard Maaranen, using Census of Canada, PUMF files, various years.

1980, recent immigrants (i.e., those arriving in the previous 10 years) in the eight largest cities on average earned 85 per cent of native-born Canadians' incomes. By 2005, this had declined to 58 per cent, a 27 per cent drop, which is even steeper in Toronto and Vancouver. This means it now takes more than 20 years for many immigrants, including Chinese immigrants, to close the earnings gap with the rest of the population—five years longer than in previous decades (Wang and Lo, 2005). This in turn fuels a similar divergence in income between members of visible minorities and the white population, the gap for which has grown by 28 per cent on average (Figure 9.3b). The racialization of poverty, and the correspondence between race and economic success, is producing new forms of social exclusion in Canada's cities (Galabuzi, 2006), not the least of which includes increased racial spatial segregation (Walks and Bourne, 2006).

Neo-Liberalism

Neo-liberalism refers to an ideological commitment to the concept of individual liberty and the institution of private property, market-based solutions to public policy, an antipathy to any form of state intervention in the economy, and, hence, privatization of state resources (see Harvey, 2005). *Neo-liberalization* refers to the transformation of state functions in line with the ideology of neo-liberalism. Peck and Tickell (2002) distinguish between two forms of neo-liberalism: (1) a "roll-back" of the welfare state, often involving the elimination or privatization of state assets and service delivery functions (public transportation, public housing); and (2) a "roll-out" form in which public policies and service delivery models are restructured according to market-based logics. Keil (2009) posits the existence of a third variant of neo-liberalism—"roll with it" neo-liberalization, in which political realities dictate that even left-leaning subjects critical of neo-liberalism must work with it in negotiating public policy reforms and pursuing public goals: in doing so, they co-construct various hybrid forms of actually existing neo-liberalism.

In Canada, neo-liberalism has been tied to the integration of Canada's economy with that of the United States, largely accomplished through the reduction of barriers to trade and flows of labour and capital between the two countries. Once the North American Free Trade Agreement (NAFTA) was implemented, authors argued that Canada would be compelled to bring many social policies in line with those of the United States in order to maintain the competitiveness of its industries (Courchene and Telmer, 1998; Hurtig, 2002). Indeed, since the 1990s federal and provincial governments have sought to limit or reduce the range of social protections inherent in Canada's welfare state, to cut taxes, and to restructure the system of benefits. While the federal government made its first small moves to "roll back" the federal state in the late 1980s, it more aggressively moved to restructure the entire welfare state system in the 1990s with the restructuring of transfers to the provinces for health and education. Reductions in employment insurance benefits, the downloading of responsibility for certain federal programs, and income tax reductions followed. These were then matched by neo-liberal policy reforms enacted by provincial government in the mid-1990s, starting with Alberta (1993) and Ontario (1995). Such changes led to drastic reductions in (and the restructuring of) welfare benefits and housing subsidies, public transit funding, public education funding, and transfers to municipalities, while outside of Quebec and British Columbia new social housing construction came to a virtual halt.

One result of neo-liberalization is that Canada's welfare state and tax structure became less redistributive and equitable. Whereas the redistributive effect of government taxes and transfers grew over the period between 1976 and 1994, largely offsetting the rise in market-based income inequality, from 1995 onwards a persistent reduction in the redistributive effects of the welfare state and taxation has been evident (Heisz, 2007: 46). This is also precisely the time when the richest 20 per cent of Canada's population saw its relative income, as well as its proportionate share of income, start to grow, while the relative incomes of the other

80 per cent remained stagnant or declined (Ibid: 33 and 43).

Neo-liberalism is also implicated in another salient phenomenon: financialization of the economy and the growth of household indebtedness. Financialization refers to the situation in which the financial sector increases in importance in relation to other economic sectors; it refers, too, to the "pattern of accumulation in which profits accrue primarily through financial channels rather than through trade and commodity production" (Krippner, 2005: 174). Neo-liberalization across the developed world has involved the deregulation of banks and of finance, the increasing importance of the financial sector within developed-nation economies, and a commitment to a low-inflation and low-interest-rate policy (Krippner, 2011). In addition to funding the carry-trade (i.e., borrowing in a low-interest-rate country like the US or Japan, and using the money to invest in growing sectors in higher-interest rate economies) and, in turn, the shift of industrial investment abroad, the easy credit facilitated by financial deregulation encourages profligate and predatory lending (i.e., the pushing of high-interest-rate debt onto those with weak ability to pay). It also encourages local speculation in housing and other asset markets (Walks, 2010).

In Canada, such processes have accompanied changes to mortgage finance and insurance rules that encourage investment in residential housing (Walks, 2012; 2013b). This has led to record levels of household debt (Figure 9.4). Unfortunately, Canada has a regressive distribution of debt: poorer households have higher levels of debt (Meh et al., 2009), and debt is associated with increasing income segregation (Walks, 2013b). The poorest quintile of debtors would have trouble paying off

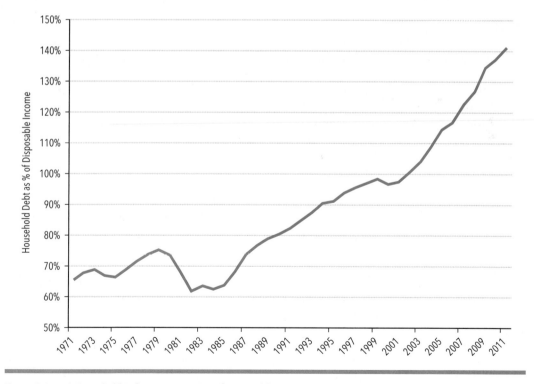

Figure 9.4   Household Debt as a Proportion of Disposable Income, Canada 1971–2011

Source: Statistics Canada, Cansim II database, Table 3800019.

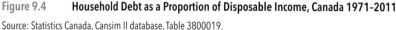

their debts if they lost their job, making them much more vulnerable to bankruptcy (Meh et al., 2009).

Furthermore, although neo-liberalism harkens back to the tenets of classical liberalism—in which those who take risks should suffer any losses—Harvey (2005) notes that in practice neo-liberalism has meant that the large lenders and investors are bailed out in the name of saving the system, while borrowers and workers have to make up for losses. The coordinated bailouts of the finance and real estate sectors that were implemented across the developed world in response to the global financial crisis, including those that took place in Canada (Walks, 2012), effectively distributed the losses of the financial system across the general public, while privatizing the gains in the hands of a few corporations and wealthy individuals (Alessandri and Haldane, 2009). In effect, the state rescued the assets of the wealthy, compelling lower-income households to pay for this through inflation, wage restraint, higher taxes, and the elimination of state benefits (including pensions) in the name of state austerity and solvency (Walks, 2010). Future research is necessary to determine the real and lasting effects of such shifts on the articulation of poverty and inequality—a task made all the more difficult by the Harper Conservative government's cancellation of the long-form of the census, which had asked questions about housing costs and income. The National Household Survey (NHS)—the voluntary online survey the Harper government put in, in place of the long-form census—has been found to be highly inaccurate (Hulchanski et al., 2013).

Shifting Household Structures

Household composition, living arrangements, aging, and other demographics (as discussed in Townshend and Walker, Chapter 7, and Moos, Chapter 20) also play a role in the articulation of inequality. The proliferation of single-person households and the growth of female lone-parent families (from 12 to 16.7 per cent of all families between 1981 and 2006) coupled with the decline of families with children (from 56 to 38.7 per cent

of all families) have introduced greater vulnerability and inequality into the urban household sector. From the perspective of inequality, a key development has been class-based marriage pairing based on employment status, with the standard one-earner household of the early postwar period—invoking the stereotypical image of a male breadwinner supporting a nuclear family with a stay-at-home housewife—now overshadowed by the growth of both two-earner and no-earner households (Figure 9.5).

Indeed, the coupling of highly educated and well-paid men and women of educated and wealthy parents is feeding class polarization (Myles, 2010). While the wealthy search out each other for mates, those less educated and less wealthy find it more difficult to meet prospective partners from different socio-economic groups, and increasingly partner with those with similar class and educational backgrounds. As family composition becomes more polarized, it is increasingly those who can draw on two or more incomes who are able to compete in housing markets, driving up housing costs and mortgage debt levels for everyone else.

Socio-Spatial Polarization of the City

Growing social inequality in Canadian society is reflected in the socio-spatial polarization of its cities. Residential segregation among neighbourhoods by class and housing tenure provides one of the most salient articulations of socio-spatial polarization. When the real estate market determines access to space, high-income households with rising incomes are able to out-bid others for housing and location (see Skaburskis and Moos, Chapter 12), displacing low-income households from desirable neighbourhoods, driving up housing values, and leading to greater neighbourhood segregation. The census tracts defined by Statistics Canada are typically used as proxies for neighbourhoods, given the lack of a consistent definition or theoretical delineation of the latter.[1] There is a clear

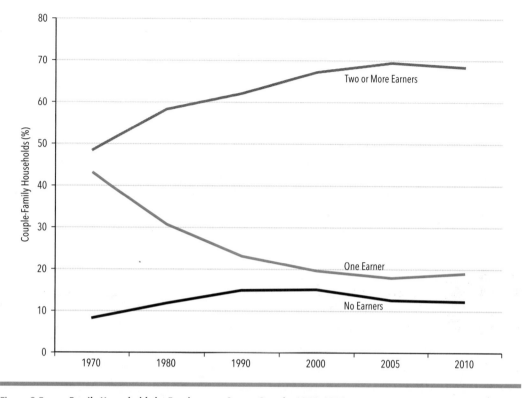

Figure 9.5   **Family Households by Employment Status, Canada, 1970–2010**

Source: Bourne (1993); Census of Canada (1991, 1996, 2001, 2006); Statistics Canada, Cansim II Tables 111-0016 through 111-0032.

trend toward socio-spatial income segregation among neighbourhoods, particularly starting in the 1990s.[2] After years of stability (and even slight declines) in income segregation over the 1970s—a period in which it has been said that looking for inequality was about as exciting as watching the grass grow (MacLachlan and Sawada, 1997)—inequality began ascending. This is particularly evident in the largest and most globally connected cities. The level of inequality as measured by the Gini coefficient—the gold standard in inequality measures—rose in Toronto and Calgary by roughly 60 per cent; and in Vancouver, by over 30 per cent (Figure 9.6).

Inequality among neighbourhoods has a specific geography in each city. The early post-war period was characterized by the spread of the middle class into the suburbs, while lower-income households remained in the inner cities, where most of the services for the poor or for new migrants to the city are traditionally located. In some Canadian cities, including Winnipeg, neighbourhoods close to the central business district have continued to house many of the poorest residents. However, since the 1970s the inner cities in most of the larger metropolitan areas have been experiencing gentrification, in which housing that once contained a mix of family types and incomes, and which once housed tenants, is converted into space for ever-wealthier households (see Bain, Chapter 14). As the rental stock is converted to owner-occupied housing and affordable rental housing disappears from the inner city, low-income households are displaced to the suburbs, where there are fewer services and where accessibility to public transit is lower.

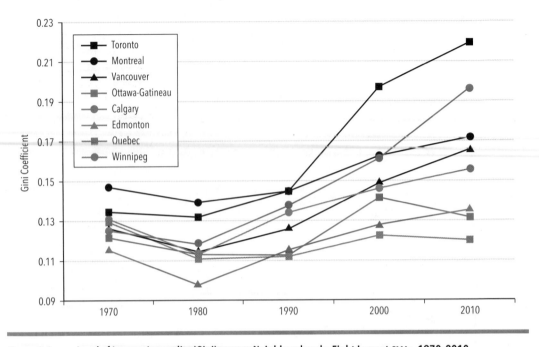

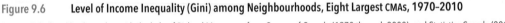

Figure 9.6   **Level of Income Inequality (Gini) among Neighbourhoods, Eight Largest CMAs, 1970–2010**

Source: Calculated by the author with the help of Richard Maaranen, from Census of Canada (1970 through 2000), and Statistics Canada (2010).

Indeed, research demonstrates that gentrification is well established in a number of Canadian cities (Ley, 1996; Walks and Maaranen, 2008a). Economic restructuring and deindustrialization as well as the neo-liberal policy reforms and the deregulation of finance, which stimulated speculation in housing, have all contributed to gentrification processes in cities (Keil, 2000; Lees, Slater, and Wyly, 2007). And as manufacturing work disappears from the inner cities and is replaced in part by high-end jobs in the FIRE sector (finance, insurance, real-estate) and other "quaternary" sector industries, the established and gentrifying neighbourhoods in the inner cities become the target of high-income households, as well as the site of new condominium development (Ley, 1996; Rosen and Walks, 2013; Walks and Maaranen, 2008a). With the gentrification of the inner-city housing stock, and the lack of significant new investments in social housing or rental apartments, low-income households and new in-migrants become concentrated in the older

suburbs, where a sizable proportion of the social housing and of the higher-density market rental housing stock is located in some Canadian cities. These areas now house the greatest proportion of low-income households, and now function as the new immigrant-reception neighbourhoods in the face of gentrification (Walks and Maaranen, 2008b).

As a result, such processes are producing new spatial patterns of urban disadvantage and neighbourhood change. This is clearly evident within the (amalgamated) City of Toronto (Figure 9.7). While traditionally wealthy areas north of Bloor St have continued to see their incomes rise, many neighbourhoods south of the Bloor-Danforth subway have witnessed gentrification and are now joining their counterparts to the north in the high-income club. At the same time, many neighbourhoods in the older ring of postwar suburbs (i.e., Etobicoke, North York, and Scarborough) have seen incomes persistently decline over time, and increasingly concentrate ever-greater proportions of low-income

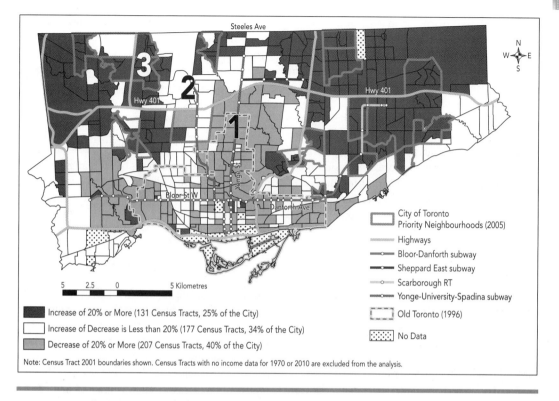

Figure 9.7   The Three Cities in Toronto: Income Change, 1970–2010

Source: Adapted and updated from Hulchanski, 2007.

households, single-parents, poor seniors, and recent immigrants (Hulchanski, 2007). As a result of such processes, poverty has been slowly shifting outward into the postwar suburbs in Toronto and a number of other Canadian cities (Ades, Apparicio, and Séguin, 2012; Walks, 2001).

From Concentrated Neighbourhood Poverty to Ghettos?

A question that often arises when discussing neighbourhood change and socio-spatial inequalities in Canadian cities is whether increasing income segregation is accompanied by rising levels of racial segregation, and whether this might be

producing **ghettos** along the lines of the black or Latino ghettos in the US. Strictly speaking, a ghetto is a neighbourhood in which a subjected racialized minority is compelled to live in a specific neighbourhood due to their ethnicity, race and/or income. The ghetto is thus a concept distinct from the **slum**—i.e., a neighbourhood in which poverty is concentrated, often due to the spatial concentration of poor-quality and under-maintained rental housing discrimination (see Johnston, Forrest, and Poulsen, 2002; Massey and Denton, 1993; Philpott, 1978). In the US, the degree of spatial overlap between the actual location and functioning of ghettos and **slums** means that high-poverty neighbourhoods and ghettos are often conflated or fused via the concepts of the "ghetto-poor" or the "outcast ghetto" (Jargowsky, 1997; Marcuse, 1997; Wilson, 1987). Kazemipur and Halli (2000) draw on this US-based discourse in suggesting that the increasing concentration of poverty—the growth of census tracts in which 40 per cent or more of the residents have incomes below the poverty line (LICO in Canada)—could be leading to a process of "ghettoization" in Canada.

The socio-spatial polarization of the city also raises important questions about "neighbourhood effects": the idea that the local neighbourhood affects the life chances of those who reside there. Neighbourhoods provide a basis for forming social relationships and networks and accessing jobs and information, are a source of amenities and services, and provide a major part of the context against which urban residents live. When poverty becomes concentrated in place, increased social needs may put pressure on local schools; and, if neighbourhoods in an urban municipality dispro-portionately concentrate residents who depend on public services, this puts pressure on the fiscal health of municipalities. Higher-poverty neighbourhoods cannot support as many retail establishments, pot-entially impacting local residents' access to quality food and other resources. Moreover, higher-poverty neighbourhoods that are geographically isolated may limit access to employment or social contact with other urban residents, producing a "spatial mismatch" between the locations of those in need and the locations of low-skill jobs and key amen-ities on which they depend (Ihlanfeldt and Sjoquist, 1998; Smith and Ley, 2008).

Some of the literature, however, suggests that benefits may flow to ethnic groups that are concen-trated in space, and that there might be both "good" and "bad" forms of segregation (Peach, 1996). Indeed, spatial concentration that is voluntary (rather than compelled) may provide greater access to job opportunities, friends and family, preferred retail amenities and religious institutions, and ser-vices in a language one understands: in such cases, ethnic concentration might on the whole provide significant benefits. Logan et al. (2002) distinguish between the traditional immigrant enclave, seen as a temporary neighbourhood of convenience until immigrants attain the social contacts and resour-ces necessary to assimilate and move out, and an emerging new form they term the "ethnic commun-ity," which is the desired residential destination of prosperous immigrants and cultural minorities who wish to live among others from the same group. Li (1998) has coined the term ethnoburb to refer to the formation of such ethnic communities in the suburbs of North American cities.

As noted in Chapter 8 by Kobayashi and Preston in this volume, while Canadian cities have been able to integrate immigrants better than many other places on the globe, visible minorities remain seg-regated, processes of racialization still occur, and new immigrants continue to face significant chal-lenges. The evidence does not, however, indicate that any process of ghettoization is occurring in Canada's cities (Table 9.1). When census tracts are classified according to the proportion of the popu-lation from racialized visible minority groups, and the proportions of such groups found in neighbour-hoods where they are concentrated (see Johnston, Forest, and Poulsen, 2002; Walks and Bourne, 2006, for discussion of the methodology), no ghettos are found anywhere in Canada's cities. Only nine metropolitan areas in 2006 contained any census tract in which visible minorities of any kind made up the majority of the population. And unlike the US, none of the latter are predominantly black or Latino. Instead, the majority of racially "polarized" neighbourhoods—in which a single minority group constitutes at least two thirds of the population—are predominantly Chinese (18 of Toronto's 22 polarized enclaves, and 13 of Vancouver's 20), or South Asian. Furthermore, many of these polar-ized neighbourhoods have middle-class incomes. Instead of being formed predominantly through discrimination, as is the case for the US ghetto, many neighbourhoods with concentrations of single ethnic groups in Canada's cities are contem-porary ethnic communities—ethnoburbs resulting from positive choice and "locational attainment" (Li, 1998; Myles and Hou, 2004).

Of course, this is not to say that there is no overlap between concentrations of racialized com-munities and poverty. However, poverty occurs in places where no single ethnic group dominates but instead where the poorest members of each

Table 9.1 Proportion of the Population, Census Tracts, and Rates of Low-Income (% below the LICO) by Neighbourhood Type; Nine Most Spatially Diverse Canadian Metropolitan Areas

CMA	Isolated	Non-Isolated	Pluralism	Mixed-Minority	Polarized-Minority	Ghetto
% of Total Population (# of Census Tracts):						
Toronto	23.3 (270)	36.9 (369)	19.6 (184)	17.9 (150)	2.3 (22)	0
Vancouver	20.4 (87)	38.1 (156)	25.9 (105)	10.9 (41)	5.0 (20)	0
Abbotsford	47.1 (17)	37.6 (14)	8.7 (2)	0	6.7 (1)	0
Winnipeg	52.1 (88)	34.6 (56)	11.6 (19)	1.7 (4)	0	0
Calgary	50.3 (110)	41.0 (79)	7.6 (11)	1.1 (2)	0	0
Montreal	67.8 (579)	27.2 (240)	4.2 (34)	0.8 (7)	0	0
Ottawa-Gatineau	65.9 (168)	31.7 (76)	2.4 (5)	0	0	0
Edmonton	44.3 (99)	55.3 (116)	0.4 (2)	0	0	0
Windsor	60.6 (41)	39.4 (29)	0	0	0	0
Rate of Low-Income (%) (# of Census Tracts with Low-Income rate > = 40%):						
Toronto	9.7 (0)	17.4 (1)	22.6 (10)	26.2 (24)	24.4 (1)	0
Vancouver	11.4 (0)	20.3 (4)	24.8 (8)	27.4 (41)	28.0 (2)	0
Abbotsford	12.1 (0)	17.0 (0)	11.8 (0)	0	13.4 (0)	0
Winnipeg	11.9 (0)	22.5 (7)	33.0 (8)	64.1 (4)	0	0
Calgary	11.2 (0)	14.8 (1)	15.0 (0)	15.7 (0)	0	0
Montreal	16.1 (34)	28.6 (56)	45.8 (22)	54.8 (7)	0	0
Ottawa-Gatineau	10.9 (3)	20.3 (9)	47.2 (4)	0	0	0
Edmonton	9.4 (0)	18.0 (2)	9.1 (0)	0	0	0
Windsor	8.8 (0)	22.2 (4)	0	0	0	0

Source: Calculated by the author from Census of Canada (2006). Adapted and updated from Walks and Bourne (2006).

Notes: Isolated = less than 20% visible minorities and/or Aboriginals; Non-Isolated = between 20% and 50% visible minorities and/or Aboriginals; Pluralism= between 50% and 70% visible minorities and/or Aboriginals; Mixed-Minority = over 70% visible minorities and/or Aboriginals but no group dominates; Polarized = over 70% visible minorities and/or Aboriginals, and one group makes up over 66% of the population, but less than 30% of this group lives in such neighbourhoods; and Ghettos = over 70% visible minorities and/or Aboriginals *and* one single group makes up over 60% *and* at least 30% of this group lives in such neighbourhoods (based on Johnston, Forrest, and Poulsen, 2002).

different minority group are compelled to live because of low incomes, often in poor-quality private rental housing, and in older social housing estates dating from the 1960s and 1970s (Walks and Bourne, 2006). It is in these neighbourhoods, many located within the inner suburbs, that spatial accessibility and isolation increasingly play important additive roles in shaping the experience of concentrated neighbourhood poverty among low-income minorities, Aboriginals, and immigrants (Smith and Ley, 2008).

Homelessness and the Canadian City

The social distribution of housing wealth and affordability is an increasingly important issue given rising socio-spatial inequality and neo-liberal approaches to finance and urban governance. As noted in Chapter 19 by Harris, the proportion of Canadian households that own their own home increased significantly and consistently over the postwar period, in large part due to access to subsidized mortgage credit. This has allowed those who can afford home ownership the ability to amass more wealth and retain more income than they otherwise would. But the flipside is that those who cannot afford to be homeowners have, as a whole, become progressively poorer and have had to find shelter in an increasingly residualized rental housing market (Figure 9.8).

One result of the divisions growing in urban society is homelessness, which is a form of extreme and often invisible poverty. The United Nations defines homelessness as either (1) having no place to call home and being forced to sleep either outside or in a temporary shelter, or (2) having access to housing that is lacking in one or more of the following: sanitation, protection from the elements, safe water, security of tenure, affordability,

personal safety, and accessibility to daily needs. Homelessness thus embodies not only those who literally have no home, but also those who do have some form of shelter but whose present housing situation is precarious and insufficient. The difference between these situations is often conceptualized as one between *absolute (or "literal")* *homelessness* (not having any home) and *relative* *homelessness* (precarious or insufficient housing). Discrepancies in precise definitions are important because alternate definitions can yield diverging estimates of the extent of homelessness; as well, they support different courses of remedial action. Those whose housing is sufficient but who are paying so much on housing that it cuts into their ability to meet other daily needs are experiencing *housing affordability stress*, and thus are considered *at risk of homelessness*. Stone (1993) calls the latter

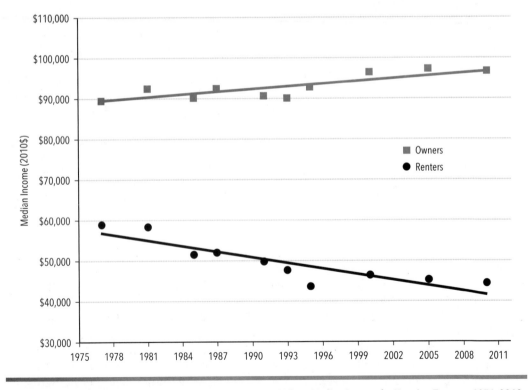

Figure 9.8   **Tenants Become Poorer, Homeowners Become Richer: Median Income by Housing Tenures, 1976–2010**

Source: CMHC (2001); Census of Canada, 1996, 2001, 2006; Survey of Household Spending, 2011.

situation shelter poverty, because in such cases housing costs are a cause of households' current poverty.

Absolute homelessness can be distinguished by its duration, with three archetypical forms (Kuhn and Culhane, 1998):

1. *Chronic homelessness* involves those who remain homeless over extended periods of time; it consumes the greatest proportion of shelter resources.
2. *Episodic homelessness* concerns repeated forays into and out of homelessness; it is the most difficult form of homelessness to treat.
3. *Temporary homelessness* typically entails brief periods of homelessness; it is the easiest form to target with preventive or emergency services.

A recent report on the state of homelessness in Canada estimates that of the roughly 200,000 people who are estimated to experience homelessness in any given year, roughly 2.0–3.5 per cent involve chronic homelessness, and between 3 and 10 per cent involve episodic forms of homelessness, with the remainder (between 86 and 95 per cent) falling into the category of temporary homelessness (Gaetz et al., 2013: 7).

Most experts acknowledge the existence of a *continuum of residential security* between homefulness at one extreme and absolute homelessness at the other (Figure 9.9). Home ownership is the housing situation that best characterizes "homefulness" in Canada, and indeed, as discussed by Harris in

Chapter 19, this form of tenure is what federal housing policy has mainly been geared to promote (see also Walks, 2012). At the other extreme is the situation most stereotypical of the homeless: "sleeping rough." This is the housing option of last resort, typically adopted when attempts to double-up with as many family and friends as possible are exhausted. Those who find themselves having to sleep rough often take refuge on park benches; under bridges; or in tents, bus shelters, parking garages, and cars. Between these extremes lie varying levels of relative homelessness, each of which can be further distinguished by the level of state or community involvement in their provision (including that provided by non-governmental organizations). State and non-market forms of housing (i.e., emergency, transitional, supportive, and social/co-operative housing) provide significant options for households to help prevent them from falling into shelter poverty and/or absolute homelessness, particularly those people with special needs and those facing problems in the labour market. Gaetz et al. (2013) estimate that in 2009 147,000 unique individuals, or 1 in 230 Canadians, stayed in an emergency shelter at least once.

The contemporary literature conceptualizes the causes of homelessness as deriving from pathways that conceptually link macro structural factors, such as major transitions affecting the economy, to individual circumstance and life worlds, that is, personal circumstances (Clapham, 2002). Such approaches bridge old debates between agency approaches that explain homelessness as the result

Options Available in the Housing Market

Options Provided by State/Non-Market Sectors

Figure 9.9   **Continuum of Homefulness to Homelessness**

of individual failings (e.g., substance abuse, job loss, disability, depression, mental-health problems, etc.) and structural explanations that pin homelessness on employment restructuring and inequitable housing markets. As O'Flaherty noted more than 20 years ago (1993), in any single city it is those individuals who suffer from one or more of the individual-level problems listed above who first fall into homelessness when the economy worsens, while the total number of homeless among different cities is strongly predicted by cities' rate and length of unemployment. Studies of the characteristics of the homeless in Canada's cities contradict stereotypes of the lazy male "hobo" with substance-abuse issues. In fact, virtually all homeless adults receive some income, and upwards of two-fifths are employed (City of Calgary, 2012; City of Toronto, 2009: 37). A common trigger inducing homelessness is the reduction or elimination of social assistance (SPCW, 2011), as well as rising rents/eviction, and loss of other forms of income (GVRSCH, 2010). While it is true that a disproportionate percentage of the homeless suffer from mental-health problems, it is unclear how much of this pre-dates, or alternatively is caused by, the homeless situation. One survey found that 42 per cent of the homeless suffered abuse as children (City of Calgary, 2012: 13). And a large proportion—upwards of one-fifth—of the homeless are children and youth (Ibid; Gaetz et al., 2013); moreover, homelessness has risen more quickly among families with children than any other group (Ibid; City of Toronto 2013b), requiring resources to be put into new specialized family shelters (Gallimore, Kreps, and Morasse, 2007). In addition, Aboriginals are over-represented among the homeless in virtually every Canadian city (Gaetz et al., 2013).

The increase in housing affordability stress and homelessness is the result of a series of changes occurring within Canadian cities (Figure 9.10). First of all are broadly based economic changes, from globalization to the demise of the family-supportive wage (in which only one wage is required to support all family members), that have produced greater income inequality. In turn, great income inequality leads to more low-income households, yet also upward pressure on the housing market caused by more high-income households in exactly those metropolitan areas experiencing gentrification and the de-conversion of rental units into owner-occupation. The second change in Canadian cities are those shifts occurring within the household sector, in which the increasing diversity of household types and sizes—the outcome of rising divorce and family dissolution rates over the postwar period—results in greater dispersion in ability to pay, with many specialized needs not easily met in the regular housing market. The third change is gentrification and the spatial restructuring of the city, which has meant the erosion of rental units in the most accessible locations, as well as new rental housing in deindustrializing cities and suburbs. This has produced a spatial mismatch between the demand and supply of rental units. With the rise of home ownership, and the shift away from building new rental housing (and toward the condominium as the preferred tenure for new high-rise buildings, see Rosen and Walks, 2013), renters have either had to pay very high rents for premium new units or have had to settle for residualized units in areas of mostly low accessibility. Spatial mismatches are exacerbated by immigrant flows that strongly favour certain cities and neighbourhoods over others.

Finally, each of these factors is exacerbated by the effects of political decisions and public policies enacted since the 1980s. These include the elimination of rent controls; declining rental subsidies; the drastic drop in new social rental construction; cutbacks in welfare support; the downloading of social housing and other social services to municipalities (which are least able to afford to maintain them); and loose credit policies that have encouraged speculation in the housing market, funded gentrification, and led to unprecedented house price inflation. This puts a squeeze on Canada's rental market, reducing the number of affordable units. In Canada, 310,000 low-rent units were lost alone during the early 1990s (Pomeroy, 2004), while Ontario lost another 45,000 during the late 1990s (Shapcott, 2004). The mismatch between the demand and

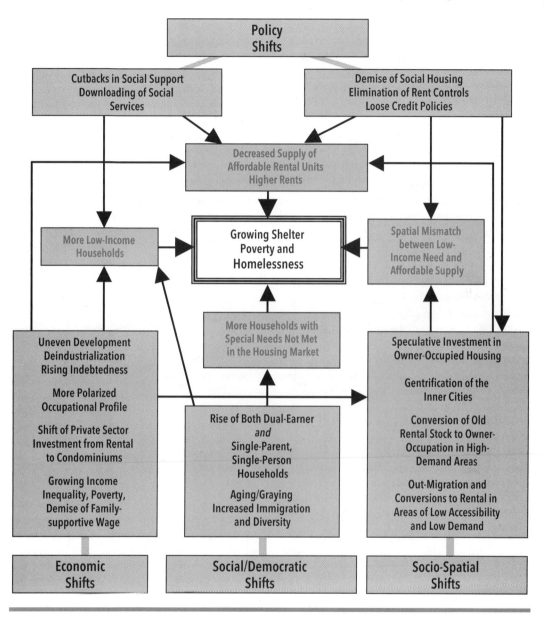

Figure 9.10   Factors Inducing Homelessness and Housing Affordability Stress

supply of affordable units is so great in Toronto that the city reported over 86,000 households on the wait list for social housing in 2012—more than the total number of such units actually existing in the city—and a 22-year wait at the going rate of absorption (City of Toronto, 2013b).

Counting and Alleviating Homelessness

In Canadian cities, the numbers of homeless present on any given night, including those in temporary shelters and those sleeping rough/doubling-up, varies between 8 and 31 per 10,000 (Table 9.2). While lower than comparable figures for US cities, which range between 21 and 77 per 10,000, this is nonetheless higher than the numbers recorded in the late 1990s and early 2000s. Some cities, including Ottawa, report rising shelter use and longer average shelter stays over the 2000s, even in the face of stable single-day snapshots (Figure 9.11). This is a worrisome trend, particularly given that cities like Ottawa did not suffer nearly to the same extent from the late-2000 recession as did other, more industrial cities. Examining annual shelter use (only), the numbers of homeless would appear to range between 50 per 10,000 in Eastern Canada, to over 100 per 10,000 in large cities such as Toronto, and in Saskatoon (Table 9.2).

However, some cities, even those with persistently high levels of homelessness, poverty, and inequality, have been able to begin reducing and even reversing the growth of homelessness in its various guises (Figure 9.12). A key principle includes applying "housing first" policies, whereby providing permanent housing is made a priority, along with better integration of public services for the homeless. In Toronto, for example, the Streets-to-Homes program, which has been implemented since the mid-2000s, is largely considered a success: 3881 people have been permanently housed through this program between 2005 and 2012, reducing the stress on the shelter system (City of Toronto, 2013b). Likewise, housing-first policies are at the centre of Calgary's 10-year plan to end homelessness, credited with reducing the level

Table 9.2   Counts of the Homeless, Canadian Cities

City	Study Year	Population (Number)	Total Annual Homeless (Number)	Number per 10,000	Unsheltered (Number)	Sheltered (Number)
On a Single Night:						
Hamilton	2006	519,949	419	8	na	419
Toronto (City)	2009	2,615,060	5,086	19	400	4,175
Winnipeg	2011	663,617	765	12	350	415
Saskatoon	2008	222,189	260	12	44	199
Edmonton	2012	812,201	2,174	27	1,070	1,104
Red Deer	2012	90,564	279	31	184	93
Calgary	2012	1,096,833	3,190	29	64	1,715
Lethbridge	2012	83,517	99	12	5	94
Kelowna	2007	117,312	279	24	150	119
Vancouver (City)	2012	603,502	1,602	27	306	1,296
Metro Vancouver	2008	2,313,328	2,660	11	1,558	849
For the Whole Year:						
Halifax	2011	390,096	1,973	51	na	1,973
Saint John	2012	70,063	341	49	na	341
Ottawa	2012	883,391	7,308	83	na	7,308
Toronto (City)	2008	2,615,060	27,256	104	na	27,256
Sudbury	2010	160,274	1,014	63	na	1,014
Saskatoon	2010	222,189	2,700	122	na	2,700

Source: ATEH (2012); City of Toronto (2009, 2013a, b); CUISR (2010); Gaetz et al. (2013); Gallimore, Kreps, and Morasse (2007); Greater Sudbury (2011); NSHHN (2012); SJHDC (2013); SPCW (2011).

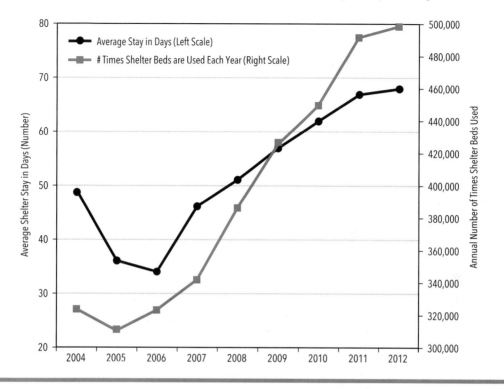

Figure 9.11   Increasing Use of Shelter Beds, and Longer Stays, Ottawa, 2004–12

Source: ATEH (various years).

,of recorded homelessness between the 2008 and 2012 snapshots, finding permanent housing for 92 per cent of those in the program within 12 months, and providing the poor with significantly improved access to health care and other public services (City of Calgary, 2012). Other cities, including Edmonton and Vancouver, have adopted similar approaches and are also seeing improvements in their state of homelessness and poverty (Gaetz et al., 2013). These efforts have been helped by the federal Affordable Housing Initiative (AHI), which targeted federal stimulus funds to build new, affordable housing. However, neither the federal government, nor any provincial government, has yet adopted the "1 per cent solution" advocated by the Federation of Canadian Municipalities (FCM), pushing for an additional 1 per cent of the annual budget on housing. This would provide for stable

funding to build upwards of 10,000 new, affordable rental units per year. If these units were built in the inner cities, they would help meet demand in exactly those places with over-heated housing markets and unaffordable rents. This would also help limit gentrification, maintain local social mix, and promote a more equitable and just city.

Conclusion

The effects of globalization, economic restructuring, deindustrialization, the racialization of poverty, demographic shifts, and neo-liberal policies have all worked to increase levels of social inequality and polarization at multiple scales throughout urban Canada. As the middle declines, the feeling that everyone is in the same boat wanes, while fears

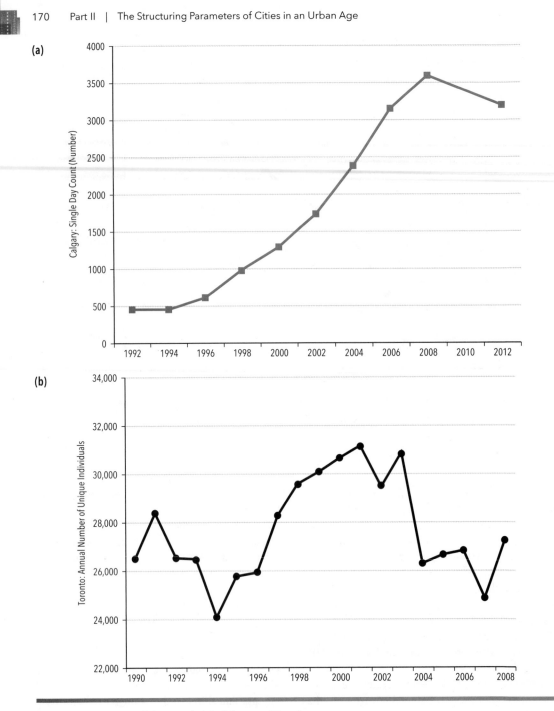

Figure 9.12   Counts of the Homeless in Calgary and Toronto

Notes: Data from Calgary represent both those sleeping rough and those in emergency shelters. Broken line in the Toronto data pertains only to those in emergency shelters. If those sleeping rough were included, the total would be approximately 5000 higher. No single-day snapshot was taken in Calgary in 2010.

Source: City of Calgary (2012); City of Toronto (2003, 2013a, b).

of those in other classes grow. Social polarization spurs a series of self-reinforcing feedback loops, in which the responses of individuals feed into the system to further aggravate the problems caused by polarization. As they become wealthier, in part from the debt payments being made by the poor, rich households attain more power to influence the political process to push for policy reforms in their favour, such as tax and public spending cuts, and shifts of public monies out of public schools and into subsidies for private schools. Such a process further drives the processes facilitating the transfer of power to the wealthy while impacting the quality of urban services that the majority depend on, thereby making poor districts all the more undesirable. The residualization of the older rental housing stock makes renting less desirable, limiting rent levels and the incentives to build new rental units while at the same time fueling the filtering of housing and concentrating the poor in increasingly stigmatized rental districts.

To reverse the growth of social polarization and inequality and ameliorate the problems such growth has caused, a multi-pronged, multi-scaled response is needed:

- Private sector investment needs to flow into productive sectors that provide sustainable jobs and an economic base upon which new economic activities can flourish, and away from non-productive sectors that encourage regressive forms of rent-taking (particularly finance and real estate).
- Wages and salaries need to be re-equalized; and decades of excessive compensation among executive and managerial staff, reversed.
- Governments need to increase the redistributive function of the tax system and public services, with top marginal tax rates increased substantially as well as minimum wages and welfare benefits (the latter to a level that meets, at very least, basic daily needs).
- Governments should work with the private sector to establish apprenticeship programs for young workers and require mandatory voting so that the marginalized—who are often disengaged and less likely to vote when it is not mandatory—are required to pass judgment on government policies that affect them.
- Items of collective consumption and public infrastructure, such as parks and public transit, upon which the majority of urban residents depend, should be maintained so that they are universally accessible, and the privatizations of strategic public infrastructure should be reversed.
- Revenue generation, particularly for social services and other "soft" services, should be shifted from property taxation and other regressive forms of taxation onto the progressive income tax.
- Special efforts are required to counter the declining incomes of new immigrants, Aboriginals, and the racialization of poverty in the larger cities, and to enhance gender and racial equity.
- Property rights must be democratized, and the right to the city, and to full participation in society, must be implemented.

Continued economic restructuring risks heavy impacts on the poor, on new immigrants, and on the young. Serious attention to these issues is required now in order to prevent Canada's cities from becoming more unequal and polarized.

Review Questions

1. What are the factors bringing about heightened income inequality in Canadian cities?
2. Is homelessness an individual or a societal problem? Explain why.
3. Is it the government's role to address income inequality? Why or why not?

Notes

1. Census tracts contain between 2000 and 8000 people and have been constructed in order to contain a similar social demographic with boundaries based on

recognizable physical features and transportation routes. Because census tract boundaries have largely been maintained over time, census tracts are the most appropriate units for examining neighbourhood changes.

2. Because of the lack of household income data (due to the cancellation of the 2011 long-form census), Figure 9.3 compares changes in individual (per-capita) income of adults aged 15 and over. The data for this income variable in 2010 is still obtainable at the census tract level from Statistics Canada (calculated from the tax returns submitted to Canada Revenue Agency).

References

Ades, J., P. Apparicio, and A-M. Séguin. 2012. "Are new patterns low-income distribution emerging in Canadian metropolitan areas?" *Canadian Geographer* 56: 339–61.

Alessandri, P., and A.G. Haldane. 2009. *Banking on the State.* London: Bank of England. At: www.bankofengland.co.uk/publications/speeches/2009/speech409.pdf

ATEH (Alliance to End Homelessness). Various years, 2004–12. *Report Card on Ending Homelessness in Ottawa.* At: www.homelesshub.ca/Search.aspx?search=Report+Card+on+ending+homelessness+in+Ottawa

Bolton, K., and S. Breau. 2012. "Growing unequal? Changes in the distribution of earnings across Canadian cities," *Urban Studies* 49: 1377–96.

Bourne, L.S. 1993. "Close together and worlds apart: An analysis of changes in the ecology of income in Canadian cities," *Urban Studies* 30: 1293–1317.

City of Calgary. 2012. *The State of Homelessness in Calgary, 2012.* At: http://calgaryhomeless.com/assets/research/The-State-of-Homelessnessonlineversion.pdf

City of Toronto. 2003. *The Toronto Report Card on Housing and Homelessness.* Toronto: City of Toronto.

City of Toronto. 2009. *Street Needs Assessment Results, 2009.* Toronto: City of Toronto, Shelter, Support and Housing Administration. At: www.toronto.ca/legdocs/mmis/2010/cd/bgrd/backgroundfile-29123.pdf

City of Toronto. 2013a. *Total Numbers of Unique Individuals Using the Shelter System 2000–2008.* Toronto: City of Toronto, official data. At: www.toronto.ca/legdocs/mmis/2009/cd/bgrd/backgroundfile-24924.pdf

City of Toronto. 2013b. *Quick Facts about Homelessness and Housing in Toronto.* Toronto: City of Toronto Shelter, Support and Housing Administration. At: www.toronto.ca/housing/pdf/quickfactsinfographic.pdf

Clapham, D. 2002. "Housing pathways: A postmodern analytical framework," *Housing, Theory and Society* 19: 57–68.

CMHC (Canada Mortgage and Housing Corporation). 2001. *Residualization of Rental Tenure: Attitudes of Private Landlords towards Low-Income Households.* Ottawa: CMHC Research Highlights, Socio-Economic Series, issue 93.

Courchene, T.J., and C. Telmer. 1998. *From Heartland to North American Region State: The Social, Fiscal and Federal Evolution of Ontario.* Toronto: Centre for Public Management, University of Toronto.

CUISR (Community-University Institute for Social Research). 2010. *Saskatoon Homeless Individuals and Families Information System (HIFIS) Report Card 2010.* Saskatoon: Community-University Institute for Social Research. At: www.homelesshub.ca/Library/Saskatoon-Homeless-Individuals-and-Families-Information-System-Report-Card-2010-53660.aspx

Gaetz, S., J. Donaldson, T. Richter, and T. Gulliver. 2013. *The State of Homelessness in Canada.* Ottawa: Canadian Homelessness Research Network Press. At: www.homelesshub.ca/Library/The-State-of-Homelessness-in-Canada-2013-55941.aspx

Galabuzi, G-E. 2006. *Canada's Economic Apartheid: The Social Exclusion of Racialized Groups in the New Century.* Toronto: Canadian Scholars Press.

Gallimore, C., B. Kreps, and T. Morasse. 2007. *On Any Given Night: Measuring Homelessness in Hamilton, 2007 Edition.* Hamilton: Social Planning and Research Council of Hamilton. At: www.homelesshub.ca/Library/On-Any-Given-Night-Measuring-Homelessness-in-Hamilton--2007-Edition-36447.aspx

Greater Sudbury. 2011. *Sudbury Report on Homelessness 2010.* Sudbury: Greater Sudbury. At: www.homelesshub.ca/Search.aspx?search=Sudbury+homelessness

GVRSCH (Greater Vancouver Regional Steering Committee on Homelessness). 2010. *Homelessness in Metro Vancouver: A Comparative Community Profile.* Vancouver: GVRSCH. At: www.homelesshub.ca/Library/Homelessness-in-Metro-Vancouver-A-Comparative-Community-Profile-53968.aspx

Harvey, D. 2005. *A Brief History of Neo-liberalism.* Oxford: Oxford University Press.

Heisz, A. 2007. *Income Inequality and Redistribution in Canada: 1976 to 2004.* Ottawa: Statistics Canada. Cat. No. 11F0019MIE Research Paper No. 298.

Hulchanski, D. 2007. *The Three Cities in Toronto.* Toronto: University of Toronto Centre for Urban and Community Studies Research Bulletin 41.

——, R. Murdie, A. Walks, and L.S. Bourne. 2013. "Canada's voluntary survey is worthless, here's why," *Globe and Mail,* October 4. At: www.theglobeandmail.com/globe-debate/canadas-voluntary-census-is-worthless-heres-why/article14674558/

Hurtig, M. 2002. *The Vanishing Country.* Toronto: McClelland and Stewart Ltd.

Ihlanfeldt, K., and D. Sjoquist. 1998. "The spatial mismatch hypothesis: A review of recent studies and their implications for welfare reform," *Housing Policy Debate* 9: 849–92.

Jargowsky, P. 1997. *Poverty and Place: Ghettos, Barrios, and the American City*. New York: Russell Sage.

Johnston, R., J. Forrest, and M. Poulsen. 2002. "Are there ethnic enclaves/ghettos in English cities?" *Urban Studies* 39: 591–618.

Kazemipur, A., and S.S. Halli. 2000. *The New Poverty in Canada: Ethnic Groups and Ghetto Neighbourhoods*. Toronto: Thompson Educational Publishing.

Keil, R. 2009. "The urban politics of roll-with-it neo-liberalization," *City* 13: 230–45.

Krippner, G. 2005. "The financialization of the American economy," *Socio-Economic Review* 3: 173–208.

———. 2011. *Capitalizing on Crisis: The Political Origins of the Rise of Finance*. Cambridge, MA: Harvard University Press.

Kuhn, R., and D.P. Culhane. 1998. "Applying cluster analysis to test a typology of homelessness by pattern of shelter utilization: results from the analysis of administrative data," *American Journal of Community Psychology* 26: 207–32.

Lees, L., T. Slater, and E. Wyly. 2007. *Gentrification*. London: Routledge.

Ley, D. 1996. *The New Middle Class and the Re-Making of the Central City*. New York: Oxford University Press.

Li, W. 1998. "Anatomy of a new ethnic settlement: The Chinese ethnoburb of Los Angeles," *Urban Studies* 35: 479–501.

Logan, J., R. Alba, and W. Zhang. 2002. "Immigrant enclaves and ethnic communities in New York and Los Angeles," *American Sociological Review* 67: 299–322.

MacLachlan, I., and R. Sawada. 1997. "Measures of income inequality and social polarization in Canadian metropolitan areas," *Canadian Geographer* 41: 377–97.

Marcuse, P. 1997. "The enclave, the citadel, and the ghetto: What has changed in the post-Fordist U.S. city?" *Urban Affairs Review* 33: 228–64.

Massey, D., and N. Denton. 1993. *American Apartheid: Segregation and the Making of the Underclass*. Cambridge, MA: Harvard University Press.

Meh, C.A., Y. Terajima, D.Z. Chen, and T. Carter. 2009. *Household Debt, Assets, and Income in Canada: A Microdata Study*. Ottawa: Bank of Canada. Discussion paper 2009-7.

Myles, J. 2010. "The inequality surge: Changes in the family life course are the main cause," *Inroads* 26 (Winter/ Spring): 66–73.

———, and F. Hou. 2004. "Changing colours: Spatial assimilation and new racial minority immigrants," *Canadian Journal of Sociology* 29: 29–58.

NSHHN (Nova Scotia Housing and Homelessness Network). 2012. *Halifax Report Card on Homelessness 2012*. Halifax: Nova Scotia Housing and Homelessness Network. At: www.homelesshub.ca/Library/Halifax-Report-Card-On-Homelessness-2012-55308.aspx

OECD (Organisation for Economic Co-operation and Development). 2008. *Growing Unequal? Income Distribution and Poverty in OECD Countries*. Zurich: OECD. Report 8108051E.

O'Flaherty, B. 1993. "Wrong person and wrong place: For homelessness, the conjunction is what matters," *Journal of Housing Economics* 13: 1–15.

Peach, C. 1996. "Good segregation, bad segregation," *Planning Perspectives* 11: 379–98.

Peck, J., and A. Tickell. 2002. "Neo-liberalizing space," *Antipode* 34: 380–404.

Philpott, T.L. 1978. *The Slum and the Ghetto: Neighbourhood Deterioration and Middle Class Reform, Chicago 1880–1930*. New York: Oxford University Press.

Pomeroy, S. 2004. "Toward a comprehensive affordable housing strategy for Canada," in D. Hulchanski and M. Shapcott, eds., *Finding Room: Policy Options for a Canadian Rental Housing Strategy*. Toronto: University of Toronto Centre for Urban and Community Studies.

Rosen, G., and R.A. Walks. 2013. "Rising cities: Condominium development and the private transformation of the metropolis," *Geoforum* 49: 160–72.

Saez, E., and M.R. Veall. 2005. "The evolution of high incomes in Northern America: Lessons from Canadian evidence," *The American Economic Review* 95: 831–49.

Sassen, S. 2001. *Global City: New York, London, Tokyo*, 2nd edn. Princeton, NJ: Princeton University Press.

Sennett, R. 1998. *The Corrosion of Character: The Personal Consequences of Work in the New Capitalism*. New York: W.W. Norton.

Shapcott, M. 2004. "Where are we going? Recent federal and provincial housing policy," in D. Hulchanski and M. Shapcott, eds., *Finding Room: Policy Options for a Canadian Rental Housing Strategy*. Toronto: University of Toronto Centre for Urban and Community Studies.

SJHDC (Saint John Human Development Council). 2013. *Experiencing Homelessness in Saint John, New Brunswick*. Saint John: Human Development Council. At: www.homelesshub.ca/Library/2013-Saint-John-Homelessness-Report-Card-55680.aspx

Smith, H., and Ley, D. 2008. Even in Canada? The multiscalar construction and experience of concentrated immigrant poverty in gateway cities. *Annals of the Association of American Geographers* 98: 686–713.

SPCW (Social Planning Council of Winnipeg). 2011. *A Place to Call Home: Homelessness in Winnipeg, 2011*. Winnipeg: Social Planning Council of Winnipeg. At: www.homelesshub.ca/ResourceFiles/A%20Place%20to%20Call%20Home_FINAL.pdf

Stone, M.E. 1993. *Shelter Poverty: New Ideas on Housing Affordability*. Philadelphia: Temple University Press.

Veblen, T. 2007 [1899]. *Theory of the Leisure Class.* Oxford: Oxford University Press.

Walks, R.A. 2001. "The social ecology of the post-Fordist/global city? Economic restructuring and socio-spatial polarization in the Toronto urban region," *Urban Studies* 38: 407–47.

——. 2010. "Bailing out the wealthy: Responses to the financial crisis, Ponzi neo-liberalism, and the city," *Human Geography* 3: 54–84.

——. 2012. "Canada's housing bubble story: Mortgage securitization, the state, and the global financial crisis," *International Journal of Urban and Regional Research* 1–30. doi: 10.1111/j.1468-2427.2012.01184.x

——. 2013a. *Income Inequality and Polarization in Canada's Cities: An Examination and New Form of Measurement.* Toronto: University of Toronto Cities Centre, Research Paper #227.

——. 2013b. "Mapping the urban debtscape: The geography of household debt in Canadian cities," *Urban Geography* 34: 153–87.

——, and L.S. Bourne. 2006. "Ghettos in Canada's cities? Racial segregation, ethnic enclaves and poverty concentration in Canadian urban areas," *The Canadian Geographer* 50: 273–97.

——, and R. Maaranen. 2008a. *The Timing, Patterning and Forms of Gentrification and Neighbourhood Upgrading in Montreal, Toronto, and Vancouver 1961 to 2001.* Toronto: University of Toronto Cities Centre Research Report 211.

——, and R. Maaranen. 2008b. "Gentrification, social mix, and social polarization: Testing the linkages in Large Canadian cities. *Urban Geography* 29: 293–326.

Wang, S.G., and L. Lo. 2005. "Chinese immigrants in Canada: Their changing composition and economic performance," *International Migration* 43(3): 35–71.

Wilson, W.J. 1987. *The Truly Disadvantaged: The Inner City, the Underclass, and Public Policy.* Chicago: University of Chicago Press.

Transport and Land-Use Interactions in Cities: Getting Closer to Opportunities

10

AHMED EL-GENEIDY,
ZACHARY PATTERSON,
AND EVELYNE ST-LOUIS

Introduction

There are many reasons why people and firms locate in cities. For some, it may be the bright lights; for others, it may be the necessity to find work—there are perhaps as many reasons to locate in a city as there are people and firms. One of the most critical reasons is that a city enables people, households, and firms to gain access to each other (see Filion and Bunting, Chapter 1). This chapter looks at Canadian cities through the lens of *accessibility,* a notion that helps in understanding and conceptualizing the complex relation between land use and transport in a city and their impacts on city organization, development, and planning to achieve more sustainable outcomes.

The following section describes and defines the key terms of *transport* and *land use* and how they relate to accessibility. The second section examines the history of transport in Canadian cities, and the role of transport and land use in their creation and development. This is followed by a discussion of the current state of transport in Canadian cities in comparison to other urban regions around the world in terms of congestion levels and mode share. The fourth section concentrates on the activity dimension of the land-use and transportation cycle: we will show how travel demand is typically modelled, how this has changed over time, and how planners and engineers seek to improve their modelling techniques today. The fifth section

moves the attention away from more mobility-focused issues to examine accessibility measures and how they are calculated. The chapter ends with a discussion of the shift in transportation planning that has been taking place in Canada in the last decade from a mobility- and car-oriented paradigm to a multi-modal sustainable approach that seeks to better integrate transportation and land use.

Transport, Land Use, and Accessibility

Alexander et al. (1977: 59) once expressed the importance of "[putting] the magic of the city within the reach of everyone in a metropolitan area." Alexander and his colleagues were promoting an ideal city in which a person could easily reach desired destinations—or *opportunities*. In the field of land use and transportation, this concept is known as *accessibility*. Both people and firms locate in cities in order to gain access to destinations (opportunities) with which they can, and want, to interact. Accessibility, or the ease of reaching valued destinations (Hansen, 1959), is often confused with mobility—defined as the ability to move from one place to another (Handy, 1994).

Since the widespread use of the private automobile, and in particular since World War II, transportation planning has been dominated by a car-oriented and mobility-focused paradigm.

Within this paradigm, speed, efficiency, and fluidity of automobile transport have been central concerns, using indicators such as congestion as one of the main measures of mobility. For example, the Texas Transportation Institute (TTI) generates an annual urban mobility report for cities in the United States that includes various measures of congestion, such as delays and total number of hours wasted per year due to congestion. In contrast, the concept of accessibility is concerned not only with how easy it is to get from one place to another, but also with what one can reach. The use of accessibility measures often leads to different conclusions about the same transport and land-use situation compared to mobility measures when they are used alone. While the concept of accessibility has been around for more than 50 years and has been a common element in the goals and objectives of transport plans (Handy, 2002), its actual adoption in transportation planning has been limited until recently.

Since accessibility evaluates not only the ease with which one can go from one place to another but also what can be reached, it is considered one of the most comprehensive planning performance measures and an important contributor to better understanding the complex relationship between land use and transportation systems in a region (Wachs and Kumagai, 1973). This relationship has been simplified by Giuliano (2004) (Figure 10.1).

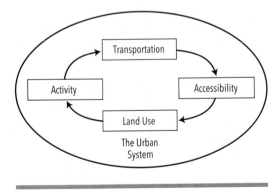

Figure 10.1   The Transportation and Land Use Cycle

Source: Giuliano, G. 2004. 'Land use impacts of transportation investments: Highway and transit', in S. Hanson & G. Giuliano, eds, *The Geography of Urban Transportation* (3rd edition). New York: The Guilford Press.

Starting with the transportation system, Figure 10.1 shows that the characteristics (i.e., network and reach) of the transportation system determine the level of accessibility in a region, given the distribution of households and firms (or land use) within the urban system. At the same time, land use itself is affected by accessibility—firms and households like to locate, all else being equal, in places with good accessibility. It is the distribution of households and firms that leads to the activity patterns (origins and destinations) within the urban system. And the interaction of activity patterns and the transport system is what determines the levels of mobility and accessibility in a region.

Transport Systems in Canadian Cities

History of Transport Systems and City Structure in Canada

Cities in Canada (and indeed everywhere) typically had their origins partly as a result of their advantages with respect to accessibility. For example, Montreal owes its origin to the fact that it was the furthest inland port that trans-Atlantic ships could reach (before the construction of the Lachine Canal, and the St Lawrence Seaway afterwards) because of the rapids surrounding the Island of Montreal (Shearmur and Rantisi, 2011). Winnipeg owes its origin to being at the junction of the Red and Assiniboine Rivers—a critical link along continental fur-trading routes (Artibise, 1977). Until the 1860s, most internal transportation within Canadian cities was done by foot, by horse, or by cart (Nader, 1975). These cities were typically quite small, dense, and characterized by juxtaposing and overlapping residential, commercial, and industrial uses, with the centres of these cities located near the terminals of long-distance transportation routes. The first public transportation systems began appearing in Canadian cities in the mid-1800s with the development of horse-drawn streetcar routes. By the end of the nineteenth century, electric streetcars replaced their horse-drawn predecessors. The streetcar systems allowed households to locate further away from the urban centres since it was now possible to travel greater distances, allowing households access to cheaper land and larger residences while still maintaining good accessibility to jobs in the urban core. Most economic activity, however, remained concentrated in the urban core because goods transportation did not experience the same improvements as public passenger transportation (i.e., freight was not moved on streetcars, so did not experience such rapid increases in mobility). This resulted in residential development around streetcar lines, creating "radial" or star-like urban development patterns. Streetcar lines also saw commercial strips along their routes, where people waiting to embark or upon disembarking took advantage of easy access to shops and services, reinforcing their commercial viability (see Filion and Bunting, Chapter 2).

The internal combustion engine, already in use at the turn of the twentieth century, did not revolutionize the transport and land-use system until the 1920s, when personal automobiles gained popularity. The internal combustion engine also allowed an increase in freight transportation by truck. The main implication of automobiles and trucks was to improve accessibility to large areas around the traditional urban cores, thus allowing for residential development and the decentralization of goods-handling activities in these areas. Since gas-powered vehicles were much less limited in where they could go compared to streetcars, development spread further and filled in areas previously undeveloped between streetcar lines, giving cities a more concentric development as in the pre-streetcar area.

After World War II, this tendency toward expanding cities was exacerbated by the construction of controlled access freeways. Even greater stretches of undeveloped land now had much greater accessibility and were developed into low-density suburbs (Perl and Kenworthy, 2010). The freeway system not only enticed households to move in great numbers to these suburban locations but also encouraged manufacturing and other

industries to suburbanize. Large regional shopping centres developed as well to serve the rapidly suburbanizing regions of urban Canada (Yeates and Garner, 1980). The result of this increasing decentralization of households and industry is commonly referred to as **urban sprawl**. *Sprawl* is a difficult term to define, but easy to recognize. While it has been characterized in many different ways, common elements to its characterization are low-density urban development, where residential, commercial, industrial, and institutional uses tend to be separated, thus requiring a private vehicle for movement between necessary daily functions in the city and making public transportation and active transportation mode choices inefficient (see Filion and Bunting, Chapter 2, and Addie, Fiedler, and Keil, Chapter 24).

Current Transport System in Canada

The proportion of trips made using different transportation modes—called mode share—is one common indicator used to describe transportation systems. Overall, Canada is an automobile-oriented country, with 80 per cent of work trips made by car or truck (Statistics Canada, 2013a). Mode share for public transportation is 12 per cent, while the combined mode share for cycling and walking is 7 per cent. Together, public transit, walking, and cycling are referred to as "sustainable" transportation modes. While the term *sustainable* can have many elements, sustainable transportation is most often referred to in the context of environmental sustainability. These modes are considered sustainable because unlike personal forms of motorized transportation they produce fewer (as in the case of public transit) or no emissions (walking and cycling).

Figure 10.2 shows the variation in 2011 public transit mode shares by the population of **census metropolitan areas** (CMAs) (Statistics Canada, 2013a). The graph indicates that a larger proportion of work commutes are done using public transit as the size of the CMA increases. Public transit mode share increases up to over 20 per cent in the largest Canadian CMAs, such as Toronto

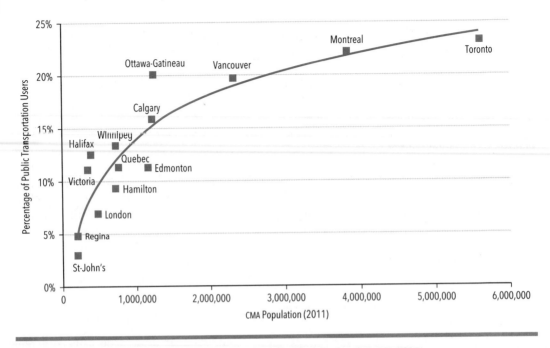

Figure 10.2   **Share of Public Transportation Users in Canadian CMAs by Population in 2011**

Data source: Statistics Canada (2013a).

(23 per cent) and Montreal (22 per cent), while it is between 10 and 20 per cent for smaller CMAs, such as Ottawa-Gatineau, Vancouver, Edmonton, and Calgary. However, the link between population and transit mode share does not hold true for all cities. Consider some of the smaller CMAs, such as Halifax and Victoria, that have public transit mode shares above 10 per cent even though their populations are approximately the same as other CMAs, like London or Regina, that have low shares of transit users (less than 8 per cent). While these city-level, "aggregate" mode share statistics are informative, they hide a great deal of variation in mode share within cities, across different demographics as well as across different kinds of trips. Within cities, public transit, cycling, and walking mode shares tend to be lowest in suburban areas, and highest toward the city core.

International comparisons can highlight areas in which the Canadian transportation system could improve, or bring to light aspects that are well advanced but may be further encouraged. Table 10.1 shows the mode share of commute trips for six Canadian cities and for other cities in the United States and Europe, focusing on the percentage of commute trips made by public transit and the two main active forms of transportation (i.e., cycling and walking). Canada's largest CMAs are roughly halfway between US and European cities in terms of public transit mode share (11 to 23 per cent). This share is higher than the typical city in the United States (except for New York), whereas it is typically much higher in Europe. We see similar patterns in terms of active modes of transportation: for the six Canadian CMAs, between 5 and 9 per cent of commutes are done by walking or cycling; in the United States, these values decrease to less than 5 per cent; in Europe, they increase considerably, up to almost 20 per cent of daily work trips. These differences in transit and active mode shares are likely related to several factors, including the age (and therefore structure) of the city, land use

Table 10.1	Percentage of Commute Trips Using Public Transportation and Active (Cycling and Walking) Modes of Transportation in Selected Major Canadian, US, and European Cities			
Country/Continent	City	Commute Mode Share: Public Transportation	Commute Mode Share: Active Transportation	Year
Canada	Toronto	23.3	5.8	2011
	Montreal	22.2	7.0	2011
	Vancouver	19.7	8.1	2011
	Ottawa-Gatineau	20.1	8.5	2011
	Calgary	15.9	6.1	2011
	Edmonton	11.3	5.2	2011
United States	New York	30.7	6.4	2010
	Chicago	11.2	3.7	2010
	Los Angeles	6.2	3.5	2010
Europe	Madrid	42.7	17.3	2008
	Paris	64.0	18.2	2008
	Stockholm	34.0	17.0	2005

Source for American cities: 2010 American Community Survey (US Census Bureau, 2010).
Source for Canadian cities: 2011 Canadian National Household Survey (Statistics Canada, 2013a).
Source for Madrid and Stockholm: Eurostat database (European Commission, 2008).
Source for Paris: 2008 Enquête nationale transports et déplacements (INSEE, 2008).

distribution, the domination of automobile culture, or the harsh winters in some Canadian cities.

It is also worthwhile to see how mode shares have been evolving over time. Figure 10.3 shows public transit mode share for commuters in CMAs with populations over one million. The data were obtained from the 1996 to 2006 censuses and from the National Household Survey for the year 2011 (Statistics Canada, 1996; 2001; 2006; 2013a).[1] For Canada's six largest CMAs, we can observe a pattern of increase in the share of daily trips by public transportation. This is encouraging as public transportation is a more sustainable form of transportation for cities than private automobiles; moreover, this shows that Canadian cities and citizens are capable of changing their mode shares. At the same time, based on a comparison with other regions around the world and with Europe in particular (Table 10.1), there is still room for improvement given that higher levels have been achieved in other cities.

Another common indicator used to characterize a transportation system is the level of congestion.[2] Issues of congestion have always been prominent in transportation planning, especially within the mobility paradigm of car-oriented North American cities. In this context, congestion is considered problematic since it compromises mobility (as well as accessibility) but also because congestion is seen today as detrimental to the environment and to public health. Indeed, high congestion means higher greenhouse gas (GHG) and other emissions from private vehicles. Congestion is, moreover, a cause of stress to road users. Table 10.2 summarizes the congestion levels for Canada's six largest CMAs, and compares the Canadian context to other cities around the world. Based on these measures, there is quite a bit of variation in how Canadian cities "perform" when compared with other cities around the world. Vancouver, the most congested in Canada, approaches the same congestion levels as Los Angeles and Paris.

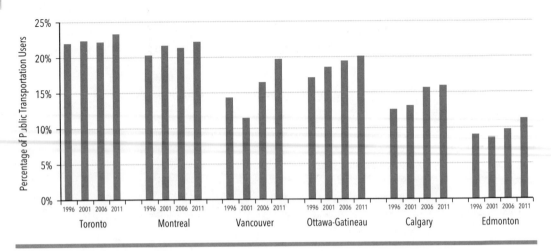

Figure 10.3   **Change in Share of Daily Trips by Public Transportation in Canadian CMAs with Populations over One Million, 1996–2011**

Source: Statistics Canada (1996, 2001, 2006, 2013a).

Table 10.2   Congestion Levels and Delay per Hour Driven in Peak Period, 2012

Country/Continent	City	Congestion Level (%)	Delay per Hour Driven in Peak Period Minutes
Canada	Toronto	22	34
	Montreal	20	30
	Vancouver	30	34
	Ottawa-Gatineau	22	39
	Calgary	17	11
	Edmonton	13	13
United States	New York	17	22
	Chicago	19	21
	Los Angeles	33	40
Europe	London	27	33
	Madrid	14	20
	Paris	33	40
	Milan	25	37
	Stockholm	28	39
	Moscow	66	74
South Africa	Johannesburg	30	43

Note: Congestion levels here are defined as the increase in overall travel times compared to a free-flow situation in minutes. For example, a congestion level of 12 per cent corresponds to 12 per cent longer travel times compared to a free-flow situation (TomTom, 2013). Free flow here refers to times of the day in which there is little or no traffic, such as at night.

Source: *TomTom North American Congestion Index*: TomTom International B.V. At: www.tomtom.com/lib/doc/trafficindex/2012-0704-TomTom-Congestion-index-2012Q1namerica-km.pdf

Travel Demand Modelling

One of the most important roles of transportation planning is to evaluate what investments should be made in the transportation system. Such an evaluation is based partly on the costs of investments or policies and partly on the potential impacts of future policies and investments. Travel demand modelling therefore involves a number of statistical and mathematical techniques designed to estimate what future travel demand will look like given different transportation policy and investment scenarios. In the past, and since the development of these techniques at the end of the 1950s, the primary indicators of interest for travel demand modelling have been concerned with mobility. As such, different transportation scenarios are evaluated based on their ability to reduce congestion and to increase speed and fluidity—particularly during peak periods. As we will show, traditional methods typically take the land-use system as a given and use this to estimate activity patterns. These activity patterns are what determine overall transport demand, and this, in conjunction with the transport system, results in various measures of mobility, such as congestion and travel times between parts of a region. While mobility is a critical part of accessibility, accessibility has not been central to traditional travel demand analysis. In fact, the link between accessibility and the land-use system has often been ignored. The traditional approach to travel demand modelling has been dominated by the four-step model, outlined in Figure 10.4 (Meyer and Miller, 2000). You can find detailed descriptions of the modelling process in many planning textbooks (e.g., Meyer and Miller, 2000; Ortuzar and Willumsen, 2011; Vuchic, 2005).

In order to go through the four-step modelling process, the region under study is first divided into transportation analysis zones (TAZs). These zones can be thought of as neighbourhoods where trips both originate and end. Note that the model is trip-based, meaning that transport demand is represented by individual and independent trips. Inputs to the model are generally forecasts of the number of people and employment in the different

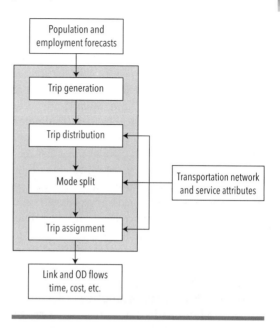

Figure 10.4   Four-Step Travel Demand Model

Source: Meyer, Michael and Eric Miller. *Urban Transportation Planning*, 2/e © 2001, McGraw Hill Education.

TAZs, as well as information on the existing transportation network, including its service attributes. The steps of the model are as follows:

1. *Trip generation* determines the number of trips produced by, and coming to, every TAZ. In other words, it predicts total flows coming into and going out of each zone without stating the origin or the destination zone of these flows.
2. *Trip distribution* matches origin with destination flows. It links the trips generated from one zone with trips ending in another zone.
3. *Mode choice* calculates the proportion of trips between all origin and destination pairs that uses a given available transportation mode (automobile, transit, walking, cycling, etc.).
4. *Route assignment* assigns trips between an origin and destination by a particular mode to a route using the respective modal network. Route assignment can be static or dynamic depending on the complexity of the model being used. Dynamic traffic assignment uses

finer increments of time (minutes instead of hours, e.g., during rush hour) and more explicitly models vehicle behaviour.

The main results of the four-step process are as follows: predicted traffic flows by mode between different zones of the urban system (origin-destination [OD] flows); predicted traffic flows along road segments (link flows); travel times between zones (OD travel times); travel times along links (link travel times) as well as link and OD measures of congestion. As mentioned above, congestion is measured as the difference between travel times during free-flow conditions (when there is little traffic, e.g., at night) and congested travel times (during rush hour). The model might be executed several times to evaluate different scenarios.

The four-step modelling process was developed, and is used, primarily for modelling passenger transportation. Freight transportation, however, is an increasingly important component of urban transportation demand. Yet it has been virtually ignored due to its complexity and lack of data for several decades. As a result, freight modelling represents an important direction for future research in transportation planning (Ortuzar and Willumsen, 2011).

Although the four-step model has been used extensively since its development, it suffers from a number of weaknesses that new methods are looking to overcome. Its first disadvantage is that it oversimplifies the complex processes involved in the travel decision-making and trip generation process. Since it concentrates on explaining trips between geographically aggregate TAZs, it is difficult (in some cases impossible) to model individual or household behaviour that is the basis of travel demand and that can be very complex. The four-step model is thus referred to as a trip-based model since it concentrates on modelling aggregate trips (aggregated to the level of the TAZ). With this approach, the trips made are abstracted from the people making them.

In response to this limitation, transportation planners and engineers have been working to improve this method by developing activity-based models. Activity-based modelling, a new approach currently used by several agencies, is built upon the behaviour and activities of individuals. As such, the activities of each individual as well as his or her trips (their number, their mode, etc.) are simulated as a function of individual characteristics, as well as of the transportation system itself. In addition to providing a richer and better understanding of travel behaviour, activity-based models address another weakness of traditional methods—that the traditional modelling framework cannot account for **induced demand**, i.e., extra trips that are made when new infrastructure is built.

Induced demand is composed of two elements. The first element refers to trips that are generated simply due to the presence of new infrastructure. Assuming this new infrastructure makes travel easier, some people will decide to make trips they did not make before. This part of induced demand cannot be captured easily by the regular travel demand model (McNally, 2000), but it can be captured through an activity-based approach. The second aspect of induced demand is related to households or firms attracted to locate near the new infrastructure to benefit from the higher levels of mobility or accessibility that is offered by its presence. This change in land use will lead to an increase in the number of trips as well. Such an increase also cannot be well captured through the regular four-step model; rather, it requires an integrated land-use and transport modelling approach.

Integrated transport and land-use models are models that help forecast the distribution of households and firms as a function of various factors, including the transportation system. While land-use forecasting has evolved more slowly than transport modelling, the availability of increasing amounts of geographic data and computing power has resulted in the development of various land use and integrated transport and land use models (for examples see Iacono, Levinson, and El-Geneidy, 2008).

Another major drawback of the four-step travel demand model has been the focus on modelling private automobile flows while ignoring other modes of transportation. To address this shortfall, engineers and planners in the past few decades have increasingly incorporated public transport in their models and, most recently, cycling and walking. This shift in focus is related to the rise of various arguments stating that cities cannot, and will not, manage to simply "build their way out" of congestion—a radical and new argument for the field of transportation and mobility studies (Downs, 2004).

Finally, some planners and engineers argue that instead of focusing on the construction of new infrastructure and its future impacts, transport planning should focus on travel demand management through better planning of land use.

Destinations are the Goal: Accessibility Measures

Although some people travel simply for the joy of it or to use a particular mode, reaching a desired destination is most often the goal of travel in urban areas. Accessibility, which is the ease of reaching these valued destinations (Hansen, 1959) is not easily communicated or measured as a number, which may explain why planners have continued, until recently, to concentrate on mobility issues. In spite of this difficulty, research has shown that accessibility within a region does have noticeable effects on travel behaviour and can have considerable economic impacts on home values (El-Geneidy and Levinson, 2006; Franklin and Waddell, 2003; Levinson, 1998; Manaugh and El-Geneidy, 2012). Accessibility is therefore important to consider in urban and transportation planning. Indeed, transportation systems are designed to help people and firms participate in activities distributed across space and over time. In order to discern whether this is occurring successfully or equitably, however, some type of measure is required. Accessibility is a useful concept for this, as it indicates the collective performance of the land use and transportation systems and thus determines how well that complex system serves its residents. As a result, a large number of review studies classify and evaluate accessibility measures (in the measurement

meaning of the word) according to various criteria (Baradaran and Ramjerdi, 2001; Cerdá and El-Geneidy, 2010; El-Geneidy and Levinson, 2006; Geurs, 2006; Geurs and Ritsema van Eck, 2001; Handy and Niemeier, 1997; Koenig, 1980).

Most accessibility measures are built around the same basic components. On the one hand, the activity component is a measure of the land use system, which is itself represented by the presence of destinations, such as jobs, restaurants, daycares, health-care facilities, and households. These destinations, or opportunities, can also be weighted to account for their attractiveness or competition effects in relation to each other. On the other hand, the transportation component consists of the transportation system using a particular mode of transport (e.g., car, walking, cycling). The transportation component is then quantified, for example by calculating the distance separating the origin and destination or by estimating the travel time between these two points, in congested and un-congested contexts. Congested travel times are generally obtained from travel demand models, as presented in the previous section. Many precise and theoretically sound measures of accessibility have been developed, but they are not necessarily based on readily available data; moreover, some are complex to calculate and interpret. Note that accessibility measures do *not* replace measures of mobility. Regions should work on generating both measures since they complement each other in generating a better picture of a region's land use and transportation system.

One of the most commonly used measures of accessibility is the cumulative opportunity measure, which was among the earliest to be developed and is also among the simplest to calculate and communicate (Vickerman, 1974; Wachs and Kumagai, 1973). Cumulative opportunity reflects the number of opportunities available from a predetermined point within a given travel time or travel distance, using a given mode of transport or combination of modes. For example, cumulative opportunity can be used to generate accessibility to jobs by car. To do so, the number of jobs that can be reached by car in a certain threshold of travel time, such as 30 minutes, is counted for a given area. Cumulative opportunity can also be used to generate, for instance, accessibility to restaurants by bicycle. This is done by counting the number of restaurants a person can reach from a given point by bicycle within a certain threshold of travel time. As an example of the cumulative opportunities measure, Figure 10.5 shows accessibility to jobs by public transit in a 45-minute travel time threshold for the Montreal metropolitan region. The number of jobs—and, thus, job accessibility—decreases as one moves out from the downtown area and away from the dense transportation network provided in the central city (the Metro [subway] network, in particular).

An alternative to the cumulative opportunity measure is the gravity-based opportunity measure (Hansen, 1959), which is also a commonly used measure of accessibility. In this measure, destinations are weighted according to their proximity to the point of origin. As a result, distance or travel time affects the value of a destination. An empirically determined distance or travel-time decay function for a given transportation mode can be derived based on travel surveys. The gravity-based measure of accessibility presents several advantages. First, it is more theoretically sound than the cumulative measure because it discounts opportunities according to their distance or travel time

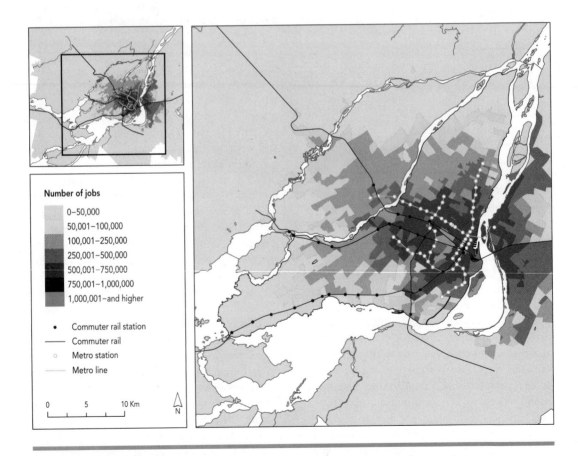

Number of jobs

- 0–50,000
- 50,001–100,000
- 100,001–250,000
- 250,001–500,000
- 500,001–750,000
- 750,001–1,000,000
- 1,000,001–and higher

- • Commuter rail station
- —— Commuter rail
- ○ Metro station
- —— Metro line

0   5   10 Km

N

Figure 10.5   **Accessibility to Jobs within 45 Minutes Travel Time by Transit, Region of Montreal**

Source: Cerdá and El-Geneidy (2010).

from an origin, rather than using an artificially determined threshold (e.g., cumulative measure includes opportunities within 30 minutes of travel time but not those requiring 31 minutes or more). Second, the gravity measure is more representative of how users perceive the transport system because it strikes a balance between the utility of a destination and the cost of travelling to it from a given origin (Miller, 2005).

The gravity measure also presents certain disadvantages compared with the cumulative measure. Although it is widely accepted in the transportation planning literature, the gravity measure is relatively complex to calculate and can be difficult to interpret and explain to the general public or to decision makers. In contrast, cumulative measures allow for easy comparison of accessibility across modes and types of destinations, thereby simplifying the interpretation of results and their discussion in public forums. Finally, cumulative opportunities, as opposed to gravity-based measures, do not rely on assumptions about the *value* of destinations to users but only assume the chosen threshold in travel time or distance. Some argue that this is a more objective approach (Geurs and Ritsema van Eck, 2001).

Walkability Scores

Accessibility can be measured at different scales (regional, sub-regional, neighbourhood, etc.) depending on the mode examined (Iacono, Krizek, and El-Geneidy, 2010). For example, one measure of local-level accessibility is the **walkability** of a given urban area (Manaugh and El-Geneidy, 2012). A walkability score represents the proximity of different amenities as well as the ease to get around as a pedestrian to reach these opportunities. There are several walkability scores generated in the transportation literature (Manaugh and El-Geneidy, 2011). A simple and easy-to-obtain measure of local accessibility is the Walk Score, obtained from walkscore.com. Walkscore.com has become a popular online source for the general public to gain insight into the walkability of an area, and is already included on property

listings on the Multiple Listing Service (MLS.ca), which is the main real estate website in Canada. The Walk Score grants a score between 0 and 100 based on the presence of nearby amenities in 13 separate categories (e.g., food, cafés, libraries, parks, cinemas, etc.). As the website itself makes clear, however, there are several limitations: for example, straight-line distances (as opposed to distances along sidewalks) are used; street design characteristics are not taken into account; and it is difficult to distinguish among types of restaurants, food stores, and retail, meaning that a convenience store is "worth" the same as a grocery store (Walk Score, 2013). Walk Score uses a simple gravity-based measure to weigh nearby locations higher than those more distant. The system's major strength is its speed: an online query takes a few seconds to complete for an inputted location. Carr, Dunzinger, and Marcus (2011) recently published research that supports the accuracy of the Walk Score algorithm, while Manaugh and El-Geneidy (2011) linked it to actual walking behaviour and found that the Walk Score explains the probability of walking in a neighbourhood just as well as other complex measures—if not better, in some cases.

Walkscore.com provides walkability scores for any address in Canada, the United States, and Australia. Figure 10.6 shows the average Walk Score by population for 15 Canadian CMAs. Since Walk Score is a location-specific value, we derived a single value for each CMA. Using the location of the city's main concert hall or opera house as the centre of every CMA, we developed 15 buffer rings around each centroid—making sure to erase water bodies and all areas falling outside the CMA boundaries. The buffer rings were situated at 1, 2, 3, 4, 5, 6, 7, 8, 9, 10, 12.5, 15, 17.5, 20, and 25 kilometres from the centroid. Within each buffer, 10 random points were generated. The Walk Score was then generated for each of these random points, resulting in a final sample of 150 Walk Score points for each CMA. The averages for each buffer ring and for each CMA were then calculated.

Toronto, Montreal, and Vancouver show average Walk Scores of 50 and above for a 25-km radius, which is relatively high. On the other hand,

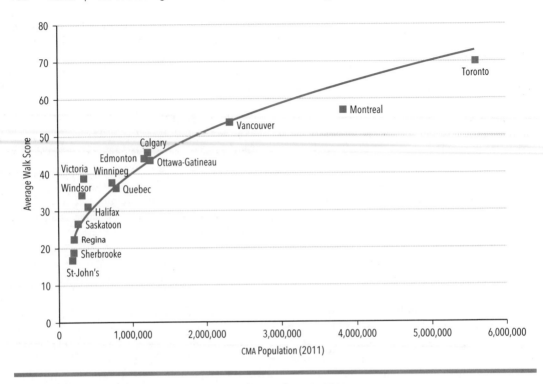

Figure 10.6   Average Walk Score in Canadian CMAs by Population in 2011

Data source: Walk Score (2013).

smaller CMAs, such as St. John's and Sherbrooke, have an average of below 20. Keep in mind that this pattern is due in part to the size of CMAs. A CMA with a small population may be small in its urban geographic extent—meaning that it does not necessarily possess a dense, walkable urban fabric for a 25-km radius around its downtown core—although it may possess this type of environment for a smaller radius.

As such, it is insightful not only to compare CMAs to each other in terms of their overall walkability but also to examine the variation of Walk Scores within each CMA. Figure 10.7 shows the Walk Score for Toronto, Montreal, and Vancouver as the distance from the centre of the CMA increases. All three cities display high walkability scores, around 90 and more, in the centre of the city as well as just a few kilometres around the core. These large CMAs are thus characterized by good accessibility by foot in their central areas. This is not surprising given

the dense street network and high concentration of amenities, including parks, businesses, restaurants, and schools, etc., in their urban cores. For Montreal and Vancouver, walkability decreases relatively quickly, down to about 50 to 60, at 10 km from the centre. However, even at further distances, such as 25 kilometres away from the centre, the walkability remains around 20, which is higher than the Walk Score average of smaller CMAs, such as St. John's. In the case of Toronto, walkability remains high even at a distance of 20 to 25 kilometres from the centre. Indeed, the Toronto CMA is a metropolitan region that spreads out over a large area as a relatively dense urban fabric. For example, Toronto has a higher walkability score than both Montreal and Vancouver in the 10- to 25-km range: Toronto's scores remain above 40, while Montreal and Vancouver show a decrease below 40. Despite having high walkability, however, total mode share for active transportation in Toronto was only around

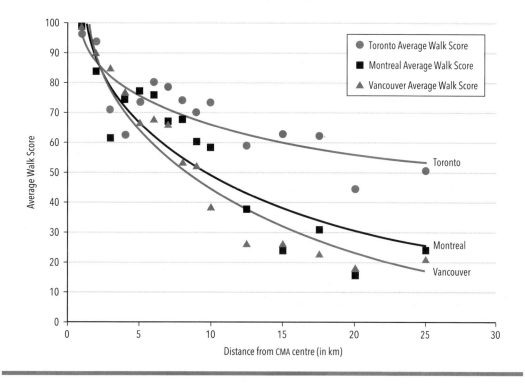

Figure 10.7   Walk Scores for the Largest Three CMAs in Canada

Data source: Walk Score (2013).

6 per cent in 2011, compared to 7 per cent and 8 per cent for Montreal and Vancouver, respectively. This indicates that factors other than the built environment come into play to determine mode share within cities. Another example is the city of Victoria, which has a high share of active transportation (16 per cent) in comparison to the average Canadian city. Although this may be partly related to the built environment and to the high average Walk Score (38.8) relative to the CMA's size, other elements may be also influencing this mode split, such as weather, culture, socio-demographic characteristics, and traveller motivations and values.

The Future of Transport in Canada

The Canadian transportation system today faces several challenges, one of the most important being the need to mitigate the environmental impacts of the transportation sector. Overall, the transportation sector contributes a large share of Canada's total CO_2 emissions. In 2010, for example, total national emissions were 701,000,000 metric tons of CO_2 equivalent, while emissions from the transportation sector amounted to 194,800,000 metric tons of CO_2, which represents about 28 per cent of total emissions (Statistics Canada, 2013b). Figure 10.8 shows rising GHG emissions per capita from private vehicle operations since the 1990s and how they have been steadily increasing over time (Statistics Canada, 2012).

Along with the realization that transportation plays a significant role in reducing GHG emissions and in mitigating climate change, a more general paradigm shift has occurred in the way planners envision transportation and in the goals they seek to achieve. City transportation plans are increasingly substituting the traditional emphasis on automobile mobility with a more progressive

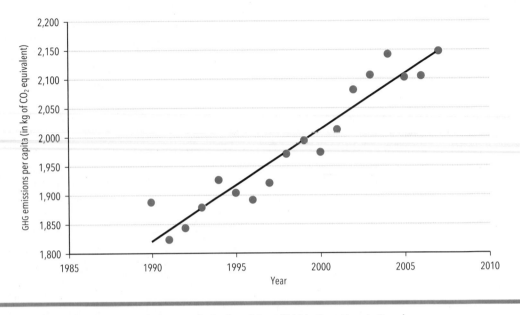

Figure 10.8   **Change in GHG Emissions per Capita from Private Vehicle Operations in Canada**

Data source: Statistics Canada (2012).

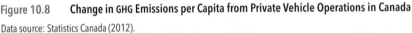

emphasis on the concept of sustainability and accessibility. Although the term *sustainability* nowadays is sometimes overused, this comprehensive concept is meant to encompass the promotion of environmental, social, cultural, and economic goals within society. Accordingly, since the end of the twentieth century transportation planners have been broadening their scope, and engaging with these issues as the founding principles of the plan-making process. By integrating the idea of the transport-land use cycle (Figure 10.1) within the plan's framework, transport plans are beginning to include goals and actions related to land use, such as accessibility. As a result, plans are increasingly moving away from acceptance or encouragement of suburban sprawl and automobile dependency, and toward density and diversity of activities and people within the urban region (Communauté métropolitaine de Montréal, 2011a; 2011b). At the same time, plans are increasingly moving toward promoting sustainable modes of transportation—especially public transit, walking, and cycling (Boston Regional Metropolitan Planning

Organization, 2009; Chicago Metropolitan Agency for Planning, 2008; City of Montreal, 2008; Metrolinx, 2008; Metropolitan Transportation Commission, 2005; SANDAG, 2007).

Examining the most recent transport plans of Canada's five largest urban regions helps us to understand the features and significance of this paradigm shift in transportation planning. The most striking pattern is the attention paid to the environmental component of the sustainability concept. Reducing GHG emissions has become a goal toward which different levels of government are seeking to contribute, including local governments (Kousky and Schneider, 2003). Considering that transportation accounts for such a significant portion of GHG emissions, and that it is a sector on which municipal and regional governments can exert a direct influence, city transport plans are one of the most important places where environmental change can be affected (Dodman, 2009). For example, the 2008 transport plan for the Vancouver metropolitan region (Translink, 2008) includes a section on climate change and highlights the fact that, within the GHG inventory of the Metro Vancouver area, 35 per cent of emissions are generated from cars and light and heavy trucks. The plan also shows the variation of GHG emissions by mode, arguing that decreasing private automobile use and increasing the use of cleaner modes will help reduce GHG emissions, and thus help mitigate climate change. Several municipalities around the world and in North America are currently adopting aggressive policies to promote the use of electric vehicles, which could partially solve the problems of GHG emissions from vehicles. However, such policies also introduce new urban challenges, such as the installation and location of charging stations or finding clean sources of electricity.

The second most noticeable trend of the recent paradigm shift in transport planning is the prioritization of public transit and active forms of transportation. In Canada's five largest cities, promoting these modes of transport is central to the goals and policies outlined in the plans. For example, the Montreal Transport Plan's (City of Montreal, 2008) main goal is to reduce automobile dependency through massive investment in public and active transportation. The plan even suggests implementing a "Pedestrian Charter" as an explicit way of increasing pedestrian safety, comfort, ease, and satisfaction around the city. Pedestrian charters are documents issued by governments giving particular rights to pedestrians, such as the Toronto pedestrian charter that "upholds the right of pedestrians of all ages and abilities to safe, convenient, direct and comfortable walking conditions" (City of Toronto, 2002: 1). Further actions are also suggested to encourage similar conditions for cyclists around Montreal. Other documents, such as the 2008 Transport Plan of Ottawa (City of Ottawa, 2008) and the 2009 Transport Plan of Calgary (City of Calgary, 2009) emphasize public investment in, and increased uptake of, public transit as well as walking and cycling. In both plans, these themes are recurrent in the stated visions and goals, as well as in concrete policy suggestions.

The 2031 transport plan for the Greater Toronto Hamilton Area (GTHA), The Big Move (Metrolinx, 2008), is another striking example of the current shift occurring in transport planning. The Big Move is a bold plan organized around the belief that transportation within the GTHA must be transformed. The plan places the priority first on public transit, second on active transportation, and only third on the efficiency of the road and highway network. Figure 10.9 shows two maps visualizing the accessibility to jobs in the Greater Toronto Hamilton Area before and after the complete implementation of The Big Move plan in the year 2031. Were the plan to be successfully implemented, workers would be positively affected, as job accessibility by transit would increase across the area. This map demonstrates the unmistakable relationship between transportation networks, accessibility, and quality of life of the city's population.

Taken together, Canadian cities seem to be embracing the shift away from the mobility-fixated approach to transportation planning and toward a comprehensive framework of sustainable accessibility. Although the automobile remains the most common mode of transport in Canadian cities, there is a growing awareness of the need for public transit and active modes. Planners and city officials are increasingly aware of the powerful impact that transportation can have on the environment, and are taking this into account in the policies put forward and the prioritization given to reducing emissions and encouraging public transit, walking, and cycling as privileged modes of transportation in the city. In addition, several of the transport plans mentioned earlier are beginning to make explicit connections between land use and transportation systems. This is essential given that the concept of sustainability combines the promotion of environmental, economic, cultural, and also social equity goals.

This last notion, social equity, refers to the distribution of benefits from transportation projects across different segments of society. Indeed, the responses of the population toward new transportation policies vary among different socio-economic groups. The idea of developing a policy that will meet all of the population's needs is no longer valid, as some groups will react differently toward certain policies based on their

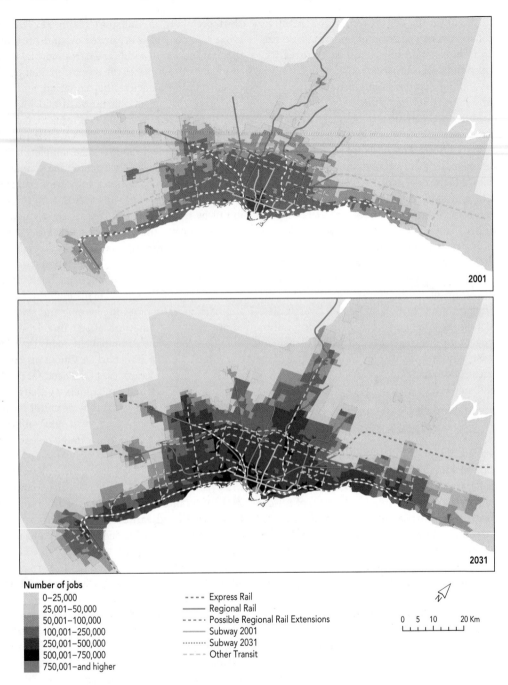

Number of jobs
- 0–25,000
- 25,001–50,000
- 50,001–100,000
- 100,001–250,000
- 250,001–500,000
- 500,001–750,000
- 750,001–and higher

- - - - Express Rail
──── Regional Rail
- - - - Possible Regional Rail Extensions
──── Subway 2001
·········· Subway 2031
- - - Other Transit

0   5   10   20 Km

Figure 10.9   Accessibility to Jobs by Fastest Transit–Based on Theoretical Project Implementations of the 2031 Regional Transportation Plan

Source: Manaugh, K, N. Foth, D. Willis and A. El-Geneidy. 2012. *Greater Toronto Destination Access: Past and Future Land Use and Transport Interaction in the GTHA*. Toronto: Metrolinx.

needs and cultures. For example, people living in socially disadvantaged neighbourhoods that have low walkability will walk more to destinations based on necessity compared to people from affluent neighbourhoods living in areas with the same low walkability (Manaugh and El-Geneidy, 2011). Another example can be seen in the policies adopted to encourage cycling in a region. Each policy implemented, such as increasing the number of bicycle lanes or removing the snow during the winter season, will have different impacts on different kinds of cyclists and how often they choose to cycle (Damant-Sirois, Grimsrud and El-Geneidy, 2014). Moreover, the effects of transportation projects are felt over long periods of time, and there is increasing evidence that they can alter the composition of surrounding populations and to whom benefits accrue over time (Grube-Cavers and Patterson, Forthcoming). Therefore, increased focus on accessibility and its relationship to transportation is one important means of addressing not only the environmental impacts of transportation, but also social equity goals in the city.

Conclusion

As concerns over climate change, air pollution, and dependency on oil sharpen, it is increasingly evident that the future lies in alternative modes of transportation rather than the private motorized vehicle, which has characterized and deeply shaped North American cities since World War II. Such alternative modes of transportation include public transport and active modes (cycling and walking). Car sharing and bicycle sharing have also become more prominent in discussions of alternatives to the private automobile. Successfully promoting these modes will require major changes in the built environment (e.g., higher density and mixed-use neighbourhoods), in people's behaviour, as well as in the approaches and priorities adopted on a political and economic level.

A first positive step toward achieving this goal is the paradigm shift that has been occurring in transport planning in the last decade—from mobility-focused planning, which consisted chiefly of car-oriented emphasis on mobility issues and concerns over how to travel in the fastest and most efficient way possible, to accessibility-focused planning, which is directed instead at the ease with which people can reach desired opportunities, where they can participate in the full spectrum of urban life and activities (see Walker and Gunn, Chapter 18).

Inspired by other cities around the world, and based on sound and innovative policies, Canadian cities must carry on toward progressive and sustainable transportation, while acknowledging the important role that the automobile is likely to play in urban transportation in the future, especially with the introduction of electric cars. In order to promote public transit, walking, and cycling, as well as the achievement of other environmental and social goals, however, action must be taken at different governmental levels. At the same time, public investment in infrastructure and facilities is necessary, but insufficient, to actually alter people's behaviour. For example, the early adoption of a given mode of transportation tends to stay with people as they age, as long as constraints related to their life-cycle changes do not vary significantly (Grimsrud and El-Geneidy, 2014). Thus, action should also be taken at other levels, such as through education and awareness or progressive change in political priorities within regional and municipal governments. However, the ideals of sustainable transportation and planning are not shared by all members of Canadian society, as demonstrated by recent and vocal calls by some people and politicians to stop "waging war" on the automobile. Often policies in favour of sustainable transportation and planning are viewed as being anti-suburban and as such are resisted in suburban locales. If sustainable transportation is to be successful in the future, such political divisions will need to be taken into consideration and efforts made to ensure that more citizens support it.

Acknowledgments

The authors would like to thank Emory Shaw for his help in conducting the literature review for the section titled "History of Transport Systems and City Structure in Canada," and Professor Craig Townsend of Concordia University for his suggestions on appropriate sources for this section. Also we would like to thank Ana Tepavac for her help in collecting some of the data used in generating the figures.

Review Questions

1. What are the different methods used in travel demand modelling?
2. What are the differences between mobility and accessibility, and what are the implications of these differences on transport planning?
3. What are the new transportation planning tendencies inspired by the sustainability movement?

Notes

1. For the 2011 Canadian Census, the obligatory "long form" of the census, in which the question on transport mode to work has traditionally been asked, was replaced with the National Household Survey (NHS). Since it was not obligatory to answer the NHS, it is unclear to what degree the 2011 figures are comparable with previous censuses.
2. Congestion levels here are defined as "the increase in overall travel times compared to a free flow situation in minutes. For example, a congestion level of 12% corresponds to 12% longer travel times compared to a free flow situation" (TomTom, 2013). *Free flow* here refers to times of the day in which there is little or no traffic, such as at night.

References

Alexander, C., S. Ishikawa, M. Silverstein, M. Jacobson, I. Fisksdahl-King, and S. Angel. 1977. *A Pattern Language: Towns, Buildings, Construction*. New York: Oxford University Press.

Artibise, A. 1977. *Winnipeg: An Illustrated History*. Toronto: James Lorimer & Company.

Baradaran, S., and F. Ramjerdi. 2001. "Performance of accessibility measures in Europe," *Journal of Transportation Statistics* 4 (2/3): 31–48.

Boston Regional Metropolitan Planning Organization. 2009. *Journey to 2040*. Boston, MA: BRMPO.

Carr, L., S. Dunsiger, and B. Marcus. 2011. "Validation of walk score for estimating access to walkable amenities," *British Journal of Sports Medicine* 45: 1144–8.

Cerdá, A., and A. El-Geneidy. 2010. *Mesures d'accessibilité: Mesures de performance pour la planification de l'utilisation du sol et du transport dans la région métropolitaine de Montréal*. Montréal: Ministère des Transports du Québec.

Chicago Metropolitan Agency for Planning. 2008. *Updated 2030 Regional Transportation Plan for Northeastern Illinois*. Chicago, IL: CMAP.

City of Calgary. 2009. *Calgary Transportation Plan*. Calgary, AB: The City of Calgary.

City of Montreal. 2008. *Plan de Transport*. Montreal: City of Montreal.

City of Ottawa. 2008. *Transportation Master Plan*. Ottawa, ON: City of Ottawa.

City of Toronto. 2002. Toronto Pedestrian Charter. At: www1.toronto.ca/city_of_toronto/transportation_services/walking/files/pdf/charter.pdf

Communauté métropolitaine de Montréal. 2011a. *Guide d'aménagement pour les aires de TOD*. Montreal : CMM. At: http://pmad.ca/fileadmin/user_upload/pmad2011/documentation/20111004_guideAiresTOD.pdf

——. (2011b). *Plan métropolitain d'aménagement et de développement*. Montréal: CMM. At: http://pmad.ca/fileadmin/user_upload/pmad2011/documentation/20111208_pmad.pdf

Damant-Sirois, G., M. Grimsrud, and A. El-Geneidy. 2014. "What's your type: A multidimensional cyclist typology." Paper presented at the 93rd Annual Meeting of the Transportation Research Board, Washington, DC.

Dodman, D. 2009. "Blaming cities for climate change? An analysis of urban greenhouse gas emissions inventories," *Environment and Urbanization* 21: 185–201.

Downs, A. 2004. *Still Stuck in Traffic*. Washington, DC: Brookins Institution.

El-Geneidy, A., and D. Levinson. 2006. *Access to Destinations: Development of Accessibility Measures*. Minnesota, MN: Minnesota Department of Transportation.

European Commission. 2008. *Eurostat Statistics Database*.

Franklin, J., and P. Waddell. 2003. "A hedonic regression of home prices in King County, Washington using activity-specific accessibility measures." Paper presented at the Transportation Research Board 82nd Annual Meeting, Washington, DC.

Geurs, K. 2006. *Accessibility, Land-use and Transport: Accessibility Evaluations of Land-use and Transport Developments and Policy Strategies*. Utrecht: Utrecht University.

——, and J. Ritsema van Eck. 2001. "Accessibility measures: Review and applications. Evaluation of accessibility impacts of land-use transport scenarios, and related social and economic impacts," in RIVM, ed., *Report*.

Bilthoven, Holland: National Institute of Public Health and the Environment.

Giuliano, G. 2004. "Land use impacts of transportation investments: Highway and transit," in S. Hanson and G. Giuliano, eds., *The Geography of Urban Transportation*, 3rd edn. New York: The Guilford Press.

Grimsrud, M., and A. El-Geneidy. 2014. "Transit to eternal youth: Lifecycle and generational trends in Greater Montreal public transport mode share," *Transportation* 41: 1–19.

Grube-Cavers, A., and Z. Patterson. Forthcoming. "Urban rapid rail transit and gentrification in Canadian urban centres—A survival analysis approach," *Urban Studies*.

Handy, S. 1994. "Highway blues: Nothing a little accessibility can't cure," *Access* 5: 3–7.

———. 2002. "Accessibility- vs mobility-enhancing strategies for addressing automobile dependence in the US." Paper presented at the European Conference of Ministers of Transport, Tokyo, Japan.

———, and D. Niemeier. 1997. "Measuring accessibility: An exploration of issues and alternatives," *Environment and Planning A* 29: 1175–94.

Hansen, W. 1959. "How accessibility shapes land use," *Journal of the American Institute of Planners* 25 (2): 73–6.

Iacono, M., K. Krizek, and A. El-Geneidy. 2010. "Measuring non-motorized accessibility: Issues, alternatives, and execution," *Journal of Transport Geography* 18: 133–40.

———, D. Levinson, and A. El-Geneidy. 2008. "Models of transportation and land use change: A guide to the territory," *Journal of Planning Literature* 22 : 323–40.

INSEE. 2008. Enquête Nationale Transports et Déplacements 2007–2008 (ENTD). Paris : INSEE.

Koenig, J. 1980. "Indicators of urban accessibility: Theory and application," *Transportation* 9: 145–72.

Kousky, C., and C. Schneider. 2003. "Global climate policy: Will cities lead the way?" *Climate Policy* 3: 359–72.

Levinson, D. 1998. "Accessibility and the journey to work," *Journal of Transport Geography* 6: 11–21.

Manaugh, K., and A. El-Geneidy. 2011. "Validating walkability indices: How do different households respond to the walkability of their neighbourhood?" *Transportation Research Part D: Transport and Environment* 16: 309–15.

———, and A. El-Geneidy. 2012. "What makes travel 'local': Defining and understanding local travel behavior," *Journal of Transport and Land Use* 5: 15–27.

———, N. Foth, D. Willis, and A. El-Geneidy. 2012. *Greater Toronto Destination Access: Past and Future Land Use and Transport Interaction in the GTHA*. Toronto: Metrolinx.

McNally, M. 2000. "The activity-based approach," in D.A. Hensher and K.J. Button, eds., *Handbook of Transport Modelling*. New York: Elsevier.

Metrolinx. 2008. *The Big Move*. Toronto: Metrolinx.

Metropolitan Transportation Commission. 2005. *Mobility for the Next Generation: Transportation 2030 Plan for the San Fransisco Bay Area*. Oakland, CA: MTC.

Meyer, M., and M. Miller. 2000. *Urban Transportation Planning*. Toronto: McGraw-Hill.

Miller, E. 2005. "An integrated framework for modelling short- and long-run household decision-making," in H.J.P. Timmermans, ed., *Progress in Activity-based Analysis*. Amsterdam: Elsevier.

Ortuzar, J., and L. Willumsen. 2011. *Modelling Transport*, 4th edn. Chippenham, Wiltshire: John Wiley and Sons.

Perl, A., and J. Kenworthy. 2010. "The Canadian city at a crossroads—between 'passage' and 'place,'" in T. Bunting, P. Filion, and R. Walker, eds., *Canadian Cities in Transition: New Directions in the Twenty-First Century*, 4th edn. Don Mills, ON: Oxford University Press.

SANDAG. 2007. *San Diego Regional Transportation Plan*. San Diego, CA: SANDAG.

Shearmur, R., and N. Rantisi. 2011. "Montreal: Rising again from the same ashes," in L.S. Bourne, T. Hutton, R. Shearmur, and J. Simmons, eds., *Canadian Urban Regions: Trajectories of Growth and Change*. Toronto: Oxford University Press Canada.

Statistics Canada. 1996. *Profile of Census Tracts*. Ottawa, ON: Statistics Canada.

———. 2001. *Profile of Census Tracts*. Ottawa, ON: Statistics Canada.

———. 2006. *Profile of Census Tracts*. Ottawa, ON: Statistics Canada.

———. 2012. *Greenhouse Gas Emissions Per Capita from Private Vehicle Operation, Canada*. Ottawa, ON: Statistics Canada. At: www.statcan.gc.ca/pub/16-001-m/2010012/t003-eng.htm

———. 2013a. *Commuting to Work: National Household Survey 2011*. Ottawa, ON: Statistics Canada.

———. 2013b. *National Inventory Report 1990–2011: Greenhouse Gas Sources and Sinks in Canada*. Ottawa, ON: Statistics Canada.

TomTom. 2013. *TomTom North American Congestion Index: TomTom Internation B.V.* At: www.tomtom.com/lib/doc/trafficindex/2012-0704-TomTom-Congestion-index-2012Q1namerica-km.pdf

Translink. 2008. *Transportation 2040*. Vancouver, BC: Translink.

US Census Bureau. 2010. *American Fact Finder: American Community Survey for Selected Cities*. Washington, DC: US Census Bureau.

Vickerman, R. 1974. "Accessibility, attraction and potential: A review of some concepts and their use in determining mobility," *Environment and Planning A*: 675–91.

Vuchic, V. 2005. *Urban Transit—Operations, Planning and Economics*. Hoboken, NJ: John Wiley and Sons.

Wachs, M., and T. Kumagai. 1973. "Physical accessibility as a social indicator," *Socioeconomic Planning Science* 7: 327–456.

Walk Score. 2013. *Walkscore*. At: www.walkscore.com/

Yeates, M., and B. Garner. 1980. *The North American City*. New York: Harper & Row.

The New Localism: Canadian Urban Governance in the Twenty-First Century

11

ZACK TAYLOR AND
NEIL BRADFORD

Introduction

In a way that would have been unthinkable a generation ago, some of the most vibrant debates in Canadian politics and policy now revolve around how cities ought to be governed and what place municipalities should occupy in the federal system. These debates have been driven by rapid economic, social, and environmental change. As discussed elsewhere in this volume, globalization's most important flows—of people, investment, and ideas—intersect primarily in cities, making urban centres focal points for major public policy challenges (Gertler, 2001). Urban economies are now understood to be the drivers of national prosperity, where creativity and innovation flourish (Hutton and Vinodrai, Chapter 6; Vinodrai, Chapter 5). At the same time, an opportunity gap between "haves" and "have-nots" widens in Canadian cities, with many residents struggling to find stable employment or affordable housing (Walks, Chapter 9). From a sustainability perspective, rapid population growth and sprawling development in the largest city-regions intensifies stress on the natural environment. As challenges of national consequence increasingly play out at the urban scale, durable solutions must be built from the bottom-up, with the participation of multiple voices. Good urban governance matters more than ever.

This chapter takes stock of debates and practices about urban governance in Canada, situating them in a twenty-first-century policy context.

Recognizing the complexity of today's urban policy dynamics and governance relations, our discussion moves across different levels of analysis and action. We explore shifts in local governance while also offering a macro-level view of various provincial and federal "New Deals" for cities. Linking these perspectives suggests that today's policy challenges require concerted action by Canadian governments and civic leaders at all levels—an approach we characterize as the "New Localism." In this spirit, the chapter begins with the ideas animating the New Localism and closes with an assessment of its prospects in Canada. Throughout we ask whether and how Canadian local governments are positioned for growing policy responsibility and governance innovation. Our narrative speaks directly to this volume's overarching theme of transition. We conclude that Canadian cities remain constrained by a historical legacy of legal and fiscal dependence on upper-level governments, yet governments and civic leaders are experimenting with various forms of local collaboration and municipal empowerment, often with promising results. The result may be a fruitful balance between local autonomy and national standards.

The New Localism: Placing Cities on the Public Policy Agenda

Traditionally, national and provincial/state governments developed uniform, "one-size-fits-all" policies that applied equally across their territories. Since the 1990s, however, a different approach—the New Localism—has emerged. The New Localism recognizes that particular geographic spaces and community contexts generate distinct policy problems that, in turn, require place-specific approaches (Dreier, Mollenkopf, and Swanstrom, 2004; Goetz and Clarke, 1993; Rodríguez-Pose, 2008; Sellers, 2002; Stoker, 2004). This approach builds on research demonstrating that today's most significant policy challenges are especially complex—interconnected in their causes and localized in their expressions—and therefore not solved unilaterally by any single government or non-governmental actor. Rather, they require joint effort whereby national and provincial governments align their policy resources with the local knowledge and networks of municipal officials, community organizations, and neighbourhood residents. The result is **place-based public policy**—collaborative, **multi-level governance** arrangements that advance national economic, social, and environmental goals through local collective action (Chisholm, 2011).

On this basis, urban scholars and think tanks have helped reorient the way policy-makers think about poverty reduction, economic growth, and environmental protection. Poverty is now seen through a wider lens of social exclusion shaped by an array of contextual factors, not only a lack of income support for individuals and households. New social risks, such as long-term unemployment, inadequate shelter, racial discrimination, and lone parenting, concentrate spatially to produce inter-generational distress in certain neighbourhoods. A social investment perspective calls for targeted, community-driven strategies to address root causes and assemble the optimal mix of services (Stone, 2011).

In parallel, a new generation of economic geographers finds that national prosperity is driven by local and regional innovation systems that link producers, suppliers, and customers (Cooke and Morgan, 1998). More than low taxes and cheap land, business productivity depends on geographically proximate firms, technology researchers, educational institutes, and venture capitalists pooling their resources to solve sector-wide problems, such as inadequate public infrastructure, skilled labour shortages, and insufficient access to finance capital.

Finally, research and policy-making on environmental sustainability increasingly focuses on the city-region as a whole, a scale where "some of the most creative and important" efforts "to integrate environmental, economic, and social concerns under the general banner of sustainability" now find expression (Portney, 2003: vii). There has been a revival of thinking about integrated regional planning as a means of preserving scarce farmland and fragile ecosystems, combatting climate change, increasing the efficiency of public infrastructure investments, reducing the economic costs of traffic congestion, and promoting social equity (Barnett, 2001; Calthorpe and Fulton, 2001; Seltzer and Carbonell, 2011).

These scholarly perspectives on how cities matter to national and individual well-being have been welcomed by think tanks and research networks close to governments (Bradford, 2009). For example, the Organisation for Economic Co-operation and Development (OECD) runs an ambitious local research program based on its recognition that "central government policies rely on dynamic communities in which business, public authorities and civic society can establish new partnerships and follow approaches adapted to their circumstances" (Johnston, 1998: 4). In the American context, the Brookings Institution now celebrates a "metro revolution" where local coalitions that were set up to solve urban problems thrive below and beyond the partisan gridlock and ideological posturing of national politics (Katz and Bradley, 2013). As well, the European Union promotes locally driven approaches to national policy by "tackling persistent underutilization of potential and reducing persistent social exclusion in specific places through external intervention and multilevel governance" (Barca, 2009: vii).

Canada has been viewed as slow to embrace the teachings of the New Localism (Horak and Young, 2012; Leo, 2006). In its 2002 country review, the OECD described "a failure to draw up an integrated urban policy" (OECD, 2002: 159) while a followup Canadian report to the prime minister concluded that Canada "lags competitors in understanding how the geographies arising from current economic and social changes shape our capacity to achieve our ambitious aims for the future" (External Advisory Committee on Cities and Communities [EACCC], 2006: 16). Scholars have investigated Canada's "shame" in ignoring the cities (Andrew, 2001), documenting both the limited policy capacity of municipalities and the extensive federal and provincial downloading of responsibilities onto local actors without the authority or resources to deliver (Eidelman and Taylor, 2010; Horak and Young, 2012; Keil, 1998). Box 11.1 discusses the position of local government in Canada's federal system; some of the limitations faced by local governments are discussed in the text.

This is changing. Since the turn of the century, a robust discussion has emerged in Canadian policy circles regarding the most appropriate distribution of powers and resources among local, provincial, and federal governments and how governments should relate to each other and engage with the public and community organizations in order to resolve pressing social, economic, and environmental problems. Canadian think tanks, foundations, and businesses have promoted a "cities agenda." For example, the Canada West Foundation, Canadian Policy Research Networks (CPRN), and the Institute for Research on Public Policy have all highlighted the weakness of Canadian municipalities in comparison with other OECD jurisdictions, and the limitations of top-down policy-making. A TD Economics study reinforces this perspective: "It is becoming overwhelmingly apparent that the long-term performance of the Canadian economy and Canadian living standards will hinge on the fortune of our cities . . . *however, Canada's cities face certain threats that, if left untended, could choke off economic expansion and gains in living standards down the road*" (TD Bank, 2002a: 4 and 9, emphasis in original).

Informed by this discussion, and as we shall see in this chapter, the federal government and several provinces have experimented with different approaches, shifting responsibilities between different levels of government, restructuring legal frameworks, and forging partnerships that span multiple levels of government to bring together traditionally separate actors (see Box 11.1). However,

---

Box 11.1   Local Government in Canadian Federalism

It is often said that municipalities are "creatures of the provinces." Under the Canadian constitution, local governments fall under provincial jurisdiction and derive all of their authority from provincial law. Provincial governments may create, dissolve, amalgamate, and alter the powers of local governments unilaterally, without consulting with local residents. After World War II, provincial governments responded to social and economic change and rapid urban growth by actively regulating what local governments could and could not do, mandating particular activities and functions, and reorganizing municipal boundaries. Municipalities and school boards effectively became administrative extensions of provincial governments, reflecting their policy priorities. As we discuss in this chapter, some provinces have in recent years moved to increase municipal autonomy; however, overall, local policymakers remain constrained in their ability to experiment and innovate. Provincial control means that the federal government has played only an indirect, yet crucial, role in urban areas through taxation, employment, and social welfare policies, the regulation and funding of major transportation infrastructure, and control over immigration.

For more information on provincial intervention in municipal affairs, both historically and today, see Crawford (1940), Sancton (2006), and Taylor (2014). To learn about provincially imposed municipal amalgamations in the 1990s and 2000s, see Sancton (2000), Garcea and LeSage (2005), and Boudreau (2000).

several questions remain unresolved: While many agree that "one size does not fit all," what might place-based policy-making actually look like in Canada's federal system? What role should non-governmental community stakeholders play in policy development and delivery? More generally, is the most appropriate response to contemporary challenges to increase the autonomy of cities to chart their own destiny in the global order, as some have advocated (Broadbent, 2008; Courchene, 2006)? Or is it to fully embrace tri-level intergovernmental collaboration—among the local, provincial, and federal levels—in pursuit of more integrated policy-making (Bradford, 2005; Stein, 2006)? Is there a viable middle ground between these ideal types?

The following sections take up these questions. We begin from the vantage point of local government and then move on to the perspective of the provincial and federal governments.

New Localism from Below: Re-Evaluating Local Government

Local governments have long been viewed as the constitutional orphans and policy afterthoughts of Canadian politics, highly constrained by provincial legal frameworks and fiscal arrangements and excluded from policy debates at other levels. From the Great Depression in the 1930s to the end of the millennium, provincial governments expanded their use of municipalities as vehicles for the delivery of provincial programs, unilaterally reorganizing municipal boundaries, "uploading" and "downloading" responsibilities and resources, and changing rules and regulations as they saw fit. Local autonomy was subordinated to provincial and, in the case of housing, federal standards and conditions.

In the 1980s and 1990s, the same top-down logic was applied as provinces rolled back the welfare state as a means of reducing chronic budget deficits. Marketed as a fiscally neutral effort to rationalize public services, the net effect of provincial–municipal "disentanglement" was to increase local responsibilities while reducing local fiscal resources (Slack, 2006). Figure 11.1

shows that municipal spending per capita has increased since disentanglement, even when inflation and population growth are taken into account. While per-capita intergovernmental transfers to municipalities increased during the recession of the early 1990s, they decreased in the period of provincial and federal retrenchment that followed. Own-source revenues (those raised by municipalities themselves) increased to compensate. Since about 2004, transfers have risen again but not by as much as total expenditure. The result: compared to the late 1980s, municipalities rely more on money they raise themselves than they do on transfer payments from upper-level governments.

In Ontario, Quebec, and Nova Scotia, disentanglement was accompanied by the imposition of municipal amalgamations. Justified on the basis that bigger government would be cheaper and more efficient (a claim that has not been borne out), these consolidations mobilized both local governments and citizens protesting violation of democratic rights and local identities (Sancton, 2000).

It is in the aftermath of these changes that the New Localism has taken root. Provincial disengagement, coupled with civic mobilization, held out the promise of greater municipal policy autonomy and subtly transformed expectations of what roles Canadian municipalities could or should play in economic, social, and environmental policy-making. Serious questions remain, however, as to whether municipal institutions as presently configured can meet these expectations.

New Actors Bring New Expectations of Local Governments

It is fair to say that there is now greater public interest in local politics and policy, especially in larger cities, than there was 20 years ago. This assertion is difficult to prove—there is little evidence that voter turnout has increased (in fact, the opposite is often true) or that ordinary people are becoming more involved in municipal policy-making. Still, there is a general sense that "real" issues are at stake and that democratic decision-making at the local level is important and desirable. This is visible in the grassroots emergence across the country of

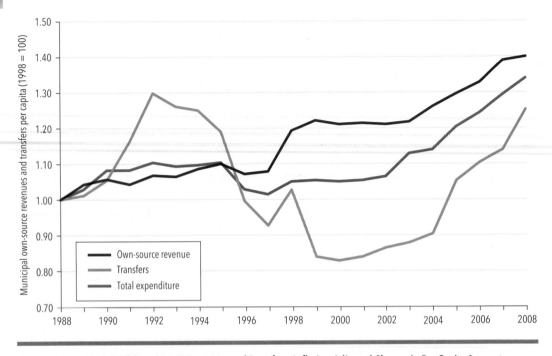

Figure 11.1   **Municipal Own-Source Revenues and Transfers, Inflation-Adjusted Change in Per Capita Amounts Relative to 1988 Levels**

Note: Unfortunately, at writing 2008 was the most recent year for which national local government financial statistics were available.

Source: Calculated from Statistics Canada, Local General Government Own-Source Revenues and Expenditures (Current Account), CANSIM Table 3850024; National Population Estimates, CANSIM Table 510001; and Consumer Price Index (2009 Basket), CANSIM Table 3260021.

new publications celebrating urban life—*Spacing* magazine being perhaps the most prominent example—which has in turn spurred the mainstream news media to expand local coverage. At least in Canada's large cities, local government is more visible, and local political information more available, than ever before. Rather than being passive "takers" of federal and provincial policies, municipalities are now seen as potentially effective policy-"makers."

At the same time, local interest groups and non-profit foundations have become increasingly active in funding policy research and advocacy. In Toronto, for example, business groups have called for new local and regional taxes to support transit expansion; the United Way and the Metcalf Foundation have promoted new public housing investment and supports for low-income residents;

the Wellesley Institute has championed urban public health issues; and the Maytree Foundation has focused on the barriers to integration faced by new immigrants. Twenty years ago, these organizations did not exist, were more nationally oriented, or were focused on traditional charitable mandates. Likewise, similar local entities are active in Calgary, Vancouver, Montreal, and other cities across the country, focusing on immigrant integration, ageing, homelessness, urban Aboriginals, and economic development (Bradford and Bramwell, 2014). In Calgary and Hamilton, business leaders have partnered with community organizations and multiple governments to mount ambitious poverty reduction strategies. In Montreal and Winnipeg, collaborations have focused on community economic development and neighbourhood **revitalization**. In high technology hubs, such as

Kitchener-Waterloo, business entrepreneurs have created partnership organizations dedicated to urban and regional economic innovation.

Local governments are perceived as key players in these new bottom-up coalitions. Whereas in the 1970s and 1980s major policy issues—such as economic growth, social equity, and immigrant integration—would have been seen as the responsibility of higher-order governments, they are increasingly seen as legitimate priorities of local governments. These new demands and expectations have challenged municipalities to pursue policy innovation and "recommit to their political role—engaging local citizens more fully, asserting themselves more forcefully, and collaborating more widely in pursuit of the local public interest" (Tindal and Tindal, 2008: 1). But to what extent have they done so? We explore this question in the next section.

Municipal Advocacy of New Intergovernmental Partnerships

Faced with a shifting policy and governance environment, Canadian municipalities have demanded more powers and resources. The call for a "New Deal for Cities" was driven by three inter-related factors:

1. A growing number of academics, journalists, and policy professionals argued that municipal governments faced growing fiscal stress. As discussed, operating expenditures had been growing faster than revenues, and transfer payments from senior governments were insufficient to fill the gap. This was exacerbated in some provinces, including Ontario, by the downloading of new responsibilities to municipalities without sufficient accompanying revenues.
2. Provincial and federal funding for capital infrastructure had shrunk at about the time that the roads, bridges, and pipes installed in the postwar boom were reaching the end of their operating life. In the 1960s, total infrastructure spending in Canada topped 6 per cent of GDP; by 2000 it had dropped below 3 per cent

(Residential and Civil Construction Alliance of Ontario [RCCAO], 2010: 14). As a result, municipalities in growing metropolitan areas found themselves with an infrastructure deficit estimated at over $100 billion, falling ever further behind on maintaining existing infrastructure systems while also having to expand them (Mirza, 2007). To overcome these constraints, municipalities needed more money, either by gaining access to new revenues or by increasing intergovernmental transfer payments.
3. Finally, evidence mounted that poverty, homelessness, and unemployment were growing in Canadian cities, especially among recent immigrants, and that deindustrialization appeared to be hollowing out the economic base of central cities and, with it, the middle class (Hulchanski and Shapcott, 2004; Lee, 2000; Lorinc, 2006; TD Bank, 2002b; 2003).

While historically municipalities would look to their provincial governments for solutions, their focus in the late 1990s was predominantly federal, and the campaign included greater autonomy and partnership. The federal focus was driven largely by money. Mounting federal budget surpluses stood in sharp contrast to deteriorating provincial finances. Only the federal government had the fiscal capacity to attack the infrastructure deficit. Moreover, the principal driver of the larger cities' policy challenges—immigration—was under federal jurisdiction. The federal government also had a political incentive to get involved: the razor-thin federalist victory in the 1995 Quebec referendum signalled the need for Ottawa to reassert its visibility and relevance through pan-Canadian policies that connected citizens, communities, and country.

Between 2000 and 2006, the Federation of Canadian Municipalities (FCM)—the national local government advocacy group—alongside Canada's large cities developed a comprehensive set of evidence-based demands for greater fiscal and legal autonomy and a seat at the federal–provincial policy table. Their demands focused on three Rs: recognition, respect, and resources (see Horak, 2008). The FCM's Big City Mayors Caucus pressed for a federal commitment to long-term predictable infrastructure funding beyond the existing application-based project-by-project model. As well, the mayors of Calgary, Montreal, Toronto, Vancouver, and Winnipeg formed the C5 group to lobby for greater federal investment in metropolitan hub cities, which, they argued, received too little of the tax revenue generated by their burgeoning economies. At the provincial level, municipalities have asked for new powers and resources and to be consulted on policy changes that affect them (Lidstone, 2004; Tindal, Tindal, Stewart, and Smith, 2013: 201–216).

The federal and provincial responses to municipal demands are discussed in greater detail in the next section. The general trend, however, is clear: people increasingly expect municipalities to do more—to be policy leaders rather than followers—and to be able to make meaningful choices on behalf of residents. Feeding these expectations and fed by them, municipal leaders have sought more authority and the resources to exercise it.

Constraints on Strategic and Creative Municipal Action

Despite advocates' optimistic discourse of empowered local government, the track record has been mixed. This is in part because the internal and external institutional frameworks and incentive structures within which municipal leaders operate work against creative local policy-making and intergovernmental partnership. Below we describe two constraints, the weakness of local political leadership, and the difficulties local politicians face in exercising their autonomy.

1. Weak and Divided Leadership

Political leadership is not merely about personality or character. As Sancton (2011: 236–40) suggests, it is also about the ability to leverage institutional and material resources. Canadian "weak mayors" lack the institutional resources available to their American "strong mayor" counterparts. The chief executive of New York or Chicago can veto council decisions, directly control the budgetary process,

hire and fire senior city staff, and direct the bureaucracy without council approval. In many large US cities, the mayor is also the local leader of a political party and can use partisan connections and control over campaign finance to exert pressure on councillors and politicians at other levels of government. The mayor of a typical Canadian city, on the other hand, has none of these powers; he or she has but one vote on council and must rely on persuasion to implement his or her vision and platform. Quebec and British Columbia are notable exceptions. In Montreal and other large Quebec cities, the mayor leads a political party and typically controls a majority of votes on council. While party cohesion is not as strong as at the federal and provincial levels, the mayor's control of election fundraising gives him or her some leverage over councillors' votes. In Vancouver and many other British Columbia cities, elections are contested by local parties and the council is elected at large. Again, this gives the mayor, as leader of the party, some measure of control over councillors. Still, even in Quebec and British Columbia, the mayor has but one vote and no veto, and the bureaucracy reports to council as a whole. Sancton (2000) argues that the weak-mayor system in Canada stacks the odds against creative policy-making. Canadian municipal institutions reward "brokers" adept at balancing competing interests and punish "entrepreneurs" who pursue policy innovation.

Is this an argument for adopting an American-style "strong mayor" system in Canadian cities, as some have advocated? In Britain, Tony Blair's 1997–2008 Labour government embraced the idea that strong mayors would increase cities' capacity for innovative and strategic policy-making. To date, there have been 48 referendums on adopting directly elected strong mayors in England and Wales; of these, 35 have been rejected by voters. Aside from London, the only cities of any size that have adopted it are Bristol and Liverpool. Britons are apparently unpersuaded of the desirability of empowering mayors and abandoning the consensual politics of coalition-building on councils. Similarly, Canadian cities are unlikely to be run by strong mayors any time soon. Recent provincial reforms (discussed next) have strengthened and increased municipal autonomy in some respects while leaving the weak-mayor system largely intact.

2. The Local Politics of Municipal Empowerment

Asking for more authority is easy; facing the political consequences of exercising it is much harder. Toronto's case is illustrative. Under new provincial legislation—the City of Toronto Act (2006), which was championed by former mayor David Miller—council gained new revenue-raising powers (see below for examples), open-ended authority to enact bylaws for the good of the city and its people, and the ability to reorganize its internal structures and create public corporations without provincial permission. At the time, this was heralded as the city's maturation as a responsible, accountable, and democratic government. City council moved to diversify its revenues away from reliance on commercial and residential property taxes by imposing two new taxes: one levied on residential property sales (the Land Transfer Tax); the other, on motor vehicle registrations. While they soon brought in hundreds of millions of dollars a year, they were unpopular. On taking office in 2010, Mayor Rob Ford cancelled the vehicle tax and pledged to eliminate the land transfer tax, effectively undoing a decade-long strategy of diversifying the city's revenue sources and dependence on the property tax. Whether this case exemplifies democratic responsiveness to unpopular taxes or the irresponsible avoidance of political costs associated with pursuing a long-term fiscal agenda depends on one's political perspective. Ultimately, local government's relative closeness to the community may inhibit its ability to make and sustain policy positions that involve short-term costs in pursuit of long-term gains.

This example and the pursuit of municipal empowerment more generally has revealed a conflict between those who embrace broader expectations of local government—we might call them the "new localists"—and the "traditionalists" who believe that local government should stick to its narrow historical role as a provider of property-related services, such as garbage collection and

local water, sewer, and transportation infrastructure (Horak, 2012: 350–1). While new localists premise their advocacy on the notion that, if appropriately empowered, municipalities can more effectively tackle major social, economic, and environmental challenges, traditionalists hold that these issues belong to other orders of government. This conflict speaks not only to expectations about local government and its interactions with community organizations and citizens, but equally to views about appropriate relations and responsibilities within Canadian federalism. Indeed, over the past decade these conflicts and questions have risen on the national political agenda as both provincial and federal governments have introduced structures and strategies to engage municipalities in wider public policy concerns.

New Localism from Above: Designing a New Deal

Toward a New Provincial–Municipal Relationship

After the rancorous provincial–municipal conflicts over amalgamations and disentanglement in the 1990s, the new political leaders who gained office at both levels in the early 2000s sought to make amends. This was driven in part by political calculation—those who had opposed unilateral provincial interventions in local affairs were attracted to opposition parties that promised respect for community identities and desires. In Quebec, the new Liberal government of Jean Charest elected in 2003 promised to undo the Parti Québécois' municipal amalgamations. In Ontario, Liberal Dalton McGuinty also promised a more constructive relationship with municipalities after his 2003 win; so too did BC premier (and former Vancouver mayor) Gordon Campbell.

In most provinces, the first decade of the 2000s saw a range of legislative changes and policy innovations consistent with municipal empowerment (Lidstone, 2004; Tindal et al., 2013: 206). Configured differently across the provinces, these changes included granting municipalities more control over their internal administrative structures, authorizing municipal action within broadly defined spheres of jurisdiction as opposed to a list of narrowly defined items, and committing to provide municipalities with the adequate resources to discharge their responsibilities. In recognition of their distinctive characteristics and problems, Toronto, Winnipeg, and Halifax have recently acquired their own city charters—special legislation pertaining only to them that grant them powers beyond those available to other municipalities. Calgary and Edmonton are now negotiating for charters of their own. The Ontario and British Columbia governments have signed agreements with municipal associations that recognize municipalities as democratic governments and establish a duty to consult them or seek their approval before making interventions that affect them; a similar agreement is under discussion in Quebec and will likely be concluded in 2014.

In sum, the provincial–municipal relationship has moved toward greater local autonomy. Provincial supremacy remains, but municipal authority and capacity have grown, especially in the largest cities.

Federal-Municipal Relations: A Seat at the Table

In comparison to provincial governments, the federal government's role in local and municipal affairs is constitutionally limited, and its engagement has been selective and episodic. The late 1960s and early 1970s saw a burst of federal interest in cities, producing a short-lived federal Ministry of State for Urban Affairs that struggled to establish a strategic focus. Overtaken by the dramatic constitutional battles of the 1980s and early 1990s, both the ministry and cities fell off the federal agenda. The federal government remained involved in selected redevelopment initiatives and pilot projects but without a policy framework.

Beginning in the early 2000s, successive federal governments embraced a cities agenda with varying degrees of enthusiasm. The project evolved gradually, in fits and starts, originating quietly within the senior bureaucracy of the Chrétien Liberal government, rapidly acquiring a public profile during the short-lived Martin Liberal government (2003–6), only to recede into the political shadows after the Harper Conservatives took power in 2006.

Ever pragmatic, Prime Minister Jean Chrétien moved cautiously, establishing a caucus task force to study urban issues and a Cities Secretariat in the Privy Council Office to review options. However, his successor Paul Martin appeared to be a more ambitious cities advocate. His abrupt departure from Cabinet in 2002 was precipitated by an address to the FCM that unveiled a New Deal for Cities and Communities. Declaring that there was "no question that the path to Canada's future runs through municipal governments large and small, urban and rural" (2003), Martin called his New Deal "a national project for our time" (2004), built through federal–local partnerships. As prime minister, Martin appointed an external advisory committee to generate a 30-year vision of Canadian progress through resilient cities and communities, and established a Ministry of State for Infrastructure and Communities to drive action along three tracks: (1) fiscal transfers to municipalities, (2) tri-level government partnerships for local interventions, and (3) pilot learning projects to strengthen federal policy knowledge of community needs and municipal capacities. The New Deal's lead minister, John Godfrey, captured the aspiration:

The New Deal is not about yielding tax room to the provinces and hoping the mayors and councils may just get lucky. What we're proposing is collaborative government and the opportunity to work together. Building Canada's cities and communities of the future requires all of us—federally, provincially and territorially, and municipally—working as equals together in what we call a collective national project. (Godfrey, 2004)

This agenda was just taking shape when the Martin Liberals were defeated in the 2006 election. The victorious Harper Conservatives avoided any talk of a cities agenda and downgraded the

Infrastructure and Communities Ministry to a branch of the Transportation Department. With a tight message about federal accountability to taxpayers, the Conservatives looked to disentangle from "messy collaborations" that intruded on provincial turf and drew Ottawa into local affairs. Subscribing to a different view of federal–local relations, Prime Minister Harper (2006) regretted that "Ottawa has stuck its nose into provincial and local matters." His "open federalism" harkened back to classical conceptions of federal and provincial areas of jurisdiction as watertight compartments:

> Of course in a perfectly balanced federation, the different levels of government wouldn't be constantly haggling with each other over taxpayers' money. Each of us would have clearly defined responsibilities, and the resources to meet them. I hope you would still invite me to your conferences, but we would have something to talk about other than funding deals, transfer payments and fiscal imbalance. This discussion is however a direct consequence of the situation that developed over the past decade. (Harper, 2006)

Despite the shift in political winds and policy rhetoric, however, the New Deal did not disappear in 2006, as we will examine next.

Innovation in Multi-Level Urban Governance

The Conservative victory spelled the end of federal leadership and political aspiration to a pan-Canadian urban policy framework. At the programmatic level, however, work on several prominent initiatives continued. Next, we highlight three examples: (1) the Gas Tax Fund, (2) Local Immigration Partnership Councils, and (3) the National Homelessness Initiative. Each is a collaboration initiated by the federal government through its spending power, implemented with provincial agreement, and directed by local stakeholders, including municipalities. Consistent with the place-based policy principles of the New Localism, each features a governance mechanism tailored to the particular policy challenge and specific local setting.

1. Hybrid Fiscal Transfer: The Gas Tax Fund

By the turn of the millenium, municipalities faced an estimated $123 billion infrastructure deficit, a large portion of it related to transportation. To fund it, municipalities asked for a share of federal and provincial taxes on fuels and gasoline. Redistribution of the federal gas tax, which generated $4 billion annually in the large city-regions, became a priority for Prime Minister Martin. Certain principles structured federal thinking: the need to provide a long-term and stable revenue stream for municipalities, to ensure that the federal transfer was a net benefit and not clawed back through provincial withdrawal, and to promote national goals on environmental sustainability while respecting local infrastructure priorities in both large cities and smaller centres (Adams, 2012).

Within these parameters, the Martin government had completed five-year Gas Tax Transfer Agreements (GTTAs) with all 13 provinces and territories by 2006. Over the five-year period covered by the original GTTAs, $5 billion—about half of the federal gas tax revenue collected—was transferred to municipalities to support locally planned investments in transportation, water, and sewers. Federal funds were allocated on a per-capita basis to the provinces and territories, which then disbursed funds to municipalities. In return, the municipalities or their representative associations submitted annual reports detailing how local plans and projects contributed to the federal policy goals of cleaner air and water, and reduction of greenhouse gas emissions. Progress was measured through an Integrated Community Sustainability Plan (ICSP) developed by each municipality "that reflected and integrated social, cultural, environmental and economic sustainability objectives in community planning" (Infrastructure Canada, 2005). The federal approach responded to local differences: capacity-building support was available to all municipalities, and where robust land use planning frameworks already existed, these could meet the ICSP requirement.

The GTTAs combined the features of a conditional transfer arrangement—whereby local governments must comply with conditions established by the upper-level government—with the project flexibility and planning support associated with more open-ended grants (Adams, 2012). Further, the agreements allowed for local discretion over how funds would be disbursed. Instead of a "one size fits all" approach, Ottawa recognized that there were different intermediaries across the provinces that could take a lead role. In Ontario, the transfer was managed by two partners, the City of Toronto and the Association of Municipalities of Ontario (AMO). In British Columbia, the Union of British Columbia Municipalities stepped forward based on demonstrated administrative and representational capacity. In Quebec, a municipal association with experience in infrastructure delivery was identified. In other cases, the provincial and territorial governments assumed direct responsibility. Across the country, the GTTA spending has been driven by local priorities. Large cities tended to use the funds for public transit, investing in buses and subways, whereas in smaller municipalities the emphasis was more on roads and bridges.

Assessments of the GTTAs have been positive (Adams, 2012). Municipal officials prefer it to traditional government infrastructure programs that require time-consuming project-by-project applications and view it as foundation for long-term national infrastructure planning. In its evaluation, the OECD concluded that the GTAA "constitutes an excellent example of an inter-governmental agreement that utilizes contractual design to optimize the effectiveness of the relationship between all levels of government" (OECD, 2007: 192). In 2007, the Harper Conservatives extended the transfer for another five years at $2 billion per year and in 2008 announced that the GTTA would become permanent.

2. Framework Agreement: Ontario's Local Immigration Partnership Councils (LIPs)

In recent years, Canada's immigrant settlement sector has experienced intense pressure (Bradford and Andrew, 2011). Global economic change, the

increasing ethno-racial diversity of newcomers, and fraying community supports have made the journey difficult (see Kobayashi and Preston, Chapter 8). Specific obstacles include service fragmentation and program gaps; inadequate links between services targeted to newcomers and "mainstream services" in health, education, and the labour market; and lack of awareness of the contributions of newcomers to their "host communities." In turn, urban researchers have shown how these gaps play out in locally specific ways across cities and within neighbourhoods (Good, 2009; Omidvar and Richmond, 2003).

Against this backdrop, the federal Department of Citizenship and Immigration Canada (CIC) in 2005 approached its Ontario government counterpart and concluded the first Canada-Ontario Immigration Agreement (COIA) to enhance services through community-based planning around the needs of newcomers. While the Martin government negotiated the agreement, it fell to the Harper Conservatives to implement and the COIA and it initially appeared to languish. However, the immigration file became a political priority for the Conservatives as they saw the newcomer vote as critical to their quest for a majority government. In 2008, CIC put out a call for "Local Immigration Partnership Councils" (LIPs) in cities and communities across Ontario. Under the terms of a federal–provincial framework agreement, LIPs receive federal funding if three criteria are met. First, there must be multi-sectoral representation that includes local government, settlement agencies, mainstream community organizations, and employers. Second, a strategic plan must identify concrete steps for better access to and coordination of immigrant services in education, health, employment, and housing sectors. Third, an implementation plan must include progress measures and transition strategies for the partnership beyond the three-year pilot stage.

The LIPs call for proposals was a success (Burr, 2011). Within three years, nearly 50 councils were established, including 15 councils in the Greater Toronto Area (GTA). Their leadership structures bridged the municipal and community sectors in locally sensitive ways, enabling different council chairing or co-chairing relationships to emerge organically (Burstein, Victoria, Lacassagne, and Nadeau, 2012). In larger cities with robust immigrant settlement networks, service providers often led, while in mid-sized cities, municipalities came forward, sometimes in partnership with mainstream organizations such as the United Way or the local economic development corporation. Importantly, the planning priorities were encouraged to vary by place—in more remote communities, immigrant attraction drove the process; in mid-sized cities, challenges of service enhancement and immigrant retention prevailed; and in the GTA, with multiple agencies in play, the priority was service integration for better immigrant settlement. The LIPs give creative expression to Ontario's varied immigration policy geography, drawing on the tacit knowledge held by frontline service providers and newcomers themselves for relevant and timely programming. For example, in London, Ontario, a city that has traditionally lagged in immigrant recruitment, the LIP forged a multi-pronged strategy that is implemented through six policy sub-councils and that draws on the research expertise of Western University.

In its recommendations to Cabinet, the Parliamentary Standing Committee on Citizenship and Immigration remarked that the "LIPs have great potential" as they "bring together diverse parties who might not otherwise collaborate on immigrant settlement initiatives" (Standing Committee on Citizenship and Immigration, 2010). In response, the federal government declared "the principles of the LIPs are in line with government priorities ... to support communities in their efforts to tackle local challenges by involving various players to partner on new approaches to address regional challenges that bring together communities across Canada" (Government of Canada, 2010).

3. Governance Partnership:
National Homelessness Initiative
Beginning in the early 1990s, homelessness became more visible in Canadian cities. Federal and provincial withdrawal from social housing,

coinciding with economic restructuring that hit urban industrial economies (See Walks, Chapter 9), left many municipal governments scrambling to provide shelter for growing numbers of residents. Research documented the scope of the problem while mayors pressed the federal government to organize a national response. In 1997, the federal government announced that it would work "with all its partners in all sectors to address the root causes of homelessness and help communities respond to their members' needs for shelter and other support" (Smith, 2004: 3). Following two years of provincial and local consultations, the $753 million National Homelessness Initiative (NHI) was launched in December 1999 at a youth shelter in Toronto, with the mayor of Toronto calling the federal minister Santa Claus.

The NHI was a multi-pronged, three-year initiative. Its cornerstone was a $305 million Supporting Communities Partnership Initiative (SCPI) that targeted areas with severe problems and provided funding for municipal and community partnerships to implement local solutions. The Liberal government renewed the initiative in 2003, and in 2008 the Harper Conservatives renamed it the Homelessness Partnering Strategy (HPS), allocating $1.9 billion over five years. In its 2013 budget, the government signed off on a further five years. While not a national affordable housing program, the successive initiatives amount to a 20-year federal–municipal partnership in providing shelter for the homeless and in planning more permanent solutions.

The initiative is geographically targeted to Canada's urban pressure points: 61 communities have been designated through a needs-based formula, and among them 10 major cities have consistently received about 80 per cent of the funding. In addition, two smaller funding streams are available for remote communities and First Nations. Governance arrangements are flexible, responding to local capacities. A community entity model delegates program authority to a local body (the municipal government or a voluntary organization). In major cities that have sophisticated social planning and service delivery networks, municipal governments have used existing plans as the basis for federal funds. In places without such planning capacity, a shared delivery model is employed whereby a local federal government office leads in consultation with the municipal and community actors.

Framing the choice of governance model are three common federal parameters: (1) production of a 10-year Community Plan with clear targets, (2) identification of a continuum of supports necessary to move individuals from the streets to shelter, and (3) strategies to engage other levels of government and the private sector. In addition, a voluntary Community Advisory Board that includes provincial and territorial representatives is required to align the Community Plan with supports from all levels of government. Finally, both the Liberal SCPI and the Conservative HPS versions have mandated knowledge development and information sharing in the form of action research and analysis of international best practices. With these multiple interactive components, Canada's homelessness collaboration is viewed by both governments and communities as "a considerable success and foundation for other approaches" (Smith, 2004: 28).

Canada's New Deal Legacy:
Place-Based Policy Pathways

The above discussion shows that Canada's decade-long experimentation with the New Localism has not resulted in an intergovernmental arrangement that makes municipalities full policy partners in the federation. Provincial empowerment of municipalities remains limited, and federal–local policy engagement has been highly selective. Yet the examples of tri-level governance in immigration, homelessness, and infrastructure policy illustrate a promising mix of strategies and mechanisms by which federal and provincial goals can be aligned with local priorities on complex urban problems.

governance and public policy. Taking our cue from international debates about the New Localism, we have explored from both local and provincial/federal perspectives whether and how Canadian municipalities are engaged in strategic governance processes or emerging as effective policy partners. Despite a decade-and-a-half of debate about a New Deal for cities, local governments remain legally subordinate to provinces. Advocacy by citizens and non-governmental actors has not changed the incentive structures that militate against strong and creative local leadership, and the initial promise of institutionalized federal–municipal partnerships has not come to fruition.

However, it would be inaccurate to conclude that these debates and policy experiments have not altered Canada's urban governance and policy landscape in interesting ways. The three place-based public policy cases we examined exemplify the New Localism in action. While modest in scope and scale, these governance innovations allow municipalities with strong leadership and strategic purpose to assume a more prominent role in Canadian federalism and local governance of public policy. It may be that Canada will chart a middle path between an overemphasis on either local autonomy or non-governmental actors to make and deliver public policies. In the United States, for example, autonomous local government has led to undesirable inequities both within metropolitan areas and between more dynamic and struggling cities. At the same time, those European jurisdictions where multi-level governance and stakeholder-led policy-making are most advanced reportedly suffer from muddled accountability and a lack of fiscal transparency. Canada's recent experience embedding **place-based public policy-making** within traditional intergovernmental relations may ease these tensions while also reconciling this country's enduring political challenge of accommodating national standards to community particularity.

Conclusion

This chapter has taken stock of recent experimentation and innovation in Canadian urban

References

Adams, E. 2012. *Intergovernmental Fiscal Transfer, Investment Decisions and Outcomes: The Case of the Gas*

Tax Fund in Ontario. Ottawa, ON: Carleton University, Ph.D. Thesis.

Andrew, C. 2001. "The shame of (ignoring) the cities," *Journal of Canadian Studies* 35(4): 100–10.

Barca, F. 2009. *An Agenda for a Reformed Cohesion Policy: A Place-based Approach to Meeting European Union Challenges and Expectations*. Brussels: European Union Commissioner for Regional Policy.

Barnett, J., ed. 2001. *Planning for a New Century: The Regional Agenda*. Washington, DC: Island Press.

Boudreau, J-A. 2000. *The MegaCity Saga: Democracy and Citizenship in the Global Age*. Montreal: Black Rose Books.

Bradford, N. 2005. *Place-based Public Policy: Towards a New Urban and Community Agenda for Canada*. Ottawa: CPRN.

———. 2009. The OECD's local turn: Innovative liberalism for the cities? in R. Mahon and S. McBride, eds., *The OECD and Transnational Governance*. Vancouver, BC: UBC Press.

———, and C. Andrew. 2011. "The Harper immigration agenda: Policy and politics in historical context," in C. Stoney & G.B. Doern, eds., *How Ottawa Spends, 2011–2012*. Montreal and Kingston: McGill-Queen's University Press.

———, and A. Bramwell, eds. 2014. *Governing Urban Economies: Innovation and Inclusion in Canadian City-Regions*. Toronto: University of Toronto Press.

Broadbent, A. 2008. *Urban Nation: Why We Need to Give Power Back to the Cities to Make Canada Strong*. Toronto: Harper Collins Canada.

Burr, K. 2011. "Local immigration partnerships: Building welcoming and inclusive communities through multi-level governance," *Horizons: Policy Research Initiative* (February).

Burstein, M., E. Victoria, A. Lacassagne, and J. Nadeau. 2012. *LIP-Municipal Interactions and CIC's Strategic Interests*. Ottawa, ON: Welcoming Communities Initiative and Citizenship and Immigration Canada.

Calthorpe, P., and W. Fulton. 2001. *The Regional City: Planning for the End of Sprawl*. Washington, DC: Island Press.

Chisholm, S., ed. 2011. *Investing in Better Places: International Perspectives*. London: Smith Institute.

Cooke, P., and K. Morgan. 1998. *The Associational Economy: Firms, Regions, and Innovation*. Oxford: Oxford University Press.

Courchene, T. 2006. "Citistates and the state of cities: Political-economy and fiscal-federalism dimensions," in R. Young and C. Leuprecht, eds., *Municipal-Federal-Provincial Relations in Canada*. Kingston, ON: Institute of Intergovernmental Relations.

Crawford, K.G. 1940. "The independence of municipal councils in Ontario," *Canadian Journal of Economics and Political Science* 6: 543–54.

Dreier, P., J. Mollenkopf, and T. Swanstrom. 2004. *Place Matters: Metropolitics for the Twenty-first Century* (2nd edn.). Kansas City, KS: University Press of Kansas.

External Advisory Committee on Cities and Communities (EACCC). 2006. *From Restless Communities to Resilient Places*. Ottawa, ON: External Advisory Committee on Cities and Communities.

Eidelman, G., and Z. Taylor. 2010. "Canadian urban politics: Another 'black hole'?" *Journal of Urban Affairs* 32: 305–20.

Garcea, J., and E.C. LeSage, eds. 2005. *Municipal Reform in Canada: Reconfiguration, Re-Empowerment, and Rebalancing*. Toronto: Oxford University Press.

Gertler, M.S. 2001. "Urban economy and society in Canada: Flows of people, capital and ideas," *Isuma: The Canadian Journal of Policy Research* 2(3): 119–30.

Godfrey, J. 2004. Address by the Honourable Minister, Infrastructure and Communities to the Association of Municipalities of Ontario (AMO) Annual Conference, Ottawa.

Goetz, E.G., and S.E. Clarke. 1993. *The New Localism: Comparative Urban Politics in a Global Era*. Newbury Park, CA: Sage Publications.

Good, K. 2009. *Municipalities and Multiculturalism: The Politics of Immigration in Toronto and Vancouver*. Toronto: University of Toronto Press.

Government of Canada. 2010. *Response to the Standing Committee on Citizenship and Immigration 2nd Report, Best Practices in Settlement Services*. Ottawa: Government of Canada.

Harper, S., Right Honourable Prime Minister. 2006. An Address by the Prime Minister on Commitments to Communities, Montreal, 2 June. At: www.pm.gc.ca/eng/news/2006/06/02/address-prime-minister-commitments-communities

Horak, M. 2008. *Governance Reform from Below: Multilevel Politics and Toronto's "New Deal" Campaign in Toronto, Canada*. Nairobi, Kenya: United Nations Human Settlements Programme (UN-HABITAT).

———. 2012. "Conclusion: Understanding multilevel governance in Canada's cities," in M. Horak and R. Young, eds., *Sites of Governance: Multilevel Governance and Policy Making in Canada's Big Cities*. Montreal and Kingston: McGill-Queen's University Press.

———, and R. Young, eds. 2012. *Sites of Governance: Multilevel Governance and Policy Making in Canada's Big Cities*. Montreal and Kingston: McGill-Queen's University Press.

Hulchanski, J.D., and M. Shapcott, eds. 2004. *Finding Room: Policy Options for Canadian Rental Housing Strategy*. Toronto: CUCS Press.

Infrastructure Canada. 2005. *Agreement for the Transfer of Federal Gas Tax Revenues under the New Deal for Cities and Communities: Canada, The Association of Municipalities of Ontario and the City of Toronto*. 17 June.

Johnston, D. 1998. "Why territorial development matters," OECD *Observer* (February/March).

Katz, B., and J. Bradley. 2013. *The Metropolitan Revolution*. Washington, DC: Brookings Institution Press.

Keil, R. 1998. "Globalization makes states: Perspectives of local governance in the age of the world city," *Review of International Political Economy* 5: 616–46.

Lee, K.K. 2000. *Urban Poverty in Canada: A Statistical Profile*. Ottawa, ON: Canadian Council on Social Development.

Leo, C. 2006. "Deep federalism: Respecting community difference in national policy," *Canadian Journal of Political Science* 39: 481–506.

Lidstone, D. 2004. *Assessment of the Municipal Acts of the Provinces and Territories*. Ottawa, ON: Federation of Canadian Municipalities.

Lorinc, J. 2006. *The New City: How the Crisis in Canada's Urban Centres is Reshaping the Nation*. Toronto: Penguin.

Martin, P., Honourable. 2003. Statement cited in D. Girard, "Martin Pledges New Deal for Cities," *Toronto Star*. 26 September.

——, Right Honourable Prime Minister. 2005. Address by Prime Minister Paul Martin to the Conference of the Federation of Canadian Municipalities, St. John's, Nfld, 5 June.

Mirza, S. 2007. *Danger Ahead: The Coming Collapse of Canada's Municipal Infrastructure*. Ottawa, ON: Federation of Canadian Municipalities.

Omidvar, R., and T. Richmond. 2003. *Immigrant Settlement and Social Inclusion in Canada*. Toronto: Laidlaw Foundation.

Organisation for Economic Co-operation and Development (OECD). 2002. *Territorial Review: Canada*. Paris: OECD.

——. 2007. *Linking Regions and Central Governments: Contracts for Regional Development*. Paris: OECD.

Portney, K. 2003. *Taking Sustainable Cities Seriously*. Cambridge, MA: MIT Press.

Residential and Civil Construction Alliance of Ontario (RCCAO). 2010. *Infrastructure Underinvestment: The Risk to Canada's Economic Growth*. Toronto: Residential and Civil Construction Alliance of Ontario.

Rodríguez-Pose, A. 2008. "The rise of the 'city-region' concept and its development policy implications," *European Planning Studies* 16: 1025–46.

Sancton, A. 2000. *Merger Mania: The Assault on Local Government*. Montreal: MQUP.

——. 2006. "City politics: Municipalities and multi-level governance," in T. Bunting and P. Filion, eds., *Canadian Cities in Transition: Local through Global Perspectives* (3rd edn.). Toronto: Oxford University Press.

——. 2011. *Canadian Local Government: An Urban Perspective*. Toronto: Oxford University Press.

Sellers, J.M. 2002. *Governing from Below: Urban Regions and the Global Economy*. Cambridge: Cambridge University Press.

Seltzer, E., and A. Carbonell, eds. 2011. *Regional Planning in America: Practice and Prospect*. Cambridge, MA: Lincoln Institute of Land Policy.

Slack, N.E. 2006. *Fiscal Imbalance: The Case for Cities*. Prepared for the Federation of Canadian Municipalities. Toronto: University of Toronto, Institute on Municipal Finance and Governance, Munk School of Global Affairs.

Smith, R. 2004. *Policy Development and Implementation in Complex Files: Lessons from the National Homelessness Initiative*. Ottawa, ON: Canada School of Public Service.

Standing Committee on Citizenship and Immigration. 2010. *Best Practices in Settlement Services*. Ottawa, ON: House of Commons.

Stein, J.G. 2006. *Canada by Mondrian: Networked Federalism in an Era of Globalization*. Toronto: Conference Board of Canada.

Stoker, G. 2004. "New localism, progressive politics and democracy," *Political Quarterly* 75: 117–29.

Stone, C.N. 2011. "Beyond the equality-efficiency tradeoff," in C.R. Hayward and T. Swanstrom, eds., *Justice and the American Metropolis*. Minneapolis, MN: University of Minnesota Press.

Taylor, Z. 2014. "If different then why? Explaining the divergent political development of Canadian and American local governance," *International Journal of Canadian Studies* 49: 53–79.

TD Bank. 2002a. *A Choice between Investing in Canada's Cities or Disinvesting in Canada's Future*. TD Economics Special Report. Toronto: TD Bank.

——. 2002b. *The Greater Toronto Area (GTA): Canada's Primary Economic Locomotive in Need of Repairs*. TD Economics Special Report. Toronto: TD Bank.

——. 2003. *The Calgary-Edmonton Corridor: Take Action Now to Ensure Tiger's Roar Doesn't Fade*. TD Economics Special Report. Toronto: TD Bank.

Tindal, C.R., and S.N. Tindal. 2008. *Local Government in Canada* (7th edn.). Toronto: McGraw-Hill Ryerson.

——, ——, K. Stewart, and P.J. Smith. 2013. *Local Government in Canada* (8th edn.). Toronto: Nelson.

Urban Economics: The Factors Shaping the Value of Land

12

ANDREJS SKABURSKIS AND
MARKUS MOOS

Introduction

You can fly over Canada for hours and see nothing but trees, lakes, and a few roads and in some parts even these disappear. We have lots of land. So why pay a million dollars for a very small lot in Vancouver? What determines the price of land, and how do land prices affect the development of the city? Who sets the price, and what are their interests in shaping the city? What are the social consequences of these processes, and what role does public policy play in shaping urban land markets? These questions are considered in this chapter.

Beginning with an overview of the factors that shape the value of land, we move on to discuss the characteristics of urban land markets in more detail. We distinguish between the rent and the price of land. Next, we highlight the structure of ownership and discuss the role of planning and politics in shaping land markets. We then go on to introduce in more detail some of the models economists use to understand the factors that affect urban land markets, and we discuss demographic, labour market, political, and societal shifts that are changing both real estate costs and land-use patterns. As we shall see, changing land markets have efficiency and equity implications.

The Value of Location

When we think of expensive locations, London, Paris, New York, and Tokyo might come to mind. In Canada, Vancouver has become almost synonymous with expensive real estate, and Calgary is not far behind. High-rise condominium apartment towers dominate the Vancouver skyline. Soon, Vancouverites will see another luxury condominium development added to their downtown, the "twisting tower" designed by Arthur Erikson. The average price is expected to be $1500 per square foot, meaning that a one-bedroom unit will cost at least $800,000 (Buzz, 2012). Old and modest single-family dwellings sell for well over $1 million, illustrating the high cost of land in the city (Figure 12.1). It may be hard to believe these figures, especially when considering that elsewhere in Canada, such as in a Quebec town on the beautiful Gaspé shoreline (Figure 12.2), a house can sell for under $50,000; one could own more than 20 homes for $1 million! But even in Canada's most expensive market, prices do not always go up: one newspaper article reports a 5.6 per cent drop in Vancouver's average house prices, down to $1.116 million (Duff, 2013).

What explains the geographic differences and the changes over time in the price of houses and the land they are built on? The quick answer to most

Figure 12.1   A Vancouver million-dollar house in the Dunbar neighbourhood. (Andrejs Skaburskis)

questions about the value of land is the realtor's mantra, "Location, location, location." We need to know more, though, about the aspects of location that matter to people and firms and the forces that determine the attractiveness of a location. The attributes of location that are of most interest to us in this chapter are formed by the relationship a place has with other places within a city and the factors that influence this relationship. These factors vary from the local to the global. The value of land and its use are determined by the conditions in the city but also by what is happening in other parts of the world. The recent economic crisis, for example, has led to devaluation, thus injecting risk into the valuation of property. Paying a high mortgage on

a Vancouver home suddenly looks less attractive when housing values begin to decline without an immediate rebound in sight. However, the economic cycles do not necessarily alter the factors that shape *relative* valuation of different locations.

The social and economic relationships that tie cities together into complex urban systems shape the relative value of location. For instance, Montreal's declining status as Canada's dominant economic centre helps explain why its property values increased no faster than the national average, whereas Toronto, Canada's economic powerhouse, had the highest property value appreciation in the years before the recent economic recession—along with the emerging regional centres of Vancouver,

Figure 12.2 $50,000 houses on the Gaspé Peninsula, Quebec. (Andrejs Skaburskis)

Calgary, and Edmonton. Historically, Montreal had an advantage in terms of the location of its port, which provided access to the West, but with the development of the railroads and the Panama Canal, western Canadian trade was increasingly captured by Vancouver (Germain and Rose, 2000). Partly because Toronto is closer to the US industrial belt, manufacturing industries grew more in Toronto than in Montreal after World War II. As well, the migration of the English out of Montreal during the 1970s reduced housing demand and hurt Montreal's property values considerably, thereby moving the gateway to English Canada to Toronto. And in the valuation of land, economic strength gained by an advantageous location matters.

Proximity and Accessibility

Richard Hurd (1903), regarded by some as the founder of urban land economics, tells us that the value characteristics of a location are determined by two sets of attributes: (1) those related to *proximity* and (2) those related to *accessibility*. People may be willing to pay more for locations close to parks, views, and quiet surroundings and less for locations close to municipal landfills or highway noise. Firms may also cluster together (proximity) to share infrastructure, local services, and communication opportunities among decision-makers. However, in many cases access rather than proximity is valued. *Access* refers to the ease of getting from one place to another. We might want to live by a lake but cannot on account of our need to access work, shops, and other facilities. Improvements in transport infrastructure raise the value of land in its vicinity as highways and public transit extensions enhance the accessibility of the locations connected by the system (see El-Geneidy, Patterson, and St-Louis, Chapter 10). Between 1986 and 1996, vacant land prices in the vicinity of Vancouver's SkyTrain stations increased by 251 per cent as compared to 133 per cent for prices as a whole (Landcor, 2008). Store owners want to locate near such transport hubs as well as each other to gain exposure to customers who are more likely to come to the shopping centres or main streets that let them reduce their overall travel costs. Polluting factories, on the other hand, are nuisances; most people do not want to live near them, but workers may have to live close by to access their workplace. The value of a location is a function of the advantages it offers in terms of proximity and in terms of its accessibility *relative* to other locations.

As was the case for the historic centre of cities whence urban development spread outward, proximity and accessibility to the downtown have remained most valued, and the highest per unit land prices are in the centre. The scatter plots in Figure 12.3 show how the value of urban land in 2001 in Toronto, Montreal, and Vancouver decreases with distance from the centre. The centre continues to provide primary employment and service functions in Canadian cities to this day, which explains why the price of land continues to be highest near the downtown and falls toward the periphery. Increases in business-related travel have made airport locations more important to many firms than downtown locations, and sub-centres have developed around the major airports that partially explain the secondary peaks in land values (Figure 12.3). Land values also increase around "suburban downtowns" and emerging employment nodes in suburban locations, where firms move for lower rents as well as to locate closer to an increasingly suburban labour force as cities continue to spread outward (Filion and Gad, 2006; Moos and Mendez, 2013).

External Factors Affecting the Value of Land

Factors external to the city also affect the value of land. For example, the Vancouver land market heated up in the late 1980s as offshore investors and immigrants bought real estate largely due to worries about the return of Hong Kong to Chinese rule. Morever, the globalization of financial markets has made it easier for foreign investors to buy real estate in distant places (see Hall, Chapter 3). Immigration has dramatically increased in recent years, thereby expanding the demand for land and housing in the large Canadian cities (Ley and Tutchener, 2001). Labour markets are closely related to housing demand, the latter being a function of household formation, income, wealth, and preferences for housing space. Our demand for housing and land is also related to how much income we earn currently, i.e., monetary income, and how much we expect to earn over a longer period of time. And, due to changes in immigration policies that evaluate migrants on a points system, recent immigrants to Canada tend to have higher permanent incomes, which increase their housing consumption (Moos and Skaburskis, 2010; see Chapter 8). Moreover, if immigrants hold strong preferences for particular locations on account of their ethnic makeup, the growth in demand for these neighbourhoods increases their land values. In this context, therefore, it would be fair to say that the federal government's immigration policy has become an important factor in shaping land markets in our largest cities.

The Influence of Demography, Planning, and Societal Factors

Changes in the population's age composition and in household and family formation rates also affect the demand for housing; smaller households buy smaller houses or, more often, condominiums. Changing lifestyles among the young have increased the relative value of inner city locations near restaurants, entertainment, and people with potentially similar interests (Skaburskis, 1999; 2012; see Moos, Chapter 20). Similarly, changes in marriage arrangements can affect the relative value of neighbourhoods: the increasing propensity of well-educated women to marry well-educated men since 1980 was observed by Picot, Miles, and Wen-Hao (2011). This propensity resulted in the increased inequality in household incomes and, therefore, in neighbourhood incomes and property values (see Walks, Chapter 9). Some firms have responded to this shift in residential location of

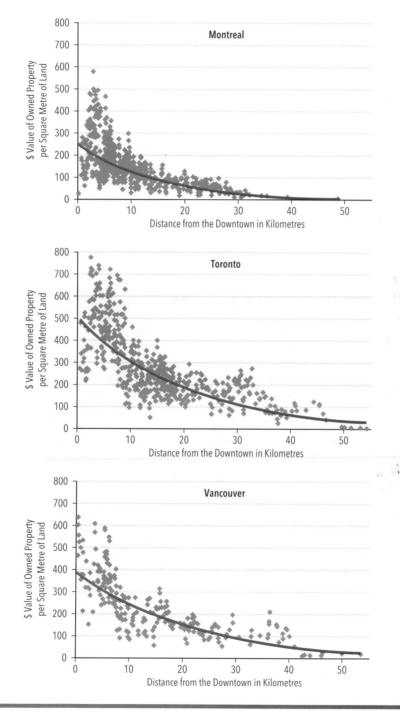

Figure 12.3   Property Value Gradients in Canada's Three Largest Cities

Source: Authors' calculations from 2001 census data.

young professionals by moving back downtown. And some developers are targeting condominiums to young, single professional women who prefer inner city locations (Kern, 2010).

Land markets are affected by planning efforts and municipal infrastructure projects that determine where public facilities are built, which waterfronts are beautified, what parts of the city are connected with roads and transit systems, and what parts of the city receive the landfills and other nuisances. Zoning, in particular, is a highly political process that sets out the pattern of land-use activities and builds expectations over the potential for land value appreciation. Decisions about zoning changes are often released only after being finalized to avoid speculative behaviour in land markets created by uncertainty. The role of government is highlighted by Charles Schultze's (1977: 30) bold assertion that the free market is "made by government": land ownership and its transactions are possible only within the protected environment formed by government.

The economic models that explain urban land values show that the land use patterns that would be formed by a perfectly competitive market place reflect the "highest and best use" of the land. In other words, in the absence of "third party effects," land markets promote the efficient use of land by ensuring that the potential users of a parcel of land are those who value and can pay the most for its location attributes. Zoning helps reduce or eliminate the negative "third party effects" one property owner can impose on a neighbour by building too high or too near the edge of the property. Fairness issues are raised when the market brings changes that hurt the more vulnerable populations by forcing them to move or by reducing the supply of lower-priced housing. Nick Blomley (2004) argues that our system of property ownership can seem definitive and even natural whereas, in fact, it is made possible by a regulatory system that favours property owners. Renters often have little to no claim to their space and are potentially harmed by changes in land prices that bring windfalls to the owners. The societal value of land is determined, therefore, not just by the price someone is willing and able to pay but also by the occupants'

emotional, cultural, and affective ties to place (see Walker and Gunn, Chapter 18).

The Characteristics of Urban Land Markets

Markets facilitate the selling and buying of goods and services, and create incentives for firms to provide the goods and services consumers most want, and to do so efficiently. Changes in prices tell producers how demand is changing. The price of a good or service is determined in the market by the interplay of demand and supply. A rise in demand unmatched by an increase in supply raises prices. Land markets are unique in that the supply of land at any location is fixed. This means that any increase in demand for land at a location will increase its price. While the supply of urban land can increase as more rural and agricultural lands are converted to urban uses, this expansion makes the inner-city locations even more desirable *relative* to the retreating peripheral locations; and, due to the fixed supply, inner-city land prices increase with city growth. As land becomes more expensive, developers use less in creating real estate, and city densities increase. The demand for land affects its price and, therefore, how it is used as well as how the city looks and functions. Understanding land markets is a key to understanding urban geography. Knowledge of property values and understanding of the dynamics that drive them are also prerequisites to informed land-use planning.

Rent and Prices

In examining land and property markets, economists distinguish between the value of *using* the property from the value of *owning* the property. In this sense, there are two markets in land: one for its use and another for its ownership. When considering the value of the use of a property, we use the concept of a "rent." The rent is the amount a household or a firm pays or would be willing to pay for the *use* of a property for a period of time. Homeowners are regarded as paying "rent" to themselves for the use of the property they themselves own. When the property is sold, a "price" is paid. The price reflects the value of owning the property and usually is determined by the expected value of the use of the property in the future or, in other words, by the rent it is expected to generate in the future. Changes in the expectation of future uses and rents will change the market price of the land much as change in expectations change the value of investments in the stock market.

The distinction between these two markets is important because the factors determining price can be different from those determining current rents, but the two measures of value are linked. In a world in which the future is known and nothing changes, the highest price someone would offer would be the present value of the expected future rents—determined by the capitalization process. If a property would yield rents starting next year, for all years into the future, the price of the land would be the rent divided by the discount rate:

$$(1) \quad \text{Price} = \text{annual rent/discount rate}$$

If we estimate the discount rate at 6 per cent and the rent on a property is $1200 per month, then the price for that property as determined by equation (1) would be as follows:

$$(2) \quad \text{Price} = (\$1200 \text{ per month} \times 12 \text{ months})/0.06 = \$240,000$$

When we look at a growing city, we see much higher prices: one cannot buy a condominium unit that would rent for $1200 a month in any of our major cities for as little as $240,000. The price is much higher because the rents are expected to increase in the future with continued city growth. The formula needs to capitalize the future increase in rents by using the "net of growth" discount rate; the simplified formula then becomes this:

$$(3) \quad \text{Price} = \text{annual rent/(discount rate} - \text{expected growth rate in rents)}$$

Using the above numerical example but adding an expected growth in rents of 2 per cent a year changes the price calculation as follows:

$$(4) \quad \text{Price} = (\$1200 \times 12)/(0.06 - 0.02) = \$360,000$$

The growth rate is not known but is guessed at by the prospective buyers. The difference in the price of the property—the difference between $240,000 and $360,000—is due to the *expectation* of a 2 per cent annual growth in rent. Equation 3 can help us illustrate two important features of the land market that affect the way cities change. First, since the growth rate is not known but is guessed at, people's expectations of their city's future affect growth rates and subsequently **urban form**. If people expect the city to keep growing, then this expectation will drive up land prices and create the incentive for developers and builders to use less land in producing real estate. Anticipated future changes in land use affect the market's view of future rents and, therefore, affect its current price. Announcing a transportation improvement, for example, offers to increase the value of the location in the future and therefore the current price. New plans that will change the use of land affect its price at the time they become known. For example, when Ontario announced plans for a greenbelt around Toronto, the price of the farmland in the greenbelt dropped because this growth boundary eliminated the possibility of gaining future urban rents. The recent 5.6 per cent drop in the average price of Vancouver houses is due to the buyers reducing their expectations of future increases in rents and prices.

The second feature revealed by Equation 3 relates to the stability of the market. The amount people will be willing to pay for land increases as their expectations of future growth rates increase. When they base their expectations on recent past trends, they may be induced to buy larger houses with the hope of increasing the amount they can gain from future price increases. As others follow, prices rise across the city and fuel expectations of an even higher future growth rate and prices increase. As the denominator in Equation 3 decreases in size, the price bubble forms until people recognize that there is no longer a connection between prices and realistic future rents. The bubble bursts and prices tumble. People who had taken mortgages they can no longer afford and households who had refinanced their homes to make other purchases find themselves underwater with a mortgage debt that is greater than the value of their homes. As in the US housing market meltdown that triggered the recent economic crisis, the viability of the banks and other financial institutions holding far too many worthless mortgages are threatened and the crisis broadens to affect the whole economy of the country and the world.

Of course, the recent economic crisis was not solely triggered by misguided expectations on the borrowers' part. The downturn has been the worst since the Great Depression of the 1930s and has drawn worldwide attention to the US sub-prime mortgage sector. Lending institutions actively pursued households who would not traditionally qualify for a mortgage in order to make money on the initial sale of the mortgage. Loans were made to working-class and racially marginalized communities with hidden costs in schemes commonly called "predatory" (Wyly et al., 2009). Most of these loans were grouped together, and shares in these bundles were sold to investors. While housing prices kept climbing, the system remained stable. A household about to default on its mortgage could sell the house at a higher price and cover all costs. However, once prices stabilized and houses were being taken back by the mortgage lenders, people began to realize that mortgages exceeded the value of their properties; as a result, the financial system began to collapse. The increase in foreclosures caused house prices to drop further, making the problem even worse by bringing bankruptcies in other sectors, loss of life savings, and widespread unemployment. Land, property markets, and the institutions that govern them can have very far-reaching consequences.

The Structure of Land Ownership

There are broad consequences to the way society determines who owns land and how to gain access to it. An understanding of the structure of ownership is therefore important for understanding the consequences of how land markets operate. "A man without land is nothing," Duddy Kravitz is told by his grandfather in Mordecai Richler's (1959) novel

about the young Duddy growing up on Montreal's St Urbain Street. Duddy becomes obsessed with the idea of attaining property, doing anything regardless of its legality or morality to attain it. Since the mid-twentieth century, the majority of young households in North America have shared his goal. Our lending institutions have engineered financial instruments to permit and encourage households to achieve home ownership. The notion that property ownership comes with elevated rights, privileges, and wealth potential has pervaded scholarly and popular Western thought for many years (Ronald, 2008); indeed, the first concept of "universal" suffrage in Western democratic societies limited voting to male property owners. Today we know that households at risk of homelessness or coping with other forms of poverty are more likely to be renters than owners (Hulchanski and Shapcott, 2004; Skaburskis, 2004). The advocates for a tax on rent, sometimes called a Ricardian land tax, argue that the value of a parcel of land at a particular location, and thus its rent, is due to its relationship with other parcels of land and the overall growth and development of the city. Hence, the value is socially constructed, raising questions as to whether the value of increases in land prices should accrue only to the owners of the land. In the late nineteenth century, Henry George was among the most vocal advocates of a land tax. Not only would such a tax be fair but also efficient since owners could do nothing to avoid paying the tax.

Clearly, property rights and the ability to gain profit from one's possessions are essential characteristics of any efficiently operating market. In order to engage in the selling and buying of goods and services, we must know who owns the good or service in question. But if the ability to attain property is unequally distributed and the status of owning property comes with elevated rights and privileges, we can begin to ask questions about the role of public policy in addressing these potential inequalities. Democratic rights are, of course, no longer defined by property ownership as they once were, but observers continue to argue that due to differential tax treatments, to wealth gain potential, and to the social status of owning, renters are at an unjust disadvantage simply because of their tenure.

Conceptualizing the Spatial Structure of Urban Land Markets

The conceptual frameworks we use to understand land markets today have evolved from classic economic theory derived from the thinking of the eighteenth-century economist Adam Smith. Examining the rents charged to tenant farmers, Smith (1970 [1776]) views rent as the residual value: the difference between the cost of growing produce and the price paid for the produce at the market. He observes that, regardless of what was grown, land rents near the market are higher than rents further from the market on account of the added cost of transportation. David Ricardo, recognized as the founder of rent theory, defines **land rent** as "that portion of the produce of the earth, which is paid to the landlord for the use of the original and indestructible powers of the soil" (Ricardo, 1969 [1817]: 33). The price of produce is set by the cost

of growing it on the least productive land. This land yields no residual value for the landowner. If we assume all produce fetches the same price in the market regardless of where it is grown (an assumption that may require revision due to growing interest in locally grown produce), the owners of more fertile land can extract a rent from their tenant farmers equal to the difference between costs and price. "Ricardian rent" levels throughout a city are set by the differences in the relative attractiveness of sites and neighbourhoods. "Fertility" can also be transformed into the "accessibility" attribute—the more accessible sites are similar to the more "fertile" plots in Ricardo's model. The base rent for urban uses is set by the least attractive land that has to be used to house the population. From a commuting point of view, these locations are at the periphery of the city. From here the urban land rent profile starts to rise from the agricultural rent level, increasing toward the centre to reflect the households' valuation of the reduced commute, as illustrated in Figure 12.4.

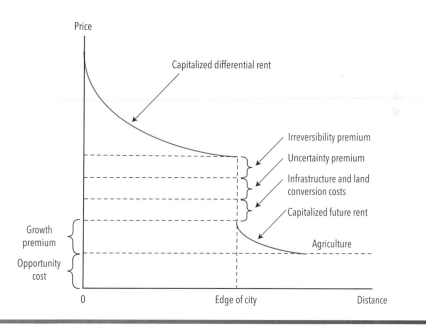

Figure 12.4   Hypothetical Land Price Gradient

Note: The price of an inner-city lot is set by the present value of the agricultural rents at the periphery plus the growth, uncertainty, and irreversibility premiums. It is set by the developer's cost of providing the on-site infrastructure plus the development cost charges for the public facilities and off-site infrastructure. Prices inside the city also are determined by the capitalized differential rents due to the relative increase in the attractiveness of locations closer to the centre.

This very simple model still pertains to the way we view the city today. Putting aside other conditions affecting the commute (an admittedly restrictive assumption) and assuming employment were concentrated in the centre of the city, as it was historically until mid-twentieth century in most Canadian and American cities, then some households would have shorter commutes than others; this difference would affect the amount they would pay for housing (see Harris, Chapter 19). Land prices near the centre are driven up by people who want to reduce their commute costs. The neo-classical models of land use and urban density are built on the classical ideas. William Alonso (1964), for instance, develops the concept of a "bid-rent" map with contours that trace the amount that a household would be willing to pay at each location while keeping its satisfaction constant (Figure 12.5). The bid-rent curves depict the rent/distance trade-off that would make the householders indifferent to their location. Households maximize their well-being by making a trade-off between better access to the city centre and lower-priced land. Since higher-income households tend to want larger lots, they are drawn toward the periphery by the lower land costs. Lower-income households occupy the more expensive inner-city land at higher densities to reduce their commute costs. Since they buy less housing and occupy less land, they would not benefit from the lower price of suburban land as much as higher-income households. Alonso's (1964) model explains the growth of the suburbs and the spread of the urban region as a function of increasing incomes and the preference for large houses. Richard Muth (1969) and Edwin Mills (1969) expand the theory and explicitly introduce housing markets.

The "New" Urban Economics

The "new" urban economics introduces the time dimension to the classical and neo-classical economic models and helps answer such questions

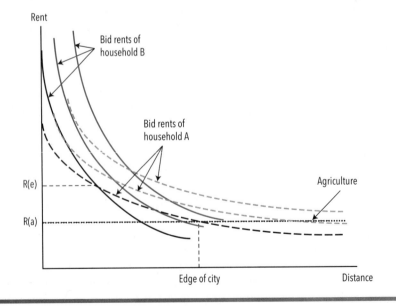

Figure 12.5   Alonso's Bid-Rent Map

Note: The figure assumes there are two households, A and B, each trying to bid for one of the two sites from agriculture for their own use. The solid lines are the bid rents of household B, and the broken lines are those of household A. Higher bid-rent curves, as indicated in green, give lower welfare to a household because the household pays more rent for the site. Lines in black represent the highest household welfare, but are the minimum rent to landowners. Land rent from agriculture is denoted by the dotted line.

as the following: Why do we find parking lots on very expensive downtown land when they clearly cannot generate the land value of a condominium tower? Why is suburban development discontiguous in places and leapfrogging into the countryside to the chagrin of most city planners? Why is the market price of agricultural land at the edge of the city so high compared to the capitalized agricultural rents? We start examining these questions through the capitalization process that links the expected future land rents with land prices and then discuss the costs and benefits of delaying development.

The market price of land at the edge of the city is set by its value in agricultural use and by the present value of the expected future growth in rents at that location. In a growing city, the boundary that sets the base rent for the rest of the city is continuously being pushed further from the centre, making the land within the built-up part of the city *relatively* more attractive. Since buyers recognize that the land at the city's current edge will command higher rents in the future, they are willing to pay a premium now to gain the future increases, as described by Equation 3 earlier in this chapter. Another complication is introduced by the possibility that development options can change over time. If a vacant lot became trapped within an expanding city, its eventual development would be different from the development that would take place when the land is at the very edge of the city. The intensity with which vacant land inside a growing city can be developed increases over time when zoning permits; and this intensity, in turn, increases the residual value of the land. It can, therefore, benefit an owner to hold the land vacant for an extended period of time before converting it to more intense use.

Hotelling's (1931) model builds the basis for understanding the process of land valuation over time. His model starts by recognizing that equilibrium in investment markets requires that assets, such as land, appreciate in value at a rate equal to the relevant interest rate (Shoup, 1970). If the rate at which the asset's price increases is lower than the rate available in other equally risky investments, then its price drops as investors sell to buy more

profitable assets. The reduction in the price of an asset increases the *rate* of return created by a given increase in price. Wicksell (1935) explains the profit-maximizing of timed decision-making with the example of a landowner waiting for trees to grow before cutting them down to sell their lumber. Waiting allows the trees to grow larger and yield more lumber when they are cut, but waiting precludes the use of the funds that would be gained by the sale of the lumber. The most profitable time to harvest the trees is when the rate of growth in their value drops to equal the rate of return on the alternative investment, as predicted by Hotelling's model. Thus, in the context of city development the models predict that the owner of a downtown lot may delay its redevelopment until demand for space in an office tower has grown enough to justify the new building. While a smaller condominium on the site might be profitable now, waiting for the site to "ripen" and allow the construction of the office tower might offer even larger profits.

Shoup (1970: 40) specifically applies the profit-maximizing timing model to urban land use and dispels the notion that "development or redevelopment would or should occur as soon as the development value of a site, net of clearance costs, exceeds the value of the existing improved property, as is sometimes stated." The most profitable development time is when the rate of change in the value of the development that can take place on a site is equal to the interest rate on equally risky alternative investments (Wicksell, 1935). Holding land vacant, or using it as a parking lot, is worthwhile when the rate of increase in the present value of the most profitable project that can be placed on the land exceeds the rate of return on alternative investments. The change in the profitability of development is due to the change in what would be built on the land and due to the fact that development freezes that use for a long time. If the development potential is not changing over time, then a site will be developed now or never. Arnott and Lewis (1979) show that waiting for development changes the density of development. As owners hold vacant land and the suburbs grow around them, land prices increase and less is used in developing real estate: higher land prices encourage higher-density development. Keeping some land vacant can help curb "sprawl" in the long run by leaving room for a new wave of much higher-density development (Peiser, 1989). Had room for infill development not been left, the new development would be at the periphery of the urban region and the total time and effort spent on commuting to the centre would be higher.

The development of land fixes its use for a long period and, thereby, prevents the property owner from taking advantage of possible future changes that could increase his or her options. The presence of uncertainty increases the value of having options, and owners will delay development until prices rise to cover their perceived cost of the uncertainty. Owners have many different reasons for holding land, as pointed out by Brown, Phillips, and Roberts (1981). Some are keeping the land for their children and have no interest in making a profit. Some may place intrinsic value on the ownership itself regardless of the returns they can get for its sale or development. Others may have different discount rates or expectations of growth rates that affect their timing of the sale or of development. The variety of reasons for owning land implies that owners will sell or develop their land at different times. The result is the discontiguous pattern of suburban development that most city planners deplore. Keeping unused land within the city's perimeter increases infrastructure costs, but it also leaves room for more intense development at a later time.

Since the development decision is irreversible, owners will wait until prices rise to cover their perceived cost of the irreversibility of the development decision (Capozza and Helsley, 1989); the resulting land price gradient is illustrated in Figure 12.4. The base price is set by the residual value of the land just outside the periphery. The growth, uncertainty, and irreversibility premiums are added along with the cost of infrastructure to determine the market price of buildable lots at the periphery. The capitalized differential rent is added only inside the city. Constraints on development or increases in development costs at the edge of the city increase the price of all land inside the city. Zoning bylaws

and differences in neighbourhood attributes create discontinuities in the rent and price profiles, resulting in a gradient that is not as smooth as the one depicted in Figure 12.4.

The Changing Profile of Cities

Canadian metropolitan areas, historically characterized by monocentric development patterns and sharply falling density gradients, have dramatically changed over the past 30 years (see Grant and Filion, Chapter 17). Not only has their reach expanded, but an amalgam of demographic, labour market, and socio-economic shifts has resulted in what many believe to be fundamental changes in the spatial and social structure of Canadian cities (see Hutton and Vinodrai, Chapter 6, Townshend and Walker, Chapter 7, and Walks, Chapter 9). The return of higher-income households to the inner city is perhaps the most important change in the structure of cities in the past half-century (see Bain, Chapter 14). The changes are spectacularly visible in Vancouver and Toronto, where high-rise condominiums have taken the place of industrial lands and rail yards (Figure 12.6). Redevelopment of the inner city, through a process called gentrification, is attributed to the growth of smaller, non-family households, the emergence of a "new middle class" of highly educated, quaternary-sector workers—employed in professional service sector occupations—who reject the suburban lifestyle, and deindustrialization that left many inner cities with undervalued properties (Ley, 1996). The incoming population tends to have specific preferences and values that translate into political lobbying for infrastructure and cultural facilities, which, when provided, further increase the value of inner-city land (as shown in Figure 12.7). In gentrification, the lower-income populations are displaced by the incoming, wealthier households. The lobbying and policies that facilitate inner-city investment, and support its upper- and middle-class residents, have even been called "revanchist" for what some describe as blatant attempts to exclude vulnerable populations

Figure 12.6   Vancouver's redeveloped inner city. (Andrejs Skaburskis)

Figure 12.7   Use of nudity by the "new middle class" to protest car culture. The ideologies of politically astute residents can shape transport and land-use policies with implications for property markets. (Andrejs Skaburskis)

(Smith, 1996) (see Siciliano, Cowen, and Smith, Chapter 16).

To be sure, most population growth is still in the suburbs. Ever since the introduction of streetcars in the early 1900s, transportation improvements have continued to permit suburban development (see Addie, Fiedler, and Keil, Chapter 24). The rate of expansion increased dramatically in the 1950s with growth in prosperity, the development of mortgage financial institutions and instruments, and the construction of intra-urban highways. The neo-classical economic models, and their focus on the trade-offs between commuting and housing costs, help explain the outward movement of the well-off and the filtering down of inner-city housing from higher- to lower-income households. The increasing income levels allow people to buy larger houses on larger lots, making them more sensitive to the per-square-metre price of lots and more willing to accept the longer commutes from the suburbs. Technological change and rising incomes increased automobile ownership, making jobs accessible from distant locations. One of the most important changes in the last half of the twentieth century was women's changing employment prospects, which in part contributed to **suburbanization**. Not only did this increase the income of households with two income earners, but it also increased their commuting costs. Some companies moved their clerical offices out into the suburbs to be closer to their predominantly female workforce, helping to intensify the emerging centres that would define the new polycentric urban region (see Hutton and Vinodrai, Chapter 6).

In turn, the spread of employment across the region increased the spread of the city. Surprising to many observers, however, was the resurgence of interest in the inner city by the well-off, leading to "the return of the café society" as some have called this trend. The filtering process in housing used to pass housing down to lower-income people as it aged and as the higher-income households moved out to newer housing of higher quality. This process has reversed in most Canadian metropolitan areas since the early 1980s (see Harris, Chapter 19). Without exception, in all Canadian metropolitan areas—small and large, growing or staying still—the average rents in the older stock, which is located in the inner city, are higher than in the newer buildings (Skaburskis, 2006). This reversal reflects a revaluation of inner-city locations by higher-income households. This revaluation can be explained by at least two viewpoints, discussed below: the neo-classical and the structuralist. Many believe, too, that the pursuit of more entrepreneurial urban policies is also partly responsible for the changes (see Taylor and Bradford, Chapter 11).

Neo-Classical Viewpoint

Wheaton (1977) shows that the perceived cost of commute time has been increasing with household income, enough to change the way the commute-cost/housing-price trade-off is made and to make some higher-income people want to move back to the inner city. Demographic changes also contribute to the displacement of lower-income households by middle- and higher-income earners when gentrification occurs. Average household sizes are declining in North America and Europe, and smaller households occupy less land and can benefit more by paying a higher per-square-foot price for land to reduce their commute costs. Employment insecurity makes central locations more attractive by reducing commute costs over the long run as job locations change. The increase in the proportion of one- and two-person households helps account for the increase in the demand for central locations. Two-worker households are more likely to locate near the urban centre to minimize joint commute costs when they work in different parts of the city. An inner-city location helps solve the co-location problem of well-educated, dual career couples and helps "preserve the marriages of dual career households" (Costa and Kahn, 2000: 1289). Women professionals are more likely to find work in the downtown (Rose and Villeneuve, 1998).

The higher density of the inner city increases the options that single people have in the marriage market. The delay in family formation since the 1950s has reduced young people's need for space and increased the time and money spent on leisure activities. Increases in the education of young people translate into a greater demand for the services and amenities generally found in the downtown, such as theatres, museums, cafés, and sushi bars. By observing that rents in cities increased faster than wages, Glaeser, Kolko, and Saiz (2001) conclude that demand for urban amenities increased faster than urban productivity. They suggest that people live in downtowns increasingly to consume, not to work. Increasing traffic congestion and gasoline costs also make inner-city locations more attractive.

Structuralist Argument

A number of geographers see the changes in inner-city land markets as linked to shifts in the social structure brought about by global economic restructuring (Badcock, 1992; Maher, 1994). The restructuring of the global economy—often labelled as a transition from **Fordism** to **post-Fordism**—has resulted in the growth of both high- and low-level service sector occupations. This two-tiered employment structure and a declining **welfare state** under **neo-liberalism** have produced an hour glass–shaped income distribution and an ever-growing income gap between high- and low-income earners, referred to as "social polarization" (Castells, 2002; Esping-Anderson, Assimakopoulou, and van Kersbergen, 1993; Hamnett and Cross, 1998; Sassen, 1990; 1991). It is this growing inequality that spurred in part the recent Occupy Wall Street movement. **Polarization** materializes in changes in the social geography of the city through segregation and neighbourhood inequalities (Marcuse and van Kempen, 2000; Walks, 2001; see El-Geneidy, Patterson, and St-Louis, Chapter 10). Those at the top end of the income structure can out-compete others in the housing market, resulting in ever-escalating markets that fewer people can attain. The trends can help to explain the declining willingness of private developers to construct rental buildings that tend to be occupied by lower-income populations. Some observers have called this the "dual" or the aforementioned "revanchist" city (Mollenkopf and Castells, 1992; Smith, 1996).

Some explanations of inner-city reinvestment draw on a Marxist perspective of investment cycles (Harvey, 1985; Smith, 1986). During Fordism, capital left downtown in favour of suburban expansion, contributing to inner-city decline. In the post-Fordist context, **revitalization/regeneration** and redevelopment through renovations and new investments returned value to inner city land.

Left with empty manufacturing buildings and polluted industrial sites, localities are devising new policies to attract and expand their workforce in the growing sectors, such as information and communications technology and cultural industries (Figure 12.8). These policies focus on securing private and public investment in urban amenities, such as beautified streetscapes and waterfront revitalization, and holding festivals and farmers' markets. It is believed that these kinds of amenities

Figure 12.8   **Construction of cultural amenities in place of manufacturing in Montreal. (Markus Moos)**

and events will be attractive to the so-called "knowledge workers" or, to borrow Richard Florida's (2002) now much-used phrase, the creative class of the new economy (Hall, 2006). A larger share of public resources is directed toward urban amenities than in the past through urban renewal projects and place-making and "place-marketing" strategies (Hackworth, 2007; Kipfer and Keil, 2002; see Bain, Chapter 14).

Urban Entrepreneurial Policies

The focus on urban amenity provision as a public policy has been labelled as "entrepreneurial" and differs in important ways from the "managerial" policies of the past, when a greater share of resources was dedicated to public services, such as housing (Harvey, 1989). The entrepreneurial policies change the amenity attributes and attractiveness of specific locations, shaping land markets differently than did the managerial policies that preceded them. Instead of investing in social infrastructure that promoted the development of stable neighbourhoods, the new policies harness the growth-generating potential of real estate markets by providing the type of infrastructure that enhances the value of land and location. Existing owners, investors, and the local tax base benefit from appreciating markets, while those wanting to enter the market or needing to pay escalating rents find it increasingly difficult to do so. Arguably, the new entrepreneurial policies cater to the consumption preferences of the workers in professional and managerial occupations, preferences not necessarily shared by those at the bottom of the income spectrum. The issue gets at fundamental ideological foundations that separate entrepreneurial from managerial urban policies and at questions of whether government should help facilitate the operations of the market or whether it should help smooth its inequities.

Conclusion

In a market framework, land values necessarily differ by location, and the land's uses and value are determined by those who have the means to pay for it. Valuing location in that manner may be efficient, but not necessarily equitable. Governments in Canada have traditionally intervened in land markets for reasons of equity and social justice when the inability to afford land and housing leads to a seriously disadvantaged social position. Whether recent increases in affordability problems and homelessness warrant renewed government programs is a question outside the scope of this chapter (see Walks, Chapter 9, and Harris, Chapter 19), but the economics of property markets clearly have broad consequences that warrant discussion about the relative role that markets and public policies ought to play in shaping our cities.

Review Questions

1. What factors—both internal and external to the city—determine the relative value of one location versus other possible locations for a home or business?
2. Why do we find expensive downtown land being held vacant or used for parking lots instead of being developed immediately at its highest and best use?

References

Alonso, W. 1964. *Location and Land Use: Toward a General Theory of Land Rent*. Cambridge, MA: Harvard University Press.

Arnott, R.J., and F. Lewis. 1979. "The transition of land to urban use," *Journal of Political Economy* 87, 4: 161–9.

Badcock, B.A. 1992. "Adelaide's heart transplant, 1970–88: 1. Creation, transfer, and capture of 'value' within the built environment," *Environment and Planning A* 24: 215–41.

Blomley, N. 2004. *Unsettling the City: Urban Land and the Politics of Property*. New York: Routledge.

Brown, J.H., R.S. Phillips, and N. Roberts. 1981. "Land markets at the urban fringe: New insights for policy makers," *Journal of the American Planning Association* 47: 131–44.

Buzz, V. 2012. "Vancouver's 2nd tallest tower on track," Vancity Buzz. At: www.vancitybuzz.com/2012/04/vancouvers-2nd-tallest-tower-back-on-track/

Capozza, D., and R. Helsley. 1989. "The fundamentals of land prices and urban growth," *Journal of Urban Economics* 26: 295–306.

Castells, M. 2002. *The Information Age: Economy, Society and Culture, Volume 1: The Rise of the Network Society*. Malden, MA: Blackwell.

Costa, D., and M. Kahn. 2000. "Power couples: Changes in the locational choice of the college educated, 1940–1990," *Quarterly Journal of Economics* 115: 1287–1315.

Duffy, A. 2013. "Housing prices drop in Victoria and Vancouver, bucking national trend," *Times Colonist* online. At: www.timescolonist.com/business/housing-prices-drop-in-victoria-and-vancouver

Esping-Anderson, G., Z. Assimakopoulou, and K. van Kersbergen. 1993. "Trends in contemporary class structuration: A six-nation comparison," in G. Esping-Anderson, ed., *Changing Classes: Stratification and Mobility in Post-Industrial Societies*. London: Sage.

Filion, P., and G. Gad. 2006. "Urban and suburban downtowns: Trajectories of growth and decline," in T. Bunting and P. Filion, eds., *Canadian Cities in Transition: Local Through Global Perspectives*. Toronto: Oxford University Press.

Florida, R. 2002. *The Rise of the Creative Class*. New York: Basic Books.

Germain, A., and D. Rose. 2000. *Montreal: The Quest for a Metropolis*. New York: John Wiley & Sons Inc.

Glaeser, E., J. Kolko, and A. Saiz. 2001. "Consumer city," *Journal of Economic Geography* 1: 27–50.

Hackworth, J. 2007. *The Neoliberal City: Governance, Ideology, and Development in American Urbanism*. Ithaca, NY: Cornell University Press.

Hall, C.M. 2006. "Urban entrepreneurship, corporate interests and sports mega-events: The thin policies of competitiveness within the hard outcomes of neoliberalism," *Sociological Review* 54: 59–70.

Hamnett, C., and D. Cross. 1998. "Social polarisation and inequality in London: The earnings evidence 1979–1995," *Environment and Planning C* 16: 659–80.

Harvey, D. 1985. *The Urbanization of Capital*. Baltimore: Johns Hopkins University Press.

——. 1989. "From managerialism to entrepreneurialism: The transformation in urban governance in late capitalism," *Geografiska Annaler* 71B: 3–17.

Hotelling, H. 1931. "The economics of exhaustible resources," *Journal of Political Economy* 39: 137–75.

Hulchanski, D., and M. Shapcott, eds. 2004. *Finding Room: Policy Options for a Canadian Rental Housing Strategy*. Toronto: Centre for Urban and Community Studies Press.

Hurd, R. 1903. *Principles of City Land Values*. New York: Record and Guide.

Kern, L. 2010. "Gendering re-urbanisation: Women and new-build gentrification in Toronto," *Population, Space and Place* 16: 363–79.

Kipfer, S., and R. Keil. 2002. "Toronto Inc? Planning the competitive city in the new Toronto," *Antipode* 34: 227–64.

Landcor. 2008. *Lessons from Expo 86 for the 2010 Winter Games*. The Landcor Report, Special Edition, 19 Aug. Vancouver: Landcor Data Corporation.

Ley, D. 1996. *The New Middle Class and the Remaking of the Central City*. Oxford: Oxford University Press.

——, and J. Tutchener. 2001. "Immigration, globalization and house prices in Canada's gateway cities," *Housing Studies* 16: 199–223.

Maher, C. 1994. "Housing prices and geographical scale: Australian cities in the 1980s," *Urban Studies* 31: 5–27.

Marcuse, P., and R. van Kempen, eds. 2000. *Globalizing Cities: A New Spatial Order?* Oxford: Blackwell.

Mason, G. 2008. "Just who is buying Vancouver's zillion-dollar condos?" *Globe and Mail*, 17 May. At: www.theglobeandmail.com/servlet/story/GAM.20080517.BCMASON17/TPStory/TPComment

Mills, E. 1969. "The value of urban land," in H. Perloff, ed., *The Quality of Urban Environment*. Baltimore, MD: Resources for the Future, John Hopkins University Press.

Mollenkopf, J.H., and M. Castells, eds. 1991. *Dual City: Restructuring New York*. New York: Russell Sage Foundation.

Moos, M., and P. Mendez. 2013. "Suburbanization and the remaking of metropolitan Canada," in R. Keil, ed., *Suburban Constellations: Governance, Land and Infrastructure in the 21st Century*. Berlin: Jovis.

Moos, M., and A. Skaburskis. 2010. "The globalization of urban housing markets: Immigration and changing housing demand in Vancouver," *Urban Geography* 31: 724–49.

Muth, R. 1969. *Cities and Housing*. Chicago, IL: University of Chicago Press.

Picot, G., J. Myles, and C. Wen-Hao. 2011. "Why have poorer neighbourhoods stagnated economically while the richer have flourished? Neighbourhood income inequality in Canadian cities," *Urban Studies* 49: 877–96.

Peiser, R.B. 1989. "Density and urban sprawl," *Land Economics* 65: 194–204.

Ricardo, D. 1969 [1817]. *The Principles of Political Economy and Taxation*. London: Everyman's Library, J.M. Dent and Sons.

Richler, M. 1959. *The Apprenticeship of Duddy Kravitz*. Don Mills, ON: A. Deutsch.

Ronald, R. 2008. *The Ideology of Home Ownership: Homeowner Societies and the Role of Housing*. New York: Palgrave Macmillan.

Rose, D., and P. Villeneuve. 1998. "Engendering class in the metropolitan city: Occupational pairings and income disparities between two-earner couples," *Urban Geography* 19: 123–59.

Sassen, S. 1990. "Economic restructuring and the American city," *Annual Review of Sociology* 16: 465–90.

———. 1991. *The Global City: New York, London, Tokyo.* Princeton, NJ: Princeton University Press.

Schultze, C. 1977. *The Public Use of Private Interest.* Washington, DC: Brookings Institution.

Shoup, D. 1970. "The optimal timing of urban land development," *Papers of the Regional Science Association* 75: 33–44.

Skaburskis, A. 1999. "Modelling the Choice of Tenure and Building Type," *Urban Studies* 36: 2199–2215.

———. 2004. "Decomposing Canada's growing housing affordability problem: Do city differences matter?" *Urban Studies* 41: 117–49.

———. 2006. "Filtering, city change and the supply of low-priced housing in Canada," *Urban Studies* 43: 533–58.

———. 2012. "Gentrification and Toronto's changing household characteristics and income distribution," *Journal of Planning Education and Research* 32: 191–203.

Smith, A. 1970 [1776]. *The Wealth of Nations.* London: Everyman's Library, J.M. Dent and Sons.

Smith, N. 1986. "Gentrification, the frontier, and the restructuring of urban space," in N. Smith and P. Williams, eds., *Gentrification of the City.* Boston, MA: Allen and Unwin.

———. 1996. *The New Urban Frontier: Gentrification and the Revanchist City.* New York: Routledge.

Walks, A. 2001. "The social ecology of the post-Fordist/global city? Economic restructuring and socio-spatial polarisation in the Toronto urban region," *Urban Studies* 38: 407–47.

Wheaton, W.C. 1977. "Income and urban residence: An analysis of consumer demand for location," *American Economic Review* 67: 620–31.

Wicksell, K. 1935. *Lectures on Political Economy.* London: Routledge.

Wyly, E., M. Moos, D. Hammel, and E. Kabahizi. 2009. "Cartographies of race and class: Mapping the class-monopoly rents of American sub-prime mortgage capital," *International Journal of Urban and Regional Research* 33: 332–54.

PART III

Planning, Policy, and Challenges in an Urban Age

Chapters in this section deal primarily with municipal policy-related concerns and contemporary challenges facing cities in an urban age. Several of the chapters engage specifically with the recent role that planning has assumed in creating the kinds of places believed to play a vital role in stimulating economic activity. In this sense, Part III is to some extent about the neo-liberal turn in urban governance and the economic role urban planning is given in this context. The chapters here describe and critically examine recent urban governance, development, planning, and lifestyle trends. The chapters also detail efforts at designing places that will "look good" and "feel good," thus attracting investments and middle- and upper-income customers with the wherewithal to generate economic activity. In addition, Part III investigates the downsides of this approach to urban development and management, as well as initiatives breaking from neo-liberal perspectives in their attempt to address these problems.

Planning-related chapters focus on contemporary issues that confront urban planners: Chapter 13, by Senbel and Lesnikowski, on the links between climate change and neighbourhood design; Chapter 15, by Donald and Hall, on slow growth and decline; Chapter 17, by Grant and Filion, on attempts at changing land use; and Chapter 23, by Blay-Palmer and Landman, on food systems. Some readers might be surprised that we feature as planning concerns topics such as the delivery or consumption of food within cities, since these matters are not directly related to traditional land-use purviews of urban planning. Indeed, only in the last few years have these kinds of issues been deemed "legitimate" by the planning and related professions. On the other hand, environmental sustainability has been on the planner's radar screen for a number of decades. But more recently, environmentalism has translated into actual planning policy mandates. Environmental inroads are visible in the planning of large and small Canadian municipalities across the country.

Ontario's 2006 *Growth Plan* policy statement and subsequent enactments, such as the Greater Toronto Area Green Belt, provide but one example (Ontario, 2006). (The reader will also note that while important in and of itself as an initial step toward environmental remediation, the *Growth Plan* also signifies a change of balance in municipal-provincial jurisdictional control over planning matters.)

Grant and Filion's chapter provides further discussion about other relatively new planning initiatives. Among other things, this chapter offers a critical view of "New Urbanism" communities, concluding that, as developed to date, undue emphasis has been given to design and "place" features of these communities at the expense of functional features, such as trip destinations and modes of travel. As another relatively new development on the urban landscape, gated communities have been generally eschewed by planners primarily due to concerns about their exclusionary nature—this contrasts with New Urbanism design, which can be said to have generally aroused some level of enthusiasm within the profession. As developed in Canadian cities, however, both types of communities raise concern about movement patterns, as well as questions as to why people choose to live in them. Reasons for choosing these alternative community types seem to be more about distinction and difference, and in the case of some gated communities about fear of and refuge from the greater urban area (see also Siciliano, Cowen, and Smith, Chapter 16), as opposed to the improvement of community planning.

Bain emphasizes place in Chapter 14, where the concept of the "spectacular" is applied to raise awareness about place-building, which is the cornerstone of regeneration in the central- or inner-city zones of Canada's largest metropolitan regions. Critics would argue that place making is a strategic social construction of "dreamscapes" and illusion. Proponents, such as developers, however, will contend that place making is the very essence of what distinguishes the twenty-first-century city from more standardized urban forms of the past, and, most importantly, that place making has made metros like Vancouver and Toronto successful competitors for world city status. And maybe unsuccessful place making could be one among other factors responsible for the stagnation or decline of no-growth urban areas (see Donald and Hall, Chapter 15). In Chapter 18, Walker and Gunn also explore notions of place making in the ways public spaces are designed and programmed. They provide a framework for measuring activity in our public spaces.

Chapter 16, by Siciliano, Cowen, and Smith, considers the city from the perspective of fear and insecurity. In this sense, the chapter is about how people living and carrying out their activities in cities perceive their urban environments. The chapter presents feelings of insecurity or danger as often constructed by interest groups benefiting from the deployment of security responses.

Chapters in Part III also identify planning concerns and urban trends and challenges that, for the most part, have been raised in the recent past, that is, in the modern city; however, these issues continue to represent problems in present-day Canadian cities. Indeed, in many cases the "neo-liberal turn" has been accused of making some of these problematic circumstances more acute than they ever were in the past—e.g., housing provision and homelessness. Certainly, like neo-liberalism itself, these concerns are ideological, so not all urbanists should be expected to agree that they are in fact problematic.

By and large, it is mostly scholars and policy-makers who affiliate themselves with centrist or left-of-centre political views, or who are otherwise committed to social justice, who have their viewpoints represented in the chapters belonging to this part of the book. Some of the issues addressed are as follows: (1) the status of Aboriginal populations in cities (Chapter 21 by Peters); (2) the differing infrastructure needs of various age groups, age segregation and ageism as a form of social exclusion, and young adults' changing economic prospects and location decisions (Chapter 20 by Moos); (3) the problems of slow-growth and declining communities (Chapter 15 by Donald and Hall); (4) the all-pervasive, continuing concern with the provision of safe and affordable housing for all Canadians, involving sectors of society currently overlooked by the private marketplace and governments alike (Chapter 19 by Harris); (5) suburbanization (Chapter 24 by Addie, Fiedler, and Keil); and (6) gender and sexuality (Chapter 22 by Rose). Some other issues—for example, those associated with racially different communities and other minority groups in the population—have been dealt with in previous chapters, or are excluded due to lack of space: for example, debates over education and the provision of schools. The concluding chapter (Chapter 25 by Moos and Vinodrai) raises the point that our historic urban models have lost predictive power due to the scope and magnitude of change occurring in our cities, and that the diversity of urban and suburban landscapes makes it more difficult to generalize. The authors put forth structure, state, and sustainability as three overarching themes that could help frame our future understanding of cities in an increasingly urban age. Finally, the appendices present select socio-economic data on our largest metropolitan areas, and discuss the challenges of obtaining quality data to study cities due to the loss of the long-form census in Canada.

References

Ontario, Ministry of Public Infrastructure Renewal. 2006. *Growth Plan for the Greater Golden Horseshoe.* Toronto: Government of Ontario.

Climate Change and Neighbourhood Design for Low-Carbon, Resilient, and Healthy Communities

13

MAGED SENBEL AND

ALEXANDRA LESNIKOWSKI

Introduction

How we design our cities and how we distribute the various functions that enable urban life have tremendous impact on the material and energy flows in those cities as well as on the economic, social, physical, and psychological well-being of their inhabitants. Two of the more difficult challenges facing contemporary urban planners and geographers are how to create neighbourhoods that go beyond mere energy efficiency to help reduce greenhouse gas emissions, and how to help create communities that contribute to residents' health and quality of life. The solutions, as this chapter argues, are interrelated.

The chapter unfolds in eight sections. The first two sections ("Linking Cities and Greenhouse Gas Emissions" and "Impacts of Climate Change in Canada") connect the urban phenomenon and the production of greenhouse gases and describe consequences of these gases on climate. The next four sections ("Neighbourhood Design and Climate Change," "Health Consequences of Neighbourhood Design," "Building Typology, Energy, and Emissions," and "Green Infrastructure and Adaptive Design") concentrate on different aspects of neighbourhood design as an instrument to reduce the emission of greenhouse gases. Finally, the two last sections ("Implementing Climate Action" and "Challenges and Opportunities for

Building Healthy, Low-Carbon Communities") concern the implementation of greenhouse reduction measures pertaining to neighbourhood design as well as circumstances affecting the effectiveness of these measures.

Linking Cities and Greenhouse Gas Emissions

Climate change is possibly the most serious challenge facing modern civilization (National Research Council, 2009) and is arguably only a symptom of a much larger overshoot of the planet's carrying capacity (Rees, 2012). Average global temperatures are increasing as greenhouse gas emission levels continue to rise. The best estimates of temperature rise produced by the Intergovernmental Panel on Climate Change project a rise in global average temperature between 1.8°C and 4°C by the end of this century (Alley et al., 2007). The National Round Table on the Environment and the Economy (NRTEE) has estimated that even if reductions in emissions are successful in limiting the global average temperature rise to under 2°C, then costs of climate change in Canada will continue to rise from $5 billion per year in 2020 to between $21 and $43 billion per year by the 2050s (NRTEE, 2011). Costs of flooding alone could be between $1 and

$8 billion per year by the 2050s. Between 16,000 and 28,000 dwelling units will be at risk of permanent flooding from sea level rise and temporary flooding by storm surges. If the objective of limiting the global average temperature rise to under 2°C is *not* met, even adaptive efforts that are many times more expensive will be unable to safeguard civilization from the devastating ravages of global warming and climate change.

While Canada produces only 2 per cent of total global emissions, it has one of the highest per capita emissions rates in the world. In 2011, Canada emitted 16.24 tonnes of CO_2 per person compared to the world average of 4.69 tonnes (US Energy Information Administration [USEIA], 2013). Cities are key drivers of GHG emission trends, and are critical to efforts to reduce national carbon footprints. The building and transportation sectors together produce 36 per cent of emissions—12 per cent from buildings, and 24 per cent from transportation. Relative to 1990 levels, emissions from these two sectors have grown by about 100 megatonnes (100 million tonnes) (Blain et al., 2013). Despite the higher per capita emissions of rural residents (Dodman, 2009), over 80 per cent of Canadians live in urban areas, so the configurations of buildings, land use, and transportation in cities are vital to GHG emissions reduction efforts.

Compact urban development patterns that increase density, make mixed land use commercially viable, and encourage alternative transportation choices through street design and transit service are widely considered to result in lower per capita greenhouse gas emissions (Bartholomew, 2005; Norman, MacLean, and Kennedy, 2006; Pataki et al., 2009; Perkins et al., 2009; VandeWeghe and Kennedy, 2007). Concentrating urban development and intensifying it in already built-up areas has the potential to reduce transportation-related emissions by 7 to 10 per cent by 2050 relative to **urban sprawl** (Ewing et al., 2008). **Urban form** and public transportation policies are therefore critical for facilitating a long-term transition toward low-carbon communities. Pricing policies on gasoline, parking, and road use can also help support behavioural changes away from automobile use toward transit, cycling, and walking in the short and medium terms (Heres-Del-Valle and Niemeier, 2011).

Impacts of Climate Change in Canada

As planners and geographers work on mitigating climate change through policies that would reduce emissions, they are simultaneously adapting to the effects of climate change that are already under way. The nature and extent of climate change is both unknown and varied across Canada (Lemmen et al., 2008). The Atlantic provinces, for example, are projected to experience more frequent and intense storm events, sea level rise, erosion, and flooding, with implications for building and transportation infrastructure and groundwater supply. Similarly in British Columbia, urban populations concentrated in vulnerable coastal regions like the Lower Mainland will experience increased risks from natural hazards, such as floods, storms, and erosion. In the Prairie provinces and in northern forests across the county, the rise in average winter temperatures above the historical lows that kept pests and diseases in check, coupled with longer and more severe summer drought conditions, are threatening vast areas of forest. Disruptions to critical infrastructure, such as water treatment systems, transportation, and energy generation and transmission, are a particular concern in the densely populated region of southern Ontario. In Canada's north, climate-induced permafrost thawing, sea level rise, changes in sea ice cover, and coastal erosion are critical threats to municipal, residential, and transportation infrastructure, and to the traditional lifestyles and heritage sites of Inuit communities (Champalle et al., 2013; Ford et al., 2010; Pearce et al., 2011).

In addition, more frequent and severe heat waves in southern Ontario and Quebec increase the risk of heat-related illnesses and death, particularly for individuals with respiratory and/or cardiovascular conditions (Belanger et al., 2008). In highly urbanized areas, the predominance of asphalt for roads and parking lots, the concentration of heat-emitting mechanical systems for buildings, and the paucity of plants and permeable surfaces that hold moisture all contribute to higher temperatures. This is known as urban heat island effect (UHI) and is particularly acute in deforested and auto-oriented urban areas. Increased levels of air pollution coupled with extreme heat events will disproportionately affect children, people with allergy symptoms, and those suffering from pulmonary and cardiovascular diseases (Belanger et al., 2008). Warmer summers and declining air quality in cities will also increase mortality and illness, and raise the costs of the health-care system.

Neighbourhood Design and Climate Change

The urban design response to climate change is an evolution of a long tradition of attempts at working within the limits and constraints of nature and natural systems. The modern application of this tradition goes back to Ian McHarg's (1969) efforts at designing urban environments that are more respectful of nature as well as the efforts of many others by the end of the twentieth century. At the beginning of the twenty-first century, urban sustainability, New Urbanism, and smart growth became popular themes among planners concerned about climate change (Farr, 2008). The New Urbanism and smart growth movements emerged in response to the proliferation of sprawling auto-oriented suburban developments throughout Canada and the United States. New Urbanism advocates for a return to traditional neighbourhood design principles, including the following: town centres that anchor the social and economic life of neighbourhoods; fine-grain and walkable streets that encourage active transportation and interaction among neighbours; architectural diversity with small building setbacks that contribute to a neighbourhood's vibrancy; and access to reliable and convenient transit that connects to other neighbourhood centres (see Grant and Filion, Chapter 17). Smart growth is similarly

concerned with integrating social, economic, and residential activity through compact mixed-use development supported by transit, bicycle, and pedestrian networks. Douglass Farr defines sustainable urbanism as "walkable and transit-served urbanism integrated with high-performance buildings and high-performance infrastructure" (Farr, 2008: 42). At the heart of these efforts is the goal of improving the quality of life of urban residents and of reducing the energy and resources dedicated to the automobile.

Informing smart growth and New Urbanism is growing evidence that neighbourhood design has an impact on transportation mode choice, and in particular on how much people choose to drive. Researchers have found that a number of neighbourhood design elements help reduce driving and encourage reliance on walking, on cycling, or on transit. These include accessibility to, and quality of, transit stops, connectivity of pedestrian and cycling paths, availability of bike parking, mixed land uses, street network density, block size, sidewalk width, building setbacks, lighting, street furniture, and engaging street frontages (Badland, Schofield, and Garrett, 2008; Berrigan, Pickle, and Dill, 2010; Bhat and Guo, 2007; Crowley, Shalaby, and Zarei, 2009; Ewing and Cervero, 2010; Frank, Kavage, and Appleyard, 2007; Frank et al., 2010; Guo, 2009; Krizek, 2003; Lee and Moudon, 2008). Designing streets to include features that are human scaled and memorable and that have a clear definition of public space, along with visual complexity, navigability, coherence, and interconnectivity between the physical elements of the street all help to increase walking as a travel choice (Ewing and Bartholomew, 2013). Streets that are treated as social spaces, in which people interact, help to improve safety, comfort, and accessibility for persons of all ages and abilities, regardless of travel mode (see El-Geneidy, Patterson, and St-Louis, Chapter 10).

Practitioners cannot rely on neighbourhood design alone, however, to reduce driving and emissions. Some studies suggest that self-selection or demographic profiles are more significant determinants than the design of different locales.

In other words, people move to walkable neighbourhoods because they are already interested in walking, cycling, and taking transit and do not become walkers or cyclists only because of the design of the neighbourhood they move to (Cao, Mokhtarian, and Handy, 2007; Schwanen and Mokhtarian, 2005). Even so, the potential for more walking and transit use increases with compact, mixed-use neighbourhoods and some causal linkages have been detected between physical environments and travel behaviour (Badland, Schofield, and Garrett, 2008; Bhat and Guo, 2007; Cao, Mokhtarian, and Handy, 2007; Ewing and Cervero, 2010).

Health Consequences of Neighbourhood Design

At the same time that planners and geographers have been working to promote walkable communities, and researchers have been gathering evidence on their merits, poor physical health has emerged as a major priority. Auto-oriented development patterns are a significant contributor to respiratory ailments, pedestrian injuries and fatalities, low levels of physical activity, and rising obesity (Maibach, Steg, and Anable, 2009). Land-use specialization, low residential density, and poor street connectivity have been significantly related to obesity outcomes, while increased walking is associated with a reduced risk of being obese (Frank, Andresen, and Schmid, 2004). Indeed, Saelens et al. (2012) found that children living in walkable neighbourhoods with access to park space and a nearby supermarket were 56 per cent less likely to be obese. Frank et al. (2005), moreover, observed that individuals living in walkable communities are 2.4 times more likely to meet the minimum recommended amount of daily physical activity than individuals living in automobile-dominated neighbourhoods. In Vancouver, evidence shows that individuals living in the most walkable neighbourhoods are half as likely to be overweight as those living in the least walkable neighbourhoods (Frank et al., 2009).

Given the large number of factors that impact mental health, understanding the relationship between urban form and mental health is difficult. Nonetheless, sprawl has been associated with various factors affecting mental health, including increased feelings of isolation, stress, and disconnect from the natural environment (Frumkin, Frank, and Jackson, 2004). Walkable and mixed-use neighbourhoods have also been shown to build social capital, in which people know their neighbours, participate politically, exhibit higher levels of trust toward other people, and are socially involved (Leyden, 2003). In addition, proximity and regular exposure to nature can help urban residents cope with stress and can even contribute to boosting their immune system (Selhub and Logan, 2012).

Large cities in Canada are recognizing the critical importance of creating pedestrian-friendly neighbourhoods for public health and safety, and of encouraging lively, sociable communities. The City of Vancouver's master transportation plan, *Transportation 2040*, prioritizes pedestrian access above all other modes of transportation, and aims to increase the share of trips taken on foot, by bike, and by transit to two-thirds of all trips by 2040. Online tools and applications like Walk Score and RateMyStreet are gaining popularity, and walking audits such as the Pedestrian Environment Review System help assess the walking accessibility of different destinations.

Building Typology, Energy, and Emissions

Another co-benefit of compact development, in addition to reduced auto-dependence and increased physical activity, is the opportunity for greater efficiencies in building energy consumption. Building emissions come from two sources: "embodied" energy consumed in the materials and construction of the building itself, and the emissions resulting from building operations (e.g., heating, cooling, and lighting). Energy requirements in residential buildings differ widely from detached single-family dwellings, to low- and mid-rise multi-family structures, to high-rise apartment buildings. The construction of compact, multi-family residential buildings is an important component of low-carbon urban development. In communities with a low existing share of compact housing, there is significant potential for energy and GHG savings (Pitt, 2013).

Life cycle assessments (LCA) track energy consumption through the construction, occupation, and decommissioning of buildings and, thereby, provide a complete and comparable profile of energy consumption across buildings. LCA and other studies that combine the embodied energy of construction with the ongoing operating energy of inhabiting the building reveal that high-rise developments are the least energy consumptive per capita (Senbel et al., 2014). Even though relative to wood frame construction, high-rise apartment buildings carry a much higher embodied energy from the steel and concrete and mechanical systems, and additional operating energy loads from lighting, heating, and cooling common rooms and hallways (Norman et al, 2006; Perkins et al., 2009; VandeWeghe & Kennedy, 2007), high rises still perform better than New Urbanism suburban communities and much better than suburbs made exclusively of large single family homes (Brown and Southworth, 2008; Senbel et al., 2014). As shown in Figure 13.1, mechanisms can be used to increase the environmental performance of relatively low-density residential areas.

Figure 13.1   Drake Landing Solar Community, Okotoks, BC

Drake Landing is the first subdivision of single-family detached dwellings in North America to derive over 90 per cent of heating needs from solar thermal energy. A district heating system generates solar thermal energy from 800 rooftop collectors and stores the energy underground during summer months for distribution to each of the 52 homes during winter. The heating system reduces annual GHG emissions from each house by an estimated five tonnes. ("Aerial photo of Drake Landing Solar Community, 2007." Natural Resources Canada, 2007. Reproduced with the permission of the Minister of Natural Resources of Canada, 2014.)

Compactness increases the number of shared walls and floors and thereby reduces the surface area of individual dwelling units exposed to the elements. Higher densities also increase the potential for district energy systems, which centralize heating and cooling equipment for several buildings or even entire urban sectors and can recycle waste heat or use waste biomass for fuel. Because district energy systems require a minimum level of density to be viable, they are more commonly found in dense downtowns like Toronto, Montreal, and Vancouver, and on university campuses like that of the University of British Columbia (Andrews, 2008).

Green Infrastructure and Adaptive Design

Green urbanism seeks to go beyond New Urbanism and smart growth to achieve zero-carbon and zero-waste urban development. It therefore emphasizes renewable resources, adaptive reuse of building stock, shared energy production, and densification within urban growth boundaries (Lehmann, 2010). Green urbanism also draws from E.O. Wilson's idea of biophilia (the existence of a bond between humans and other forms of life) to ensure that urban environments are integrated with natural systems, and that urban dwellers have access to green spaces, such as parks, urban forests, and waterfronts. The integration of high-quality and well-connected patches of habitat for native plants and animals throughout neighbourhoods allows functioning ecosystems to live alongside urban residents. The psychological and educational benefits of urban nature are well documented. Green spaces in the fabric of urban life promote both ecosystem functioning, and the health and well-being of urban residents (Selhub and Logan, 2012).

Parc du Mont-Royal in Montreal, Stanley Park in Vancouver, and High Park in Toronto provide both recreational space and habitat for local wildlife and plant species. Cities across Canada have more recently begun integrating urban forests and "wild areas" in parks to create ecological corridors that integrate native species into the urban fabric (Figure 13.2). Framing urban systems as embedded within natural systems also helps to facilitate urban design that minimizes the adverse impacts of the natural hazards that come with climate change. For example, landscape elements like bioswales (the use of vegetation, compost, and stones to purify runoff water) and permeable surface materials are now considered essential to stormwater management efforts. Unlike pipes and concrete culverts, bioswales and permeable surfaces work to naturally reduce runoff during high precipitation events; they also filter pollutants while allowing stormwater to percolate into the ground. These stormwater management systems reduce flood damage during storms, and improve the environmental performance of urban infrastructure.

Regenerative design theory argues for a more fundamental restructuring of the city's relationship with nature so that our cities are designed to benefit native ecosystems. Rather than simply "doing less harm," regenerative design suggests that if we were to build neighbourhoods based on patterns identified in native ecosystems, we would begin to erase the artificial boundary between the built and natural environments. Urban development would seek to restore rather than destroy ecosystem habitats. This has implications for watershed management, urban agriculture, urban ecology, and energy and water resource management.

In Vancouver, the conversion of former industrial lands along False Creek to residential and commercial space has culminated in increasing levels of habitat restoration. With the beginning of high-rise residential construction in the 1980s, remediation of shoreline habitat included the gradual phasing out of the combined (storm and sanitary) sewer overflow system that drains into the creek. The development of the Olympic Village in Southeast False Creek saw more ambitious restoration with the creation of Habitat Island (Figure 13.3). Using a design that emphasizes native vegetation and tree snags, the island attracts waterfowl and bald eagles. In the fall of 2008, herring returned to spawn along one kilometre of the

Figure 13.2   Urban Forest Management Plan, Edmonton, AB.

Edmonton is home to about 300,000 publicly owned trees. Since 2000, the city has lost over 30,000 trees due to drought and pests, problems that are expected to increase under changing climatic conditions. Recognition of the importance of the urban forest in keeping neighbourhoods cool, improving air quality, sequestering CO_2 emissions, and reducing storm water runoff has encouraged the city to proactively plan for tree replacement, fire and disaster management, and planting strategies. The urban forest plan has also set a target to double the city's tree canopy from 10.3 to 20 per cent. (Adapted from flickr/Aaron, under Creative Commons License Attribution 2.0–www.flickr.com/photos/egoant/3840275074/)

shoreline for the first time in decades. However, industrial waste trapped in the ground around the creek remains a problem. Toxic chemicals continue to leak into the creek bed, preventing marine life from utilizing the bottom of the creek. Difficulties in dealing with these chemicals underscore complexities inherent in the regenerative process.

On land, restoring habitat helps to revive tree canopies, which improves rainfall retention and in turn helps reduce the urban heat island effect. Surface temperatures beneath individual and clustered trees and over grassy surfaces are typically cooler than over concrete or asphalt. Parks, for example, have been shown to be on average 0.95°C cooler during the day than non-green sites (Bowler et al., 2010). Integration of green roofs and living walls into buildings also provides an opportunity

to increase urban micro ecosystems while improving buildings' energy performance (Smith and Levermore, 2008).

Restoration of natural ecosystems when combined with urban design responses can help cities adapt to climate change conditions, including sea level rise and flooding. Adaptive building designs that accommodate flooding (for example, by locating all vital systems and functioning to higher floors) and floating residential developments are important design opportunities for vulnerable coastal and floodplain communities. Additionally, restoration and preservation of natural habitats along shorelines is a common strategy to protect communities from sea level rise, erosion, storms, and flooding. Living shorelines, as they are called, are flexible and cost-effective alternatives to hard

Figure 13.3   Olympic Village, Vancouver, BC.
Southeast False Creek in Vancouver was selected as the site for the Olympic Village for the 2010 Olympic and Paralympic Winter Games. A former industrial district comprising sawmills, port operations, and shipping, the area was redeveloped into a mixed-use, mixed-income neighbourhood designed for 11,000–13,000 residents. The neighbourhood is connected with the False Creek seawall pedestrian and cycling network, is served by two light rapid transit stations, and features Habitat Island. (Maged Senbel)

adaptations like dikes, dams, or locks that some communities are pursuing in tandem with environmental protection. In some cases, communities are resorting to managed retreat from vulnerable land and relocating homes, businesses, and recreational facilities away from areas at risk of flood and erosion.

Implementing Climate Action

A number of factors impact the success of local climate action. Leadership from municipal staff and elected officials, jurisdictional powers, organizational capacity, and adequate financing are critical factors in local climate action (Robinson and Gore, 2005). Mandates from senior levels of government tend to motivate local jurisdictions to address climate change (Senbel, Fergusson, and Stevens, 2013), especially where municipalities previously considered climate change to be a regional rather than a local problem (Tang et al., 2010). In 2008, for example, the province of British Columbia passed Bill 27, requiring local governments to set targets to reduce GHG emissions and identify implementable policies and actions in their official community plans. Despite the absence of any enforcement mechanism in the legislation, BC municipalities registered high rates of compliance by setting emission reduction targets (Senbel, Fergusson, and Stevens, 2013; Stevens and Senbel, 2012).

To date, every Canadian province, except Saskatchewan, has created and implemented a climate action plan (Holmes et al., 2012). Alberta was the first Canadian province to pass legislation on GHG emissions reduction, but targets focus on large industrial emitters and the province's climate change action plan allows emissions to continue growing until 2020. The strategy focuses largely on achieving emissions reductions through energy efficiency gains, greening energy production, and carbon sequestration. *Go Green: Ontario's Action Plan on Climate Change* set an emissions reduction target of 15 per cent below 1990 levels, and launched a $17.5 billion rapid transit investment in the Greater Toronto and Hamilton Area. As well, the Ontario Greenbelt Act was passed to protect undeveloped land around Toronto by limiting urban sprawl. Ontario has also mandated the closure of all coal-fired power plants. The province of Quebec has set an emissions reduction target of 20 per cent below 1990 levels, the highest emissions reduction target of any Canadian province or territory. The Quebec Climate Change Action Plan emphasizes transitions to sustainable land use planning, including densification around public transit corridors, mixed-use planning, and enhancement of existing town cores. Quebec also plans to develop a sustainable building strategy.

Community environmental activism affects how proactive local governments are on climate planning (Millard-Ball, 2012; Pitt, 2010). Having a history of disasters, proximity to coastal areas, and population concentration all influence perceptions of risk and willingness to engage in climate change planning (Tang et al., 2010). Non-governmental organizations (NGOs) also play an important role in mobilizing and supporting Canadian municipalities on climate change planning. The Federation of Canadian Municipalities and ICLEI Canada—Local Governments for Sustainability (formerly the International Council for Local Environmental Initiatives)—formed the Partners for Climate Protection (PCP) network among municipalities that have committed to acting on climate change. Municipalities are supported through a five-milestone framework toward developing a local action plan to reduce GHG emissions. By 2013, there were 240 Canadian cities participating in the PCP network.

Local governments face a number of challenges in their efforts to mitigate, and adapt to, climate change. A major impediment confronting mitigation is the difficulty of reducing total emissions through higher density developments that reduce *per capita* emissions but that, because of the growing population, fail to reduce *total* emissions or prevent an increase of total emissions (Senbel et al., 2013). An absence of reliable data and forecasting tools for the local scale, methodological uncertainties in tracking emissions and projecting impacts, and resource constraints further challenge local efforts to design low-carbon neighbourhoods (Measham et al., 2011; Pitt and Randolph, 2009). Planning for adaptation is made difficult by uncertainty about climate change futures and their impact on human systems. The complexity and global nature of climate-change science challenge efforts at raising awareness of climate change and interest in mediation and adaptation. Public engagement strategies that employ visualizations of neighbourhoods under different possible scenarios can help simplify the complexity of climate-change issues, and thus facilitate understanding and favour more effective climate action (Sheppard et al., 2011).

Challenges and Opportunities for Building Healthy, Low-Carbon Communities

Confounding the climate-change challenge is the potential for conflict in implementing both adaptation and mitigation. Hamin and Gurran (2009) point to a "density conundrum" in climate planning, where emissions reduction requires high-density urban environments that reduce driving and building energy use, and adaptation requires open spaces for stormwater management, migration of species, and cooling in urban areas. Optimal urban forms must therefore minimize conflicts between mitigation and adaptation by setting urban growth boundaries, designing open spaces to achieve multiple goals—such as urban agriculture and floodplain protection—and building green transportation routes that enable public transit (Hamin and Gurran, 2009). A strong bias in civic agendas toward mitigation over adaptation means that neighbourhood design approaches have generally not considered intersections between these two approaches to climate change (Measham et al., 2011).

A common challenge with increased density is the public perception of a dichotomy between sustainability and livability. High costs of housing in transit-rich neighbourhoods; perceptions of poor environmental quality in urban centres; and increased noise, traffic, crowding and crime: these all make it difficult to promote density (Ancell and Thompson-Fawcett, 2008; Howley, Scott, and Redmond, 2009). Higher density neighbourhoods must therefore achieve a high quality of urban design to appeal to residents. Neighbourhood design that emphasizes green space and the adaptation of space to the presence of children can help to cast a positive light on compact neighbourhoods. However, while quality materials and amenities might help make density more desirable, they exacerbate the affordability problem.

Involving community residents in climate change planning is important to address resistance to higher density developments and large investments in public transit infrastructure. Visualization media, such as film, along with digital 3-D and energy consumption modelling may also make relationships between climate change and urban form more accessible to community residents.

Figure 13.4   Adaptation Planning for Sea Level Rise, Halifax, NS.

The Halifax Regional Municipality has undertaken an extensive adaptation planning process to address risks of sea level rise in Halifax Harbour. Using LiDAR mapping for Digital Elevation Models, future flood hazard maps, vulnerability analysis, and community consultations, Halifax is drafting a comprehensive adaptation strategy. In the meantime, the Municipal Planning Strategy and Land Use Bylaw requires coastal developments to be at least 2.5 metres above the current high-water mark, subject to ongoing sea level rise monitoring and analysis. (Adapted from flickr/Gavin Langille, under Creative Commons License Attribution 2.0–www.flickr.com/photos/langille/7571302486/)

Senbel and Church (2011) found that these approaches must be embedded in a broader effort to build trust and dialogue between communities and decision-makers if they are to contribute to abating community opposition to changes in neighbourhood form. The Demain Montréal example (Figure 13.5) points to broad public support for measures promoting the greening of neighbourhoods.

Emphasizing the co-benefits of urban planning for climate change whereby compact development also provides other benefits for municipalities and their residents helps to make the case more compelling. For example, higher densities result in lower per capita costs for public infrastructure and services. The same goes for health promotion through transportation, land use, and building design decisions, which generates a range of positive side-effects: public safety, air quality, physical activity, accessibility, local food production, preservation of natural resources, urban greening, and contact with nature (Younger et al., 2008). For example, urban design practices that increase shading and green space in neighbourhoods, enhance walkability and cycling infrastructure, and improve access to public transportation lead to increases in physical activity, improved social connectivity and mental-health outcomes, and decreased cardiovascular and respiratory diseases (Cheng and Berry, 2013; Frank et al., 2010).

Figure 13.5   Montreal Development Plan–Demain Montréal.

Montreal is developing a 20-year vision that integrates economic, land use, transportation, and sustainability priorities. Demain Montréal emphasizes neighbourhood design for pedestrians and cyclists, aiming to expand the cycling network from 600km to 800km by 2016. The city intends to grow the Quartiers verts program, which implements traffic calming in neighbourhoods, greening with native plant species, significant increases in the tree canopy, creation of new space for active transportation, and collaboration with community groups and local artists. (Adapted from flickr/Montroyaler, under Creative Commons License Attribution 2.0–www.flickr.com/photos/puertodelacruz/4851566352/)

Conclusion

Structural changes in the way we design our neighbourhoods can improve public health outcomes, as well as reduce GHG emissions. Changing the dominant pattern of sprawling urban development in Canadian cities may go a long way toward addressing some of the major challenges that urban areas face. Urban design that mixes land uses alongside safe and enjoyable pedestrian and cycling pathways can help. Building compact, mixed-use, transit-oriented communities with networks of streets that are safe for walking and cycling, and creating networks of parks that provide habitat for native flora and fauna and have the capacity to filter, store, and absorb storm water is how Canadian cities can create low-carbon, resilient, and healthy neighbourhoods.

Review Questions

1. Why is it important to take measures that reduce the environmental impact of urban areas?
2. What approaches are most apt to minimize the environmental damages caused by cities?
3. What is your opinion on the different examples presented in the chapter? Which are most likely to achieve their environmental objectives?

References

Alley, R.B., T. Berntsen, N.L. Bindoff, Z. Chen, A. Chidthaisong, J.M. Gregory, and G.C. Hegerl. 2007. "Technical summary," in S. Solomon, D. Qin, and M. Manning , eds., *Climate Change 2007: The Physical Science Basis. Contribution of Working Group I to the Fourth Assessment Report of the Intergovernmental Panel on Climate Change.* Cambridge: Cambridge University Press.

Ancell, S., and M. Thompson-Fawcet. 2008. "The social sustainability of medium density housing: A conceptual model and Christchurch case study," *Housing Studies* 23: 423–41.

Andrews, C.J. 2008. "Greenhouse gas emissions along the rural-urban gradient," *Journal of Environmental Planning and Management* 51: 847–70.

Badland, H.M., G.M. Schofield, and N. Garrett. 2008. "Travel behavior and objectively measured urban design variables: associations for adults traveling to work," *Health & Place* 14: 85–95.

Bartholomew, K. 2005. *Integrating Land Use Issues into Transportation Planning: Scenario Planning.* Salt Lake City, UT: University of Utah.

Belanger, D., P. Berry, V. Bouchet, D. Charron, K-L. Clarke, B. Doyon, and M. Fleury. 2008. *Human Health in a Changing Climate: A Canadian Assessment of Vulnerabilities and Adaptive Capacity.* Ottawa: Health Canada.

Berrigan, D., L.W. Pickle, and J. Dill. 2010. "Associations between street connectivity and active transportation," *International Journal of Health Geographics* 9. At: www.ij-healthgeographics.com/content/9/1/20

Betsill, M.M. 2001. "Mitigating climate change in US cities: Opportunities and obstacles," *Local Environment* 6: 393–406.

Bhat, C.R., and J.Y. Guo. 2007. "A comprehensive analysis of built environment characteristics on household residential choice and auto ownership levels," *Transportation Research Part B: Methodological* 41: 506–26.

Blain, D., A. Matin, M. McGovern, S. McKibbon, D. Moore, F. Neitzert, and L. Pratt. 2013. "National inventory report 1990–2011: Greenhouse gas sources and sinks in Canada," in *National Inventory Report 1990–2011: Greenhouse Gas Sources and Sinks in Canada* (Vol. Part 1). Ottawa: Environment Canada.

Bowler, D.E., L. Buyung-Ali., T.M. Knight, and A.S. Pullin. 2010. "Urban greening to cool towns and cities: A systematic review of the empirical evidence," *Landscape and Urban Planning* 97: 147–55.

Brown, M., and F. Southworth. 2008. "Mitigating climate change through green buildings and smart growth," *Environment and Planning A* 40: 653–75.

Cao, X., P.L. Mokhtarian, and S.L. Handy. 2007. "Do changes in neighborhood characteristics lead to changes in travel behavior ? A structural equations modeling approach," *Transportation* 34: 535–56.

Champalle, C., P. Tudge, E. Sparling, R. Riedlsperger, J. Ford, T. Bell, and M. Tremblay. 2013. *Adapting the Built Environment in a Changing Northern Climate: A Review of Climate Hazard-Related Mapping and Vulnerability Assessments of the Built Environment in Canada's North to Inform Climate Change Adaptation.* Ottawa: Natural Resources Canada.

Cheng, J.J., and P. Berry. 2013. "Health co-benefits and risks of public health adaptation strategies to climate change: A review of current literature," *International Journal of Public Health* 58: 305–11.

Crowley, D.F., A.S. Shalaby, and H. Zarei. 2009. "Access walking distance, transit use, and transit-oriented development in North York City Center, Toronto, Canada," *Transportation Research Record* 2110: 96–105.

Dodman, D. 2009. "Blaming cities for climate change? An analysis of urban greenhouse gas emissions inventories," *Environment and Urbanization* 21: 185–201.

Ewing, R., and K. Bartholomew. 2013. *Pedestrian- and Transit-Oriented Design.* Washington, DC: Urban Land Institute and American Planning Association.

——, K. Bartholomew, S. Winkelman, J. Walters, and G. Anderson. 2008. "Urban development and climate change," *Journal of Urbanism* 1: 201–16.

——, and R. Cervero. 2010. "Travel and the built environment," *Journal of the American Planning Association* 76: 265–94.

Farr, D. 2008. *Sustainable Urbanism: Urban Design with Nature.* Hoboken, NJ: John Wiley & Sons.

Ford, J.D., T. Pearce, F. Duerden, C. Furgal, and B. Smit. 2010. "Climate change policy responses for Canada's Inuit population: The importance of and opportunities for adaptation," *Global Environmental Change* 20: 177–91.

Frank, L.D., M. Andresen, and T.L. Schmid. 2004. "Obesity relationships with community design, physical activity, and time spent in cars," *American Journal of Preventive Medicine* 27: 87–96.

——, M.J. Greenwald, S. Winkelman, J. Chapman, and S. Kavage. 2010. "Carbonless footprints: Promoting health and climate stabilization through active transportation," *Preventive Medicine* 50: S99–105.

——, S. Kavage, and B. Appleyard. 2007. "The urban form and climate change gamble," *Planning* 73 (8): 18–23.

——, T.L. Schmid, J.F. Sallis, J. Chapman, and B.E. Saelens. 2005. "Linking objectively measured physical activity with objectively measured urban form: Findings from SMARTRAQ," *American Journal of Preventive Medicine* 28: 117–25.

——, M. Winters, B. Patterson, and C.L. Craig. 2009. *Promoting Physical Activity through Health Community Design.* Vancouver, BC: Faculty of Medicine, University of British Columbia.

Frumkin, H., L. Frank, and R. Jackson. 2004. *Urban Sprawl and Public Health: Designing, Planning, and Building for Healthy Communities.* Washington, DC: Island Press.

Guo, Z. 2009. "Does the pedestrian environment affect the utility of walking? A case of path choice in downtown Boston," *Transportation Research Part D* 14: 343–52.

Hamin, E.M., and N. Gurran. 2009. "Urban form and climate change: Balancing adaptation and mitigation in the U.S. and Australia," *Habitat International* 33: 238–45.

Heres-Del-Valle, D., and D. Niemeier. 2011. "CO_2 emissions: Are land-use changes enough for California to reduce VMT? Specification of a two-part model with instrumental variables," *Transportation Research Part B: Methodological* 45: 150–61.

Holmes, M., D.M. Lingl, I. Bruce, M. Carter, and F. Moola. 2012. *All Over the Map 2012.* Vancouver, BC: David Suzuki Foundation.

Howley, P., M. Scott, and D. Redmond. 2009. "Sustainability versus liveability: An investigation of neighbourhood satisfaction," *Journal of Environmental Planning and Management* 52: 847–64.

Krizek, K.J. 2003. "Relocation and changes in urban travel," *Journal of the American Planning Association* 69: 265–81.

Lee, C., and A.V. Moudon. 2008. "Neighbourhood design and physical activity," *Building Research & Information* 36: 395–411.

Lehmann, S. 2010. *The Principles of Green Urbanism: Transforming the City for Sustainability.* London: Earthscan.

Lemmen, D.S., F.J Warren, J. Lacroix, and E. Bush. 2008. *From Impacts to Adaptation: Canada in a Changing Climate 2007.* Ottawa: Natural Resources Canada.

Levine, J., and A. Inam. 2004. "The market for transportation-land use integration: Do developers want smarter growth than regulations allow?" *Transportation* 31: 409–27.

Leyden, K.M. 2003. "Social capital and the built environment: The importance of walkable neighborhoods," *American Journal of Public Health* 93: 1546–51.

Maibach, E., L. Steg, and J. Anable. 2009. "Promoting physical activity and reducing climate change: Opportunities to replace short car trips with active transportation," *Preventive Medicine* 49: 326–7.

McHarg, I. 1969. *Design with Nature.* New York: The Natural History Press.

Measham, T.G., B.L. Preston, T.F. Smith, C. Brooke, R. Gorddard, G. Withycombe and C. Morrison. 2011. "Adapting to climate change through local municipal planning: Barriers and challenges," *Mitigation and Adaptation Strategies for Global Change* 16: 889–909.

Millard-Ball, A. 2012. "Do city climate plans reduce emissions?" *Journal of Urban Economics* 71: 289–311.

National Research Council. 2009. *Restructuring Federal Climate Research to Meet the Challenges of Climate Change.* Washington, DC: The National Academies Press.

Norman, J., H.L. MacLean, and C.A. Kennedy. 2006. "Comparing high and low residential density: Life-cycle analysis of energy use and greenhouse gas emissions," *Journal of Urban Planning and Development* 132: 10–21.

NRTEE (National Round Table on the Environment and the Economy). 2011. *Paying the Price: The Economic Impacts of Climate Change for Canada.* Ottawa: NRTEE.

Pataki, D.E., P.C. Emmi, C.B. Forster, J.I. Mills, E.R. Pardyjak, T.R. Peterson, and J.D. Thompson. 2009. "An integrated approach to improving fossil fuel emissions scenarios with urban ecosystem studies," *Ecological Complexity* 6: 1–14.

Pearce, T., J.D. Ford, F. Duerden, B. Smit, M. Andrachuk, L. Berrang-Ford, and T. Smith. 2011. "Advancing adaptation planning for climate change in the Inuvialuit Settlement Region (ISR): A review and critique," *Regional Environmental Change*, 11: 1–17.

Perkins, A., S. Hamnett, S. Pullen, R. Zito, and D. Trebilcock. 2009. "Transport, housing and urban form: The life cycle energy consumption and emissions of city centre apartments compared with suburban dwellings," *Urban Policy and Research* 27: 377–96.

Pitt, D. 2010. "The impact of internal and external characteristics on the adoption of climate mitigation policies by US municipalities," *Environment and Planning* C 28: 851–71.

———. 2013. "Evaluating the greenhouse gas reduction benefits of compact housing development," *Journal of Environmental Planning and Management* 56: 588–606.

———, and J. Randolph. 2009. "Identifying obstacles to community climate protection planning," *Environment and Planning* C 27: 841–57.

Rees, W. 2012. "The way forward: Survival 2100," *Solutions for a Sustainable and Desirable Future* 3(2). At: www.thesolutionsjournal.com/node/1113

Robinson, P.J., and C.D. Gore. 2005. "Barriers to Canadian municipal response to climate change," *Canadian Journal of Urban Research* 14: 102–20.

Saelens, B.E., J.F. Sallis, L.D. Frank, S.C. Couch, C. Zhou, T. Colburn, and K.L. Cain. 2012. "Obesogenic neighborhood environments, child and parent obesity: The Neighborhood Impact on Kids study," *American Journal of Preventive Medicine* 42: 57–64.

Schwanen, T., and P.L. Mokhtarian. 2005. "What affects commute mode choice: Neighborhood physical structure or preferences toward neighborhoods?" *Journal of Transport Geography* 13: 83–99.

Selhub, E.M., and A.C. Logan. 2012. *Your Brain on Nature.* New York: John Wiley & Sons.

Senbel, M., and S.P. Church. 2011. "Design empowerment: The limits of accessible visualization media in neighborhood densification," *Journal of Planning Education and Research* 31: 423–37.

———, D. Fergusson, and M. Stevens. 2013. "Local responses to regional mandates: Assessing municipal greenhouse gas emissions reduction targets in British Columbia," *Sustainability: Science, Practice, & Policy* 9: 28–41.

———, W. Giratallah, K. Zhang, and M. Kissinger. 2014. "Compact development without transit: GHG emissions from three versions of high-density residential neighbourhoods in Vancouver," *Environment and Planning A.* forthcoming.

———, M. van der Laan, R. Kellett, C. Girling, and J. Stuart. 2013b. "Can form based code help reduce municipal GHG emissions in small towns? The case of Revelstoke, British Columbia," *Canadian Planning and Policy* annual special issue of *Canadian Journal of Urban Research.* Forthcoming.

Sheppard, S.R.J., A. Shaw, D. Flanders, S. Burch, A. Wiek, J. Carmichael, and J. Robinson. 2011. "Future visioning of local climate change: A framework for community engagement and planning with scenarios and visualisation," *Futures* 43: 400–12.

Smith, C., and G. Levermore. 2008. "Designing urban spaces and buildings to improve sustainability and quality of life in a warmer world," *Energy Policy* 36: 4558–62.

Stevens, M., and M. Senbel. 2012. "Examining municipal response to a provincial climate action planning mandate in British Columbia, Canada," *Local Environment* 17: 837–61.

Tang, Z., S.D. Brody, C. Quinn, L. Chang, and T. Wei. 2010. "Moving from agenda to action: Evaluating local climate change action plans," *Journal of Environmental Planning and Management* 53: 41–62.

USEIA (US Energy Information Administration). 2013. *International Energy Statistics.* Washington, DC: U.S. Energy Information Administration. At: www.eia.gov/cfapps/ipdbproject/iedindex3.cfm?tid=90&pid=45&aid=8&cid=regions&syid=2007&eyid=2011&unit=MMTCD

VandeWeghe, J.R., and C. Kennedy. 2007. "A spatial analysis of residential greenhouse gas emissions in the Toronto census metropolitan area," *Journal of Industrial Ecology* 11: 133–44.

Younger, M., H.R. Morrow-Almeida, S.M. Vindigni, and A.L. Dannenberg. 2008. "The built environment, climate change, and health: Opportunities for co-benefits," *American Journal of Preventive Medicine* 35: 517–26.

Re-Imaging, Re-Elevating, and Re-Placing the Urban: The Cultural Transformation of Canadian Inner Cities

14

ALISON BAIN

Introduction

This chapter explores the new structural dynamics of metropolitan change at work in the inner cities of large Canadian cities. As introductory chapters in this volume illustrate, it is inner cities that have shown the most transformative changes over the past quarter-century. And in the past decade, with the apparent dominance of the new neo-liberal urban agenda, this transformation process has accelerated.

In this chapter, the prefix *re-* (meaning "once more," "again," or "afresh") is used to emphasize that cities, and neighbourhoods within them, are works in progress shaped by, and reflective of, prevailing political, economic, and social forces. In the case of inner cities in many large Canadian metropolitan areas, this chapter demonstrates how cultural forces have transformed formerly industrialized and centralized portions of cityscapes into up-scale and fashionable post-industrial places. The reader should be aware that interpretations of this "cultural turn" range from celebratory (Florida, 2002, 2005; Hall, 2003; Montgomery, 2008) to critically concerned (Kipfer and Keil, 2002; Ley, 2003; Peck, 2005, 2011; Walks, 2001; Wilson and Keil, 2008). The current discussion leans towards the latter perspective. This chapter asks what the contemporary built landscapes of core parts of Canada's largest urban centres reveal about who and what are privileged there. Conclusions are filtered through a social justice lens that reveals the vulnerable underbelly of spectacular but exclusive socio-spatial processes that (re)produce inequalities between people and places.

The argument asserted in this chapter is threefold. First, the twenty-first-century metropolitan quest for civic renewal in large Canadian cities has been dominated by a creative capital model of privately sponsored urban development (see Taylor and Bradford, Chapter 11). Second, that while culture can be used strategically to foster the development of place identities, high-profile cultural initiatives can exacerbate social divisions by creating consumption-driven urban environments with the potential to produce elitist and exclusionary experiences. Third, this chapter proposes that a more socially inclusive urban future may be possible for large Canadian cities if urban decision-makers aim for a finer balance between the production of spectacle and the production of possibility in the informal spaces of everyday life.

Urban Development in Transition

A Neighbourhood Typology

In an earlier edition of this book, Ley and Frost (2006) document the historical development of the Canadian inner city as concept, region, and object of study. They present a fourfold typology of different kinds of districts: (1) declining; (2) stable; (3) revitalized; and (4) redeveloped.

Neighbourhoods experiencing decline usually have the following: housing stock that is physically deteriorated; declining property values; a greater proportion of rental rather than home ownership; population loss from the out migration of higher income groups; high deprivation indicators (e.g., high unemployment, single-parent households, low-levels of high school completion, and elevated levels of social assistance); and an increasing presence of marginalized social groups (e.g., immigrants, refugees, mentally ill, substance abusers, sex-trade workers, homeless) and the services to support them (e.g., dollar stores, charity shops, food banks, and drop-in centres). In contrast, more stable neighbourhoods tend to have low population turnover, high levels of home ownership, well-maintained properties, dynamic voluntary organizations and community institutions that support durable social networks, and a strong sense of place.

All neighbourhoods sit somewhere on a continuum of decline to stability to revitalization. The extent of change that a neighbourhood experiences depends upon the age of the physical environment, the age of the residents, and the movement of households (Knox and McCarthy, 2012). Differences usually exist between neighbourhoods in terms of the rate and type of change, and the investment opportunities available. For example, a neighbourhood with a good physical stock of properties that is socially and demographically stable is unlikely to attract significant reinvestment. If, however, a profit can be made by changing the character of a neighbourhood or land use within it to better meet market demand, then developers and planners may consider it ripe for redevelopment and reinvestment.

Although the inner city is at no time homogeneous, Ley and Frost's typology represents a useful transitional view of inner city neighbourhoods. They move from a discussion of the 1960s late-modern period, when deterioration and decline seemed all-pervasive across inner-city zones, to the early twenty-first century when inner-city redevelopment and revitalization/ regeneration have become the celebrated characteristics of the new, creative city.

A Temporal Framework of Neighbourhood Change

When we examine large Canadian cities, it becomes clear that members of each generation of citizens, decision-makers, and scholars have used their experiences, ideas, labour, and capital to intellectually and materially re-imagine and rebuild the urban fabric. The following is a brief historical overview of urban development within a temporal framework of pre- and post-1945 and pre- and post-1975 (see also Filion and Bunting, Chapter 2).

Pre-1945 Period

In Canada, the pre-1945 period has been referred to by Filion and Bunting, in Chapter 2, as an era of inner-city development driven by industrial production. At the close of the nineteenth century, municipal governments focused on building the basic infrastructure of cities: sidewalks, roads, bridges, sewer systems, and water filtration plants. In the early twentieth century, the role of municipal government expanded further to include the establishment of housing programs and parks and recreation facilities. Urban growth became focused on the central business district; industrial corridors radiated along waterways and railways, and high-density residential neighbourhoods segregated by income and ethnicity developed along public transit lines and roads close to retail and other educational, religious, and health-care institutions. With the creation of the welfare state in the 1940s, urban problems were framed as national problems, and federal and provincial governments became heavily involved in municipal affairs.

Post-WWII Period

In the ensuing post–World War II period, 1945–75, metropolitan growth accelerated to include suburbs. This was a time of massive government-led restructuring of urban space, underwritten by the increasing professionalization and bureaucratization of the urban planning process (Grant, 2006).

At the same time, decline was becoming prevalent in many parts of the inner city. New-Marxists, such as Neil Smith (1996), have theorized central-city decline and revitalization as revanchist reinvestment of capital in property, a form of spatialized revenge by the privileged middle class against the poor and minorities, who supposedly "stole the inner city" from them (see Siciliano, Cowen, and Smith, Chapter 16). Out of concern for central-city decline in the face of dramatic **suburbanization**, the public sector invested heavily in downtown redevelopment. To improve the image of the core of many large Canadian cities, roads were widened, public transit was funded, and symbolic buildings were constructed. In Montreal, for example, during his nearly three-decade tenure as mayor, Jean Drapeau supported the construction of mega-projects that would increase the city's international profile and create highly visible urban landmarks: the Montreal Metro subway system; the Expo 67 site; and the 1976 Olympic Stadium (Germain and Rose, 2000; Lortie, 2004). In Montreal and other large agglomerations, the 1960–75 period was also a time of major private-sector investment in office buildings, plazas, underground shopping concourses, and downtown shopping malls, which together dramatically altered the built fabric and character of the central city (Filion and Gad, 2006).

Latter Twentieth Century

The last quarter of the twentieth century was a period of economic restructuring and urban transition for large Canadian cities, with an emphasis on suburban domination (Bourne, 1989). Loss of traditional industrial manufacturing and warehouse functions has reoriented downtowns toward recreational, cultural, educational, and residential functions. The 1970s witnessed the politicization of city spaces in Canadian urban centres. Citizen groups mobilized to preserve neighbourhoods and green spaces threatened by **urban renewal**, development projects, and highway expansions (Grant, 2006).

While urban planning may have become more democratic and participatory through increased public consultation, the financial constraints wrought by the 1980s recession, the 1990s downloading of programs to municipalities (e.g., housing, welfare, transit), and the most recent global economic downturn have produced cash-strapped cities struggling to manage infrastructural decline. Cities have turned to the private sector for financial support, and the participatory era of the 1970s has given way to an entrepreneurial era of urban development that yields authority to market forces (see Walks, Chapter 9; Taylor and Bradford, Chapter 11). The twenty-first century marks a new era wherein cities are run more like businesses and local governments rely on risk-taking, inventiveness, self-promotion, and profit-maximization.

The Optics of the Twenty-First-Century Competitive City

The most recent distinctive and self-consciously entrepreneurial phase of urban development is characterized by "flagship" strategies centred on profit, spectacle, and consumption (Hall, 2003; Logan and Molotch, 1987). Cities now take great care to use architectural form and urban design to promote a positive and high-quality image of place (Harvey, 1989; Zukin, 1995; Walker and Gunn, Chapter 18). This attention to **place-making** creates a distinctive development style that is notable in Canada's largest and fastest-growing metropolitan areas, where branding is applied to whole cities in an effort to develop a distinctive civic image appealing to tourists, investors, and members of the **creative class** (Bradley, Hall, and Harrison, 2002). The "boosterist" goal of many municipalities is to replace perceptions of the city as a place of disinvestment, decay, crime, and poverty left behind by the post–World War II suburban transitions with images of growth, vitality, and prosperity (Avraham, 2004; Short, 1999). In a global economy, city image is of concern, particularly in the best-known and most central parts of the metropolitan region, because it influences where businesses locate. This, in turn, impacts inward investment and the infrastructure of daily life for residents. But it is not just the built and physical environments that are central to imaging a city; the lifestyles and symbolic economies that exist in these spaces through recreation, leisure, and cultural activities also contribute to a city's image and perceived quality of life (Zukin, 1995, 2004).

Culture, in particular, has become an instrument of economic development and "urban spectacularisation, which serves both for real-estate speculation and for political propaganda" (Vaz and Jacques, 2007: 249). In addition to a bias toward the better-off in society, spectacle can have an inversely proportional relationship to popular participation: the more spectacular the interventions in urban revitalization, the less the participation of the population (Vaz and Jacques, 2007). Thus, who is included and who is excluded, who wins and who loses in the urban revitalization process are important considerations. Is this so-called "circus" serving those in need of "bread" and other necessities of life (Kipfer and Keil, 2002)? The assumed trickle-down mechanisms may not work: poorer local residents may become further marginalized, their visions of less exclusive, corporate, or authoritarian urban futures sidelined or ignored by urban elites (see Walks, Chapter 9).

Re-Imaging Canadian Cities through Spectacle

Over the past two decades, academics, urban planners, and municipal politicians across North America and Europe have enthusiastically favoured a flexible "creative capital" model of urban development that privileges knowledge, creativity, and commodified difference as a means of civic renewal (Gertler et al., 2002; Markusen and King, 2003). Turning away from the more traditional primary and secondary sectors of the economy for support, this new model seeks instead to use urban amenities as "honey pots" to attract a broad creative class of mobile and educated professionals (Florida, 2002; 2005; Pratt 2009; Vinodrai, Chapter 5). The iconic citizens of the new knowledge-based economy are presented

as the "storm troopers" of city branding; they are said to be attracted to cities that offer "the 3Ts": technology, talent, and tolerance. But as Wilson and Keil (2008) question, tolerance of whom and by whom? They argue that the "real" creative class is the poor—who use everyday resourcefulness to navigate torn social safety nets, make homes in neglected neighbourhoods, and work in low-wage service-sector jobs. For Wilson and Keil (2008: 846), the concept of the creative class is a perverse fantasy in which "the white affluent are the historic and current bearers of civility, tradition, and good culture"; and the creative capital model of urban development is just another fast-track public policy option that privileges "the desires and aspirations of capital and the affluent."

In a quest to lure members of the creative class, Canadian cities are remaking themselves as centres of arts and culture and marketing themselves as places that provide stimulation, diversity, and a richness of experience that inspire creativity and innovation. Culture has been co-opted to the agenda of marketization (Miles, 2005). Nowhere is this more apparent in Canada than in Toronto.

Since the turn of the twenty-first century, Toronto has witnessed an urban cultural building boom in which cultural spaces have been given new social and architectural prominence in the city. Financial assistance from provincial and federal governments and wealthy private sponsors has supported "starchitectural" makeovers of high-culture institutions (e.g., the Royal Ontario Museum, the Gardiner Museum of Ceramic Art, the Four Seasons Centre for the Performing Arts, the National Ballet School, the Royal Conservatory of Music, and the Art Gallery of Ontario) by internationally renowned architects, including Frank Gehry, Daniel Libeskind, Lord Norman Foster, and Will Alsop. This trend of creating iconic architectural landmarks began with the completion in 1997 of the franchised Guggenheim Museum in the industrial city of Bilbao, Spain, by Frank Gehry (Marshall, 2001). Glen Murray, the former mayor of Winnipeg turned urban strategist and Liberal Member of Provincial Parliament (MPP) in Ontario, has humorously referred to civic enthusiasts' mistaken belief that building iconic museums can be a shortcut to urban revitalization as the "Irritable Bilbao Syndrome." Instead of developing cultural planning strategies that use grassroots economic and cultural assets for new uses, many urban decision-makers in Canada's biggest and wealthiest cities are busy with large-scale redevelopment initiatives. Such strategies may augment the provision of cultural infrastructure for consumption, but they do not provide adequate support for "the experimental, non-market-led production of new work" by cultural producers, such as artists, writers, and performers (Miles, 2005: 893).

The centrepiece of Toronto's cultural promotion package, initiated in the fall of 2005, was the $4 million, two-year, street-banner branding campaign—"T.O. live with culture"—and its accompanying website that listed arts events in the city (www.LiveWithCulture.ca). This marketing campaign was conceived of as a means to increase local and tourist awareness of the extent of Toronto's cultural activities (e.g., corporate-sponsored events such as Scotiabank Nuit Blanche and L'Oréal Luminato). While such short-term events continue to draw crowds and have increased local cultural awareness, members of Toronto's arts communities have argued that city funding would be better spent on capital grants that would allow arts organizations and cultural workers to purchase permanent affordable workspace, thus breaking the cycle that displaces them from gentrifying neighbourhoods (Bain and McLean, 2013). Without such financial support, Toronto's street banners could become a misnomer: future cultural workers may not be able to afford to live downtown. Instead, the inner city may be left to developers to infill with condominium towers.

Growing Sky High: The Condominium Boom

In large Canadian cities where significant inner-city redevelopment has occurred, the nineteenth-century, middle-class stigma once associated with living among the supposed deprivation, pollution, and pathologies of the working classes has lost some of its potency. Canadian urban geographer David Ley (1988, 1993, 1996a, 1996b) has studied how, since the 1970s, the romanticized cosmopolitan character of downtown living has gained a cachet among the "new middle class"; he persuasively argues that their residential preferences, investment decisions, and cultural values have facilitated substantial gentrification and upgrading in many Canadian cities.

Unlike some American (e.g., Cleveland and Detroit) and European (e.g., Liverpool and Leipzig) "shrinking city" counterparts that have witnessed urban population decline (www.shrinkingcities.com), large cities in Canada's urban system have not lost population nor become hollowed out because of racial tensions, violence, or poor schools. In fact, some of urban Canada's most expensive real estate can be found in core-area neighbourhoods (see Skaburskis and Moos, Chapter 12). Recognizing that land is a finite resource, many sizeable Canadian cities have focused development on brownfield and infill sites, a process often referred to as intensification. In the Province of Ontario's Growth Plan for the Greater Golden Horseshoe prepared under the Places to Grow Act (2005), intensification is defined as "the development of property, site or area at a higher density than currently exists through redevelopment, including the reuse of brownfield sites; the development of vacant and/or underutilized lots within previously developed areas; infill development, or the expansion or conversion of existing buildings" (www.placestogrow.ca). The Growth Plan establishes intensification and density targets for 25 urban growth centres (400, 200, and 150 people and jobs per hectare) as part of an integrated package of policies to foster the creation of more compact, mixed-use, and transit-supportive communities. The highest density target has been applied to the City of Toronto (Downtown Toronto, Etobicoke Centre, North York Centre, Scarborough Centre, and Yonge-Eglinton Centre), which has a large population and high-frequency subway service. Much of this intensification, particularly in Toronto, has taken the form of privately developed condominiums.

Condo-mania has a firm grip on large cities across the country. Many urban planning departments are overrun with proposals for high-density residential living and must contend with condominium development as a major component of municipal comprehensive plans (Kern, 2007; Lehrer, 2008). Inevitably, such intensive residential development involves substantial physical and social change to the fabric of the city.

There are many potential benefits associated with increased residential densities: improved energy and land conservation; maximization of existing infrastructure; reduced reliance on the private automobile; improved economic capacity through the increased circulation of money in the local economy; an increased tax base; and the social and safety dimensions of a more vibrant street life. But drawbacks exist, also. It has been argued, for example, that intensification in the form of high-rise condominium towers that commonly cater to childless singles or couples from the middle and upper classes who seek maintenance-free living has created "vertical gated communities" (see Townshend and Walker, Chapter 7). Condominium fees cover the costs of residents-only facilities (e.g., gym, swimming pool, spa, games room, movie theatre) and security systems, creating islands of wealth and privilege where residents may seldom interact with each other or with the people and spaces of the surrounding neighbourhood. People insulated from one another lose a sense of community and of commitment to a common social project with shared social justice and social sustainability goals (e.g., equity, inclusion, participatory processes, and access to services, housing, and employment) (Quastel, Moos, and Lynch, 2012). As a result, planners must consider ways of fostering social interaction at the neighbourhood scale over the longer term, perhaps by providing accessible, inclusive, well-maintained public spaces (e.g., parks, parkettes, and squares) that support a variety of uses and involve a range of different social groups. Intensified residential development can be a positive contribution to city life if cities have the financial means and the political will to adequately invest in providing and maintaining public infrastructure (e.g., developing dedicated cycle routes and public transit). Indeed, Danyluk and Ley (2007) have shown that higher density central city neighbourhoods in Canada tend to be home to walkers and cyclists who rely on non-motorized modes of commuting.

In his book *Cities for People*, Danish architect and urban designer Jan Gehl (2010) advocates that urban planners attend to the human scale by creating cities that are pedestrian- and bicycle-friendly. Built environments where attention has been paid to details in the "experience zone" encourage people to walk slowly, stop frequently, and linger. Widening sidewalks and removing interruptions, laying textured surfaces, planting shade trees, improving street crossings, and providing comfortable street furniture and good lighting are all practical recommendations for improving the public realm and increasing the amount of time that people spend in public space.

The quality of the public realm is a key component of livability (see **livable cities**), which, in conjunction more recently with sustainability goals (e.g., densification, social mixing, and transit accessibility) has driven twenty-first-century urban planning policy agendas in North America. Livability, in contrast to sustainability, does not refer to the future but, rather, to the current state of the environment and the quality of life it offers to local residents. Cities like Vancouver, that often appear high on world rankings of livable cities, have paid attention to retaining a distinctive local character, ensuring connectivity and ease of movement, promoting higher density living, supporting a diversity of land uses, and creating a high-quality public realm. In privileging a sustainability agenda, Vancouver has established the Greenest Capital Action Team (GCAT) with the intent of becoming the greenest city in the world by 2020.

But for whom are cities livable and sustainable? While densification may lay "at the heart of a process of cultural and economic restructuring," it can also lead "to the gentrification and revalorization of walkable and transit-accessible spaces" that privilege middle-class priorities (Quastel, Moos, and Lynch, 2012: 1077). Thus, the potential exists to exacerbate spatial injustice and offer few environmental benefits for more marginal social groups.

Place-Making at the Water's Edge

Much condominium construction is concentrated along river-, lake-, or oceanfront property. The reclaiming of waterfront sites began in the 1980s, and today these sites are considered valuable urban amenities with a central role to play in contemporary city-making (Marshall, 2001). Waterfronts are complex places that have hosted a plurality of functions over time. Historically, the working part of the city was on the waterfront: the waterfront was where industry located and ship and rail yards interfaced. Urban waterfronts consisted of dirty, messy, and contaminated sites and so were largely undervalued in the collective conscience. As a result, for much of the twentieth century, Canada's urban waterfronts were under-utilized parcels of land separated from the rest of the city by transportation corridors. Today, however, waterfronts have been revalued as city assets, and efforts are underway to "recapture" these areas by reconfiguring connections between the older, original city centre and the water's edge (Bunce, 2009; Desfor and Ledley, 2011).

A noteworthy example of post-industrial city-making through waterfront redevelopment is Vancouver. Since the 1990s, Vancouver has gained an international reputation for its high standard of urban planning and design practice, so much so that when North American architects and planners promote the idea of a high-residential density, high-public amenity central city they call it "Vancouverism" (Boddy, 2005). In Vancouver, the ocean is brought right into the heart of the city and together with the mountains provides the raw material for the "cult of the view," which, in conjunction with a series of overlapping official "view corridors," has driven high-rise residential development in the inner city for the past 50 years (Berelowitz, 2005). Historic neighbourhoods in the inner city (e.g., Strathcona, Gastown, and Chinatown) remain largely intact as

pedestrian-friendly, bicycle-friendly places because Vancouver has managed to avoid the worst of traditional North American urban renewal: highways, elevated and underground pedestrian systems, large shopping malls, and big-box retail. For example, within the city's municipal boundaries, no highways disrupt the regular street grid or cut the city off from its waterfront. Since the 1970s and accelerating after Expo 86 and into the 2010 Winter Olympics, Vancouver's waterfront has been strategically transformed from industrial and railway use to residential and recreational use (Hutton, 2004). The construction of public pathways along the seawall has repositioned recreational activity in a continuous corridor along the inner-city waterfront. The downtown street grid and urban fabric have gradually been extended to the water's edge and filled in with tall, glass condominium towers known locally as "see-throughs" (Coupland, 2000). But the city has also faced criticism for privileging residential development over office development, thus jeopardizing its commercial land base, elevating land values, and creating more of a recreational resort than a working city.

A centrepiece of Vancouver's waterfront renewal is Granville Island. This former industrial site beneath the southern viaduct of the Granville Bridge was transformed in the 1980s into a commercial, arts, entertainment, and recreation destination. The foci of this complex are a public farmers' market and the Emily Carr University of Art + Design, combined with an eclectic mix of studios, galleries, theatres, restaurants, and specialty shops in converted warehouses. Granville Island has been characterized as a privatized public place of conspicuous consumption and play (Ley, 1996a). This island of wealth, investment, and pleasure stands in contrast to the poverty, homelessness, and health crises of drug use and HIV transmission experienced in Vancouver's Downtown Eastside (DTES), perhaps Canada's poorest inner-city neighbourhood (Ley and Dobson, 2008; Smith, 2003). Stigmatized as a "skid row" district of concentrated poverty and inadequate single-room occupancy hotel housing, the DTES gained international notoriety for the disappearance and murder of 69 sex-trade workers (Robertson, 2007). The DTES is a diverse neighbourhood that has housed a variety of populations over time, each attaching different social meanings to the neighbourhood (Burke, 2006). Yet gentrification and property development processes unfolding here work through policy-makers, service providers, and police to discipline places and racialized and sexualized bodies into a more uniform, middle- and upper-class urban landscape (Robertson 2007).

While Vancouver may arguably be North America's most livable city, this positive affinity for the city is likely only shared by those who can afford the high real estate costs. As in most other fast-growing, large Canadian cities, the process of urban redevelopment and modernist planning practice has physically reorganized poverty and affluence in the city, often concentrating poor residents in neighbourhoods that are poorly serviced, far from employment opportunities, and physically separated from the rest of the city (Walks, 2001). The image of a new, affluent city of leisure seeks to hide such marginal spaces from view.

What Lies Behind the Shimmering Facades and Visual Noise?

In a neo-liberal era of municipal financial constraint, where discourses of urban entrepreneurialism and competitiveness dominate and business elites hold the reins of power in public–private partnerships, market forces are readily accommodated while social justice objectives that could help to meet the basic needs of the most marginal populations are all too easily abandoned (Miles, 2005). The large-scale cultural and residential redevelopment projects discussed in this chapter can create huge commercial gains for developers and landlords and increase the city's tax base. However, "[w]hat this branding of commodified space also shares over time is the fact that little or none of the increased values accrue to the residents who have been decanted and displaced" (Evans, 2007: 198–200). Social displacements and dramatic inequities are particularly apparent in

western Canada, where the oil boom has accelerated urban growth.

The inflow of workers and money to cities such as Saskatoon, Calgary, and Vancouver has caused local housing markets to climb to record highs, thus minimizing the availability of affordable accommodation (see Walks, Chapter 9). In Calgary, rental apartments have been converted into luxury condominiums and blocks of lower-end residences have been bulldozed to make room for condominium towers, some of which remain incomplete because labour and material shortages have caused construction delays and cost overruns. According to one journalist, in the past half-decade Calgary has lost 220 modest downtown units, experienced a rent increase of 67 per cent, and seen increases in homelessness of 264 per cent (MacGregor, 2008: A2). In an effort to combat homelessness, the Calgary Committee to End Homelessness was established in 2007, releasing, a year later, a *10-Year Plan to End Homelessness*, which is being implemented by the Calgary Homeless Foundation through public–private partnerships (calgaryhomeless.com). Five years into the plan, the city has prioritized a housing-first strategy that focuses on the most vulnerable subpopulations (e.g., youth, women, families, and Aboriginal people). A key component of the plan has involved the development of a Homeless Management Information System, which makes data on homelessness and affordable housing available in real time to facilitate inter-agency co-ordination in the design and implementation of programs.

Artistic Interventions in the Gentrifying Urban Landscape

The story of inner-city neighbourhood change through gentrification and other kinds of upgrading is not a new one. It is a story that is national in scope, impacting cities diverse in population, age, size, and location. The following discussion focuses on the role of the arts and cultural workers in the transformation of one of Toronto's inner-city neighbourhoods; this discussion reflects on how the generalizations of urban development trajectories made at the outset of the chapter play out in the spaces of one neighbourhood and suggests alternative approaches to urban change. This case study also raises questions about displacement, social justice, equity, and balance. If there is a moral to the story, it comes in the form of a question: Does inner city revitalization that is driven almost entirely by private-sector profit-making threaten "to kill the goose that lays the golden egg"?

Inner cities have long been celebrated by urban theorists as the places where the arts, culture, and creativity flourish. Cultural or creative activities tend to cluster in places with an "urban edge: that is, a mix of old and new buildings, an active streetscape, mixed use development, contemporary design, cafés and bars, nightclubs" (Montgomery, 2008: xviii). This has been the case in Toronto. Art districts have formed and reformed in different neighbourhoods in the city as artists have discovered the character and potential for inexpensive work spaces in declining neighbourhoods ahead of developers and the "new middle class" (Ley, 1996; 2003). Since the 1960s, however, gentrification has spread across most residential neighbourhoods in downtown Toronto. The process has exiled risk-taking and trend-setting households, such as those of artists, from the more centrally located Yorkville district to Queen Street West, then to King Street West, out to the Junction (i.e., Dundas Street West and Keele Street), over to Queen Street East, and out to the inner suburbs of Etobicoke and Scarborough (Bain, 2003, 2013). This sequence of relocations closely parallels the "stage theory" of gentrification (Gale, 1980).

Researchers have developed a typology that seeks to explain who is involved in the gentrification process through various stages (Caulfield, 1994). The first stage includes "marginal gentrifiers" (Rose, 1984), a lower-middle class of professionals (including artists) and students who are often non-family groups who rent inexpensive housing in socially diverse inner city neighbourhoods. The second stage includes "early gentrifiers," a group of highly educated social and cultural workers, who may be first-time homeowners using

sweat equity to renovate their homes. The third stage, "gentrification proper," includes increasingly affluent middle-class professional households and developers exploiting the "rent gap" to maximize the greatest profit from the land. The "advanced gentrification" stage includes major redevelopment projects funded by "super-gentrifying" financiers who re-gentrify areas previously gentrified (Butler and Lees, 2006). One of the drawbacks of stage theory, however, is that it fails to concern itself with the location and welfare of displaced incumbents. Artists—often referred to as the storm troopers of gentrification—while resourceful and adaptable, are one such displaced group.

In the central city, Queen Street West is Toronto's main arts axis. Extending westward from University Avenue, this street has the largest concentration of art galleries in the city and an extensively developed network of artist-run spaces, arts organizations, studios, and art-supportive cafés, bars, and restaurants. Since the 1950s this neighbourhood has been transformed from an economically depressed, largely immigrant community in the light industrial garment district into a trendy "new Soho." The name was first applied by local 1970s journalists who noted similarities with the development of SoHo in New York. Both areas were vibrant city neighbourhoods of avant-garde arts activity with residential lofts in former warehouses, stores, and galleries. In 1979, the Soho Merchants Association was formed on Queen Street West and "Welcome to Soho" signs appeared in store windows. The signs incurred the wrath of some residents who saw it as an embarrassing derivative and a ploy to increase rents. Through the 1980s, rents increased and artists were displaced as developers converted warehouses into condominiums and offices.

The continued migration of artists exiled from Queen West proper has inspired the westward development of an eclectic retail mix of high-end independent and chain stores. But despite consumer hyperactivity, residual poverty is apparent in the mix of Parkdale residents who call Queen West home: the precariously housed; newcomers to Canada; psychiatric survivors; sex-trade workers; methadone-clinic users; and cultural workers

(Slater, 2004). In 2003, with the city's support, the neighbourhood was officially re-branded by the local business improvement area (BIA) as the West Queen West Art and Design District. A website (westqueenwest.ca), pocket maps, and unique street signs and banners all have helped to reinforce the neighbourhood brand. Refurbished hotels with bars (e.g., The Cameron House, The Drake, and The Gladstone), host well-publicized cultural events and function as cultural lynchpins in the area. While The Drake is a small player in the local real estate market, it has the symbolic cultural capital through artist-in-residency programs, music, lectures, performances, exhibitions, and sponsorship to make the arts community complicit in the processes of gentrification and displacement at work in the neighbourhood. The creation of these high-profile cultural destination points has helped to push up residential and commercial real estate values, leading one graffiti artist to scrawl on the side of a Starbuck's coffee shop, "Drake, you pimp, it's all your fault!" (Blackwell, 2008).

Gentrification is hard at work on Queen Street West, physically restructuring the neighbourhood and displacing marginalized residents, such as cultural workers, rooming-house residents, and refugees. Luxury condominiums, like the Bohemian Embassy, are going up one after another, capitalizing on the trendy counterculture first established by the very artists who have been displaced. Condominium branding campaigns co-opt the language of the arts and use cultural workers as bait to lure new buyers. These condominiums do not cater to real Bohemians, however, but to "fauxhemians" (Kingwell, 2008) and "neo-Bohemians" (Lloyd, 2006). In nineteenth century Paris, the term *Bohemian* was used pejoratively in conjunction with words like *beggar* and *Gypsy* to describe self-chosen social outcasts who sacrificed money, job security, and social status for the freedom to pursue creative practice. In the early twentieth-century North American context, *Bohemia* was associated with the countercultural movements that opposed the rationalized organization of labour and commerce under industrial capitalism. Bohemia materialized in artistic districts (e.g., Greenwich, New York City; Venice Beach, Los Angeles; Haight-Ashbury, San Francisco). However, the new Bohemia of the twenty-first century is not as marginal to the urban economy or to society; it has a central role to play in enhancing property speculation. Fauxhemians and neo-Bohemians, then, are "hipsters" (a catch-all term for urbane, anti-conformist conformist city dwellers who self-style as the harbingers of cool) with superficial Bohemian lifestyles who may have corporate jobs, trust funds, and upscale tastes.

But gentrification has not gone unchallenged. For years, cultural workers on Queen Street West have protested their forced evictions with demonstrations, petitions, exhibitions, and urban interventions. Ute Lehrer (2008) has documented how Active 18, a coalition of local residents and business owners who work in the cultural industries, opposed development proposals for the area that were out of scale with the neighbourhood and provided little in the way of mixed-use or mixed-income opportunities. Active 18 successfully obtained some concessions from developers with respect to building height, contributions for arts-related community improvement projects, and affordable housing.

As well, the non-profit organization Artscape has been heavily involved in cultural regeneration in Toronto since the mid-1980s. Functioning as a cultural intermediary between artists, developers, and municipal politicians, Artscape oversees the development and management of building conversions (e.g., the former police station at 1313 Queen Street West; the Distillery District; a streetcar repair yard at Wychwood Barns; and a decommissioned school at Artscape Youngplace) into multi-tenant facilities. Such facilities position artists as agents of change at the centre of urban development and embed them in the landscape by providing affordable living, work, exhibition, and performance spaces (www.torontoartscape.on.ca).

But more such "adaptive re-use" projects (Caulfield, 2005) need to be undertaken across the city, particularly in suburban neighbourhoods, if the exodus of artists to small-, mid-size, and rural areas is to be slowed. Without continued urban cultural activism, the city will continue to witness "a massive art-brain-drain" (LeBlanc, 2008):

cultural workers and creative industries will likely continue to be displaced in favour of the purchasing preferences of the middle class, and inner-city neighbourhoods likely will struggle to function productively as incubators for culture and entrepreneurship. As productive as Artscape has been at creating a bulwark for cultural workers to withstand gentrification, its overshadowing effect and privileging of one low-income group (artists) over countless others with more pressing needs is of concern. Artscape's mandate aligns with the creative capital model of development, and its signature cultural hub projects are frequently prioritized despite serious issues of racialized poverty and an affordable housing crisis in Toronto. Indeed, in the same week that Artscape opened to positive critical acclaim, for example, the Ontario Non-Profit Housing Association reported the longest waiting list for affordable housing in the past decade (Whyte, 2013). There is a danger that culture does not make space for all; that Artscape is "a symbolic salve" in a "nefarious process" of gentrification and real estate development that continues to displace low-income earners of all kinds from the inner city (Whyte, 2013).

In the Queen Street West neighbourhood of Parkdale, some artists have worked collaboratively with BIAs, art councils, private sponsors, and boutique hotels to facilitate small-scale urban performance interventions to reanimate Queen Street West and to reveal complex layers, histories, and narratives about the neighbourhood. The artist Darren O'Donnell (2006) and his company Mammalian Diving Reflex use "social acupuncture" to transform social life into art as a way to make the world a more just and equitable place. In the project Parkdale Public School vs. Queen West, low-income schoolchildren from new immigrant families theatrically competed in six rounds of culinary, visual art, and music challenges at the Gladstone Hotel against adult "artser" gentrifiers (McLean, 2009). This project facilitated communication between social groups from the same neighbourhood usually divided by age, ethnicity, and class. Such local initiatives by countercultural communities add "cumulative texture" to cities in ways that

cannot be reproduced by urban elites through macro-scale policy initiatives (Lloyd, 2006). Site-specific performances in everyday spaces create opportunities for participatory dialogue and engagement with diverse audiences. As David Pinder (2005) explains, artists and cultural practitioners who intervene in cities through creative practice have the ability to "challenge norms about how urban space is framed and represented" and to disrupt routines of use, meaning, and value. In so doing, artists help to question and to re-envision who can claim a "right to the city" (Staehli, Mitchell and Gibson, 2002).

For Henri Lefebvre (1991), *le droit à la ville* is earned through the everyday routines of people living in the city. "The right to the city" is a form of urban citizenship that involves two main entitlements: to appropriate urban space and to participate in decision-making about the production of urban space (Mitchell, 2003). These rights of appropriation and participation are about use value rather than exchange value. The idea of urban space as property, as a commodity to be exchanged on the real estate market for profit, is antithetical to these rights. When urban space is privileged for its exchange value it mutes what Lefebvre refers to as "the city as oeuvre"—by this, he means the city as a work of art (re)created out of the collective daily routines of citizens. Each person who lives his or her life in urban space helps to make the city an oeuvre and is entitled to rights of appropriation and participation. In Lefebvre's framework, residents should play a central role in policy and planning decisions that produce urban space, and property ownership should not be the principal voice in decisions about what to do with urban land. Thus the phrase "the right to the city" references the ongoing and radical need for all users of the city to have an active presence in urban life to ensure that the city is produced *by* residents rather than *for* residents. As Mitchell (2003: 42) reminds us, though, the "right to the city is never guaranteed and certainly never freely given." Rather, that right must be earned through social and political action challenging urban planning and policy decisions that produce spatial injustices (Soja, 2010).

Conclusions and Improvisational Alternatives

To withstand waves of national and international competitive urbanism, Canadian cities have relied heavily on branding and spectacularization to reinvent and redevelop inner-city spaces. Across the country we see the creation of cultural mega-projects, luxury condominiums, hotel and retail districts, and festival waterfronts in redundant industrial areas. Such urban development and policy choices have a consequential geography that creates lasting structures of unevenly distributed advantage and disadvantage (Soja, 2010). In the face of such apparent consensus on how Canada's largest cities should be re-imaged, re-elevated, and re-placed, one sees the danger of creating generic, homogenizing, single-thought cities where differences and conflict are neither tolerated nor valued. For it is the people "excluded from this spectacularisation process [who] possess perhaps the key to its reversal, which would entail . . . popular participation . . . and deep acquaintance with urban spaces" (Vaz and Jacques, 2007: 250). This suggestion is persuasive and reflective of the right to the city agenda.

Popular participation and a deep, rather than a shallow, engagement with urban spaces can be encouraged through urban interventions that both produce and are a product of improvisational space. Improvisational space can be understood as space that is changeable, malleable, and affordable, that encourages spontaneous and intuitive activities, and that supports risk-taking (Bain, 2003). It supports small-scale experiential initiatives and local interventions in the urban fabric that allow for unexpected encounters with differences. Moreover, improvisational space can be occupied and used in ways that "not only . . . disrupt the authoritative structures that govern them, but also . . . encourage a dialogue about the possibility for other forms of being and behaving" (Jonsson, 2006: 37). As in-between space with the potential for plurality and contradiction within it, improvisational space could be interpreted as a more socially sustainable alternative to spectacular space. Such localized spaces of possibility (whether they be informal community cultural hubs, storefronts, community gardens, or tool libraries) are the sites from which grassroots urban activism, optimism, and creativity that resist dominant ideologies and practices can emerge.

However, the opportunities for finding and securing affordable improvisational space in cities are rapidly diminishing. Such space used to be found in lower-income, working-class, inner-city neighbourhoods (e.g., in empty storefronts and abandoned warehouses). But cultural commodification, sustainability discourses, the condominium boom, and waterfront redevelopment projects have intensified residential development in the downtown core to meet middle- and upper-class consumptive and experiential practices, and in the process marginal social groups and cultural workers have been displaced. Such processes of displacement need to be continually and actively challenged, if inner-city neighbourhoods are to remain socially diverse, equitable, and inclusive places that can function as incubators for culture and entrepreneurship for more than just the middle class.

Review Questions

1. Why is the prefix *re-* (as in *re-imaging*, *re-elevating*, and *re-placing*) used with regard to inner-city change?
2. Explain the relationship between the competitive city and the inner city as "spectacle."

References

Avraham, E. 2004. "Media strategies for improving an unfavorable city image," *Cities* 21, 6: 471–9.

Bain, A.L. 2003. "Constructing contemporary artistic identities in Toronto neighbourhoods," *Canadian Geographer* 47: 303–17.

———. 2006. "Resisting the creation of forgotten places: Artistic production in Toronto neighbourhoods," *Canadian Geographer* 50: 417–31.

———. 2009. "Creative suburbs: Cultural 'popcorn' pioneering in multi-purpose spaces," in Edensor et al. (2009).

——. 2013. *Creative Margins: Cultural Production in Canadian Suburbs.* Toronto: University of Toronto Press.

——, and McLean, H. 2013. "The artistic precariat," *Cambridge Journal of Regions, Economy, and Society* 6, 93–111.

Berelowitz, L. 2005. *Dream City: Vancouver and the Global Imagination.* Vancouver: Douglas & McIntyre.

Blackwell, A. 2008. "The gentrification of gentrification and other strategies of Toronto's creative class," *Fuse Magazine* 29, 1: 28–37.

Boddy, T. 2005. "Vancouverism and its discontents," *Vancouver Review.* At: www.vancouverreview.com/past_articles/vancouverism.htm

Bourne, L. 1989. "Are new urban forms emerging? Empirical tests for Canadian urban areas," *Canadian Geographer* 33: 312–28.

Bradley, A., T. Hall, and M. Harrison. 2002. "Selling cities: Promoting new images for meetings tourism," *Cities* 19: 61–70.

Bunce, S. 2009 "Developing sustainability: Sustainability policy and gentrification on Toronto's waterfront," *Local Environments* 17: 651–67.

Bunting, T., and P. Filion, eds. 2006. *Canadian Cities in Transition: Local through Global Perspectives.* Toronto: Oxford University Press.

Burk, A. 2006. "Beneath and before: Continuum of publicness in public art," *Social and Cultural Geography* 7: 949–64.

Butler, T., and L. Lees. 2006. "Super-gentrification in Barnsbury, London: Globalisation and gentrifying global elites at the neighbourhood level," *Transactions of the Institute of British Geographers* 31: 467–87.

Caulfield, J. 1994. *City Form and Everyday Life: Toronto's Gentrification and Critical Social Practice.* Toronto: University of Toronto Press.

——. 2005. "Toronto: The form of the city," in H. Hiller, ed., *Urban Canada: Sociological Perspectives.* Toronto: Oxford University Press.

Coupland, D. 2000. *City of Glass: Douglas Coupland's Vancouver.* Vancouver: Douglas & McIntyre.

Danyluk, M., and D. Ley (2007) "Modalities of the new middle class: Ideology and behavior in the journey to work from gentrified neighbourhoods in Canada," *Urban Studies* 44: 2195–2210.

Desfor, G., and J. Ledley, eds. 2011 *Reshaping Toronto's Waterfront.* Toronto: University of Toronto Press.

Edensor, T., D. Leslie, S. Millington, and N. Rantisi, eds. 2009. *Spaces of Vernacular Creativity: Rethinking the Cultural Economy.* London: Routledge.

Evans, G. 2007. "Branding the city of culture—The death of city planning?" in J. Monclus and M. Guardia, eds., *Culture, Urbanism and Planning.* Aldershot: Ashgate.

Filion, P., and G. Gad. 2006. "Urban and suburban downtowns: Trajectories of growth and decline," in Bunting and Filion (2006).

Florida, R. 2002. *The Rise of the Creative Class: And How It's Transforming Work, Leisure, Community and Everyday Life.* New York: Basic Books.

——. 2005. *The Flight of the Creative Class.* New York: Harper Business.

Gale, D. 1980. "Neighbourhood resettlement: Washington, DC," in S. Laska and D. Spain, eds., *Back to the City.* New York: Pergamon.

Gehl, J. 2010. *Cities for People.* Washington: Island Press.

Germain, A., and D. Rose. 2000. *Montréal: The Quest for a Metropolis.* Toronto: John Wiley and Sons.

Gertler, M., R. Florida, G. Gates, and T. Vinodrai. 2002. *Competing on Creativity: Placing Ontario's Cities in a North American Context.* Toronto: Ontario Ministry of Enterprise, Opportunity, and Innovation.

Grant, J. 2006. "Shaped by planning: The Canadian city through time," in T. Bunting and P. Filion, eds., *Canadian Cities in Transition: Local through Global Perspectives.* Don Mills, ON: Oxford University Press.

Hall, T. 2003. "Art and urban change: Public art in urban regeneration," in A. Blunt et al., eds., *Cultural Geography in Practice.* New York: Arnold.

Harvey, D. 1989. "From managerialism to entrepreneurialism: The transformation in urban governance in late capitalism," *Geografiska Annaler: Series B, Human Geography* 71: 3–17.

Hutton, T. 2004. "Post-industrialism, post-modernism and the reproduction of Vancouver's central area: Retheorising the 21st-century city," *Urban Studies* 41: 1953–82.

Jonsson, T. 2006. "Space invaders: There goes the neighbourhood," *In/Site* 15: 37–9.

Kern, L. 2007. "Reshaping the boundaries of public and private life: Gender, condominium development, and the neo-liberalization of urban living," *Urban Geography* 28: 657–81.

Kingwell, M. 2008. *Concrete Reveries: Consciousness and the City.* Toronto: Viking Canada.

Kipfer, S., and R. Keil. 2002. "Toronto Inc? Planning the competitive city in the new Toronto," *Antipode* 34: 227–64.

Knox, P., and L. McCarthy. 2012. *Urbanization: An Introduction to Urban Geography* (3rd edn.). Boston, MA: Pearson.

LeBlanc, D. 2008. "In constant exile, artists seek next colony," *Globe and Mail*, 21 Nov., G4.

Lehrer, U. 2008. "Urban renaissance and resistance in Toronto," in L. Porter and K. Shaw, eds., *Whose Urban Renaissance? An International Comparison of Urban Regeneration Strategies.* London: Routledge.

Lefebvre, H. 1991. *The Production of Space.* London: Blackwell.

Ley, D. 1988. "Social upgrading in six Canadian inner cities," *Canadian Geographer* 32: 31–45.

——. 1993. "Past elites and present gentry: Neighbourhoods of privilege in Canadian cities," in L. Bourne and D. Ley, eds., *The Changing Social Geography of Canadian Cities.*

Montreal and Kingston: McGill-Queen's University Press.

——. 1994. "The Downtown Eastside: One hundred years of struggle," in S. Hasson and D. Ley, eds., *Neighbourhood Organizations and the Welfare State*. Toronto: University of Toronto Press.

——. 1996a. *The New Middle Class and the Remaking of the Central City*. Oxford: Oxford University Press.

——. 1996b. "The new middle class in Canadian central cities," in J. Caulfield and L. Peake, eds., *City Lives and City Forms: Critical Research and Canadian Urbanism*. Toronto: University of Toronto Press.

——. 2003. "Artists, aestheticisation and the field of gentrification," *Urban Studies* 40: 2527–44.

——, and H. Frost. 2006. "The inner city," in Bunting and Filion (2006).

——, and C. Dobson. 2008. "Are there limits to gentrification? The contexts of impeded gentrification in Vancouver," *Urban Studies* 45: 2471–98.

Lloyd, R. 2006. *Neo-Bohemia: Art and Commerce in the Post-Industrial City*. New York: Routledge.

Logan, J., and H. Molotch. 1987. *Urban Fortunes: The Political Economy of Place*. Berkeley, CA: University of California Press.

Lortie, A. 2004. *The 60s: Montreal Thinks Big*. Montreal: Canadian Centre for Architecture.

Macgregor, R. 2008. "The boom's ugly underside," *Globe and Mail*, 18 Feb., A2.

McLean, H. 2009. "The politics of creative performance in public space," in Edensor et al. (2009).

Markusen, A., and D. King. 2003. *The Artistic Dividend: The Hidden Contributions of the Arts to the Regional Economy*. Minneapolis, MN: Project on Regional and Industrial Economics, Humphrey Institute, University of Minnesota.

Marshall, R., ed. 2001. *Waterfronts in Post-Industrial Cities*. London: Spon Press.

——. 2001a. "Connection to the waterfront: Vancouver and Sydney," in Marshall (2001).

——. 2001b. "Remaking the image of the city: Bilbao and Shanghai," in Marshall (2001).

Miles, M. 2005. "Interruptions: testing the rhetoric of culturally led urban redevelopment," *Urban Studies* 42: 889–911.

Miles, S. 2005. "Creativity, culture and urban development: Toronto examined," *disP—The Planning Review* 162, 3: 70–87.

Mitchell, D. 2003. *The Right to the City: Social Justice and the Fight for Public Space*. New York: Guilford Press.

Montgomery, J. 2008. *The New Wealth of Cities: City Dynamics and the Fifth Wave*. Aldershot: Ashgate.

O'Donnell, D. 2006. *Social Acupuncture: A Guide to Suicide, Performance and Utopia*. Toronto: Coach House.

Peck, J. 2005. "Struggling with the creative class," *International Journal of Urban and Regional Research* 29: 740–70.

——. 2011. "Creative moments: Working culture through municipal socialism and neoliberal urbanism," in E. McCann and K. Ward, eds., *Mobile Urbanism: Cities and Policymaking in the Global Age*. Minneapolis, MN: University of Minnesota Press.

Pinder, D. 2005. "Arts of urban exploration," *Cultural Geographies* 12: 383–411.

Pratt, A. 2009. "Urban regeneration: From the arts 'feel good' factor to the cultural economy," *Urban Studies* 46: 1041–61.

Quastel, N., M. Moos, and N. Lynch. 2012. "Sustainability-as-density and the return of the social: The case of Vancouver, British Columbia," *Urban Geography* 33: 1055–84.

Robertson, L. 2007. "Taming space: Drug use, HIV, and homemaking in Downtown Eastside, Vancouver," *Gender, Place and Culture* 14: 527–49.

Rose, D. 1984. "Rethinking gentrification: Beyond the uneven development of Marxist urban theory," *Environment and Planning D: Society and Space* 2: 47–74.

Short, J.R. 1999. "Urban imagineers: Boosterism and the representation of cities," in A. Jonas and D. Wilson, eds., *The Urban Growth Machine: Critical Perspectives Two Decades Later*. Albany, NY: State University of New York Press.

Slater, T. 2004. "Municipally managed gentrification in South Parkdale," *Canadian Geographer* 48: 303–25.

Smith, H. 2003. "Planning, policy and polarization in Vancouver's Downtown Eastside," *Tijdschrift voor Economische en Sociale Geografie* 94: 496–509.

Smith, N. 1996. *The New Urban Frontier: Gentrification and the Revanchist City*. New York: Routledge.

Soja, E. 2010. *Seeking Spatial Justice*. Minneapolis, MN: University of Minnesota Press.

Staehli, L., D. Mitchell, and K. Gibson. 2002. "Conflicting rights to the city in New York's community gardens," *GeoJournal* 58: 197–205.

Vaz, L.F., and P.B. Jacques. 2007. "Contemporary urban spectacularisation," in J. Monclus and M. Guardia, eds., *Culture, Urbanism and Planning*. Aldershot: Ashgate.

Walks, A. 2001. "The social ecology of the post-Fordist/global city? Economic restructuring and socio-spatial polarization in the Toronto urban region," *Urban Studies* 38: 407–47.

Whyte, M. 2013. "Art schools now in session," *Toronto Star*, November 24, E1, E11.

Wilson, D., and R. Keil. 2008. "The real creative class," *Social and Cultural Geography* 9: 841–7.

Zukin, S. 1995. *The Cultures of Cities*. Cambridge, MA: Blackwell.

——. 2004. *Point of Purchase: How Shopping Changed American Culture*. New York: Routledge.

Slow Growth and Decline in Canadian Cities

15

BETSY DONALD AND
HEATHER M. HALL

Introduction

One notable finding from the 2011 Canadian census is that over 57 per cent of the Canadian urban system is either growing slowly (40.1 per cent) or declining (17.7 per cent). Geographers, planners, and policy-makers have been involved in planning for decline *within* the city for several decades. This is not new. Research on intra-urban declivity has examined downtown and inner-city deterioration along with derelict brownfields sites, waterfronts, and industrial lands. What is new, however, is a heightened awareness, and growing reality, of rising disparities *between* cities—those that are rapidly growing and those that are not. This uneven inter-urban geography is confronting all developed countries to a greater or lesser degree; it is increasingly attracting attention across Canada, Germany, and the United States (Bontje, 2004; Bourne and Rose, 2001; Bourne and Simmons, 2003; Bunting and Filion, 2001; Cocks and Couch, 2012; Downs, 1994; Hall, 2009; Hall and Hall, 2008; Hollander and Nemeth, 2011; Hollander et al., 2009; Hospers, 2013; Leo and Anderson, 2006; Lötscher, 2005; Martinez-Fernandez et al., 2012a, 2012b; Müller and Siedentop, 2004; Oswalt, 2005; Popper and Popper, 2002; Rybczynski and Linneman, 1999; Simmons, 2003). This literature shares a common view that if current demographic, economic, and policy trends persist, then the gap between cities that are rapidly growing and those that are not will become increasingly accentuated. The uneven inter-urban geography among Canadian cities will challenge the way we think about urban development issues because the dominant discourse in Canada is about planning for growth, not decline. How we manage decline in many of our Canadian cities will become one of the most pressing urban policy issues of the twenty-first century.

This chapter is organized into four sections. The first section provides a typology of urban decline and includes a description of the broader demographic, economic, and policy trends producing this new and accentuated pattern of uneven growth. In the next section, we focus on the negative perceptions and "psychology of failure" that often accompany academic or political labelling of a "slow-growth" or "declining city." A discussion of the challenges and opportunities associated with different growth trajectories constitutes the third section. In the fourth section, we focus on the geographic, planning, and policy implications for Canadian cities experiencing slow growth and decline. We conclude with a discussion of further challenges confronting urban areas in Canada.

Terminology, Trends, and Discourse

What Are "Slow-Growth" and "Declining" Cities?

In the Canadian urban geography literature, cities experiencing slower or declining rates of growth are referred to as "slow-growth" or "declining" (Bourne and Simmons, 2003; Bunting and Filion, 2001; Hall, 2009; Hall and Hall, 2008; Leo and Anderson, 2006; Simmons, 2003). In Europe and the United States, the term "shrinking cities" is commonly used, along with "stagnating cities" or "urban areas in difficulty" (Atkinson, 2001; Bontje, 2004; ECOTEC Research and Consulting, 2007; Lötscher, 2005; Rybczynski and Linneman, 1999). While these different terms incorporate a number of trends, the common measurement for slow growth and decline is population change over time. No concise method exists for measuring this change, however, which produces a variety of results. For example, American policy analyst Anthony Downs classifies cities based on population change in a 10-year period as rapidly declining if they lost more than 4.9 per cent of their population, slowly declining if they lost between 0.1 and 4.9 per cent, slowly growing if they gained less than 10 per cent, and rapidly growing if they gained more than 10 per cent. In Canada, five-year periods are frequently used, although this method only considers short-term trends and may not provide an accurate depiction of long-term trajectories of change (Bourne and Simmons, 2003; Bunting and Filion, 2001; Hall and Hall, 2008; Leo and Anderson, 2006; Simmons, 2003).

Where Are Slow-Growth and Declining Cities?

Canadian declining cities are not alone. Similar patterns of slow growth and decline are emerging across Europe, Australia, South America, and the United States. A recent working report on demographic change and local development from the Organisation for Economic Co-operation and Development (OECD) Local Economic and Employment Development (LEED) Programme makes reference to a number of countries, including the following: the US, Australia, Japan, Finland, Poland, Germany, Portugal, Spain, Italy, France, Latvia, Slovak Republic, Czech Republic, Slovenia, Switzerland, Brazil, Netherlands, the United Kingdom, and Canada (see Martinez-Fernandez et al., 2012b). In fact, prior to the 2007 American subprime mortgage crisis and the 2008 global economic slowdown, Oswalt and Rienitz (2006) estimated that 25 per cent of world cities with populations over 100,000 were in decline (see also Hollander and Nemeth, 2011). This trend has most likely intensified since the global economic slowdown. In the United States, for example, land abandonment has once again become a significant issue in cities like Detroit, Michigan, and Gary, Indiana. In the most severe cases, residential and commercial property owners abandon their property, leading to drastic decreases in land prices, home values, and municipal revenue (Hackworth, 2012).

Meanwhile, in Canada, 85 of 147 census agglomerations (CAs) and **census metropolitan areas (CMAs)** experienced slow growth or decline between 2001 and 2011 (Table 15.1). As seen in Figure 15.1, this uneven pattern of growth in Canada is more pronounced in small and mid-size urban areas. Prince Rupert, BC, for example, had the largest decline, at -14.7 per cent, followed by Cape Breton, NS (-7.1 per cent), and Terrace, BC (-6.5 per cent). Meanwhile, most large city-regions, such as Toronto, Calgary, and Vancouver (with the exception of Winnipeg and Hamilton), as well as small and mid-size cities in oil and mineral-rich regions, grew rapidly.

In most developed countries, this uneven inter-urban geography is largely a result of several powerful demographic, economic, and policy trends (Bourne and Rose, 2001; Bourne and Simmons, 2003; Hall and Hall, 2008; Hollander and Nemeth, 2011; Hospers, 2013; Lötscher, 2005; Mäding, 2004; Martinez-Fernandez 2012a, 2012b; Müller, 2004; Müller and Siedentop, 2004; Oswalt, 2005; Popper and Popper, 2002). In Canada, we are in the final stages of the demographic transition in which

Table 15.1   Trends in the Canadian Urban System, 2001–11

	Large Urban Areas (>500,000)	Mid-Size Urban Areas (50,000–500,000)	Small Urban Areas (10,000–50,000)	All Urban Areas
Number of urban areas	9	53	85	147
Total pop. 2001	15,109,380	7,054,858	1,948,550	24,112,788*
Total pop. 2011	17,548,422	7,813,057	2,073,486	27,434,965*
Overall % pop. change, 2001–11	16.1	10.7	6.4	13.8*
Number of slowly growing areas**	2	19	38	59
% slowly growing	22.2	35.9	44.7	40.1
Number of declining urban areas**	0	6	20	26
% declining	0	11.3	23.5	17.7
Lowest % pop. change	Winnipeg, MB (7.9)	Cape Breton, NS (−7.1)	Prince Rupert, BC (−14.7)	Prince Rupert, BC (−14.7)
Highest % pop. change	Calgary, AB (27.7)	Wood Buffalo, AB (57.1)	Okotoks, AB (109.9)	Okotoks, AB (109.9)

*   The Canadian population grew by 11.6 per cent between 2001 and 2011, from 30,007,094 to 33,476,688.

**   Slowly growing cities are defined as cities that grew by less than 10 per cent while declining cities are those that lost population between 2001 and 2011.

Source: Statistics Canada (2013a, 2013b, 2013c).

lower fertility rates are resulting in the decreased role of natural increase for population growth (see Townshend and Walker, Chapter 7). As a result, immigration is the major source of demographic change; it is well documented that the majority of domestic and international migrants locate in large city-regions like Toronto and Vancouver, further accentuating the uneven population distribution between cities (Bourne and Rose, 2001; Bourne and Simmons, 2003; see Kobayashi and Preston, Chapter 8). In some cities, especially on the Prairies, another major source of demographic change is the rising Aboriginal population (see Peters, Chapter 21). These demographic trends are expected to continue in the foreseeable future.

Economic restructuring and technological changes in Canada have also led to fewer jobs in the resource and manufacturing sectors while job growth related to the knowledge economy has concentrated primarily in large city-regions as well as areas within their zone of influence (Barnes et al.,

2000; Bourne and Simmons, 2003; Gertler, 2001; Norcliffe, 1994; see Vinodrai, Chapter 5; Hutton and Vinodrai, Chapter 6). In their work on Atlantic Canada and Quebec, Polèse and Shearmur (2002) argue that having a resource-dependent economic base is another precondition for decline. This might appear to contradict the current growth in resource rich cities; however, resource dependency is an issue because the economies of many smaller peripheral cities often lack the economic diversification to counteract the volatile boom-bust cycle of a natural resources–based economy. More importantly, these cities have little local control over resource decision-making and often receive few royalties or value-added development.

Other conditions contributing to decline relate to changing state policies and geography. In Canada, shifting national capital flows to the United States along with the changing role of government through trade liberalization and increased provincial responsibilities have contributed to

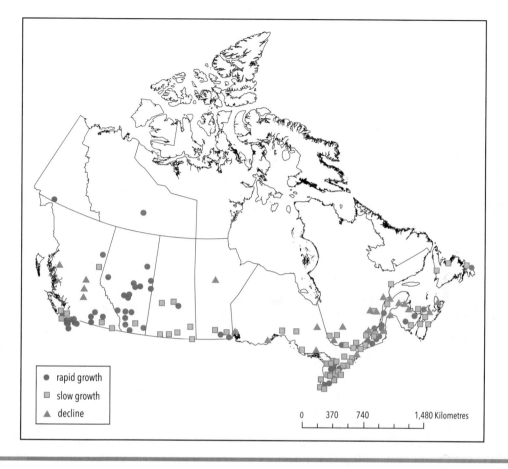

Figure 15.1   Pattern of Growth and Decline in the Canadian Urban System, 2001-11

what Bourne and Simmons (2003) refer to as "new fault lines" between cities that are rapidly growing and those that are not. Added to this is the shift away from state redistribution policies aimed at reducing spatial inequalities and toward policies that stress competitiveness, innovation, and development from within urban areas. In Canada, a peripheral location in the national or continental space economy or a location away from a major transportation axis or trade route are also cited as preconditions for decline (Polèse and Shearmur, 2006: 42). Thus, all of these macro social, economic, and political factors have accumulated to produce a new pattern of uneven growth, which has further accentuated existing patterns between

a small number of cities and regions that are rapidly growing and a larger number of those that are not (Table 15.2).

Who Cares about "Declining" Cities?

The literature on slow growth and decline is relatively small, although it is growing, especially in Europe, Australia, and the United States. Articles on decline have appeared in the *Journal of the American Planning Association*, the *International Journal of Urban and Regional Research*, *International Planning Studies*, *European Planning Studies* and *Plan Canada*. A number of research networks and projects have also been developed, including the

Table 15.2	Summary of Macro Trends Contributing to the Pattern of Uneven Growth
Trend	Description
Demographic	• Canada in the final stages of the demographic transition • Lower fertility rates and decreasing natural increase • Immigration to and migration within Canada major source of demographic growth • Demographic concentration occurring in large Canadian city-regions
Economic	• Economic restructuring and technological changes in manufacturing and resource sectors • Shift to a more knowledge-intensive economy • Resource dependency and limits of (profitable) resource exploitation • Economic concentration in large Canadian city-regions
State policy	• Shifting national trade to the United States • Shifting Canadian capital flows • National trade liberalization and devolved responsibilities to lower levels of government • Shift away from state redistribution policies aimed at reducing spatial inequalities
Locational	• Peripheral location in the Canadian urban system • Location away from a major transportation axis or trade route • Outside the influence zone of a large city-region • Size: small and mid-size cities

German government-funded Shrinking Cities research project (www.shrinkingcities.com) and Shrink Smart—a European Union Framework VII—funded research project (www.shrinksmart.eu) (Cocks and Couch, 2012; Hollander and Nemeth, 2011; Hospers, 2013).

Much of the early writing on decline was focused on describing the causes, characteristics, and consequences of decline or slow growth (Bourne and Rose, 2001; Bourne and Simmons, 2003; Bunting and Filion, 2001; Leo and Anderson, 2006; Leo and Brown, 2000; Lötscher, 2005; Lötscher, Howest, and Basten, 2004; Martinez-Fernandez et al., 2012a; Müller, 2004; Müller and Siedentop, 2004; Oswalt, 2005; Polèse and Shearmur, 2006; Reckien and Martinez-Fernandez, 2011; Simmons, 2003). These scholars initiated the discussion by providing detailed national accounts of the causes and by depicting the pattern of growth and decline. More recent research has examined the social, fiscal, economic, spatial, planning, and policy challenges and responses associated with shrinkage or decline (Bontje, 2004; Cocks and Couch 2013; Franz,

2004; Hackworth 2012; Hall, 2009; Hollander and Nemeth, 2011; Hospers 2013; Mäding, 2004; Müller and Siedentop, 2004; Simmons and Bourne, 2007; Wiechmann, 2008; Wiechmann and Pallagst, 2012). Research has also explored the psychological dimension of open public discussion of the topic due to the growth-centric mentality that permeates civic politics and planning (Hall, 2009; Hollander and Nemeth, 2011; Hospers 2013; Leo and Anderson, 2006; Oswalt, 2005; Popper and Popper, 2002; Seasons, 2007). A common thread running throughout all of this research is that the current demographic, economic, and policy trends most likely will persist and the spatial fallout of these trends will deepen the uneven inter-urban geography across Canada and internationally.

Psychology of Failure and Political Sensitivity

How is the topic of decline perceived in the conduct of urban affairs? In a recent study on the social dynamics of economic performance in Kingston, Ontario, a slowly growing city, a key informant explained that the city has a "psychology of failure" that plays a strong role in its economic governance (Lewis and Donald, 2010: 36).

> If a place has a personality, it can also have a psychology. Just as individual psychologies reflect their experiences, their traumas, and upbringing and raising and so on, Kingston has had, one can argue, a psychology of loss, of failure. It didn't grow, it wasn't industrialized, it was bypassed by commerce, the military left, the capital left.

This psychology of failure and government malaise that often accompanies these slow-growth and declining cities is a pressing issue that influences all aspects of decision-making from land-use planning to economic development. Likewise, Hospers (2013: 5) describes the "urban mindware" or image of a city and the impacts of being labelled a shrinking city. He notes that this "negatively loaded term" can discourage local empowerment and make people feel inferior.

In the local policy arena the issue of decline is rarely broached unless the discussion is focused on reversing the trend (Müller and Siedentop, 2004; Seasons, 2007). Seasons (2007: 6) refers to decline as the "policy elephant in the living room" while Hall (2009) found that planners, economic developers, and policy-makers were uncomfortable discussing the topic at the local level. This discomfort is a direct result of the negative perceptions and psychology that accompany decline (Robinson, 1981). For example, Leo and Anderson (2006: 393), in their research on Winnipeg, argue that there is a perception that "any city that is not growing rapidly is being 'left behind.'" Hall (2007) discovered that local officials in Greater Sudbury associated decline with death, producing a negative image that would counteract investment and local economic development. One key informant suggested that "if you're not growing, you're dying." Put simply, cities view growth as expected, desirable, and necessary, while any trajectory other than

growth is seen as failure. Moreover, anticipating decline is equivalent to accepting this failure.

This obsession with urban growth is firmly rooted in the politics of local economic development. From the early days of North American cities, demographic and economic growth and new urban development have been perceived essentially as ingredients for maintaining and improving urban quality of life. Harvey Molotch (1976) emphasized the entrenched attachment to growth in his now classic framing of the city as a "growth machine." Molotch (1976: 310) further stated that "the clearest indication of success at growth is a constantly rising urban area population." Growth is depicted as the magic potion that creates jobs, reinforces the tax base, and provides resources to solve social problems (Logan and Molotch, 1987). In the current economic context, a positive urban image is perceived to be a vital component for urban competitiveness; no city wants to be labelled as declining (Avraham, 2004).

Decline creates a policy dilemma for those cities experiencing it. Yet, if current trends persist, some cities will be unable to reverse their demographic situation and may have to make the best of what is perceived to be a non-ideal situation. Incessantly planning for future growth in its absence, however, may prove to be more costly in the long term. We argue that approaches reflecting place-based realities are essential because slow growth and no growth do not necessarily have to be viewed as problems if they are managed and planned for. As an example, Greater Sudbury has changed and improved dramatically over the last few decades without population growth, suggesting that city decline is different, but not deadly. Over the 40-year period between 1971 and 2011, the population of Sudbury has grown and declined cyclically, from about 170,000 to just over 160,000. Despite this trend, the economic base has expanded so that Sudbury has become a regional service centre for northeastern Ontario for medical care, retail, tourism, government, and education. In 2005, the Northern Ontario School of Medicine was opened with a campus in Sudbury. This is the first medical school to be opened in Canada in over 30 years. More recently, the Laurentian University School of Architecture was opened in downtown Sudbury. Like the medical school, it is the first school of architecture to open in Canada in over 40 years (Laurentian University, 2013). When the city was rapidly growing during the 1960s, the natural environment was barren and polluted due to smelting techniques used by the mining industry. Indeed, a widespread rumour claimed that US astronauts, in preparation for landing on the moon, trained on the supposedly similar barren terrain that Sudbury provided. While this rumour has since been dispelled, it gives some indication of the former state of the landscape. Since that time, key agents in the city have planted over eight million trees, earning a United Nations commendation, among other distinctions. The Sudbury case depicts how communities can change and improve without demographic growth. As we discuss further in the following section, both declining *and* growing cities have unique opportunities and challenges.

Growth, Slow Growth, and Decline: Challenges and Opportunities

A common perception exists that rapid growth is the desideratum of urban development. There are challenges, however, associated with this type of development trajectory. Hall and Hall (2008) discuss how urban growth can lead to environmental concerns, such as rural fringe development and the loss of prime agricultural land. Furthermore, challenges arise related to the provision and maintenance costs of infrastructure and municipal services as a city grows. Conflicts may arise between urban and rural land uses or other community social tensions, such as has occurred in Fort McMurray, located within the Regional Municipality of Wood Buffalo, Alberta. Between 2001 and 2011, the population of this region increased by 57 per cent, from 42,580 to 66,896 people (Statistics Canada, 2013a). This

rapid growth is a direct result of the region's proximity to the Athabasca oil sands and the booming oil and gas industry. Hoernig et al. (2005) discuss the social impacts of this rapid growth. High wages due to labour shortages in the oil sands development industry lead to shortages in other sectors that are unable to match the high oil wages. Other issues related to the quick demographic changes include a serious shortage of affordable housing, a high cost of living, homelessness, social and individual stresses, and, of course, environmental degradation on a massive scale. Thus, rapid growth is not a panacea but has challenges and opportunities that require realistic planning solutions.

On the positive side, large, growing cities often offer demographic and cultural diversity as a result of their large immigrant populations, economic diversity in terms of employment opportunities and choices, and urban diversity, which includes more selection in dwelling types, such as lofts and condominiums (Gertler et al., 2002). In slow-growth or declining cities, on the other hand, the populations tend to be relatively homogeneous, with a higher proportion of aging residents due to limited economic opportunities, which lead to youth out-migration and low immigrant settlement (Hanlon and Halseth, 2005; Simard and Simard, 2005). Declining cities can also become increasingly dependent on grants from provincial and federal governments as a result of their shrinking tax base. However, slow-growth and declining cities in peripheral locations often boast an abundance of landscapes rich in natural amenities: lakes and forests, better air quality, and less traffic congestion (Hall, 2009; Simard and Simard, 2005).

Leo and Anderson (2006) compared Vancouver, a fast-growing urban area, with Winnipeg, a slow-growing urban area. They found that housing costs are cheaper in Winnipeg, yet Vancouver has more ability to pay for its infrastructure and services. Vancouver also has sharper contrasts between the rich and poor. A remarkable characteristic of some **slow-growth cities** is evident in Winnipeg, where dispersion has occurred despite its slow growth. This contrasts with Vancouver, a fast-growing city, which has had more success in limiting the region's outward growth. This dispersion pattern in Winnipeg is related to decisions made by city officials who are more accepting of pro-development proposals in their desire to grow at any cost. Often these developments are unsuitable with regard to location, densities, and land uses and may place further pressure on services and infrastructure. In Greater Sudbury, Hall (2007) identifies a similar planning practice to "take anything anywhere," in which decline is used as an opportunity to push through proposals. This trend has also occurred in Kingston, where a sprawl-like spatial pattern has emerged over the last 10 years without a significant population increase. This "any growth is good growth" mentality becomes a problem, however, when city officials fail to see that more development also produces more pressure on municipal services and increased expenditures (Siegel, 2002).

Growth is an important component in municipal budgeting for infrastructure and services, presenting a challenge for cities in decline. Indeed, growth brings money into municipal accounts. In Canadian municipal budgeting, the three main sources of revenue are user fees; unconditional or conditional grants; and taxes on the assessed value of property (see Taylor and Bradford, Chapter 11). Complicating municipal financing, moreover, has been the downloading in recent years of responsibilities from senior levels of government to municipalities, without augmenting municipalities' capacity to secure new revenue streams (Bradford, 2002, 2004; Federation of Canadian Municipalities [FCM], 2006; Kitchen, 2002; Mintz and Roberts, 2006; Sancton, 2000, 2006; Vojnovic and Poel, 2000). For example, Mintz and Roberts (2006) describe how the Ontario government downloaded various social welfare programs, including social assistance, child care, immigration services, social housing, and homelessness. Kitchen (2002: 5) argues that this downloading was the "largest redistribution of services between a province and its municipalities ever witnessed in Canada," thereby further fuelling a growth mentality because new property development increases the tax base and, ultimately, municipal revenue. Without substantial new growth, the purse strings

on the municipal budget become tighter and the challenge becomes how to deliver up-to-date and quality services and infrastructure without considerable new growth occurring.

One last opportunity associated with slow growth and decline is the option to manage land resources in a more efficient and forward-looking manner (Robinson, 1981). In rapidly growing cities, policies can be reactive, whereas in slow-growth and declining cities, the potential exists to become more proactive. Strategies like impact analyses and strategic assessments can be employed before making development decisions to determine how foreseeable changes will affect the city presently *and* over time. In reality, however, declining cities are not necessarily using that time to practice proactive planning. Thus, a variety of place-based opportunities and challenges are associated with rapid-growth, slow-growth, and declining communities (Table 15.3).

Implications for Urban Geography, Planning, and Policy

We argue that urban experts and urban policies have failed to consider the realities of slow-growth and declining cities. The 1950s and 1960s were a time of rapid economic and demographic growth, and during these decades "most Canadian planning standards, norms and zoning practices were developed" (Wolfe, 1995: 55). Historically, then, planning has been tied to growth, and the current framework does not provide the proper tools for urban areas experiencing anything other than rapid growth at the urban scale.[1] Nevertheless, planners do have experience managing areas in decline, such as inner cities, brownfields, and core areas, to increase livability and attract investment. Most planning concepts, policies, and statutes, however, are devoid of the word *decline*, with common approaches like smart growth and the *Places to Grow Act* 2005 in Ontario focused on growth. For example, the recent Growth Plan for Northern Ontario (2011) includes no reference to demographic decline facing many communities

Table 15.3   Summary of Challenges and Opportunities

	Rapid-Growth Cities	Slow-Growth and Declining Cities
Opportunities	• Demographic and cultural diversity • Employment diversity • Variety in housing options and the built form • Higher tax base	• Lower cost of living • Housing affordability • Less traffic congestion • Better air quality • Natural amenities • Opportunities to be more proactive about decision-making
Challenges	• Sharper contrasts between rich and poor • Environmental concerns related to increased dispersion • Land-use conflicts • Social conflicts • Extreme pressure on infrastructure and services • Pollution (air quality) • Congestion	• Aging population • Homogeneous population • Youth out-migration • Limited economic opportunities • "Any growth is good growth" mentality for urban development • Grant dependency • Less ability to pay for infrastructure and services • Land abandonment

Source: Compiled by authors. For similar summary tables, see Bourne and Simmons (2007) and Robinson (1981).

across the region. A similar tale is told for the United States and Germany. Popper and Popper (2002) argue that US planning tools are designed to manage a rising economy and population. In Germany, municipal, regional, and state planning approaches are unprepared to meet the challenges of demographic decline (Bontje, 2004; Müller, 2004; Müller and Siedentop, 2004). More fundamentally, growth-centred solutions to no-growth scenarios are unrealistic and prevent the acceptance and management of decline as an acceptable trajectory. In the following sections we offer some solutions to ignite the search for alternatives.

Creating a New Decline Discourse

Canadian urbanists and policy-makers must turn their attention to the certainty that decline or slower growth will continue in some places and begin in others. Hall and Hall (2008: 14) argue that the Canadian urban literature "repeats, and

arguably reinforces, the message that quantitative [population] growth is the only legitimate response to decline" and that "[c]onsumers of this research are implicitly dared to concede defeat if they disagree with this perspective." If we expect places to realistically plan for decline, then the topic can no longer be avoided (Bunting and Filion, 2001). Focus must now turn to how cities in decline can maintain quality of life when revenue sources depend on growth. This may require alternative financial tools and policies for slow-growth and declining cities. For example, many European cities rely much less on the property tax base. In fact, Canadian municipalities have one of the highest dependencies on property taxes in the world. Alternative revenue sources more prominent in other jurisdictions include user fees, sales taxes, and income-based taxes. These alternative sources—especially the income tax—may diminish the pressure on cities to continuously seek land-development-related growth (see Slack, 2005, and Courchene, 2005, for discussions of fiscal constraints in Canadian cities.) At a more fundamental level, the perceived notion that slow-growing or declining places are "failing" in the metropolitan growth competition needs to change if we expect the political sensitivity of discussing the issue to diminish and become a more solutions-oriented conversation.

"Smart Decline" and "Qualitative Development"

Hospers (2013: 5) identifies four policy responses to decline in Europe: (1) trivializing shrinkage, (2) countering shrinkage, (3) accepting shrinkage, and (4) utilizing shrinkage. Canadian planning legislation and policy tools have ignored decline, however, and are largely ill-equipped to manage decline at the urban scale. Existing concepts like growth management, growth controls, and smart growth all imply the existence of substantial growth to manage. Müller and Siedentop (2004) call for a decline paradigm to establish more decline-oriented planning tools. Their suggestions include but are not limited to focusing on redevelopment, recycling land and buildings, adapting infrastructure, and planning strategically. Likewise, Popper and Popper (2002: 22) argue that we need a "smart decline" strategy requiring us to think "about who and what remains," and that this "may entail reorganizing or eliminating some services and providing different ones." In Germany, Hospers (2013) identifies *Gesundschrumpfen*, or healthy shrinking, while in the Netherlands he identifies *slimpen,* or smart shrinking. Hollander et al. (2009) point out that the corporate expression of "right-sizing" is being touted in the United States, while Pallagst (2013) discusses the notion of "palliative planning."

Based on previous research, we offer a number of alternative planning approaches to assist urban geographers, planners, and city officials (Hall, 2009). Our hope is to kick-start conversations on how to accept, manage, and plan for decline. We start with qualitative development, a concept used by Sudbury in the 1980s, which centres on the existing built form, promoting redevelopment, infilling, and conservation. These concepts

are simple to implement and already essential to good planning. The challenge, however, is to forget about the growth mentality associated with quantitative development or expanding growth, services, and infrastructure in the city. An expansive urban boundary is *not* a metaphor for success. Other decline-oriented approaches involve realigned development, where settlement boundaries and services actually are scaled back or reduced to reflect current expectations while maintaining and improving the existing built form. Controlled development would mean halting municipal infrastructure or service expansions to facilitate new growth, with developers paying the costs associated with development and identifying spaces for redevelopment and infilling. A final decline-oriented technique that we offer is internal zoning, whereby a hierarchy of limited settlement areas are predetermined for development. Each zone or settlement area slated for urbanization or re-urbanization would be developed before another zone could be selected. Essentially, the key is not to overdevelop but to think strategically about where growth should occur within the city, which is something all cities should be doing. A summary of these approaches is provided in Table 15.4.

Hollander and Nemeth (2011: 358–62) make five recommendations for smart decline planning processes. They can be summarized as follows:

1. Include and recognize multiple voices.
2. Be political and deliberative.
3. Be aware of various communication techniques, and provide information to mobilize citizens.
4. Be transparent and utilize different types and sources of information.
5. Be regional in scope but ensure local control and implementation.

Focusing upon the complexity of the process, Hospers (2013: 13) argues that "responding to urban shrinkage is a complex urban governance issue. A range of actors, groups and institutions (e.g. local government, corporations, schools, business networks, local associations and citizens) have a role to play."

Table 15.4   Summary of Decline-Oriented Techniques

Decline-Oriented Technique	Description
Decline-oriented planning/ decline paradigm	• Focus on redevelopment, recycling land and buildings, adapting infrastructure, and strategic planning
Smart decline	• Plan for who and what remains • Might involve reorganizing or eliminating some services and providing alternatives
Qualitative development	• A concept used by Sudbury, ON, in the 1980s • Focus on the existing built form, promoting redevelopment, infilling, and conservation
Realigned development	• Settlement boundaries and services are scaled back to reflect current expectations • Focus on maintaining and improving the existing built form
Controlled development	• No infrastructure or services expansion to facilitate new growth • Developers pay the costs associated with development • Identify spaces for redevelopment and infilling
Internal zoning	• Hierarchy of limited settlement areas are predetermined for development

Source: Compiled by authors from Müller and Siedentop (2004); Popper and Popper (2002); and Hall (2009).

Fischler and Wolfe (2006: 348) describe efforts of the Montreal Metropolitan Community (MMC), which is planning for a smaller population by the year 2050.[2] They explain that the MMC approach is to "consolidate already urbanized areas, to rationalize regional infrastructure investment, and to arbitrate the inter-municipal competition for households and businesses by restricting development on greenfield sites." Arguably, little risk befalls a city that plans for decline but experiences growth, other than negative image. If a city plans for growth and experiences decline, however, the risk is overbuilding and extending services and infrastructure that will be too costly to manage and upgrade in the future.

Moving Away from One-Size-Fits-All

In recent decades, government has become more concerned with large city-regions and their competition on a global scale (Donald, 2005). As Bürkner (2005) explains, state intervention policies that once aimed to *balance* spatial disparities between cities have shifted to *targeting* cities and regions that are already economically competitive or that are perceived to have potential. However, Atkinson (2001) cautions that this focus on competition may actually accentuate disparities and create more place-based winners and losers. In Ontario recently, most government policy has paid attention to the Greater Toronto Area and its surrounding region, exemplified through the City of Toronto Act, 2006, and the 2006 Growth Plan for the Greater Golden Horseshoe. The first provides the city with powers and legislative freedoms that other municipalities do not have, while the latter was designed to guide where and how growth should occur in order to promote healthy, strong, and prosperous communities in this large conurbation (Ontario Ministry of Municipal Affairs and Housing, 2009; Ontario Ministry of Public Infrastructure Renewal, 2006). More recently, a report published for the Ontario government by the Martin Prosperity Institute promotes the Greater Toronto Area as pivotal to a secure future for Ontario, centred on the creative economy (Florida and Martin, 2009).

We are not suggesting that Toronto and the broader Golden Horseshoe region are undeserving of attention. We are suggesting, however, that as the rift between have and have-not cities in the Canadian urban system widens, a new way of thinking will be needed to balance the needs of large, growing city-regions and their slow-growing and declining counterparts. This will require place-based, locally or regionally sensitive policies. It will require us to move beyond supply-side policies aimed at competitiveness that do little to manage spatial disparities between cities.

A similar spatial penchant for large city-regions is seen in much of the contemporary economic geography literature. The creative economy literature is biased by design to favour large cities like Toronto and Vancouver, while much of the literature on regional innovation systems and clusters is focused on economically advanced regions like Silicon Valley, Boston, Baden-Württemberg, and Toronto (Hall and Donald, 2009; see Vinodrai, Chapter 5). Unfortunately, this spatial bias creates a dualistic depiction that shows large cities, on the one hand, as creative and cosmopolitan economic drivers, and, on the other hand, many smaller peripheral places as economic failures. Hayter, Barnes, and Bradshaw (2003: 18) remind us that "[t]here is a whole world out there and not just a few cores or clusters."

Determining if Population Growth Matters

As described earlier in the chapter, growth is commonly measured in terms of population change. But is population growth everything? Is there a better way to measure a city's prosperity? Given the current economic realities and the expected demographic situation in many Canadian cities, we contend that these questions will require future attention. Population growth is important for municipal revenue generation but little is known about savings that could be made by planning for a smaller population. Rybczynski and Linneman (1999) believe that cities experiencing decline should not be trying to grow big again but, rather, should find out how to prosper as great, smaller cities. Other suggestions include planning

for sustainability, livability, and quality of life (Gonzáles, 2006). Furthermore, Molotch (1976: 328) foresees opportunities in the city that asks "what it can do for its people rather than what it can do to attract more people."

In Germany, Oswalt (2005: 13) describes a new slogan, "shrinking as a new potential," to suggest that decline can result in a new compact urban core, which is an ideal European urban form. Meanwhile, the concept of Slow Cities or Cittaslow evolved out of the slow food movement in Italy. These two movements are responses to the fast-paced growth and cultural standardization most often associated with the broader trend of globalization (Knox, 2005: 6). The slow cities movement encourages "local, traditional cultures, a relaxed pace of life, and conviviality" (Knox, 2005: 6). The founding principles of Cittaslow include "working towards calmer and less polluted physical environments, conserving local aesthetic traditions and fostering local crafts, produce, and cuisine" (Knox, 2005: 6). At the heart of the movement are the concepts of health, sustainability, and the environment (see Rees, Chapter 4). Interestingly, participating cities are required to have populations of less than 50,000 (Knox, 2005). This model moves away from the obsession with rapid growth and instead encourages slow growth as the ideal trajectory for cities. Declining and slow-growing cities in Canada could draw on the Cittaslow movement for inspiring a new reality in which quality of life, quality of place, quality of employment opportunities, and sustainability become central to any policy-making, regardless of size. Thus, emphasizing local strengths and a *better* place, rather than a bigger place, could provide the opportunity for an alternative vision: one that ignores the obsession with growth and promotes urban quality (see Walker and Gunn, Chapter 18).

Conclusions: Moving Forward on a New Urban Agenda

Population growth remains concentrated in major urban centres across Canada, from Toronto to Calgary to Vancouver and Saskatoon. Many of the reasons behind this growth are linked more fundamentally to broader changes in the global economy and to increased flows of people, capital, and ideas from around the world to Canada (see Hall, Chapter 3). As a consequence, researchers and policy-makers interested in the Canadian urban system have become fascinated with documenting and promoting the dynamic, diverse, and creative Canadian urban centres. As detailed in this chapter, new research projects have explored the social dynamics of economic performance in these fast-growing cities, and politicians have called for more explicit urban-based policies at the national level. However, this spatial bias accentuates inter-urban differences that are increasing across Canada.

As we have demonstrated, over 57 per cent of the Canadian urban system is either growing slowly (40.1 per cent) or declining (17.7 per cent). The questions we must ask are as follows: How are we going to plan for Canadian cities in decline? What are the realistic urban scenarios and what are the effective policy tools at our disposal? Now is the time for urban scholars to turn more actively to insights from the environmental, green, sustainable, and quality-of-life literatures for ideas on how to plan for slow growth and decline (see Rees, Chapter 4). Before doing this, however, we must first permit ourselves to face this reality and find new ways of constructively conversing about preparing for slow growth and decline in our Canadian cities. Only then can we enhance our collective capacity to respond to policy problems that are increasingly defined by the complex interdependence and spatially concentrated expression of the dynamic Canadian urban system. Coming to the aid of Canada's slow-growing or declining cities does not necessarily have to be a "zero-sum" view of power relations between Canada's have and have-not places. Rather, doing so can be aligned with our ability and history as a nation to embed place-based public policies that are sensitive to the realities of different regions across space and with our reputation as a nation to deal with deeper economic unevenness with broader multi-scaled policy effects.

Acknowledgements

We would like to thank Marcel Boudreau and Laurent Martel from Statistics Canada for their statistical assistance as well as Charlie Conway from Memorial University for his mapping assistance.

Review Questions

1. What is a "slow-growth" or "declining" city, and where are they located in the Canadian urban system?
2. Is a "qualitative development" strategy a good idea for municipalities in order to foster growth, or is it strictly a strategy for managing decline?

Notes

1. Our definition of the Canadian urban system includes all census agglomerations (CAs) and census metropolitan areas (CMAs) (see also Simmons and Bourne, 2013).
2. The MMC is a planning and funding body that represents 82 municipalities (Communauté métropolitaine de Montréal, 2013).

References

Atkinson, R. 2001. "The emerging 'urban agenda' and the European spatial development perspective: Towards an EU urban policy?" *European Planning Studies* 9: 385–406.

Avraham, E. 2004. "Media strategies for improving an unfavorable city image," *Cities* 21: 471–9.

Barnes, T.J., W.J. Coffey, D.W. Edgington, M.S. Gertler, and G. Norcliffe. 2000. "Canadian economic geography at the millennium," *Canadian Geographer* 44: 4–24.

Beckstead, D., and G. Gellatly. 2003. "The growth and development of new economy industries," *The Canadian Economy in Transition Series*. Ottawa, ON: Statistics Canada Catalogue no. 11–622–MIE2003002.

Bontje, M. 2004. "Facing the challenge of shrinking cities in East Germany: The case of Leipzig," *GeoJournal* 61: 13–21.

Bourne, L.S., and D. Rose. 2001. "The changing face of Canada: The uneven geographies of population and social change," *Canadian Geographer* 45: 105–19.

——, and J. Simmons. 2003. "New fault lines? Recent trends in the Canadian urban system and their implications for planning and public policy," *Canadian Journal of Urban Research* 12, 1 (suppl.): 22–47.

Bradford, N. 2002. *Why Cities Matter: Policy Research Perspectives for Canada*. Ottawa, ON: Canadian Policy Research Networks. At: www.cprn.org/documents/29277_en.pdf

——. 2004. *Place Matters and Multi-level Governance: Perspectives on a New Urban Policy Paradigm*. Ottawa, ON: Canadian Policy Research Networks. At: www.cprn.org/documents/26856_fr.pdf

Bunting, T., and P. Filion. 2001. "Uneven cities: Addressing rising inequality in the twenty-first century," *Canadian Geographer* 45: 126–31.

——, and ——, eds. 2006. *Canadian Cities in Transition: Local through Global Perspectives* (3rd edn.). Toronto: Oxford University Press.

Bürkner, H.J. 2005. "Polarization and Peripherization," in Oswalt (2005).

Cocks, M., and Couch, C. 2012. "The governance of a shrinking city: Housing renewal in the Liverpool conurbation, UK," *International Planning Studies* 17: 277–301.

Communauté métropolitaine de Montréal. 2013. *Who Are We—Establishment*. At: http://cmm.qc.ca/who-are-we/establishment/

Courchene, T.J. 2005. *Citistates and the State of Cities: Political-Economy and Fiscal-Federalism Dimensions*. Montreal: Institute for Research in Public Policy (IRPP Working Paper Series no. 2005–03).

Donald, B. 2005. "The politics of local economic development in Canada's city-regions: New dependencies, new deals, and a new politics of scale," *Space and Polity* 9: 261–81.

——. 2006. "From growth machine to ideas machine: The new politics of local economic development in the knowledge-intensive city," in D.G. Tremblay and R. Tremblay, eds., *The Competitive City in the New Economy*. Montreal: University of Quebec Press, Political Economy Collection.

——, and D. Morrow, with A. Athanasiu. 2003. *Competing for Talent: Implications for Social and Cultural Policy in Canadian City-Regions*. Ottawa, ON: Department of Canadian Heritage, Report prepared for Strategic Research and Analysis (SRA) Strategic Planning and Policy Coordination.

Downs, A. 1994. *New Visions for Metropolitan America*. Washington, DC: Brookings Institution.

ECOTEC Research and Consulting Ltd. 2007. *State of European Cities Report: Adding Value to the European Urban Audit*. Birmingham: ECOTEC Research and Consulting Ltd. At: http://ec.europa.eu/regional_policy/sources/docgener/studies/pdf/urban/stateof cities_2007.pdf

Federation of Canadian Municipalities (FCM). 2006. *Building Prosperity from the Ground Up: Restoring Municipal Fiscal Imbalance*. Ottawa: FCM. At: www.fpeim.ca/2006_FCM_Building_Prosperity_from_the_Ground_Up.pdf

Fischler, R., and J.M. Wolfe. 2006. "Contemporary planning," in Bunting and Filion (2006).

Florida, R. 2002. *The Rise of the Creative Class*. New York: Basic Books.

——. 2005. *Cities and the Creative Class*. New York: Routledge.

——, and R. Martin. 2009. *Ontario in the Creative Age*. Toronto: Martin Prosperity Institute. At: http://martinprosperity.org/media/pdfs/MPI%20Ontario%20Report%202009%20v3.pdf

Franz, P. 2004. "Shrinking cities–shrinking economy? The case of East Germany," *German Journal of Urban Studies* 44, 1: online journal.

Gertler, M.S. 2001. "Urban economy and society in Canada: Flows of people, capital and ideas," *ISUMA: The Canadian Journal of Policy Research* 2 (3): 119–30.

——, R. Florida, G. Gates, and T. Vinodrai. 2002. *Competing on Creativity: Placing Ontario's Cities in North American Context*. Toronto: Ontario Ministry of Enterprise, Opportunity and Innovation and the Institute for Competitiveness and Prosperity. At: www.competeprosper.ca/research/CompetingOnCreativity_061202.pdf

Gonzáles, S. 2006. *The Northern Way: A Celebration or a Victim of the New City-Regional Government Policy?* Swindon: Economic and Social Research Council Postgraduate Research Programme, Working Paper 28.

Grant, J. 2006. "Shaped by planning: The Canadian city through time," in Bunting and Filion (2006).

Hackworth, J. 2012. *A Critical Examination of Market-Centred Land Abandonment Policies in Shrinking American Cities*. Toronto: University of Toronto (Working Paper Geography & Program in Planning).

Hall, H.M. 2007. *Being Realistic about Planning in No Growth Communities: Challenges, Opportunities, and Foundations for a New Agenda*. Waterloo, ON: University of Waterloo, MA thesis.

——. 2009. "Slow growth and decline in Greater Sudbury: Challenges, opportunities, and foundations for a new planning agenda," *Canadian Journal of Urban Research* 18: 1–26.

——, and B. Donald. 2009. *Innovation and Creativity on the Periphery: Challenges and Opportunities in Northern Ontario*. Toronto: Martin Prosperity Institute Working Paper. At: http://martinprosperity.org/media/pdfs/Innovation_and_creativity_on_the_Periphery-H_Hall-B_Donald.pdf

Hall, H., and P. Hall. 2008. "Decline and no growth: Canada's forgotten urban interior," *Canadian Journal of Regional Studies* 31: 1–18.

Hanlon, N., and G. Halseth. 2005. "The greying of resource communities in northern British Columbia: Implications for health care delivery in already-underserviced communities," *Canadian Geographer* 49: 1–24.

Hayter, R., T.J. Barnes, and M.J. Bradshaw. 2003. "Relocating resource peripheries to the core of economic geography's theorizing: Rationale and agenda," *Area* 25, 1: 15–23.

Hoernig, H., D. Leahy, Z.X. Zhuang, R. Early, L. Randall, and G Whitelaw. 2005. "Planning for people: Integrating social issues and processes into planning practice," *Berkeley Planning Journal* 18: 35–55.

Hollander, J.B., K.M. Pallagst, T. Schwarz, and F.J. Popper. 2009. "Chapter 4: Planning shrinking cities," *Progress in Planning,* 72 (4): 223–32.

———, and Nemeth, J. 2011. "The bounds of smart decline: a foundational theory for planning shrinking cities," *Housing Policy Debate,* 21: 349–67.

Hospers, G. 2013. "Policy responses to urban shrinkage: From growth thinking to civic engagement," *European Planning Studies* (in press, published online).

Kitchen, H.M. 2002. *Municipal Revenue and Expenditure Issues in Canada* (Canadian Tax Paper No. 107). Toronto: Canadian Tax Foundation.

Knox, P.L. 2005. "Creating ordinary places: Slow cities in a fast world," *Journal of Urban Design* 10: 1–11.

Laurentian University. 2013. School of Architecture. Sudbury, ON: Laurentian University. At: laurentian.ca/content/school-architecture-0

Leo, C., and K. Anderson. 2006. "Being realistic about urban growth," in Bunting and Filion (2006).

———, and W. Brown. 2000. "Slow growth and urban development policy," *Journal of Urban Affairs* 22: 193–213.

Lewis, N., and B. Donald. 2010. "A new rubric for 'creative city' potential in Canada's smaller cities," *Urban Studies* 47: 29–54.

Logan, W., and H. Molotch. 1987. *Urban Fortunes: The Political Economy of Place.* Berkeley, CA: University of California Press.

Lötscher, L. 2005. "Shrinking East German cities?" *Geographia Polonica* 78: 79–98.

———, F. Howest, and L. Basten. 2004. "Eisenhüttenstadt: Monitoring a shrinking German city," *Dela* 21: 361–70.

Mäding, H. 2004. "Demographic change and local government finance—Trends and expectations," *German Journal of Urban Studies* 44, 1: online journal.

Martinez-Fernandez, C., I. Audirac, S. Fol, and E. Cunningham-Sabot. 2012a. "Shrinking cities: Urban challenges of globalization," *International Journal of Urban and Regional Research,* 36: 213–25.

———, N. Kubo, A. Noya, and T. Weyman. 2012b. *Demographic Change and Local Development: Shrinkage, Regeneration and Social Dynamics.* Paris: OECD (Working Paper from the OECD Local Economic and Employment Development [LEED] Programme).

Mintz, J.M., and T. Roberts. 2006. *Running on Empty: A Proposal to Improve City Finances.* Toronto: C.D. Howe Institute.

Molotch, H.L. 1976. "The city as a growth machine: Toward a political economy of place," *American Journal of Sociology* 82: 309–32.

Müller, B. 2004. "Demographic change and its consequences for cities—Introduction and overview," *German Journal of Urban Studies* 44: online journal.

———, and S. Siedentop. 2004. "Growth and shrinkage in Germany—Trends, perspectives and challenges for spatial planning and development," *German Journal of Urban Studies* 44, 1: online journal.

Norcliffe, G. 1994. "Regional labour market adjustments in a period of structural transformation: An assessment of the Canadian case," *Canadian Geographer* 38: 2–17.

Ontario Ministry of Municipal Affairs and Housing. 2009. City of Toronto Act, 2006. At: www.mah.gov.on.ca/Page343.aspx

Ontario Ministry of Public Infrastructure Renewal. 2006. *Growth Plan for the Greater Golden Horseshoe.* Toronto: Ontario Ministry of Public Infrastructure Renewal. At: www.placestogrow.ca/images/pdfs/FPLAN-ENG-WEB-ALL.pdf

Oswalt, P., ed. 2005. *Shrinking Cities: Volume 1— International Research.* Ostfildern-Ruit, Germany: Hatje Cantz.

———. 2005. "Introduction," in Oswalt (2005).

———, and T. Rienitz, ed. 2006. *Shrinking Cities, Volume 2: Interventions.* Ostfildern, Germany: Hatje Cantz Verlag.

Pallagst, K. 2013. "A Review of 'Design after Decline: How America Rebuilds Shrinking Cities,'" *Journal of the American Planning Association,* 79 (2): 11.

Polèse, M., and R. Shearmur, with P.M. Desjardins and M. Johnson. 2002. *The Periphery in the Knowledge Economy: The Spatial Dynamics of the Canadian Economy and the Future of Non-Metropolitan Regions in Quebec and the Atlantic Provinces.* Montreal and Moncton: Institut national de la recherche scientifique and the Canadian Institute for Research on Regional Development.

———, and ———. 2006. "Why some regions will decline: A Canadian case study with thoughts on local development strategies," *Papers in Regional Science* 85: 23–46.

Popper, D.E., and F.J. Popper. 2002. "Small can be beautiful: Coming to terms with decline—Americans tend to think that places, once settled, stay settled," *Planning* 68, 7: 20–3.

Reckien, D., and C. Martinez-Fernandez. 2011. "Why Do Cities Shrink?" *European Planning Studies,* 19: 1375–97.

Robinson, I.M. 1981. *Canadian Urban Growth Trends: Implications for a National Settlement Policy.* Vancouver, BC: University of British Columbia Press.

Rybczynski, W., and P.D. Linneman. 1999. "How to save our shrinking cities," *The Public Interest* 135: 30–44.

Sancton, A. 2000. "Amalgamations, service realignment, and property taxes: Did the Harris government have a plan for Ontario's municipalities?" *Canadian Journal of Regional Science* 23: 135–56.

——. 2006. "City politics: Municipalities and multi-level governance," in Bunting and Filion (2006).

Seasons, M. 2007. "Planning for uneven growth," *Plan Canada* 47 (2): 6.

Siegel, D. 2002. "Urban finance at the turn of the century: Be careful what you wish for," in E.P. Fowler and D. Siegel, eds., *Urban Policy Issues: Canadian Perspectives* (2nd edn.). Toronto: Oxford University Press.

Simard, M., and C. Simard. 2005. "Toward a culturalist city: A planning agenda for peripheral mid-size cities," *Canadian Journal of Urban Research* 14: 38–56.

Simmons, J. 2003. *Cities in Decline: The Future of Urban Canada*. Toronto: Ryerson University, Centre for the Study of Commercial Activity.

——, and L.S. Bourne. 2007. "Living with population growth and decline," *Plan Canada* 47, 2: 13–21.

——, and L.S. Bourne. 2013. *The Canadian Urban System in 2011: Looking Back and Projecting Forward*. Research Paper 228. Toronto: Cities Centre University of Toronto.

Slack, E. 2005. "Easing the fiscal restraints on Canadian cities," *Dialogues: Canada West Foundation* (Spring): 19–20.

Statistics Canada. 2013a. Based on one dataset showing 2001 CA populations in 2011 geography and another showing 2001 CMA populations in 2011 geography.

——. 2013b. Population and dwelling counts, for Canada, provinces and territories, 2011 and 2006 censuses. At: www12.statcan.gc.ca/census-recensement/2011/dp-pd/hlt-fst/pd-pl/Table-Tableau.cfm?LANG=Eng&T=101&S=50&O=A

——. 2013c. Population and dwelling counts, for Canada, provinces and territories, 2001 and 1996 censuses—100% data. At: www12.statcan.gc.ca/English/census01/products/standard/popdwell/Table-PR.cfm

Vojnovic, I., and D. Poel. 2000. "Provincial and municipal restructuring in Canada: Assessing expectations and outcomes," *Canadian Journal of Regional Science* 23: 1–6.

Wiechmann, T. 2008. "Errors expected-aligning urban strategy with demographic uncertainty in shrinking cities," *International Planning Studies*, 13: 431–46.

——, and K.M. Pallagst. 2012. "Urban shrinkage in Germany and the USA: A comparison of transformation patterns and local strategies," *International Journal of Urban and Regional Research* 36: 261–80.

Wolfe, J.M. 1995. "Canada," in D. Lyddon, ed., *International Manual of Planning Practice* (2nd edn.). The Hague: International Society of City and Regional Planners.

Fear, Insecurity, and the Canadian City

AMY SICILIANO,
DEBORAH COWEN,
AND NEIL SMITH

16

No matter how many valuable functions the city has furthered, it has also served throughout most of its history as a container of organized violence and a transmitter of war. (Mumford, 1961)

Introduction

On 4 December 2005, Vancouver's SkyTrain police became the first armed transit security force in Canadian history. Prompted by the perception of growing insecurity in and around the elevated light-rail system, Vancouver's municipal transit authority, TransLink, granted SkyTrain police the power to carry semi-automatic weapons along the 49.5-kilometre track. In 2007, tasers were added to the SkyTrain police arsenal, while the power to carry guns was extended to police on select bus lines. More recently, in 2009, private security guards working on contract for TransLink also were granted the power to carry guns.[1] These urban security initiatives are not without their critics. The Vancouver Bus Riders Union (BRU), a group of over 900 transit advocates, concluded that transit police are *the source* of insecurity for many transit-dependent women. Following extensive research on riders' experiences of the transit system, the BRU released a report that asserted, "many women feel unsafe around SkyTrain police and have experienced harassment, intimidation and racial profiling." If the city justifies its expansion of transit police authority as a protection of passengers, the BRU (2006) challenges this securitization, arguing that "the real safety issues for women in transit are long waits at poorly lit bus stops, overcrowded buses, and the recent purchase of polluting, dirty diesel buses." On the first day the SkyTrain police were armed, the Canadian Press (2005) reported that many riders "didn't think the system was threatening or dangerous, but giving the officers more powers could make them feel safer." One passenger, Robert Smith, echoed this intriguing logic when he said, "I guess it makes me feel a little bit more secure although I didn't feel all that insecure" (Carmichael, 2005). Securitization may in fact *create* insecurity, heightening anxieties about fear in the city.

The arming of public transit guards in Vancouver highlights three crucial insights: the extent, contestation, and effects of security. First, this case demonstrates how public spaces like the transit system increasingly are defined as *insecure* and in need of *more security*. More and more, state and corporate initiatives in Canadian cities are oriented toward achieving "security." As Mariana Valverde (2009) points out, everyday issues become securitized: hunger is now a problem of "food security"; homelessness, a problem of "housing security." Increased surveillance, new fencing and gating, the creation of "secure areas," and expanded police, paramilitary, and even military power in cities are increasingly the norm.

Second, the case of the SkyTrain police and the response from the Bus Riders Union reveal the *contested nature* of securitization. Security projects impact people differently and social groups define the very meaning of security in dramatically varying ways. Thus, while security—rarely ever explained or defined—is presented as an objective public good, the BRU's challenge to the arming of transit police reveals the political nature of securitization. The BRU critique also points to specific ways that securitization reproduces established patterns of marginalization and stigmatization, in this case creating more insecurity for transit-dependent women. In addition, the BRU response highlights a broader shift underway in cities: from *welfarist approaches* to *security responses* to social problems (on "welfarism," see Walks, Chapter 9; Addie, Fiedler, and Keil, Chapter 24).

Third, and finally, this case reveals some complicated *effects of security*. If we move beyond the question of the extent of security in Canadian cities and its contestation, some very challenging questions about securitization emerge. The SkyTrain rider's response to the arming of guards suggests that efforts to secure the city can in fact produce *greater insecurity*. This transit rider admits that he did not feel insecure prior to these events, and yet he still describes feeling *more secure* once the transit police were armed. The paradox of securitization is that it can *create* insecurities that may not have existed before, and by doing so may also stimulate real demands for still more security initiatives. In a sense, securitization fuels itself. This raises a crucial point: it is nearly impossible to distinguish between "real" and "constructed" feelings of insecurity. Indeed, we take as our starting point that actual and perceived insecurities are impossibly entangled, while we contend that the relationship between the two demands careful investigation.

This chapter builds on these three themes: the extent, contestation, and effects of securitization. Everyday urban life presents genuine dangers and risk. Economic crises, contaminated water supplies, and epidemics have created disruptions to everyday life in Canadian cities. However, the translation from actual risk to urban fear is complicated, requiring critical scrutiny. Fear is mobile, rarely reflecting actual risks that may arise in particular places. For instance, many women feel fear on city streets at night when the most likely place they will encounter violence is at home with men they already know. As we explore below, fear in public space is often expressed as a fear of racialized male strangers, an expression that takes up and reproduces racist stereotypes circulating in popular culture. Thus, fear may be motivated by actual risks, but, typically, fear is ordered by established social imaginaries. Fear sanctions the securitization of the city, but it tends to reproduce classed, gendered, and racialized relations of power. We further suggest that the particular kinds of uncertainty and risks generated by contemporary urban life in a globalized world are at once fuelling securitization of the city *and* pervasive insecurity. Securitization provides a promise of stability in a fundamentally precarious urban world but at the same time generates its own rationale, namely, insecurity.

The chapter unfolds as follows. In the next section we provide a brief and selective historical sketch of the securitization of cities, highlighting the changing contexts for urban insecurity and tactics of securitization. We pose the complicated but unavoidable question "How real is fear?" in order to explore the relationships between insecurity and securitization in contemporary Canadian cities. In the third section, to open some alternative ways of making sense of insecurity, we shift to look at different forms of urban fear governed under the rubric of security. We investigate forms of fear that are playing a profound role in reshaping urban space and governance: biohazards, terrorism, street crime, gendered violence, and security associated with property (such as the home). Each of these discussions addresses how actual risks are organized into security responses, revealing different aspects of the displacement of social and economic anxieties by fear and securitization. In a concluding section, we reflect on this tango of fear and security in contemporary Canadian urbanism.

Social Anxiety and the Securitization of Urban Space

Concern for security in Canadian cities is not a new phenomenon, but it has changed form over time. In fact, it could be said that cities have long been centres for security and defence. Taking a more global perspective, the city-states of Europe, Asia, and North Africa that predate nation-states were walled and heavily fortified, and were the primary spaces of sovereignty and protection (Graham, 2004a: 166; Mumford, 1961: 44). Our common-sense association of security issues with *nation-states,* then, is a product of the modern system of nation-states and only 200–300 years old (Cowen and Smith, 2009; Singer, 2003). During the era of colonial settlement of North America, cities played crucial roles as administrative but also as defensive centres. With the consolidation of the nation-state system, cities increasingly performed as spaces "inside" sovereign national borders. With this shift, military and police authority were assigned separate spheres—the police kept order "inside" while the military operated "outside" the national borders (Giddens, 1985).

Hence, domestic military deployments in cities seem shocking; they trespass the foundational mythologies of the nation-state and national territoriality. However, it is crucial to remember that in colonial and indeed in many post-colonial contexts, police and military authority remain thoroughly entangled in *paramilitary* forces. In Canada, the domestic deployment of military forces in response to Aboriginal land claim struggles, which have become increasingly urban affairs, reminds us of the persistent colonial politics of settler societies. The 1970 October Crisis in Quebec is another example of a deployment of military forces into city streets that was deeply startling to the public. The crisis unfolded when the Front de Libération du Québec (FLQ), a revolutionary socialist movement that sought sovereignty for

the province, kidnapped the British trade commissioner in Montreal as well as a provincial minister. In response, the federal government declared a state of "apprehended insurrection" under the War Measures Act, deployed the armed forces in city streets, and authorized arrests without charge. More than 450 people were detained. The 1970 deployment also raised questions about a persistent colonial relationship between Québécois people and the Canadian state.

The Royal Canadian Mounted Police's changing form demonstrates this entanglement of "inside" and "outside" security and how security threats—both real and imagined—generate the perceived need for more security. In 1873, British imperialists established Canada's first police force, then called the North West Mounted Police (NWMP), to defend colonial interests and sovereignty claims on the nation's western frontier. The "taming" of the frontier saw the colonization of outside space transformed into the domestication of inside space. As the frontier became more densely settled, the role of the NWMP (which had *Royal* added to its name in 1904 and later, in 1920, became the more generic Royal Canadian Mounted Police, or RCMP), initially imagined to be a temporary force, shifted from a militaristic focus bringing colonial "rule of law" in the West, to policing its rapidly expanding urban and rural settlements. The external mutated into the internal as colonialization proceeded.

With the declaration of World War I and the passing of the War Measures Act in 1914, the Royal North West Mounted Police were granted special powers to monitor and detain Austrian and German settlers, or "enemy aliens." Soon after the war, and on the heels of the Russian Revolution, perceived threats posed by "radical and revolutionary" unions in Canada's rapidly industrializing cities again rejuvenated the force with the establishment of a secret security division designed to infiltrate union organizing. When 30,000+ workers walked off the job to protest poor working conditions during Winnipeg's General Strike in 1919, the RNWMP responded with the takeover of the city. Known as "Bloody Saturday," the massive riot resulted in the death of one civilian, and hundreds of others were injured. Because municipal and provincial police forces actually were sympathetic to the workers—and with the military, exhausted after World War I—the national government decided to reinvest in the federal police force, which otherwise might have been disbanded, to bridge instead the military–police-security divide. The government "looked to the Force's unique character as a semimilitary organization, whose discipline and traditions would make it a dependable arm of authority" (RCMP, 2009).

By the early 1970s, investigative journalists had exposed illegal "disruption tactics" committed by the RCMP secret service in Vancouver and Montreal. The result was the formal separation of policing and security wings of the RCMP and the creation of the Canadian Security Intelligence Service (CSIS) (Security Intelligence Review Committee, 2005). Today, while CSIS is responsible for state intelligence, the passage of anti-terrorist legislation in Canada grants "special powers" to police and orients them toward a more proactive, "intelligence-led" model. The line between security, police, and military is once again blurring (Murphy, 2007). The expanded powers of surveillance and information-sharing within and between different security forces, especially after 2001, have led to unwarranted detentions, extraditions, and the violation of basic human rights, especially for racialized people. The case of Maher Arar, unlawfully deported by the US to several years of torture in Syria, all as a result of erroneous RCMP "intelligence," serves as a vivid example of the consequences of inflated fears on public policy, policing, and security.

Since the mid-twentieth century, cities again became more explicitly entangled in matters of security (Murphy, 2007). During World War II, cities in Europe and Asia became the targets of intentional air strikes. We can think of the devastation of cities like London, Hamburg, Dresden, Hiroshima, and Nagasaki. Air strikes clearly had immediate impacts on targeted cities, but they also had lasting effects on urban planning practice. Density became associated with danger; urban concentration became a source of acute vulnerability to attack. Postwar city planning in North America was impacted such that dispersal and decentralization became important planning principles (Farish, 2003; Light, 2003). Suburbanization can therefore be understood in part as a security response to the Cold War.

Security "in" Cities

Security has been an issue not simply *of* cities but also *in* cities for a long time. Policing is often an important element in efforts to improve urban security, but as the BRU reminds us, *police can be the source of fear and insecurity* for many groups, particularly poor and racialized people, who may experience violence and intimidation associated with racial profiling and targeted policing. We will return to the question of policing shortly, but first, some key moments in urban insecurity demand scrutiny because they have transformed the boundaries of police and military authority. Starting in 1956, the US government declared a form of open warfare against a number of activist groups that posed a direct challenge to the social and economic status quo. Under the banner of COINTELPRO, for "Counter Intelligence Program," the FBI engaged in a range of illegal and extreme practices, a form of domestic warfare against civil groups, that included the assassination of movement leaders including the Black Panthers, women's rights groups, the American Indian Movement (AIM), and socialist and communist groups (Glick, 1989). Government response to riots in American cities in the 1960s also exceeded the boundaries of legal civilian law enforcement. National Guard forces were deployed into city streets, while the government initiated military planning for civilian unrest in US cities. A bitter irony: the riots of the 1960s were a direct response to racist police violence against African Americans. The US War on Drugs, initiated in 1971 under President Nixon, was largely responsible for the unprecedented rates of incarceration of black and Latino men. It also sanctioned a dramatic expansion of military and intelligence work inside national borders and the militarization of policing, and in this way set new precedents in the blurring of police and military authority and jurisdiction (Burghardt, 2002).

In the wake of numerous acts of terrorism in urban settings, such as the 1995 Oklahoma City bombing, the 9/11 terrorist attacks of 2001 in the US, the 7/7 bombings of the London public transit system on 7 July 2005, and Israeli attacks on urban areas in Gaza and Fallujah, cities, globally, have become deliberate targets of terrorism by state and non-state actors (Graham, 2010; Sassen, 2010). This urbanization of warfare has been particularly noticeable since the end of the Cold War and has enormous implications for violence against civilian populations and military preparations for urban warfare (Graham, 2004b). As one Australian Defence College report (Evans, 2007) suggests, globalization and urbanization processes are together responsible for the intensification of urban warfare. The report argues that military planners should take the work of human geographers very seriously. Quite extraordinarily, the report is premised on the argument that, from the perspective of military forces, urban warfare raises *"the problem of a civilian presence in cities."* A curious problem indeed!

Globalizing "Insecurity"?

Alongside the urbanization of the global population, warfare, too, is urbanizing. Urban security practices have changed in response to events like anti-globalization protests, anti-war protests, union organizing, and public health crises. From Vancouver to Genoa and from Seattle to Quebec City, anti-globalization protests have provoked massive experimentation in urban security strategies (Fernandez, 2008). Disruption to trade summits has led governments to crack down on protests, sometimes banning activists entirely by creating special "no-protest zones" or more permanent "secure areas" where civic rights are severely circumscribed (Németh, 2009, 2010). And sometimes, world leaders organize their meetings far from the crowds of large cities to avoid protests: the 2002 G8 summit, for example, was held at a secure and remote resort in Kananaskis, Alberta,

and in February 2010 finance ministers and their entourages representing the G7 countries converged on Iqaluit, Nunavut. Security planning for world trade summits has extended co-operation and information—sharing practices between national governments, and between governments and private security companies. Paramilitary units proliferate in cities, and military technologies are regularly imported into urban policing (Balko 2013; Kraska, 2001; Rygiel, 2009).

Globalization has created particular kinds of risks that make people less secure but that may not register as "security" issues. The fact that terrorism receives extraordinary public attention does not mean it is actually the most pressing source of insecurity. The Worldwatch Institute reminds us that far more people die from car accidents (more than 43,000 a year in the US) or even from accidental falls (approximately 15,000) than from such terrorist acts as the events of 9/11 (2975). This emphasis on particular types of threats suggests that we need to consider the issues that create social, economic, and biological precariousness but may not feature in debates about security. If we do consider such issues, we see that contemporary forms of precariousness are linked through processes of globalization.

On the one hand, economic globalization increases polarization in Canadian cities. The movement of production to the global South has led to the decline of stable industrial employment for working-class populations in the North and the rise of an urban economy characterized by high-wage professions and low-wage service work. The proliferation of "McJobs" has led to the expansion of the working poor while the gentrification of the city by the professional classes denies this group access to housing and services in the core. As we will explore, official responses to social polarization have relied increasingly on social discipline, policing, and even expanded prison sentencing in place of the welfarist approaches that dominated the post-World War II period (Friedman and Wolff, 2006 [1982]).

The movement of production to the global South is paired with the movement of people from these regions to countries like Canada in search of opportunities or to escape violence and instability. However, once in Canada, even highly skilled immigrant populations are concentrated in low-wage and precarious work (Vosko, 2000), such that social polarization and the racialization of poverty are two sides of the same coin (Galabuzzi, 2006; see Kobayashi and Preston, Chapter 8). The global South, now literally "at home" in the cities of the global North, experiences forms of security that were once more sharply delineated by national borders; they have been rescaled in the city, giving rise to new forms of *urban geopolitics* (Fregonese 2012; Graham, 2004a). Of course, we also might identify the post-2008 financial crisis as a "security problem" that emerged directly from the globalization of particular high-risk practices of finance and property capital. Even war is understood today as a means of policing globalization (Smith, 2004).

The brief sketch of changes in this chapter highlights pivotal events in the historical geography of urban securitization and, specifically, some of the socio-economic context for urban *insecurity*. However, insecurity cannot be *reduced* to social and economic fear. It may be impossible to identify definitively sources of insecurity, and such a quest can miss more important questions about the form and effects of specific *security projects* (see Valverde, 2009). Nevertheless, the relationship between *sources of fear* and *security responses* is important precisely because fear is at once real and manufactured. We have already seen with the Vancouver transit police that insecurity can be created by securitization. While fear is not a new phenomenon in cities, security projects have proliferated in recent years. Insecurity is not "unreal"—fear stems from actual events and has powerful effects on urban life. Real threats exist, certainly; but fear also can be cultivated and channeled into particular kinds of responses.

Securing the City?

How do we make sense of the fears that define Canadian urbanism today, and what is the relationship between fear and insecurity? Through a series of brief vignettes, we explore the ways in which insecurity is animated by anxieties over changing social and economic geographies at multiple spatial scales, from the local to the transnational. While urban fear can stem from a vast range of sources (e.g., communicable disease, gun violence, dark and empty streets, hunger) and can take an expansive number of forms when channeled into security projects (e.g., food security, community safety, bio-security), the major shifts provoking security responses stem from the changes in the population and economy of Canadian cities brought about by globalization. We examine six different issues that are conceptualized as problems of security: terror, crime, everyday urban life, property, gendered violence, and biohazards. The fact that such diverse issues can all be managed as matters of "security" is not benign. As a number of scholars have argued, "security" is a powerful but depoliticizing way of conceptualizing and governing social problems (Gaonkar 2010; Neocleous 2007; Stasiulis and Ross, 2006).

Terror

Terror has become the issue that first comes to mind when we think about cities and security; however, an enormous dissonance exists between sources of terror and efforts to secure cities against it. The fear of terrorist attack has fuelled the widespread securitization of urban space, with national borders actively "re-scaled" within cities today (Graham, 2004a; 2004b). The threat of terrorism—typically categorized as a matter of *national* security—is managed within urban space in a number of different forms. The physical securitization of public transportation systems in the name of counter-terrorism—the SkyTrain in Vancouver, for example, and other spaces and infrastructure devoted to the circulation of people and goods—has been striking. Port spaces in Canadian cities are subject to a host of new security regulations largely inspired by the US-led "War on Terror." Concern for terrorism has provoked the Canadian government to deem ports "secure areas," where access is heavily restricted by fencing, bollards, closed-circuit television cameras, and the extreme and possibly unconstitutional scrutiny of transportation workers' lives (Cowen, 2007; Cowen and Bunce, 2006). The creation of special secure areas has advanced rapidly in Canadian cities, although this does not compare to the US where as much as 40 per cent of urban land in Los Angeles is under special security regulations (Németh, 2009).

Concern for urban terror has prompted shifts in the organization of the security state. CSIS, the RCMP, and the military have seen their domestic authority extended under the 2001 Anti-Terrorism Act. Counter-terror work south of the border saw the Los Angeles police develop a plan to map Muslim communities in the city in an effort "to identify at-risk communities" (Winton, Renaud, and Pringle, 2007). This plan was eventually dropped because of widespread outrage over such stark racial profiling; however, targeted police surveillance proceeds on both sides of the border, even when it is not explicit public policy. The arrest of the "Toronto 18" made an enormous media splash in 2006 when young Muslim men in Brampton were arrested on charges of "homegrown terrorism," including a supposed plot to assassinate the prime minister. But the subsequent court hearings have done more to expose racial profiling and police incompetence than any terrorist activity in cities. In fact, as the trial became increasingly farcical, David Charters, an expert member of the Advisory Council on National Security, conceded that "Canada's biggest case of alleged homegrown terrorism—the "Toronto 18"—is turning out to be little more than a bunch of 'wanna-be jihadists.'" To "anyone the least bit familiar with security," he added, "their so-called 'plans' were scarcely credible" (*Ottawa Citizen*, 2008). Nonetheless, a number of these "wanna-be jihadists" have been tried and convicted, with the so-called "mastermind" receiving a life sentence for his part in the plot and offering an extensive apology in court for his role, stating that he deserved the "absolute contempt" of Canadians (CBC News, 2010).

Whatever the ubiquitous talk about terror (Katz, 2001) and the fact that it has had enormous impacts on everyday life—particularly for people of colour, who are subject to racial profiling—terrorism is one of the least likely threats to life in Canadian cities. The discrepancy between terror talk and terror reality is vast. There is only one common thread that links several major terrorist acts in the US in the last 10 years—Timothy McVeigh, the Oklahoma bomber, who killed 168 people in 2002; Al-Qaeda and Osama bin Laden; Saddam Hussein: all, at some point in their past, were employed by or financially aided and politically supported by the US military and security apparatus.

Crime

In 2012, Canada's national crime rate reached its lowest point since 1972 (Perreault, 2013). Yet judging from media reports, political discourse, and recent changes to the Criminal Code, fear would seem to be on the rise. Perception of crime and violence is inextricably linked to the geographies of race and class. Kelling and Wilson's influential 1982 "broken windows" thesis illustrates this connection succinctly. It argues that minor issues of "social disorder" lead to more serious forms of crime and violence if left unchecked. "The citizen who fears the ill-smelling drunk, the rowdy teenager, or the importuning beggar is not merely expressing his distaste for unseemly behavior," they assert, but "is also giving voice to a bit of folk wisdom that happens to be a correct generalization—namely, that serious street crime flourishes in areas in which disorderly behavior goes unchecked. The unchecked panhandler is, in effect, the first broken window." Kelling and Wilson argue that policing should address issues that are *not quite criminal* in order to pre-empt actual crime. This argument had dramatic impact in many cities, most notably New York but also Canadian cities like Windsor (Lippert, 2007), and around the world, and entailed the widespread criminalization of people (such as panhandlers) and activities (such as graffiti). "Broken windows policing" extends the authority of the police well beyond the law, much as Kelling and Wilson intended: "arresting a single drunk or a single vagrant who has harmed no identifiable person seems unjust, and in a sense it is." Yet "failing to do anything about a score of drunks or a hundred vagrants may destroy an entire community." They acknowledge the danger of police use of "discretionary powers," namely that they could be used to "maintain the racial or ethnic purity of a neighborhood."

While many have critiqued the basic logic of the broken windows thesis, the dangers of pre-emptive police power, and the racist and class violence that such a policy is premised upon, another element to broken windows policing has received less critical scrutiny in its original articulation: *geographical targeting* in police operations. Kelling and Wilson (1982) argue that additional police resources should be devoted to areas of the city that appear to be experiencing a breakdown of social order, evident to them in the physical deterioration of property, which they argue is "vulnerable to criminal invasion."

"Broken windows" helped rationalize targeted policing, yet the language and practice of targeting comes from military practice. As Kaplan (2006) argues, police "targeting" mobilizes the same logic of "precise positioning" and containment as the military—the definition of a social problem as one of *location*.

Everyday Urban Life

The adoption and use of bylaws, business improvement areas, and neighbourhood watch programs at first glance can seem benign feature of everyday urban life. However such methods of designating and controlling urban space often result in pernicious consequences, particularly for marginalized populations, including the racialized, the poor, and the mentally ill (see, for instance, Mitchell, 2003). While regulatory mechanisms have long played a central role in urban governance, they are increasingly being used as means of responding to fear arising from growing concentrations of social inequality in our cities.

For instance, equal access to education for First Nations has long been area of concern for many of Canada's indigenous people. Currently, thousands of youth from remote reserves migrate to larger urban centres with the hope of attaining a high school diploma because this right is unavailable anywhere in or near their home communities. Thunder Bay, a city of about 120,000 in north-western Ontario, hosts approximately 200 of these students a year. In response, in 2000 a secondary school dedicated to serving First Nations youth opened in the city. However, since its opening, seven students have died prematurely during their studies—most found in the rivers that cut across the city (see Porter, 2013; Weinstein, 2011).

School administrators introduced a "three strikes" student curfew policy to improve safety and quell fears in the broader community. Paradoxically, rather than addressing the *source* of insecurity—namely funding and access for indigenous education—such a punitive policy contributes to feelings of *insecurity*. Curfews have been shown to increase racial profiling of youth and decrease youth mobility and socialization as well as feelings of happiness and well-being (see Siciliano, 2011, for an overview of social impacts of youth curfews). For instance, in Thunder Bay, one First Nations student falsely alleged that local police took him on a "Starlight Tour" (picking him up and dropping him off at the edge of town) to evade punishment for a curfew breech (CBC News, 2013; see also Brass, 2004, on the practice of Starlight Tours). Thus, while the curfew appears to have done little to address the social issues underpinning student safety and access to education, it contributes to strained relations between indigenous and settler communities in the city (Mansbridge, 2013).

Youth curfews are just one example of everyday regulations used to monitor or limit access for certain citizens in the name of public safety. Since its North American introduction in the late 1800s, zoning has been used to regulate access to land use: from bylaws used to regulate Vancouver's Chinese community at the turn of the nineteenth century (Anderson, 1987) to Toronto's current zoning regulations restricting the location of supportive housing. Such municipal zoning regulations—although often neutral in appearance—can exclude based on social class, ability, race, or ethnicity (Leisk, 2012).

For instance, as the number of people struggling with drug- and opiate-related addiction climbs, several medium and smaller sized cities have used zoning to limit access to public health services. Despite evidence demonstrating that harm reduction programs can improve safety and reduce crime (Bell et al., 1997; Killias and Rabasa, 1997; Stevens, 2013), zoning bylaws are being used in several cities to prohibit their existence based on fear of "undesirables" in neighbourhoods—typically gentrifying downtown cores (Bernstein and Bennett, 2013; Smith, 2010).

A lack of regulations can also have exclusionary effects. Between 1991 and 2005, the private security industry—which is often funded by public tax dollars through the support of **business improvement areas (BIAs)**—grew by nearly 70 per cent. Currently, the ratio of private to public police is approximately three to one. Such exponential growth in the absence of regulatory oversight profoundly affects the rights and freedom of movement of many citizens, as a study by Pivot Legal Society demonstrated (Bennett et al., 2008). Kelly Gorkoff, of the University of Winnipeg's Criminal Justice Department, states this of the city's Business Improvement Zone programs: "They are not a community support network offering assistance. . . . Instead, they move people around so business owners can operate without customers feeling fearful of street people" (Cable, 2011).

Property

As the 2008 economic crash suggests, the greatest threat to the "security" of private property may stem from volatility in the global financial markets. However, growing fear regarding the home has fuelled the rapid expansion of the home security industry. The spread of gated communities exemplifies this manifestation of fear; they now house at least 9 million Americans, and 40 per cent of new homes in California are behind walls (Low, 2006). Lang and Danielson (1997) found that many people choose gated communities because they believe such places reduce risks, ranging from "unwanted social exchange" to "decline in property value." Jill Grant suggests that gated communities in Canada have a complicated relationship to security. She writes, "The gate is advertised as a security feature, but our observations indicate that gates mostly function to keep casual visitors and sight-seers out" (Grant, n.d.). She argues that there is a direct connection between socio-economic anxieties and security responses; gated communities are a reaction to "urban problems that show no sign of easing" and become an option when "people feel they cannot rely on public regulations and political processes to protect their neighbourhoods from unwanted uses (or people)" (Grant, 2005).

Mike Davis (1990) argues that the expansion of security is a response to growing social polarization. This sentiment is echoed by the World Urban Forum (2006) in its document *The Secure City*, produced for a Vancouver meeting in 2006, which describes urban fear as a result of the growing gap between "haves" and "have-nots." Indeed, social **polarization** in Canadian cities is generating more spatial segregation and the formation of "citadel" spaces in gentrified downtown cores (Hulchanski, 2007). Citadel spaces are often fortified and create border zones within the city that become spaces of conflict. Moreover, citadel spaces are emerging in the construction of heavily securitized condominiums in gentrifying areas like Vancouver's Downtown Eastside, where security gates and surveillance cameras control access to residential and recreation spaces. But subtler forms of securitized elite spaces are becoming common in other Canadian cities. Toronto's gentrifying Cabbagetown neighbourhood, for example, has few visible signs of gating or cameras, yet the area is rife with conflicts over security. In 2007, out of concern for the protection of their property, middle-class Cabbagetown residents hired off-duty police to bring under surveillance the poor and working-class spaces in the neighbourhood.

Gendered Violence

Desolate city streets, parking lots, and other public spaces dominate popular imaginaries of dangerous urban spaces, especially in perceptions of women's safety. However, it is not in the public space but in the home where women are most likely to encounter violence (Bowman, 1993; Day, 1999, 2001; Valentine, 1992). And while fear of public spaces may not reflect the actual risks of gendered violence, such fear is nonetheless "real" in the sense that it fuels concrete actions. On the one hand, gendered fear of public spaces often translates into fear of particular people and places. Day argues that racialized communities, and especially racialized men, are often branded as dangerous and the source of women's insecurity (Day, 2001: 114), which rationalizes intensive and targeted policing of young racialized men in public spaces (Siciliano, 2007; Tanovich, 2006). Targeted policing has further impact: it *creates* insecurity for racialized men (Day, 1999).

Indeed, fear shapes the feelings people have about city spaces, the travel routes they take, and the demands they place on elected officials (Day, 2001). For instance, a 1976 transit safety audit by the Toronto Transit Commission illustrates this point: despite a very low crime rate, many women saw the subway as unsafe, causing them to limit "their lives very dramatically by stopping their use of the public transit system altogether or at certain times, especially at night" (quoted in Shulz and Gilbert, 2003: 554). However, concerns for women's safety in public can also be mobilized for other purposes. Concern for women's safety was accentuated with the opening of the first mass transportation systems in North America. In 1909, five years after the opening of New York's Interborough Rapid Transit, women's groups expressed safety concerns (Shulz and Gilbert, 2003). The Women's Municipal League proposed that the last car of every rush-hour train should be reserved exclusively for women to protect them from "fearful crushes" and sexual aggression. However, as Shulz and Gilbert argue, "a secondary purpose of [the] demand for segregated cars was less benevolent." The Municipal League, "representing the views of many upper-class women of the time, believed that some working-class women were willing participants in this subway rowdiness, and that creation of women-only cars would lead to more ladylike behaviour by those who needed such reforming." In this case, class perspectives were plainly evident in the Women's Municipal League's efforts to protect working-class women *from themselves.*

These complicated politics of "protection"—specifically, the use of "women's security" as a rationale for social control of poor and racialized people—have important parallels at other spatial scales. Much international warfare is today premised on the need to *protect women's safety,* but this rationale helps produce the racial and gendered violence it claims to contest. Spivak (1985) famously described instances of gendered colonial violence as "white men saving brown women from brown men." The military mission in Afghanistan, where Canada played a leading role, provides parallels. Today, the language of "urban security" frames debates about women's safety in the city, and this framing supports more securitized and even militarized responses to fear.

Biohazards

Biohazards cover a wide range of events and processes, from bio-terror to oil spills, from the results of climate change to a broad array of everyday environmental hazards. Here we focus on threats from communicable disease as they affect urban life. The dense concentration of populations and the rapid circulation of people between cities worldwide enable the geographical transmission of disease (Ali and Keil, 2006). Outbreaks of infectious disease are not new to urban life: plague, cholera, tuberculosis, HIV, and many other contagious diseases all have had an impact on urban history. What distinguishes the present situation is that infectious disease is being brought under the rubric of security planning and management. Bio-security has become the official framework through which governments, **non-governmental organizations** (NGOs), and corporations conceptualize epidemics and emergency response. However, bio-security approaches can displace effective prevention efforts, such as investment in public health, by resorting to expensive security initiatives that do little to mitigate contagion (Fearnley, 2008; Hooker and Ali, 2006).

The 2003 outbreak of severe acute respiratory syndrome (SARS) provides a perfect example. SARS is understood to have emerged in southern China. It spread around the world, impacting a series of globally networked cities, including Toronto. Encountering an unprepared public health system, SARS had a big impact on Toronto. As a result, the World Health Organization (WHO) issued a warning against any but essential travel to Canada's largest city. Federal authorities adopted stricter monitoring of international travellers, and almost 30,000 people in the city were voluntarily quarantined. In total, 44 people died as a result of the outbreak in Toronto.

The SARS outbreak took place less than three years after another environmental tragedy: the 2000 Walkerton, Ontario, *E. coli* outbreak, in which several people died and many became ill after provincial cuts to water inspection services contributed to undetected *E.coli* contamination of the town's drinking water. There are important political parallels between Walkerton's water and Toronto's SARS outbreak. As Hooker and Ali (2006: 14) argue, Walkerton "received a great deal of national and international media coverage and the accompanying inquiry commission identified many neoliberal structural influences common to the SARS outbreak." Like Walkerton, responsibility for the strained response to SARS can be placed squarely on the retrenchment of investment in public health. Three major commissions of inquiry into the SARS outbreak led by different levels of government concurred that the response failed because of underfunding of health infrastructure. All three recommended renewed public health investment (Sanford and Ali, 2005).

As with other "security issues," the SARS outbreak reveals how human welfare approaches have been reframed and even displaced by the lens of security. Managing SARS as a security issue contributed to a "geopolitical" response to the outbreak. Containing SARS, moreover, became an occasion for racism against Chinese and other East Asian people, with many incidents of official and unofficial anti-Asian sentiment reported daily. Popular racism became so salient that Ontario's

commissioner of public health was compelled to speak out (Wharry, 2003), stating that "It is both wrong and prejudicial to fear or shun any or all people in the Asian community based on the assumption that they must have SARS." People avoided Chinese businesses, and racial slurs were reported on the streets, but as Hung (2004: 8) writes, official responses also were characterized by racism: "Many immigration officers wore face masks when attending audits for Chinese migrants applying for citizenship, though all eligible applicants must have resided in Canada for at least two years before the interview."

Conclusion

On 13 October 2007, soon after SkyTrain police obtained tasers, officers in the Vancouver airport encountered a newly arrived visitor from Poland. Robert Dziekanski spoke no English, was held alone in a security area for nearly nine hours, seemed disoriented and combative, and was tasered by RCMP officers, soon after which he was declared dead. The Dziekanski case exemplifies key problems with the securitization of cities. On the one hand, Dziekanski's arrival in Vancouver had everything to do with new global patterns of migration—in his case, a post–Berlin Wall world. The case became an important news item in Poland and around the world and a major embarrassment in Canada. On the other hand, it was a highly localized event in the Vancouver airport terminal. The geography of fear and security in Canadian cities can be studied as a question of scale: what happens in Canadian cities is part of a global story of movement and flows (see Hall, Chapter 3), and what happens globally may land locally. We have seen that traditional matters of national security are rescaled in the city. Indeed, global patterns of movement are directly connected to the securitization of Canadian cities, which are increasingly managed as insecure border spaces.

Three conclusions stand out. First, securitization often entails a displacement of real social and economic fears, refocused against surrogate social targets. Second, attempts at securitization breed their own very real experiences of insecurity. Third, the geography of fear and insecurity is central to both of these shifts insofar as the sources of insecurity are routinely displaced by implanting that insecurity in a specific place—identified by class or race or national or other forms of social difference—whether at global or local scales. The question of fear and insecurity in the Canadian city is only going to intensify, and critical responses to this intensification need to develop apace.

Review Questions

1. What groups are most targeted by urban security measures? How are they affected by these measures?
2. Why does the public demand additional urban security?
3. In what ways is globalization linked to urban securitization?

Note

1. In addition to arming police and security guards in an effort to secure the system for the 2010 Olympics, TransLink spent upward of $23 million on the "physical hardening" of the system, including new cameras and video software, lights, "smart fences" able to detect human motion, chemical sensors for SkyTrain and the West Coast Express (the area's commuter rail service), and counter-terrorism training for transit police (Keast, 2008).

References

Ali, S.H., and R. Keil. 2006. "Global cities and the spread of infectious disease: The case of severe acute respiratory syndrome (SARS) in Toronto, Canada," *Urban Studies* 43: 1–19.

Anderson, K. 1987. "The idea of Chinatown: The power of place and institutional practice in the making of a racial category," *Annals of the Association of American Geographers* 77: 580–98.

Balko, R. 2013. *Rise of the Warrior Cop: The Militarization of America's Police Forces.* New York: Perseus Books.

Bell J., R. Mattick, A. Hay, J. Chan, and W. Hall. 1997. "Methadone maintenance and drug related crime," *Journal of Substance Abuse* 9: 15–25.

Bennet, D., D. Eby, J. Richardson, and K. Tilley. 2008. "Security before justice: A study of the impacts of private security on homeless and under-housed Vancouver residents." Pivot Legal Society, November. At: pivotlegal.org/pivot-points/publications/security-before-justice

Bernstein, S.E., and D. Bennett. 2013. "Zoned out: 'NIMBYism,' addiction services and municipal governance in British Columbia," *International Journal of Drug Policy* 24 (6): 61–5.

Brass, Mervin. 2004. "In Depth: Aboriginal Canadians, Starlight Tours." *The National Magazine.* CBC News. At: cbc.ca/news/background/aboriginals/starlighttours.html

Bowman, C. 1993. "Street harassment and the informal ghettoization of women," *Harvard Law Review* 106: 517–80.

Burghardt, T. 2002. *Police State America: US Military "Civil Disturbance" Planning.* Toronto: Arm the Spirit Press.

Bus Riders Union (BRU). 2006. "SkyTrain police pose threat to bus riders," press release. At: http://BRU.vcn.bc.ca

Cable, E. 2011. "Downtown BIZ Hires New Watch Ambassadors." *The UNITER: Winnipeg's Weekly Urban Journal.* 8 Sept. At: uniter.ca/view/6365

Canadian Press. 2005. "They have guns, will travel: Vancouver becomes first city in Canada to specially train, arm transit police force," *Kitchener-Waterloo Record,* 6 Dec.

Carmichael, A. 2005. "Vancouver arms transit cops," *Globe and Mail,* Dec 5.

CBC News. 2010. "Toronto 18 co-leader apologizes to Canadians," 14 Jan. At: www.cbc.ca/canada/toronto/story/2010/01/14/amara-trial.html

CBC News. 2013. "Investigate allegations to avoid 'tragedies,' lawyer says," Jan 7. At: cbc.ca/news/canada/thunder-bay/story/2013/01/07/tby-allegations-of-starlight-tours-thunder-bay.html

Cowen, D. 2007. "Struggling with 'security': National security and labour in the ports," *Just Labour* 10: 30–44.

———, and S. Bunce. 2006. "Competitive cities and secure nations: Conflict and convergence in urban waterfront agendas after 9/11," *International Journal of Urban and Regional Research* 30: 427–39.

———, and N. Smith. 2009. "After geopolitics? From the geopolitical social to geoeconomics," *Antipode* 41: 22–48.

Davis, M. 1990. *City of Quartz: Excavating the Future of Los Angeles.* London: Verso.

Day, K. 1999. "Embassies and sanctuaries: Race and women's fear and welcome in privatized public space," *Environment and Planning D: Society and Space* 17: 307–28.

——. 2001. "Constructing masculinity and women's fear in public space in Irvine, California," *Gender, Place and Culture* 8: 109–27.

Evans, M. 2007. *City without Joy: Urban Military Operations into the 21st Century*. Canberra, Australia: Australian Defence College, Occasional Paper No. 2.

Farish, M. 2003. "Disaster and decentralization: American cities and the Cold War," *Cultural Geographies* 10: 125–48.

Fearnley, L. 2008. "Signals come and go: Syndromic surveillance and styles of biosecurity," *Environment and Planning A* 40: 1615–32.

Fernandez, L. 2008. *Policing Dissent: Social Control and the Anti-Globalization Movement*. Brunswick, NJ: Rutgers University Press.

Fregonese, S. 2012. "Urban geopolitics 8 years on: Hybrid sovereignties, the everyday, and geographies of peace," *Geography Compass* 6.5: 290–303.

Friedman, J., and G. Wolff. 2006 [1982]. "World city formation: An agenda for research and action," in R. Keil and N. Brenner, eds., *The Global Cities Reader*. New York: Routledge.

Galabuzzi, G. 2006. *Canada's Economic Apartheid: The Social Exclusion of Racialized Groups in the New Century*. Toronto: Canadian Scholars' Press.

Gaonkar, D. 2010. "Whose fears? Which life? What security?" *Public Culture* 22.3: 405–10.

Giddens, A. 1985. *The Nation-state and Violence*. Cambridge: Polity.

Glick, B. 1989. *War at Home: Covert Action against U.S. Activists and What We Can Do About It*. Cambridge, MA: South End Press.

Graham, S. 2004a. "Postmortem city: Towards an urban geopolitics," *City* 8: 165–96.

——. 2004b. "Introduction: Cities, warfare and states of emergency," in S. Graham, ed., *Cities, War and Terrorism*. Oxford: Blackwell.

——. 2010. "Laboratories of war: United States–Israeli collaboration in urban war and securitization," *Brown Journal of World Affairs* 17: 35.

Grant, J. 2005. "The function of the gates: The social construction of security in gated developments," *Town Planning Review* 76: 339–61.

——. n.d. "Gated Communities in Canada," project website. At: http://gated.architectureandplanning.dal.ca/welcome.htm

Hooker, C., and S. Ali. 2006. "SARS and security: Public health in the 'new normal,'" paper presented at the annual meeting of the American Sociological Association, Montreal.

Hulchanski, D. 2007. *The Three Cities within Toronto: Income Polarization among Torontoès Neighbourhoods, 1970–2000*. Toronto: University of Toronto, Centre for Urban and Community Studies, Research Bulletin No. 40.

Hung, H-F. 2004. "The politics of SARS: Containing the perils of globalization by more globalization," *Asian Perspective* 28: 19–44.

Kaplan, C. 2006. "Precision targets: GPS and the militarization of U.S. consumer identity," *American Quarterly* 58: 693–714.

Katz, C. 2001. "Vagabond capitalism and the necessity for social reproduction," *Antipode* 33: 709–28.

Keast, K. 2008. "B.C. Transit security and 2010," *Vancouver Sun*, 13 Aug.

Kelling, G., and J. Wilson. 1982. "Broken windows," *Atlantic Monthly* (Mar.): 29–38. At: www.theatlantic.com/magazine/archive/1982/03/broken-windows/4465/

Killias, M., and J. Rabasa. 1997. "Less crime in the cities through heroin prescription? Preliminary results from the evaluation of the Swiss Heroin Prescription Projects," *The Howard Journal of Criminal Justice* 36: 424–9.

Kormarnicki, J. 2008. "Crime rate hits 30-year low, Statscan says," *Globe and Mail*, 17 July.

Kraska, P. 2001. *Militarizing the American Criminal Justice System: The Changing Roles of the Armed Forces and the Police*. Boston, MA: Northeastern University Press.

Lang, R., and K. Danielson. 1997. "Gated communities in America: Walling out the world?" *Housing Policy Debate* 8: 867–99.

Leisk, S. 2012. "Zoning by-laws: Human rights and charter considerations respecting the regulation of the use of land," *Municipal Lawyer: The Journal of Local Government Law* January/Feb: 14–16.

Light, J. 2003. *From Warfare to Welfare: Defense Intellectuals and Urban Problems in Cold War America*. Baltimore: Johns Hopkins University Press.

Lippert, R. 2007. "Urban revitalization, security and knowledge transfer: The case of broken windows and kiddie bars," *Canadian Journal of Law and Society* 22: 29–54.

Low, S. 2006. *Behind the Gates: Life, Security, and the Pursuit of Happiness in Fortress America*. New York: Routledge.

Mansbridge, P. 2013. "Thunder Bay's Aboriginal population fears racism and violence." *The National*. CBC Television. At: cbc.ca/news/canada/story/2013/02/20/thunder-bay-aboriginal-abuse-racism-violence-police

Marcuse, P. 1997. "The enclave, the citadel, and the ghetto," *Urban Affairs Review* 33: 228–64.

Mitchell, D. 2003. *The Right to the City: Social Justice and the Fight for Public Space*. New York: Gilford Press.

Mumford, L. 1961. *The City in History: Its Origins, Its Transformations, and Its Prospects*. New York: Harcourt, Brace and World.

Murphy, C. 2007. "Securitizing Canadian policing: A new policing paradigm for the post 9-11 security state?" *Canadian Journal of Sociology* 32: 449–73.

Németh, J. 2009. "The closed city: Downtown security zones and the loss of public space," paper presented to the

Association of American Geographers annual meeting, Las Vegas.

———. 2010. "Security in public space: An empirical assessment of three US cities," *Environment and Planning A*, 42 (10): 2487–2507.

Neocleous, M. 2007. "Security, liberty and the myth of balance: Towards a critique of security politics," *Contemporary Political Theory* 6 (2): 131–49.

Ottawa Citizen. 2008. "Toronto 18 terror suspects posed little danger: analyst," 6 Mar. At: www.canada.com/topics/news/story.html?id=7e6e2029-447a-4181-bc52-d5ed06044bc2

Perreault, S. 2013. "Police Reported Crime Statistics in Canada, 2012," component of Statistics Canada, catalogue no. 85-002-X; *Juristat*.

Porter, J. 2013. "Hearing starts for First Nations student deaths inquest." *CBC News*. At: cbc.ca/news/canada/thunder-bay/story/2013/06/11/tby-thunder-bay-first-nations-youth-drowing-inquest.html

Royal Canadian Mounted Police (RCMP). 2009. *An Interactive History 1873–1973*. At: www.RCMPhistory.ca/

Rygiel, K. 2009. "The securitized citizen," in E. Isin, ed., *Recasting the Social in Citizenship*. Toronto: University of Toronto Press.

Sanford, S., and S.H. Ali. 2005. "The new public health hegemony: Response to severe acute respiratory syndrome (SARS) in Toronto," *Social Theory and Health* 3: 105–25.

Security Intelligence Review Committee. 2005. *Reflections: Twenty Years of Independent External Review of Security Intelligence in Canada*. Ottawa: Government of Canada.

Sassen, S. 2010. "When the city itself becomes a technology of war," *Theory, Culture and Society* 27 (6): 33–50.

Shulz, D., and S. Gilbert. 2003. *Women and Transit Security*. At: www.fhwa.dot. gov/ohim/womens/chap30.pdf

Siciliano, A. 2007. "The cultural politics of control: The 'year of the gun' in Toronto," paper presented to the Association of American Geographers annual meeting, San Francisco.

Siciliano, A. 2011. *Youth Curfew Report: Effectiveness, Social Impacts, and Community Perspectives*. Thunder Bay, Ontario: City of Thunder Bay (Corporate Report 2011.51).

Singer, P. 2003. *Corporate Warriors: The Rise of the Privatized Military Industry*. Ithaca, NY: Cornell University Press.

Smith, N. 2004. *Endgame of Globalization*. New York: Routledge.

Smith C.B.R. 2010. "Socio-spatial stigmatization and the contested space of addiction treatment: Remapping the strategies of opposition to the disorder of drugs," *Social Science and Medicine* 70: 859–66.

Spivak, G. 1985. "Can the subaltern speak? Speculations on widow-sacrifice," *Wedge* 7–8 (Winter–Spring): 120–30.

Stasiulis, D., and D. Ross. 2006. "Security, flexible sovereignty, and the perils of multiple citizenship," *Citizenship Studies* 10: 329–48.

Stevens, A. 2013. *Applying Harm Reduction Principals to the Policing of Retail Drug Markets*. London: International Drug Policy Consortium (Modernising Drug Law Enforcement Report 3).

Tanovich, D. 2006. *The Colour of Justice*. Toronto: Irwin Law.

Valentine, G. 1992. "Images of danger: Women's source of information about the spatial distribution of male violence," *Area* 24: 22–36.

Valverde, M. 2009. "Questions of security," unpublished paper available from author, at: m.valverde@utoronto.ca

Vosko, L. 2000. *Temporary Work: The Gendered Rise of a Precarious Employment Relationship*. Toronto: University of Toronto Press.

Weinstein, T. 2011. Stories from the River's Edge. CBC Television, Fifth Estate. At: cbc.ca/fifth/2011-2012/storiesfromtheriversedge

Wharry, S. 2003. "Health officials warn against SARS racism," *Canadian Medical Association Journal*, 4 April. At: www.cmaj.ca/news/04_04_03.shtml

Winton, R., J-P. Renaud, and P. Pringle. 2007. "LAPD to build data on Muslim areas—Anti-terrorism unit wants to identify sites 'at risk' for extremism," *Los Angeles Times*, 9 Nov.

World Urban Forum. 2006. *The Secure City*. Vancouver: Vancouver Working Group Discussion Papers. At: www.cd.gov.bc.ca/LGD/intergov_relations/library/wuf_the_secure_city.pdf

Emerging Urban Forms in the Canadian City

17

JILL L. GRANT AND
PIERRE FILION

Introduction

How have cities changed over the past two or three decades, and what factors have shaped the transformation? Chapter 2 described the 1950s as a period of urban transition as development accommodated widespread automobile use and consequently reshaped the city. By the 1970s, optimism and faith in modernism gradually gave way to concerns about the environment and the quality of urban life. Critics like Jane Jacobs (1961) argued that the form of the city mattered to the health and well-being of residents. New theories of sustainable development, New Urbanism, and smart growth gradually gained adherents and began to influence public policy and market trends. Although conventional patterns of car-oriented development persisted in many parts of Canada, and new ones emerged, the last decades have produced innovative urban forms, some of which respond to critiques of postwar urban form. In this chapter we survey the Canadian urban environment to identify and explain the innovative urban forms that developed over the past decades.

We begin by discussing the key processes and factors that have affected the emergence of new physical forms in the Canadian city in recent experience. Then, we explain some ways that government policy has responded to changing economic and cultural processes to frame the legal and regulatory contexts within which urban development occurs. Finally, we describe the new urban forms emerging as a result of policy and market dynamics. The new physical forms include multi-functional developments like mixed nodes and complete communities, and segregated patterns like auto-oriented pods and private communities.[1]

Factors Contributing to Urban Change

We might expect components of the city that are sold or rented to behave like other consumer products, which are the object of constant efforts at innovation in response to changing circumstances or simply to cravings for novelty (Baudrillard, 1994; McDonald and McMillen, 2007). Cities are inherently stable because innovations must jibe with infrastructure networks and dominant technologies while conforming to regulations, such as building codes, zoning bylaws, and infrastructure standards. Moreover, the home-purchasing process itself induces conservatism (Lipson, 2006; Steacy, 1987); a home is not just a commodity but also an investment. Accordingly, the cautious homebuyer considers the potential preferences of the subsequent purchaser who will determine the house's resale value. Lending institutions, moreover, shy away from unusual house designs, preferring proven styles. Buzzelli and Harris (2006) suggest that local builders tend to avoid innovations that may increase their risks, and Harris (2004) documented the role of the Canada Mortgage and Housing Corporation (CMHC) in standardizing suburban development after the 1940s.

These circumstances account for a rate of change in the city that lags behind most consumer products. While consumers typically replace computers every three or four years, for instance, houses last many decades, even centuries. In cities, circumstances favour urban stability, not innovation. Yet major forces of change can challenge the inherent inertia of cities.

Over the past decades, economic transformations have had profound impacts on cities. For example, the decline in manufacturing changed demand for land in urban areas while altering employment structure. Rising consumption of services represents a related economic change with powerful urban reverberations (Gallouj, 2002; Industry Canada, 1996). The mushrooming of restaurants, gyms, health centres, and countless other categories of service establishments reveals the effects of the transition. In many cities, rising levels of service consumption contribute to the growing appeal of "revitalized" residential areas in the core and the inner city (Meligrana and Skaburskis, 2005; Skaburskis and Moos, 2008). Deepening income polarization resulting from the loss of middle-class jobs and reduced transfer payments is having a dramatic effect on the social geography of Canadian cities, as the number of middle-class neighbourhoods dwindles (Apparicio, Séguin, and Leloup, 2007; Hackworth, 2006; Hulchanski, 2007; Keil, 2002; Walks, 2001; Walks and Bourne, 2006; see Walks, Chapter 9).

In the competitive context of urban development in high-growth areas, some developers and builders responded by targeting projects at particular niche markets. New urban forms and practices have emerged as developers have looked for ways to reduce development costs, achieve economies of scale, control the chain of production, and improve the marketability of projects. To lower the costs of urban infrastructure, some developers turn to building private streets and services sold to occupants through condominium corporations. These various economic factors contribute to new patterns of social and spatial sorting in urban landscapes.

Although technological innovations—like the bulldozer and the automobile—significantly affected the development of new urban forms in the early and mid-twentieth century, technology figured less prominently among sources of new urban forms over the past decades. The recent past has not seen the rapid spread of any new technology that could have had such a dramatic impact. For instance, we find little evidence that computer and Internet use are transforming dominant spatial patterns. Construction techniques have remained remarkably consistent over the last decades. Cities have stayed car-dependent, despite public transit holding its own in large centres. Some industrial and retailing innovations of an organizational nature are, however, having an impact on the city. We might argue that "just-in-time" inventory systems via truck delivery are beginning to render some spaces surplus in the city, as warehouses become open to transformation to new uses. Also, the shift in retailing to auto-oriented big-box vendors has influenced the distribution and uses of commercial spaces in many cities.

Changing cultural values and practices have had significant effects on urban form over the past two or three decades. Demographic shifts induced some forms of urban innovation. Over the period under consideration, several demographic trends had a major impact on housing (Bourne and Rose, 2001; Foot with Stoffman, 1996; Isaacs et al., 2007). First, the demographic structure changed as birth rates fell and longevity increased, leading to aging of the population (see Moos, Chapter 20). Second, household size dropped steadily as more people chose to live alone and divorce rates increased (see Townshend and Walker, Chapter 7). Third, immigration levels increased with more immigrants coming from Asia and other parts of the world; these immigrants were accustomed to high-density living (see Kobayashi and Preston, Chapter 8). These trends influenced options for recent forms of residential development. For instance, households with no children or with older members constitute a significant proportion of the target market for gated communities (Maxwell, 2004). As well, the popularity of condominium developments during the last few decades owes a debt to the growth in small and immigrant households.

Consumer preferences reflect cultural values. While many Canadians continue to look for homes in car-oriented conventional suburbs, recent decades have shown that a segment of the population shifted its priorities. Urbanism—a commitment to participating in urban life—inspired a resurgence of interest in downtown and inner-city living (Meligrana and Skaburskis, 2005; Skaburskis, 2006). These consumers want specialty services like coffee shops; they seek access to public transportation; they willingly give up residential space for urban amenities; they drive the growth in the development of mixed nodes. Other households appreciate elements of traditional towns and provide a market for New Urbanism communities. Households seeking privacy and security may purchase homes in private or gated enclaves. The greater diversity in values associated with residential choices supports the trend toward niche markets and specialization in urban forms.

In the immediate postwar period, consumers and governments seemed to believe that energy and materials were endless, technology could solve any problem, and the future promised unlimited opportunities. For many Canadians, that optimism has succumbed to concerns about pollution, climate change, dwindling fossil fuels, economic recession, urban gridlock, and health risks from urban living. Cultural values associated with environmentalism—commitment to environmental protection and appreciation—have increasingly influenced public policy and local planning. Environmentalism supports efforts to limit land consumption and to reduce reliance on the automobile. Recent trends to protect waterways, wetlands, and forested areas reflect, in part, the shift to these values. At the same time, however, Canadians have proven remarkably resistant to the idea of giving up their cars and trucks.

Public Policy Responses

Governments respond to prevailing economic and cultural trends. As early as the 1970s, cities like Toronto, Vancouver, and Ottawa were adopting policies promoting urban intensification and environmental protection. Those policies took some time—and changing economic conditions—to influence urban outcomes. Over the past 40 years, governments have strengthened policies and improved implementation mechanisms. Dominant philosophies of what it takes to make cities and economies thrive shifted: whereas at one time economic development strategies recommended land-use segregation, decongestion, and garden suburbs, contemporary development strategies advocate density and a mix in land use. Spatial planning at a large scale—including amalgamated city regions—is making a comeback as cities seek to improve their competitiveness in a global market.

Laws, policies, and regulations have influenced urban form outcomes in various ways. For instance, one legal innovation had a profound effect on urban form outcomes over the past decades. In the late 1960s and 1970s, provincial governments across Canada adopted legislation to permit condominium tenure—a form of property ownership that allows people to own units within shared property managed by a corporation of which they are members. By the 1980s, condominium tenure had become the predominant form of high-density residential development (Hulchanski, 1988). High housing costs and declining household sizes confirmed the trend during the 1990s and 2000s. And by 2006 almost 11 per cent of Canadian households lived in condominiums: 40 per cent of those units were townhouses (Canadian Mortgage and Housing Commission [CMHC], 2008). With almost 35 per cent of housing starts in 2012 in condominium tenure, the potential for private residential enclaves—whether gated communities in the suburbs, private courts in redeveloped urban brownfield sites, or high-rise towers near transit stations—was growing rapidly (CMHC, 2013).

The rise of neo-liberal philosophies in the 1980s and 1990s encouraged governments to change their ways of managing urban development. Many municipalities transferred responsibility for building urban infrastructure to developers, who then passed on the costs to purchasers. To reduce the cost of roads in large development sites zoned for multi-family housing, developers often created bare-land condominium projects with attached or free-standing homes sharing private access streets. The condominium projects offered the additional attraction to municipalities that residents would remain responsible for road maintenance, snow clearing, and garbage collection. In an era when municipalities were struggling to meet their financial obligations while keeping property taxes as low as possible, private communities proved attractive.

By the 1990s plans and policies in most Canadian cities promoted greater densities, compact form, multi-functionality, mixed housing, environmental protection, quality urban design, and transportation options to promote the values of efficiency, competitiveness, and diversity. Demonstration projects and master planned developments provided opportunities to introduce innovative planning and design practices, like complete communities. Responding to economic and demographic pressures and to changing values on the part of the public, governments adopted plans that called for urban intensification and reduced dependence on the car (e.g., Metro Vancouver, 2007; Ontario, 2006). At the same time, however, market forces continued to fight for space for auto-oriented development forms that met the needs of business.

The Emergence of New Urban Forms

In response to the factors driving urban change, we see several important emerging urban forms in Canada. The forms differ according to three criteria:

1. The extent to which they mix a range of uses or tend toward reproducing a segregated pattern of uses

2. The degree to which commercial or residential uses dominate the mix of uses
3. The location within the city (urban core or suburban fringe)

Figure 17.1 illustrates the new forms that are emerging. New forms cluster in two general types: predominantly mixed use (left side of graphic), and predominantly segregated use (right side). Public policy and planning agendas advocate mixing uses; public investment in infrastructure in urban areas experiencing rapid growth promotes mixed-use urban forms. The new, segregated use patterns reflect the persistent strength of economic and market forces even in the face of policy efforts to shift development paradigms away from auto-dependency.

Within the general types, are further categories of new forms that differ according to the types of uses that dominate within them, and depending on where they are in the city. Mixed-use projects include mixed nodes and complete communities. Segregated use forms include auto-oriented pods and private communities.

Mixed-Use Forms

Governments seek to integrate uses by enabling mixed-use development. Mixed-use forms reflect the philosophy of Jane Jacobs (1961) and the growing influence of sustainable development, New Urbanism, and smart-growth principles in urban planning. Mixed-use projects are most common in high-growth areas seeking to facilitate higher density land use and transportation options. In some cases, the projects reuse parts of cities hollowed out by the decline in manufacturing. Most projects combine residential and commercial uses, and sometimes add civic uses. Uses may be vertically integrated (within the building) and/or horizontally mixed (within the block). In mixed nodes, commercial uses represent the more common use, with residential being ancillary. In complete communities, residential uses tend to occupy more territory, but commercial and other uses are planned to provide the range of services needed for daily living.

New Urban Forms Emerging

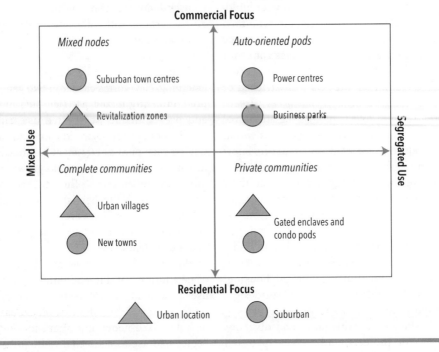

Figure 17.1   Emerging New Urban Forms

New urban forms vary by the degree of integration of uses, by the type of use that dominates the mix, and by location in the city.

Mixed Nodes

In this chapter, nodes are understood as medium- to high-density multi-functional developments, usually with planned access to public transportation networks. Plans see nodes as transit-oriented developments linked to each other by high-quality public transportation networks, an objective that is, however, generally unmet. The planning and implementation of nodes stem from the adherence of governments since the 1970s to urban intensification in an effort to manage sprawl and accommodate more residents and uses within developed areas. The public sector thus played a key role in launching nodes.

We consider two types of nodes: suburban and downtown. Suburban nodes (variously labelled suburban town centre, sub-centre, suburban downtown, or regional city centre) purport to reproduce the dynamics found in successful traditional downtowns, characterized by intense pedestrian-based interaction between diverse land uses. The second type of nodal development involves the premier node of major metropolitan regions, the downtown area. We demonstrate how the large-scale redevelopment of abandoned or under-utilized industrial, commercial, or institutional sites recently enhanced the density and diversity of downtowns. These efforts enriched downtowns with new residential, recreational, and cultural uses.

Suburban Town Centres

Suburban town centres are planned intensification nodes located in large suburbs on the periphery of major city regions. Local authorities attempt to mimic the dynamics of traditional downtowns, typically by including retail, office space, public-sector institutions and services, and housing uses. In order to encourage public transit patronage, nodes may include rail transit stations and/or assume the role of bus service hubs. Their multi-functionality and density distinguish these nodes from the suburban low-density and segregated land-use norm.

The nodal approach is a keystone of metropolitan region planning across North America, often linked to the ideal of transit-oriented development (Filion and Kramer, 2012). Calgary and Edmonton, for example, promote transit-oriented development around certain stations of their light-rail systems, and Ottawa does the same for stations on its Transitway, a system of roads for the exclusive use of buses (Calgary, 2008; Edmonton, 2009; Ottawa, 2007). Transit-oriented development remains in its initial stages in Canada, although suburban town centres can be perceived as large transit-oriented developments.

Virtually all North American urban regions that engage in metropolitan-scale planning adopt some version of the nodal model used by Atlanta, Boston, Chicago, Los Angeles, Miami, Minneapolis–St Paul, Montreal, Portland (Oregon), San Francisco, Seattle, Toronto, Vancouver, and Washington, DC. Toronto and Vancouver, where regional administrations have pursued a nodal strategy for over 25 years, are among those North American metropolitan regions where nodal development is most advanced (Davis and Perkins, 1993; Greater Vancouver Regional District [GVRD], 1994; Metro Toronto, 1981; Metro Vancouver, 2008; Ontario, 2006; Raad, 2006).

Toronto features three major suburban nodes— North York City Centre, Scarborough Town Centre, and Mississauga City Centre—as well as many smaller ones (Figure 17.2). An additional major

Figure 17.2   Mississauga City Centre.
Like many suburban nodes, Mississauga City Centre developed around a regional mall and its parking area. (Pierre Filion)

node, Markham City Centre, is growing quickly. In the Vancouver metropolitan region eight major nodes or regional town centres are at different stages of development: Lonsdale, Richmond City Centre, Metrotown, New Westminster, Coquitlam Town Centre, Surrey Centre, Maple Ridge Town Centre, and Langley Town Centre. In Montreal, the current metropolitan plan continues earlier traditions of proposing a nodal structure (Communauté Métropolitaine de Montréal [CMM], 2012), but the limited mixture of uses at Carrefour Laval, Fairview in Pointe-Claire, and Galleries d'Anjou reveals the challenges of implementing the plan.

How well do the suburban centres function? Toronto's major nodes meet some of their objectives but not to the extent anticipated in planning documents (Filion, 2007). Over the past 20 years a near-stalling of high-density office development threatened their multi-functionality. Meanwhile, residential development, in the form of high-rise condominiums, boomed between 2000 and 2009, causing an imbalance between an expanding residential function and a stagnating employment base. Moreover, while suburban nodes offer more transit options than other suburban areas, workers and residents remain dependent on automobiles. Nodes suffer from Canadians' enduring reliance on driving for shopping, and from poor access to public transit in the suburban environments that constitute local catchment areas. Indeed, much of the space in nodes serves the automobile, with deleterious effects on walking: for example, office workers within Scarborough Town Centre and Mississauga City Centre do not patronize local restaurants as much as they could if large expanses of surface parking did not separate offices from restaurants (Filion, 2001). The best-laid plans to induce mixed use and to reduce auto-oriented development patterns continue to face significant challenges in practice.

Downtown Revitalization Zones

The traditional postwar image of the downtown entailed a **central business district (CBD)** occupied exclusively by offices, retailing, and ancillary activities. While zoning contributed to land-use specialization, market forces drove the process. Until recently, office buildings, retail uses, and hotels outbid other activities and thus collectively took over downtowns. Middle- and upper-income households migrated to uniformly residential suburban districts (Murphy, 1972). Downtown Calgary comes close to retaining the conventional CBD model, although residential development has recently dotted its edges. The financial districts of Toronto and Montreal (where the highest office buildings are found) remain highly specialized (Gad, 1991). Other areas have moved increasingly to a nodal model of mixed uses downtown.

Planning attempts to depart from the CBD model began in Toronto in the 1970s as the city responded to the infrastructure overload caused by a massive wave of office development. Authorities attributed worsening traffic and transit congestion to the growing concentration of downtown employment. Planners argued that housing more residents downtown would reduce in-bound commuting. Downtown residents could walk to work and other core area activities. The presence of housing would ensure that the downtown would remain lively in the evenings rather than emptying after office hours (Toronto, 1974). Developers received bonuses allowing them to build higher and larger buildings if they included housing components in their projects. As a result, the mid- to late-1980s witnessed a surge in downtown residential development, followed by massive condominium construction in the 2000s. Railway and industrial lands left fallow for decades now feature condominium developments.

Vancouver also actively encouraged high-density housing development in its core area. It first allowed high-rise residential redevelopment in the West End, an amenity-rich neighbourhood between Stanley Park and downtown. High-rise apartment construction proceeded apace in the 1960s and 1970s. A second high-rise residential boom occurred in the 1990s with redevelopment of the Expo 86 site and of other waterfront land adjacent to downtown (Berelowitz, 2005; Punter, 2003). New high-rise residential buildings spread through the downtown. With the most rapid growth of downtown housing in Canada, Vancouver, like Toronto, registers accelerated downtown residential growth and a 2011 downtown population above 100,000 (Table 17.1). It developed its own style of high-density residential development, referred to as "Vancouverism": narrow glass towers of condominium units sit on podiums that provide three- or four-storey facades at street level. Ground-level uses include townhouses, stores, cafés, and restaurants. Public policy requires that developers provide affordable housing and family units in downtown condominium structures. In some cases, new downtown schools have been integrated in the developments. Downtown Vancouver arguably offers one of the most livable high-density residential formulas (Punter, 2003) (Figure 17.3).

Downtown residential intensification strategies have largely achieved their planning objectives in the largest cities. Downtown nodes have become livelier with a wide range of activities (including supermarkets) that cater to the growing resident population. Also, transportation objectives have been met. In downtown Toronto, for example, 35.6 per cent of home-based journeys are made on foot, more than combined auto-driver and auto-passenger modal shares (29.2 per cent). Fostering downtown residential concentrations thus offers a clear environmental benefit in reduced vehicle use. Lively downtowns attract young professionals and the employers seeking their services: some

indicators suggest that the kinds of businesses and workers occupying downtown offices differ from those selecting suburban highway-related locations (Gad, 1985; Ley, 1996) (see Moos, Chapter 20).

However, urban nodes are not without problems. Despite Vancouver's attempts to promote social diversity, its downtown has become mainly an upper- and middle-income enclave due to the high cost of most condo units and the replacement of low-income housing with new condominium towers. Threats to social diversity are even more serious in Toronto, where little effort was made to vary the units in new condominium developments (see Bain, Chapter 14). In addition, the growing presence of condominium developments may limit downtown functional diversity as housing crowds out office buildings (Boddy, 2005; McCullough, 2005). And, unfortunately, nodal development has not alleviated social polarization, nor can it guarantee continuing diversity of uses in the context of market processes that may favour specialization.

As shown in Table 17.1, other large Canadian metropolitan regions have not experienced anything close to the downtown residential intensification that took place in Toronto and Vancouver. These findings suggest that large-scale, condominium-based downtown intensification requires particular conditions. These include rich downtown amenities (entertainment and culture in Toronto and natural features in Vancouver),

Table 17.1	Downtown Population in Large Canadian Census Metropolitan Areas (CMAs) (with a 2011 Population Exceeding One Million), 1971–2011*							
CMA	1971	1991	2001	2011	1971–1991	1991–2011	2001–2011	1971–2011
Toronto	63,110	81,646	111,122	150,967	29.4%	84.9%	35.9%	139.2%
Montreal	95,619	54,747	80,378	91,002	−42.7%	66.2%	13.2%	−4.8%
Vancouver	42,499	34,442	51,340	100,187	−19%	190.9%	95.1%	135.7%
Ottawa	92,737	73,972	79,506	78,917	−20.2%	6.7%	−0.7%	−14.9%
Calgary	68,742	66,604	70,263	77,211	−3.1%	15.9%	9.9%	12.3%
Edmonton	39,041	27,594	36,005	44,236	−29.3%	60.3%	22.9%	13.3%

*Includes census tracts mostly located within 2 km of the peak value intersection.

Source: Compiled by authors from 1971, 1991, 2001, and 2011 Statistics Canada census data.

Figure 17.3   High-rise condominiums, Vancouver. Vancouver has experienced massive downtown residential growth, much of it in the form of high-rise condominium buildings. (Pierre Filion)

sustained demographic and economic growth, high real estate values due to land scarcity, and accommodating planning interventions. Mid-size cities have similarly struggled to try to reverse processes hollowing their cores. While cities like London, Ontario, and Winnipeg struggle with the revitalization of their centres, others, such as Halifax and Kingston, have had some success in luring new residents downtown (Burayidi, 2001; Filion et al., 2004).

Complete Communities

While nodes reflect attempts at creating or enhancing poles of attraction within the urban environment, complete communities are new areas envisioned as complete small towns or urban villages. In contrast to conventional development trends that generated homogeneously residential suburbs, complete communities plan for a mix of uses, housing, and densities. Most involve suburban locations, but some entail comprehensive redevelopment of brownfield sites. The new complete communities reflect largely interchangeable principles associated with the contemporary development paradigms of New Urbanism, sustainable development, and smart growth (Grant and Scott, 2012). The complete community creates a miniature urban structure with a town centre of commercial and office uses, sets high design standards, implements a mix of housing types, creates a connected street network (often supplemented with rear service lanes), and includes a system of open and public spaces. These are large master-planned projects intended to house hundreds to thousands of homes and the services residents require to meet their daily needs. Despite the effort to be "complete," however, most plan few employment opportunities within the development.

In some cases, like Cornell in Markham (in the Toronto metropolitan region), provincial and municipal governments played a significant role in assisting with planning and developing projects. In other cases, like Calgary and Surrey (to the east of Vancouver), municipal policy adopted the principles promoting complete communities advocated by project developers. In the 2000s, Ontario made smart growth principles provincial policy for the Greater Golden Horseshoe area. While most of the development and building of new communities remains in the hands of the private sector, various levels of government set a policy context that promotes complete communities as a desired form of urban development.

Since the mid-1990s, New Urbanism principles have influenced residential development in many parts of Canada (Grant, 2003). New Urbanism originated in the US with the development of projects such as Seaside, Florida, and Kentlands, Maryland. Its proponents advocate building complete and compact communities with a mix of uses and housing types, pedestrian-oriented streets, and an attractive public realm (Duany, Plater-Zyberk, and Speck, 2000). Many of the projects feature traditional architectural and urban design qualities. A recent study identified 42 New Urbanist communities in Canada, mostly in rapidly growing suburban areas in Ontario, Alberta, and British Columbia (Grant and Bohdanow, 2008).

In Ontario the provincial government set the policy context for promoting New Urbanism in the early 1990s by arranging for design competitions and providing a large parcel in Markham for a demonstration project. Cornell, designed by Duany Plater-Zyberk Associates, soon revealed the potential of New Urbanism to support environmental policies and objectives to protect sensitive areas (Gordon and Tamminga, 2002).

The East Clayton community in Surrey established an ambitious environmental agenda in its construction. Designers employed sustainable development principles to guide the site and landscape design. Green infrastructure manages storm water on the site, and park designations protect waterways from development (Condon, 2003). New Urbanism principles influenced the urban design: small lots, traditional architectural designs, and rear service lanes are common features throughout the project.

Developers began work on McKenzie Towne in southeast Calgary in the mid-1990s. Creating a New Urbanism community was a private-sector marketing strategy to give the project a strong identity in a region where many developments constructed artificial lakes to anchor subdivisions. Despite a promising start, however, McKenzie Towne struggled in the marketplace. The distance of the development from Calgary's city centre and the continuing lure of large suburban houses with attached garages made small homes on small lots a challenge to sell. The developer returned to a conventional development concept after building three phases. Another Calgary new community, Garrison Woods, proved more successful in the market. Its development was launched in the late 1990s, when Canada Lands began planning to transform a former military base in Calgary into New Urbanism communities. The commercial centre, built adjacent to a successful commercial district and existing transportation networks, attracted a range of uses. The project sold out two years ahead of schedule. Property values increased rapidly, though, pricing homes out of the range of the average Calgary household.

Complete communities ideally contain a robust mix of uses and housing types, and enjoy good access to transportation options. In addition, an attractive and well-connected street network encourages walking. Each community includes a town centre with civic, commercial, office, and residential uses. Businesses in the town centres in developments like McKenzie Towne and Cornell, however, struggled to survive on the limited trade available within the developments.

In early applications of the New Urbanism model, the mixed-use area was located centrally in the development, but later developments moved the commercial district close to major arterials to take advantage of larger markets (Figure 17.4). While many of the projects have some access to public transportation, few are well-sited for rapid transit to major employment centres. The mix of housing types provided has not resulted in the degree of socio-economic diversity that planners hoped to achieve in designing "complete" communities (Grant and Perrott, 2009). Although the projects attract a range of household types (from single persons to multi-generational families), they produce relatively homogeneous income levels. Indeed, McKenzie Towne and Cornell offered reasonably affordable housing in their early years

of development, but escalation of prices in the Toronto and Calgary markets soon priced homes out of range of many households. Apart from a small number of well-known projects, few of the Canadian New Urbanism communities have lived up to the potential of the concept. None of the projects, in fact, is fully "complete" in terms of the original design.

Segregated-Use Forms

While government policy over the past decades has generally encouraged mixing uses, market pressures continue to promote conventional forms of segregated use—as in suburban residential pods—and to develop new forms of separation.

Figure 17.4   **The commercial area of Cornell (Markham, Ontario). The amount and range of retailing is very limited in New Urbanism developments, as seen here in Cornell's commercial area. (Pierre Filion)**

New segregated-use forms reflect developers' continuing efforts to find niche markets to appeal to consumers and to raise returns on development. The forms presume that most users will have access to private automobiles.

Although we classify these forms as segregated, we recognize that some projects may involve a small admixture of uses other than the dominant ones. The projects are occurring in cities of varying sizes across Canada. While the forms reflect market dynamics at work, they occur because government policies have made space for them. New practices in retail and commercial developments may take advantage of land that local governments previously designated for future industrial use.

Auto-Oriented Pods

In the 1960s through the 1980s, many cities designated, zoned, or developed land for industrial use. The decline in manufacturing in Canada over the last few decades, however, slowed demand for industrial land; many communities were oversupplied in land they originally hoped would house industrial uses. Looking for alternative uses for the surplus land, many accepted proposals for big-box retail outlets or for business parks.

Power Centres

Most mid- and large-sized cities now feature one or more power centres: concentrations of big-box and factory outlet retail stores, entertainment and recreational facilities, and hotels. The new power centres generally locate on the urban periphery near major highway transportation corridors and junctions. They feature large parking areas, sometimes shared by several retailers. By contrast with the suburban nodes promoted by public policy and investment, power centres continue the tradition of auto-oriented land-use segregation. They become significant shopping destinations, catering to consumers looking for bargains and willing to drive some distance to find what they want (Lorch, 2005).

The power centre reflects a new form in its scale and particular mix of commercial uses. The pattern and location of retail uses in cities is constantly

changing in response to economic conditions and consumer behaviour (Zukin, 2005). A century ago, residential neighbourhoods enjoyed a wide mix of uses, including local grocers and barbers. By the early twenty-first century, the neighbourhood mom-and-pop corner store struggled to survive in the face of competition from chain outlets on arterial streets. The shopping malls of the postwar economic boom looked frayed around the edges: some closed or converted to discount outlets or call centres; others renovated in the hopes of staving off redundancy. The pattern of commercial uses transformed over the decades not only in the largest urban centres, but even in smaller settlements. Consumers looking for bargains and variety drove the success of the new power centres.

Most of the power centres have appeared in suburban or urban fringe locations. For instance, in Halifax, the Bayer's Lake big-box centre was developed in the 1980s on land prepared for industrial uses. With industry and warehouses in the region preferring to buy land in Burnside Industrial Park in Dartmouth (across the harbour), Halifax council decided to permit a big-box retailer to open in Bayer's Lake. Within a decade the area had become a big-box power centre subject to considerable traffic congestion. In the early 2000s, now amalgamated as a regional municipality with Dartmouth and the county, Halifax approved a new power centre at Dartmouth Crossing: the new site dwarfs other regional shopping facilities and serves as a tourism destination for the Maritimes region. In 2009, the project developers applied to Halifax Regional Municipality for a zoning change to permit them to add a residential component to the project. Most Canadian power centres have limited residential uses, but many "leisure centres" in American cities have added condominium projects.

While the power centres in Canada are generally in the suburbs, developers have shown some interest in proposing them in central places, even in Toronto. The City of Toronto opposed an effort to transform a former film studio in Leslieville into a power centre, citing policy aimed at protecting the area for employment uses (Vincent, 2009). Even in contexts where municipal policy clearly discourages such auto-oriented commercial concentrations, developers continue to promote segregated development models.

Business Parks

The growth in business parks—sometimes called office parks or research parks—similarly involves new uses for lands previously held for industrial activities. Searching for less expensive land with ample parking for employees, office developers have looked to the periphery of urban regions to create upscale business parks since the 1980s (Lang, 2003). These projects do not include warehousing or heavy manufacturing facilities. Many feature natural or environmental amenities; the business parks house growing concentrations of office uses, accompanied by business-oriented retail and service uses. Landscaping and design standards in business parks may screen parking lots from view, but these developments generally are low density and auto-oriented. The campus configuration of business parks and their easy car access by a wide suburban labour pool have proved especially popular with businesses. The stalling of office development in many downtowns and suburban nodes is in part a consequence of the success of business parks.

Private Communities

While government policy in many larger cities advocates complete communities, market factors are creating new types of developments in cities of varying sizes. The popularity of condominium tenure underpins the building of private communities. Private communities involve clusters of buildings in areas zoned for medium- to high-density housing with land held in common ownership. Sometimes units share recreational amenities, but the communities are not complete because they rarely contain commercial or civic uses. Many of these residential districts have private streets, and some are gated. Private enclaves are appearing in urban cores and suburban areas.

For most of the twentieth century, open-concept community designs were popular in Canada.

Postwar subdivisions often avoided fences or hedges, preferring unbounded lawns that facilitated views and access. By the 1980s, though, gated communities—developments restricting public access to internal streets—began to appear in parts of British Columbia. The popularity of gated communities in the US at this time arguably inspired their development in Canada. The trend accelerated by the late 1990s, with some development companies exploiting a niche market for affluent retirees choosing to move into condominium townhouse projects. By 2003, Canada had thousands of private communities and hundreds of gated enclaves (Grant, Greene, and Maxwell, 2004). Two-thirds of Canadian gated projects are in British Columbia: provincial laws in BC and Alberta make it possible for developers to target projects for seniors, a population that finds private enclaves attractive.

Municipal authorities eager to reduce the costs of providing services such as garbage collection, snow removal, and road maintenance have proven sympathetic to private townhouse condominium developments and have directly or indirectly facilitated gating. In high-growth areas, medium-density townhouse projects have become a common development form providing more affordable housing options. Many such projects employ private streets built by developers and managed by condominium corporations. Those private streets, which some municipalities call "shared access driveways," can easily be gated to restrict access when residents decide the cost of doing so is worthwhile.

Most enclaves occur in suburban areas, but some appear in urban districts where sites are redeveloped for high-end residential use. The smallest private enclaves have only a few homes around a cul-de-sac, but the largest have more than a thousand units. Most enclaves, however, have fewer than 100 units and feature modest clubhouses or pool facilities for the exclusive use of residents. Many involve small households of high socio-economic status seeking privacy, exclusivity, and a degree of security. Large gated projects may house social elites and sometimes include recreational amenities, such as private golf courses, lakes, or marinas. Few Canadian gated communities, in contrast to their US counterparts, employ guards.

Critics suggest that private communities exacerbate social and spatial fragmentation in suburban landscapes and encourage automobile use (Grant and Curran, 2007). Certainly the growth in gated communities parallels advancing social polarization in Canadian society and exacerbates the spatial fragmentation that already characterizes suburban areas (see Walks, Chapter 9; Addie, Fiedler, and Keil, Chapter 24). Gated developments like Swan Lake in Markham, with over 1000 homes planned, force pedestrians, cyclists, and drivers to go around a large enclosed area. As an urban form, the private enclave constitutes a space marked for privacy and social distance.

Planning policies that promote urban connectivity, social integration, and mixed uses have slowed but not prevented the proliferation of private and gated communities. Developers continue to respond to consumer demands for privacy. Having permitted ground-oriented condominium development originally as a way to address the need for more affordable housing for Canadians, governments now find themselves unable to prevent an urban form that generates some significant social and spatial concerns (Figure 17.5).

Conclusion

The urban forms that have appeared over the past decades reflect different strategies that local governments have employed to address the fiscal and

Figure 17.5   **A gated community in Calgary. (J.L. Grant)**

environmental challenges they face. The desire to promote urban efficiency has led to plans for new community forms that are denser, mixed in use, and accessible by transit. The most populous cities with rapid growth and high rates of immigration have seen some progress in making new forms of mixed-use nodes and complete communities happen, both in their core areas and in suburban town centres. Cities with low rates of growth or with population decline have often adopted similar ideals and prescriptions in their plans, but show few examples of successful mixed-use projects. While intensification suits the interests of government and of land developers in high-growth areas, the dynamics to promote greater urban densities do not exist in many regions. Urban patterns in the largest cities are changing in ways that are different from those in smaller settlements.

Local governments anxious to find resources to provide services and programs continue to respond to the imperative to find uses for land they have available for development. They need development to provide property tax revenues. They rely on development strategies that reduce the costs of delivering infrastructure. These pressures lead governments—especially those in **slow-growth** and smaller cities—to make compromises with development interests that result in segregated land-use forms, such as auto-oriented pods and private communities (see Donald and Hall, Chapter 15). As long as consumers shop in big-box stores and buy homes in private communities, developers will produce segregated land-use forms. Rising gasoline prices may eventually limit such sprawl, but in the interim it continues unabated.

Our account of new urban forms has a strong transportation dimension that points to the lingering predominance of the car and its impact on land use. We pointed to Canadian attempts at creating multi-functional environments in order to abate dependence on the automobile. Predictably, these efforts have met with more success in transit- and walking-oriented core areas than in car-dependent suburbs. Meanwhile, despite their inconsistency with prevailing planning objectives, segregated uses enjoy strong growth

potential by virtue of their adaptation to high levels of car use.

Review Questions

1. What emerging trends are influencing public policy responses in cities? What forms are local responses taking?
2. What urban forms are surfacing in the contemporary city? To what extent are these new urban forms likely to alter the course of urban development?
3. Among the new urban forms described in the chapter, which are likely to most influence future urban patterns?

Note

1. To place the issues discussed in the chapter within the broader context of contemporary Canadian planning, see Raphaël Fischler and Jeanne M. Wolfe, "Contemporary Planning," Chapter 19 in Bunting and Filion (2006), at: www.oupcanada.com/filion

References

Apparicio, P., A.-M. Séguin, and X. Leloup. 2007. "Modélisation spatiale de la pauvreté à Montréal: Apports méthodologiques de la régression géographiquement pondérée," *Canadian Geographer* 51: 412–27.

Baudrillard, J. 1994. *Simulacra and Simulation*. Ann Arbor, MI: University of Michigan Press.

Berelowitz, L. 2005. *Dream City: Vancouver and the Global Imagination*. Vancouver, BC: Douglas &McIntyre.

Boddy, T. 2005. "'Downtown' a fool's paradise? Council policy has encouraged the construction of new condos but not new office towers," *Vancouver Sun*, 10 Aug., B2.

Bourne, L.S., and D. Rose. 2001. "The changing face of Canada: The uneven geographies of population and social change," *Canadian Geographer* 45: 105–19.

Burayidi, M., ed. 2001. *Downtowns: Revitalizing the Centers of Small Communities*. New York: Routledge.

Buzzelli, M., and R. Harris. 2006. "Cities as the industrial districts of housebuilding," *International Journal of Urban and Regional Research* 30: 894–917.

Calgary, City of. 2008. *Transit Oriented Development (TOD): Development around Rapid Transit Stations*. Calgary: City of Calgary, Mar. At: www.calgary.ca/portal/server.pt/gate way/PTARGS_0_2_527219_0_0_18/Transit+Oriented+ Development+.htm

Canada Mortgage and Housing Corporation (CMHC). 2008. "Changing patterns in homeownership and shelter costs in Canada: Information from the 2006 census," *National Housing Research Committee Newsletter* (Fall): 8.

——. 2013. *Housing Information Monthly* January. Ottawa, ON: CMHC.

Communauté Métropolitaine de Montréal (CMM). 2012. *An attractive, competitive and sustainable Greater Montréal.* Montreal: CMM. At: http://cmm.qc.ca/fileadmin/user_ upload/pmad2012/documentation/20120813_PMAD_ eng.pdf

Condon, P. 2003. "Green municipal engineering for sustainable communities," *Municipal Engineer* 156: 3–10.

Davis, H.C., and R.A. Perkins. 1993. "The promotion of metropolitan polynucleation: Lessons to be learned from the Vancouver and Melbourne experience," *Canadian Journal of Urban Research* 1: 16–38.

Duany, A., E. Plater-Zyberk, and J. Speck. 2000. *Suburban Nation: The Rise of Sprawl and the Decline of the American Dream.* New York: North Point Press.

Edmonton, City of. 2009. *Stadium Station Transit Oriented Development.* Edmonton: City of Edmonton. Mar. At: www. edmonton.ca/city_government/planning_development/ stadium-station-transit-oriented-development.aspx

Filion, P. 2001. "Suburban mixed-use centres and urban dispersion: What difference do they make," *Environment and Planning A* 33: 141–60.

——. 2007. *The Urban Growth Centre Strategy in the Greater Golden Horseshoe: Lessons from Downtowns, Nodes and Corridors.* Toronto: Neptis Foundation.

——, H. Hoernig, T. Bunting, and G. Sands. 2004. "The successful few: Healthy downtowns of small metropolitan regions," *Journal of the American Planning Association* 70: 328–43.

——, and A. Kramer. 2012. "Transformative metropolitan development models in large Canadian urban areas: The predominance of nodes," *Urban Studies* 49: 2237–64.

Foot, D.K., with D. Stoffman. 1996. *Boom, Bust and Echo: Profiting from the Demographic Shift in the New Millennium.* Toronto: Macfarlane Walter and Ross.

Gad, G. 1991. "Toronto's financial district," *Canadian Geographer* 35: 203–7.

Gallouj, F. 2002. *Innovation in the Service Economy: The New Wealth of Nations.* Cheltenham, UK: Edward Elgar.

Gordon, D.L.A., and K. Tamminga. 2002. "Large-scale traditional neighbourhood development and pre-emptive ecosystem planning: The Markham experience 1989–2001," *Journal of Urban Design* 7 (2): 41–54.

Grant, J. 2003. "Exploring the influence of new urbanism in community planning practice," *Journal of Architectural and Planning Research* 20: 234–53.

——, and S. Bohdanow. 2008. "New urbanism communities in Canada: A survey," *Journal of Urbanism* 1: 111–30.

——, and A. Curran. 2007. "Privatised suburbia: The planning implications of private roads," *Environment and Planning B: Planning and Design* 34: 740–54.

——, K. Greene, and D.K. Maxwell. 2004. "The planning and policy implications of gated communities," *Canadian Journal of Urban Research, Canadian Planning and Policy* 13, 1 (suppl.): 70–88.

——, and K. Perrott. 2009. "Producing diversity in a new urbanism community: Policy and practice," *Town Planning Review* 80: 267–89.

——, and D.E. Scott. 2012. "Complete communities and the Canadian dream: Representations of suburban aspirations," *Canadian Journal of Urban Research* 21, 1 (Supplement), 132–57.

Greater Vancouver Regional District (GVRD). 1994. *Livable Region Strategic Plan.* Burnaby, BC: GVRD.

Hackworth, J. 2006. *The Neoliberal City: Governance, Ideology, and Development in American Urbanism.* Ithaca, NY: Cornell University Press.

Harris, R. 2004. *Creeping Conformity: How Canada Became Suburban, 1900–1960.* Toronto: University of Toronto Press.

Hulchanski, J.D. 1988. "The evolution of property rights and housing tenure in postwar Canada: Implications for housing policy," *Urban Law and Policy* 9: 1350–6.

——. 2007. *The Three Cities within Toronto: Income Polarization among Toronto's Neighbourhoods, 1970–2000.* Toronto: Centre for Urban and Community Studies, University of Toronto (Research Bulletin 41). At: www.urbancentre.utoronto.ca/pdfs/researchbulletins/ CUCSRB41_Hulchanski_Three_Cities_Toronto.pdf

Industry Canada. 1996. *Canada's Service Economy.* Ottawa: Industry Canada.

Isaacs, B., G. Miller, G. Harris, and I. Ferguson. 2007. "Bracing for the demographic tsunami: How will seniors fare in an aging society," *Plan Canada* 47, 4: 20–1.

Jacobs, J. 1961. *The Death and Life of Great American Cities.* New York: Random House.

Keil, R. 2002. "'Common-sense' liberalism: Progressive conservative urbanism in Toronto, Canada," *Antipode* 34: 541–601.

Lang, R.E. 2003. *Edgeless Cities: Exploring the Elusive Metropolis.* Washington: Brookings Institution Press.

Ley, D. 1996. *The New Middle Class and the Remaking of the Central City.* Oxford: Oxford University Press.

Lipson, B.D. 2006. *The Art of the Real Estate Deal.* Toronto: Thomson Carswell.

Lorch, B. 2005. "Auto-dependent induced shopping: Exploring the relationship between power centre morphology and consumer spatial behaviour," *Canadian Journal of Urban Research* 14: 364–83.

Maxwell, D.K. 2004. "Gated communities: Selling the good life," *Plan Canada* 44, 4: 20–2.

McCullough, M. 2005. "Office space suffers lack of demand: Real Estate 1 Cheapest condos now worth more per square foot than the priciest office space," *Vancouver Sun*, 30 Apr., G3.

McDonald, J.F., and P. McMillen. 2007. *Urban Economics and Real Estate: Theory and Policy*. Malden, MA: Blackwell.

Meligrana, J., and A. Skaburskis. 2005. "Extent, location and profiles of continuing gentrification in Canadian metropolitan areas, 1981–2001," *Urban Studies* 42: 1569–92.

Metro Toronto. 1981. *Official Plan for the Urban Structure*. Toronto: Metro Toronto.

Metro Vancouver. 2007. *Choosing a Sustainable Future for Metro Vancouver: Options for Metro Vancouver's Growth Management Strategy*. Burnaby, BC: Metro Vancouver. At: www.metrovancouver.org/about/publications/Publications/RGS_Options.pdf

———. 2008. *Our Livable Region 2040: Metro Vancouver Growth Strategy (Preliminary Draft)*. Burnaby, BC: Metro Vancouver.

Murphy, R.E. 1972. *The Central Business District*. Chicago: Aldine-Atherton.

Ontario, Ministry of Public Infrastructure Renewal. 2006. *Growth Plan for the Greater Golden Horseshoe*. Toronto: Government of Ontario.

Ottawa, City of. 2007. *Transit-oriented Development Guidelines*. Ottawa, ON: City of Ottawa. At: www.ottawa.ca/residents/planning/design_plan_guidelines/completed/transit/index_en.html

Punter, J. 2003. *The Vancouver Achievement: Urban Planning and Design*. Vancouver, BC: University of British Columbia Press.

Raad, T. 2006. "Turning transit stations into transit villages: Examples from Greater Vancouver," *Plan Canada* 46 (2): 25–8.

Skaburskis, A. 2006. "Filtering, city change and the supply of low-priced housing in Canada," *Urban Studies* 43: 533–58.

———, and M. Moos. 2008. "The redistribution of residential property values in Montreal, Toronto, and Vancouver: Examining neoclassical and Marxist views on changing investment patterns," *Environment and Planning A* 40: 905–27.

Steacy, R. 1987. *Canadian Real Estate*. Toronto: Stoddart.

Toronto, City of, Planning Board. 1974. *Core Area Task Force: Report and Recommendations*. Toronto: City of Toronto, Planning Board.

Vincent, D. 2009. "OMB rejects big box plans in Leslieville," *Toronto Star*, 5 Mar. At: www.thestar.com/news/gta/article/596848

Walks, R.A. 2001. "The social ecology of the post-Fordist/global city? Economic restructuring and socio-spatial polarization in the Toronto urban region," *Urban Studies* 38: 407–47.

———, and L.S. Bourne. 2006. "Ghettos in Canada's cities? Racial segregation, ethnic enclaves and poverty concentration in Canadian urban areas," *Canadian Geographer* 50: 273–97.

Zukin, S. 2005. *Point of Purchase: How Shopping Changed American Culture*. New York: Routledge.

Public Space in the City Centre: Design, Activity, and Measurement

18

RYAN WALKER AND
JILL GUNN

Introduction

Our chapter examines one of the most dynamic aspects of our urban age—public space. Jan Gehl and Lars Gemzoe (2008) characterize the uses of public space by referring to its three Ms: movement, market, and meeting. The most well-known public space in western history may be the agora of the ancient Greeks, serving as the main public square for meeting and assembly and as the central marketplace (Madanipour, 2003). Canada's oldest public market, Market Square in Kingston, has served in that lineage of function in the socio-cultural, political, and economic lives of citizens for hundreds of years, and before that as a First Nations meeting place (Lynch and Ley, 2010). Today you will find people shopping at its public market and, depending on the season, meeting to ice-skate or watch open-air films. Such programming and management of activities in public spaces is a key feature that we return to throughout the chapter. The same physical space can vary remarkably over time and between seasons based on its programming.

The most prominent of public spaces in any city is its streets. In Regina on 24 November 2013, Albert Street—known in the city centre as the Green Mile in honour of the province's Canadian Football League (CFL) team—came alive with thousands of people to celebrate the Saskatchewan Roughriders'

victory in the Grey Cup match against the Hamilton Tiger-Cats. It was the first time the Grey Cup had been won by the Saskatchewan team while playing at their home stadium. Young and old, families, friends, strangers from across Saskatchewan gathered in the streets of the capital city to share with each other the victory of their team and to trumpet their pride of place to the rest of Canada. A couple of months prior, on 14 September 2013, tens of thousands of citizens marched through the streets of Montreal's city centre to protest against the Charter of Values proposal, ending their march at Place du Canada in front of the monument of Canada's first prime minister, Sir John A. Macdonald. Indeed, practising citizenship—the active animation of state–society relations—is a principal purpose of public space. While streets are most commonly associated with movement, it is critical that we understand their role equally as a meeting place for protest, for celebration, and for public life generally, including commerce.

In the next two sections we discuss the concept of public space and some of the measurement and metrics for better understanding how our public spaces are functioning. We then focus on the physical design of public space and programming of activities (e.g., arts, commerce, recreation, debate) for enhancing the movement, market, and meeting dimensions of public life in Canadian cities. The design and programming of streets is our main focus, followed by a shorter examination of squares. We look at city centres—the heart of a city's identity and image, commerce, and neighbourhoods—although the ideas transfer in many ways to other areas of the city (also see Senbel and Lesnikowski, Chapter 13; Bain, Chapter 14; and Siciliano, Cowen, and Smith, Chapter 16). We return to the three Ms of public space throughout as a useful tool for structuring our discussion. While we use examples from across Canada, most are from Saskatoon and Montreal, the two cities where we have directed our most recent empirical attention. Some important public space topics are not covered in this chapter. One is waterfront re-development, which is an important aspect of post-industrial public space (re-)design (e.g., Galland and Hansen, 2012; Gordon, 1997; Greenberg, 2011; see Vinodrai, Chapter 5, and Hutton and Vinodrai, Chapter 6, for discussions of the post-industrial urban economy). Another topic on public space that this chapter does not address is the design of urban parks and their integration with regional natural processes (e.g., Hough, 2004; McHarg, 1969; see Rees, Chapter 4).

The Role of Public Space

> The values attaching to public space are those with which the generality of the citizenry endows it. Citizens create meaningful public space by expressing their attitudes, asserting their claims and using it for their own purposes. It thereby becomes a meaningful public resource. The process is a dynamic one, for meanings and uses are always liable to change. Renegotiation of understandings is ongoing; contention accompanies the process. (Goheen, 1998: 479)

Peter Goheen (1998), a well-respected urban historical geographer, attributes much importance to the role of public space in modern urbanism. Citing Haussmann's massive urban re-development of historic central Paris in the mid- to late-nineteenth century, Goheen explains how the city became

available to ordinary citizens to a much greater and unrestricted extent than before. Streets or boulevards, in particular, became the places of regular and uncontrolled encounters among the citizenry (Goheen, 1998). Today there is concern that the practice of citizenship in streets and squares is diminishing, replaced in prominence by the passive citizen-spectator, spectacle, and a commodification of public space, where citizen-consumers engage in individualized pursuits for leisure offered as much by private companies as by public authorities (e.g., Goheen, 1998; Madanipour, 2003; Zukin, 2003). Public space is also a receptacle for the structural failures of our modern economy and social welfare state, when seen through the rise in homelessness over the past two decades in the cities of Canada, a wealthy country (see Walks, Chapter 9).

The importance of symbolism in constructing social reality looms large in the design of public spaces in our cities. For example, state power and authority are asserted symbolically through selections of who or what to commemorate in the naming and monuments of public spaces (Madanipour, 2003). State power and authority are also asserted overtly, perhaps no more starkly than in 2001, when federal, provincial, and municipal governments erected a three-metre-high concrete and chain-link barricade around the centre of Quebec City and brought in police and military personnel in riot gear, supported by helicopters and armoured vehicles. This state control of public space was done to keep the public away from heads of state and their officials gathered for the third Summit of the Americas. Different social groups, private corporations, and public authorities construct different layers of meaning in public spaces and their uses, symbols, monuments, and heritage in dynamic and continuous ways over time (Madanipour, 2003). Contention does indeed accompany the process (Goheen, 1998).

Public space is best understood in conjunction with the concept of "place," which encompasses a meeting point for social and cultural relations with physical form. As Nicholas Lynch and David Ley (2010) explain, place is connected intimately to identity and belonging (Relph, 1976). They discuss how people's love of place flourishes from their attachment of meaning to relationships between culture, environment, and time in space (Tuan, 1974). Lynch and Ley (2010: 327) argue that a sense of place is created by a combination of many facets of the built and socio-cultural environment and is physically and socially constructed "with continuously circulating meanings among different groups reflecting history and supporting identities."

Place-making and the value of urban design has become a priority of many public authorities, citizens, and the private sector. This is particularly true in an era of city-"concepting," branding, and marketing in a competitive effort to attract and retain a population of workers seen to fuel a post-industrial international economy, often referred to as the creative class, and to augment urban tourism (Carmona, de Magalhaes, and Edwards, 2002; Florida, 2004; see Hall, Chapter 3, and Vinodrai, Chapter 5). Project for Public Spaces (PPS), a non-profit organization based in New York City, argues that about 80 per cent of the success of most public spaces is attributable to their management and programming by responsible authorities (e.g., municipality, community or other non-profit organization) (PPS, 2005). The drawing power of public spaces—where not only will people move through for necessary activities, but will also stay for optional activities (Gehl, 2010)—requires good design, management, and programming. In the following section, we move away from our conceptual discussion and look instead at how direct observation and empirical measurement can enhance our understanding of how public spaces function.

Measurement and Metrics of How Public Spaces Are Functioning

The urbanists whose conceptual insights into city spaces and public life we treasure in the classroom learned most of what they know by direct observation. Jane Jacobs, Jan Gehl, William Whyte, and Allan Jacobs, for example, did a lot of walking around, sitting, watching, measuring, taking film and photographs, making notes, sketching, and speaking with citizens using the spaces. In our own public space and activity research program (e.g., City of Saskatoon, 2011), we use a set of methods that have much in common with—and were inspired by—those used by Gehl and his team (see Gehl and Svarre, 2013, for an introduction to their toolkit) and by PPS (2005). Our methods are grouped into three categories: site survey, direct observation, and public surveys.

In the first category (i.e., site survey) are inventories of street furniture, window and sidewalk displays, public art placement, landmarks, street trees, soft and hard landscaping, and snow clearance, among other things. Also included are evaluations of ground-floor frontage, test-runs through cycling and pedestrian infrastructure, transit stop improvements, and revitalized laneways. Our research team also conducts sensory perception surveys that develop understanding of comfort, safety, and enjoyment in the public realm.

In the second category of methods (i.e., direct observation), we include active transport counts in winter and summer of pedestrians and cyclists, and intersection studies that examine how cyclists, pedestrians, and motorists are interacting at intersections, including the frequency of use at different times of day (Figure 18.1). Stationary activity mapping of public spaces is done to examine how people are using them; where they situate themselves, for how long, and at what times of the day; and changes in the use of public space by season.

Some cities have introduced automated approaches as a substitute for direct observation to understand how the cycling network is being used. Montreal, for example, has nine permanent counters (i.e., Eco-counters) installed along some of its cycling lanes, providing daily cyclist counts for every day of the year since 2008. The city plans to install 10 more in the near future. In 2013 the city also launched Mon RésoVélo, a free smartphone application where cyclists record their route on a given day and send it to the city. Use of this route-tracking technology has risen since its introduction, and after a few months 200 to 300 trips per day were being submitted by cyclists.

Figure 18.1   Direct observation methods in public space and activity research, Saskatoon city centre. (Jill Gunn)

For the third category of methods (i.e., public surveys), we use intercept surveys of people moving through or staying in public spaces to learn about their perceptions of comfort, safety, and enjoyment, as well as their mode of travel to the city centre. Finally, participatory mapping is done with people in the city centre to learn which areas they perceive as being safe or dangerous, and which areas they treasure and dislike most.

The composite understanding developed through this series of methods provides an updatable longitudinal database that can be used to target improvements to the public realm (e.g., new cycling infrastructure), measure the impact of new investments in the public (e.g., a parklet) and private realms (e.g., re-development of a prominent corner parcel on a block). The results of these methods can also be used to monitor at regular intervals (e.g., every five years) how public space, activity, and **urban form** are interacting in the city centre and whether public space planning goals are being met.

The Design and Programming of Streets

Streets and their sidewalks, the main public places of a city, are its most vital organs. Think of a city and what comes to mind? Its streets. If a city's streets look interesting, the city looks interesting; if they look dull, the city looks dull. (Jacobs, 1961: 29)

In the previous section, we provided an overview of measurements and metrics used to understand how public spaces are functioning. In this section we examine what these approaches have taught scholars and practitioners about the movement, market, and meeting functions of streets, the primary public space of any city.

Many cities still plan for the efficient movement of private automobiles but give only secondary consideration to public transit, and a very distant third consideration to bicycle network infrastructure. The pedestrian experience and active transportation options are generally subsumed in the Canadian quest to move more cars, more quickly. For public-health, financial, and environmental reasons, cities need to accelerate the superimposition upon the already well-designed automobile infrastructure of an equally effective infrastructure for transit, cycling, and pedestrian travel. For example, a study of the safety of different types of cycling infrastructure in Toronto and Vancouver showed that cyclists are nine times more likely to be injured on a major street with parked cars and no bike infrastructure than on a dedicated cycling lane on a major street separated by a physical barrier, such as a curb, median, or bollards (Teschke et al., 2012). Major streets with bike lanes marked with solid or dotted lines and no parked cars presented about half the risk to cyclists compared to those with parked cars and no cycling infrastructure. By comparison, shared lane

infrastructure, like "sharrows" or shared bike-bus lanes, showed negligible risk reductions to cyclists (Teschke et al., 2012).[1]

Montreal ranks first in North America, and eleventh world-wide, in the 2013 Copenhagenize Index of bicycle-friendly cities, based on its review of 150 cities (Copenhagenize Design Co., 2013). Montreal created some of the north–south segments of its cycling network in the mid-1980s, from the Old Port to near Laval; however, its current approach to transportation planning was catalyzed by the launch of its *Réinventer Montréal: Transportation Plan 2008* (City of Montreal, 2008). As a result, active transportation and transit became the focus of significant new investment (see El-Geneidy, Patterson, and St-Louis, Chapter 10). The city's network of cycling infrastructure includes lanes separated from vehicle traffic by medians (Figure 18.2); lanes painted on streets between parked and moving vehicles and next to moving vehicles without parked cars; sharrows; and, along the

Figure 18.2   Bicycle lanes separated from vehicle traffic by median, rue University, Montreal. (Ville de Montréal)

Quartier des Spectacles, a bike lane that is adjacent to pedestrians on the sidewalk. Montreal's cycling infrastructure network has very good connectivity and continuity and is expanding yearly.

One action put forward in *Réinventer Montréal* was to create a self-service bicycle system. In 2008 BIXI was implemented by a private non-profit company created by the City of Montreal. Now, there are hundreds of BIXI stations and thousands of bikes around the city. Each station has a pay station and a series of bike docks that house the bikes. Bikes are rented for short intervals (e.g., up to 45 minutes) at one dock, then ridden and returned to any dock in the system. There are over 50,000 BIXI members in Montreal, and usage has gone from just over one million single trips in 2009 to over four million trips in 2011 (Damant-Sirois, Grimsrud, and El-Geneidy, 2014). The BIXI system has since been exported to cities around North America (e.g., Boston, Toronto) and overseas (e.g., London, Melbourne). However, despite rising patronage, BIXI has not achieved profitability. In 2014 the company was under bankruptcy protection and the City of Montreal stepped in to operate it for a year, after which time it will determine whether to add BIXI permanently to the City's public transportation infrastructure.

Another action that came out of *Réinventer Montréal* is keeping a portion of the cycling lane network clear during the winter. This *Réseau Blanc* comprises areas of the city centre where cycling is most prevalent, which has helped increase ridership numbers during winter months. City centres typically have higher cycling trips than other areas of the city. Saskatoon is similar in this regard and has twice as many residents in the city centre who choose cycling as their means of travel (i.e., 5 per cent) as the city overall (City of Saskatoon, 2011). Cities that want to get a toehold for improving cycling infrastructure overall start in the city centre.

Complete Streets

A progressive model for creating a full spectrum of movement infrastructure on our streets is known as **complete street design**. The Toronto Centre for Active Transportation (2012a: 4) defines it as

follows: "Complete Streets provide for all road users—pedestrians, bicyclists, transit users, and motorists of all ages and abilities." Faced with transforming current city-centre streets—from automobile and parking lanes to complete streets with vehicle, parking, cycling, and transit lanes—political will can be difficult to muster. As more cities achieve success, however, other jurisdictions are emboldened into action. In 2010, for example, the City of Winnipeg re-designed Assiniboine Avenue in its city centre as a complete street. Assiniboine Avenue includes the city's first separated bike lanes and improvements to the pedestrian infrastructure, such as corner bulbs (i.e., curb extensions) at intersections to reduce the crossing distance. Count data collected in 2009, 2011, and 2012 have shown a 65 per cent increase in cyclists during the afternoon rush hour (Toronto Centre for Active Transportation, 2012b).

Re-apportioning the street right-of-way to provide safe and dedicated passage to multiple modes can involve removing one or more vehicle lanes in order to accommodate new bike or bus lanes, or removing some on-street parking to improve pedestrian infrastructure, such as corner bulbs at intersections and mid-block crossings, bus bulbs, new or improved medians, or widened sidewalks (Figure 18.3). There are many possible reconfigurations, and the design of a particular street requires an empirical understanding of the users, the street's role in the city's transportation system, and spatial parameters of the particular site. Complete streets have the capacity to move more people through the street on the full spectrum of properly appointed transportation infrastructure, each inducing new demand to match the infrastructure supplied for it.

Shared Streets

The concept of complete street design only addresses movement, one of the public space functions of streets. So it could be said that the complete street design concept is, in fact, incomplete. Streets are public spaces that include meeting and market functions as well. **Shared street design** is a complementary concept to complete streets, and there

Existing Street Section

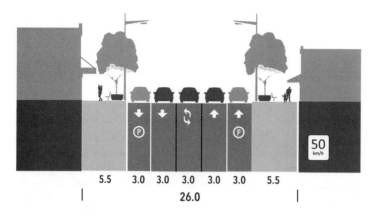

Complete Street Section

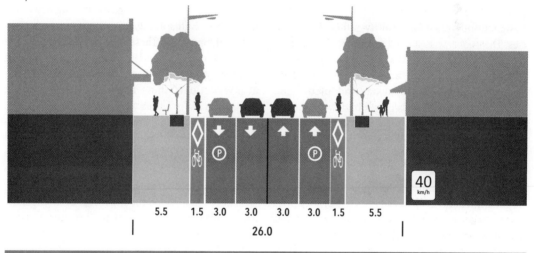

Figure 18.3   Example of Re-Design to "Complete Street" Standards

Source: Toronto Centre for Active Transportation, 2012a: 10–11.

is room for both models of street recalibration in any city.

The shared street concept designs for its most vulnerable user, the pedestrian, although it is also used by other modes, including bikes and cars. Rather than designating separate lanes for cyclists and for cars, and sidewalks for pedestrians, the design is open and the right-of-way shared by all users. Curbs and lane markings are either nonexistent or very subtle. To demarcate areas where vehicles are *not* permitted, bollards may be used.

Paving materials and patterns are selected that are aesthetically pleasing in appearance, texture, and sometimes even in the sound they make as vehicles and bicycles drive over them. The paving is used for the full width of the street right-of-way to evoke urban quality at a human scale and invite pedestrians to make full use of the street. The same is true of street lights and other street furniture. Places for people to congregate and stay, with public art and other interpretive elements often punctuate the space along the street. All are geared to the human scale, with lower speed limits and design cues that tame vehicle traffic with the intrigue and uncertainty created by the shared and active space (Engwicht, 1993). Popular city centre examples include the stretch of Sainte-Catherine Street in Montreal that runs through the Quartier des Spectacles and of King Street in Kitchener in front of City Hall. Both are highly used as event and festival spaces, blending the movement, meeting, and market functions of public space.

Perhaps the most famous type of shared street design is the *woonerf*, which originated about 40 years ago in the Netherlands (Ben-Joseph, 1995). This type of shared street design is most common in areas with high residential use, combining neighbourhood-scale social space that is safe for children to play in with movement of local traffic, designed for pedestrian-priority rather than vehicles. The *woonerf* has started to appear in Canadian cities. Ottawa (e.g., a section of Cambridge Street), Montreal (Saint-Pierre), and Toronto (West Don Lands) are three cities that have adopted them, while other cities (e.g., Calgary's Inglewood neighbourhood) are poised to introduce them.

Design Qualities of Great Streets

Based on his examination of "great streets" internationally, Allan Jacobs (1993: 270–92) identifies eight categories of design qualities that he argues great streets require: (1) places for people to walk with some leisure; (2) physical comfort; (3) definition; (4) qualities that engage the eyes; (5) transparency; (6) complementarity; (7) maintenance; and (8) quality of construction and design. We adapt and elaborate upon some of those qualities next.

1. Places for People to Walk with Comfort

Sidewalks must accommodate people who walk at varying paces: those in a hurry; those at leisure; those who wish to stop mid-course to look more closely through a window, at public art, or at a building; or those who wish to stop to chat with other people. City planners need to carefully consider whether the city-centre sidewalks are wide enough to enable the kinds of public space improvements,

movement, and stationary activities they aim to foster. If the space is overcrowded, neither leisurely nor hurried pedestrian travel is feasible (Jacobs, 1993). But sidewalks that are slightly overcrowded are better than sidewalks that are empty. Put another way, it is better to be too lively for the space available than to be lifeless (Gehl, 2010). People are attracted to spaces full of other people.

Sidewalks need separation from vehicles to keep the pedestrian environment secure and pleasant, with curbs, trees that are planted sufficiently close in succession, other landscaping, and perhaps a row for parked cars or a cycling lane to create a buffer between pedestrians and those using the street for rapid movement. The 20th Street West Streetscape Improvement Project in Saskatoon's city centre, for example, began installing bus bulbs and corner bulbs along this commercial street in 2013 (Figure 18.4). These design features improve transit efficiency and pedestrian safety when embarking and alighting from buses and crossing at intersections. These features also improve the pedestrian realm with a variety of associated public art installations and amenity strips. Heated sidewalks and outdoor fireplaces in some locations, and heated transit shelters are proposed in Saskatoon's new City Centre Plan (City of Saskatoon, 2013) to enhance streets in this winter city.

Safety and trust on a street full of strangers is an important dimension of walking comfortably through city streets. Jane Jacobs (1961) explains how sidewalks with people at all times of the day can create the conditions for safety and trust. Her now famous concept of having many "eyes upon the street" from the windows and doorways of buildings with a variety of uses oriented to the street is fundamental to its safety. Participatory mapping undertaken with people in Saskatoon's city centre showed that the streets with the highest residential density—where windows, doorways, and balconies are oriented to the street—were perceived to be most safe. Areas with surface parking lots lining a significant portion of the block-face and little residential density were perceived as unsafe (City of Saskatoon, 2011) (see Siciliano, Cowen, and Smith, Chapter 16).

Figure 18.4 **Corner bus bulb nearing end of construction, 20th Street West Streetscape Improvement Project, Saskatoon. (City of Saskatoon)**

2. Definition

Streets should create a sense of being in an "urban room." Christopher Alexander, Sara Ishikawa, and Murray Silverstein explain that outdoor spaces—of which the street is the most prominent—can be either positively or negatively defined:

> Outdoor space is negative when it is shapeless, the residue left behind when buildings— which are generally viewed as positive—are placed on the land. An outdoor space is positive when it has a distinct and definite shape, as definite as the shape of a room, and when its shape is as important as the shapes of the buildings which surround it. (1977: 518)

Streets are defined in combination between their vertical (e.g., height of buildings) and horizontal dimensions (e.g., street width from building facades on one side of the street to the buildings on the other side) (Jacobs, 1993). The wider a street gets, the more building height and mass it takes to define the street and create the human-scale sensory perception of enclosure within an urban room. On wide streets, closely spaced trees on medians and sidewalks can have an intervening influence and enhance definition. From his observation of great streets around the world, Jacobs (1993: 279–80) concludes that "buildings along streets are likely to provide a sense of definition when height to horizontal distance ratios are at least 1:4 with the viewer looking at a 30-degree angle to the right or left of the direction of the street." At a ratio of 1:5 or smaller, the street will not have a sense of definition (Figure 18.5).

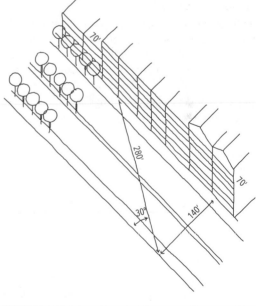

Figure 18.5 **Street Definition: Height to Horizontal Distance Ratio**

Source: Jacobs, Allan B. *Great Streets, Street Definition: Height to Horizontal Distance Ratio,* © 1993 Massachusetts Institute of Technology, by permission of The MIT Press.

Terminal vistas also help create definition. Examples include a sightline to a prominent natural feature or landscape, a roundabout with a sculpture, a building or landmark, or a public square. Serial views that emerge as one moves down a gradually curving street (e.g., due to physical topography or street pattern) are another way that definition is enhanced with visual endpoints along the street wall. Finally, gateways can enhance street definition and improve the legibility of movement into and out of distinctive urban precincts (Alexander, Ishikawa, and Silverstein, 1977). They can be literal gateways, for which many Chinatown precincts in Canadian cities are famous, or they can be created by using building design guidelines (e.g., directing the prominence of massing and facade at the lot line, roof treatment, materials, lighting) to create distinction on corner lots at intersections that mark the entryway to precincts and thus frame the street beyond. As Jacobs (1961: 380) explains, many streets "need visual interruptions, cutting off the indefinite distant view and at the same time visually heightening and celebrating intense street use by giving it a hint of enclosure and entity."

A challenge to street definition in some Canadian cities is the prevalence of surface parking lots in places where buildings should be. These holes in the street wall can undermine the urban quality of an entire block, which would otherwise be well defined. Saskatoon faces a remarkable challenge in this regard, with surface parking covering roughly 26 per cent of developable land in its city centre (City of Saskatoon, 2011). Unfortunately, its property tax assessment structure does not include a premium on the inherent value of zoned developable land in the city centre. This and the absence of regulations against using building land as surface parking lead to the demolition, rather than up-keeping, of older buildings in the commercial rental market. As well, there is a tendency to hold land indefinitely to use as under-capitalized, income-generating (often gravel) parking lots (see Skaburskis and Moos, Chapter 12).

3. Design Qualities that Stimulate and Create Transparency

The human field of vision has evolved to observe the world on a frontal horizontal plane while moving through it on foot at an average of roughly 5 km/h, ranging from slightly faster in the winter to a little bit slower in the summer (Gehl, 2010). By shifting our eyes, without tilting our head, our vertical field of vision is roughly 50–55 degrees upward from horizontal, and 70–80 degrees downward. Our eyes naturally shift their focal point as many as a hundred times over the course of a minute, communicating curiosity and interest psychologically in proportion to changing visual stimuli. Quality physical design promotes activity in the public realm by being a draw for people. And, in turn, people are the item of most interest and greatest stimulation to other people (Gehl, 2010; Whyte, 1980).

Many units, windows, doorways, and street furniture are important design features, where we can see, hear, and (when close enough) smell people inside, outside, and in liminal spaces throughout our 100-metre horizontal "social field of vision" (Gehl, 2010). Stimulating paving surfaces, vegetation, awnings, and a complexity of lines and texture in building facades all determine the degree to which we experience quality in our streetscapes. And the design of the first three stories of buildings matters most in defining the urban room, given the field of vision we have as human beings. Vertical relief in building facades with narrow and active shop-fronts—rather than long, horizontally undifferentiated passive walls—have the effect of creating a good sensory rhythm for the pedestrian as visual stimuli change more often and walking distances seem shorter as well as more interesting (Gehl, 2010). The kinds of cities that are memorable and that retain residents and attract visitors are those that put time into urban quality considerations. Vancouver is a good example of this with its high-quality public space design, framing mountain views, and high-rises constructed to have a narrow tower and street-oriented podium (base) designed to enhance the streetscape at ground level and preserve significant sightlines.

Window displays, signage, doorways with people shuffling in and out between the private and public realms of the street enhance public life on both sides of the threshold (Whyte, 1980). The sight of activity is an incentive for activity; as a result, seeing inside buildings that frame the street has the effect of enlarging the pedestrian realm and making it richer (Alexander, Ishikawa, and Silverstein, 1977). The City of Saskatoon has operationalized transparency as one of the key dimensions of an attractive exchange zone at the ground floor between buildings and the street (City of Saskatoon, 2011; Gehl, 2010). In Saskatoon, attractive ground-floor frontages along street blocks in the city centre have 11–20 units, or shop fronts, per 100 metres, with many entrances and few or no closed or passive units (e.g., bank or law-office windows with blinds drawn). Neutral frontages have 6–10 units per 100 metres, with some closed or passive units; dull frontages have 1–5 units per 100 metres with many closed or passive units (Figure 18.6). On the best commercial streets, the edges between private and public space will be soft, and merchandise or services will be displayed or performed in the area of sidewalk or street in front of the shops (e.g., books from the bookshop on display on the sidewalk, café seating on the street or sidewalk, clothing racks brought outside the shop doorway on nice days, sandwich-board signage with a restaurant's daily specials) (Alexander, Ishikawa, and Silverstein, 1977; Gehl, 2010; Jacobs, 1993; Whyte, 1980).

4. Complementarity

To create a streetscape that is a positively defined and transparent, buildings must be respectful of the street character overall and re-enforce that character. Having no prescriptive guidelines on building size, massing, lot coverage, materials, or placement pattern of windows and doorways can leave a streetscape at serious risk of long-term damage when individual building projects treat their site as though it existed in isolation. The vast majority of users of the public realm will not set foot within any specific building within this realm; most public realm users only engage with the exterior a building contributes to the streetscape it helps to frame. As a result, meeting the needs

☺ **Attractive frontages in the City Centre**

Active frontages are predominantly found in the core of the retail and entertainment district along 2nd Avenue South and 21st Street East, as well as parts of Broadway Avenue and 20th Street West. These streets are busy with shops, restaurants and bars, as well as attractive streetscapes. In total there are over 5.3 km of attractive street frontages in the City Centre.

Evaluation:

Narrow units	Few closed or passive units
Many entrances	Interesting facades
(10–20 units per 100 m)	Quality materials & details
A diversity of functions	

☹ **Neutral frontages in the City Centre**

The City Centre has a notable amount of neutral ground floor frontages. Many of these buildings are found in the commercial district, some are office uses. Most of the neutral frontages are medium-sized buildings, with fewer units and entrances, with some fenestration and architectural detail.

Evaluation:

Mixture of small/large units	Some closed, passive units
(6–10 units per 100 m)	Average facades
Some diversity of functions	Decent materials & details

☹ **Dull frontages in the City Centre**

The City Centre has many inactive and dull ground floor frontages. Most of these are found along the western edge of the downtown where larger buildings have been developed along the former railway lands. The long blank walls of the Midtown Plaza present a significant challenge as vital and active urban edge. The recently built Galaxy Cinemas, although smaller in size, similarly lacks active frontage along 20th Street and most of 2nd Avenue.

Evaluation:

Larger units, few entrances	Mostly unattractive facades
(1–5 units per 100 m)	Few or no details
Little diversity of functions	
Many closed, passive units	

Figure 18.6   Ground floor frontage typology for Saskatoon's city centre. (City of Saskatoon, 2011: 74)

of the users of the public realm outside the building—just like meeting the needs of tenants inside the building—is part of the responsibility of developing real estate in a city. Property developers have every right to develop their land parcel, but, we would argue, do not have the right to side-step the public interest in maintaining a high-quality streetscape in so doing.

Canadian cities have been devising tools to protect complementarity in urban design. The Halifax Regional Municipality's HRMbyDesign downtown design plan and Design Review Committee (DRC), for example, ensures that development applications comply with minimum standards set for built form and public space. The DRC has approval authority for the qualitative aspects of built form; it is rare if not unique in Canada for a DRC to have authority rather than serving in an advisory capacity to the municipality's development officer. Advisory DRCs are more common, and they can work very well, especially when they provide formative input in early stages of the development proposal. They can also provide a summative recommendation to the city's development officer when the application and site plan is submitted.

The City of Saskatoon's new architectural control overlay zoning district for the Broadway Avenue commercial area in the city centre—a 2011 "Great Street" winner in the Great Places in Canada competition—is an example of design guidelines to safeguard the public interest. The initiative originated out of the community-driven Broadway 360° Development Plan. The DRC advises the city's development officer on building projects according to 14 design guidelines, which include building expression, orientation and placement, street wall, heritage contexts, corner sites, storefronts, residential street access units, roof treatment, above-grade parking, material and architectural quality, sidewalk cafés, building lighting, signage, and sustainable design.

Although complementarity is critically important, Jane Jacobs (1961) has argued convincingly for the role of landmarks—most often buildings—sited sparingly through streetscapes to enhance overall urban quality. Examples might include a historic church, court house, library, or heritage building that sits differently on its lot than its neighbours. The overall positive effect of landmarks like these on enhancing streetscapes will be better if they are not clustered together—in a civic complex for example—and are instead spread throughout different streets (Jacobs, 1961). Not only the buildings themselves but the uses they house within them are best spread widely. A block that contains mostly civic buildings, and little else, neither assists with a diversity of uses at the fine-grained scale that creates urban vitality nor assists with spreading landmark buildings through the city to provide well-conceived punctuation to streetscapes.

We must end the discussion on complementarity with a return to the fundamentals for city life: density and diversity. One cannot expect to have a great street—with vitality, safety, and public life—if there is insufficient density and diversity of residents, commerce, and institutional uses to "give each other close-grained and lively support" (Jacobs, 1961: 377). No design treatment will make up for the absence of these things, although these things can make up for deficits in design.

Programming Streets–Art, Culture, and Commerce

Lively streets will be well-designed with the physical attributes discussed above, will be supported by density and diversity along and in adjacent areas, and will be enhanced with programming in art and design, culture, and commerce. Together, these will augment the street's meeting and market functions.

Street furniture itself can be artfully conceived and built to carry through design elements that create a street identity using tactics of emphasis and suggestion (Jacobs, 1961). The design of garbage bins, benches, bus shelters, street lights, bollards, and maps or historic interpretive panels can all be designed in a style that carries through a theme enhancing the spirit of place. For example, tree grates along the street at River Landing, the signature public space of Saskatoon's city centre, were designed in consultation with Cree and Dakota

First Nation Elders to reflect the secular activities that would have been undertaken at that place prior to urbanization (see Peters, Chapter 21). In downtown Kitchener, bike racks are in the shape of bicycles and painted in vibrant colours, providing both public art and bike parking. The main street in Kitchener's downtown has been designed so that it can be easily closed off to traffic for concerts, markets, and festivals as part of the city's regular programming of events. With thoughtful placement, the advantage of triangulation can occur, where a bench next to a map or interpretive panel or next to a bike rack, garbage bin, or an intriguing tree grate can prompt casual encounters between strangers, whether a conversation or only a smile or nod (Whyte, 1980). Each encounter is a contribution to public activity and the relations of trust so fundamental to vibrant and safe streets.

The streetscape design joining the pavilions of the Musée des Beaux Arts along rue Sherbrooke and Avenue du Musée in Montreal provides an excellent example of place-specific public art (Cartiere, 2010). Undertaken by the City of Montreal, the Place du Musée project was inspired by the cultural presence of this eminent art gallery and the nearby northern backdrop of Mont-Royal, one of the city's most distinctive place-making natural landmarks (Figure 18.7). City urban design staff worked with an artist to inspire concepts and create models for limestone blocks that would serve as seating and areas for play, and as plinths for sculptures. The limestone blocks mirror the geological composition of Mont-Royal and are situated to emerge out of the ground along the sidewalks as though extending from the mountain itself. Some blocks are cut with a five-degree angle and are clustered in groups of six, interspersed with vegetation and trees that mirror species from the mountain. A terraced sidewalk along Avenue du Musée serves as a sculpture garden that leads

Figure 18.7   Place du Musée project, avenue du Musée, Montreal. (Denise Caron/Ville de Montréal)

toward Mont-Royal, carrying the art gallery into the street. At night, the sculptures are lit by street lights that are directed as spotlights on each sculpture, creating a theatrical effect much as you would see in an exhibit inside the gallery. The segment of Avenue du Musée closest to Sherbrooke is closed to vehicle traffic in summer and itself becomes the set for an additional installation of street art. The project creates a brilliant backdrop for public activity, triangulation prompting casual encounters among strangers, and an artful interpretation and re-enforcement of this specific cultural and natural place. In "winter cities" particularly, the use of light in urban design initiatives is an effective way to bring a feeling of warmth to the public realm when daylight hours are short and the display of light can be very powerful and heartening.

Streets and laneways are becoming some of the most exciting places for art and performance in Canadian city centres. Public art is diversifying beyond the occasional sculpture, mural, fountain, or monument, and it is enhancing public life in interactive and place-specific ways (see Bain, Chapter 14). Contemporary art and performance of a scale often confined to museums, galleries, and auditoriums are flowing into public space and producing "an in-between space where the divisions between contemporary art, audiences and everyday life are, at least temporarily, re-imagined and considerably altered" (Borsa, 2004; 2006: 132). In Saskatoon, for example, the Free Flow Dance Theatre Company has transformed rear laneways in the city centre into the site for its show, Back Alley Antics. In it the lines between audience and performer blur, and the intimate human scale of the laneway streetscape becomes the setting for the production of space through public art and activity (Figure 18.8). Similarly, rear laneways and fire escapes in the city centres of Edmonton and Calgary have been transformed by the Mercury Opera company into sites for public enjoyment of opera.

Rear laneways are one of the great underused public spaces of our city centres. Artists have figured this out, as indicated above, but others are catching on. The intimate human-scale of laneways, and their ability to provide better shelter and more

Figure 18.8   **Free Flow Dance Theatre Company's "Back Alley Antics," Saskatoon. (Marcia Provenzano)**

direct mid-block routes in the cold of winter makes them attractive year-round prospects for enhancing movement, market, and meeting (Akkerman, 2013; City of Saskatoon, 2011). Behind commercial streets with rising rents like Broadway Avenue in Saskatoon, they offer the possibility of new commercial frontage that hits a price point accessible to small-scaled or start-up businesses that can no longer afford the front-of-house.

Initiatives led by local shop owners and **business improvement areas** have also tapped into new vessels for culture and commerce on the streets. For four weeks spanning August–September 2012, the Downtown Yonge Business Improvement Area in conjunction with Toronto Ward 27 Councillor Kristyn Wong-Tam hosted "Celebrate Yonge." Lanes were reduced from four to two in order to expand the pedestrian space and create 11 themed event areas that contained art installations, street furniture, lounges, and patios for the segment of Yonge Street between Queen Street and Gerrard Street in the city centre (City of Toronto, 2013). Pedestrian traffic increased, vehicle traffic decreased, and there was roughly a 40 per cent increase in sales (Greenberg, 2013), supporting the argument that people—not cars—drive commerce.

In September 2013, Saskatoon businessman Dave Denny celebrated the one-hundredth anniversary of his Drinkle No. 3 building on Third Avenue downtown by closing the block between 21st and 22nd Streets for a day to hold DrinkleFest (Figure 18.9). He worked with local organizations like Saskatoon Cycles and Great Places to install a temporary bike lane and bike box as a demonstration project for complete street design, and stage a variety of other place-making initiatives

to engage citizens. Street performances and a talk by Better Block co-founder and tactical urbanist Jason Roberts were held. A restaurant in the building moved patio seating onto the street, occupying on-street parking spaces along the shopfront. While the street was only closed to vehicle traffic for the one-day DrinkleFest celebration, the restaurant was permitted by the City to keep its on-street dining installed for two weeks as a demonstration project, an initiative that was profitable for both the restaurant and public life. Examples like DrinkleFest and Celebrate Yonge teach us how interconnected the movement, market and meeting functions of the street should be. It is only in our recent past that we separated these functions and privileged movement (of cars) over the others. Initiatives like these help to repair the damage done by the disaggregation of the three *M*s.

The creation of parklets provides a final example of a street-side public space intervention—again by

Figure 18.9   **DrinkleFest Better Block party, Third Avenue, Saskatoon. (Michelle Berg/*The StarPhoenix*)**

reclaiming on-street parking spaces—that is catching on in Canadian cities. San Francisco is often given pioneering credit for formalizing the parklet as a type of permanent (or at least seasonally recurrent) public space starting in 2010. The City of San Francisco (2013: 1) defines it thus:

> A parklet repurposes part of the street into a public space for people. They are intended as aesthetic enhancements to the streetscape, providing an economical solution to the need for increased public open space. Parklets provide amenities like seating, planting, bike parking, and art.

Parklets are typically funded and maintained in some type of partnership between local businesses, residents, community organizations, and civic authorities. An important distinction between parklets and on-street café dining, for example, is that parklets are public spaces. Anyone can enjoy them without buying anything. Montreal's first (seasonally) permanent parklet was created in 2013 along boulevard Saint-Laurent in the Plateau-Mont-Royal neighbourhood. It occupies the space of three on-street parking spots and comprises a painted shipping container with openings throughout, with seating, and with planter boxes.

This ends our discussion of the functions of streets. We continue our examination of what the observation of the movement, market, and meeting functions of public spaces have taught scholars and practitioners by discussing public squares, one of the signature spaces of cities.

The Design and Programming of Squares

Squares are public spaces at the intersection of two or more streets in an urban area where people can sit and relax, walk, people-watch, and meet others. They may serve variously as a hard-scaped marketplace or space for ceremony and civics, or an area of lush and landscaped trees, grass, and gardens. Like streets, good physical design is necessary but insufficient on its own to ensure a vibrant square: "What stands out most is that design is only a small fraction of what goes into making a great square. To really succeed, a square must take into account a host of factors that extend beyond its physical dimensions" (PPS, 2013: n.p.).

Factors present in great squares include a key landmark feature, such as a fountain or other touchable water feature, or a prominent sculpture or civic building (PPS, 2005; Whyte, 1980). A great square will have several smaller places within it that attract a variety of different people at different times of the day, such as cafés, food vendors, play areas for children, enclosed off-leash areas for dogs, or performance spaces. If a square is one-dimensional, it will be empty most of the time. Thoughtful placement of amenities like public art, lighting, benches, and garbage bins are all important, some of which can be movable (e.g., some of the seating, tables, games) to accommodate seasonal changes in programming (PPS, 2013). A square may house a skating rink in the winter and open-air movies in the summer (like Kingston's Market Square); it may have a market space that shifts over the course of the year from an open-air food and produce market in the summer to covered (e.g., heated tents) selling local artisanal crafts and gifts during the holiday season in winter.

Easy access for pedestrians is important for a vibrant square, with transit and cycling infrastructure nearby and pedestrian-scale street design at crossings that form the entry points to the square, as well as along the edges. Attention to the movement functions of streets nearby will enhance the meeting and market functions of a square. Specifically, vehicle traffic should be tamed along the edges. A square is not something for vehicles to drive by quickly. It is, rather, a feature of the urban environment that must invite slow, safe, and deliberate attention to movement at a pedestrian's scale.

Management of the space—its upkeep, safety, and programming—is fundamental to success, and often this comes with a partnership between public (e.g., city hall, community association) and private (e.g., local business improvement district) sectors (PPS, 2013). Local community members who use and value the space are a key source of expertise on the features of the square that work best and what improvements might be made to design and programming.

"The life of a public square forms naturally around its edge. If the edge fails, then the space never becomes lively" (Alexander, Ishikawa and Silverstein, 1977: 600). The edges of a square, then, require much attention, in both design and programming. People naturally gravitate toward the edges of public space to linger. They like to have their back to something and look outward toward the space before them and beyond. Creating pockets of activity (e.g., food and craft vendors, heritage and art installations) around the edges, starting at points of entry to the square, are a technique for building vibrancy and use (Alexander, Ishikawa, and Silverstein, 1977). People will enter, linger, and perhaps then move out into other areas of the square. One common error in the design of squares is that they are too large and undifferentiated. With people most focused upon the edges and entry points, vast expanses of open space can defeat the human-scale required for comfortable enjoyment. On the other hand, if a larger overall space is designed in such a way as to create precincts of different uses, attractions, and amenities throughout, then the effect can be positive. Many of the principles of definition that are relevant in great streets are also transferable to squares.

Edges should provide shade when it is warm and sunlight when it is cold, and primary (e.g., benches) and secondary seating (e.g., ledges along planters, niches in walls, steps) where people can stay and engage with the public space in front of them (Gehl, 2010; Whyte, 1980). People tend to want to linger in a square, standing or sitting, in the direct line of movement through the space (Whyte, 1980), to have lunch, read a book. Most of all, people want to see and be seen by other people. Just as in streets, edges of a square can be important exchange zones between adjacent buildings and the square's public space (Gehl, 2010). Café seating can spill out of a building fronting a square in the spring, summer, and fall. In the winter the seating is all indoors, but the presence of hot

chocolate so close by makes skating in the square that much more enjoyable. This is certainly the case at one of the most popular wintertime public spaces in Saskatoon's city centre, the Meewasin Valley Authority's public skating rink in the plaza next to the Bessborough Hotel, named the best outdoor skating rink in Canada by *Reader's Digest* in 2006 (Figure 18.10). With hot drinks available across the street and edges created by an outdoor fireplace, warming hut with wood-burning stove, ornate lighting (including coloured tree lights), and the magnificent hotel defining one side and the river valley another, the invitation to public activity even on the coldest days and evenings of winter is irresistible. It is not uncommon to see brides and grooms skating on it for wedding photos. The raw materials of urban design—including two of the most potent for winter cities, i.e., colour and light—are masterfully combined.

Finally, the density and diversity of residents, commerce, and institutional uses that surround the square are fundamental to populating it with people at all times of the day (Jacobs, 1961). William Whyte (1980: 16) estimates that the "market radius" around a square is about three blocks for people working in the area. Within that distance, workers looking to sit outside for lunch will populate the square. Adult and children residents of the area will also walk with some frequency within that radius, making a square a regular node in their common living patterns. Square Saint-Louis—a popular and vibrant public space—and its surroundings in Montreal provide a good example of the "close-grained and lively support" discussed by Jacobs (1961: 377) that is so pivotal in thriving city spaces. Immediately bordering the square are medium-density housing, food, retail and office shop fronts, and BIXI docks. One block away is a Metro (subway) station. Well within three blocks of the square is high-density housing, a university satellite campus, a military regiment, government offices for health and social services, a tourism institute, two schools, a rehabilitation hospital, and vibrant commercial streets connecting on the north and south (Saint-Denis) and west (Prince-Arthur, a pedestrian street) sides of the square. The design

Figure 18.10   Cameco Meewasin Skating Rink at PotashCorp Plaza, Saskatoon. (Nola Stein/Meewasin Valley Authority)

of the square itself includes, with excellence, most of the features described in this section for vibrant squares.

Conclusion

The Canadian Institute of Planners started the annual Great Places in Canada contest in 2011 to highlight the best public spaces in communities across the country. Hundreds of thousands of ballots have been cast to choose winners during the past three years. In addition, Canada's most popular urbanism magazine, *Spacing*, assembled a panel of urbanists across the country to rank the 100 best public spaces in Canadian cities in its 2011 national issue (e.g., University Avenue in Charlottetown; Place d'Youville in Quebec City; Nathan Phillips Square in Toronto; 13th Avenue in Regina; Fernwood Square in Victoria). Public

space ignites our emotions and attachment to place. It continues to be the connective tissue of our cities, our local economy, and our citizenship. The balance of proportions may have shifted over time between the movement, market, and meeting functions of public space, with vehicle movement dominating the street in the past several decades and consumption (market) and spectacle overtaking citizenship practices (meeting) in the public square. But all the functions of public space remain, much as in the agora and the streets of the ancient Greeks, or Haussmann's boulevards in Paris. Our knowledge of public space in the context of social and cultural theory is constantly evolving. It is contentious precisely because all of the currents of the urban age take the stage at one point or another in public space, whether it is homelessness, celebration, leisure, or protest. While knowledge of physical design is well developed, the programming and management dimension of public space research has received far less attention, and is one of the areas where further empirical and educational focus would be highly valuable (Nikitin, 2011).

The study of the interaction between public space, activity, and urban form is fascinating, and some of the methods introduced here, and the lessons learned, will hopefully inspire readers to undertake field observation as a necessary (and enjoyable) dimension of understanding how Canadian cities function. Adding new layers of depth and complexity to the conceptualization, design, and programming of public spaces will enrich Canada's comparatively young (by international standards) cities. We hope this chapter motivates further exploration of public space theory and practice in all of its fascinating intricacy.

Acknowledgements

Walker thanks the School of Urban Planning at McGill University for hosting him as a visiting professor during the semester when this chapter was written. The authors appreciate the assistance given by Nancy Shoiry, Yannick Roy (cycling infrastructure), Wade Eide (Place du Musée), and François Gagné at Ville de Montréal. The authors thank David Gordon at Queen's University for sharing his perspective on light as a winter design treatment and Mike Velonas at Meewasin Valley Authority for his insight on street design. The authors recognize Jan Gehl at Gehl Architects for inspiring a deeper knowledge of how public spaces function on his visit to Saskatoon in 2009 and acknowledge Jeanna South and Rick Howse at City of Saskatoon, and Chris Hardwicke and Mark Sterling at Sweeny Sterling Finlayson &Co Architects for their collaboration on the public spaces, activity, and urban form work in Saskatoon.

Note

1. A "sharrow" is a shared lane marking to communicate to both cyclists and motorists the lateral positioning of cyclists in the centre of the shared traffic lane. A "sharrow" does *not* denote a dedicated cycling lane, a common misconception. It simply informs motorists (and cyclists) that cyclists may ride in the full lane of traffic and need not ride pressed up closely against the curb. The word "sharrow" combines *share* and *arrow*, and the name is credited to a cycling-program official in San Francisco.

Review Questions

1. The concept of "complete streets" focuses predominantly on only one of the three Ms of public space. Which one is it, and how might this influential concept in street design become truly "complete"?

2. Programming is an often overlooked dimension of enhancing public life and activity in public space. What are local artists, citizens, and business people teaching us about successfully programming public space?

3. Think of examples in your city centre of streets that exhibit good "definition," "stimulating design quality," and "complementarity." Think of examples that do not.

4. Describe some of the features that a square in the city centre requires in order to induce public life and activity. Do you have any in your city centre that exhibit these features or that fail to do so?

References

Akkerman, A. 2013. "Reclaiming the back alley," *Public Sector Digest: Intelligence for the Public Sector* Fall: 6–10.

Alexander, C., S. Ishikawa, M. Silverstein, with M. Jacobson, I. Fiksdahl-King, and S. Angel. 1977. *A Pattern Language: Towns, Buildings, Construction.* New York: Oxford University Press.

Ben-Joseph, E. 1995. "Changing the residential street scene: Adapting the shared street (woonerf) concept to the suburban environment," *Journal of the American Planning Association* 61: 504–15.

Borsa, J. 2004. "The ephemeral collection: Public repositories or sites for creative endeavour," in A. Kiendl, ed., *Obsession, Compulsion, Collection: On Objects, Display Culture, and Interpretation.* Banff, AB: The Banff Centre Press.

———. 2006. *Site- and Context-oriented Curating: Staging Encounters between Art and Everyday Realities.* Montreal: Concordia University, unpublished PhD thesis.

Carmona, M., C. de Magalhaes, and M. Edwards. 2002. "Stakeholder views on value and urban design," *Journal of Urban Design* 7: 145–69.

Cartiere, C. 2010. *Re/Placing Public Art: The Role of Place-specificity in New Genre Public Art*. Saarbrucken: VDM Verlag Dr. Muller.

City of Montreal. 2008. *Réinventer Montréal: Transportation Plan 2008*. Montreal: City of Montreal.

City of San Francisco. 2013. *San Francisco Parklet Manual*. San Francisco: City of San Francisco.

City of Saskatoon. 2011. *Public Spaces, Activity and Urban Form: Strategic Framework—City Centre Plan Phase 1*. Saskatoon: City of Saskatoon.

———. 2013. *City Centre Plan: Strategic Framework—City Centre Plan Phase 3*. Saskatoon: City of Saskatoon.

City of Toronto. 2013. *Celebrate Yonge—Post-event Review*. Toronto: City of Toronto.

Copenhagenize Design Co. 2013. *The Copenhagenize Index 2013: Bicycle Friendly Cities*. At: http://copenhagenize.eu/index/

Damant-Sirois, G., M. Grimsrud, and A. El-Geneidy. 2014. "What's your type: A multidimensional cyclist typology," paper presented at Transportation Research Board annual meeting. Washington, DC: January.

Engwicht, D. 1993. *Reclaiming Our Cities and Towns: Better Living with Less Traffic*. Gabriola Island, BC: New Society Publishers.

Florida, R. 2004. *Cities and the Creative Class*. London: Routledge.

Galland, D., and C. Hansen. 2012. "The roles of planning in waterfront redevelopment: From plan-led and market-driven styles to hybrid planning?" *Planning Practice and Research* 27: 203–25.

Gehl, J. 2010. *Cities for People*. Washington, DC: Island Press.

———, and L. Gemzoe. 2008. *New City Spaces*. Copenhagen: Danish Architectural Press.

———, and B. Svarre. 2013. *How to Study Public Life*. Washington, DC: Island Press.

Goheen, P. 1998. "Public space and the geography of the modern city," *Progress in Human Geography* 22: 479–96.

Gordon, D. 1997. "Managing the changing political environment in urban waterfront redevelopment," *Urban Studies* 34: 61–83.

Greenberg, K. 2011. *Walking Home: The Life and Lessons of a City Builder*. Toronto: Vintage Canada.

———. 2013. "Students and emerging leaders," presentation at Council for Canadian Urbanism National City-building Leadership Summit. Halifax, NS: September.

Hough, M. 2004. *Cities and Natural Process: A Basis for Sustainability*. London: Routledge.

Jacobs, A. 1993. *Great Streets*. Cambridge: MIT Press.

Jacobs, J. 1961. *The Death and Life of Great American Cities*. New York: Vintage Books.

Lynch, N., and D. Ley. 2010. "The changing meanings of urban places," in T. Bunting, P. Filion, and R. Walker, eds., *Canadian Cities in Transition: New Directions in the Twenty-first Century* (4th edn.). Toronto: Oxford University Press.

Madanipour, A. 2003. "Why are the design and development of public spaces significant for cities?" in A. Cuthbert, ed., *Designing Cities: Critical Readings in Urban Design*. Malden: Blackwell Publishing.

McHarg, I. 1969. *Design with Nature*. Garden City, NY: Natural History Press.

Nikitin, C. 2011. *Personal Communication*, March 1, Vice-President for Downtowns, Project for Public Spaces and 2011 Planner in Residence, University of Saskatchewan, Saskatoon.

Project for Public Spaces. 2005. *How to Turn a Place Around: A Handbook for Creating Successful Public Spaces*. New York: Project for Public Spaces, Inc.

———. 2013. *10 Principles for Successful Squares*. At: www.pps.org/reference/squareprinciples/

Relph, E. 1976. *Place and Placelessness*. London: Pion.

Teschke, K., M. Harris, C. Reynolds, M. Winters, S. Babul, M. Chipman, M. Cusimano, J. Brubacher, G. Hunte, S. Friedman, M. Monro, H. Shen, L. Vernich, and P. Cripton. 2012. "Route infrastructure and the risk of injuries to bicyclists: A case-crossover study," *American Journal of Public Health* 102: 2336–43.

Toronto Centre for Active Transportation. 2012a. *Complete Streets by Design: Toronto Streets Re-designed for All Ages and Abilities*. Toronto: Toronto Centre for Active Transportation.

———. 2012b. "Assiniboine Avenue, Winnipeg," *Complete Streets for Canada*. At: www.completestreetsforcanada.ca/examples/assiniboine-avenue-winnipeg

Tuan, Y. 1974. "Space and place: Humanistic perspective," *Progress in Geography* 6: 211–52.

Whyte, W. 1980. *The Social Life of Small Urban Spaces*. New York: Project for Public Spaces.

Zukin, S. 2003. "The urban landscape," in A. Cuthbert, ed., *Designing Cities: Critical Readings in Urban Design*. Malden, MA: Blackwell Publishing.

Housing: Dreams and Nightmares

19

RICHARD HARRIS

Introduction

Housing occupies 30 per cent of the land area of Canadian towns and cities, and so dwellings help frame the character of each place: the urbane **row plexes** of Montreal, the graceful limestone homes of old Kingston, the interwar bungalows of Vancouver, the modern condominiums of Toronto, and the garage-fronted homes that characterize postwar suburbs from coast to coast. But these dwellings have other kinds of significance. Owning a home is the Canadian dream; however, including furnishings, appliances, utilities, and property taxes, home ownership absorbs a quarter of household income as it is the owner's largest asset. Most Canadians value the comfort, privacy, and autonomy that housing provides, but four walls can also hide loneliness and abuse. For better or worse, we spend most of our lives at home and we care a lot about how we are housed.

This chapter surveys the subject of housing from various angles. It considers the way housing has been produced, financed, and sold, and how it is occupied and used by different types of people. The chapter goes on to highlight geographical variations at the regional and local scales. Housing is, finally, a concern of public policy, and issues of affordability, energy use, and public health keep it in the public eye.

The Production, Financing, and Sale of Housing

Critics have complained that house-building resists innovation (Harris and Buzzelli, 2005). True, most dwellings are still erected on site (McKellar, 1993), and the pace of technological change has been slow. But such change does happen: a century ago, electrical wiring became the norm; later, iron pipes were replaced by plastic while wallboard supplanted lath and plaster; insulation has improved; roof trusses are now assembled off-site; and, after 1945, power tools became ubiquitous. It is also true, on the other hand, that many builders remain small and apparently inefficient. In Ontario in 1998, more than 98 per cent of them erected fewer than 100 units/year and were responsible for 74 per cent of all housing starts (Buzzelli, 2001). Builders rely on subcontractors, both for physical tasks such as digging basements and for professional services, like accounting (Harris and Buzzelli, 2005). For this reason, they operate with little capital equipment: a truck, some power tools, and a cellphone. It is still easy to become—and to fail as—a builder: during the 1990s in Ontario, on average one-third of the builders active in any year had entered the industry in the previous 12 months; another third would be gone in a year's time (Harris and Buzzelli, 2003). And yet the industry is surprisingly efficient.

Subcontracting enables entrepreneurs and tradesmen to specialize, reaping economies of scale. Suppliers deliver to sites just-in-time and, with builders and contractors, form a dense and flexible production network, akin to those found in other industries that operate in industrial districts.

More dramatic shifts have affected building organization, finance, and land development (Figure 19.1). Three changes are noteworthy. First, speculative builders (those who build first and then seek buyers) have grown in importance. Once, many households commissioned homes from

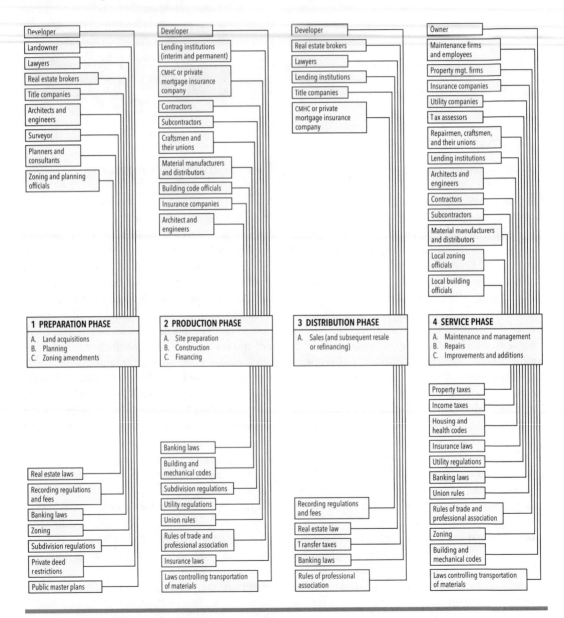

Figure 19.1   The Structures of Residential Building Provision

Source: Adapted from Report of the President's Committee on Urban Housing (the Kaiser Committee), *A Decent Home* (Washington, 1968), 115.

architects and/or custom builders. Low-income households built their own, with help from family or neighbours. In the building boom of the 1900s, in fact, a third of all new homes in Toronto were self-built, and in western cities the proportion was probably higher (Harris, 2004). Today, custom work makes up a small fraction of new construction, and owner-building is important only in the Atlantic region (Rowe, 1989).

A second change has been the elaboration of housing finance. As late as the 1940s, many households relied on savings to buy their first home. Few borrowed more than half the value of their property: mortgage ratios were below 50 per cent. Borrowers obtained credit from other individuals, including family, friends, or people contacted through local lawyers or, in Quebec, *notaires publiques* (Harris, 2004). In the 1930s, to revive construction and hence the wider economy, the federal government passed the first in a series of Housing Acts that revolutionized home finance. In 1946 the Central (now Canada) Mortgage and Housing Corporation (CMHC) was set up, mainly to grant and insure mortgages. Buyers were encouraged to borrow; mortgage terms were relaxed to allow 25-year loans on high ratio (80–90 per cent) mortgages. This helped to restore and then exceed the level of urban home ownership achieved before 1945 (Figure 19.2). With federal encouragement, institutional lenders—i.e., insurance companies and, after 1954, banks—soon dominated the mortgage market, except among some immigrant groups (Murdie, 1986). By 2012, banks alone held

75 per cent of residential mortgage debt (Canadian Mortgage and Housing Corporation [CMHC], 2012).

A third change has been the rise of the developer. A century ago, land was subdivided, sold in parcels to speculators, sold again to small builders, built upon, and eventually sold to the first occupants. The result was a varied landscape where small and large dwellings might be juxtaposed. This still happens in some **exurban** areas. But, especially within large metropolitan areas, most house-building is supervised by developers who control the process from land subdivision to final sale. Developers emerged in the 1920s, shaping areas like Kingsway Park in Etobicoke (Toronto) (Paterson, 1984) and Westdale in Hamilton (Weaver, 1978). After World War II, developers became dominant in building offices, shopping centres, apartments and condominiums, as well as suburban homes. Everywhere, the result was the planned subdivision.

Balancing the uniformity of large-scale development has been the growth of home renovation. In 1966, renovations and repairs to the existing housing stock accounted for 18 per cent of housing investment. (The remainder was for new construction.) By 1976, this proportion had increased to 23 per cent; and by 2002, to 47 per cent (Fallis, 1993). If the land component of new housing is excluded, renovation expenditures exceeded new construction by 1981 (Clayton Research Associates, 1988: 6). Renovations are more significant than published data suggest since much occurs through do-it-yourself (DIY). And renovations are supported by building suppliers who are oriented to

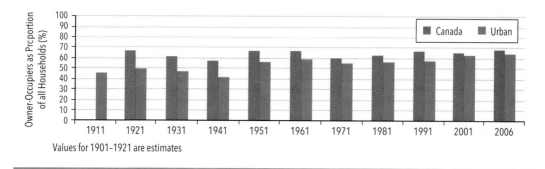

Figure 19.2   The Historical Trend in Home Ownership in Canada, 1901–2006

Source: Canadian Census, various years.

consumers, not contractors, and offer advice as well as materials. Home Depot and Lowe's are US chains that have made incursions into Canada, but are resisted by Canadian Tire and RONA, a Quebec-based company (Yakabuski, 2004). Other renovations are done by contractors, whose receipts are unrecorded and not declared for tax purposes: the underground economy accounts for about 15 per cent of new construction, 56 per cent of renovations, and 67 per cent of repairs (Canadian Home Builders' Association, 2003). Hard to measure, demand for the services of small contractors and subcontractors remains strong.

The growth of speculative builders has made marketing more important. In the early twentieth century, builders and homeowners used the classified section of the local newspaper to sell houses. From the 1920s, speculative builders built model homes. Today, builders blur the lines with custom building: offering variations on a few basic models, they build only when a client has signed a contract. Some new homes and most existing homes are sold, while many apartments are rented, through agents. In major cities, "multiple listing services" (MLS) are owned by local real estate boards. They record and display information on the price and characteristics of dwellings that are on the market. Member agents use these listings to identify properties that might interest their clients. Using MLS guarantees that a property will be seen by many agents and potential buyers. This advantage comes at a price to the seller, however: a commission of 5–6 per cent of the selling price. This cost is one reason why homeowners move less often than tenants. In 2011, the federal Competition Bureau forced boards to share some of their proprietary information, making it possible for agents to offer varying, and cheaper, mixes of services. By mid-2013, the impact was still limited.

Factors that Affect Housing Occupation

By definition, housing units are occupied by households (Miron, 1988; 1993). The household may be a social entity—an individual, a couple, or a nuclear family—but not always. In the past, many families took in lodgers or lodging families, although this practice became uncommon after the 1940s (Harris, 1994: 35). Then, too, "the family" might include grandparents or siblings of the parents, especially among immigrants. The household then is malleable, responding to changes in economic circumstances, in social mores, and in market conditions (see Townshend and Walker, Chapter 7).

Household formation depends on incomes and the age composition of the population. High rates of household growth after 1945 were due to rising incomes: one-third of the increase in households in 1951–1981 was due to new living arrangements enabled by affluence (Miron, 1988). In time, the high rates also reflected the maturation of the baby-boom generation. This age cohort sought rental accommodation, fueling the apartment boom of the 1960s. As they married, saved, and had children (although fewer than their parents) they acquired homes, pushing prices up rapidly but ensuring that ownership rates remained high (Foot and Stoffman, 1996: Chapter 2). In the 1990s, however, as the "echo" generation entered the housing market, high prices compelled many to stay or return home (Mitchell and Gee, 1996). Between 1991 and 2001, the proportion of 20- to 29-year-olds living at home increased from 33 per cent to 41 per cent. However, during the 2000s prosperity enabled large numbers to enter the homeowner market, many as singles. The latter included young women, a growing force in professional occupations. The result was a major condo boom (Kern, 2006).

Filtering and Neighbourhood Change

Condominiums have changed the way a part of the housing market works. Traditionally, new households rarely occupied new housing. Young people with modest incomes and savings bought starter homes that were typically older and deteriorating, lacking some conveniences, and therefore cheaper. So did moderate-income households, of whatever age. For decades, experts and policy-makers assumed that this "filtering down" process could be relied upon to deliver housing to those unable to afford new homes (Bourne, 1981: 149–60) (Figure 19.3). In the 1920s, the concept of filtering (although not the term) influenced Chicago sociologists, who assumed that immigrants must occupy inner-city housing that had filtered far down market.

Until the 1970s, filtering was common. In Vancouver, the Chinatown and Eastside districts, in Toronto the Kensington–Spadina neighbourhoods, and in Montreal the Saint-Urbain corridor exemplify this process. And in cities like Hamilton and Winnipeg, this pattern continues. Elsewhere, the **gentrification** of inner neighbourhoods, including those just mentioned, has slowed or reversed the filtering process (Ley, 1997; Walks and Maaranen, 2008). Classic gentrification involved the upgrading of existing dwellings; notably in

Vancouver and Toronto, it has segued into a condo boom that has seen redevelopment, sometimes of industrial and commercial land (D. Harris, 2011; Lehrer and Wieditz, 2009). One consequence has been the loss of cheap rental housing, together with the displacement of immigrants, single parents, and others with low incomes. Some of the demand for inexpensive housing has been displaced into inner suburbs, where filtering apparently does occur. In many central neighborhoods, however, reverse-filtering has disrupted the fragile market mechanism by which the poor were housed.

Residential Mobility and Neighbourhood Change

People move when they perceive their existing dwelling to be much less desirable than an

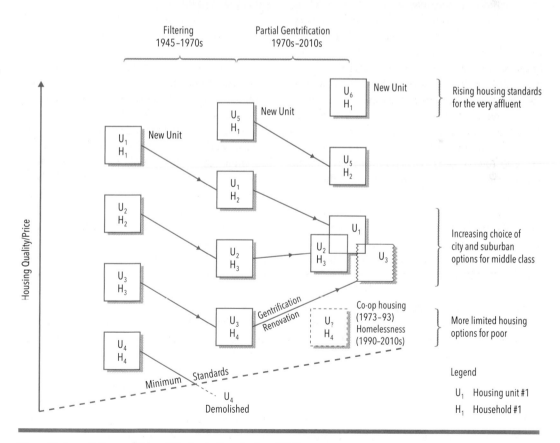

Figure 19.3   Patterns of Urban Filtering in Canada since 1945

alternative. Many factors can contribute to dissatisfaction (Brown and Moore, 1970), including job relocation, changes in income or family size, or a deteriorating neighbourhood. In moving to the suburbs after 1945, Canadians often moved closer to suburbanizing jobs, acquiring larger homes in quieter and more spacious surroundings that growing families needed and that rising incomes could support (Clark, 1966; Michelson, 1977). The decline of some inner-city neighbourhoods added another push. Immigrants from diverse backgrounds, moreover, endorsing home ownership and family-focused values, have helped perpetuate the suburban trend (Hiebert, 2009; Teixeira, 2006), a preference that often carries into the second generation (Kataure and Walton-Roberts, 2013; see Kobayashi and Preston, Chapter 8).

Gentrification, too, may be explained by changes in job location and household structure (Ley, 1997). Its more visible aspects—singles and gay bars, upscale specialty stores, cosmopolitan restaurants—reflect a new lifestyle of discriminating consumerism. These patterns have been shaped by office growth in central cities, and by the desire of employees to live close by. Between 2006 and 2011, for example, employment in Toronto's downtown core grew by 14.2 per cent, with a net growth of 3600 businesses (TD Economics, 2013). The resident population increased by about the same amount. Then, too, changes in household structure have caused many to re-evaluate inner city living. More households consist of singles or two earners with no children. Schools and open space—except perhaps somewhere to walk a dog—are low priorities; walkability, street life, and meeting-places are what matter. A fairly central location also makes sense for single parents, since inner areas are better served by transit and the community services (notably daycare) that such households need (Rose, 1989; Rose and Le Bourdais, 1986; see Bain, Chapter 14).

The growing labour-force participation of women has had complicated effects on the household's decision about where and when to move (Hanson and Pratt, 1995; Jarvis, Pratt and Wu, 2001). With two earners and two workplaces, adults must compromise about where to live. Women, however, still compromise more than men. Many are employed part-time or in jobs—such as clerical work, nursing, and teaching—that are available in scattered locations (Armstrong and Armstrong, 1994). Most households still decide where to live mainly on the basis of where the man works. The woman may then seek employment nearby to avoid interfering with her greater responsibilities for housework and child-rearing (Michelson, 1984). As more women build careers or live alone, however, their preferences and options change. Without a "wife" at home they minimize commuting to leave time for household chores and are attracted to easily maintained condominiums, whether in the city or the suburbs (Rose, 1989). Still, then, for various reasons women do not commute as far as men.

Social Differences in Housing Occupancy

Social groups occupy different types of housing. Some "social" housing is provided to the needy (as discussed below), but most is allocated via the market, which allocates on the basis of price. Income differences determine what type of housing—and in what location—households can afford.

Owners, managers, and, to a lesser extent, middle-class professionals live in relatively large and well-equipped homes, and tend to own them. In Canada there is a strong tax incentive for home ownership. Unlike other assets, homes are exempt from capital gains tax. For this and other reasons, across Canada in 2009 the average homeowner received seven times the government subsidy of the average tenant; in Ontario, total subsidies to homeowners were four times greater than expenditures on social housing (Clayton, 2010). Not surprisingly, then, except for those who move often or who find property maintenance burdensome, households prefer to buy. Since they can afford to, most owners and managers do in fact own their own homes. Home ownership rates among blue-collar workers are lower, although higher than their income might suggest: workers have especially strong aspirations to own their own home.

Vulnerable to layoff, with little control over their work environment and with manual skills, they view the home as a source of financial security and a place of personal autonomy (Harris, 2003). Those with the lowest incomes, including the unskilled and welfare poor, occupy the worst, typically rental, accommodation. Some districts of such housing are badly deteriorated. Slums that result in housing abandonment, however, are uncommon in Canada.

Differences in the housing situation of men and women began to receive serious attention in the 1980s (McClain and Doyle, 1983). In the 1950s, most adults lived in husband-wife households so that men and women occupied the same dwellings. The home meant something different to each: women experienced it as a domestic workplace and perhaps as a showplace for homemaking talents, while men viewed it as a haven from work and sometimes as a DIY project (Strong-Boag, 1991; Strong-Boag, England and Johnson, 1999). But both lived in the same structure. With rising divorce rates and more single-parent households, mostly headed by women, this is no longer true. An increasing proportion of households living below the poverty line, typically in poor-quality rental housing, are headed by women (Rose and Wexler, 1993; Watson, 1986).

Immigrants and ethnic minorities also differ in their housing situation. In the past—although not always today—immigrants had low incomes and occupied modest housing. They brought a strong desire to establish themselves in their adopted country, and tolerated crowding to save capital to acquire property. As a result, until the 1990s immigrants were more likely than the native-born to own their own home. Over the past two decades, however, immigrants have fared worse in the job markets, and by the 2000s their home-ownership edge had disappeared (Haan, 2005). Even so, by saving money by pooling resources in large households, they are able to improve their owner-ship position rapidly, year by year. In Hamilton, Ontario, in 2001 for example, only 26 per cent of recent immigrants (those who arrived 1996–2001) owned their own home. Those who emigrated

between 1991 and 1995 were in a better position (48 per cent), while those who came to Canada before 1985 had a higher home-ownership rate (72 per cent) than the Canadian-born (69 per cent) (Schellenberg, 2004). The same pattern was apparent across the country (Hiebert, 2009). Even refugees are able to substantially improve their housing conditions and ownership position within three years of arrival (Carter, Polevychok, and Osborne, 2009).

But generalizing can be misleading. Some recent immigrants, notably those from Hong Kong, are in fact affluent. Some groups, including Italians and Portuguese, have attached special value to home ownership. Observers have suggested that there is a cultural difference between Canada's two "charter" groups and that Montreal once had a lower home-ownership rate than Toronto because French-Canadians did not value home ownership. Research has challenged this view (Choko and Harris, 1990), but, in general, cultural as well as economic factors influence the types of housing people aspire to and occupy.

The Meaning and Uses of the Home

Once built and occupied, houses acquire meaning. Consumers use material goods like houses to construct and express their identities, and to signal their membership in socially distinct groups (Bourdieu, 1984; Jackson, 1999; Miller, 1987). Dwellings are important in this regard because they are valuable and permanently visible. Front exteriors present the social self; interiors embody personal traits, especially for women (Belk, 1988; Leslie and Reimer, 2003; Sadella, Verschure, and Burroughs, 1987). The balance has shifted as the home has become more important for recreation. Indeed, gas barbeques and swimming pools testify to the recreational uses of the back yard, while radio, television, computers, and the Internet have made home leisure more attractive. Homes have grown and developed new rooms, in part to house this technology (Simon and Holdsworth, 1993). As feminists have emphasized, however, the home is also important as a place of work.

Unpaid Work

The home has always been a workplace, especially for women (Bradbury, 1993; MacKenzie and Rose, 1983). Running a household takes work; people, clothes, floors, and dishes have to be kept (fairly) clean. Food has to be bought, and sometimes cooked. Moreover, children create additional tasks: changing diapers, teaching, ferrying, and consoling. It is true that some technologies have reduced the amount of housework done in the home: doing the wash by hand, or fetching water from a well, took time. But the differences between past and present may be overstated (Cowan, 1983). Today, there is more to keep clean: single-detached homes built in the 2000s were over 50 per cent larger than those built in the years 1946–60, even though households have declined in size, from an average of 3.9 persons in 1961 to 2.1 in 2001 (but assume a rising trend to 2.5 in 2011). As well, appliances have raised standards—of cleanliness and culinary expertise—and created new work. Dishwashers must be bought and maintained. Automobiles have encouraged us to build at lower densities, and sprawl compels us to buy and maintain cars in order to live. Today we spend less time cleaning, but more time shopping, than our parents. To consume more than earlier generations we have to work hard.

Unpaid work is also performed *on* the home, chiefly by men. As late as the 1950s, many families built homes with their own hands (Harris, 2004). Today, more modest DIY projects are common. Some maintenance is carried out by almost every household, including tenants when their landlords offer rent discounts (Krohn, Fleming, and Manzer, 1977), but owner-occupiers have the greatest opportunities and incentives to do such work. Many buyers hope that DIY will save them money, build capital, and allow self-expression. Then, too, ownership can change people's lifestyle, encouraging DIY as part of a more home-centred life (Michelson, 1977: 268–9).

Paid Work

The home has also been a place of paid employment. Historically, many women earned income by taking in lodgers. Recently, other types of home employment have increased. Licensed daycare has lagged behind the number of young mothers in the labour force, so many children go to home daycare, part of the underground economy (MacKenzie and Truelove, 1993). There has also been a resurgence of industrial "homework," especially in the garment industry in Toronto and Montreal, while technology has made possible new types of home employment. The recent growth of small businesses, many run out of the home, has been supplemented by telework. In 2000, 10.2 per cent of employees did at least some of their work from home (on average, eight hours a week), as did 50 per cent of the self-employed. By 2008 these percentages had increased to 11.2 per cent and 60 per cent, respectively (Turcotte, 2011). Combined, the number of teleworkers had risen to 3.5 million.

Homeworkers place new demands on homes and on neighbourhoods. Many alter homes to accommodate work needs, typically by improving lighting and wiring (Gurstein, 1995: 34). Almost a third of respondents to a survey in 1994 had renovated existing space, while 12 per cent had added a new room for home-based work purposes. Use of neighbourhood facilities also changed. Home-based workers make more use of post offices and copy centres, while many contravene local zoning regulations. In terms of public health and safety, paid work in the home is a growing issue.

Work at home is part of a gender division of labour. Since the nineteenth century, men have commuted, and worked *on* the home, while women have laboured *in* it, whether for love or for money. This pattern is weakening, but does persist. Even though women spend a good deal of time working outside the home, surveys show that they continue to do most of the housework, even in households where both adults work full-time (Armstrong and Armstrong, 1994; Michelson, 1984). In 2010, for example, in dual earner households women did 13.9 hours of unpaid housework a week while men did 8.6 hours; those caring for children spent 50 hours and 27.2 hours a week, respectively (Milan, Keown, and Urquijo, 2011). More than men, women juggle work to accommodate domestic responsibilities (Hanson and Pratt, 1995). Some are attracted to teleworking for this reason: in the mid-1990s women made up about 45 per cent of the labour force but 55 per cent of those who worked for pay at home (Gurstein, 1995: 12). The persistence of differences between men and women is nowhere more apparent than in the use of the home.

A Geographical Perspective

Especially in Canada, it can be misleading to generalize about housing. True, Canadians occupy some of the best, and best-equipped, housing in the world: almost all urban dwellings are structurally sound and can boast piped water, electricity, and central heating. But the form these houses take, and how much they cost, varies greatly from place to place.

The Uniqueness of Each Place

The size of Canada, and the immobility of housing, guarantees that housing market conditions vary enormously from place to place (Bourne and Bunting, 1993). A local shortage cannot be met from a surplus elsewhere, especially since most major urban areas are beyond commuting distance of one another. This affects vacancies, rents, and house prices. Across metropolitan areas, rental vacancy rates averaged 2.5 per cent in 2011, but ranged from a low of 1.1 per cent in Kingston, Winnipeg, and Guelph to a high of 8.1 per cent in Windsor (CMHC, 2012). House prices are also variable and often out of sync. Prices in Calgary, for example, rose rapidly during the OPEC-induced oil boom of the 1970s and slumped in the early 1980s; in Toronto and southern Ontario, prices boomed in the prosperous 1980s, but dropped sharply in the early 1990s; in Montreal, they were depressed for a generation after the Parti Québécois's first victory in 1976. Recently, economic growth and low interest rates have pushed prices up everywhere. Five-year mortgage rates fell from 9 per cent in 1995 to 7 per cent in 2002, and by March 2013 had reached 2.99 per cent. The result was a sellers' market, as indicated by the high ratio of sales to new listings on the Multiple Listings Service (Figure 19.4). Canada-wide MLS house prices increased 111 per cent between 2001 and 2011 (CMHC, 2012). But this nation-wide boom has been

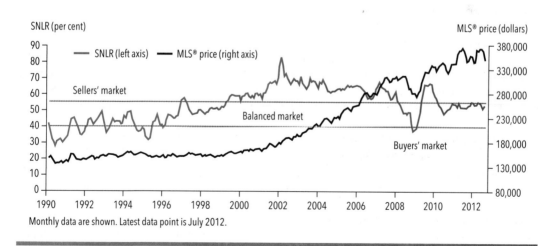

Monthly data are shown. Latest data point is July 2012.

Figure 19.4 **The Rise of a Seller's Market in Urban Housing since 1990**

Source: Canada Mortgage and Housing Corporation (CMHC). Data from the Canadian Real Estate Association.

unusual, and average prices still vary widely from place to place: they are currently twice as high in Vancouver as in Montreal. Single-industry towns have the most volatile housing markets, but even the largest centres are susceptible to price variations, booms, and busts.

The progression of European settlement in Canada has helped distinguish urban housing submarkets. Eastern cities have the highest proportion of older housing, developed before the automobile, and hence a higher proportion of dense, multi-occupancy housing with higher levels of tenancy. In western cities, neighbourhoods of single-detached homes may be found close to the **central business district (CBD)**. As each city was settled by different immigrants, varying architectural styles predominated. Nineteenth century Montrealers, for example, favoured "plexes," superimposed dwellings with separate entrances; Torontonians favoured gabled row houses style; while Vancouverites drew on California bungalow and British "Tudorbethan" models (Holdsworth, 1977). The historical geography of the country helped create a unique housing stock, and different housing markets, in each centre.

Generic Differences between Places

If each place is unique, some geographical variations are generic, being specific to certain types of places. The most basic difference is that between rural and urban areas. Urban land is more expensive than rural, and so urban housing requires a high proportion of residents' incomes, is less likely to be owner-occupied, and includes more multi-family dwellings. In 2001 the home ownership rate was lower in **census metropolitan areas (CMAs)** (61 per cent) than in smaller urban centres (68 per cent), and much lower than in rural areas and places with a population of less than 10,000 (76 per cent). Contrasts in the proportion of multi-unit dwellings—respectively 52, 36, and 18 per cent—were even more striking.

The difference between urban and rural housing is one of degree, and suburbs lie in between. During the 1960s, proportionately more apartments were built in Canadian than in US suburbs, but even in this country suburbs contain a relatively high proportion of detached, owner-occupied homes (Harris, 2004: Chapter 2). This is due to lower land prices and the fact that postwar suburbs developed when incomes were relatively high. City–suburban differences in home ownership are associated with variations in the uses to which the home is put. Owners do more unpaid work around the home than tenants, partly because they are more likely to have children, and are more likely to become active in the community (Cox, 1982). Generic differences between city and suburban housing are bound up with different ways of life.

Because of urban–rural differences, urbanization affected the types of housing that Canadians occupied until the trend tapered off in the 1970s.[1] Urbanization raised the proportion of multi-unit structures during the 1920s and 1960s and depressed the level of owner-occupation, although this was counteracted by rising incomes and the suburban trend. In Canada as a whole, the home-ownership rate fell from 66 per cent to 62 per cent between 1951 and 1981. Since then, it has rebounded to 68.4 per cent in 2006 (Figure 19.2). This recent trend reflects the popularity of condominiums, which enable households to own real estate in multi-unit structures. Across all CMAs, one-third of dwellings completed in 2011 were condo units, the share being highest in the largest centres, notably Toronto (51 per cent), Montreal (56 per cent), and Vancouver (58 per cent) (CMHC, 2012). A significant minority of condo units are bought speculatively and rented out, but most are owner-occupied and are helping to transform the geography of housing tenure in Canadian cities.

After 1945, suburban development eroded the character of each place. Everywhere, suburbs looked much the same: the generic term *suburbia* first appeared in the *Globe and Mail* in 1946 (Harris, 2004). A new National Building Code, the growth of municipal planning and of large land developers, and the popularity of ranch and split-level styles produced a standard environment (Relph, 1987). Today, much of Mississauga and Kingston Township in Ontario and Richmond, BC, look alike. Since the 1970s, however, neo-historical styles have become increasingly popular (Harris and Dostrovsky, 2008). These draw on local and regional architectural traditions: in Toronto, more "Victorian" homes date from the late twentieth than from the late nineteenth century. Beneath the surface variety, however, methods of land development have become more streamlined than ever.

Housing and the State

In Canada, housing is produced by the private sector and mostly owned by private corporations or individuals, but its character and use are profoundly influenced by the state. The rights associated with owner-occupation and tenancy, for example, are defined by government and enforced in the courts. And, through political lobbying, they can be changed, as is illustrated by the continuing evolution of tenant law and the creation of condominium and co-operative tenures.

The Growth, and Faltering, of Government Activity

All three levels of government have played a growing role in the housing market over the past century. Municipalities were the first to become involved because they were most directly affected by poor conditions. Industrial urbanization, coupled with low wages, led to overcrowding and poor sanitation; infectious diseases threatened everyone, including the middle class; frame construction led to serious fires. From after World War II, municipalities began to control the way houses were built, maintained, and occupied (Hodge and Gordon, 2008). Suburbs, especially those of immigrants and workers, adopted controls slowly, but most had done so by the 1950s.

After 1900, municipalities also took control of land use. Once, land was developed piecemeal, with stores or small factories built in residential areas. The value of a fine home, as a result, might be undermined by a neighbour's shack or warehouse. Subdividers perceived a demand for

subdivisions where undesirable users were prohibited. They used legal covenants to prohibit certain uses or building materials and, sometimes, specific residents. On the west coast, the Chinese were targeted; down east, African-Canadians; frequently, Jews (Harris, 2004). In 1948, the Supreme Court declared ethnic covenants illegal, and in the same period the provinces began to require municipalities to develop systematic land use plans. Recently, these have been supplemented again by private covenants, although not as commonly as in the US (Filion and Alexander, 1994). Some are associated with **common interest developments (CID)**, where, rather like condominiums, buyers acquire a stake in (and responsibility for) shared facilities as well as their own unit. Especially on the west coast, some are age-restricted for retirees; a few are gated (Grant, 2005; see Grant and Filion, Chapter 17). The CID trend may continue as the proportion of households headed by people aged 65+ rises from 21 per cent in 2006 to a projected level of 31 per cent in 2026.

Everywhere, municipal zoning controls how land parcels may be used (Hodge and Gordon, 2013). However, these regulations are not always followed. In older districts, "nonconforming" uses persist. Anywhere, zoning may be changed if developers or local residents make a strong case. Such changes require public hearings, an everyday staple of grass-roots politics. Just as significant as overt controls are implicit biases in property taxes and development charges that favour single-family as opposed to multi-family dwellings, and suburban sprawl over urban redevelopment (Blais, 2010). Some of the most important effects of policy, such as those of property taxation and infrastructure funding, are unintended.

Permanent federal involvement in housing dates from the Great Depression (Bacher, 1993; Harris, 2004). In 1935, the government passed a Dominion Housing Act (DHA) that provided insured, amortized mortgage loans to boost demand for the building industry; most buyers were affluent (Belec, 1997). In 1946, the Canadian Mortgage and Housing Corporation (CMHC) was created in order to administer federal policy.

Its mortgage loan activity has shaped suburban development ever since (Poapst, 1993; Pomeroy and Falvo, 2013; Walks, 2013).

Unlike the US, Canada did not build public housing during the Depression, and only in 1964 did it make the financing of this type of housing attractive enough for provinces to participate. In the next five years, there was a short boom in public housing construction, that is, of subsidized rental accommodation owned by public agencies (Patterson, 1993). Units for seniors were well received but those for families were opposed. Large schemes exacerbated social problems and attracted stigma, especially those that housed visible minorities. In Toronto, blacks at first occupied only 4 per cent of units managed by the Metro Toronto Housing Authority (Murdie, 1994). By 1986, the figure had soared to 27 per cent, five times this group's proportion of the Toronto population. By the early 1970s, opposition, and high unit costs, led to the federal program's demise (Patterson, 1993).

In the early 1970s, innovative programs encouraged the rehabilitation of existing housing and the construction of new types of social housing, chiefly co-operatives and municipal non-profits (Patterson, 1993). (Social housing refers to units subsidized for lower-income households.) In co-ops, ownership is shared and projects are often socially mixed. Since most co-ops were built in older, mixed neighbourhoods, they avoided social stigma (Skelton, 1994). However, project mix reduced the number of low-income families housed. In the late 1980s, the federal government reduced support for social housing and in 1993 froze funding for new projects, except on First Nations reserves (Pomeroy and Falvo, 2013). Few provincial governments picked up the slack, and Ontario devolved responsibility for project management to municipalities. Commonly, the construction of social housing virtually ceased (Carter, 1997; Shapcott, 2004; Wolfe, 1998). In Hamilton, Ontario, for example, no units were built between 1996 and 2003 (Hamilton, 2004: 37–9).

One consequence of funding cuts was the growth of homelessness, broadly defined (see Walks, Chapter 9). Many of those who are not on the street are, nevertheless, housed precariously. Without a place of their own, they surf the couches of friends and extended kin (Peters, 2012). Rates of homelessness are highest among the mentally disabled and among Aboriginal Canadians. Deinstitutionalized in the 1970s, many with mental disabilities have had to fend for themselves, comprising a large proportion of people on the street or in prison (Schiff, Schiff and Schneider, 2010). Aboriginal people are not much better off. In 2008, they comprised 2.5 per cent of Calgary's population but 36 per cent of its visible homeless (Belanger, Head, and Awosoga, 2012: 30). They made up 15 per cent of the homeless population in Toronto, 30 per cent in Ottawa, 80 per cent in Regina, and 95 per cent in Yellowknife. In part for this reason, in 1999 the federal government developed a National Homelessness Initiative. In 2000, social housing programs were reframed as an Affordable Housing Initiative (AHI) that avoided long-term subsidies or financial commitments (Pomeroy and Falvo, 2013). The federal government committed $680 million over five years for affordable housing; in 2003 the government raised this to $1 billion. Following the financial crisis in 2008, additional funds were earmarked as part of Canada's Economic Action Plan. Substantial commitments were made to affordable housing, to a home renovation tax credit, and in assistance for municipal infrastructure (Pomeroy and Falvo, 2013). By 2012, 51,843 affordable units had been funded under the AHI, accounting for about 3 per cent of housing starts during the 2000s (CMHC, 2012: 5-3).

To access federal funds, provinces entered cost-sharing agreements, with varying consequences. Quebec and BC acted promptly, but, even under Liberal governments, other provinces lagged, including Ontario (Hackworth, 2008). Overall, although Canadians pride themselves on their social safety net, their governments have built and subsidized less social housing than those of most other industrialized nations—including the United States (Harris, 2000; Shapcott, 2004).

The Purposes and Consequences of Housing Policy

In Canada, the main purposes of housing policy have been economic, a fact implied in the naming of CMHC: it is a "corporation" concerned as much with "mortgages" as with housing. This is not surprising. Building 10,000 new homes creates 19,337 person-years of work, including 10,533 in construction and 3087 in manufacturing (CMHC, 2010: 19). Federal policy has consistently sought to strengthen the private sector, including corporate land development (Bacher, 1993; Hackworth, 2008). Actions during the 1930s were designed primarily to revive the building industry and facilitate mortgage lending. The first president of CMHC had been an executive at Sun Life. After 1945, policies favoured large developers over small builders, and financial institutions over individual lenders, although the latter held half of all mortgage debt into the early 1950s (Harris, 2004). CMHC has consistently made a profit from its mortgage operations (Shapcott, 2004). However, it arguably received a bailout in 2008 and may be troubled if the current housing bubble bursts (Pomeroy and Falvo, 2013; Walks, 2013).

The market bias of policy is a mixed blessing. It has helped produce safe, energy-efficient, and roomy housing for most Canadians, but at a price: the promotion of mortgages has created a nation of indebted consumers living in low-density suburban homes. This has boosted demand for other goods (Belec, Holmes, and Rutherford, 1987), with unfortunate environmental and health consequences. Policy has also been socially regressive, notably through the subsidies to owner-occupation (Clayton, 2010; Steele, 1993). Moreover, housing policy has not been an important part of Canada's social safety net, neglecting many of those who cannot help themselves. Past policy biases towards home ownership rather than social housing have become self-perpetuating. Most Canadian households own their own home and would resist any attack on the subsidies they enjoy. Indeed, periodically, conservative politicians promise new subsidies, although economists deplore the idea. The constituency for the status quo is both numerous and powerful.

Current Issues

Currently, three issues dominate the public debate about housing in Canada: (1) conditions for the mentally disabled and for Aboriginal people; (2) the real estate boom of the 2000s, which threatens affordability and financial stability, turning dreams to nightmares; and (3) effects on the environment and on health.

Until the 1950s, the housing problem was one of poor housing conditions and overcrowding. Since then, municipal regulations have raised standards of construction and maintenance. Today, disabled and Aboriginal peoples are the only groups who commonly experience substandard or crowded housing, a fact dramatized by media coverage of conditions in Attawapiskat, and by the "Idle No More" movement in 2012–13. In 2001, only 2.5 per cent of the units occupied by non-Aboriginal households was inadequate (in need of major repairs), and 1.4 per cent failed the National Occupancy Standard (NOS) (CMHC, 2004).[2] The equivalent ratios for Aboriginal households off reserves were 6.8 and 4.9 per cent, respectively; for those on reserves the proportions were 22.5 and 10.3 per cent (see Peters, Chapter 21).

Mostly, however, the key issue is affordability. For individual households, the greatest challenge is felt by tenants and those on low incomes. **Core housing need** exists when a household must spend at least 30 per cent of before-tax income for an adequate, uncrowded dwelling. According to this criterion, 13.5 per cent of all urban Canadian households were in need in 2009, a proportion that remained stable over a decade (CMHC, 2012: 5–12). At 20.4 per cent in 2006, however, the incidence of need among Aboriginal people was almost double that of other Canadians (Belanger, Head, and Awosoga, 2012). Among tenants in the lowest-income quintile, the incidence of core housing need in 2009 was 60.5 per cent; on average, they paid 38.7 per cent of their income in rent (CMHC, 2012: 5–11). The equivalent ratios for homeowners in the same income quintile, many of whom were elderly persons with no mortgages, was 40.4 per cent and 27.5 per cent, respectively.

In the longer run, affordability issues and the high level of indebtedness of homeowners may pose a larger economic problem. The level of household debt has risen steadily since the 1980s, exceeding an unprecedented 160 per cent of **gross domestic product (GDP)** by 2010 (Walks, 2013). Exceptionally low interest rates have kept manageable the level of personal debt as a proportion of disposable income (CMHC, 2012). But if the economy stalls, if house prices dip, as many believe they will, and if interest rates rise, as they will eventually, many borrowers, lenders, and the CMHC, as the country's largest insurer of mortgage debt, may be in trouble. As the world learned in 2008, the fallout from a burst house price bubble affects everyone.

Canadians have viewed larger houses as a sign of progress, but researchers now challenge this view. Oil price increases in the early 1970s made energy costs an issue. The federal government funded a short-lived program to promote energy conservation in existing dwellings; in 1973, this criterion was added to the National Building Code; in 1981 the National Home Builders' Association and National Resources Canada initiated the "R2000" building program for new homes, which has helped make house-builders unusually effective in limiting **greenhouse gas emissions** (Canadian Home Builders' Association, 2012; 2013). Today, international awareness of the links between energy consumption and global warming has grown. Oil and gas are the main fuels used for home heating, and home energy consumption is an environmental issue. A federal program offers property owners loans and grants to improve energy efficiency. But most Canadian dwellings are detached and, per cubic metre, these use 80 per cent more energy than those in multi-unit structures. High-rise condominiums, and **New Urbanist** suburbs that include row dwellings, are more environmentally friendly, but carbon emissions will remain a housing-related issue in Canadian cities (Gordon and Tamminga, 2002; Grant, 2006; see Senbel and Lesnikowski, Chapter 13).

Large homes and reliance on the automobile are associated with low-density suburban development. Lately, we have learned that they bring with them health and environmental problems (Frumkin, Frank and Jackson, 2004). Homes and subdivisions save effort: we drive to the store for a carton of milk; order fast food from the driver's seat; and change channels from the couch. As a result, Canadians do less, eat more, and grow fatter, on average, by the year, raising the incidences of heart disease and other health problems. Such issues can be mitigated, however, through urban design that promotes walking, cycling, and public transit. Such change requires higher densities and will affect the size and type of dwellings that are built (see Senbel and Lesnikowski, Chapter 13). Apart from building more affordable and energy-efficient housing, Canadians will have to change their expectations. Less is sometimes more.

Review Questions

1. How did the meaning and uses of the home evolve over time? How did this evolution reflect Canadian value and lifestyle changes?
2. What have been the main stages of housing policy evolution in Canada? What is the present trajectory of this evolution?
3. Who is most advantaged and disadvantaged by present housing market trends in Canada?

Notes

1. The number of people living in cities continues to grow, but the proportion has changed little since the 1970s.
2. The definition of the NOS is complex. See CMHC (2012: 5–16).

Recommended Websites

Canadian Housing and Renewal Association (CHRA)
www.chra-achru.ca/en/

Canada Mortgage and Housing Corporation (CMHC)
www03.cmhc-schl.gc.ca/catalog/home.cfm?lang=en&fr=
1363812019812

Canadian Real Estate Association (CREA)
www.crea.ca/

References

Armstrong, P., and H. Armstrong. 1994. *The Double Ghetto*, 3rd edn. Toronto: McClelland & Stewart.

Bacher, J. 1993. *Keeping to the Marketplace: The Evolution of Canadian Housing Policy*. Montreal and Kingston: McGill-Queen's University Press.

Belanger, Y., G.W. Head, O. Awosoga. 2012. *Assessing urban aboriginal housing and homelessness in Canada*. Ottawa: National Association of Friendship Centres and the Office of the Federal Interlocutor for Métis and Non-Status Indians. At: www.homelesshub.ca/Library/Assessing-Urban-Aboriginal-Housing-and-Homelessness-in-Canada-54375.aspx

Belec, J. 1997. "The Dominion Housing Act," *Urban History Review* 25 (2): 53–62.

———, J. Holmes, and T. Rutherford. 1987. "The rise of Fordism and the transformation of consumption norms: Mass consumption and housing in Canada, 1930–1945," in R. Harris and G. Pratt, eds., *Social Class and Housing Tenure*. Gavle, Sweden: National Swedish Institute for Building Research.

Belk, R. 1988. "Possessions and the extended self," *Journal of Consumer Research* 15: 139–68.

Blais, P. 2010. *Perverse Cities: Hidden Subsidies, Wonky Policy, and Urban Sprawl*. Vancouver: UBC Press.

Bourdieu, P. 1984. *Distinction. A Social Critique of the Judgment of Taste*. London: Routledge Kegan Paul.

Bourne, L.S. 1981. *The Geography of Housing*. London: Edward Arnold.

———, and T. Bunting. 1993. "Housing provision, residential development and neighbourhood dynamics," in L.S. Bourne and D. Ley, eds., *The Social Geography of Canadian Cities*. Montreal and Kingston: McGill-Queen's University Press.

Bradbury, B. 1993. *Working Families: Age, Gender, and Daily Survival in Industrializing Montreal*. Toronto: McClelland & Stewart.

Brown, L.A., and E.G. Moore. 1970. "The intra-urban migration process: A perspective," *Geografiska Annaler* 28: 1–13.

Buzzelli, M. 2001. "Firm size structure in North American housebuilding. Persistent deconcentration, 1945–98," *Environment and Planning A* 33: 533–50.

Canada Mortgage and Housing Corporation. 2004. *2001 Census Housing Series Issue 6: Aboriginal Households*.

Research Highlight. Socio-Economic Series 04-036. Ottawa: CMHC. At: www.cmhc-schl.gc.ca:50104/b2c/b2c/init.do?language=en

———. 2010. "Housing and the Economy," in *Canadian Housing Observer*. Ottawa: CMHC. At: www.cmhc.ca/en/corp/about/cahoob/upload/chapter2_housing_economy_2010.pdf (last accessed 20 March 2013).

———. 2012. *Canadian Housing Observer*. Ottawa: CMHC. At: www.cmhc.ca/en/corp/about/cahoob/cahoob_001.cfm

Canadian Home Builders' Association (CHBA). 2003. *The Need for Action. Pre-Budget Submission*. Ottawa: CHBA.

———. 2012. *Recognizing the Residential Sector's Contribution to Greenhouse Gas Reduction*. Ottawa: CHBA. At: http://chba.ca/uploads/policy%20archive/2012/Housing%20and%20Canada%27s%20GHG%20Emission%20Targets.pdf

———. 2013. *Welcome Home to R2000*. Ottawa: CHBA. At: www.chba.ca/r-2000.aspx

Carter, T. 1997. "Current practices for procuring affordable housing. The Canadian context," *Housing Policy Debate* 8: 593–631.

Carter, T.S., C. Polevychok, and J. Osborne. 2009. "The role of housing and neighborhood in the re-settlement process. A case study of refugee households in Winnipeg," *The Canadian Geographer* 53: 305–22.

Choko, M., and R. Harris. 1990. "The local culture of property: A comparative history of housing tenure in Montreal and Toronto," *Annals of the Association of American Geographers* 80: 73–95.

Clark, S.D. 1966. *The Suburban Society*. Toronto: University of Toronto Press.

Clayton Research Associates. 1988. *The Changing Housing Industry in Canada, 1946–2001*. Ottawa: CMHC. At: www.chba.ca/uploads/Policy%20Archive/1988/1988-ChangingIndustry.pdf

Clayton, F.A. 2010. *Government Subsidies to Homeowners versus Renters in Ontario and Canada*. At: www.cfaa-fcapi.org/pd2/Submission.Supplementary_Eng.pdf

Cowan, R. 1983. *More Work for Mother: The Ironies of Household Technology from the Open Hearth to the Microwave*. New York: Basic Books.

Cox, K. 1982. "Housing tenure and neighborhood activism," *Urban Affairs Quarterly* 18: 107–29.

Fallis, G. 1993. "Postwar Changes in the Supply-Side of Housing," in Miron (1993a).

Filion, P., and M. Alexander. 1994. "Restrictive covenants: Hidden obstacles," *Plan Canada* 35 (1): 33–7.

Foot, D., and D. Stoffman. 1996. *Boom, Bust, and Echo: How to Profit from the Coming Demographic Shift*. Toronto: Macfarlane, Walter and Ross.

Frumkin, H., L. Frank, and R. Jackson. 2004. *Urban Sprawl and Public Health. Designing, Planning and Building for Healthy Communities*. Washington, DC: Island Press.

Gordon, D., and K. Tamminga. 2002. "Large-scale traditional neighborhood development and pre-emptive ecosystem planning. The Markham experience, 1989–2001," *Journal of Urban Design* 7: 321–40.

Grant, J. 2005. "Planning responses to gated communities in Canada," *Housing Studies* 20: 273–85.

———. 2006. *Planning the Good Community: New Urbanism in Theory and Practice*. New York: Routledge.

Gurstein, P. 1995. *Planning for Telework and Home-based Employment: A Canadian Survey on Integrating Work into Residential Environments*. Ottawa and Vancouver: CMHC and Centre for Human Settlements, University of British Columbia.

Haan, M. 2005. *The Decline of the Immigrant Homeownership Advantage. Life Cycle, Declining Fortunes and Changing Housing Careers in Montreal, Toronto and Vancouver, 1981–2001*. Ottawa: Statistics Canada. At: http://dspace.cigilibrary.org/jspui/bitstream/123456789/301/1/The%20Decline%20of%20the%20Immigrant%20Homeownership%20Advantage.pdf?

Hackworth, J. 2008. "The durability of roll-out neoliberalism under centre-left governance. The case of Ontario's social housing sector," *Studies in Political Economy* 81: 7–26.

Hamilton (City of). 2004. *Keys to the Home. A Housing Strategy for Hamilton*. Hamilton: The City. At: www.hamilton.ca/NR/rdonlyres/0ED608D0-7D8F-4CBF-83F5-B6B88102A689/0/KeystotheHome.pdf

Hanson, S., and G. Pratt. 1995. *Gender, Work, and Space*. New York: Routledge.

Harris, D.C. 2011. "Condominium and the city. The rise of property in Vancouver," *Law and Social Inquiry* 36: 694–726.

Harris, R. 1994. "The flexible house: The housing backlog and the persistence of lodging, 1891–1951," *Social Science History* 18: 31–53.

———. 2000. "More American than the United States: Housing in urban Canada in the twentieth century," *Journal of Urban History* 26: 456–78.

———. 2003. "The suburban worker in the history of labor," *International Labor and Working Class History* 64: 8–24.

———. 2004. *Creeping Conformity. How Canada Became Suburban, 1900–1960*. Toronto: University of Toronto Press.

———, and M. Buzzelli. 2003. "Small is transient. Housebuilding firms in Ontario, Canada 1978–1998," *Housing Studies* 18: 369–86.

———, and M. Buzzelli. 2005. "House building in the machine age, 1920s–1970s. Realities and perceptions of modernisation in North America and Australia," *Business History* 47 (1): 59–85.

———, and N. Dostrovsky. 2008. "The suburban culture of building and the reassuring revival of historicist architecture since 1970," *Home Cultures* 5: 167–96.

Hiebert, D. 2009. "Newcomers in the Canadian housing market. A longitudinal study, 2001–2005," *The Canadian Geographer* 53: 268–87.

Hodge, G. and D. Gordon. 2013. *Planning Canadian Communities*. Toronto: Nelson.

Holdsworth, D. 1977. "House and home in Vancouver: Images of West Coast urbanism, 1881–1929," in A.F.J. Artibise and G. Stelter, eds., *The Canadian City: Essays in Urban History*. Toronto: McClelland & Stewart.

Jackson, P. 1999. "Commodity cultures: The traffic in things," *Transactions, Institute of British Geographers* 24: 95–108.

Jarvis, H., A.C. Pratt, and P. Wu. 2001. *The Secret Life of Cities: The Social Reproduction of Everyday Life*. Harlow: Prentice Hall.

Kataure, V., and M. Walton-Roberts. 2013. "The housing preferences and location choices of second-generation South Asians living in ethnic enclaves," *South Asian Diaspora* 5 (1): 57–76.

Kern, L. 2010. *Sex and the Revitalized City. Gender, Condominium Development, and Urban Citizenship*. Vancouver: UBC Press.

Krohn, R.G., B. Fleming, and M. Manzer. 1977. *The Other Economy: The Internal Logic of Local Rental Housing*. Toronto: Peter Martin.

Lehrer, U., and T. Wieditz. 2009. "Condominium development and gentrification. The relationship between policies, building activities and socio-economic development in Toronto," *Canadian Journal of Urban Research* 18: 82–13.

Leslie, D., and S. Reimer. 2003. "Gender, modern design, and home consumption," *Environment and Planning D Society and Space* 21: 293–316.

Ley, D. 1997. *The New Middle Class and the Remaking of the Central City*. New York: Oxford University Press.

McClain, J. 1993. "Housing as a human service: Accommodating special needs," in J. Miron, ed., *House, Home and Community. Housing Progress in Canada since 1945*. Montreal and Kingston: McGill-Queen's University Press.

McClain, J., and C. Doyle. 1983. *Women as Housing Consumers*. Ottawa: Canada Mortgage and Housing Corporation.

McKellar, J. 1993. "Building technology and the production process," in J. Miron, ed., *House, Home and Community: Housing Progress in Canada since 1945*. Montreal and Kingston: McGill-Queen's University Press.

MacKenzie, S., and D. Rose. 1983. "Industrial change, the domestic economy and home life," in J. Anderson et al., eds., *Redundant Spaces in Cities and Regions*. London: Academic Press.

———, and M. Truelove. 1993. "Access to public services: The case of day care," in L.S. Bourne and D. Ley, eds., *The Social Geography of the Canadian City*. Montreal and Kingston: McGill-Queen's University Press.

Michelson, W. 1977. *Environmental Choice, Human Behavior and Residential Satisfaction*. New York: Oxford University Press.

——. 1984. *From Sun to Sun: Daily Obligations and Community Structure in the Lives of Employed Mothers and Their Families*. Totowa, NJ: Rowman and Allanheld.

Milan, A., L-A. Keown, and C.R. Urquijo. 2011. *Families, Living Arrangements and Unpaid Work*. Ottawa: Statistics Canada. At: www.statcan.gc.ca/pub/89-503-x/2010001/article/11546-eng.pdf

Miller, D. 1987. *Material Culture and Mass Consumption*. Oxford: Blackwell.

Miron, J. 1988. *Demographic Change, Household Formation and Housing Demand: Canada's Postwar Experience*. Montreal and Kingston: McGill-Queen's University Press.

——. 1993. "Demographic change, household formation and housing demand: Canada's postwar experience," in J. Miron, ed., *House, Home and Community. Housing Progress in Canada since 1945*. Montreal and Kingston: McGill-Queen's University Press.

Mitchell, B., and E.M. Gee. 1996. "Young adults returning home: Implications for social policy," in B. Galaway and J. Hudson, eds., *Youth in Transition: Perspectives on Research and Policy*. Toronto: Thompson.

Murdie, R.A. 1986. "Local strategies in resale home financing in the Toronto housing market," *Urban Studies* 28: 465–83.

——. 1994. "Blacks in near-ghettoes? Black visible minority population in Metropolitan Toronto Housing Authority public housing units," *Housing Studies* 9: 435–58.

Paterson, R. 1984. "The development of an interwar suburb: Kingsway Park, Etobicoke," *Urban History Review* 13: 225–35.

Patterson, J. 1993. "Housing and community development policies," in J. Miron, ed., *House, Home and Community. Housing Progress in Canada since 1945*. Montreal and Kingston: McGill-Queen's University Press.

Peters, E. 2012. "'I like to let them have their time.' Hidden homeless First Nations people in the city and their management of household relationships," *Social and Cultural Geography* 13: 321–38.

Poapst, J.V. 1993. "Financing of postwar housing," in J. Miron, ed., *House, Home and Community. Housing Progress in Canada since 1945*. Montreal and Kingston: McGill-Queen's University Press.

Pomeroy, S., and N. Falvo. 2013. "Pragmatism and political expediency: Housing policy under the Harper regime," in G.B. Doern and C. Stoney, eds., *How Ottawa Spends*. Kingston and Montreal: McGill-Queen's University Press.

Relph, E.C. 1987. *The Modern Urban Landscape*. Baltimore, MD: Johns Hopkins University Press.

Report of the President's Committee on Urban Housing (the Kaiser Committee). 1968. *A Decent Home*. Washington: President's Committee on Urban Housing.

Rose, D. 1989. "A feminist perspective on employment restructuring and gentrification: The case of Montreal," in J. Wolch and M. Dear, eds., *The Power of Geography: How Territory Shapes Social Life*. Boston, MA: Unwin Hyman.

——, and C. Le Bourdais. 1986. "Changing conditions of female single parenthood in Montreal's inner city and suburban neighborhoods," *Urban Resources* 3 (2): 45–52.

——, and M. Wexler. 1993. "Post-war social and economic changes and housing adequacy," in J. Miron, ed., *House, Home and Community. Housing Progress in Canada since 1945*. Montreal and Kingston: McGill-Queen's University Press.

Rowe, A. 1989. "Self-help housing provision: Production, consumption, accumulation and policy in Atlantic Canada," *Housing Studies* 4: 75–91.

Sadella, E.K., B. Verschure, and J. Burroughs. 1987. "Identity symbolism in housing," *Environment and Behavior* 19: 569–87.

Schellenberg, G. 2004. *Immigrants in Canada's Census Metropolitan Areas*. Ottawa: Statistics Canada. At: www.statcan.gc.ca/pub/89-613-m/2004003/4224946-eng.pdf

Schiff, R., J.W. Schiff, and B. Schneider. 2010. "Housing for the disabled mentally ill: Moving beyond homogeneity," *Canadian Journal of Urban Research* 19: 108–28.

Shapcott, M. 2004. "Where are we going? Recent federal and provincial housing policy," in J.D. Hulchanski and M. Shapcott, eds., *Finding Room: Policy Options for a Canadian Rental Housing Strategy*. Toronto: University of Toronto, Centre for Urban and Community Studies.

Simon, J., and D. Holdsworth. 1993. "Housing form and use of domestic space," in J. Miron, ed., *House, Home and Community. Housing Progress in Canada since 1945*. Montreal and Kingston: McGill-Queen's University Press.

Skelton, I. 1994. "The geographic distribution of social housing in Ontario, Canada: Comparing public housing and locally sponsored, third sector housing," *Housing Studies* 11: 189–206.

Statistics Canada. 2007. *Households and the Environment. Energy Use*. Ottawa: Statistics Canada. At: www.statcan.gc.ca/pub/11-526-s/11-526-s2010001-eng.pdf

Steele, M. 1993. "Incomes, prices and tenure choice," in J. Miron, ed., *House, Home and Community. Housing Progress in Canada since 1945*. Montreal and Kingston: McGill-Queen's University Press.

Strong-Boag, V. 1991. "Home dreams: Women and the suburban experiment in Canada, 1945–60," *Canadian Historical Review* 72: 471–504.

——, K. England, and L. Johnson. 1999. "What women's spaces? Women in Australian, British, Canadian and US suburbs," in R. Harris and P. Larkham, eds., *Changing Suburbs: Foundation, Form, and Function*. London: E and FN Spon.

TD Economics. 2013. *Toronto—a return to the core*. Toronto: TD Bank. At: www.td.com/document/PDF/economics/special/ff0113_toronto.pdf

Teixeira, C. 2006. "Residential experiences and the culture of suburbanization: A case study of Portuguese home-buyers in Mississauga," *Housing Studies* 22: 495–521.

Turcotte, M. 2011. *Working at home: An update*. Canadian Social Trends No. 91. Ottawa: Statistics Canada. At: www.statcan.gc.ca/pub/11-008-x/2011001/article/11366-eng.pdf

Walks, A. 2013. "Canada's housing bubble story: Mortgage securitization, the state and the global financial crisis," *International Journal of Urban and Regional Research* (forthcoming).

——, and R. Maaranen. 2008. "Gentrification, social mix, and social polarization: Testing the linkages in large Canadian cities," *Urban Geography* 29: 293–326.

Walton-Roberts, M., and D. Hiebert. 1997. "Immigration, entrepreneurship, and the family. Indo-Canadian entrepreneurship in the construction industry of Greater Vancouver," *Canadian Journal of Regional Science* 20: 119–40.

Watson, S. 1986. *Housing and Homelessness: A Feminist Perspective*. London: Routledge and Kegan Paul.

Weaver, J. 1978. "From land assembly to social maturity: The suburban life of Westdale (Hamilton), Ontario, 1911–1951," *Histoire sociale/Social History* 11: 411–40.

Wolfe, J. 1998. "Canadian housing policy in the 1990s," *Housing Studies* 13: 121–34.

Yakabuski, K. 2004. "Bob the builder," *Report on Business* October: 84–92, 94, 96.

Generational Change and the City: How Age Defines the Urban Landscape[1]

20

MARKUS MOOS

Introduction

"How old are you?" We have all been asked this question, perhaps most often when we were children or as young adults when buying beverages that have age restrictions. As we get older, some see it as impolite to ask somebody's age, and in job interviews doing so is even against the law. Sometimes the question is also used sarcastically when we see someone act in a manner that we think is "immature." In her article, "Act Your Age," sociologist Cheryl Laz (1998) describes how we hold specific expectations of the responsibilities and roles people should fill at different ages. What it means to be "old" or "young" differs across cultures and over time. In other words, Laz distinguishes between the biological and the social meanings of age (also see Pain and Hopkins, 2010). The biological experience of aging is important to consider as our needs for housing, infrastructure, amenities, and services change throughout our lives. But age also defines us socially, for instance by placing us into specific generations that are believed to have different values, preferences, and lifestyles. The social roles we tend to fill at particular ages shape where and how we reside and spend our time in the city. This chapter considers the importance and relevance of age, and the related concept of generation, in studying and understanding urban landscapes.

The chapter begins with an overview of how the cohort approach can be utilized as a method to study generational differences. It compares age groups in different time periods. The discussion considers the kinds of urban environments in which different generations grew up in Canada, followed by an analysis of the geographies of age and age segregation in the largest metropolitan areas. Ageism is discussed as a form of inequality. The chapter then focuses on young adults growing up in different time periods. It tracks changes in employment opportunities and housing decisions of different generations of young adults over time. The chapter ends with a discussion of planning for an aging society and considerations of age-friendly community design.

Generational Differences and the Cohort Approach

There is much discussion in the media today about generational differences. Writers often compare the baby boomers—born between the mid-1940s and 1960s—to Generation Y, or Millennials—born since the early 1980s—on work ethic, spending patterns, environmental values, and other characteristics. Such generational comparisons assume that each generation is distinguished from those preceding it because people in the same generation are confronted with "similar opportunities and constraints" (Carr, 2004: 453; Myers, 1999; Twenge, 2006). This assumption is the basis for the cohort approach, a common research method used in the social sciences, particularly in housing studies, economics, sociology, and demography (Ryder, 1965). Comparing people of the same age in different time periods is also a useful measure of changing standards of living (Osberg, 2003). The terms cohort and *generation* are often used interchangeably to refer to people born in the same time period (Riley, 1987).

Riley's (1987) description perhaps best elucidates the basis of the cohort approach. She explains two "dynamisms" that make aging a process of social change: First, since everyone ages there are necessarily "successive cohorts" aging together. Second, at any given time, societies, and their institutions, are composed of numerous "age strata." Riley describes how these two processes

can be visualized as a series of diagonal (cohorts) and horizontal (strata) lines in a two dimensional space of time (x-axis) and age (y-axis) (Figure 20.1). The implication is that as time passes, society and our cities change simply due to the "dynamisms of aging" (Riley, 1987: 4). As Riley (1987: 4) notes, "the people in a particular age strata are no longer the same people: they have been replaced by younger entrants from more recent cohorts, with more recent life experiences."

Younger cohorts replace older ones in the age strata and selectively transfer emerging behaviours into existing settings, such as the workplace, housing markets, or political institutions. Behaviours and trends that may have been seen as "deviant" or unconventional by one generation become socially acceptable by the next (Mills, 2004). Some of these

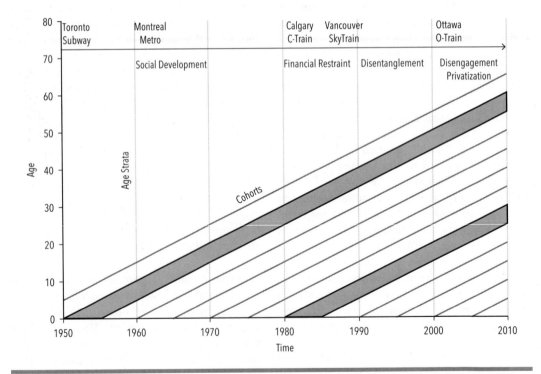

Figure 20.1   **Society as Composed of Age Strata and Cohorts**

Note: Society is composed of age strata, which consist of different cohorts that age together over time (e.g., green shading indicates two generations aging over time). Each cohort experiences unique challenges–for instance, different housing policy contexts (Carroll and Jones, 2000)–and opportunities–for instance, the availability of new public transportation systems.

Source: Based on Riley (1987).

behaviours will alter the **urban form** as new generations have different ideas about where to live and how to get around the city than previous ones. But it also means that different generations are presented with unique challenges. For instance, Figure 20.1 shows four characterizations of the housing policy context in Canada during different time periods, ranging from heavy investment in housing as part of "social development" in the 1960s to subsequently decreasing levels of support and eventual "disengagement and privatization" during the 1990s and 2000s (Carroll and Jones, 2000: 279; see Harris, Chapter 19). As a result, someone looking for housing in the 2000s would encounter higher prices, more condominium apartments, and less government support for assisted housing than someone did in the 1960s. Another example, also shown in Figure 20.1, is transit investment that happens over time so that different generations have different transportation options available to them.

Generational differences are also highly context specific because they are contingent upon the pace of societal change itself (Constable, 1996). In other words, if society changes more slowly, succeeding generations will be more similar than if society changes very quickly. Generational differences are not new. But some have argued that because of rapid changes in technology and social and economic organization in recent years, a period that Giddens (1984) calls "high modernity," generational differences are more amplified than in the past (Furlong and Cartmel, 2007). Two people, one born in 1880 and the other in 1900, experienced cities differently, but the difference is arguably even larger between one born in 1980 and the other in 2000. As Ryder (1965: 855) argued, "In an epoch of change, each person is dominated by his birth date. He derives his philosophy from his historical world, the subculture of his cohort."

However, a growing diversity of **life courses** may also render age a somewhat less useful criterion in understanding socio-spatial differentiation (see Townshend and Walker, Chapter 7). The social construction of the life cycle leads us to associate young adulthood with getting married and having children, which sociologists refer to as "transition markers" (Calvert, 2010). But the decline of traditional norms regarding family formation and marriage, growing educational attainment, and young adults' own changing and varying perception of adulthood question any universality the markers may have held. This "destandardization argument" does remain subject to debate since some scholars suggest that it is a delay in the attainment of markers rather than an increase in the diversity of life courses that is occurring (see Calvert, 2010: 9; Elchardus and Smits, 2006; Shanahan, 2000). Even if our social roles are less connected to age today, not fitting societal expectations remains a source of exclusion as preconceptions remain regarding what someone "should be doing" at a given age (Laz, 1998).

One issue with comparing generations is that doing so can have the unintended effect of overlooking other changes that differentiate society over time, for instance the growth in global migration patterns that has increased the share of immigrants in Canada (see Kobayashi and Preston, Chapter 8). Aging and generational differences help to define the city, but we need to acknowledge that they are not the only factors that determine the characteristics of urban space. Even though not everyone within a generation necessarily has the same history (Pred, 1984)—for instance, having grown up in different places or having been brought up with different values—comparing generations over time is useful because it helps us understand how people's decisions are shaped and constrained by a particular urban and societal context (McDaniel, 2004). For example, unlike an individual born in the 1980s, someone born in the 1950s in Vancouver would not have been able to choose a residential location based on the presence of rapid transit (Figure 20.1). Changing housing policies and transportation contexts shape location and commuting decisions of different cohorts in unique ways.

Growing Up in the City

The theory of generational change suggests that our preferences and values are shaped—at least in part—by the context within which we grow up.

Studies have shown links between our residential experiences as children and our residential preferences as adults (Blaauboer, 2011). For instance, Feijten, Hooimeijer, and Mulder (2008: 156), studying households in the Netherlands, found that moves away from the city are triggered by "life events," such as having children, but that "the place of birth turns out to play a decisive part in shaping residential environment choices later in life." Social ties bring people back to the cities or the suburbs where they grew up. In this same vein, growing up in a rural area also made households in the study more likely to move to any rural area. This makes it important to consider the changes in the structure and size of cities experienced by different generations over time. However, residential decisions are influenced by several factors, including income, household composition, ethnicity, and the location of jobs (see Townshend and Walker, Chapter 7). Younger generations also have different values and ideals that create new preferences and location patterns, as was the case in the countercultural movement of the 1960s that brought young artists to the inner city (Ley, 1996). Therefore, where someone grows up is only one variable among others predicting future residential preferences.

Successive generations of residents living in Canada since the beginning of European settlement experienced the country in quite different ways. Until the early 1920s, Canada was primarily a rural nation. Indeed, in 1851, before Confederation, 87 per cent of Canada's population lived in places with fewer than 1000 residents (Statistics Canada, 2011a). Most of the population growth since then has occurred in larger towns, cities, and metropolitan areas. The rural population dropped to 51 per cent in 1921, 30 per cent in 1961, 23 per cent in 1991, and 19 per cent in 2011. Those born in the 1950s and 1960s are now in their late fifties and early sixties—a larger share of this population may hold affinity for rural and small-town living than those growing up today in a more urbanized context. Although not everyone in the non-rural population resides in large urban centres, these changes mean that a much larger share of Canada's population today is growing up in proximity to large cities. Some argue that because presently a larger share of the population lives in urban areas near restaurants, shopping, and schools, their experience could continue to fuel demands for municipal services and urban amenities.

To further help us understand the different residential experiences of successive generations, we can compare the location of people from different age groups in two periods (Figure 20.2). The first thing to note here is that there is a growing share of the population residing in larger metropolitan areas (Bourne, 2007). Forty-seven per cent of those 17 and younger in 1976, the oldest of which are in their fifties today, grew up in places with populations of less than 100,000. By 2012, this share had shrunk to 28 per cent. On the other hand, the percentage of those 17 years or younger residing in places with a population of 1 million or more increased from 27 to 46 per cent; in other words, more young people and children are growing up in large metropolitan areas. Increasing immigration played an important role in these changes since most immigrants and their families have settled in the largest metropolitan areas (see Kobayashi and Preston, Chapter 8).

The second thing to note is that young adults and the working age population in general are more likely to live in larger urban centers (Figure 20.2). They are attracted to larger urban centers by job prospects, lifestyle and entertainment amenities (see Skaburskis and Moos, Chapter 12; Bain, Chapter 14). It is noteworthy, however, that the young and working age population has become more concentrated in large cities than the population 65 and older. That is to say that the percentage residing in the largest metropolitan areas increased less among those 65 and older than among the rest of the population. We might attribute this to seniors' own past experiences, since they were more likely to have resided in smaller cities and towns when they were younger than is the case for more recent generations. For instance, some have argued that concerns over rapid growth are contributing to the move of some Canadian born residents away from large metropolitan areas (Ley, 2007).

There have also been widespread changes in the internal structure of cities since the 1960s. Downtowns have transitioned from primarily

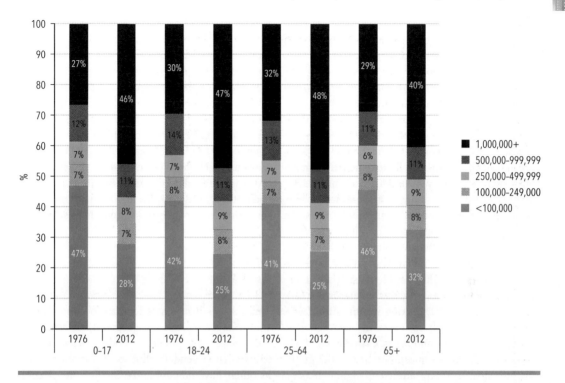

Figure 20.2   The Percentage of Different Age Groups by Community Population Size, 1976 and 2012

Note: The figure shows the percentage of an age group that lives in an urban area (census agglomeration or census metropolitan area) of a particular size. For instance, in 1976, 47 per cent of 0- to 17-year-olds were living in places where the population is less than 100,000, whereas by 2012 this percentage had decreased to 28 per cent.

Source: Statistics Canada (1976; 2013).

being places of employment, experiencing decline in manufacturing and warehousing employment, to include more residential and recreational amenities (see Bain, Chapter 14; Ley, 1996). Young adults in particular have been associated with the growth of core area population (see Townshend and Walker, Chapter 7). A decline in number of young people holding a driver's licence has led to speculations as to whether this is due to the change in their residential location (i.e., more young adults living in walkable, urban neighbourhoods), to emerging environmental concerns, to declining employment prospects, or to a combination of these factors (Badger, 2013). For instance, a survey by Vancouver's transit agency, TransLink, showed that in 2011, 50 per cent of those 16–19 years of age and 80 per cent of those 20–29 years of age had

a driver's licence, a decrease of 10 per cent since 1999 in each age group (Sinoski, 2013). TransLink points to the increasing availability of transit and the high cost of car ownership as explanations.

Since transit use, walking, and cycling are associated with living in higher density, urban environments (see Senbel and Lesnikowski, Chapter 13), whether or not young adults will continue to register lower car use than previous generations have will depend in part on where they decide to move as they have children (Badger, 2013). Historically at least, urban lifestyles were generally associated with young and non-family households (Van Diepen and Musterd, 2009) although the presence of households with children is increasing somewhat in some downtowns, such as those of Vancouver and Toronto (Willcocks,

2011). A shortage of daycare, schools, playgrounds and other family-oriented amenities is sometimes seen as a barrier to families wanting to raise children downtown. Another factor accounting for a low proportion of families in core areas is the persistence of traditional cultural norms that continue to associate the suburbs, and the availability of private yards, with greater "family friendliness." Recent political discourse in the City of Toronto highlighted this polarizing issue. One side argued for greater availability of larger sized apartments in the downtown to allow more families to live there, and the other side deemed an urban environment to be unsuitable to raising children (Zerbisias, 2012). Notwithstanding cultural norms, families with children remain more likely to reside in suburbs because the cost of housing and land (per area) decreases with distance from urban amenities and transit, making it more affordable for larger households to locate in lower density areas (see Skaburskis and Moos, Chapter 12).

There is reason to question whether the growing presence of young adults in higher density neighbourhoods actually signals a lasting change in preference for urban living, implying that young populations will remain downtown as they age. Figure 20.3 shows the correlation between the percentages of young adults, aged 25–34, residing in Vancouver census tracts (used to define neighbourhoods by Statistics Canada) in 1991 versus 2006 (Figure 20.3a). The figures show a strong association, as evidenced by the high R^2 value, indicating that the percentage of young adults tends to remain high in the same neighbourhoods over time. Figure 20.3 also shows that the correlation between the percentage of young adults in 1991 and those 40 to 49 years old in 2006 (Figure 20.3b). If the young adults had remained in the same neighbourhoods between 1991 and 2006, the correlation between these two age groups would be positive. But the correlation is weak, as evidenced by the R^2 value near zero, indicating that there is no relationship between the residential location of 25- to 34-year-olds in 1991 and those 40 to 49 years old in 2006. From this we can at least tentatively infer that new young adults are moving into neighbourhoods where there are already young

people and that they change location as they age (Moos, 2014). The growing presence of young adults in the downtowns of Canadian metropolitan areas is therefore at least in part a reflection of the delay of child-bearing and an extended young adult life stage (Champion, 2001; Chatterton and Hollands, 2002). Some people may even have fewer or no children to facilitate an urban lifestyle choice (Lauster, 2010; Skaburskis, 1994). As Van Diepen and Musterd (2009: 344) note, "Household structure and urbanity are indisputably related to each other." And, despite important changes, age remains closely connected to household structure.

Geographies of Age and Age Segregation

The linkages between residential location and life stages imply a particular geography of age. There are fewer studies of age than other societal dimensions, such as gender, ethnicity, or social class, and as others have noted the existing literature focuses largely on either the young or the old (Chatterton, 1999; Pain and Hopkins, 2010; Vanderbeck, 2007). Rosenberg and Wilson (2010), in a previous edition of this book, distinguish between "younger and older cities" and between places for youth and older populations within Canadian cities. Some cities, such as Victoria and Quebec City, have a higher share of older residents, while other cities have more children and people of working age, such as Kitchener-Waterloo and Ottawa-Gatineau. At the intra-urban scale, public spaces are also defined by age. Within cities, Rosenberg and Wilson describe how few public places are fully exclusive to any one age group. But there are some spaces that are more frequented by certain age groups, for instance the presence of young parents with children in playgrounds or teenagers in skateboard parks. Rosenberg and Wilson also describe the challenges of accommodating youth populations in public spaces in cities—that is, those who are too old for playgrounds but too young to spend time in establishments where age of majority is required. They note that young people spending time in public parks or shopping malls can encounter exclusion and stereotyping,

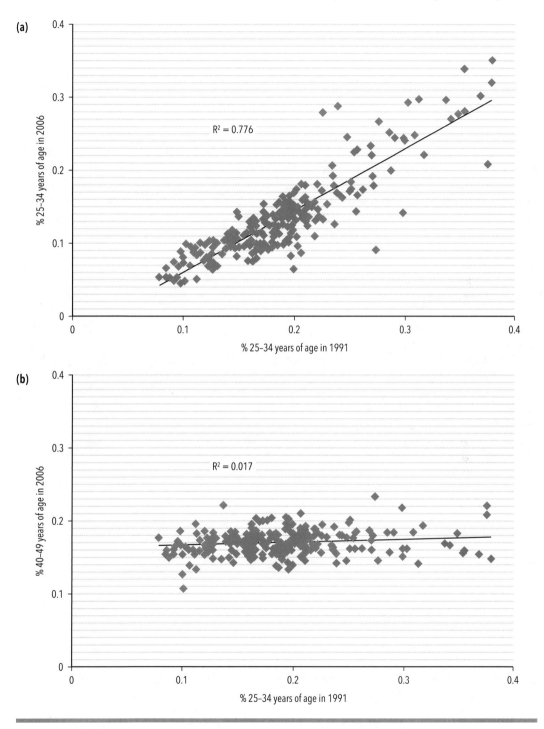

Figure 20.3 **Correlation between Age Groups in Vancouver Census Tracts in 1991 and 2006**

Source: Statistics Canada (1991; 2006a).

being depicted as loiterers or thugs. In response, several Canadian cities have specific programs to help foster youth spaces and activities. One example is a new skateboarding park in Waterloo, Ontario. In the US, New York City enacted specific measures to counter "discrimination against young people in public places such as restaurants and movie theatres" (Phillips, 2010: 381).

Age segregation is multifaceted because it is both a spatial and temporal phenomenon. The separation of home, work, and schooling means that during the day, many of us interact more with people our own age, while we may interact with all different kinds of age groups within our households (Hagestad and Uhlenberg, 2006; Vanderbeck, 2007), particularly in multigenerational households

that are today more common among recent immigrants than among those Canadian born (see Kobayashi and Preston, Chapter 8). Integration of daycares into the workplace and the location of schools, universities, and senior homes in central areas can also increase inter-generational interactions in public places or restaurants. However, the co-location of older and younger residents does not necessarily result in increased social interaction. In fact, such co-location can even lead to tensions, for instance due to the noise from night-time activities in cities where the downtown can be home to both young adults and seniors (Bromley, Tallon, and Thomas, 2005; Chatterton, 1999).

The residential geography of young adults (25 to 29 years of age) and seniors (65 years of age and

Figure 20.4   **The Residential Location of Young Adults in Six Canadian Cities Measured Using Location Quotients, 2011**

Source: Robert Walter-Joseph.

over) in six of Canada's largest metropolitan areas shows that young adults are most concentrated in the inner cities (Figure 20.4) while seniors are more likely to reside in suburban areas (Figure 20.5). Figure 20.4 and 20.5 use a location quotient to analyze concentration—it measures the percentage of an age group in a census tract divided by the percentage of the same age group in the metropolitan area. In the largest metropolitan areas, the geography of young adults aligns with higher density housing, the availability of public transit, and walkable urban areas (see Figure 20.6). In Vancouver, the pattern of young adults extends from the **central business district (CBD)** into the suburbs along the SkyTrain transit corridor that connects several urban growth centres (Moos,

2014). While young adults have concentrated in the inner city in the past, this phenomenon has intensified considerably over the last decades, as shown in Toronto (Figure 20.7).

Intensification of land uses also means that the housing stock in the inner city is most suitable for younger households who are delaying marriage and child-bearing or choosing alternate lifestyles altogether. Seniors are most concentrated in old suburbs built between the 1950s and 1970s, in more recent outer suburbs, and in the smaller towns at the outskirts of metropolitan areas (Figures 20.5 and 20.6). But note that young adults are also concentrated in some lower density outer suburban areas, particularly in the smaller metropolitan areas, such as in Quebec City, where seniors

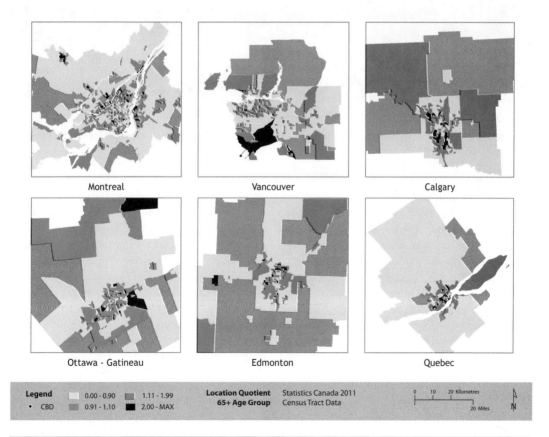

Figure 20.5   The Residential Location of Seniors Measured in Six Canadian Cities Using Location Quotients, 2011

Source: Robert Walter-Joseph.

Figure 20.6   Contrasting Residential Landscapes of Young Adults and Seniors

Left: Toronto neighbourhoods with high concentrations of young adults. Right: Ottawa neighbourhoods with high concentrations of seniors. (Robert Walter-Joseph)

are more present in the inner city. Among young adults, suburban areas are correlated with married households and the presence of children. In some cases the increased presence of young adults in suburbs, as visible in some areas of Toronto, may also relate to the growing share of such individuals still living at home or reporting their parents' home address while attending post-secondary education (Figure 20.7).

We can measure the degree of, and changes in, age segregation using a coefficient of localization, which gauges the over- or under-representation of a particular age group in different parts of an urban area (Table 20.1). The higher the magnitude of the coefficient, the larger the degree of residential segregation. The results show that residential space is segregated by age but the degree of segregation is certainly not as strong as found with

other variables of social differentiation, such as income, immigration, or occupation (Walks, 2001). Across the seven largest metropolitan areas, age segregation is largest for young adults and seniors. The changes over time are modest in magnitude; the largest increases are visible among young adults, which is an outcome of planning policies and demographic changes that have produced high-density residential neighbourhoods in inner cities that are largely targeted at the young. The older populations show the largest decrease in the coefficient of localization, which may be in part a product of the extended time seniors now remain in their own homes, which would increase the variety of age groups found in residential neighbourhoods, and of the dispersal of older populations from the inner cities (Seguin, Apparicio, and Negron, 2008).

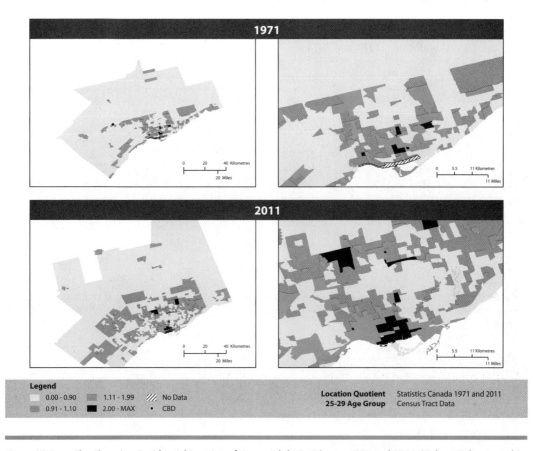

Location Quotient   Statistics Canada 1971 and 2011
25-29 Age Group   Census Tract Data

Figure 20.7   The Changing Residential Location of Young Adults in Toronto, 1971 and 2011. (Robert Walter-Joseph)

For the most part, the segregation of different age groups in the city is mainly a reflection of different lifestyles and not so much an indicator of inequality. Ageism is one form of discrimination based on age that produces inequalities (Bisom-Rapp and Sargeant, 2013), and ageism can have a spatial dimension. As Blaikie (2013) notes, the Charter of Rights and Freedoms protects against "discrimination based on age." Any age group can experience age discrimination but often it is the young and the old that experience it. Phillips (2010) indicates that age discrimination is more prevalent in societies placing greater value on economic productivity, as this marginalizes those who are not participating in the workforce. As others have noted, ageism is a somewhat perplexing type

of discrimination because it is targeted at one's past or future self (Joenson, 2013). North and Fiske (2012: 982) point out that "only age encompasses categories that every living person potentially joins" but that we still know little about "prejudice" on the basis of age. Ageism is commonly studied in the context of the workplace. For instance, younger workers are sometimes viewed as less able to handle managerial responsibilities whereas older workers are portrayed as less competent in technological domains despite their actual qualifications (Sargeant, 2013). One recent survey claims that ageism is "widespread" in Canada and manifests itself in seniors being "seen as less important" or "more ignored than younger generations" (CTV, 2012). Ageism will likely become a more important

Table 20.1   Age Segregation in Canadian Metropolitan Areas Measured Using a Coefficient of Localization, 1971 and 2011

	Toronto		Montreal		Vancouver		Ottawa		Calgary		Edmonton		Quebec City	
Age groups	Δ1971	2011	Δ1971	2011	Δ1971	2011	Δ1971	2011	Δ1971	2011	Δ1971	2011	Δ1971	2011
<18	0	11	0	11	−1	11	2	12	0	12	−1	10	4	15
18–24	−1	8	0	8	−5	7	0	10	−8	9	−8	8	2	10
25–29	0	14	5	17	2	16	6	17	4	17	3	16	7	16
30–34	0	7	3	8	1	8	3	9	2	9	1	8	3	8
35–39	0	7	3	8	1	8	3	9	2	9	1	8	3	8
40–44	0	7	3	8	1	8	3	9	2	9	1	8	3	8
45–49	0	7	3	8	1	8	3	9	2	9	1	8	3	8
50–54	−4	8	−4	7	−3	6	−5	8	−4	11	−5	8	−7	6
55–59	−6	10	−9	8	−5	7	−10	10	−8	13	−10	9	−11	7
60–64	−8	11	−10	10	−7	9	−12	12	−12	14	−12	11	−13	9
65+	−8	17	−6	18	−6	15	−11	20	−12	22	−7	19	−7	21

The table shows the change in coefficient of localization between 1971 and 2011 (Δ1971) and the coefficient of localization in 2011. The coefficient of localization is a measure of segregation of an age group from the rest of the population (see Walks, 2001). It was calculated as follows:

$$CL_g = \sum_{i=1}^{n} |T_i - B_i| / 2$$

Where CL is the coefficient of localization
g is the age group under observation
i is the census tract
n the number of census tracts
T is the percentage share of the age group under consideration
B is the percentage share of the total population

Source: Statistics Canada (1971, 2011b).

topic of conversation as the size of the older population grows, i.e., as baby boomers age (e.g., CBC, 2012).

Generation F*CK*D: Debt, Expensive Housing, and Fewer Jobs

The Occupy Wall Street protests, starting in New York and spreading around the globe in 2011, were first and foremost concerned with growing income inequalities (Figure 20.8). But the protests also revealed that some emerging inequalities were in essence generational (Kershaw, 2011). Young adults today are facing more expensive housing markets, lower wages, higher unemployment rates, greater employment uncertainty, higher student and consumer debt, and fewer social services than young adults did in past decades (Moos, 2012; 2013; see Walks, Chapter 9). In Canada, the unemployment rate for youth 15 to 24 was 2.4 times higher in 2012 than for those 25 to 54 years of age, which is the largest generational difference since 1977 (Bernard, 2013). These trends have led some to come up with creative names like "generation squeeze" or "generation F*CK*D" to describe the difficult context faced by young generations today (Bridge, 2011; Kershaw, 2013). Millennials are also labelled by some as "lazy," "whiners," "entitled," and "self-absorbed," but this seems misguided, as others have noted, when in fact many more than in previous generations are university educated yet are working in minimum-wage retail and sales jobs (Fawcett, 2007; Kolm, 2013; Mason, 2011). It may be the case that young peoples' attitudes and expectations are not in line with actual outcomes. As the phrase "oh, young people today . . ." suggests, generational differences have of course long been a source of discussion and, at times, even contempt. One can argue that the many conveniences and opportunities life offers today perhaps lead us to forget the difficulties faced by previous generations. At the same time, economic and social indicators do point to severe challenges confronting the Millennials.

The generational wage gap, the difference in earnings between younger and older cohorts in a given time period, is one indicator of the changing economic conditions. Figure 20.9 shows the wage gap and young adults' changing household income from the mid-1970s to 2008 in Canada (adjusted for inflation). Household income has increased over this time period, notwithstanding the decrease during the 1990s due to recessionary times. Significantly, several societal changes took place over this time period that influenced household earnings. For example, there has been an increase in dual earner households as more women entered the labour force (Osberg, 2003). More young adults today are also completing post-secondary education, which raises their incomes, as education is associated with higher earnings; however, higher educational attainment also delays entry into the labour force (Boudarbat, Lemieux, and Riddell, 2010). This means that those 25 to 34 years of age would have lower incomes today than people at the same age did 20 or 30 years ago in part because of increasing educational attainment, which tends to increase earnings later in life (Mincer, 1974).

Figure 20.9 shows the wage gap as a ratio by measuring young adults' incomes as a share of the income of the population 35 years of age and older.

Figure 20.8   Occupy Wall Street Protestor in Vancouver

Use of profanity by protestors to voice their concern that the world left behind for future generations is "doomed" due to bleak employment outlooks, rising income inequalities, and environmental deterioration. (Elvin Wyly)

The figure indicates that young adults' incomes were 97 per cent of those of the older population in the late 1970s. While it is not unexpected that young adults' incomes would be lower than for older workers with more experience, the sustained increase in the wage gap over time points to systematic changes. By 2008, young adults' incomes were down to 85 per cent of the incomes of the older population. Statistical analysis of individual earnings shows that this generational wage gap remains even when other changes, such as increasing educational attainment, are taken into account (Boudarbat, Lemieux, and Riddell, 2010). In the Vancouver metropolitan area, for example, young adults are earning about $12,600 less than older workers with otherwise similar characteristics, an increase in the wage gap of $4800 since 1981 (Moos, 2013). The changes have been attributed to economic restructuring and the neo-liberalization

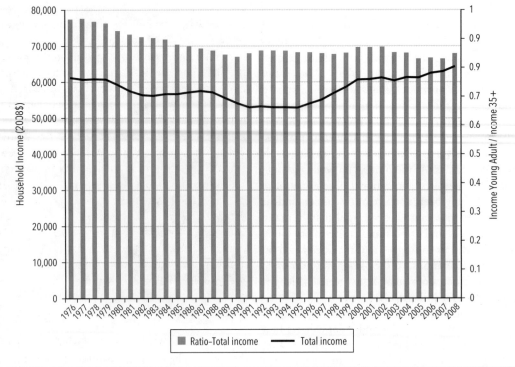

Figure 20.9   **Young Adults' Changing Household Income: Total and Ratio Compared to the Older Population in Canada, 1976 to 2008**

Source: Survey of Consumer Finance (1976–1993) and Survey of Labour and Income Dynamics (1993–2008) available through Statistics Canada's (2008) analysis series.

(see neo-liberalism) of the welfare state that increased employment insecurity and the share of so-called "precarious" and "flexible" employment, where jobs are often less secure and wages generally lower (Myles, 1993; Vosko, 2006). Educational attainment has become ever more important to gain access to the labour market in a knowledge- and information-based economy (Wesson, 2007). But those left out of educational opportunities also face greater obstacles and exclusion than in the past (Hall, 1996).

The increasing wage gap translates into greater difficulties as young adults enter housing markets, competing with the older generations that have greater spending power—although they may not be entering the same local housing markets as we have seen in the geographies of age. One ramification

has been the increase of young adults returning to their parental home or remaining there for longer periods than in the past. From 1981 to 2001, the percentage living with parents increased from 12 to 24 per cent for 25- to 29-year-olds and from 5 to 11 per cent for those aged 30 to 34 (Beaupré, Turcotte, and Milan, 2006). Deteriorating economic conditions, rising housing costs, increasing educational attainment, and an increase in the length of the young adult life stage are contributing to this trend (Boyd and Norris, 1999; Chatterton and Hollands, 2002). Moreover, adult children remain at home longer in some immigrant households from Asia and South America in part due to cultural differences (Turcotte, 2006). Also, the growing housing affordability difficulty for young adults is a common issue, widely discussed in the media in Canada's largest cities, where housing prices are highest (Beers, 2007; Rotberg, 2008). Table 20.2 shows that the percentage of young adults spending more than 30 per cent of their income on shelter costs, a common measure of unaffordability (Lefebvre, 2003), has increased in Toronto and Vancouver between 1986 and 2006. The share of young adults spending more than 30 per cent on housing actually decreased slightly in Montreal due to lesser price and rent increases and a greater retention of government support to housing affordability programs in Quebec (Germain and Rose, 2000; Walks and Maaranen, 2008).

Interestingly, despite the growing affordability concerns, home ownership among young adults has actually increased in all three major cities. This is in part an outcome of the growth of the condominium apartment stock now available in most major cities, which was not available to past generations when home ownership was much more directly associated with single-family homes (Harris, 2011). In Montreal, where there are fewer condos than in Vancouver and Toronto, increases in ownership rates among young adults continue to be more directly related to suburban expansion.

But in Vancouver and Toronto, there have been large shifts in the housing types of young adults, from single-family housing to apartment dwellings—not an unexpected phenomenon given the shifts in residential location patterns toward higher density areas. The high share of apartment dwellings is not too surprising in and of itself given young adults early stage in the housing and labour markets and their smaller household size (Bailey, 2009; McLeod and Ellis, 1983; Thomas, 2005). Remarkable, however, is the dramatic decline from 42 per cent in 1986 to 18 per cent in 2006 of the proportion of young adults residing in single-detached houses in Vancouver. The percentage living in single-family homes was almost 50 per cent in 1981. A similar trend is visible in Toronto, although less pronounced, whereas in Montreal the share of young adults in single-family homes remained almost constant over the 20-year period.

The trends reflect important differences among metropolitan areas due to unique housing markets and planning contexts. Prices increased more rapidly in Vancouver and Toronto, while Montreal has had a longer tradition of renting in the central city and fewer planning constraints on suburban

Table 20.2   Changing Housing Affordability, Home Ownership, and Housing Types among Young Adults, 1986 and 2006

25- to 34-year-olds	Toronto		Montreal		Vancouver	
	% 1986	% 2006	% 1986	% 2006	% 1986	% 2006
Shelter cost exceeding 30% of income	21.0	36.6	21.8	20.3	31.5	38.5
Owners	40.5	48.7	33.3	35.6	38.5	43.7
Housing types (both rented and owner-occupied):						
Single-detached house	32.2	23.2	22.8	21.5	42.0	18.1
Apartment, five or more storeys	32.9	36.6	6.7	6.5	11.0	18.2
Apartment, fewer than five storeys	17.2	18.1	58.3	57.1	31.4	37.8
Semi-detached house	8.3	7.5	4.6	3.5	2.8	1.6
Apartment, duplex	1.7	5.0	3.5	8.5	6.4	15.4
Row house	7.1	9.5	2.7	2.3	5.8	8.5
Other dwellings	0.6	0.1	1.3	0.5	0.7	0.2

Source: Statistics Canada (1986; 2006b; 2006c).

expansion (Filion et al., 2010). In Vancouver, some observers have noted that the condominium apartment has become the new bungalow that used to be the stereotypical starter home for baby boomers. Young adults are opting to purchase smaller dwellings in a context of rising costs (Skaburskis, 2001). However, in 2006 about 51 per cent of young adults in Toronto, 56 per cent in Vancouver, and 64 per cent in Montreal were renters. Some have argued that increases in owner-occupied higher density housing forms are an extension of home-ownership ideals to the central city (Kern, 2010). However, the data also indicate that not only is a large share of young adults not, or not yet, able to participate in the home-ownership market, but also that rental markets may provide one way to access an urban lifestyle in the context of rising inner city housing costs.

Planning for an Aging Society

The large size of the baby boom generation has steered interest among policy-makers regarding the implications of an aging population for cities. For instance, the Ontario Professional Planners Institute (OPPI) published a report called *Age Friendly Communities: A Call to Action* that outlines anticipated challenges for local community planning (OPPI, 2009). In the document, the OPPI discusses the growing need for more diverse housing options as baby boomers begin to downsize their households. There is also an increasing need for accessibility improvements to accommodate seniors who may be less mobile. The report anticipates growing public transit reliance as people age and lose their ability to keep a driver's licence due to health conditions. Accessibility improvements to sidewalks, streetscapes, parks, and public buildings are called for to ensure that seniors with mobility impairments can still go about their day-to-day activities. The OPPI notes that baby boomers differ from previous generations of seniors in that they have more discretionary income, longer life expectancy, and higher demand for active recreational activities. Florida (2013) argues that seniors

today are increasingly moving to large cities to be able to access urban amenities and recreational opportunities. Planning, therefore, can accommodate seniors by locating age-targeted communities and care facilities in central locations near parks, public transit, shopping, and health-care facilities (Figure 20.10). Indeed, particularly in medium-sized cities, baby boomers are a growing target demographic for new downtown condominium apartments. But as we have seen, the overall residential geography of seniors remains associated with suburban landscapes. This raises particular challenges for delivering health-care services and meeting accessibility challenges of seniors aging in place, which is a growing phenomenon (Garvin, 2012). We should also not forget that income is distributed unevenly within older generations and that governments have cut social service provisions (see Walks, Chapter 9), which will make it more difficult for some seniors to afford housing and to maintain consumption-oriented lifestyles.

The research on age-friendly community design discusses the need to consider the ways people are able to participate in their communities and engage with other people as they age (Lui et al., 2009; Menec et al., 2011). This literature commonly notes that good health is an important consideration of successful aging but that it is not sufficient. Lui et al. (2009) review various frameworks for age-friendly community design. While details of the frameworks vary, all include physical as well as social dimensions of the urban environment. One framework they review is from the World Health Organization (WHO), which has launched the "Global Age Friendly Cities Project." The WHO framework focuses on "Outdoor spaces and buildings," "Transportation," "Housing," "Communication and information," "Social participation," "Respect and social inclusion," and "Civic participation and employment" (Lui et al., 2009: 118). According to the WHO (2013),

> [i]n an age-friendly community, policies, services and structures related to the physical and social environment are designed to support and enable older people to "age

Figure 20.10   A retirement community in Waterloo near a park, shopping, recreational amenities, and a future light-rail transit stop, all contributing to age-friendly design. (Michael Seasons)

actively"—that is, to live in security, enjoy good health and continue to participate fully in society.

Age-friendly community design thus requires considerations of how people in different age groups can access the physical urban environment as well as of their ability to participate in their communities, employment, and decision-making. The municipality of Saanich, British Columbia, which participated in the WHO project, identified the importance to "provide opportunities for meaningful participation," "recognize the diverse needs," and identify "barriers" to seniors in the community (District of Saanich, 2013). Professor John Lewis, who studies age-friendly community design in the City of Waterloo, which recently received the WHO's age-friendly city designation, argues that barriers are also often attitudinal—people have to become more receptive to having seniors, and people of all

ages, participate regularly in all aspects of daily life (Csanday, 2012; Lewis, 2013). As Lui et al. (2009: 119) note, a growing "focus on active participation and engagement of older people is an antidote to the conception of old age as an inevitable period of withdrawal from social roles and relationships."

Conclusion

This chapter dealt with the age and generational dimensions of the urban landscape. Increased spatial segregation of young adults is an indication of the city's growing fragmentation and may be a sign of growing "social distance" between generations that can lead to challenges in social interaction (Hagestad and Uhlenberg, 2006). An example is the workplace, where there may be tensions between younger and older workers, which can even lead to age-specific discrimination or systemic ageism. The growing discourse on generational change deals in part with the challenges of finding common ground between generations (Kolm, 2013; Mason, 2011; Twenge, 2006). It speaks to larger societal challenges of "how to live together" and foster mutual understanding in a metropolitan context, where differences—whether age, class, gender, or ethnicity—are producing stronger socio-spatial divisions.

The study of age cohorts reveals the dramatic structural changes in the inner cities of Canada's major metropolitan areas, which have attracted large shares of young adults to new housing and recreational opportunities. The younger generations in Canada today are better educated than any prior generation and live in a society where standards of living are high. Housing choices are more abundant, particularly in inner cities. At the same time, young adults are facing greater difficulties in the job market in a context of growing employment uncertainties. Meanwhile, the cost of housing escalates. Young adults live close to public transit and in more walkable neighbourhoods than in the past and compared to other age groups. On average, the aging baby boomers have higher incomes and more housing wealth than any previous generation. In part this wealth is still tied up in their suburban homes, but in some cities baby boomers are beginning to downsize and move into central areas. The context makes it more difficult for younger generations (Beer et al., 2011), and also for those baby boomers with lower incomes, to compete in the housing market. Moreover, the increasing share of seniors produces new challenges in ensuring that our communities remain accessible for all generations. These generational changes reveal how age is socially constructed, as new generations take on different roles, responsibilities, and lifestyles than those in the past. The study of the city through the lens of age helps reveal the unique challenges we face as we inevitably get older.

Review Questions

1. How have young adults' residential locations and housing decisions changed over the past several decades? Do the changes suggest there is increasing age segregation in Canadian cities? What are the implications?

2. Have you ever experienced or witnessed a case of ageism? What is it about the incident that suggests there was discrimination based on age?

3. What is the generational wage gap? And how can it help us understand young adults' changing economic fortunes?

Note

1. Parts of this chapter are based on research and writing from the author's doctoral thesis (Moos, 2012). The author thanks Robert Walter-Joseph and Michael Seasons for research assistance.

References

Badger, E. 2013. "Millenials lead the trend to less driving, but what happens as they get older?" *The Atlantic Cities* (online magazine), May. At: www.theatlanticcities.com/commute/2013/05/planning-our-transportation-future-millennials-mind/5575/

Bailey, A. 2009. "Population geography: Lifecourse matters," *Progress in Human Geography* 33: 407–18.

Beaupré, P., T. Turcotte, and A. Milan. 2006. "When is junior moving out? Transitions from the parental home to independence," *Canadian Social Trends* 82: 9–16.

Beer, A., T. Clower, D. Faulkner, and C. Paris. 2011. *Consuming Housing? Transitions through the Housing Market in the 21st Century*. Bristol: The Policy Press.

Beers, D. 2007. "Vancouver eats its young," *The Tyee* (online magazine), October. At: http://thetyee.ca/Views/2007/10/23/Vancouver/

Bernard, A. 2013. "Unemployment dynamics among Canada's youth," *Economic Insights* 24: 1–7.

Bisom-Rapp, S. and M. Sargeant. 2013. "Diverging doctrine, converging outcomes: Evaluating age discrimination law in the United Kingdom and the United States," *Loyola University Chicago Law Journal* 44: 717–70.

Blaauboer, M. 2011. "The impact of childhood experiences and family members outside the household on residential environment choices," *Urban Studies* 48: 1635–50.

Blaikie, H. 2013. "Age discrimination internationally: Canada," *Agediscriminaiton.info*. At: www.agediscrimination.info

Boudarbat, B., T. Lemieux, and C. Riddell. 2010. "The evolution of the returns to human capital in Canada, 1980–2005," *Canadian Public Policy* 36: 63–89.

Bourne, L. 2007. *New Urban Divides: How Economic, Social and Demographic Trends Are Creating New Sources of Urban Difference in Canada (Research Bulletin No. 33)*. Toronto: Centre for Urban and Community Studies, University of Toronto.

Boyd, M., and D. Norris. 1999. "The crowded nest: Young adults at home," *Canadian Social Trends* 52: 2–5.

Bridge, T. 2011. "Going gone," *Vancouver Magazine*, November. At: www.vanmag.com/News_and_Features/Gone?page=0%2C0

Bromley, R., A. Tallon, and C. Thomas. 2005. "City centre regeneration through residential development: Contributing to sustainability," *Urban Studies* 42: 2407–29.

Calvert, E. 2010. *Young People's Housing Transitions in Context* (working paper). Southampton: Centre for Population Change, University of Southampton.

Canadian Press. 2012. "Baby boomers push back against age discrimination," *CBC News*, May. At: www.cbc.ca/news/canada/story/2012/05/29/census-age-discrimination.html

Carroll, B., and R. Jones. 2000. "The road to innovation, convergence or inertia: Devolution in housing policy in Canada," *Canadian Public Policy* 26: 277–93.

Carr, D.S. 2004. "Psychological well-being across three cohorts: A response to shifting work-family opportunities and expectations? Work and well-being across three cohorts," in O.G. Brim, C.D. Ryff, and R.C. Kessler, eds., *How Healthy Are We? A National Study of Well-being at Midlife*. Chicago, IL: University of Chicago Press.

Champion, A.G. 2001. "A changing demographic regime and evolving polycentric urban regions: Consequences for the size, composition and distribution of city populations," *Urban Studies* 38: 657–77.

Chatterton, P. 1999. "University students and city centres: The formation of exclusive geographies," *Geoforum* 30: 117–33.

Chatterton, P., and R. Hollands. 2002. "Theorizing urban playscapes: Producing, regulating and consuming youthful nightlife city spaces," *Urban Studies* 39: 95–116.

Constable, G. 1996. *The Reformation of the Twelfth Century*. New York: Cambridge University Press.

Csanady, A. 2012. "World Health Organization declares Waterloo an 'age-friendly' city," *The Record*, January. At: www.therecord.com/news-story/2597007-world-health-organization-declares-waterloo-an-age-friendly-city/

CTV. 2012. "Ageism widespread in Canada, survey finds," *CTV News*, November. At: www.ctvnews.ca/canada/ageism-widespread-in-canada-survey-finds-1.1021641

District of Saanich. 2013. "Age friendly cities and the municipality of Saanich," *District of Saanich*. At: www.saanich.ca/parkrec/community/agefriendly.html

Elchardus, M., and W. Smits. 2006. "The persistence of the standardized life cycle," *Time and Society* 15: 303.

Fawcett, M. 2007. "Hey boomers, stop banging on us: Young people are tired of your baseless lectures," *The Tyee*, September. At: http://thetyee.ca/Views/2007/09/26/Boomers/

Feijten, P., P. Hooimeijer, and C. Mulder. 2008. "Residential experience and residential environment choice over the life-course," *Urban Studies* 45: 141–62.

Filion, P., T. Bunting, D. Pavlic, and P. Langlois. 2010. "Intensification and sprawl: Residential density trajectories in Canada's largest metropolitan regions," *Urban Geography* 31: 541–69.

Florida, R. 2013. "Why no city can afford to forget about seniors," *The Atlantic Cities*, January. At: www.theatlanticcities.com/neighborhoods/2013/06/why-no-city-can-afford-forget-about-seniors/5789/

Furlong, A., and F. Cartmel. 2007. *Young People and Social Change: New Perspectives* (2nd edn.). Berkshire: McGraw-Hill.

Garvin, T. 2012. "Can we get old here? Senior's perceptions of seasonal constraints of neighbourhood built environments in a northern, winter city," *Geografiska Annaler: Series B, Human Geography* 94: 369–89.

Germain, A., and D. Rose. 2000. *Montreal: The Quest for a Metropolis*. New York: John Wiley & Sons Inc.

Giddens, A. 1984. *The Constitution of Society*. Cambridge: Polity.

Hagestad, G., and P. Uhlenberg. 2006. "Should we be concerned about age segregation? Some theoretical and empirical explorations," *Research on Aging* 28: 638–53.

Hall, P. 1996. *Cities of Tomorrow: An Intellectual History of Urban Planning and Design in the Twentieth Century* (Updated edn.). Cambridge: Blackwell.

Harris, D. 2011. "Condominium and the city: The rise of property in Vancouver," *Law & Social Inquiry* 36: 694–726.

Joenson, H. 2013. "We will be different! Ageism and the temporal construction of old age," *The Gerontologist* 53: 198–204.

Kern, L. 2010. "Gendering re-urbanisation: Women and new-build gentrification in Toronto," *Population, Space and Place* 16: 363–79.

Kershaw, P. 2011. "Movement should change focus: Occupy Wall Street zeros in on 'fat cats,' but this thinking overlooks important generational realities," *The Vancouver Sun*, 18 October: A11.

Kershaw, P. 2013. *Generation squeeze*. At: http://gensqueeze.ca/

Kolm, K. 2013. "Why are so many of Canada's young people out of work?" *CBC News*, June. At: www.cbc.ca

/news/canada/story/2013/06/12/f-millennial-youth-unemployment.html

Lauster, N. 2010. "A room to grow: The residential density-dependence of childbearing in Europe and the United States," *Canadian Studies in Population* 37: 475–96.

Laz, C. 1998. "Act your age," *Sociological Forum* 13: 85–113.

Lefebvre, S. 2003. "Housing: An income issue," *Canadian Social Trends* 68: 15–18.

Lewis, J. 2013. "Creating age-friendly communities. Diversity and inclusion events: Dialogues on diversity," *Region of Waterloo.* At: www.regionofwaterloo.ca/en/regionalGovernment/resources/DOCS_ADMIN-1374206-v1-john_Lewis_presentation_-_creating_age_friendly_communities.pdf

Ley, D. 2007. "Countervailing immigration and domestic migration in gateway cities: Australian and Canadian variations on an American theme," *Economic Geography* 83: 231–54.

——. 1996. *The New Middle Class and the Remaking of the Central City.* Oxford: Oxford University Press.

Lui, C-W., J.A. Everingham, J. Wrburton, M. Cuthill, and H. Bartlett. 2009. "What makes a community age-friendly: A review of international literature," *Australasian Journal of Ageing* 28, 3: 116–21.

Mason, G. 2011. "Gen Y's pampered losers are just a myth," *The Globe and Mail,* September. At: www.theglobeandmail.com/news/opinions/opinion/gen-ys-pampered-losers-are-just-a-myth/article2175084/

McDaniel, S. 2004. "Generationing gender: Justice and the division of welfare," *Journal of Aging Studies* 18: 27–44.

McLeod, P.B., and J.R. Ellis. 1983. "Alternative approaches to the family life cycle in the analysis of housing consumption," *Journal of Marriage and Family* 45: 699–708.

Menec, V., R. Means, N. Keating, G. Parkhurst, and J. Eales. 2011. "Conceptualizing agefriendly communities," *Canadian Journal on Aging* 30: 479–93.

Mills, M. 2004. "Stability and change: The structuration of partnership histories in Canada, the Netherlands, and the Russian Federation," *European Journal of Population* 20: 141–75.

Mincer, J. 1974. *Schooling, Experience and Earnings.* New York: Columbia University Press.

Moos, M. 2012. *Housing and Location of Young Adults, Then and Now: Consequences of Urban Restructuring in Montreal and Vancouver.* Vancouver, BC: University of British Columbia, Ph.D. thesis.

——. (2014). "'Generationed' space: Societal restructuring and young adults' changing residential location patterns," *The Canadian Geographer* 58: 11-33.

——. (2013). "Generational dimensions of neo-liberal and post-Fordist restructuring: The changing characteristics of young adults and growing income inequality in Vancouver and Montreal," *International Journal of Urban and Regional Research* Early view: http://onlinelibrary.wiley.com/doi/10.1111/1468-2427.12088/abstract

Myers, D. 1999. "Cohort longitudinal estimation of housing careers," *Housing Studies* 14: 473–90.

Myles, J., G. Picot, and T. Wannell. 1993. "Does post-industrialism matter? The Canadian experience," in Esping-Andersen, G., ed., *Changing Classes: Stratification and Mobility in Post-industrial Societies.* London: Sage.

North, M., and S. Fiske. 2012. "An inconvenienced youth? Ageism and its potential intergenerational roots," *Psychological Bulletin* 138: 982–97.

Ontario Professional Planners Institute (OPPI). 2009. "Age friendly communities: A call to action," *Ontario Professional Planners Institute.* At: http://ontarioplanners.ca/PDF/Healthy-Communities/2009/Call-to-Action-Age-Friendly-Communities-June-18-20.aspx

Osberg, L. 2003. "Long run trends in income inequality in the United States, UK, Sweden, Germany and Canada: A birth cohort view," *Easter Economic Journal* 29, 1: 2003.

Pain, R., and P. Hopkins. 2010. "Social geographies of age and ageism," in S. Smith, R. Pain, S. Marston, and J. Jones III, eds., *The Sage Handbook of Social Geographies.* Los Angeles: Sage.

Phillips, B. 2010. *City Lights: Urban-suburban Life in the Global Society.* New York: Oxford University Press.

Pred, A. 1984. "Place as historically contingent process: Structuration and the time-geography of becoming," *Annals of the Association of American Geographers* 74: 279–97.

Riley, M. 1987. "On the significance of age in sociology," *American Sociological Review* 52: 1–14.

Rosenberg, M., and D. Wilson. 2010. "Younger cities, older cities, and cities in the balance: Spaces and places of the younger and older populations," in T. Bunting, P. Filion, and R. Walker, eds., *Canadian Cities in Transition: New Directions in the Twenty-First Century* (4th edn.). New York: Oxford University Press.

Rotberg, H. 2008. *Exploring Vancouverism: The Political Culture of Canada's Lotus Land.* Toronto: Mantua Books.

Ryder, N. 1965. "The cohort as a concept in the study of social change," *American Sociological Review* 30: 843–61.

Sargeant, M. 2013. "Young people and age discrimination," *E-Journal of International and Comparative Labour Studies* 2: 2–16.

Séguin, A-M., P. Apparicio, and P. Negron. 2008. *The Changing Spatial Distribution of the Elderly Population in Eight Canadian Metropolises: A Decreasing Segregation (Working paper No. 2008-10).* Montreal: Centre Urbanisation Culture Société (INRS).

Shanahan, M. 2000. "Pathways to adulthood in changing societies: Variability and mechanisms in life course perspective," *Annual Review of Sociology* 26: 667–92.

Sinoski, K. 2013. "Fewer drivers among urban youth in Metro Vancouver," *Vancouver Sun,* March. At: www.vancouver

sun.com/Fewer+drivers+among+urban+youth+Metro+Vancouver/8128997/story.html

Skaburskis, A. 1994. "Determinants of Canadian headship rates," *Urban Studies* 31: 1377–89.

——. 2001. "Housing prices and housing density: Do higher prices make more compact cities," *Canadian Journal of Regional Science* 23: 455–80.

Statistics Canada. 1971. Census of Canada—Profiles of census tracts. Accessed through the Canadian Census Analyzer at the University of Toronto. At: http://dc1.chass.utoronto.ca/census/

——. 1976. Census of Canada, 1976: Public use sample tapes on individuals. Accessed through the Canadian Census Analyzer at the University of Toronto. At: http://dc1.chass.utoronto.ca/census/

——. 1986. Census of Canada, 1986: Public use microdata on households and housing. Accessed through the Canadian Census Analyzer at the University of Toronto. At: http://dc1.chass.utoronto.ca/census/

——. 1991. Census of Canada—Profiles of census tracts. Accessed through the Canadian Census Analyzer at the University of Toronto. At: http://dc1.chass.utoronto.ca/census/

——. 2006a. Census of Canada—Profiles of census tracts. Accessed through the Canadian Census Analyzer at the University of Toronto. At: http://dc1.chass.utoronto.ca/census/

——. 2006b. Census of population, topic-based tabulations. Household Income Groups, Owner's Major Payments, Housing Affordability, Presence of Mortgage, Age Groups of Primary Household Maintainer, Condition of Dwelling and Housing Tenure for the Private Households with Household Income Greater than Zero, in Owner-occupied Private Non-farm, Non-reserve Dwellings of Canada, Provinces, Territories and Census Metropolitan Areas, 2006 Census—20% Sample Data (No. 97-554-XCB2006052). Ottawa, ON: Ministry of Industry.

——. 2006c. Census of population, topic-based tabulations. Household Income Groups, Housing Affordability, Gross Rent, Condition of Dwelling and Household Type for the Private Households with Household Income Greater than Zero, in Tenant-occupied Private Non-farm, Non-reserve Dwellings of Canada, Provinces, Territories and Census Metropolitan Areas, 2006 Census—20% Sample Data (No. 97-554-XCB2006053). Ottawa, ON: Ministry of Industry.

——. 2011a. "Population, urban and rural, by province and territory," *Statistics Canada: Summary Tables*. At: www.statcan.gc.ca/tables-tableaux/sum-som/l01/cst01/demo62a-eng.htm

——. 2011b. Census of Canada—Profiles of census tracts. Accessed through the Canadian Census Analyzer at the University of Toronto. At: http://dc1.chass.utoronto.ca/census/

——. 2013. "Annual population estimates by census metropolitan area, Canada—Population by age group and sex at July 1, 2012," *Statistics Canada*. At: www.statcan.gc.ca/pub/91-214-x/2011000/t142-eng.htm

Thomas, D. 2005. "Socio-demographic factors in the current housing market," *Canadian Economic Observer* 18 (10): 3.1–3.9.

Turcotte, M. 2006. "Parents with adult children living at home," *Canadian Social Trends* 80: 2–10.

Twenge, J. 2006. *Why Today's Young Americans Are More Confident, Assertive, Entitled—and More Miserable than ever before.* New York: Free Press.

Vanderbeck, R.M. 2007. "Intergenerational geographies: Age relations, segregation and re-engagements," *Geography Compass* 1: 200–21.

Van Diepen, A., & Musterd, S. 2009. "Lifestyles and the city: Connecting daily life to urbanity," *Journal of Housing and the Built Environment* 24: 331–45.

Vosko, L., ed. 2006. *Precarious Employment: Understanding Labour Market Insecurity in Canada.* Montreal: McGill-Queens University Press.

Walks, A. 2001. "The social ecology of the post-Fordist/Global city? Economic restructuring and socio-spatial polarisation in the Toronto urban region," *Urban Studies* 38: 407–47.

——, and R. Maaranen. 2008. *The Timing, Patterning, and Forms of Gentrification and Neighbourhood Upgrading in Montreal, Toronto, and Vancouver, 1961 to 2001.* Toronto: Centre for Urban and Community Studies, University of Toronto.

Wesson, T. 2007. "The sectoral structure of Canada's economy," in T. Wesson, ed., *Canada and the New World Economic Order: Strategic Briefings for Canadian Enterprise* (3rd edn.). Concord, ON: Captus Press Inc.

Willcocks, C. 2011. *Encouraging Family-friendly Condominium Development and Creating Complete Communities in Downtown Toronto.* Waterloo, ON: University of Waterloo, M.A. Thesis.

World Health Organization (WHO). 2013. "Global age-friendly cities project," *World Health Organization*. At: www.who.int/ageing/projects/age_friendly_cities/en/index.html

Zerbisias, A. 2012. "Downtown Toronto kids lead enviable lives, their parents tell Holyday," *Toronto Star*, July. At: www.thestar.com/news/gta/2012/07/16/downtown_toronto_kids_lead_enviable_lives_their_parents_tell_holyday.html

Aboriginal People in Canadian Cities

21

EVELYN J. PETERS

Introduction

Perspectives of Indigenous[1] realities rarely focus on life lived in major metropolitan centres. Instead, the tendency is to frame rural and remote locations as central to the survival of Indigenous cultures and societies. However, recent censuses show that in many countries Indigenous populations are now mainly urban populations (Peters and Andersen, 2013). Rural land claims and settlement, as well as treaties remain important for many Indigenous peoples, as the recent *Idle No More* movement in Canada demonstrates. However, the Indigenous experience is increasingly an urban one.

According to the 2006 Canadian census, 53.2 per cent of Aboriginal people live in urban areas (Statistics Canada, 2008a). Comparative data are not available for 2011 yet, but the steady increase in urbanization rates since the 1950s suggests that the proportion is currently even higher. Aboriginal populations comprise the largest minority group in many prairie cities, and their social and economic conditions are central to the future of these cities. While researchers and popular accounts document Aboriginal urbanization and their "migration" to urban areas, many Aboriginal people are travelling *within* their traditional territories, and the urban centres they migrate to are often built on traditional Aboriginal settlement places. In fact, the earlier absence of Aboriginal people in urban areas was the result of explicit policies to remove them from growing urban centres (Wilson and Peters, 2005).

Despite the importance of urban life to contemporary Aboriginal people and their importance in many Canadian cities, very little work in geography or in other disciplines explores these realities. Without recognizing the presence and experiences of urban Aboriginal peoples, it is difficult to understand how many cities, particularly those on the Prairies and in the North, function (see Townshend and Walker, Chapter 7). Many Aboriginal people arrive in cities expecting their histories and their status as Aboriginal people to make a difference to their access to institutions and services. In this way, Aboriginal people are not like other urban residents. These characteristics pose unique challenges to policy and to urban theory.

The following sections examine three main aspects of urban Aboriginal life and their associated challenges to public policy. The first section examines assumptions about Aboriginal peoples' abandonment of reserves and rural communities and subsequent concentration in cities. Then the issues raised by an emphasis on Aboriginal cultures and rights to self-government in the city are explored. Finally, the chapter considers the challenges associated with the socio-economic diversity of urban Aboriginal communities.

An explanation about terminology is in order at the outset. According to Section 35.1 of the

Constitution Act, 1982, Aboriginal peoples are the "Indian, Inuit and Métis peoples of Canada." Most contemporary writers use "First Nations" instead of "Indian," although many official government policy documents and statistics still use the colonial terms "North American Indian" and "registered Indian." The former refers to all individuals who identify themselves as such in censuses and other situations, while the latter refers to First Nations peoples who are registered pursuant to the Indian Act. However, these general terms homogenize particular Aboriginal identities and cultures. Many First Nations, for example, identify with their particular cultural groups, for example Mi'kmaq, Cree, and Algonquin. The general term *Inuit* includes a variety of different cultural groups. The term *Métis* also has different and contested meanings. Sometimes it is used to refer to descendants of First Nations and European people regardless of geographical location or historical period, and sometimes it refers specifically to descendants of the Métis Nation that emerged in the Prairie provinces, was centred on the Red River settlement in Manitoba, and was a consequence of relations between Aboriginal women and European fur traders.

Urbanization Processes

Expectations that Aboriginal people would leave their reserve and rural communities and move to urban areas have a long history in Canada. Until the mid-twentieth century, "Indian" policy assumed that reserve lands would be abandoned as First Nations peoples assimilated (Tobias, 1983). Urbanization was seen as a partial solution for reserve and rural poverty, and the Department of Indian Affairs organized a relocation program in 1956 designed to assist First Nations to move to urban areas (Peters, 2002). Urbanization rates began to increase in 1950 and climbed sharply in the 1970s and 1980s (Kalbach, 1987: 102). Since then the proportion of Aboriginal people living in cities has increased for each census period. Table 21.1 describes recent population growth and urbanization rates. Census counts document considerable growth in Aboriginal populations in recent years. Between 1996 and 2006, the proportion of the Aboriginal population living in urban areas increased from 46.8 to 53.2 per cent. (These data are not available yet for the 2011 National Household Survey).

Table 21.1	Urbanization Patterns for Different Groups of Aboriginal People, 1996-2011				
	Total Aboriginal Identity*	Métis**	First Nations	Inuit	Registered Indian
Total population, 1996	1,101,960	204,115	529,040	40,220	488,040
Total population, 2006	1,172,790	389,780	698,025	50,480	623,780
Total population, 2011	1,400,690	451,795	851,560	59,440	697,510
On reserve, 1996 (%)	32.8	1.5	47.4		46.0
On reserve, 2006 (%)	26.3	1.1	43.1	0.9	48.1
On reserve, 2011 (%)	23.2	0.7	37.6	0.4	45.3
Urban, 1996 (%)	46.8	67.1	40.0	28.0	41.0
Urban, 2006 (%)	53.2	69.4	44.7	37.6	40.6

* The total Aboriginal identity population includes persons who reported more than one Aboriginal identity group and those who reported being a registered Indian and/or band member without reporting an Aboriginal identity.

** The counts for Métis, First Nations, and Inuit were based on single responses to census questions about Aboriginal identity. Some individuals identifying as Aboriginal claimed more than one Aboriginal identity.

Sources: Statistics Canada (2003; 2006; 2013).

Urbanization rates vary for different legal categories of Aboriginal peoples. Métis people, for example, are most highly urbanized, with almost 70 per cent living in urban areas, as defined by Statistics Canada. While this is lower than the Canadian urbanization rate, which is above 80 per cent, it is substantially higher than the rate for other Aboriginal groups. The Inuit have the lowest proportion living in cities. Urbanization for First Nations increased from 40 per cent to almost 45 per cent between 1996 and 2006. However, the proportion of registered Indians (First Nations people registered under the Indian Act) living in cities remained relatively constant at close to 40 per cent in that time period. For several census periods, a number of reserves have refused to participate in census taking, with the result that the number and proportion of First Nations people, and especially registered Indians, living on reserves are underestimated. Norris and Clatworthy (2003: 54) suggested that if un-enumerated reserve populations had been included in 1996, approximately 60 per cent of registered Indians would live on reserves.

Aboriginal urbanization rates cannot be explained solely by population measures, such as fertility, mortality, and migration (Guimond, Robitaille, and Senécal, 2009). Legislation passed in 1985 allowed for the reinstatement of First Nations people who had lost their status through a variety of processes, and this accounts for part of the increase. However, another component of the increase is the result of individuals who did not identify as Aboriginal in previous census years now choosing to do so. Researchers have documented a similar phenomenon in the US, identifying as contributing factors US ethnic polities that embraced ethnic pride and Indian activism (Nagel, 1995). Siggner (2003) indicates that shifting attitudes toward Aboriginal peoples in Canada are important in changing patterns of self-identification. US researchers suggest that urban residents are more likely to reclaim their Indian identities, and similar processes may be occurring in Canadian cities.

An examination of absolute numbers shows that, despite increasing urbanization rates, the number of First Nations people living in reserve areas also increased between 1996 and 2011. In other words, reserves are not being depopulated as urban Aboriginal populations grow. Migration data from 1986 to 2001 show a substantial movement back and forth between cities and reserves and rural areas (Norris and Clatworthy, 2009). While some migrants may return to reserve and rural communities because of problems with urban life, researchers found that these communities of origin remain important for individuals (Wilson and Peters, 2005). Many Aboriginal people emphasize ties to the land as a continuing element of their cultural identity, and migration may be one reflection of these ties (Todd, 2000–1). Migration back to rural and reserve communities may also represent an attempt to maintain vital and purposeful community relationships.

The continuing importance of reserves and the migration between them and urban areas have some important policy implications. Clearly, early assumptions about the depopulation of reserves have not materialized. The continuing connections many urban Aboriginal people have with these rural communities raise questions about the appropriate scale of policy interventions. A recent study of First Nations homelessness in Prince Albert, Saskatchewan, found that First Nations homelessness in urban areas was linked to the poor condition and crowding of reserve housing (Peters and Robillard, 2007). Initiatives only in cities or only in rural/reserve areas may not address significant factors at work among urban Aboriginal people. Migration back and forth also raises the importance of interface mechanisms that connect urban and rural populations. The appropriate geographies for addressing issues facing urban Aboriginal people may extend beyond urban boundaries.

Aboriginal Cultures and Rights in Urban Areas

A long history in Western thought sees urban and Aboriginal cultures as incompatible (Berkhoffer, 1979). Early writing about Aboriginal migrants to urban areas reflected ideas that Aboriginal cultures were an impediment to successful adjustment to urban society. As a result, services to Aboriginal migrants emphasized integration (Peters, 2002). More recent perspectives, however, view urban Aboriginal identities and communities as dynamically constructed in response to the challenges and opportunities of urban life (see Peters 2011 for a review of this work). In this perspective, urban Aboriginal residents draw on cultural traditions and identities, but these are consciously and systematically being reconstructed differently in cities (see for example Howard and Proulx, 2011; Newhouse, 2011; Peters and Andersen, 2013). Ramirez (2007) suggested that urban Native American communities were "hubs" from which cultural innovations were transmitted to tribal communities. Andersen and Denis (2003: 385) argued that urban Aboriginal communities "are the source of new forms of culture, association and self-perception—both individual and collective—about what it means to be Aboriginal."

An important challenge for policy-makers is to recognize that vibrant Aboriginal cultures can contribute positively, not only to Aboriginal communities in cities but also to non-Aboriginal communities. Researchers have found that skilled workers are attracted to particular cities both for economic and for social reasons. And cultural diversity is one of the elements that make cities attractive (Bradford, 2002). Aboriginal cultures have the potential to be part of this cultural diversity, contributing not only to elements such as art, dance, theatre, music, food, and media, but new perspectives on governance, a greater depth to urban histories, and different approaches to environmental issues and educational practices (Walker, 2008a).

The Indigenous right to self-determination is an important component of Aboriginal identities, and as a result Aboriginal people distinguish themselves from other minority cultural groups, rejecting approaches based on multiculturalism (Johnson, 2008; Walker, 2008b). Increasingly, Aboriginal people in urban areas strive to express this right by attempting to define a role in policy-making and by determining and delivering programs and services to urban populations. And while the Canadian government has recognized the Aboriginal right to self-government as an inherent right of all Aboriginal people (Canada, 1997), practical and political challenges face the implementation of the right to self-government in urban areas.

Not all urban Aboriginal people are represented by existing Aboriginal political bodies, and consequently they are denied a strong political voice in this arena. This lack of representation derives both from geographic variations in organizational structures and from differential access to these organizations for different categories of Aboriginal people. The Congress of Aboriginal Peoples (CAP), formerly the Native Council of Canada, has defined itself as the voice of off-reserve Aboriginal people in Canada since 1971. CAP currently has very limited support in the Prairies and Ontario, however. And the Assembly of First Nations' (AFN) stated interest in urban issues is relatively recent, sparked in part by assumption of responsibility for off-reserve member services by some First Nations governments and tribal councils. At present, though, the AFN has little involvement in urban First Nations issues. The Métis National Council, which is working to affirm Métis rights more generally, also does not have a strong presence in providing services in urban areas. Provincial First Nations and Métis organizations similarly do not have a well-developed focus on urban Aboriginal affairs.

At the level of particular cities, however, some political organizations have emerged with a specific focus on urban Aboriginal issues. Arrangements are extremely variable geographically. One approach is an urban-focused organization that represents all Aboriginal people (First Nations, Métis, and Inuit) in the city, such as the Aboriginal Council of Winnipeg (ACW). Founded in 1990 with the union of the Urban Indian Association and the Winnipeg Council of Treaty and Status Indians, it serves as a political and advocacy voice representing the interests of Aboriginal people of Winnipeg regardless of their legal status. While there have been attempts to establish similar organizations in other cities, none appears to have been as stable as the ACW. In addition, in some cities individual First Nations have set up urban offices to represent and provide services to their members in the city. In a few cities, separate organizations represent and provide services for urban First Nations and Métis people. For example, in Saskatoon, political representation for First Nations is provided by the Saskatoon Tribal Council, which also delivers a wide range of services, some to First Nations and some to all Aboriginal people living in Saskatoon. The Central Urban Métis Federation Inc. (CUMFI) is a Métis local of the Métis Nation-Saskatchewan that provides a political voice as well as programs and services to Métis people in Saskatoon. Finally, the location of some reserves within the city boundaries of a few urban areas means that members of those First Nations have political representation within the city.

In most cities, though, urban Aboriginal people do not have political representation. Even where there are urban-focused organizations, such as the ones in Saskatoon, they do not provide a voice for all urban Aboriginal people, leaving out First Nations people who are not registered or who do not belong to First Nations that are represented on the tribal council. Moreover, as Walker (2003; 2006) has described, urban Aboriginal people, like many other urban residents, often do not participate in non-Aboriginal community organizations and consultations. This, in addition to their uneven access to political representative bodies, means that they often do not have a direct voice in public policy-making.

Most urban Aboriginal people experience some level of self-government through a variety of urban Aboriginal organizations that deliver programs and services in a wide range of policy sectors. The emergence of many urban Aboriginal organizations marked the increase in migration to the city around 1950. Like ethnic groups in Canadian cities, Aboriginal people worked to develop formal and informal institutions to meet the needs of migrants (Ouart, 2013). Unlike ethnic organizations, though, these institutions are often

viewed as steps toward self-government. The Royal Commission suggested that the development of urban Aboriginal organizations created meaningful levels of control over some of the issues that affect urban Aboriginal residents' everyday lives (Royal Commission on Aboriginal Peoples [RCAP], 1996a: 584). Aboriginal-controlled social services generally have greater scope in delivering programs that incorporate Aboriginal principles, beliefs, and traditions, they create important employment opportunities for urban Aboriginal residents, and they result in significant economic benefits for Aboriginal communities (Hylton, 1999: 85–6).

Heather Howard-Bobiwash's (2003: 567) account of the strategies of Aboriginal women in Toronto between 1950 and 1975 describes how Aboriginal women "utilized their class mobility to support the development of Native community organizations and promote positive pride in Native cultural identities" in the city. Similar to the emergence of "pan-tribal" urban organizations in US cities (Straus and Valentino, 2001), small numbers and the nature of federal policies meant that early organizations in Canadian cities were "pan-Aboriginal"; in other words, they did not distinguish by legal status or different Aboriginal cultures. The emphasis was on programs to facilitate integration and address poverty (Peters, 2002). While some cultural programming was supported as a way of providing a familiar milieu for urban Aboriginal residents, there was no room at that time for programming based on rights or targeted to particular Aboriginal cultural groups.

Friendship Centres represent the earliest formal urban Aboriginal organizations. The first Friendship Centre opened in Winnipeg in April 1959. At present there are 119 Friendship Centres in cities throughout the country. Since the 1950s many other Aboriginal organizations have emerged to address a wide variety of issues. Some recent research in Edmonton, Winnipeg, and Saskatoon found that, in addition to Friendship Centres, non-profit housing organizations have existed for many decades (Peters, 2005). In larger cities, urban Aboriginal organizations are now found in a wide variety of policy sectors, including economic development, child, youth, family, and senior services, education, and justice, as well as in cultural fields (e.g., language, dance, theatre, music, and media).

As the urban Aboriginal populations grew in many cities, the emphasis increasingly shifted away from pan-Aboriginal approaches to particular cultures and histories. Especially in prairie cities, separate First Nations and Métis organizations emerged to provide services for community members and to encourage a sense of strong cultural identity. A recent study of First Nations and Métis identities in Saskatoon found that most respondents identified with a particular First Nation origin (Cree, Saulteaux, Dene, etc.) and that they also differentiated between western prairie Métis Nation identity and the definition of Métis as "mixed-blood" (Peters et al., 2013). Because many urban Aboriginal people want to practise their particular cultures, pan-Aboriginal organizations often attempt to involve Elders and representatives from a variety of cultures in their programs and services. Nevertheless, urban Aboriginal people who live in cities where their culture of origin is a minority in the urban Aboriginal population sometimes find that, to access culturally specific services, they need to visit or return to their communities of origin (Wilson and Peters, 2005).

The size of the urban Aboriginal population influences the number and diversity of organizations that a particular city can support. Table 21.2 provides information from the 2011 National Household Survey for census metropolitan areas (CMAs) with Aboriginal populations of 10,000 or more. Winnipeg had the largest Aboriginal population (more than 78,000) in 2011. The next largest urban Aboriginal populations were found in Edmonton and Vancouver, respectively. The composition of the urban Aboriginal population is also an important influence on the structure of urban Aboriginal organizations. In some prairie cities, half or more of this population self-identifies as Métis, and in many of these cities Métis organizations have emerged to provide culturally specific services.

Obtaining predictable and adequate funding is a challenge to urban Aboriginal organizations. The federal government has maintained that it is responsible only for registered Indians and that these responsibilities are limited to reserve borders. The federal government has regarded all other Aboriginal people as a provincial responsibility. In turn, the provinces have argued that the federal government has responsibility for all Aboriginal people. The Royal Commission on Aboriginal Peoples (RCAP) (1996a: 538) noted that the result is a "policy vacuum." Although some urban programs have been established through federal, provincial, and municipal funding, these initiatives are unevenly distributed, with short-term and often limited funding (Hanselmann, 2001). Annual grants place an enormous administrative burden on Aboriginal organizations and limit their ability to build successful programs over time. Dependence on government funding creates concerns about sustainability and the ability to shape aspects of programming to reflect cultural needs (Tomiak, 2010).

The emphasis on culture, rights, and self-government raises some unique challenges for policy-making for urban Aboriginal peoples. The rationale for government funding for most urban Aboriginal programming is the amelioration of poverty and unemployment, not the promotion of Aboriginal rights to self-government. Although the RCAP (1996a) suggested several models through which urban Aboriginal people could have access to self-government, there has been virtually no progress on this front since the release of the report. While urban Aboriginal organizations have some scope for decision-making, it is severely circumscribed by program regulations and underfunding. Moreover, jurisdictional disputes between federal and provincial governments continue to generate complex and fragmented programming. The emphasis on the importance of culture and self-government results in a focus on particular cultural groups and histories, with the result that the configuration of Aboriginal organizations is complex and varies in different cities. Policy-making for urban Aboriginal communities, then, has some

Table 21.2   Cultural Characteristics of the Aboriginal Identity Population in Selected Cities, 2011

	Victoria	Vancouver	Edmonton	Calgary	Prince Albert	Saskatoon	Regina	Winnipeg	Thunder Bay	Sudbury	Brantford	Hamilton	Toronto	Ottawa-Gatineau	Montreal
Total Aboriginal	14,200	52,375	61,765	33,370	15,775	23,895	19,785	78,420	11,670	13,405	11,120	11,980	36,990	30,565	26,285
% of CMA	4.2	2.3	5.4	2.8	38.5	9.3	9.6	11	9.8	8.5	8.4	1.7	0.7	2.5	0.7
% First Nations*	62.7	60.5	43.6	43.8	49.1	49.2	56.5	38.8	77	48.4	92.6	74.7	64.8	53.2	56.1
% Métis	33.8	35.3	51.4	51.1	50.1	48.2	41.6	59.1	21	48.2	5.1	19.7	27	40.1	33.6
% Inuit	0.7	0.7	1.8	0.7	0.1	0.4	0	0.5	0.2	0.3	0	0.6	1.7	2.8	3.4

* Totals do not add up to 100 per cent because of rounding, because some individuals identified with more than one category, and because some individuals identified themselves as Aboriginal but did not identify as First Nations, Métis, or Inuit.

Source: Statistics Canada (2013).

distinct elements associated with Aboriginal cultures, rights, and status.

Socio-economic Diversity in Urban Areas

Urban Aboriginal people are most often depicted as socio-economically marginalized populations, and most programs and services in urban areas address this marginalization. A literature beginning around the 1940s suggests that Aboriginal migration to cities creates challenges for those migrants and that, because of their poverty, their movement into cities also challenges the capacity of municipal governments to provide for them (Peters, 2000). The homogenization of urban Aboriginal communities primarily in terms of their socio-economic status hides the socio-economic diversity of these people, both within and between cities.

A comparison of socio-economic indicators for Aboriginal and non-Aboriginal people in Canada's largest cities suggests that urban Aboriginal people are, in aggregate, less well-off than non-Aboriginal people (Table 21.3). A word of caution is in order concerning the 2011 National Household Survey data, however. While there is no official analysis available of biases in response rates, the very low responses in some of the poorest areas of cities (and subsequent suppression of data) suggest that marginalized populations were less likely to participate. As a result, I suspect that the degree of socio-economic marginalization in the Aboriginal population is seriously underestimated in these data. The unemployment rate among urban Aboriginal people is more than double that of the non-Aboriginal population in most cities. Median incomes, moreover, are lower for Aboriginal than for non-Aboriginal people. Furthermore, Aboriginal people are much less likely than others to have a university degree. In addition to these statistical descriptions, increased vulnerability to homelessness, addictions, violence, and incarceration also mark the lives of many urban Aboriginal people (Belanger et al., 2012; Culhane, 2009; LaPrairie, 2002). Aboriginal gang membership is a growing issue, especially in prairie cities. In a new book based on interviews with Winnipeg gang members themselves, Comack et al. (2013) argue that existing studies miss the larger dynamics of racialized and spatialized poverty and the colonial histories that contribute to the emergence of Aboriginal gangs. Gang formation is a form of resistance to these conditions, but the results are extremely destructive both to individual gang members and to the inner-city Aboriginal community. Comack et al. (2013) found, as have others, that prisons played a key role in the recruitment of gang members and that getting sent to prison was a marker of status and street credibility. The sale of illegal drugs represents a major source of income for gang members, but this income benefited neither the inner city economy nor gang members in the long run. Drugs were sold mainly to other Aboriginal people, sucking up money needed for necessities, and profits were quickly spent on consumer goods and partying.

It is important to provide a context for urban Aboriginal socio-economic marginalization. Interviews by Silver et al. (2006: 11–15) with 26 urban Aboriginal community leaders identified a number of factors affecting Aboriginal people's economic situation in urban areas, including the failure of both residential and non-residential schools to provide them with the skills required in urban employment; the experience of racism, often on a daily basis; and the resulting destruction of self-esteem and identity. The urbanization of Aboriginal people in Canada occurred at a time when urban economies increasingly required education levels and skills that relatively few Aboriginal people received during their schooling. Challenges facing urban Aboriginal people also need to be situated within the larger context of colonization, which dispossessed them of their lands and languages, sent many children to residential schools, and impoverished reserves and rural Métis communities (RCAP, 1996b).

There are, however, variations within urban Aboriginal populations. Siggner and Costa's (2005) study of urban Aboriginal people in large cities reports that between 1981 and 2001 school attendance among Aboriginal youth improved and rates of post-secondary completion increased. As

Table 21.3   Socio-Economic Characteristics, Aboriginal Identity Population, Selected Cities, 2011

		Vancouver	Victoria	Edmonton	Calgary	Prince Albert	Regina	Saskatoon	Winnipeg	Thunder Bay	Greater Sudbury	Brantford	Hamilton	Toronto	Ottawa-Gatineau	Montreal
Unemployment rates (%)	Aboriginal	21.6	11.6	11.7	10.8	17	12.2	12.2	10.3	19.5	11.8	17.7	9.9	11.9	9.2	7.7
	Non-Aboriginal	7	5.9	5.3	5.8	6.3	4.3	5	5.3	7.4	7.5	6.9	7.9	8.6	6.5	7.7
Median individual income ($)	Aboriginal	21,568	21,679	25,291	28,012	No data	25,314	21,901	21,968	18,747	25,322	19,057	25,408	25,408	28,198	22,814
	Non-Aboriginal	26,796	30,506	33,503	34,259	No data	32,933	30,775	27,503	28,956	30,154	26,911	27,390	27,390	34,062	25,806
% with university degree or certificate	Aboriginal	10.7	12.4	8.2	11.0	8.2	11.7	12.1	9.4	9.1	8.4	6.4	9.4	16.1	17.0	12.7
	Non-Aboriginal	28.1	27.2	22.6	29.3	15.3	22.0	23.9	23.6	18.1	16.3	12.6	20.5	30.0	31.9	23.6

Source: Statistics Canada (2011).

well, employment rates improved in most cities, dependence on government transfer payments decreased, and there was a 28 per cent growth of Aboriginal income earners making $40,000 or more in annual income (adjusted for comparison with 1981). Silver et al. (2006: 18) identify three important strategies—adult education, employment in Aboriginal organizations, and involvement in their children's activities—that Aboriginal community leaders in Winnipeg used to gain socio-economic mobility. Several recent studies have begun to explore the development of an urban Aboriginal middle class. The 2007 Urban Aboriginal Task Force (2007: 171–7) study in Thunder Bay, Ottawa, Sudbury, Barrie-Midland, and Kenora found that some members of the middle class did not participate in urban Aboriginal organizations because of their emphasis on meeting the needs of the poor and at-risk Aboriginal clients. Middle-class respondents indicated that there were few relevant services focusing on their needs with respect to traditional cultural learning, language classes, and interests in Aboriginal art. McCaskill, FitzMaurice, and Cidro's (2011) Toronto study found that middle-class residents were scattered throughout the city, contributing to the difficulty in creating organizations to meet their needs. They (2011: 236) point out the importance of the creation of a new set of Aboriginal institutions, including cultural, social and recreational organizations, created to cater to the aspirations of the middle class. If such organization supports are not established it is fair to assume that increasing numbers of economically successful Aboriginal individuals will leave or distance themselves from the larger Aboriginal community.

In contrast, middle-class employees of the Saskatoon Tribal Council (Peters and Lafond, 2013: 137) found that working in an Aboriginal organization was positive, because it provided them with access to Aboriginal ceremonies. For example, one participant said this:

Working here I still get to the smudging ceremonies and the powwows. If you need time off to attend one of those ceremonies you can usually get it pretty easy. They have no problem with a guy taking off in the afternoon to go to a sweat, so that's pretty good.

We must recognize this socio-economic diversity in the design and delivery of programs and services. Emphasizing only marginalization can perpetuate negative stereotypes that view all urban Aboriginal people as destitute, deflect attention from the success that many urban Aboriginal residents experience, and create the perception that there is no capacity among Aboriginal people to contribute to both the Aboriginal and the non-Aboriginal communities in urban areas. An emphasis on socio-economic marginalization can also homogenize the design and delivery of programs and services within and between cities and fail to respond to the aspirations of Aboriginal peoples who do not fall into this group.

The homogenization of urban Aboriginal peoples as economically marginalized is linked to a history of concern about their settlement patterns by governments, social agencies, and a variety of academic researchers. With increasing numbers in cities, researchers and policy-makers expected that they would create poverty-stricken concentrations in inner-city areas (Peters, 2005). Concern about Aboriginal concentration has roots, explicitly or implicitly, in a literature on the emergence of inner-city ghettos in large US cities. In the US, the concept of the "underclass" was developed to describe intense poverty, its concentration over very large areas, and the resulting social isolation from mainstream society and values. Wilson (1987) described how the movement of employment opportunities to suburban locations drew away working- and middle-class families, leaving behind an increasingly isolated and politically powerless "underclass." Inner-city disinvestment, coupled with growing welfare dependence and illicit economies in response to the lack of employment opportunities, resulted in the collapse of public institutions and the development of a set of attitudes and practices of everyday life that isolated populations from the rest of urban society. Other work has explored "neighbourhood effects," suggesting that concentration itself can have negative impacts, such as the development of antagonistic cultures and isolation from the rest of urban society (Buck, 2001).

Aboriginal people are over-represented among the urban poor in Canadian cities and are more likely than the non-Aboriginal population to live in poor urban neighbourhoods (Heisz and McLeod, 2004: 7). Yet researchers have consistently found relatively low rates of segregation among urban Aboriginal and non-Aboriginal peoples (Walks and Bourne, 2006). A recent study (Peters and Starchenko, 2008) assesses levels of segregation and explores whether the neighbourhood effects identified with levels of racialized segregation in the US and in studies of other ethnic groups are found with urban Aboriginal people in Canadian cities. The study employed the five classical indices identified by Massey and Denton (1988)—evenness, exposure, concentration, clustering, and centralization—and compared the Aboriginal identity population and the white Caucasian population as defined by the Canadian Employment Equity Act of 1986. The study found that Aboriginal settlement patterns were generally characterized by the following:

- Even to moderately even distribution across census tracts (evenness)
- Low likelihoods of exposure only to other Aboriginal people (exposure)
- Relatively high levels of concentration; in other words, Aboriginal people occupy a relatively small amount of urban space (concentration)
- Low likelihood that census tracts inhabited by Aboriginal people adjoin each other (clustering)
- High tendencies to live close to the city centre in prairie cities and moderate tendencies to live near the city centre in eastern cities and in Vancouver (centralization)

In combination, these dimensions of the settlement patterns of urban Aboriginal people suggest that characteristics linked to the emergence of ghettos in the US—isolation from the mainstream as a result of large numbers of contiguous census tracts with a high proportion of the population

being black or Hispanic (Hughes, 1990)—are not characteristics of the Canadian situation.

Table 21.4 provides more information about Aboriginal settlement patterns over time, describing changes in patterns of urban Aboriginal residency in inner-city areas of the prairie cities of Edmonton, Saskatoon, Regina, and Winnipeg between 1996 and 2006. (The poor quality of the 2011 National Household Survey data and the fact that information is suppressed for some census tracts in the inner city make it impossible to analyze patterns for 2011.) These are cities with relatively large numbers of Aboriginal residents representing a relatively large proportion of the total population. Inner-city areas were defined as those census tracts where the proportion of housing built before 1946 was twice the metropolitan average in 2006. Census tracts that did not meet these criteria but were surrounded on three sides by inner-city tracts were included to incorporate areas that have been redeveloped. Table 21.4 shows that between 1996 and 2006 the proportion of the inner-city Aboriginal population did not increase as much as the total Aboriginal population did. In other words, many of the individuals who contributed to the increase in urban Aboriginal populations over that decade are found in areas outside the core. This is reflected in the drop in the total proportion of the Aboriginal population living in the core in Edmonton, Saskatoon, and Winnipeg, with the proportion remaining the same in Regina.

Table 21.4 also addresses perceptions that urban Aboriginal residents are overwhelmingly represented in high-poverty neighbourhoods. Following Jargowsky's (1997) definition, high-poverty neighbourhoods are those where 40 per cent or more of individuals have incomes below the poverty line. Clearly, Aboriginal people are over-represented in high-poverty neighbourhoods, compared to the proportion they represent of the total population of these cities. However, they comprise considerably less than half of the population in those areas; in other words, the majority of residents in high-poverty areas are non-Aboriginal. Moreover, a relatively small proportion of the

Table 21.4   Aboriginal Identity Population in Relation to Prairie Inner-City and High Poverty Areas, 1996–2006

	Edmonton	Saskatoon	Regina	Winnipeg
% increase in Aboriginal identity population, 1996–2006	39.4	33.3	25.7	49.5
% of inner city that is Aboriginal, 1996	6.6	11.2	14.8	15.7
% of inner city that is Aboriginal, 2006	6.5	13.2	18.6	18.5
% of total CMA Aboriginal population in inner city, 1996	22.6	19.5	16.8	51.6
% of total CMA Aboriginal population in inner city, 2006	16.9	16.8	16.9	40.4
% of CMA that is Aboriginal, 2006	5.1	9.3	8.9	10.0
% of high-poverty tract population that is Aboriginal, 2006	12.7	33.5	40.8	28.1
% of total Aboriginal population in high-poverty tracts, 2006	1.5	17.0	15.3	22.5

Source: Statistics Canada (2008b).

total Aboriginal population lives in poor neighbourhoods. Clearly programs and services need to address the over-representation of Aboriginal people in high-poverty areas. At the same time, it is important to recognize that urban Aboriginal people are not homogeneously poor or residing in core areas or in neighbourhoods with a high concentration of Aboriginal people.

The fact that Aboriginal people are relatively dispersed in urban areas indicates that Aboriginal issues in cities are not only inner-city issues, and raises questions for targeting programs and services. Located in inner-city areas, programs and services may not be accessible to middle- and upper-class Aboriginal residents living in more suburban areas. If programs *and* services for Aboriginal people are found only in inner-city areas, they can lead to the inadvertent clustering of Aboriginal people in those areas. Finally, initiatives that target areas of high poverty need to recognize that the majority of people living in those areas are not Aboriginal people.

Conclusion

The analysis in this chapter suggests a number of challenges for public policy concerning Aboriginal urbanization. First, the perception that Aboriginal people are leaving reserves and rural communities and moving to urban areas needs to be carefully examined. Census data show that an increasing proportion of the Aboriginal population lives in cities, but there are variations by Aboriginal group, as well as under-enumeration, back-and-forth movement between cities and reserves, and changing patterns of self-identification that complicate that picture. While the proportion of Aboriginal people living in the city has increased according to census data, rural areas and particularly reserves continue to have importance in many Aboriginal peoples' lives, raising questions about the appropriate geographies for public-policy intervention.

Aboriginal cultures can facilitate successful adaptation to urban life for Aboriginal residents. These cultures can also contribute to the richness of urban cultural life. Like other cultural groups, urban Aboriginal cultures are dynamic and creative in attempts to adapt values and practices to a new environment. Urban Aboriginal cultures are reflected in, and reinforced by, a variety of urban Aboriginal organizations, and these organizations continue to be the main way urban Aboriginal people experience self-government. While these organizations face challenges related to cultural complexity and unstable government funding, they are an important element of contemporary urban Aboriginal communities. Challenges for public policy emerging from the importance of Aboriginal cultures in urban areas include promoting these cultures as contributors to cultural liveliness in cities; recognizing the diversity of urban Aboriginal cultures; creating transparent, stable, and adequate funding; and finding ways to recognize Aboriginal rights to self-government.

Many depictions of urban Aboriginal people view them primarily as poor and service-dependent. Clearly, poverty is a serious issue in urban Aboriginal communities, and programs and services addressing poverty amelioration are essential. However, a focus only on marginalization can hide the history of colonialism that failed in the economic and cultural development of reserves and rural communities, education systems that did not teach Aboriginal children the skills necessary for economic success in contemporary economies, and racism and discrimination in urban areas. Emphasizing marginalization can also hide the successes of urban Aboriginal people. Finally, despite continuing concerns about Aboriginal peoples' concentration in inner-city areas, their settlement patterns are quite different from those of minority groups in US inner cities. Inner-city areas continue to have Aboriginal and non-Aboriginal residents, and, increasingly, Aboriginal people are found in all areas of cities. These settlement patterns challenge policy-makers to develop programs and services for diverse and dispersed populations.

Aboriginal cultures have the potential to make unique and valuable contributions to the cultural life of cities. Their status as Aboriginal peoples with Aboriginal rights makes them unique from other urban residents. The poor socio-economic conditions of many urban Aboriginal people and the often negative relationships between them and majority populations mean that the challenges associated with Aboriginal urbanization need to be taken very seriously. Relatively little research, however, has focused on urban Aboriginal people. As a result, academics and policy-makers assume that studies of other cultural groups (ethnic groups, immigrants, US inner-city populations, marginalized peoples) are directly applicable to the situation of urban Aboriginal people in Canada. We must examine the

demographics and experiences of urban Aboriginal people in specific places in order to evaluate whether these models are appropriate. This work will add to our understanding of the social, economic, and political dynamics of these cities.

Review Questions

1. Why do Aboriginal peoples move to cities?
2. What are the situations Aboriginal peoples face in cities in terms of access to services and cultural identity?
3. What urban problems are specific to Aboriginal peoples? What can be done about them— by Aboriginal peoples themselves or by governments?
4. What do you know about the issues the *Idle No More* movement has tried to address?

Note

1. I use the terms *Indigenous* and *Aboriginal* to refer to the original inhabitants of North America and their descendants. I capitalize the terms *Indigenous* and *Aboriginal* in the same manner that words such as *European* and *American* are capitalized when referring to specific peoples (Johnson et al., 2007).

References

Andersen, C., and C. Denis. 2003. "Urban native communities and the nation model: Before and after the Royal Commission on Aboriginal Peoples," *Canadian Review of Sociology and Anthropology* 40: 373–90.

Belanger, Y., G. Weasel Head, and O. Awasoga. 2012. *Urban Aboriginal Housing and Homelessness in Canada.* Ottawa, ON: National Association of Friendship Centres (NAFC) and the Office of the Federal Interlocutor (OFI).

Bradford, N. 2002. *Why Cities Matter: Policy Research Perspectives for Canada.* cprn Discussion Paper No. F/23. Ottawa, ON: Canadian Policy Research Networks.

———. 2005. *Place-based Public Policy: Towards a New Urban and Community Agenda for Canada.* Ottawa, ON: Canadian Policy Research Network.

Buck, N. 2001. "Identifying neighbourhood effects on social exclusion," *Urban Studies* 38: 2251–75.

Canada. 1997. *Gathering Strength: Canada's Aboriginal Action Plan*. Ottawa, ON: Minister of Public Works and Government Services Canada.

Comack, E., L. Deanne, L. Morrissett, and J. Silver. 2013. *Indians Wear Red: Colonialism, Resistance and Aboriginal Street Gangs*. Winnipeg, MB: Fernwood Press.

Culhane, D. 2009. "Narratives of hope and despair in Downtown Eastside Vancouver," in L.J. Kirmayer and G.G. Valaskakis, eds., *Healing Traditions: The Mental Health of Aboriginal Peoples in Canada*. Vancouver, BC: UBC Press.

Guimond, E., N. Robitaille, and S. Senécal. 2009. "Aboriginal populations in Canadian cities: Why are they growing so fast?" *Canadian Issues* (Winter): 11–17.

Hanselmann, C. 2001. *Urban Aboriginal People in Western Canada*. Calgary, AB: Canada West Foundation.

Heisz, A., and L. McLeod. 2004. *Low Income in Census Metropolitan Areas, 1980–2000*. Catalogue no. 75–001–XIE. Ottawa, ON: Statistics Canada.

Howard, H.A., and C. Proulx, eds. 2011. *Aboriginal Peoples in Canadian Cities: Transformations and Continuities*. Waterloo, ON: Wilfrid Laurier Press.

Howard-Bobiwash, H. 2003. "Women's class strategies as activism in Native community building in Toronto," *American Indian Quarterly* 27: 566–82.

Hughes, M.A. 1990. "Formation of the impacted ghetto: Evidence from large metropolitan areas, 1970–1980," *Urban Geography* 11: 265–84.

Hylton, J.H. 1999. "The case for self-government: A social policy perspective," in J.H. Hylton, ed., *Aboriginal Self-Government in Canada*. Saskatoon, SK: Purich Publishing.

Johnson, J.T. 2008. "Indigeneity's challenges to the white settler-state: Creating a third space for dynamic citizenship," *Alternatives* 33: 29–52.

——, G. Cant, R. Howitt, and E.J. Peters, eds. 2007. *Geographical Research: Journal of the Institute of Australian Geographers* 45: 117–210.

Jargowsky, P.A. 1997. *Poverty and Place: Ghettos, Barrios and the American City*. New York: Russell Sage Foundation.

Kalbach, W.E. 1987. "Growth and distribution of Canada's ethnic populations, 1871–1981," in L. Dreidger, ed., *Ethnic Canada: Identities and Inequalities*. Toronto: Copp Clark Pitman.

LaPrairie, C.P. 2002. "Aboriginal over-representation in the criminal justice system: A tale of nine cities," *Canadian Journal of Criminology* 44: 181–208.

Massey, D.S., and N. Denton. 1988. "The dimensions of residential segregation," *Social Forces* 67: 281–315.

McCaskill, D., K. FitzMaurice, and J. Cidro. 2012. *Toronto Aboriginal Research Project*. Toronto: Toronto Aboriginal Support Services Council (TASSC).

Nagel, J. 1995. "American Indian ethnic renewal: Politics and the resurgence of identity," *American Sociological Review* 60: 947–65.

Newhouse, D.R. 2011. "Urban life: Reflections of a middle-class Indian," in H.A. Howard and C. Proulx, eds., *Aboriginal Peoples in Canadian Cities: Transformations and Continuities*. Waterloo, ON: Wilfrid Laurier Press.

Norris, M.J., and S. Clatworthy. 2009. "Urbanization and migration patterns of Aboriginal peoples in Canada: A half century in review (1951–2006)," Paper presented at the workshop on Indigenous Urbanization Internationally, Saskatoon, 29–30 Oct.

——, and ——. 2003. "Aboriginal mobility and migration within urban Canada: Outcomes, factors and implications," in D. Newhouse and E. Peters, eds., *Not Strangers in These Parts: Aboriginal People in Cities*. Ottawa, ON: Policy Research Initiative.

Ouart, P., and the Saskatoon Indian and Metis Friendship Centre. 2013. "Laying the groundwork for co-production: The Saskatoon Indian and Métis Friendship Centre, 1968–82," in E.J. Peters and C. Andersen, eds., *Indigenous in the City: Contemporary Identities and Cultural Innovation*. Vancouver, BC: UBC Press.

Peters, E.J. 2000. "Aboriginal people in urban areas," in D. Long and O.P. Dickason, eds., *Visions of the Heart: Canadian Aboriginal Issues*. Toronto: Harcourt Canada.

——. 2002. "'Our city Indians': Negotiating the meaning of First Nations urbanisation in Canada, 1945–1975," *Historical Geography* 30: 75–92.

——. 2005. "Indigeneity and marginalisation: Planning for and with urban Aboriginal communities in Canada," *Progress in Planning* 63: 325–404.

——. 2011 "Emerging themes in academic research in urban Aboriginal identities in Canada, 1996–2010," *Aboriginal Policy Studies* 1: 78–105.

——, and C. Andersen, eds. 2013. *Indigenous in the City: Contemporary Identities and Cultural Innovation*. Vancouver, BC: UBC Press.

——, and C. Lafond. 2013. "'I basically mostly stick with my own kind': First Nations appropriation of urban space in Saskatoon, Saskatchewan, Canada," in E.J. Peters and C. Andersen, eds., *Indigenous in the City: Contemporary Identities and Cultural Innovation*. Vancouver, BC: UBC Press.

——, R. Maaka, and R. Laliberte. 2013. "I'm sweating with Cree culture not Saulteaux culture and there goes the beginning of pan-Indianism," in F. Trovato and A. Romanik, eds., *Aboriginal Populations—Social, Demographic and Epidemiological Perspectives*. Toronto: University of Toronto Press.

——, and V. Robillard. 2007. "Urban hidden homelessness and reserve housing," in J.P. White, P. Maxim, and D. Beavon, eds., *Aboriginal Policy Research*. Toronto: Thompson Educational Publishing.

——, and O. Starchenko. 2008. *Neighbourhood Effects and Levels of Segregation of Aboriginal People in Large Cities in Canada*. Ottawa, ON: Canada Mortgage and Housing Corporation.

Proulx, C. 2006. "Aboriginal identification in North American cities," *Canadian Journal of Native Studies* 26: 405–39.

Ramirez, R.K. 2007. *Native Hubs: Culture, Community and Belonging in Silicon Valley and Beyond*. Durham, NC: Duke University Press.

Royal Commission on Aboriginal Peoples (RCAP). 1996a. *Perspectives and Realities: Report of the Royal Commission on Aboriginal Peoples*, vol. 4. Ottawa, ON: Minister of Supply and Services.

——. 1996b. *Looking Forward, Looking Back. Report of the Royal Commission on Aboriginal Peoples*, vol. 1. Ottawa, ON: Minister of Supply and Services.

Siggner, A. 2003. "The challenge of measuring the demographic and socio-economic condition of the urban aboriginal population," in D. Newhouse and E. Peters, eds., *Not Strangers in These Parts: Aboriginal People in Cities*. Ottawa, ON: Policy Research Initiative.

——, and R. Costa. 2005. *Aboriginal Conditions in Census Metropolitan Areas, 1981–2001*. Catalogue no. 89–613–MIE, No. 008. Ottawa, ON: Statistics Canada.

Silver, J., P. Ghorayshi, J. Hay, and D. Klyne. 2006. *In a Voice of Their Own: Urban Aboriginal Community Development*. Winnipeg, MB: Canadian Centre for Policy Alternatives.

Statistics Canada. 2003. *Aboriginal Peoples of Canada*. At: www12.statcan.ca/English/census01/products/analytic/companion/abor/Canada.cfm

——. 2006. *Aboriginal Identity, Area of Residence, Age Groups and Sex for the Population of Canada, Provinces and Territories, 2006 Census of Population*. Catalogue no. 97–558–XCB2006006. Ottawa, ON: Statistics Canada.

——. 2008a. *Aboriginal Peoples in Canada in 2006: Inuit, Métis and First Nations, 2006 Census*. At: www12.statcan.ca/english/census06/analysis/aboriginal/index.cfm (June 2009)

——. 2008b. *Aboriginal Population Profile, 2006 Census of Population*. Catalogue no. 92–594–XWE. Ottawa: Statistics Canada. At: www12.statcan.ca/english/census06/data/profiles/aboriginal/index.cfm?Lang=E (June 2009)

——. 2011 *National Household Survey*, Statistics Canada Catalogue no. 99-012-X2011039.

——. 2012. *Census Profile. 2011 Census*. Statistics Canada Catalogue no. 98-316-XWE. Ottawa, ON: Statistics Canada. At: www12.statcan.gc.ca/census-ecensement/2011/dp-pd/prof/index.cfm?Lang=E

——. 2013. *NHS Profile*. 2011 Census. Catalogue no. 99-004-XWE2011001-201. At: www12.statcan.gc.ca/nhs-enm/2011/dp-pd/prof/details/download-telecharger/comprehensive/comp-csv-tab-nhs-enm.cfm?Lang=E

Straus, A.T., and D. Valentino. 2001. "Retribalization in urban Indian communities," in L. Susan and K. Peters, eds., *American Indians and the Urban Experience*. New York: Altamira Press.

Tobias, J.L. 1983. "Protection, civilization, assimilation: An outline history of Canada's Indian policy," in A.L. Getty and A.S. Lussier, eds., *As Long as the Sun Shines and Water Flows: A Reader in Canadian Native Studies*. Vancouver, BC: UBC Press.

Todd, R. 2000–1. "Between the land and the city: Aboriginal agency, culture, and governance in urban areas," *London Journal of Canadian Studies* 16: 48–66.

Tomiak, J. 2010. "Indigenous governance in Winnipeg and Ottawa: Making space for self-determination," in J.P. White and J. Bruhn, eds., *Aboriginal Policy Research: Exploring the Urban Landscape*. Toronto: Thompson Educational Publishing, Inc.

Urban Aboriginal Task Force. 2007. *Urban Aboriginal Task Force. Final Report*. Toronto: Ontario Federation of Indian Friendship Centres.

Walker, R. 2003. "Engaging the urban Aboriginal population in low-cost housing initiatives: Lessons from Winnipeg," *Canadian Journal of Urban Research* 12: 99–118.

——. 2006. "Searching for Aboriginal/Indigenous self-determination: Urban citizenship in the Winnipeg low-cost housing sector, Canada," *Environment and Planning A* 38: 2345–63.

——. 2008a. "Improving the interface between urban municipalities and Aboriginal communities," *Canadian Journal of Urban Research* 17: 20–36.

——. 2008b. "Aboriginal self-determination and social housing in urban Canada: A story of convergence and divergence," *Urban Studies* 54: 185–205.

Walks, R.A., and L.S. Bourne. 2006. "Ghettos in Canada's cities? Racial segregation, ethnic enclaves and poverty concentration in Canadian urban areas," *Canadian Geographer* 50: 273–97.

Wilson, K., and E.J. Peters. 2005. "'You can make a place for it': Remapping urban First Nations spaces of identity," *Society and Space* 23: 395–413.

Wilson, W.J. 1987. *The Truly Disadvantaged: The Inner City, the "Underclass" and Public Policy*. Chicago, IL: University of Chicago Press.

Gender, Sexuality, and the City

22

DAMARIS ROSE

Introduction

Ever since the early twentieth century, the urban spaces of cities, transformed by mass urbanization and economic diversification, have been key arenas for the destabilization, reinforcement, and renegotiation of society's prevailing visions about two of the crucial ways in which society classifies people and judges their behaviour. The first concerns visions about *gender*. This concept refers to the roles, behaviour, activities, and responsibilities that societies and cultures deem appropriate for people biologically sexed as women and men to fulfill in their key arenas and institutions—such as the family, the workplace, the community, civic and political bodies, and public space. Likewise, people take on gender identities based on their internalization, or their contestation, of these social and cultural norms. The second concerns society's visions about *sexuality*. This concept refers not just to biologically driven expressions of sexual desire, but to the sets of sexual behaviours that societies and cultures either expect or consider to be "normal" or "abnormal" (in both private and public domains) based on biological sex differences, and to the identities that people take on based on these expectations. In fact, many of the topics and urban processes that form the subject of chapters in this book are undergirded and crosscut by questions of gender and sexuality.

Since the late 1970s, a diverse body of research in urban geography and related fields from a feminist perspective has studied the gendered qualities of urban life with a view to understanding the roles of the urban in dynamics of gender equity/inequity and in shaping gendered dimensions of identity (for reviews, see Bondi and Rose, 2003; McDowell, 1999). Major themes addressed have included the challenges of a legacy of spatial arrangements based on a gendered breadwinner/homemaker divide that no longer corresponds to the realities of today's urban households; gendered aspects of urban fear in public space; and how gendered constructions of space and place intersect with those based on social class and racialization (see Siciliano, Cowen, and Smith, Chapter 16). More recently, the field of urban studies has also been enriched by a mushrooming body of literature on sexualities and urban space (for reviews, see Oswin, 2008; Peake, 2010). Many scholars in this field identify with the goal of "queer-ing" geographic analysis, meaning that they seek to uncover and critique the ways that the organization of urban life is shaped by heteronormativity. This concept refers to the entrenchment of heterosexual forms of attachment, sex, and reproduction in institutions, policies, and expectations of behaviour such that non-heterosexuals are made to feel, at best, like outsiders. This entrenchment translates into heterosexism by implicitly inscribing or "coding" urban spaces as heterosexual, leading researchers in this field to study how lesbians, gays, bisexuals, and transgender people adapt to, make use of, and contest their "outsider" status by creating their own urban "scenes" (Valentine and Skelton, 2003).

Feminist urban studies and the sexualities and space literatures have had a tendency to move along parallel tracks (Domosh, 1999; Knopp, 2007). However, bridges are beginning to be built by researchers who highlight how heteronormativity corresponds to a "moral heartland" at the intersection of what society deems to be "good" or "normal" gender relations and "good" or "normal" sexualities (Hubbard, 2008; Oswin, 2010; Wright, 2010). In western, highly urbanized societies, such as Canada's, for most of the twentieth century the landscape of this "moral centre" was dominated by the patriarchal heterosexual nuclear family with a strongly gender-typed role division between male authority-figure and breadwinner and female nurturer and homemaker. Placed outside this intersection of gender and sexual norms were all non-heterosexuals, but also heterosexual men and women who never married and lived autonomously from their parental or extended family. They faced various forms of "othering," marginalization, or social ostracism (such as that of "unwed mothers") depending on the perceived threat they posed to prevailing norms. This of course extended to outright repression in the case of homosexual practices, which were fully illegal until the partial victories of the gay rights movements, which began, like second-wave feminism, in the context of the social and cultural ferment associated with the decade of the 1960s.

Two dominant narratives, in creative tension with each other, traverse both the feminist geography and sexualities and space literatures: the liberating potential associated with life in a large metropolitan centre compared to rural and small town living, versus the constraining and controlling qualities of the heteronormative organization of space within the metropolis (Bondi and Rose, 2003; Cattan and Leroy, 2010; Muller Myrdal, 2013; Wilson, 2001). In this chapter I explore this interplay of "freedom" and "constraint" within topic areas that have received considerable attention in feminist or queer geographies. I begin with a discussion of the linkages between metropolitan urbanization over the twentieth century and women's opportunities for economic autonomy via the labour market, as well as an examination, using recent census data, of the widely held view in sexuality studies that large cities are a magnet for homosexuals. Second, I review and update research on a key dimension of metropolitan, especially suburban, life in which gender-based spatial constraints have been extensively documented—urban mobility, in particular travel-to-work. I follow this up with a discussion of the challenges facing lone-parent families in metropolitan space—a family form that has been widely subjected to economic marginality, in large part because of its outsider status in a heteronormative society geared toward the two-parent nuclear family. I also examine gendered dimensions of gentrification, and go on to discuss central city neighbourhoods as resources for sexual minorities.

Metropolitan Urbanization and Departures from the Heteronormal in Historical Perspective

It is common to see the social, cultural, and political upheavals of the 1960s (Campbell, Clément, and Kealey, 2012) as a turning point in the situation of women in Canadian society in terms of what sociologists refer to as "individualization" (Jones, Marsden, and Tepperman, 1990)—their ability to implement their own choices about their sexuality, fertility, marital arrangements, and, of course, their opportunities for paid work and career employment. However, key precursors of these changes were already incubating throughout the first half of the twentieth century, an era of major socio-economic and demographic upheavals punctuated by the two world wars and the Great Depression. Over this period, Canadian cities from coast to coast experienced massive growth in a context of out-migration from struggling agricultural communities combined with successive waves of international immigration. Among the many consequences of these upheavals were major changes in the lives of single women. In the major urban centres of central Canada, the expansion of the garment and other light industries plus the demand for domestic service workers were major factors in rural–urban and international migration of young single women, who would often board with relatives or employers while sending remittances to their parental families (Gauvreau, Olson, and Thornton, 2008). After World War I, urban growth accelerated across the country. The rise of corporate capitalism, technological changes in white-collar work, and the rise of the consumer society among the expanding urban middle classes all fuelled the growth of the service economy—generating a steady increase in work opportunities in clerical, sales, and consumer services for young women, both from middle-class backgrounds and those from upwardly mobile working-class families (England and Boyer, 2009; Srigley, 2010). As

we can see from Figure 22.1, in the first half of the twentieth century the rate of increase in feminization of clerical work paralleled that of urban growth and exceeded that of the feminization of the labour force as a whole.

However, prior to World War II, women were shut out of almost all Canadian workplaces once they married, and in the social and cultural climate of the times, most middle-class women and those in upwardly mobile working-class households accepted this situation as normal and inevitable (Strong-Boag, 1988). Big labour unions, corporate employers, and governments supported mass production with labour relations based on the concept of a "family wage," earned by a single male breadwinner. The application of this concept would generate enough disposable income to fuel the spread of a middle-class consumer society based on home ownership and mass consumption of standardized goods. Integral to this economic and cultural paradigm (referred to in political-economic theory as Fordism) was an ethos of conformity, epitomized by the spread of

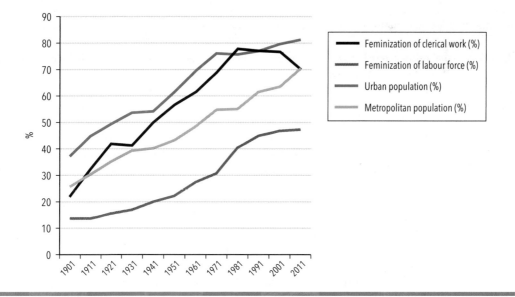

Figure 22.1   Urbanization, Metropolitan Growth, and the Feminization of the Labour Force and of Clerical Work, Canada 1901–2011

Source: England and Boyer, 2009; Statistics Canada, censuses and CANSIM, various years.

tract suburbs where women devoted themselves exclusively to raising heterosexual families. And, of course, the automobile was central to this paradigm. In poorer working-class families, married women often engaged in home-based employment to make ends meet, such as taking in paying boarders, laundry work, or piece-work in the garment industry (Baillargeon, 1999).

While the patriarchal nuclear family was well entrenched across social classes in early twentieth-century urban society and became increasingly inscribed in space in residential suburbs designed to isolate private from public life (Mackenzie and Rose, 1983), this was simultaneously a time when, at least in metropolitan cities, young single women gained new freedoms (Peiss, 1986). The 1900–30 decades saw a surge in "moral panics" among bourgeois social reformers, clergy, and public-opinion shapers about young rural women deemed at risk of drifting into areas of the city associated with prostitution as well as about young urban women who might become "too independent" and lose interest in marriage (Myers, 2006; Strange, 1995). These "moral panics" led to religious and philanthropic organizations setting up supervised boarding homes and institutional residences for young working women who could not live with their parental families, as well as outreach programs to prepare them for a life of motherhood and running a family household (Kirkland, 2006; Piché, 1999a). However, young working women did not necessarily buy into the paternalism inherent in such programs: they strove to use their living arrangements as resources for forging companionship with their peers, creating safe but autonomous spaces, and overcoming the isolation of the metropolitan city (Beer, 1939; McMaster, 2002). Increasing numbers of single women began sharing flats as the supply of apartment buildings increased rapidly in Canadian cities beginning in the 1920s (Dennis, 2006/7). Young white-collar women, even when they continued to live with and help support their parental families, increasingly asserted their rights to join in urban consumer culture, and their presence in the city's public spaces, socializing with peers, became increasingly socially acceptable (Boyer, 1998;

Srigley, 2010), although far less so in francophone Quebec milieus (Piché, 1999b). Both residential and public spaces were thus key sites for negotiating individualized identities as "modern girls" or "business girls," as women office workers were then known (Beer, 1939). For most of these young women, however, their assertion of economic and personal autonomy was still framed within a vision of marriage and inevitable eventual departure from the workforce (Kirkland, 2006; Strange, 1995: 179–85). Those who remained unmarried over the longer term were still very much at the margins of heteronormative urban society. Not only did they rarely make a living wage, but maintaining their professional career also meant ensuring that their housing arrangements were perceived as "respectable"—sharing with another woman of similar age and status or in a boarding house run by a widow, for example (O'Hanlon, 2002; Tallentire, 2006).

Overall, these diverse metropolitan environments could be conducive to ways of life that did not conform to normative visions of heterosexual femininity and masculinity maintained through the traditional nuclear family, and so including not only single women but also gays and lesbians (Garber, 2000). Historically grounded scholarship on sexualities and urban life as well as gay and lesbian fiction have emphasized how both the metropolitan city's modern cultural qualities and its diversified employment opportunities have made it a magnet for gays and lesbians seeking refuge from rural communities and small towns characterized by strictly enforced heterosexual nuclear family norms (Chauncey, 1994; Lewis, 2013; Muller Myrdal, 2013; Podmore, 2006). As well, the patriarchal extended family structures of rural communities limited the freedoms of long-term single men and women (Christie, 2004). In contrast, as the early twentieth century sociologist Georg Simmel argued, the modern metropolis facilitates individual self-development without reference to the norms of family-based rural and small-town society (Simmel, 1950 [1903]). The big city was seen to afford anonymity, but also the opportunity to make oneself visible to others with whom one has affinities. The size and diversity of metropolitan populations and the high densities of streetscapes created favourable conditions for a critical mass of gays and lesbians who could organize themselves into subcultures that were visible to themselves—but not necessarily visible to heterosexual individuals or to the police and other institutions involved in punishing transgressive sexualities.

Post-World War II research on the history of gay male communities in the US indicates that their migration to large metropolitan centres was linked to the growth and diversification of service sector employment, which was less associated with traditional expressions of masculinity than was work in heavy industries (D'Emilio, 1998[1983]; Lauria and Knopp, 1985). Some of these cities were also cultural and artistic hubs, sectors long associated with gay communities. Government services, whose highest concentrations are in national and state or provincial capitals, are also a key sector of professional and white-collar employment. The Cold War period of the 1950s and 1960s was a time of government surveillance and exclusion of presumed homosexuals, but subsequently Ottawa, for example, became a hub of gay activism for legal rights, and its government services sector acquired a reputation for relative tolerance of "responsible" middle-class gay men (Lewis, 2012). Scholarship on lesbian communities has also pointed to pressures to concentrate in larger urban centres, emphasizing the issue of isolation in small towns and rural areas and the difficulties of organizing support groups and political movements for lesbian rights in a widely dispersed spatial context (Millward, 2012; Muller Myrdal, 2013).

Since 2001, the Canadian census has included a question enabling people to identify if they live in a same-sex relationship. The published data (Figure 22.2) allow us to take as the denominator the total numbers of individuals of each sex who are living in a spousal relationship and calculate what percentage of them are same-sex spouses. For Canada as a whole, the 2011 percentages are 0.89 per cent for males and 0.75 per cent for females. The CMAs (census metropolitan areas) with the highest reported rates of same-sex spouses differ by gender: in the case of men, Montreal (1.54 per cent), Vancouver (1.40 per cent), and Quebec City (1.33 per cent) report the highest rates. In the case

of women, however, Victoria (a provincial capital, but also the CMA with the highest share of seniors, an age group where women predominate) ranks highest (1.45 per cent), followed by the Gatineau (Quebec) part of the Ottawa-Gatineau CMA (1.31 per cent), and another provincial capital, Halifax (1.30 per cent). When we plot the percentages for men (y-axis of Figure 22.2) against population size for all 33 Canadian CMAs (x-axis, using the natural log so that we can include large and small CMAs on the same chart), we find a modest positive relationship ($R^2 = 0.4692$). Outliers at the high end are Montreal and Vancouver, consistent with their "gay-friendly" reputation, followed by a cluster of provincial capitals and the national capital CMA. CMAs with low rates of men in same-sex couples relative to their population size include numerous mid-size and small CMAs whose economy is manufacturing-based, as well as BC's two smallest CMAs, which have a reputation for social conservatism. In the case of Toronto, cultural diversity may play a role in reducing the reporting of gay domestic partnerships.

The portrait changes completely for women: the frequency of female same-sex domestic partnerships is totally unrelated to CMA population size ($R^2 = 0.013$) (Figure 22.3). This could be in part due to the gendered dimensions of employment segmentation: women are concentrated in service sector employment regardless of where they live. As well, it is only gay men, not homosexuals in general, that are historically associated with the arts and culture sectors. The findings become even more interesting when we use as the denominator for the y-axis all persons living in same-sex couples, then calculate the percentage of these couples that are comprised of two women and chart this percentage against CMA population size. This time we get a moderately ($R^2 = 0.498$) negative correlation with CMA size. Gay male couples are distinctly more prevalent than lesbian couples in the larger CMAs, with the exception of Winnipeg. The balance shifts toward lesbian couples in a wide variety of mid-size and small CMAs. The most important high-end outliers are two small "university-town" CMAs: Kingston and Guelph. In a context where most research on homosexuality

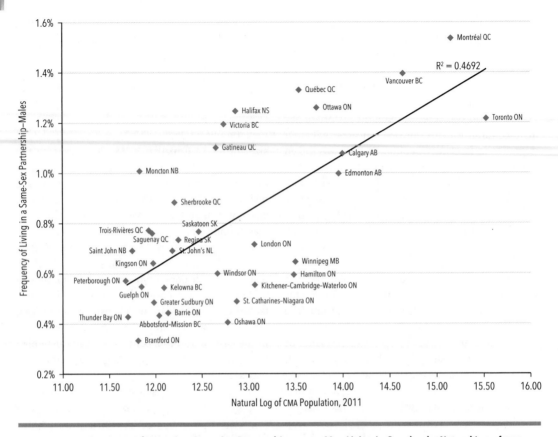

Figure 22.2   **Frequency of Living in a Same-Sex Partnership among Men Living in Couples, by Natural Log of CMA Population, 2011**

Source: Statistics Canada, 2012. 2011 Census, Topic-based tabulation: Catalogue no. 98-312-XCB2011045; Statistics Canada, 2012; Population and dwelling counts, for Canada, provinces and territories, census metropolitan areas and census agglomerations, 2011 and 2006 censuses (table); Population and Dwelling Count Highlight Tables, 2011 Census. Statistics Canada Catalogue no. 98-310-XWE2011002. Ottawa: Statistics Canada.

and urban life (which we discuss later) still focuses on large cities, these results support a recent call to pay more attention to how non-heterosexuals, and lesbians in particular, negotiate their identities in "ordinary cities," including small urban settings where non-heterosexuals face unique challenges in building social networks (Muller Myrdal, 2013).

Gender and Urban Mobility

The rapidity of metropolitan growth, the increasing demographic, socio-economic, and ethnocultural diversification of suburbs, and the rising interest in urban sustainability have all contributed in recent years to renewed interest in the relationships between transportation and mobility, individual opportunity, and systemic social exclusion. Transportation was one of the first fields of urban studies to be extensively studied from a feminist perspective; it is opportune to revisit this discussion.

Every five years in the Greater Montreal area, as in other large metropolitan cities, a government agency conducts a detailed travel behaviour survey. In recent years, reports from this study have

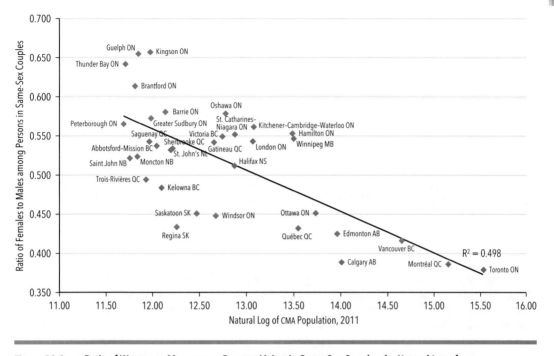

Figure 22.3   **Ratio of Women to Men among Persons Living in Same-Sex Couples, by Natural Log of CMA Population, 2011**

Source: Statistics Canada, 2012. 2011 Census, Topic-based tabulation: Catalogue no. 98-312-XCB2011045; Statistics Canada, 2012; Population and dwelling counts, for Canada, provinces and territories, census metropolitan areas and census agglomerations, 2011 and 2006 censuses (table); Population and Dwelling Count Highlight Tables, 2011 Census. Statistics Canada Catalogue no. 98-310-XWE2011002. Ottawa: Statistics Canada.

highlighted findings presented as quite startling: women are responsible for most of the increase, from one survey to the next, in the number of trips from home to work taken by private car in the peak morning rush hour; yet men are beginning to shift toward greater use of public transportation (St-Pierre, 2007). Gender, the government analysts point out, will be a key parameter for transportation planning in the coming years because women's participation in the labour force is continuing to increase along with their rate of car ownership, whereas both of these have peaked for men. The attention paid to these findings by government planners highlights some important ways that everyday life has changed for a large segment of Canadian women in recent decades, and points out how changes in women's lives can affect key dimensions of urban development and

change. Yet 30 years ago, feminist urban geographers found themselves having to critique a tradition of journey-to-work studies that only took account of men's commuting patterns (Monk and Hanson, 1982)! Most of the increase in Greater Montreal women's work trips by car is coming from the region's sprawling and fast-growing outer suburbs, which have even lower residential densities than the outer suburbs of most other large Canadian metropolitan areas (Filion et al., 2010), and are mostly still poorly served by public transit. Families raising children still predominate in these newer outer suburbs although this is beginning to change with population aging and condominium construction.

While this increased **automobility** (Featherstone, 2004) of middle-class women symbolizes a type of freedom associated with their individualization, for those with family responsibilities this freedom is deeply embedded in gender-typed constraints. Such constraints are heightened in contexts of strong spatial separation between different functional land uses, which has been a characteristic of outer suburban morphology since the post-World War II boom. Within heterosexual nuclear families, women devote far more time than men to child-rearing activities and domestic tasks, even though this gender gap has narrowed as fathers take on more responsibilities for children (Dyck, 2005; Statistics Canada, 2012b). From the late 1940s to early 1960s, when most suburban married mothers of young and school-aged children did not do paid work outside the home, their daytime weekday mobility was very limited because their husbands usually took the family car to work; indeed, mass media, advertisers, government agencies, and urban planners strongly encouraged this confined, home-centred way of life as the best way to reinforce the heterosexual nuclear family (Mendes, 2010; Strong-Boag, 2002 [1991]). Yet married women joined the paid workforce—especially clerical work—in rapidly increasing numbers from 1941 onwards (Dominion Bureau of Statistics, 1954: 702–3), in part due to middle-class families' financial needs in the context of the rising cost of living, but also in a context of rising educational attainment as well as mounting frustration with what Betty Friedan, the American pioneer of second-wave feminism, famously called "the problem with no name." Their employment was very often part-time, and many relied on husbands for rides to work, but a growing number of families could afford—and found they could not do without—two cars. For the period between the mid-1970s and mid-1990s, a study in Quebec City, where the configuration of highway corridors has led to scattered linear patterns of employment growth, showed quite convincingly that the rise in women's labour force participation was in part made possible by their increased car ownership (Vandersmissen, Villeneuve, and Thériault, 2001).

In general, late-twentieth-century suburban women took jobs that were closer to home than were jobs that suburban men took or that involved shorter driving distances (Preston and McLafferty,

1993). Overall, even today women who drive to work still have slightly shorter trip times than men, according to estimates from Statistics Canada's 2011 National Household Survey (NHS)—27 minutes versus 31 minutes on average in the Toronto case (Statistics Canada, 2012a). Qualitative research has found that suburban women often seek to reduce their commute times in order to make time for domestic responsibilities, many of which require additional driving time to make stops to drop off/collect children or the babysitter, pick up groceries, and so on. Indeed, travel survey data clearly show that women with children at home make far more daily trips by car then those without children at home, and this is also true for those who use public transportation (Bernard et al., 1997). As well, the types of jobs in which women have traditionally been concentrated, especially for part-time work, such as retail sales and personal services, but also for predominantly female professions, such as elementary school teaching, are typically quite accessible from suburban residential neighbourhoods. However, the better-paying clerical jobs as well as professional employment in finance, government services, specialized health care, or high-technology sectors are generally located in the urban core or in science parks quite far from residential suburbs (Villeneuve and Rose, 1988). Consequently, as more suburban-based women need a "breadwinner's" salary or move into professional and non-traditional fields, their commuting trips will tend to lengthen, increasing the challenges of juggling work and domestic responsibilities, especially if the spouse/domestic partner is not available to take on an increased share of these tasks due to extended working hours or shift work (Preston et al., 2000).

We now step back to examine the bigger picture of travel modes in metropolitan Canada. Figure 22.4 presents National Household Survey (NHS) estimates for 2011, for a selection of large CMAs, of the percentage of employed women and men who used various modes of transportation as their main means of getting to work. The figure shows that women are still far more likely to travel to work by public transportation than are men. The NHS data also show that those who commute by public transportation have much longer travel times, on average, than car commuters. For example, in Montreal average transit commute times are 43 minutes for both men and women versus 28 minutes for male drivers and 26 minutes for female drivers (Figure 22.4). However, the quality of transit users' commuting experiences varies depending on mode and the state of maintenance of these forms of public infrastructure—we can think of the contrast between using a high-speed commuter line versus making two or three slow bus connections. In Canada's large metropolitan areas, gender, social class, and immigrant status can intersect to produce a variegated network of advantaged and disadvantaged travel patterns. Those living in poor and underserviced apartment districts, which are often interspersed with more affluent neighbourhoods (Fiedler, Schuurman, and Hyndman, 2006), may well face what labour-market geographers refer to as "spatial mismatch" on account of the great distance and poor connectivity between neighbourhoods of affordable rental housing and areas where jobs paying a living wage are available (see Walks, Chapter 9).

Transportation use and disadvantage are also related to immigrant status intersecting with gender (Uteng, 2009). A detailed analysis of

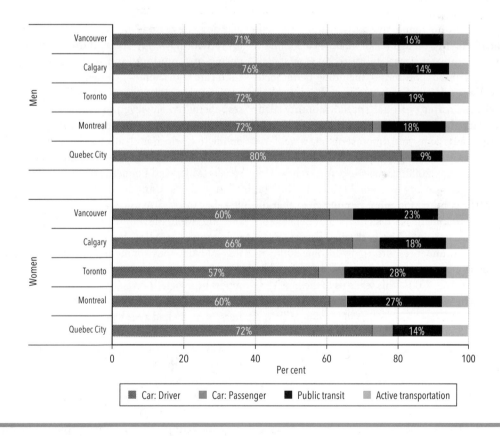

Figure 22.4 **Main Mode of Travel to Work, for Selected CMAs, 2011**

Source: Source: Statistics Canada, 2011. National Household Survey, NHS Data Tables, 99-012-X2011031.

Note: Data should be interpreted with caution due to non-response bias resulting from the voluntary character of the NHS. Overall non-response rates: Quebec City, 21.4 per cent; Montreal, 19.7 per cent; Toronto, 25.4 per cent; Calgary, 23.6 per cent; Vancouver, 24.4 per cent.

2001 data for Toronto, Montreal, and Vancouver showed that recent immigrants, many of whom are known to experience severe difficulties in finding both suitable, affordable housing and suitable employment are far more likely to rely on public transportation to get to work than other groups, even when they live far away from their work (see Kobayashi and Preston, Chapter 8). This is especially true for low-earning workers. Recent immigrant women are even more likely than recent immigrant men to rely on public transportation (Heisz and Schellenberg, 2004). As well, fear about personal safety while using public transportation is both gendered and racialized (see Siciliano, Cowen, and Smith, Chapter 16).

Placing a gendered lens on urban transportation issues thus highlights how greater personal spatial mobility, though it can be time-consuming, generates greater accessibility to diverse social resources and opportunities, including better jobs and a wider range of community and commercial services. Greater personal spatial mobility also generates the less tangible benefits of a greater sense of autonomy and empowerment, which are important for immigrant women, for example (Ray and Rose, 2000). Conversely, researchers are increasingly focusing on "mobility deprivation" (a term that is becoming more popular than that of "spatial entrapment") as a significant dimension of social exclusion. In this respect, sole-support mothers living in under-resourced low-income suburbs comprise one group that is particularly vulnerable (Morency et al., 2011). This leads us to the next section, where we examine lone-parent families.

The Gendered Challenges of Lone Parenthood in Urban Settings

The past few decades have seen a broad societal shift toward more fluidity in conjugal relationships, a turning point being the liberalization of divorce laws in Canada in 1968. This has had major consequences for family types and parenting arrangements. A key change has been the growth in the number of lone-parent families compared to two-parent families. In the first half of the twentieth century, widowhood was an important source of lone-parent family formation (Bradbury, 2000), and so with rising life expectancy after World War II the percentage of lone-parent families declined to a low of 8.4 per cent of census families in 1961 before starting to rise again, reaching 16.3 per cent by 2011. Today just over half of single parents are divorced or legally separated, and almost one-third have never married (Milan and Bohnert, 2012a). What has changed little, however, is the highly gendered nature of lone parenthood. The ratio of female- to male-led lone-parent families has remained at about four to one for the past five decades. The reasons for this are complex but have to do with powerful and enduring socio-cultural norms of femininity and masculinity in which child-care in the home and other "routine" aspects of parenting are still deemed to be primarily women's responsibility. However, in the new millennium, shared custody arrangements following divorce are on the rise, which is creating a slight upward trend in the share of male lone parents enumerated in the census (Milan and Bohnert, 2012b).

In today's Canadian society there is less stigma attached to lone-parent families than in the mid-twentieth century, but beliefs persist that they are not "normal" families and are inherently less adequate environments for child-raising than the two-parent nuclear family. Indeed, in a recent report by a socially conservative think-tank ranking Canadian cities according to their "family-friendliness," if a city had a high percentage of lone-parent families its score was lowered (Walberg and Mrozek, 2010)! As well as being heteronormative, there is an ethnocentric bias in such a viewpoint, because the cultural groups with the highest rates of lone parenthood (those with Caribbean origins and urban aboriginals) have strong traditions of supporting child-raising through extended family networks (Mata, 2011; Peters, 2000). It is undeniable that in the absence of social supports and services geared to their needs, lone parents face more challenges than two-parent families.

However, analyses from a feminist perspective point out that the materially and socially deprived domestic and neighbourhood environments that many lone-parent families have to deal with are essentially the consequence of gendered poverty and not related to family type as such. In fact, the children of lone-parent households in the middle-income category—to which some female lone parents and most male lone parents belong—do not experience a higher rate of problems in their schooling and social integration than those growing up in two-parent families (Ambert, 2006).

The economic situation of female lone parents varies greatly depending on education and age. Far more have a university degree compared to three decades ago, which greatly reduces the risk of poverty (LaRochelle-Côté, Gougeon, and Pinard, 2009). Lone parents under 25 form a small minority of the total, but have very high poverty rates due to dependence on social assistance; they typically have not been able to complete their education and face further barriers to employment due to the young age of their children and lack of affordable child-care. Although poverty can be a

lifetime experience for some, overall lone-parent poverty rates decrease in each successive age group over 25. Becoming a lone parent later in the life cycle is associated with divorce after a number of years in a marriage where family assets were built up and then divided between the ex-spouses (Ambert, 2006).

Female lone parents face greater financial challenges than their male counterparts because their incomes are almost 40 per cent lower (based on 2006 data for lone parents aged under 65) (LaRochelle-Côté, Gougeon, and Pinard, 2009). The gender gap in income persists regardless of education level or age group (Canada Mortgage and Housing Corporation, 2012). We can see this from the first two sets of bars in Figure 22.5, showing after-tax low-income rates of male and female lone parents in Canada in 2006 (the most recent year available) by age group.

Since more than 70 per cent of households consisting of a lone-parent family live in **census metropolitan areas** (Canada Mortgage and Housing Corporation, 2012), I also present data in this chart for female lone parents by age group

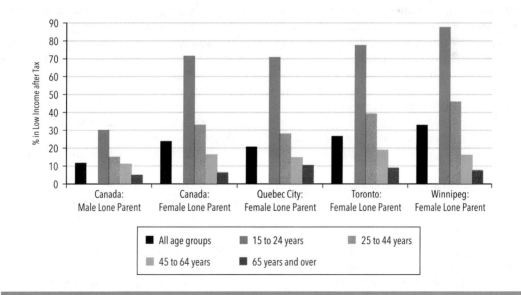

Figure 22.5   **Low Income Rates among Lone Parents, after Tax, by Age Group, 2006**

Source: Statistics Canada, 2007. 2006 Census, Topic-Based Tabulations, 2006, Catalogue no. 97-563-XCB2006029.

in three large CMAs: Quebec City, Toronto, and Winnipeg. (I do not present the data for male lone parents by CMA due to their very small numbers in the younger age groups.) I selected these three CMAs to illustrate different characteristics that explain variations in poverty rates among female lone parents. Quebec City's lower rates no doubt reflect the extensive and good quality white-collar employment opportunities (many being permanent positions with flexible working hours) available to women in government services industries in a provincial capital, and no doubt also the greater availability of affordable daycare due to provincial government policy. The high rates in Winnipeg in the 15–24 and 25–44 age groups reflect the high concentration of poor Aboriginal women in this CMA (see Peters, Chapter 21), and may also indicate the long duration of lone parenthood in the life course in this group. Toronto lies in between these extremes, with its diversified work opportunities for women being offset by high numbers of those visible minority groups in which both lone motherhood and poverty are prevalent.

Since the 1970s, female lone parents' employment rates have not increased as fast as those of mothers in two-parent families. As well, the age of the youngest child has more impact in reducing the employment rate for lone mothers compared to mothers in two-parent families (based on our analysis of Table 6 in Williams, 2010), which is undoubtedly due to difficulties in access to suitable and affordable child-care arrangements. Since the Quebec government implemented a $5 per day daycare program in 1997 (later raised to $7), the labour force participation of women in that province with very young children has overtaken the rates in the other three largest provinces, and poverty rates of lone-mother families have fallen considerably (Friendly and Prentice, 2009; Proulx et al., 2011).

The economic and emotional precariousness often associated with becoming a lone parent has important repercussions for their housing situations and needs. If the family has to move to a different neighbourhood in order to find a cheaper, easier-to-maintain home, this can be disruptive for children's social networks. In the extreme scenario of flight from domestic violence, non-profit organizations (supported by government and charitable funding) play a crucial role in providing safe and supportive temporary shelter and transitional accommodation. Core housing need is common among lone mothers (see Harris, Chapter 19), but rare among lone fathers (Canada Mortgage and Housing Corporation, 2012). A shelter cost-to-income ratio of 50 per cent or more is not uncommon, making families vulnerable to losing their housing if there is an unexpected drop in income from one month to the next (see Walks, Chapter 9). In other cases, their poverty leads to having to live in conditions that fall below acceptable environmental health standards or that are overcrowded; recent immigrant and refugee women may be especially vulnerable to such situations (Rose and Charette, 2014). Finally, although illegal under provincial human rights codes, lone parents may still find their housing choices limited by discrimination by private landlords (Lauster and Easterbrook, 2011). Social housing can provide security of tenure, rent stability, and, sometimes, companionship and mutual support to low- and modest-income lone parents, who are often given priority on waiting lists by social housing providers (Wekerle, 1993) (see Harris, Chapter 19).

A way to sum up these intersecting differences among lone parents in terms of gender, socio-economic status, and racialization is by examining the spatial distributions of male and female lone parents within a metropolitan area. The two maps comprising Figure 22.6 present the relative concentration of female- and male-headed lone-parent families in the Montreal CMA in 2011. Comparing these maps to the map of average incomes for the entire population for 2010 (in Figure 22.7) allows us to see whether the areas where lone parents are under- or over-represented (compared to their share of the population as a whole) are low-, middle-, or high-income neighbourhoods. The maps show that although lone-parent families are found in a wide variety of neighbourhoods, from inner city to outer suburban and from low to high income, there is still an association of female lone parents with low-income neighbourhoods. The census tracts of highest relative concentration are in fact those with

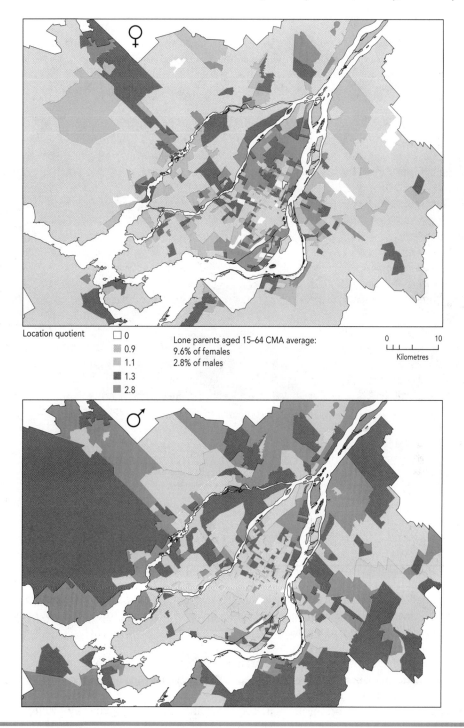

Figure 22.6   Relative Concentration of Female and Male Lone Parents in the Montreal CMA, 2011, by Census Tracts

Source: Statistics Canada, *2011 Census of Population*, Statistics Canada Catalogue no. 98-312-XCB2011029.

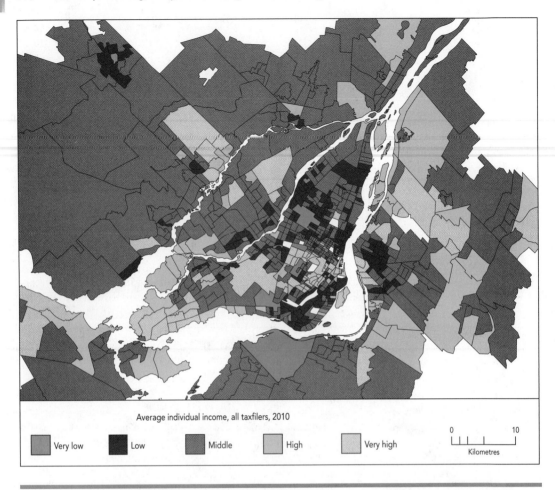

Average individual income, all taxfilers, 2010

Very low   Low   Middle   High   Very high

0   10
Kilometres

Figure 22.7   Economic Status of Census Tracts in the Montreal CMA, 2010, Based on Tax Filers' Average Incomes

Source: Canada Revenue Agency, Taxfiler Data, 2010. Individual income in 2010 is from all sources, before tax. Data used by permission of the Neighbourhood Change Research Partnership, University of Toronto.

high concentrations of public housing. In addition, high concentrations are found in parts of NE and SW Montreal, where Caribbean-origin populations are concentrated. Male lone parents, however, are more associated with middle- and high-income neighbourhoods—including parts of the Plateau Mont-Royal, where gentrification is very advanced (many of these high-income male lone parents are no doubt in shared custody arrangements). This last finding contrasts with the situation back in the 1980s, when such neighbourhoods were in a

very early stage of gentrification and appealed to well-educated female lone parents with precarious employment status (Rose and Le Bourdais, 1986).

Gendered Dimensions of Gentrification

Scholars such as David Ley (1996) have convincingly shown how the settlement of "new bohemians"—artists, students, and others rooted in the "countercultural" social movements of the 1960s—in a good number of inner-city neighbourhoods in Canadian cities was an important factor in paving the way for those neighbourhoods' subsequent gentrification (see Bain, Chapter 14). In the context of debates around gentrification in the 1980s and 1990s, feminist geographers argued that the changes in gender relations and identities that also began to foment in the 1960s and accelerate in the next two decades also contributed to early stages of gentrification (Bondi, 1999; Rose, 2010 [1984]). In a modern variant of the early-twentieth century pattern of single women establishing their independence in metropolitan urban space, discussed earlier in this chapter, this research pointed to a sub-group of highly educated and economically self-supporting women, on their own or with children, attracted to diverse and affordable inner city neighbourhoods. These neighbourhoods were located close to downtown professional employment in advanced tertiary sectors, such as government services, specialized education, and health institutions, where career opportunities for female professionals expanded from the 1970s to 1990s (Rose and Villeneuve, 1993). Many of these professional positions were, however, precarious (e.g., short-term contracts). Both functionally and culturally, such neighbourhoods were more comfortable spaces for these "non-traditional" women compared to classic postwar suburbia. In such neighbourhoods, compared to lower-density suburbs, mothers of young children, without access to a car, could more easily participate in informal networks, thereby reducing isolation and fostering mutual aid. Such women were among the key players in collective urban movements to develop their supportive qualities for themselves and for other modest-income households—such as parent-run daycare centres, food and housing co-operatives, or "alternative" low-cost forms of home ownership (Rose, 2010 [1984]; Wekerle, 1985; 1993).

In this vein, a study in Montreal showed that during the early stages of gentrification in the Plateau Mont-Royal district, women were over-represented among professionals living there, and those women professionals were more likely to be single or lone parents compared to women professionals overall in the Montreal CMA (Rose, 1989). A more contemporary version of this phenomenon has been identified in a "pre-gentrifying" Toronto neighbourhood where small, female-led commercial enterprises are embedded in gender-typed mutual aid networks that also outreach to the area's most precarious residents severely hit by neo-liberal social services cuts (Kern, 2012). However, in many cases, and especially in cities that have successfully converted their economic base to a post-industrial one with a strong downtown employment core, the gentrification of these types of neighbourhoods has accelerated and become much more upscale, decreasing their socio-economic diversity. Influxes of affluent dual-earner professional/managerial couples have helped fuel inflation in local real estate markets, contributing to displacement of low-income households and increasing the polarization of household incomes within the inner city (see Walks, Chapter 9). As well, mothers of young children in these affluent couples have less of a stake in non-profit service provision compared to the early-stage gentrifiers, since they can afford to purchase child-care and other resources at market rates. Gendered understandings of gentrification thus always need to be placed in relation to dynamics associated with social class.

The ways that gentrification takes place have diversified since the mid-1990s with the increasingly widespread phenomenon of new-build gentrification, wherein the local state primes the redevelopment of former industrial sites, including large tracts adjacent to downtown cores, by inviting and offering incentives to private developers to create new residential zones comprised essentially of high- or low-rise condominium buildings. This is part of a broader urban-economic revitalization strategy of "densification" aimed at supporting the emergence of post-industrial "consumption landscapes" that are supposed to reboot urban economies on the basis of leisure, tourism, cultural, and other new economy industries (see Vinodrai, Chapter 5). Such residential densification has reawakened interest in gendered aspects of gentrification because it not only targets the affluent but also builds "affordable" condos for the growing number of middle-income men and women living alone. They are now the fastest growing segment of first-time homebuyers in Canada—especially single women. In the past, they would have followed the classic residential life-cycle pattern by remaining renters until marriage or until a long-term relationship, or would often return to renting if they did not keep the family home after a marital break-up (Rose, 2010). What has changed is not only the expansion of choice via the booming condo market, offering low maintenance and the promise of an "urban lifestyle," but the increased appeal of home ownership as a source of future economic security and symbol of personal self-esteem and individual responsibility, framed by the wider political economic context of neo-liberalism (Kern, 2010).

These motives for condo ownership among single people cross gender lines (Rose, 2009), but Kern (2010) focused on how developers marketing downtown condos in Toronto primarily targeted women, playing on dual narratives of freedom and constraint associated with the downtown lives of middle-class heterosexual women. These narratives, as we saw earlier in this chapter, go back to the early decades of the twentieth century. On the one hand, advertisements stressed the freedom of these women to frequent safe after-hours meeting places, such as wine bars, though such ads sometimes represented women in a sexually objectified way. On the other hand, the ads played on gendered experiences of urban fear (see Siciliano, Cowen, and Smith, Chapter 16) through the marketing of the buildings' security features. Finally, while the single women and men in the Kern and Rose studies expressed a strong anti-suburban discourse, densification has now become an important trend in the suburbs, and a growing number of new "suburban downtowns" are being populated with "urban lifestyle" condo developments (see Filion and Bunting, Chapter 2). How these are marketed and why they might appeal to sub-groups of single men and women is a new and interesting direction for research about gender and urban lifestyles.

Central City Neighbourhoods as Resources for Sexual Minorities

Decades before the legalization of private homosexuality, gay and lesbian communities took shape in major US, European, Canadian, and other settler colonial cities via the clubs and other social institutions on a clandestine basis; as well, various "mainstream" public spaces were coded as "furtive" and anonymous meeting places for casual male homosexual encounters (Cattan and Leroy, 2013; Podmore, 2006). Gay and lesbian subcultures developed in districts adjacent to the downtowns of major metropolitan cities that were characterized by transient populations, and mixes of household types, socio-economic status, and land uses. Neighbourhoods of furnished rooms and boarding houses were home to diverse subcultures, including artists and other bohemians, but also to discreet lesbian residential communities in accommodations catering to middle-class and working-class women (Meyerowitz, 1990).

"Gay villages," however, are a much more recent phenomenon. While their histories and geographies vary from city to city, the gay liberation movement of the 1960s—which involved struggles for legal and political recognition of gay and lesbian rights and for cultural identity—was an important impetus in encouraging gay and lesbian establishments to make their presence more visible both at the scale of the city and in society at large. Creating strong spatial concentrations of gay residents and critical mass of social venues and businesses was also a way to gain representation of their interests in local politics and economic development (Castells, 1983). Thus, gay villages would foster pride and empowerment; they would facilitate "coming out" in a non-threatening context; and, through "safety in numbers," they would afford some protection against homophobic oppression and violence (a recent newspaper article by Burnett [2014] recalls the violence inflicted on gays before the advent of gay villages and the recent liberalization of views on sexual preference). The spatial concentration of gay nightlife establishments was also a consequence of police repression on the basis of local laws about "public morality" (long after the legalization of homosexual acts in private) when these businesses had set up in downtown entertainment districts. Their presence amounted to a transgression of the "normal" role of these nightlife districts, which were supposed to be for heterosexual meeting, dating, and coupling (Hubbard, 2008). Gay establishments were thus often forced to relocate to more economically marginal neighbourhoods somewhat removed from the downtown core (Podmore, 2006).

Criminal attacks against LGBT (lesbian, gay, bisexual, transgender) individuals are far from a thing of the past even in Canada, which has officially embraced politically progressive policies toward sexual minorities. In Ottawa, for example, some gay men feel that the absence of a gay village—which means that they have no public places to socialize in couples without standing out as "different"—makes them vulnerable to "gay-bashing" by vigilantes from outlying socially conservative communities (Lewis, 2012). Restaurants and bars still tend to be implicitly coded as heterosexual spaces unless they are located in identifiably gay enclaves, such that lesbian and gay couples expressing ordinary gestures of affection in everyday settings in such locales may be made to feel out of place (Browne, 2007). However, the strategy of consolidating resources for the support and self-realization of people with non-heterosexual identities within a gay spatial enclave has never been unanimous within LGBT communities. In some cities, lesbian, bisexual, and transgender people as well as LGBT people belonging to racialized minorities have come to feel marginalized by the perceived masculine and white middle-class culture of gay villages, or that gay enclaves do not offer them sufficient protection. This has led to the creation of more subtle and discreet queer territorialities elsewhere in the city (for reviews of research and debates on these questions, see Cattan and Clerval, 2011; Oswin, 2008; Podmore, 2006). Gay villages, then, are sites of contestation and negotiation around different meanings of homosexuality (Nash, 2006), and a key issue for

LGBT organizations is how to share material and cultural space in gay villages such that they are, or remain, inclusive spaces for all sexual minorities—regardless of gender, class, and ethno-racial background, and regardless of whether the wider society still considers their sexualities to be dissident or socially acceptable. The legalization of gay marriage in 2005 in Canada and the gaining by same-sex couples of many other rights associated with families is a huge gain in terms of equity and justice, but it potentially heightens the contrasts in rights and social status between same-sex "normal families" and other non-heterosexuals still considered as outsiders.

Gay villages were initially characterized by socio-economic mix. That remains the case for some, such as the one in Montreal, which is located in an old working-class neighbourhood with strong community organizations and a high proportion of public housing. Even though the Montreal gay village is today a regional, national, and international destination, many of its commercial and cultural establishments still cater to gays, lesbians, and bisexual and transgender people with limited financial resources (Giraud, forthcoming). Nevertheless, both residential and commercial gentrification are powerful forces shaping gay villages. One scenario is that where spatially concentrated gay and lesbian communities do not manage to establish a strong economic and symbolic power base, they may be displaced by heterosexual gentrification (Doan and Higgins, 2011). Podmore (2006) sees this as one reason for the decline in stores and bars identified with the lesbian community in Montreal's Plateau Mont-Royal neighbourhood after the 1990s. Dual-professional gay male couples, on the other hand, may be important players in accelerating gentrification, on account of their very high disposable incomes. Personal preference and life-cycle stage affect whether such couples opt to locate in gay villages or in gentrifying neighbourhoods not strongly associated with gay communities (Giraud, forthcoming; Ray and Rose, 2000). Whether or not they live in gay villages, more affluent gay individuals and households also contribute significantly to the gentrification of their retail businesses because of the importance of these neighbourhoods as places for affirming gay identity on an aesthetic as well as social level. With such retail gentrification, not only do less affluent LGBT households run the risk of residential displacement, but so do establishments catering to members of LGBT communities with fewer financial resources (Ray, 2004).

Since the mid-1990s, policies for the revitalization of the economies and central-city landscapes of old metropolitan cities have increasingly leaned toward developing specialized consumer items and services and cultural production to appeal to residents and visitors with high disposable incomes (see Bain, Chapter 14). Municipal governments have thus come to value and embrace gay villages, gay pride events, and other cultural manifestations of gay and lesbian identities for their contributions to urban economic renewal, and with an eye on the growth of revenues as cities become national and international gay tourism destinations. Where urban policies promote gay villages as tourist attractions, this often draws in heterosexual visitors as well, which raises the question as to whether these places then remain as LGBT "safe spaces" (Doan, 2011). In a broader context of neo-liberal economic globalization, city administrations—needing to generate revenues to maintain infrastructure and environmental and social services for their residents—seek to establish their city as a competitive location in the international "knowledge economy" (see Hall, Chapter 3).

This quest helps to explain the extraordinarily widespread appeal of Richard Florida's (2002) "creative cities" thesis over the past decade. This thesis posits that in every economic and social epoch, certain sub-groups of the population that were trained or had inherent talents in particular kinds of occupations and industrial sectors were the "carriers of creativity." For urban economies to flourish, then, cities needed to attract this creative class by offering them an excellent quality of life both in terms of environmental amenities and in terms of a social climate embracing "diversity" and a cosmopolitan ethos. Florida attracted particular attention for his "diversity index" of major North American

and world cities in which a major element weighting the score favourably was the presence of a large gay population; he argued that this increased the city's attractiveness to creative class members (of all sexual identities). This thesis has been subject to many critiques (Peck, 2005) (see also Vinodrai, Chapter 5), but sexualities and urban space researchers express serious concerns with two aspects in particular (Muller Myrdal, 2011; Nash, 2013). First, although the recognition of gay and lesbian contributions to the economic and cultural mainstream is welcome, Florida's approach appropriates gay and lesbian identity struggles as instruments for economic gain. Second, the supposedly inclusive "brand identity" of the creative city in reality only includes white middle-class gays and lesbians, and only those whose practices differ little from those of the heterosexual mainstream. In sum, in terms of equity and justice, we need to critically examine whether these types of policies really do "promote and preserve diverse understandings of identity and sexual expression" (Doan, 2011: 15).

Conclusion

We have seen in this chapter that the subjects of many chapters in the present volume are crosscut by issues of gender and sexuality. By this, I mean three things. First, we see that new insights can be gained on numerous aspects of urban development and socio-spatial dynamics by analyzing them with the aid of concepts developed by researchers in the feminist geography and "sexualities and space" traditions. Second, we see that urban contexts shape experiences of inequality and injustice related to gender and sexuality in important ways. Third, over recent decades, the accumulation of individual and collective endeavours to challenge and overcome barriers to gender equity in the public and private spheres and to contest cultural and political exclusions based on sexual identity has significantly changed the social, cultural, and economic dynamics of Canadian cities and neighbourhoods.

Review Questions

1. How are changes in gender roles and especially in the participation of women in the labour force reflected in the social geography of cities and in their journey patterns?
2. What are the causes and consequences of higher poverty levels among women?
3. What are the reasons for the appearance of gay villages in some large Canadian cities? What are the impacts of these villages on the LGBT community and on the economy of cities?

References

Ambert, A-M. 2006. *One Parent Families: Characteristics, Causes, Consequences, and Issues, Contemporary Family Trends*. Ottawa: Vanier Institute of the Family.

Baillargeon, D. 1999. *Making Do: Women, Family and Home in Montreal during the Great Depression*. Waterloo, ON: Wilfrid Laurier University Press.

Beer, E.S. 1939. "The Social Life of the Business Girl," *Social Forces* 17: 546–50.

Bernard, A., A-M. Séguin, Y. Bussière, and A. Polacchini. 1997. "Household structure and mobility patterns of women in O-D surveys: Methods and results based on the case studies of Montreal and Paris," in Federal Highway Administration United States Department of Transportation, Office of Highway Policy Information, ed., *Women's Travel Issues: Proceedings from the Second National Conference* (held in Baltimore, Oct. 1996). Washington, DC: Federal Highway Administration.

Bondi, L. 1999. "Gender, class, and gentrification: Enriching the debate," *Environment and Planning D: Society and Space* 17: 261–82.

Bondi, L., and D. Rose. 2003. "Constructing gender, constructing the urban: A review of Anglo-American feminist urban geography," *Gender, Place and Culture* 10: 229–45.

Boyer, K. 1998. "Place and the politics of virtue: Clerical work, corporate anxiety, and changing meanings of public womanhood in early twentieth-century Montreal," *Gender, Place & Culture* 5: 261–75.

Bradbury, B. 2000. "Single parenthood in the past: Canadian census categories, 1891–1951, and the 'normal' family," *Historical Methods: A Journal of Quantitative and Interdisciplinary History* 33: 211–17.

Browne, K. 2007. "(Re)making the other, heterosexualising everyday space," *Environment and Planning A* 39: 996–1014.

Burnett, R. 2014. "Prejudice to pride: The forgotten murder of Joe Rose," *Montreal Gazette*, 16 March.

Campbell, L., D. Clément, and G.S. Kealey, eds. 2012. *Debating Dissent: Canada and the 1960s*. Toronto: University of Toronto Press.

Canada Mortgage and Housing Corporation. 2012. *2006 Census Housing Series: Issue 18—Housing Conditions of Lone-Parent-Led Households, Research Highlight* (Socio-economic Series 12-003). Ottawa, ON: CMHC.

Castells, M. 1983. *The City and the Grassroots*. Berkeley, CA: University of California Press.

Cattan, N., and A. Clerval. 2011. "A right to the city? Virtual networks and ephemeral centralities for lesbians in Paris," *Justice spatiale/Spatial Justice* 2011 3: 1–16.

——, and S. Leroy. 2010. "La ville négociée : Les homosexuel(le)s dans l'espace public parisien," *Cahiers de géographie du Québec* 54 (151): 9–24.

——, and S. Leroy. 2013. *Atlas mondiale des sexualités. Libertés, plaisirs et interdits*. Paris: Éditions Autrement.

Chauncey, G. 1994. *Gay New York : Gender, Urban Culture, and the Makings of the Gay Male World, 1890–1940*. New York: Basic Books.

Christie, N. 2004. "Bachelors and spinsters: Introduction," in N. Christie and M. Gauvreau, eds., *Mapping the Margins: The Family and Social Discipline in Canada, 1700–1975*. Montreal and Kingston: McGill-Queen's University Press.

D'Emilio, J. 1998 [1983]. *Sexual Politics, Sexual Communities: The Making of a Homosexual Minority in the United States, 1940–1970* (2nd edn.). Chicago, IL: University of Chicago Press.

Dennis, R. 2006/7. "Working women downtown: Single women in Toronto 1900–1930," *London Journal of Canadian Studies* 22: 35–58.

Doan, P.L., ed. 2011. *Queerying Planning: Challenging Heteronormative Assumptions and Reframing Planning Practice*. Farnham: Ashgate.

——, and H. Higgins. 2011. "The demise of queer space? Resurgent gentrification and the assimilation of LGBT neighborhoods," *Journal of Planning Education and Research* 3: 6–25.

Dominion Bureau of Statistics. 1954. *Canada Year Book, 1954*. Ottawa: DBS.

Domosh, M. 1999. "Sexing feminist geography," *Progress in Human Geography* 23: 429–36.

Dyck, I. 2005. "Feminist geography, the 'everyday,' and local-global relations: Hidden spaces of place-making," *The Canadian Geographer* 49: 233–43.

England, K., and K. Boyer. 2009. "Women's work: The feminization and shifting meanings of clerical work," *Journal of Social History* 43: 307–40.

Featherstone, M. 2004. "Automobilities: An introduction," *Theory, Culture & Society* 21: 1–24.

Fiedler, R., N. Schuurman, and J. Hyndman. 2006. "Hidden homelessness: An indicator-based approach for examining the geographies of recent immigrants at-risk of homelessness in Greater Vancouver," *Cities* 23: 205–16.

Filion, P., T. Bunting, D. Pavlic, and P. Langlois. 2010. "Intensification and sprawl: Residential density trajectories in Canada's largest metropolitan regions," *Urban Geography* 31: 541–69.

Florida, R. 2002. *The Rise of the Creative Class: And How It's Transforming Work, Leisure, Community and Everyday Life.* New York: Basic Books.

Friendly, M., and S. Prentice. 2009. *About Canada: Childcare.* Winnipeg, MB: Fernwood.

Garber, J.A. 2000. "'Not named or identified': Politics and the search for anonymity in the city," in K.B. Miranne and A.H. Young, eds., *Gendering the City: Women, Boundaries, and Visions or Urban Life.* Lanham, MD: Rowman and Littlefield.

Gauvreau, D., S. Olson, and P. Thornton. 2008. "The harsh welcome of an industrial city: Immigrant women in Montreal, 1880–1902," *Social History/Histoire sociale* 40 (80): 345–80.

Giraud, C. forthcoming. "Le 'Village Gai' de Montréal. Une aventure urbaine minoritaire." *Espaces et sociétés.*

Heisz, A., and G. Schellenberg. 2004. *Public Transit Use among Immigrants.* Ottawa, ON: Statistics Canada, Analytical Studies Branch research paper series, Catalogue no. 11F0019MIE—No. 224.

Hubbard, P. 2008. "Here, there, everywhere: The ubiquitous geographies of heteronormativity," *Geography Compass* 2 : 640–58.

Jones, C.L., L.R. Marsden, and L. Tepperman. 1990. *Lives of their Own: The Individualization of Women's Lives, Studies in Canadian Sociology.* Toronto: Oxford University Press.

Kern, L. 2010. *Sex and the Revitalized City: Gender, Condominium Development, and Urban Citizenship.* Vancouver, BC: University of British Columbia Press.

———. 2012. "All aboard? Women working the spaces of gentrification in Toronto's Junction," *Gender, Place & Culture* 20: 510–27.

Kirkland, E. 2006. "A home away from home: Defining, regulating, and challenging femininity at the Julia Drummond residence in Montreal, 1920–1971," *Urban History Review* 34: 3–16.

Knopp, L. 2007. "On the relationship between queer and feminist geographies," *The Professional Geographer* 59: 47–55.

LaRochelle-Côté, S., P. Gougeon, and D. Pinard. 2009. "Changes in parental work time and earnings," *Perspectives on Labour and Income* (Statistics Canada, Cat. no. 75-001-X) (October): 5–16.

Lauria, M., and L. Knopp. 1985. "Toward an analysis of the role of gay communities in the urban renaissance," *Urban Geography* 6: 152–69.

Lauster, N., and A. Easterbrook. 2011. "No room for new families? A field experiment measuring rental discrimination against same-sex couples and single parents," *Social Problems* 58: 389–409.

Lewis, N.M. 2012. "Gay in a 'government town': The settlement and regulation of gay-identified men in Ottawa, Canada," *Gender, Place & Culture* 19: 291–312.

———. 2013. "Beyond binary places: The social and spatial dynamics of coming out in Canada," *ACME: An International E-Journal for Critical Geographies* 12: 305–30.

Ley, D. 1996. *The New Middle Class and the Remaking of the Central City.* London: Oxford University Press.

Mackenzie, S., and D. Rose. 1983. "Industrial change, the domestic economy and home life," in J. Anderson, S. Duncan, and R. Hudson, eds., *Redundant Spaces in Cities and Regions.* London: Academic Press.

Mata, F. 2011. *Lone-Parent Status among Ethnic Groups in Canada: Data Explorations on its Prevalence, Composition and Generational Persistence Aspects, Working Paper Series.* Vancouver, BC: Metropolis British Columbia (Working Paper Series, 11-17).

McDowell, L. 1999. *Gender, Identity and Place: Understanding Feminist Geographies.* Minneapolis, MN: University of Minnesota Press.

McMaster, L. 2002. "The urban working girl in turn-of-the-century Canadian fiction," *Essays on Canadian Writing* 77 (Fall):1–25.

Mendes, K. 2010. "Reading *Chatelaine*: Dr. Marion Hilliard and 1950s women's health advice," *Canadian Journal of Communication* 35: 515–31.

Meyerowitz, J. 1990. "Sexual geography and gender economy: The furnished room districts of Chicago, 1890–1930," *Gender & History* 2: 174–296.

Milan, A., and N. Bohnert. 2012a. *Fifty years of families in Canada: 1961 to 2011. Families, households and marital status, 2011 Census of Population, Census in Brief.* Ottawa, ON: Statistics Canada (Catalogue no. 98-312-X2011003).

———, ———. 2012b. *Portrait of Families and Living Arrangements in Canada. Families, Households and Marital Status, 2011 Census of Population, Analytical Document.* Ottawa, ON: Statistics Canada (Catalogue no. 98-312-X2011001).

Millward, L. 2012. "Making a scene: Struggles over lesbian place-making in anglophone Canada, 1964–1984," *Women's History Review* 21: 553–69.

Monk, J., and S. Hanson. 1982. "On not excluding half the human in human geography," *The Professional Geographer* 34: 11–23.

Morency, C., A. Paez, M.J. Roorda, R. Mercado, and S. Farber. 2011. "Distance traveled in three Canadian cities: Spatial analysis from the perspective of vulnerable population segments," *Journal of Transport Geography* 19: 39–50.

Muller Myrdal, T. 2011. "Queerying creative cities," in P.L. Doan, ed., *Queerying Planning: Challenging Heteronormative Assumptions and Reframing Planning Practice.* Farnham: Ashgate.

——. 2013. "Ordinary (small) cities and LGBQ lives.," *ACME: An International E-Journal for Critical Geographies* 12: 279–304.

Myers, T. 2006. *Caught: Montreal's Modern Girls and the Law, 1869–1945, Studies in Gender and History.* Toronto: University of Toronto Press.

Nash, C.J. 2006. "Toronto's gay village (1969–1982): Plotting the politics of gay identity," *The Canadian Geographer* 50:1–16.

Nash, C.J. 2013. "Queering neighbourhoods: Politics and practice in Toronto," *ACME: An International E-Journal for Critical Geographies* 12: 193–219.

O'Hanlon, S. 2002. "'All found they used to call it': Genteel boarding houses in early twentieth-century Melbourne," *Urban History* 29: 239–53.

Oswin, N. 2008. "Critical geographies and the uses of sexuality: Deconstructing queer space," *Progress in Human Geography* 32: 89–103.

——. 2010. "The modern model family at home in Singapore: A queer geography," *Transactions of the Institute of British Geographers* 35: 256–68.

Peake, L. 2010. "Gender, race, sexuality," in S.J. Smith, R. Pain, S.A. Marston, and J.P. Jones III, eds., *The Sage Handbook of Social Geographies.* London: Sage.

Peck, J. 2005. "Struggling with the creative class," *International Journal of Urban and Regional Research* 29: 740–70.

Peiss, K.L. 1986. *Cheap Amusements: Working Women and Leisure in Turn-of-the-century New York.* Philadelphia, PA: Temple University Press.

Peters, E. 2000. "'The two major living realities': Urban service needs of First Nations women in Canadian cities," in K.B. Miranne and A.H. Young, eds., *Gendering the City: Women, Boundaries, and Visions or Urban Life.* Lanham, MD: Rowman and Littlefield.

Piché, L. 1999a. "La jeunesse ouvrière catholique féminine un lieu de formation sociale et d'action communautaire, 1931–1966," *Revue d'histoire de l'Amérique française* 52: 481–506.

——. 1999b. "La jeunesse ouvrière catholique féminine, un lieu de formation sociale et d'action communautaire, 1931–1966," *Revue d'histoire de l'Amérique française* 52: 481–506.

Podmore, J. 2006. "Gone 'underground'? Lesbian visibility and the consolidation of queer space in Montreal," *Social and Cultural Geography* 7: 595–625.

Preston, V., and S. McLafferty. 1993. "Gender differences in commuting at suburban and central locations," *Canadian Journal of Regional Science* 16: 237–59.

——, D. Rose, J. Holmes, and G. Norcliffe. 2000. "Shift work, childcare and domestic work: Divisions of labour in Canadian paper mill communities," *Gender, Place and Culture* 7: 5–29.

Proulx, C., S. Faustmann, H. Raiq, and A. van den Berg. 2011. "Internal diversity in social policy regimes: The case of Canada's four major provinces," in G. Fréchet, D. Gauvreau, and J. Poirier, eds., *Statistiques sociales, pauvreté et exclusion sociale: Hommage à Paul Bernard.* Montreal: Presses de l'Université de Montréal.

Ray, B. 2004. "A diversity paradox: Montréal's gay village," *Our Diverse Cities* 2004 (1): 72–5.

——, and D. Rose. 2000. "Cities of the everyday: Socio-spatial perspectives on gender, difference and diversity," in T. Bunting and P. Filion, eds., *Canadian Cities in Transition: The Twenty-First Century* (3rd edn.). Toronto: Oxford University Press Canada.

Rose, D. 1989. "A feminist perspective of employment restructuring and gentrification: The case of Montréal," in J. Wolch and M. Dear, eds., *The Power of Geography: How Territory Shapes Social Life.* Boston: Unwin Hyman

——. 2009. "L'accès à la propriété et ses significations chez les ménages d'une seule personne: Une étude de cas montréalaise," in J. Charbonneau, A. Germain, and M. Molgat, eds., *Habiter seul: Un nouveau mode de vie?* Quebec: Presses de l'Université Laval.

——. 2010. "Vivre seul et devenir propriétaire au centre de Montréal: Au-delà de la trajectoire résidentielle normée," in J-Y. Authier, J-P. Lévy, and C. Bonvalet, eds., *Élir domicile. La construction sociale des choix résidentiels.* Lyon: Presses de l'Université de Lyon.

——. 2010 [1984]. "Rethinking gentrification: Beyond the uneven development of marxist urban theory," in L. Lees, T. Slater, and E. Wyly, eds., *The Gentrification Reader.* London & New York: Routledge.

——, and A. Charette. 2014. "Housing experiences of users of settlement services for newcomers in Montréal: Does immigration status matter?" In K. Kilbride, ed., *Immigrant Integration: Research Implications for Public Policy*, pages TBA. Toronto: Canadian Scholars' Press.

——, and C. Le Bourdais. 1986. "The changing conditions of female single parenthood in Montréal's inner city and suburban neighborhood," *Urban Resources* 3(2): 45–52.

——, and Paul Villeneuve. 1993. "Work, labour markets and households in transition," in L.S. Bourne and D. Ley, eds., *The Changing Social Geography of Canadian Cities.* Montreal and Kingston: McGill-Queen's University Press.

Simmel, G. 1950 [1903]. "The Metropolis and mental life," in K.H. Wolff, ed., *The Sociology of Georg Simmel.* New York: Free Press.

Srigley, K. 2010. *Breadwinning Daughters: Young Working Women in a Depression-era City, 1929–1939, Studies in Gender & History.* Toronto: University of Toronto Press.

St-Pierre, B. 2007. *Déplacements des personnes dans la grande région de Montréal. Scénario prévisionnel 2026 tendanciel* (Mtl03-26T_DGMO2006n). Quebec, QC: Ministère des transports du Québec, Service de la modélisation des systèmes de transport. At: www.mtq.gouv.qc.ca/portal/page/portal/Librairie/Publications/fr/ministere/recherche/enquetes/montreal/previsions2007.pdf

Statistics Canada. 2012a. *2011 National Household Survey, NHS Data Tables, 99-012-X2011031.* Ottawa, ON: Statistics Canada. At: www12.statcan.gc.ca/nhs-enm/2011/dp-pd/dt-td/Rp-eng.cfm?LANG=E&APATH=3&DETAIL=0&DIM=0&FL=A&FREE=0&GC=0&GID=0&GK=0&GRP=0&PID=105619&PRID=0&PTYPE=105277&S=0&SHOWALL=1&SUB=0&Temporal=2013&THEME=96&VID=0&VNAMEE=&VNAMEF=

Statistics Canada. 2012b. *General Social Survey: Table 7: Time spent on household domestic work, by working arrangement, Canada, 2010.* Ottawa, ON: Statistics Canada. At: www.statcan.gc.ca/pub/89-503-x/2010001/article/11546/tbl/tbl007-eng.htm

Strange, C. 1995. *Toronto's Girl Problem: The Perils and Pleasures of the City, 1880–1930, Studies in Gender and History.* Toronto: University of Toronto Press.

Strong-Boag, V. 2002 [1991]. "Home dreams: Women and the suburban experiment in Canada, 1945–60," in V. Strong-Boag, M. Gleason, and A. Perry, eds., *Rethinking Canada: The Promise of Women's History* (4th edn.). Oxford, UK: Oxford University Press.

——. 1988. *The New Day Recalled: Lives of Girls and Women in English Canada, 1919–1939.* Toronto: Copp Clark Pitman.

Tallentire, J. 2006. *Everyday Athenas: Strategies of Survival and Identity for Ever-Single Women in British Columbia, 1880–1930.* Vancouver, BC: University of British Columbia, PhD thesis.

Uteng, T.P. 2009. "Gender, ethnicity, and constrained mobility: Insights into the resultant social exclusion," *Environment and Planning A* 41: 1055–71.

Valentine, G., and T. Skelton. 2003. "Finding oneself, losing oneself: The lesbian and gay 'scene' as a paradoxical space," *International Journal of Urban and Regional Research* 27: 849–66.

Vandersmissen, M-H., P. Villeneuve, and M. Thériault. 2001. "Mobilité et accessibilité: Leurs effets sur l'insertion professionnelle des femmes," *L'Espace géographique* 30: 289–305.

Villeneuve, P., and D. Rose. 1988. "Gender and the separation of employment from home in metropolitan Montreal, 1971–1981," *Urban Geography* 9: 155–79.

Walberg, R., and A. Mrozek. 2010. *Canada's Top Family-friendly Cities. Canada Is a Great Place to Live. But What Are the Best Cities for Families? A New Report Card Finds Out.* Ottawa, ON: Institute of Marriage and Family Canada.

Wekerle, G.R. 1985. "From refuge to service center: Neighborhoods that support women," *Sociological Focus* 18 (2):79–85.

——. 1993. "Responding to diversity: Housing developed by and for women," *Canadian Journal of Urban Research* 2: 95–111.

Williams, C. 2010. *Economic Well-being, Women in Canada: A Gender-based Statistical Report.* Ottawa, ON: Statistics Canada (Catalogue no. 89-503-X).

Wilson, E. 2001. "The invisible flâneur (revised version)," in E. Wilson, ed., *The Contradictions of Culture: Cities, Culture, Women.* London: Sage.

Wright, M.W. 2010. "Gender and geography II: Bridging the gap—feminist, queer, and the geographical imaginary," *Progress in Human Geography* 34: 56–66.

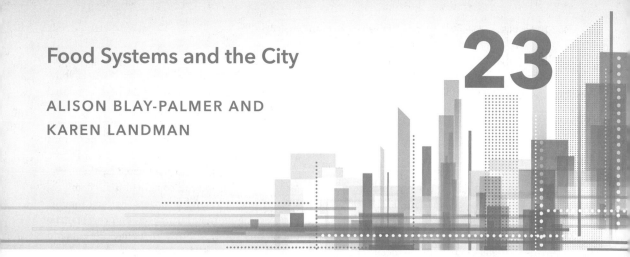

Food Systems and the City

23

ALISON BLAY-PALMER AND KAREN LANDMAN

Food is a sustaining and enduring necessity. Yet among the basic essentials for life—air, water, shelter, and food—only food has been absent over the years as a focus of serious professional planning interest. This is a puzzling omission because, as a discipline, planning marks its distinctiveness by being comprehensive in scope and attentive to the temporal dimensions and spatial interconnections among important facets of community life. (American Planning Association, 2007: 1)

Introduction

Food offers a prism for understanding more about the challenges faced in cities and regions (Born and Purcell, 2006; Morgan, 2008). Food can help us envision more sustainable, livable urban spaces that are better integrated with their adjacent landscapes. Urban geography, planning, and sociology contribute to rethinking the role of food as we move to more sustainable communities. By placing food at the centre of thinking about quality and the (re)imagining of producer–consumer linkages, we are able to conceive of space and relationships in new ways (Donald, 2008; Hinrichs and Lyson, 2008; Marsden, 2008; Morgan, Marsden, and Murdoch, 2006). As planners and others clamour

for new approaches and tools, food has surfaced as a missing link in the urban (re)creation project. While the evolution of agriculture and urban life are linked (Steel, 2008), in the past century in North America agriculture has traditionally been considered a rural preoccupation, separate from urban issues. Engaging with food as an integral part of the urban system is still considered by some to be unusual. Based on the recognition of the potential for a more integrated approach to food, this chapter addresses how our cities could and should be fed; as such, it also delivers a strong rationale for using food as a lens to frame policy and develop even more relevant perspectives on urban growth and development.

The chapter unfolds in three parts. First, to provide a meaningful context, the issue of food and planning in Canada is tackled. Next, we explore innovative moves by planning and policy groups that signal a radical change in the role of food as a theoretical and policy framing tool. We then turn to case studies that offer examples of different initiatives that can assist academics and practitioners interested in putting food on the agenda. In many ways, academic and policy concerns about how a city feeds itself reflect the most profound changes within the nascent transition from modern to coherent postmodern world views. The evolution of land-use practices, community well-being, and the rise of science and technology are all well represented in the Canadian food story. These shifts provide us with a context for the evolution of planning for food systems as a consideration in Canadian cities.

Food and Urban Spaces in Canada

The history of food in Canada encapsulates many changes in our society since the mid-1800s. The place of rural, urban, and food communities in our planning traditions also reflect these shifts. In a broader societal context, the association of food with rural landscapes is founded in our farm community roots. At the turn of the twentieth century, some 63 per cent of Canadians lived in rural areas (Statistics Canada, 2007). As modern society took hold, however, there was a gradual shift in population from rural to urban communities. As the economy became much more deeply entrenched in manufacturing, farm size expanded, partially in response to rural depopulation. Planning and food intersected peripherally through land preservation initiatives as people attempted to protect fertile rural land from development. This was also the time when increased mechanization and the application of nitrogen-based fertilizers and chemical pesticides meant that fewer people were needed to farm bigger tracts of land. By 2006, Canada had 229,373 farms remaining, with an average of 728 acres per farm, an increase in acreage per farm of 73 per cent from the early twentieth century (Statistics Canada, 2007). With fewer links to food producers, places of food production and food consumption became increasingly disconnected.

In addition to demographic changes, food systems also reflect technological changes and help us understand the challenges that innovation poses to planners. Since the mid-nineteenth century, the transformation of food production from a local, small-scale, manual activity to a predominately technologically complex, industrial, monoculture production system mirrors key changes in our relationship to nature. The "green revolution" that began in the 1950s marked a technological shift, with increased reliance on irrigation, chemicals, and sophisticated seed technology packages for food production, plus distribution via new, long-distance, refrigerated modes of transport. The stated goal was to eliminate famines by mass-producing food. Coincident with this green revolution was the reorientation of large chemical companies away from wartime production and toward more domestic markets, a shift dominated by the manufacture and distribution of agricultural chemicals, such as pesticides and fertilizers. As food production became more industrialized and corporatized under this food production regime (Friedmann and McMichael, 1989; Goodman and Redclift, 1989), urban and rural spaces became increasingly separate, and people became physically and psychologically distanced from their food sources (Kneen, 1995). This has accelerated so that most of our food now comes from a global industrial food system where produce travels on average over 2400 kilometres from field to fork (Pirog et al., 2001).

In the past, planners have been challenged to reconcile conflicting needs across jurisdictions and across interest groups. On the one hand, there is a need to preserve valuable farmland, often in the shadow of urban development; on the other, are urbanites who leave cities for suburban, peri-urban, and rural areas, bringing along their idealized visions of rural landscapes. These idyllic imaginaries must be reconciled with the realities of farming, which includes odours; access to roadways for the movement of machinery, livestock and crops; and the conservation of agriculturally productive lands (Bryant, Russwurm, and McLennan, 1982). In the face of pressures from "city folk" to gentrify the countryside and turn more land from food production to housing development, golf courses, and other amenities, the primary provincial response has been to preserve agricultural land. The 1976 Ontario Agricultural Code of Practice (Caldwell, 2000), the Agricultural Land Reserve (ALR) enacted in British Columbia in 1973, and the Greenbelt legislation enacted in Ontario in 2005 (Wilson, 2008) all reflect the desire to set aside land for food production. The closer one gets to urban centres, the more intense the conflict—as of 2001, half of Canadian urban centres were built on agriculturally viable land (Statistics Canada, 2001, cited in Campbell, 2006). However, despite provincial initiatives to protect land, urban pressures for outward expansion and development frequently supersede the need to protect quality land for food production. The case of the British Columbia ALR is instructive. Despite the provincial government's having set aside land for agriculture in the 1970s, the reality is that poor-quality land in remote parts of the province has been swapped by developers for high-quality land closer to urban centres for the purposes of development, such as second homes in "cottage" communities in Invermere (Campell, 2006). In this way, development trumps the protection of fertile farmland.

Our lifestyles also affect how we eat. In recent times in Canada the pace of life has accelerated—families, often out of economic necessity, moved from one to two incomes, exerting pressure for food preparation to be faster and more efficient. This has produced tension in Canadians' attitudes to food, which is captured through the debate about affordable access to quality food, such as organically grown foods. This is contrasted against the trade-offs linked to large-scale retail developments, our reliance on a suburban car culture, and the apparent efficiency offered by large retailers that regularly opt for quantity over quality. Locally based food production, consumption linkages, new health and fitness awareness, and environmental concerns all are reflections of individual attempts to redress some of these challenges.

As part of the move to healthier living, in the last decade we have witnessed an increased desire on the part of consumers to reconnect with and understand what they are putting into their bodies (Whatmore, 2002). This desire has created opportunities for many innovative relationships between people and their food. For example, the creation of community-supported agriculture (CSA), farmers' markets, the slow food movement, and the 100-mile diet (Smith and MacKinnon, 2006) all demand that spaces exist in or near urban centres for consumers and farmers to connect. The recent move by the Canadian Medical Association calling for calorie counts on fast-food meals is

another facet of the quest to eat better and regain an understanding of what we are consuming. Other emerging trends are linked to urban food production. These include a suite of garden types, including rooftops, backyards, and community gardens, as well as the emergence of urban farms. For this change to be significant and lasting, a reconceptualization of how people get access to food will ultimately be required. This, in turn, is connected to how we conceive of city spaces.

As the archetypical big-box store, Wal-Mart provides interesting insights into food and retail (Donald, 2008). Wal-Mart's motto is "Save money. Live better." The company honours this commitment by being fiercely competitive through its "lean retailing" strategy that (1) concentrates purchasing power; (2) vertically integrates global production–delivery chains; and (3) maintains low-wage operations (Christopherson, 2007: 453). When Wal-Mart entered the organic food market in 2006, it used its global connections to access fresh produce and encouraged its multinational corporate suppliers, such as Kellogg's, to develop lines of organic processed food. The move by Wal-Mart into organics provoked widespread controversy about alternative food systems, specifically organics (Donald and Blay-Palmer, 2006). Organic supporters' vision is founded on small-scale, trust-based, locally rooted ecological production. Wal-Mart, on the other hand, sees organic food as a new niche opportunity and has revved up its suppliers to produce more of what Guthman (2003; 2007) has dubbed "yuppie chow." While organic production methods lower the use of chemicals, other core organic/sustainability principles, including ecologically sound production methods, fair labour standards, and animal welfare, are not on Wal-Mart's table (see Rees, Chapter 4). As well, to get access to Wal-Mart's organics, consumers need to be part of the sprawling suburban car culture (Donald and Blay-Palmer, 2006; Dupuis, 2000; Guthman, 2003).

Clearly, then, food represents a complex and nuanced challenge. But nothing hits closer to home than food. Given the growing advocacy on the part of some consumer groups,[1] food could shape how we see the future of cities. In the case of food in the cityscape, there is considerable public stakeholder support for locally produced foods but not a lot of knowledge. Food offers a unique lens for rethinking city spaces as it integrates land-use planning, transportation, water management, and environmental quality, as well as regulations and regulatory regimes concerned with human and environmental health. While conservation initiatives are important and have resulted in planning regulations to address tensions related to agriculture and food production as well as urban/rural tensions, most policies contain nothing that directly relates to the food system per se (Mackenzie, 2008). Given the environmental impact of food production, urban sprawl, the need for green infrastructure, and heightened consumer awareness about food safety and food-related health issues, relevant public policy is pressing. In addition, ground-up initiatives remain disjointed, fragmented, and small-scale. A synthesizing approach is urgently needed, as is a large-scale, integrated model such as smart growth that could empower municipalities and encourage city officials to take steps in new directions (see Grant and Filion, Chapter 17). As a group, planners may well be in a unique position to offer this direction.

To understand how food can help make linkages to more sustainable cities, we need to understand how food and cities are connected. If we adopt a food perspective to frame urban challenges, food accounts for a substantial level of a city's ecological footprint (see Rees, Chapter 4). For example, food accounts for 40 per cent of the ecological footprint of London, England. Every year its residents and citizens consume 2.5 million tons of food, which in turn generate 883,000 tons of organic waste (Petts, 2001). As we have now crossed the threshold where globally more people live in urban areas than in rural areas, planning for food as part of the urban environment promises to make cities greener in many ways. In recent years there has been concern about the following:

- Environmental impacts of cities and their growing greenhouse gas footprints

- The escalating cost of transporting food, particularly in the context of the food-for-fuel debate
- The need to recycle waste/nutrients within the urban system

As experts at the Global Footprint Network explain:

The global effort for sustainability will be won, or lost, in the world's cities, where urban design may influence over 70 per cent of people's Ecological Footprint. High-Footprint cities can reduce this demand on nature greatly with existing technology. Many of these savings also cut costs and make cities more livable. (Wackernagel et al., 2006)

Research on food issues clarifies changing relationships between people, food, and the city, particularly in the context of creating alternative food networks through shorter, increasingly trust-based food chains. Central to these discussions are farmers' markets (Connell, Smithers, and A. Joseph, 2008; Feagan, 2008), alternative supply chains (Goodman, 2003; Maye, Holloway, and Kneafsey, 2007; Morgan, Marsden, and Murdoch, 2006), and the role of retailers as supply chains shift in the existing food system. Food planning and policy can help address all of these challenges.

Food, Planning, and Policy

Various bodies within North America and the European Union (EU) have incorporated food into their planning agendas. The most notable accomplishment at the organizational level is that of the American Planning Association (APA), which in 2007 produced the highly influential Policy Guide on Community and Regional Food Planning. The inclusion of food in planning is not exclusive to the United States, however. In 2008, the Association of European Schools of Planning (AESOP) established a special thematic group to study food and planning, marking another pivotal point. Food became another critical planning issue along with property rights, new technologies, urban design, ethics, transportation, and risk mitigation. Food is an essential addition to planning, as it offers a lens to see and understand the entire urban-to-rural landscape as a system. As such, this new focus can contribute to the creation of healthy communities. Thus, the importance of getting planners to respond immediately to food in broad-based policy initiatives cannot be underestimated.

In Canada, planning for food is increasingly evident in policy formation. Organizations, most notably the Toronto Food Policy Council (TFPC), have helped pave the way for planners to include food policy in their toolboxes. Early initiatives opened up opportunities and inspired others to use food as a vehicle to deal with a range of challenges, from community beautification to improving youth self-esteem. As TFPC manager Wayne Roberts explains,

> food security is good for Toronto's integrity, cohesion and reputation as "the city that works" which in turn attracts tourists and business. Everyone benefits when fresh, local food is available at vibrant farmers' markets, lively main street grocery stores and picturesque community gardens. (Roberts, 2013)

One recent initiative reflects this multi-faceted policy approach to food: "healthy" food-vending carts are being introduced as a way to add to the progressive image of the city and contribute to the health of Toronto citizens and visitors. The TFPC's vision has spread to other cities in North America and the EU, as many municipalities have adopted food charters and/or created food policy councils of their own. The appeal of this approach is the integrative perspective that comes from having a food policy council.

With this holistic approach in mind, planners at the Region of Waterloo Public Health Unit take a systems approach to food at a regional scale. They have produced groundbreaking work on food miles, the distance travelled from farm to fork, as they connect the dots between what the region could produce for local consumption, what food the region exported, and the resulting unnecessary food miles due to a mismatch between the two. Using data about existing production capacity, Xuereb (2005) estimated that if the region ate what it could produce, it would reduce its greenhouse gas emissions by the equivalent of over 16,000 cars every year. Waterloo's public-health planners have also been leaders in producing local food maps, showing where nearby producers are located as part of their broader undertaking to understand the linkages between health, food prices, local sustainability, and rural–urban relationships.

Increasingly, municipal governments have raised the profile of food by taking on various aspects of the food cause. For example, in June 2008, the mayor of Markham, Ontario, announced a local food procurement initiative that would "help support Ontario's farm economy, address climate change, reduce greenhouse gas emissions and pesticide use, curb urban sprawl, protect Ontario farm lands and promote sustainable farming practices" (Scarpitti, 2008). The City of Toronto (2009) announced a similar plan in the fall of 2008 for 37 daycares with the potential to expand the program to senior citizen homes and homeless shelters. The directive to purchase up to 50 per cent of food from local sources was unanimously approved by Toronto City Council. Local environmental groups claimed that "[i]ncreasing the amount of local produce will support farmers in the Greenbelt and Southern Ontario and the decrease in greenhouse gases emitted from food being transported to Toronto from the other side of the globe will improve air quality" (Hanes, 2008). The EU is far ahead of North America on issues of public procurement—an excellent summary is available in Morgan and Sonnino's *The School Food Revolution* (2008). For example, Rome undertakes to purchase local, organic ingredients, where possible, for meals made from scratch and served in its public schools (Morgan and Sonnino, 2008).

In this regard, the intersection of policy and food reflects the importance of good governance (see Taylor and Bradford, Chapter 11). In the cases of both Toronto and Markham, public input and discussion preceded the creation of the purchasing policies. In the short term, this produced thoughtful policy and is helping to reshape government so that it supports more sustainable procurement in the long term. The hierarchical, silo approach that dominates much of current policy and planning results in disconnected outcomes that serve the needs of a few and often create more problems than solutions. A systemic approach founded on networks and informed by a broad grasp of challenges that include economic, social, environmental, policy, and design considerations could improve the urban environment.

In Canada, we have begun the work to achieve planning for this broad-based and integrative city. In 2007, Duany Plater-Zyberk and Company developed an agrarian urban masterplan for Southlands, a 200 hectare site outside Vancouver. Four years later Duany's book *Garden Cities: Theory & Practice of Agrarian Urbanism* (Duany, 2011) captured this vision for the integration of agriculture at all levels of development. Also in 2011, de la Salle and Holland published *Agricultural Urbanism*, which proposes that all aspects of the food system be made visible in our cities. In June, 2011, the Ontario Professional Planners Institute (OPPI) released *Healthy Communities and Planning for Food Systems in Ontario—A Call to Action* to raise awareness of the need to consciously plan for healthy food systems at the community level. We are beginning to make progress on a number of urban food fronts, as illustrated by the case studies in the following section.

Case Studies

Numerous projects in Canada currently capture the reality and/or potential offered by strengthening local food systems. The few examples offered here are from multiple perspectives—production, distribution, and consumption—and illustrate how more sustainable food initiatives could fit into a systematic urban regeneration context.

Community Gardens

Community gardens are not new in North America. During World War I and especially World War II,

households and neighbourhoods were encouraged to plant Victory Gardens; communal plots were set aside so that food could be produced locally. The success of community gardens lies in the ability to meet a range of community needs, including the provision of beautiful and safe community spaces, informal meeting places, and personal well-being. Community gardens can be found across Canada. In Montreal, the first community garden was created in 1936. Today the city has 97 community gardens with over 8200 plots. The gardens are multi-functional, meeting recreational, food, accessibility, and community needs of Montreal citizens. The city provides seeds, soil, flowers, tool storage facilities, and access to water to support these initiatives (Montreal, 2008).

In Winnipeg, community gardens can be rented from the city for a nominal amount every year ($28.35 for an unserviced plot and $42.20 for a serviced plot). Plots are managed by the Public Works Department, which stipulates strict conditions of use (Winnipeg, 2013). Vancouver also offers community gardening opportunities, primarily on its own parkland. In this case the city prepares the garden space—breaking ground, applying compost, and setting out individual plots—and the community is expected to manage the land in an open and inclusive way (Vancouver, 2009).

In Toronto, community gardens are viewed as places to build safe community spaces where people can interact, create beauty, and get some physical activity and mental peace (Parker, 2008). As part of its network, Toronto has an eight-acre urban farm, Black Creek Community Farm, that operates in one of the most economically disadvantaged areas of the city. This farm provides youth with leadership opportunities. It also aims to break down barriers between gangs as youth get to know their peers from other parts of the city.[2]

Despite the value of these community gardens, there are typically two problems. First, the costs associated with infrastructure and maintenance include the need to insure gardens; second, pressures from land development are unavoidable. In the first case, basic infrastructure must be provided to gardeners, including reliable access to water, compost, mulch, and general maintenance. In some instances, gardens are made available to communities at no charge and municipalities absorb operational expenses. The most onerous cost is insurance, which is in fact such a burden that it has prevented some gardens from getting off the ground. In Kingston, Ontario, urban agriculture and community gardening activities are being proposed as part of the Official Plan. As part of this initiative, the designation of urban agriculture (UA) as a "community facility" is being recommended so that gardens could be covered under city insurance policies.

With respect to development threats, the benefits and success of community gardens can also be their downfall. The classic case in this regard comes from New York City. Starting in the mid-1990s with the bulldozing of 20 community gardens, the city moved to sell land used by communities as gardens since 1918 as part of efforts to revitalize communities. The rationale to sell garden land was that the lots had previously been building sites, so they were only temporary gardens. Ironically, once "blighted" neighbourhoods were revived in part by community gardens and witnessed increasing land prices and gentrification, these lands came under pressure for housing and retail space. A second issue was the need for affordable housing lands. In 2002, a settlement was reached between the city and the state, protecting over 200 gardens, some of which ended up in land trusts, while the rest were designated as parkland (Elder, 2005).

Urban Farms

Positive economic considerations also are emerging from urban farms. A fascinating initiative is SPIN (small plot intensive) farming, a new farming model that is taking hold in cities across North America. The first SPIN "farm" was developed in Saskatoon on half an acre of land pieced together from a number of arable residential plots, accessed via a handshake agreement or through payment in vegetables, with each plot ranging in size from 45 to 275 square metres. SPIN farmers report benefits from reduced wind and pest damage, more frequent harvests of fast-growing produce (e.g., lettuce and radishes) due to the urban microclimate, and a market literally at the doorstep. A government-funded pilot SPIN project in Philadelphia documented that gross revenue of over $50,000 can be earned from half an acre of urban land using SPIN techniques. SPIN farming has also been reported in British Columbia, Ontario, and Iowa (SPIN Farming, 2009). The most-cited benefits of SPIN farming are the low start-up costs, profitability, and the maintenance of urban green spaces. New forms of urban farming such as SPIN offer economic alternatives as well, providing a positive and empowering way to move from urban blight to beautification.

Non-profit farms, such as that of Just Food in the Ottawa region, work on community-based initiatives for social justice. In the Ottawa Greenbelt, on the former grounds of the National Capital Commission's tree nursery, the Just Food Farm offers access to land, training, and shared infrastructure and equipment to help foster viable small-scale agriculture. Just Food also offers support for other initiatives, such as the Karen Community Farm Project, Permaculture Ottawa's Community Urban Food Forest (CUFF), and the Ottawa Food Bank Community Harvest Program (Just Food, 2013).

Rooftop Production

Rooftops offer another opportunity for cities to foster urban food production. In 2011, Montreal's Lufa Farms built a 3000-square-metre commercial rooftop greenhouse with the goal to recycle water, reduce energy consumption, and grow food without using synthetic pesticides. Produce is sold through a weekly-box subscription model, with delivery to over 100 drop-off points in and around the city. Lufa Farms partners with 25 other food producers to offer their subscribers an extensive product line beyond their own 40 varieties of vegetables. From the Quebec landscape, partners provide such items as maple syrup, jams and jellies, mustards and oils—even wild foods, such as cattail hearts and marinated milkweed pods (Lufa, 2013). In spite of having to overcome zoning, building code, engineering, and lease and taxation issues, Lufa Farms is building a new greenhouse in Laval, and plans to scout for possibilities in Toronto, Boston, Chicago, and New York (Meeting of Minds, 2013).

The Carrot Common (2013) in Toronto developed from a partnership between a workers co-operative and a private developer interested in community development. Profits go to social-justice food initiatives and organic agriculture projects. The Big Carrot, an organic food store, is on the main floor of the Carrot Common, along with 17 other stores. The second floor is a holistic health centre, and on the roof is the Carrot Green Roof, a food-producing garden where many community events take place and workshops on urban agriculture are held. While not focused on rooftop food production as a primary goal, the rooftop offers a space for the diffusion of food production knowledge and methods throughout the city.

The YWCA Metro Vancouver, in partnership with the Society Promoting Environmental Conservation, offers urban agriculture courses at the YWCA Rooftop Food Garden. Their goal is to provide training for sustainable urban agriculture, on topics such as urban soil management, season extension, growing in small spaces, and small-business planning. At the same time, volunteers have experimented with 40 different varieties of fruits, herbs, and vegetables, and have grown over four tonnes of food since the Rooftop Food Garden began in the summer of 2006. The food is provided to low-income single mothers and their children through the YWCA programs in Vancouver (YWCA Metro Vancouver, 2013).

Elimination of the Food Desert

Important work has been going on in North America and the UK in the last decade to identify and find solutions to problems associated with food deserts (for the UK, see Wrigley, 2002; for Chicago, Block and Kouba, 2006; for Alberta, Smoyer-Tomic, Spence, and Amrhein, 2006). According to work done in the UK, a food desert exists in "areas of relative exclusion where people experience physical and economic barriers to accessing healthy food" (Reisig and Hobbiss,

2000: 138). Food deserts are linked with poor diet, which in turn is linked to compromised health. In North America, food deserts are often related to the advent of big-box stores that require car access and can result in diminished food access in urban areas. Planners can address food access challenges through better design. The move to walkable communities, including higher-density urban use, is part of the solution. A recent study in Saskatoon highlights useful strategies on the potential of zoning to encourage multi-purpose neighbourhoods of high population density with incentives for retailers to establish food outlets in "food desert" areas (Peters and MacCreary, 2008).

While radical shifts to more livable cities are being established, interim measures can be adopted. Small farmers' markets, for example, can be located where commuters congregate and/or in under-used spaces in low-income areas. The Region of Waterloo Public Health Department is experimenting with this option. Weekly summer markets were set up in parking lots around the City of Waterloo. Community centres, hospitals, and other public venues were included. Disadvantaged communities were targeted as a way to provide ready access to fresh, healthy food. While the project is still being assessed, preliminary results indicate that people who had access to the markets increased the quantity and variety of food they ate. The markets also became a meeting place and helped to build a stronger sense of community.

Another example involves taking food to people, or people to food. Both solutions offer ways to reconnect people with their food; a pilot project funded by the New York State Health Department illustrates this approach (Figures 23.1 and 23.2). In this case, Veggie Mobiles provide low-income communities with much-needed fresh produce. The concept is simple and allows people such as diabetics, who need fresh, low-sodium food, access to appropriate produce. They also provide food education by offering a "Taste and Take" event on Wednesdays when people can sample and take home a selected produce item.

Santropol Roulant (2006) in Montreal is another example of creative food delivery. This

Figure 23.1   The Veggie Mobile™, a travelling produce market operated by Capital District Community Gardens in New York's Capital Region. (Capital District Community Gardens)

project also targets disadvantaged citizens, in this case people who are elderly and/or have mobility challenges. Affiliated with McGill University, the project provides "Meals on Wheels" by delivering hot meals using bicycles and bringing together youth and senior citizens. Santropol Roulant (2006) grows its own produce as much as possible on rooftops and in small urban spaces, such as balconies. By using intense growing techniques that combine hydroponics with biodynamic and permaculture growing strategies, project members are able to produce up to six times more food than normally would be expected from the small areas under "cultivation."

Other jurisdictions are addressing poverty through food access programs. In this vein, the Toronto FoodShare program is among the most

recognized of its kind in Canada. Established in 1985, FoodShare improves access to food through school meal programs, the good food box, incubator kitchen facilities, youth programs, and food education programs (FoodShare, 2009). The Child Hunger Eradication Program (CHEP) in Saskatoon is another Canadian success story. By focusing on food security and child poverty issues, the program mobilizes parents, school groups, volunteers, and the local business community to improve food education and access to children living in poverty (CHEP, 2009). Both FoodShare and CHEP work to build linkages with local farmers as part of their food security strategies. However, while these programs are remarkable initiatives that reflect people's ability to work with limited resources, they are also small in scale and exist largely outside

Figure 23.2   Interior of The Veggie Mobile™, operated by Capital District Community Gardens. (Capital District Community Gardens)

the main operations of cities; as such, they reflect fundamental problems in urban environments and highlight the pressing need to make food access an integrated consideration for urban development.

Vertical Farming

While the idea of a sustainable vertical farm is futuristic at the moment, due to the challenges of producing food in vertical conditions, there are interesting ideas being generated on this type of production. Dickson Despommiers and his students at Columbia University have worked to conceptualize **vertical farms** (Despommiers, 2009). While still on the drawing board, they combine principles of urban agriculture and hydroponics in multi-storey indoor farms (Figure 23.3).

Vertical farms, they suggest, would be able to provide food year-round while using space more efficiently. Depending on the crop, a hectare could be 4 to 6 times as productive as a hectare of outdoor land, while for crops such as strawberries, indoor cultivation would be 30 times as productive per hectare. Growing indoors also addresses issues of drought and other weather-related challenges faced by farmers. Proposed water recirculation systems would make vertical farms closed-loop food production systems as waste and water could be captured and reflowed into the system. Vertical farms could also offer urban employment opportunities as this type of food production would be labour-intensive. The proposal for vertical farms offers interesting possible scenarios for the future of healthy food production within more sustainable cities.

Conclusion

Clearly, food offers an integrative lens to urban geographers, planners, policy-makers, and other practitioners who seek to move cities in more sustainable directions. This chapter outlined the trajectory Canada and its cities have taken in addressing food issues. The overview makes it clear that planners have lost sight of food systems in the urban context in the recent past and that food connections to peri-urban and rural communities are tenuous at best. While the case studies point to places where food is making its way onto the urban planning, policy, and design agenda, much more is needed.

Through food we can develop progressive dialogues about and address issues facing urban centres. A food prism allows us to examine challenges, such as production, distribution, and waste management in terms that are relevant to many members in a community. The need for food is something we all have in common. Planning for food therefore provides a language and a space for uniting seemingly disparate interests. Food provides a place from which to appreciate the extent of connectivity within and beyond city systems and to situate urban areas within their foodsheds (Kloppenberg et al., 1996). This

Figure 23.3 **Prototypical model of a vertical farm. (Courtesy of Blake Kurasek)**

connects consumers to producers, and urban landscapes to rural ones. Food offers the chance to break down the silos between health, social justice, environmental well-being, and economic development. Recalling the emphasis that the American Planning Association (APA) has placed on the positive role food can play for planners, we can begin to understand how food can help us to address the most pressing issues for cities—deteriorating urban environments (see Rees, Chapter 4), crumbling and declining economies (see Donald and Hall, Chapter 15), and social decay (see Walks, Chapter 9)—to create more robust and resilient living spaces. While it is essential to recognize the pressures on urban resources and capacities, integrated food systems offer solutions to many related and pressing problems.

For this to take place, large-scale integration and incorporation with policies such as sustainability and smart-growth plans are necessary. Specific references to food are needed in official plans to give food-based initiatives traction. Planners and municipal officials can help move food onto the agenda. In a newspaper interview, Paula Jones, a San Francisco food activist, explains,

> All the individual efforts are super important, but we need policymakers and business at the table, too. . . . Government can bring in not only the policy but also the funding and technical expertise that it takes to drive large-scale, systemic changes. (Rich, 2008)

Food, then, can provide the basis for partnerships between public and private interests as we conceive of and make real our cities of the future. Bringing projects such as rooftop greenhouses from the drawing board into urban centres requires many partners at the table. To facilitate this process, we will need to legitimize, integrate, and standardize the role of food in urban planning, design, and policy. As recognized by the APA, food needs to be accorded a policy home so citizens, policy-makers, and bureaucrats can be given a food-centric mandate. As this chapter has demonstrated, this is happening in some jurisdictions.

However, a permanent set of champions could bring food onto the agenda and ensure that hard dollars are committed to food-based initiatives so that we avoid relying largely or entirely on soft money and volunteers. This task calls for professional engagement at all scales—from the local to the international—to take ownership of food and to provide mandates that need to be entrenched in law. With these points in mind, it appears that the realm of planning may offer the best place for food. Planning could offer the integrated perspective now missing for food. While food will continue to be connected to issues of rurality, communities, and health, urban planning may be a way to bring food forward as a focal point for a new understanding of planning, design, environmental quality, and quality of life in urban areas.

Food provides a rallying point to re-imagine cities so they are truly "just cities" (Fainstein, 2010). Planning for food can give us the chance to redefine our cities in sustainable terms and to empower citizens to be engaged in everyday acts of change, lifting common, daily acts to ones of transformation (Lefebvre, 1991). Indeed, food can provide a platform in the creation of the "new city."

Review Questions

1. Why should professional planners be concerned with urban food supplies and distribution?
2. How have urban food systems changed over the past 100 years?
3. How is the urban food system changing today?

Notes

1. Sales of organic food increased an average of 20 per cent annually from the early 1990s into the twenty-first century. Knudson (2007) reported that organic sales in

the US were set to increase by 71 per cent between 2006 and 2011.
2. See also the award-winning work by Will Allen, "Growing Power in Milwaukee and Chicago," at www. macfound.org/site/c.lkLXJ8MQKrH/b.4537249/k.29CA/ Will_Allen.htm

References

American Planning Association. 2007. *Policy Guide on Community and Regional Food Planning*. At: www. planning.org/policy/guides/adopted/food.htm

Ayalon, O. 2006. *Making Rooftops Bloom: Strategies for Encouraging Rooftop Greening in Montréal*. Montreal: McGill University, MA Thesis.

Block, D., and J. Kouba. 2006. "A comparison of the affordability of a market basket in two communities in the Chicago area," *Public Health and Nutrition* 9: 837–45.

Born, B., and M. Purcell. 2006. "Avoiding the local food trap: Scale and food systems in planning research," *Journal of Planning Education and Research* 26: 195–207.

Bryant, C.R., L.H. Russwurm, and A.G. McLennan. 1982. *The City's Countryside: Land and Its Management in the Rural–Urban Fringe*. London: Longman.

Caldwell, W. 2000. *Rural Non-Farm Development: Its Impact on the Viability and Sustainability of Agricultural and Rural Communities*. Toronto: Government of Ontario, Ministry of Agriculture, Food and Rural Affairs, Research and Corporate Services Division Research Branch.

Campbell, C. 2006. *Forever Farmland: Reshaping the Agricultural Land Reserve for the 21st Century*. Vancouver, BC: David Suzuki Foundation.

Carrot Common. 2013. Carrot Common—Home of the Big Carrot! At: www.carrotcommon.com

Child Hunger Eradication Program (CHEP). 2009. "Good food incorporated." At: www.chep.org/index.html

Christopherson, S. 2007. "Barriers to 'US Style' lean retailing: The case of Wal-Mart's failure in Germany," *Journal of Economic Geography* 7: 451–69.

Connell, D., J. Smithers, and A. Joseph. 2008. "Farmers' markets and the 'good food' value chain: A preliminary study," *Local Environment* 13: 169–85.

de la Salle, J., and M. Holland, eds. 2011. *Agricultural Urbanism: Handbook for Building Sustainable Food Systems in 21st Century Cities*. Winnipeg, MB: Green Frigate Books.

Despommiers, D. 2009. "Vertical farms: Home." At: www. verticalfarm.com/

Donald, B. 2008. "Food systems planning and sustainable cities and regions: The role of the firm in sustainable food capitalism," *Regional Studies* 42: 1251–62.

——, and A. Blay-Palmer. 2006. "The urban food economy: Cultural consumption for the urban elite or social inclusion opportunity?" *Environment and Planning A* 38: 1901–20.

Duany, A. 2011. *Garden Cities: Theory & Practice of Agrarian Urbanism*. London: The Prince's Foundation for the Built Environment, Duany Plater-Zyberk & Company.

Dupuis, M. 2000. "Not in my body: BGH and the rise of organic milk," *Agriculture and Human Values* 17: 285–95.

Elder, R.F. 2005. "Protecting New York City's community gardens," *New York University Environmental Law Journal* 13: 769–800. At: www3.law.nyu.edu/journals/envtllaw/issues/vol13/3/v13_n3_elder.pdf

Fainstein, S. 2010. *The Just City*. Ithaca, NY: Cornell University Press.

Feagan, R. 2008. "Direct marketing: Towards sustainable local food systems?" *Local Environment* 13: 161–7.

FoodShare. 2009. "Good, healthy food for all." At: www.food share.net/index.htm

Friedmann, H., and P. McMichael. 1989. "Agriculture and the state system: The rise and decline of national agri-cultures, 1870 to the present," *Sociologia Ruralis* 29: 93–117.

Goodman, D. 2003. "The quality 'turn' and alternative food practices: Reflections and agenda," *Journal of Rural Studies* 19: 1–7.

——, and M. Redclift. 1989. *From Peasant to Proletarian: Capitalist Development and Agrarian Transitions*. New York: Blackwell.

Gutham, J. 2007. "The Polanyian Way? Voluntary Food Labels as Neoliberal Governance," *Antipode* 39: 456–78. doi: 10.1111/j.1467-8330.2007.00535.x

Guthman, J. 2003. "Fast food/organic food: Reflexive tastes and the making of 'yuppie chow,'" *Social and Cultural Geography* 4: 45–58.

Hanes, A. 2008. "Toronto's target: 50% local food," *National Post*, 31 Oct. At: http://network.nationalpost.com/np/blogs/toronto/archive/tags/Local+food/default.aspx

Hinrichs, C., and T. Lyson, eds. 2008. *Remaking the North American Food System: Strategies for Sustainability*. Lincoln, NE: University of Nebraska Press.

Just Food. 2013. *The Just Food Farm: A Community Food and Sustainable Agriculture Hub*. At: www.justfood.ca/just-food-farm/

Kloppenberg, J., et al. 1996. "Coming into the foodshed," *Agriculture and Human Values* 13, 3: 33–41.

Kneen, B. 1995. *From Land to Mouth: Understanding the Food System* (2nd edn.). Toronto: NC Press.

Knudson, W. 2007. *The Organic Food Market*. East Lansing, MI: Michigan State University, Strategic Marketing Institute Working Paper 01-0407.

Lefebvre, H. 1991. *The Production of Space*. London: Blackwell.

Lufa Farms. 2013. *Lufa Farms: Farming for a Better Future*. At: http://lufa.com/en/

Marsden, T., ed. 2008. *Sustainable Communities: New Spaces for Planning, Participation and Engagement*. London: Elsevier.

Maye, D., L. Holloway, and M. Kneafsey, eds. 2007. *Alternative Food Geographies: Representation and Practice*. Oxford: Elsevier

Meeting of Minds. 2013. *Beyond the Green Roof: Greenhouses Grow Possibilities for Urban Building Owners*. At: http://cityminded.org/greenhouses-grow-possibilities-for-urban-building-owners-5809

Montreal, City of. 2008. "Montreal, living in Montreal, community gardens." At: http://ville.montreal.qc.ca/pls/portal/docs/page/plan_urbanisme_en/media/documents/061030_2_1_en.pdf

Morgan, K. 2008. "Greening the realm: Sustainable food chains and the public plate," *Regional Studies* 42: 1237–50.

——, T. Marsden, and J. Murdoch. 2006. *Worlds of Food: Place, Power and Provenance in the Food Chain*. London: Oxford University Press.

——, and R. Sonnino. 2008. *The School Food Revolution: Public Food and the Challenge of Sustainable Development*. London: Earthscan.

Peters, E., and T. McCreary. 2008. "Poor neighbourhoods and the changing geography of food retailing in Saskatoon, Saskatchewan, 1984–2004," *Canadian Journal of Urban Research* 17: 78–106.

Petts, J. 2001. *Urban Agriculture in London*. Copenhagen: World Health Organization, Regional Office for Europe. Series on Urban Food Security—Case Study 2. At: www.euro.who.int/__data/assets/pdf_file/0015/101625/E724 21.pdf

Pirog, R., T. Van Pelt, K. Enshayan, and E. Cook. 2001. *Food, Fuel, and Freeways: An Iowa Perspective on How Far Food Travels, Fuel Usage, and Greenhouse Gas Emissions*. Ames, IA: Iowa State University, Leopold Center for Sustainable Agriculture, June.

Rich, D. 2008. "Farming the city: Planners start thinking of how to feed us," *San Francisco Chronicle*, 22 Mar., F-1.

Reisig, V., and A. Hobbiss. 2000. "Food deserts and how to tackle item: A study of one city's approach," *Health Education Journal* 59: 137–49.

Roberts, W. 2013. *No Nonsense Guide to World Food*. Toronto: Between the Lines.

Santropol Roulant. 2006. "Mission." At: http://santropol roulant.org/about-us/mission/

Scarpitti, F. 2008. "Announcement on Markham's agreement with Local Food Plus to adopt LFP standards and zero waste program for municipal catering and food servi-ces," Markham, ON: Municipality of Markham, 4 June, 2008 Smog Summit, Toronto. At: www.organicfood council.org/files/downloads/Announcement%20on%20 Markham.pdf

Smith, A., and J. MacKinnon. 2006. *The 100-Mile Diet: A Year of Local Eating*. Toronto: Vintage.

Smoyer-Tomic, K., J. Spence, and C. Amrhein. 2006. "Food deserts in the prairies? Supermarket accessibility and neighbourhood need in Edmonton, Canada," *Professional Geographer* 58: 307–26.

SPIN Farming. 2009. "SPIN makes agriculture accessible to anyone, anywhere." At: www.spinfarming.com/whats Spin/

Statistics Canada. 2007. "A statistical portrait of agriculture, Canada and provinces: Census years 1921 to 2006. At: www.statcan.gc.ca/pub/95-632-x/2007000/t/4185571-eng.htm

Steel, Carolyn. 2008. *Hungry City: How Food Shapes Our Lives*. London: Catto & Windus.

Toronto, City of. 2009. "Living in Toronto: Green Bin Program." At: www.toronto.ca/greenbin/index.htm

Vancouver, City of. 2008. "City of Vancouver fact sheet: Green building made easier." At: www.vancouver-ecodensity.ca/webupload/File/Green%20Barriers%20 Fact%20Sheet.pdf

———. 2009. Vancouver's Community Gardens. "Parks and recreation." At: http://vancouver.ca/parks/parks/comgardn.htm

Wackernagel, M., J. Kitzes, D. Moran, S. Goldfinger, M. Thomas. 2006. "The ecological footprint of cities and regions: Comparing resource availability with resource demand," *Environment and Urbanization* 18: 103–12. At: www.footprintnetwork.org/en/index.php/GFN/page/footprint_for_cities/

Whatmore, S. 2002. *Hybrid Geographies: Natures, Cultures, Spaces*. London: Sage.

Wilson, S.J. 2008. *Ontario's Wealth, Canada's Future: Appreciating the Value of the Greenbelt's Eco-Services*. Vancouver, BC: David Suzuki Foundation.

Winnipeg, City of. 2013. "Allotment gardens/Community gardens." At: www.winnipeg.ca/publicworks/parksand fields/CommunityGardens/communitygardens.asp

Wrigley, N. 2002. "'Food deserts' in British cities: Policy context and research priorities," *Urban Studies* 39: 2029–40. At: www.informaworld.com/smpp/content~db=all~content=a713707798

Xuereb, M. 2005. *Food Miles: Environmental Implications of Food Imports to Waterloo Region*. Waterloo, ON: Region of Waterloo Public Health. At: http://chd.region.waterloo.on.ca/web/health.nsf/0/54ED787F44 ACA44C852571410056AEB0/$file/FOOD_MILES_REPORT.pdf

YWCA Metro Vancouver. 2013. *YWCA Metro Vancouver Rooftop Food Garden*. At: www.ywcavan.org/content/YWCA_Metro_Vancouver_Rooftop_Food_Garden_/605

Cities on the Edge: Emerging Suburban Constellations in Canada

24

JEAN-PAUL D. ADDIE,
ROBERT S. FIEDLER,
AND ROGER KEIL

Introduction

Canada is a suburban nation. While, statistically, a majority of the population now lives in urban environments, that majority for the most part is found in places that are "suburban" in terms of built form or location at the periphery of large urban centres, small towns, or even villages. If we take into account exurban sprawl, there is even more dispersion of habitat. This is not to diminish the trend, at least in some of our urban centres, toward re-urbanization (i.e., the increase in population and density in traditional inner cities). We have all heard stories of walkability, downtown living, creative economies, increased transit use, condominiums, and revived cultural scenes in downtowns and adjacent inner city neighbourhoods. This chapter aims to demonstrate that this is only one side of the story. Most Canadians live in suburban constellations (Table 24.1). Those who move to major urban areas from elsewhere in Canada (rural and remote areas, as well as small towns) and those who arrive from distant shores (the majority of the approximately 250,000 immigrants who arrive each year) also tend to settle directly in suburban and exurban areas found around the country's largest cities.[1] That latter trend, which started in the final decades of the last century, has changed not only the face of our urban peripheries, but also the demographic and cultural composition of Canada overall.

In this chapter, we speak about suburbanization and suburbanisms. In simple terms, we define suburbanization "as the combination of non-central population and economic growth with urban spatial expansion." By suburbanism(s) we refer to "a growing prevalence of qualitatively distinct 'suburban ways of life'" (Ekers, Hamel, and Keil, 2012: 407). By this, we refer to emerging modes of heterogeneous, non-traditional ways of living at the urban periphery that are distinct from those classically understood in relation to both the city and the countryside. To better understand suburbanisms as a "plural phenomenon," an *Atlas of Suburbanisms*, created at the University of Waterloo, mapped its dimensions across the Canadian metropolitan landscape—city, suburb, exurb, and rural fringe. To distinguish between suburbs as places, and suburbanisms as ways of living, the project mapped the 25 largest metropolitan areas in Canada at the dissemination area (DA) level using three sets of variables: (1) the built-form/commute-mode dimension, (2) the domesticity dimension, and (3) the social status dimension (Moos and Kramer, 2012; also see Moos and Mendez, 2014).[2] The resulting maps, shown in Figure 24.1, make it apparent that characteristics associated with suburbs and suburban living are found across the entire metropolitan fabric of Canada, including in central cities or urban core areas (albeit less intensely than elsewhere in

Table 24.1	Population Distribution in Different Urban and Suburban Realms in Canada				
CMA	2011 Population	Active Core (%)	Transit Suburb (%)	Auto Suburb (%)	Exurban (%)
Toronto	5,583,064	11.0	14.0	72.0	3.0
Montreal	3,824,221	10.5	13.5	72.0	4.0
Vancouver	2,313,328	16.0	12.0	67.0	6.0
Ottawa	1,236,324	12.0	10.5	65.0	12.5
Calgary	1,214,839	12.9	2.6	80.0	4.6
Edmonton	1,159,869	11.0	12.0	66.0	11.0
Quebec City	765,706	15.0	6.0	65.0	14.0
Winnipeg	730,018	12.0	5.0	75.0	8.0
Hamilton	721,053	11.0	10.0	71.0	8.0
Kitchener-Waterloo	477,160	10.0	9.0	77.0	4.0
London	474,786	14.0	14.0	58.0	14.0
St.Catherines	392,184	15.0	2.0	69.0	14.0
Halifax	390,317	14.0	18.0	44.0	24.0
Oshawa	356,177	3.0	13.0	77.0	7.0
Victoria	344,615	17.0	11.0	67.0	4.0

Source: Statistics Canada, 2011 Census; www.canada.com/news/infographics/suburbs/suburbs.html (based analysis by David Gordon, Professor and Director: Queen's University School of Urban and Regional Planning)

metropolitan space). In these terms, we are a suburban nation in an urbanized country.

Uncovering the Historical Geographies of Canadian Suburbs and Suburbanization

How did we get to be a suburban nation? In the far-reaching postwar transformation of Canadian cities, no change has been more impactful than the shift from relatively compact forms of urban development, built when walking or public transit were the principal means for getting around, to the more sprawling, large-scale suburban forms that emerged alongside the mass adoption of private automobile-based travel after World War II. The changes were drastic and abrupt. They altered society, the economy, and governance at all scales. As urban historian Robert Fishman (1987: 183) has noted, the postwar suburban building boom "was so powerful that it was like a tide that washed

over all precedents. It was as if suburbanization *began* in 1945."

The prominence of postwar suburbanization has a number of implications for how we typically see our suburbs. Periodic calls to "re-invent the suburbs" (see Bourne, 1996) are inevitably directed at the multiple stereotypes and clichés that have attached themselves to postwar suburbia. In the 1950s, young families flooded into new suburban developments filled with modest homes, automobile usage proliferated, and television extended the reach of mass culture and consumerism. Chain stores in shopping plazas and suburban malls began to replace independent shops and street-based retailing in newly built suburban areas. The newness and initial sameness of postwar suburbs led urban-based intellectuals, writers, artists, and social commentators to deride them as sterile, banal, and conformist places. Initially viewed as the solution to urban problems, such as poverty, crime, vice, and pollution, the suburb now seemed to urbanists to be a hellish place devoid of culture and home to all manner of new social pathologies

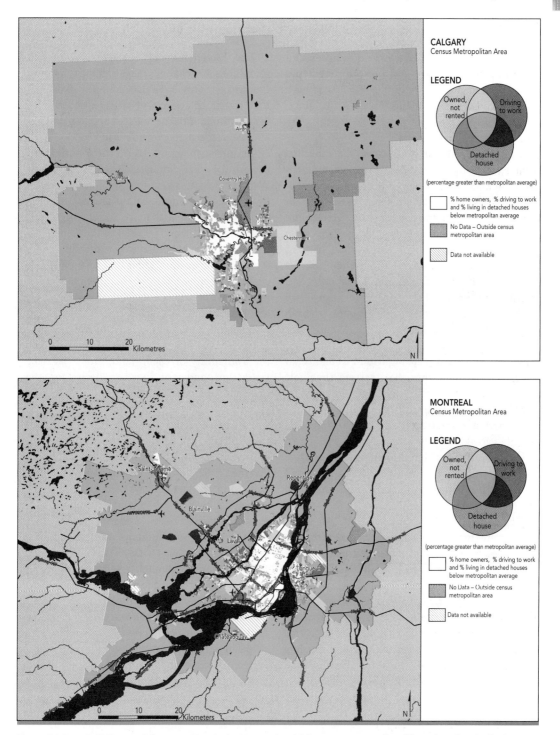

Figure 24.1 **Built Form and Commute Type in the Montreal and Calgary CMAs, Reproduced from the *Atlas of Suburbanisms***

Source: Moos and Kramer (2012). Note: Colour maps available on-line http://env-blogs.uwaterloo.ca/atlas/

(Nicolaides, 2006). Since the 1970s, however, various attempts have been made to demonstrate that "the suburbs" have evolved into a complex and variegated socio-spatial landscape. But stereotypes and clichés that originated in the 1950s, and have gained almost mythical status in the decades since, continue to powerfully shape how suburbs are represented and understood.

Rather than attempt to disprove "the suburban myth" (see Donaldson, 1969), it is more productive to see cities and their suburbs as both real and imagined places, and to consider why certain representations of them endure as well as the degree to which such representations reflect the realities of "actually existing" suburbs (past and present). A vital task, therefore, is to question the often taken-for-granted assumption that cities and suburbs are socio-spatial opposites. If instead we conceive of suburbs as transitional spaces—a middle landscape between city and open countryside (Rowe, 1991)—then it becomes easier to consider "city" and "suburb" as existing within a continuum of urban spaces, rather than setting them off against each other as categorically different places. Viewing suburbs this way also encourages us to view them as places that evolve: in response to the life cycle of residents; as political, economic, or social conditions change; and as their relative location within a metropolitan region is altered by continued urban growth and spatial expansion (McManus and Ethington, 2007).

The challenge is to better understand when and where stereotypes and clichés, often masquerading as conventional wisdom, obscure contemporary suburban realities and distort suburban histories. German planning theorist Tomas Sieverts (2003) argues that the "myth of the old city" or a "one-sided love for the historical city" among urbanists distorts how suburbs are perceived. In North America, a preoccupation with the vast, sprawling landscapes built around cities after World War II colours how we understand prior waves of suburbanization. This is particularly true when older suburban landscapes, such as streetcar suburbs, are folded into the urban realm and washed of their suburban-ness. We need to understand that

many areas now within the city limits were once peripheral and suburban (see Harris and Lewis, 1998a). Though it is impossible to know the transformations and changes that await today's suburbs, the urban past tells us that they will evolve—and that transformation and change will occur in response to internal needs, metropolitan pressures, and wider social and economic forces.

Recent scholarship on North American suburbanization has emphasized that prior to World War II "differences between cities and the suburbs as a whole were quite minor and were dwarfed by variations within the city and among suburbs" (Harris and Lewis, 2001: 284). Further, texts and commentary on suburbanization and metropolitan development from the first half of the twentieth century unsettle the notion that the only (or even main) participants in the suburban trend were affluent commuters (Wunsch, 1995). Rather, multiple factors converge to explain the diversity of Canadian suburbia prior to World War II, including the availability of cheap land, industrial decentralization, and working-class desire for home ownership (Harris 1996; Lewis 2000; 2001). Street railways also played an important role in allowing urban development to extend further outwards from the core, and enabled a wider range of workers to live beyond the limits of the walking city (Warner, 1962). In addition to the development and expansion of street railways in Canadian cities, the episodic nature of urban land development—real estate booms and busts—underwrote the variation in lot sizes and housing styles found in many pre–World War II suburban districts (McCann, 1999). Revisionist (mostly American) suburban histories increasingly demonstrate that an over-emphasis on elite or middle-class suburbanization in suburban histories has distorted who and what is to be found in the suburban periphery. The suburb as a landscape of residential privilege and exclusion has long co-existed with "other" forms of suburban life, including lower income, self-built, industrial, ethnically segregated, and new-immigrant suburbs.

That "other" suburbs existed does not mean that individual suburbs were diverse, however. Historical research suggests that the metropolitan periphery during first half of the twentieth century was a segmented social space in which individual suburbs could be relatively homogeneous at the same time as the whole (suburbia) was diverse. Rather than resembling the simple zonal pattern of increasing affluence with distance from the urban core, an assumption built into the concentric model of the Chicago School (see Harris and Lewis, 1998b), the complexity of the Canadian metropolis prior to World War II was shaped by the decentralization of industry along rail corridors and by the segmentation of social space along class, ethnic/racial, and religious lines (Harris 1996; 2004; Lewis 2000; 2001). The conventional image of suburban affluence and conformity, shaped heavily by postwar suburban stereotypes, has made it easier to elide the historical importance of industrial and working-class suburbanization.

Richard Harris's *Unplanned Suburbs* (1996) provides a rich account of blue-collar British immigrant settlement in unserviced fringe areas around Toronto during the first decades of the twentieth century. Made possible by unregulated development of cheap land on the urban periphery, the unplanned suburbs that resulted had little in common with the bourgeois utopias, borderlands, or streetcar suburbs that have led most historians and urbanists to cast suburbanization solely in relation to middle- or upper-class proclivities. Sharing the desire for home ownership with more affluent suburbanites, working-class suburbanization rested upon a willingness to settle marginal land and upon the ability to substitute thrift and sweat equity for capital (see also Nicolaides, 2002; Wiese, 2004). It also rested upon a willingness to forgo amenities and comforts offered in the city. Unplanned suburbs had at best limited transit service and few, if any, municipal services, such as water, sewage, power, and police and fire protection. Continued urban growth eventually led to unplanned districts being swallowed up by the rest of the metropolis, and the costs of providing municipal infrastructure and services to inefficiently planned areas and poorly constructed self-built homes led to tighter regulation of development and a greater emphasis on planning.

The fall of self-built, unplanned suburbs after World War II and their seemingly sudden replacement by standardized, large-scale suburban tract housing developments has been captured in the expression "creeping conformity" (Harris, 2004). An important part of that narrative points to the growing influence of the state in the twentieth century: first, in response to speculative land subdivision prior to World War I and later more profoundly in response to the Great Depression of the 1930s and wartime housing needs in the 1940s. By the 1950s, national housing standards developed by the Canada Mortgage and Housing Corporation (CMHC) (enforced via its role in mortgage finance) and new planning legislation enacted by provincial governments in the mid- to late-1940s worked to produce more standardized suburban built environments (Harris, 2004; Miron, 1988).

When considering the evolution of Canadian suburbia, we must remember that it has been characterized by regional diversity (McCann, 2006). Differences in provincial planning practices and the role of the distinctive suburban strategies employed by large regional land syndicates (notably the Hudson's Bay Company and the Canadian Pacific Railroad) in the pre-World War I era shaped the overall suburban form we now find everywhere. Postwar suburbanization did not simply happen in the form that it did because of world-historical forces, though broad structural factors—such as social class stratification (emergence of the middle class), patterns of industrialization (large-scale, Fordist production facilities), technological change (automobilization), and the governance of land ownership (far-reaching government programs such as mortgage subsidies)—did play a significant role. The suburbs were also forged by various interests, values, and beliefs—of suburban residents, land developers, builders, planners, financial organizations, and governments—that combined to change the "pluralistic" character of early Canadian suburbs, usually toward a more regulated, planned, and middle-class (though not completely) urban space. In most cases, this led to lower-income, self-built forms of suburbanization being squeezed out (McCann, 1999). Despite the appeal to a growing middle-class, the suburbs remained more diverse than is often acknowledged.

The suburbs also reveal much about societal trends and norms. One aspect of this is the gender dimension. Feminist geographers have long argued that "suburban studies" largely fail to consider suburbs as "women's spaces" or to critically examine the gendered nature of discourses on suburbanization (Strong-Boag et al., 1999). Conventional accounts have focused on the suburbs as a male paradise, a haven from the hustle and bustle of the city and a separation of work life from family life. The suburbs were closely implicated in the Victorian defense of the ideal middle-class family through the spatial separation of "private" homes and "public" cities. Accordingly, the inner city came to represent locales of the deviant, the poor, the recent immigrant and racially marginalized, and, in particular, came to represent a place of female sin.

The design of suburbs and suburban housing has also enacted (and reinforced) gendered divisions of labour. "Traditional" suburbia was underpinned by women's unpaid domestic work. Over time, these "bourgeois utopias" have become harder to find as women increasingly entered the paid workforce in order to maintain middle-class lifestyles in the face of rising costs and stagnant or declining real wages (Rose and Villeneuve, 1998). Paradoxically, women's increased work outside the home has resulted in contradictions between the ". . . assumptions underpinning suburban communities and the reality of female residents' lives" (Strong-Boag et al., 1999: 178). These contradictions include the increased isolation of stay-at-home mothers and the difficulties experienced by working mothers trying to manage the multiple demands of family life, wage labour, and long commutes. This contrasts with the active role of women in negotiating and constructing the suburban landscape and highlights the differing experiences of women in the suburbs, with some women finding the "burden of being 'good' wives and mothers worsened by a landscape that has regularly ignored them," while "[o]thers have flourished, able to mobilize community and kin resources in ways they experience as rewarding"

(Strong-Boag et al., 1999: 179). In the absence of traditional family structures, social relationships had to be reconfigured in new suburban neighbourhoods. For example, women whose child-care needs were not being met in these emerging communities engaged in reciprocal economies to perform the "invisible work" done at home (Pratt, 2003). New Urbanist developments like Cornell in the Toronto suburb of Markham have done little to change the overall patterns of gender relations seen in classical suburban neighbourhood (Markovich and Hendler, 2006). While such developments post higher density patterns and different design features, which could suggest different lifestyles, in reality their residents behave just like their counterparts in conventional suburbs.

There is much controversy about the gender aspects of the suburban landscape. In terms of safety, some groups of women have been found to have a preference for inner city urban design, for an abundance of "populated" public spaces and sense of community that makes them feel safer—more at home—in contrast with images of bleak, unpopulated suburban landscapes that makes them feel isolated and vulnerable. But race and class privilege may act as a blindspot to urban violence more broadly. Spaces of whiteness or middle-classness are constructed in Toronto through associating urban violence with "other" neighbourhoods like inner suburban Jane-Finch or inner-city Parkdale (Kern, 2005).

The Diverse Canadian Suburb: Suburbanization and Suburbanisms Redefined

Although Canadian suburban development adopted a more regulated planned and institutional form in the postwar era, there is now a broad picture of suburban social diversity that has decisively moved suburban Canada from the classical trajectory of Anglo-American suburbanization to a remarkable new model of peripheral development (Fong, Luk, and Ooka, 2005; Rose, 2010; Walks,

2013). Canadian suburbs are now increasingly defined by the immigrant experience and the heterogeneity of new suburban populations. No longer are the outskirts of cities more homogeneous and straightforwardly wealthier than cities. Whereas previously new immigrants settled in the inner city and moved to the suburbs as their economic situation permitted, the contemporary pattern is for (notably non-European) immigrants to move directly to the suburbs. Immigrants are therefore responsible for qualitative changes to suburban lives, which destabilize stereotypes of white middle-class nuclear families living in single-family homes as the suburban norm. This trend takes two main forms. In the old, formerly white, and middle-class suburbs of the postwar years, there are now large and remarkably diverse non-white and immigrant populations attracted by low-rent apartments, affordable single-family homes, and the availability of public transit. Here change is registered visually by the appearance of new places of worship and via the now kaleidoscopic diversity of signage for ethnic businesses found in strip malls and modest plazas located along major arterial roads (Figure 24.2). In newer, outer suburbs, more affluent immigrant households are shaping new suburban spaces, rather than adapting existing ones to meet new needs. In Toronto and Vancouver, one manifestation of this is a novel form of suburban development: the **ethnoburb** (see Kobayashi and Preston, Chapter 8).

Chinese immigration, for example, has altered the suburban landscape in both Toronto and Vancouver in profound ways. In both cities, new Chinese immigrants increasingly bypass

Figure 24.2   Evolving Social Diversity in Postwar Canadian Suburbs

The Canada Kanthaswamy Temple, Birchmount Road, in the inner Toronto suburb of Scarborough. (Roger Keil)

traditional reception areas in the inner city and settle directly in peripheral communities. In Richmond (south of Vancouver) and Markham (north of Toronto) significant concentrations of Chinese immigrant populations have formed. Accompanying the development of these places into ethnoburbs has been the emergence of distinctive and novel suburban forms, such as "Asian theme malls" (Preston and Lo, 2000). This reflects a shift away from traditional geographies of Chinese business and commercial activity, which concentrated in inner-city "Chinatowns" (Wang, 1999). Now well established as ethnoburbs, the initial transformations in Richmond and Markham revealed tensions between official multiculturalism (the ideology and policy) and its actual practice as an everyday urban reality on-the-ground in Canadian communities (Ray, Halseth, and Johnson 1997; Wood and Gilbert, 2005; see Kobayashi and Preston, Chapter 8).

Traditional understandings of home and neighbourhood may explain the resistance of established suburban residents to the changes prompted by the influx of newcomers to previously white suburban areas. In two (quite different) residential subdivision developments in Surrey (a mostly lower-middle-class or working-class suburban city about 40 minutes east of Vancouver), white residents avoided the use of explicitly racialized language to explain their residential locational choices and preferences (Dowling, 1998). Feelings about perceived "others"—non-traditional families or Indo-Canadians—were made apparent, instead, through the use of a local "sociospatial vocabulary" that linked specific suburban places to marginalized or racialized groups.

In north Scarborough, in Richmond Hill, and in Markham, the transformation of the suburban landscape in the 1980s and 1990s was marked by planning conflicts over proposals for new Chinese-oriented shopping centres (Preston and Lo, 2000). Opposition was usually framed by residents around traffic, parking, and character/scale of the proposed developments, but political debate and newspaper coverage at the time reveal at least an undercurrent of racial intolerance; anxiety about

the scale and pace of ethnic change was also a factor. Proposals to establish new places of worship in the suburbs by minority groups can also spur community opposition, though increasingly ethnic communities in the suburbs are locating their churches, temples, gurdwaras, mosques, and other cultural institutions in industrial areas (Hackworth and Stein, 2012).

The diverse suburb also takes other more subtle, less visible forms. It involves the diversification of everyday life and socio-cultural patterns through niche building and novel suburbanisms. A case in point is the socio-spatial clustering of suburban mothers and children whose husbands/fathers live permanently abroad for employment—a trend documented in suburban Mississauga (Aulakh, 2011). In suburban Vancouver and Toronto, the term "astronaut families" is used to describe immigrant families where the husband continues to work in Hong Kong (see Kobayashi and Preston, Chapter 8). It is the emergence of these everyday practices, introduced by immigrant, non-European suburban populations that marks most tangibly a contrast between suburbanization as a readily identifiable built environment (allegedly white picket-fenced single-family homes for nuclear families in cul-de-sac neighbourhoods) and suburbanisms as rapidly diversifying ways of life.

Given the heavy Canadian reliance on immigration for population growth, the anticipated flow of newcomers into mostly suburban environments has far-reaching implications (Lo, 2011; Teixeira, 2008). This is particularly the case if we consider the social, economic, and political context into which immigrants arrive. These are fragile neo-liberal times characterized by widening income inequality, the growth of precarious employment, and rising levels of housing stress and homelessness (See Walks, Chapter 9; Walks, 2009). Among South-Asian and Chinese Canadians, there is a clear trend toward suburban residency (Hiebert, 2000), which may be at least partly explained by higher incidences of multi-generational and/or multi-family living arrangements. It is likely that these households find larger suburban homes a preferred form of accommodation. But the diversity of immigrants arriving results in highly uneven suburban geographies of poverty and housing stress. For example, low-rent apartments in suburban areas are often highly localized within large tracts of mostly single-family homes, creating micro-geographies of acute housing need and poverty in otherwise comfortably housed areas (Bunting, Walks, and Filion, 2004; Fiedler, Schuurman,and Hyndman, 2006). The picture is further complicated by evidence of housing need and poverty that is thinly distributed across areas where residents are generally well-housed—a phenomenon that may be explained by the growing role of basement and secondary suites as a form of low-rent housing in suburban areas, though this is somewhat speculative (see Ransford, 2003; Tanasescu, 2009).

This is not to suggest that the inner city no longer faces problems. Indeed, social problems such as poverty, homelessness, food insecurity, and so forth have become suburban problems, too—albeit with different implications for policy-makers, service providers, and those who are marginalized, poor, and suburban. As well, structural changes have occurred to postwar, inner suburban areas, which have experienced considerable **deindustrialization** since the 1980s (Walks, 2001). These changes have been identified, particularly as they relate to income inequality and neighbourhood poverty, in influential reports and studies (Hulchanski, 2010; United Way Toronto, 2004).

Thus far, the focus has been on older, inner suburban areas as places where so-called "urban" problems have emerged in recent decades. The suburbanization of poverty's leading edge, however, continues to move outward; it is an emergent reality in newer, outlying suburban areas. The concept of "priority neighbourhoods," introduced as part of Toronto's Strong Neighbourhoods Strategy, has been exported to allegedly wealthy suburbs where social distress has not previously been acknowledged or presumed to exist (Baluja, 2011). This has yet to translate, as it has in relation to older, closer-in suburban areas, into the talk of suburban **ghettos**, as is sometimes evoked in media coverage of certain neighbourhoods, such as Toronto's Jane and Finch, Kingston-Galloway, or Malvern

neighbourhoods. These have become objects of perhaps misguided top-down policies transferred from other cases to pump resources into places that are considered breeding grounds of poverty, educational failure, and crime (Black, 2011). Putting this aside, it would seem that poverty and social exclusion are on the radar of policy-makers, which is important given that suburban municipalities have been slow to build the kinds of social infrastructure available in inner city areas (Cowen and Parlette, 2011; Lo, 2011).

Complicating Suburban Form and Function: Post-Suburbia and the in-between City

Contemporary suburbanization has been characterized by a qualitative transformation and diversification of the structure and functions of Canadian urban peripheries (Addie and Fiedler, 2013; Keil and Addie, under review). New suburban forms such as **edge cities** (Garreau, 1991) or **technoburbs** (Fishman, 1987) and suburban downtowns (Filion and Gad, 2006)—the sprawling mixed-use suburban zones on the urban periphery that are automobile dependent, highway oriented, computer network-enabled, and relatively autonomous from older central cities—have been identified over the past two decades and are receiving increased attention in relation to contemporary concerns with suburban sustainability (Atkinson, 2007; Kruse and Sugrue, 2006). The social differentiation of the suburb challenges prior perceptions and conceptions of peripheral development (Harris, 2010). Most suburban development now takes place in a dynamic landscape that resembles neither the old inner city nor the glamorous cookie-cutter suburbs. Significantly transformed since their original development, these "in-between" spaces have often become neglected as the focus of urban growth has been on the densification of the downtown and the continued sprawl of subdivisions across greenfields in the outer reaches of Canadian cities. Yet, most Canadians now live, work, and play in quite undefined and nondescript middle landscapes, where everything seems to happen at once: large-scale infrastructure, such as highways and airports, are next to residential quarters; all manner of service infrastructures, including universities and high-tech corridors, sit adjacent to low-rent apartments; parks and parking are side by side; high-speed highways, food and transit deserts define the same space; religious mega-structures sit across the street from ethnic mini-malls (Young, Wood and Keil, 2011).

We can also call these spaces "post-suburbia" (Teaford, 1997). Post-suburbs are dynamic and diverse spaces and, as a consequence, are difficult to pin down: "The problem of adequately *placing* postsuburbia is part of its analytical attraction and potentially a key distinctive element of it when compared with established notions of cities, suburbs, and the rural" (Phelps, Wood, and Valler, 2010: 370). Indeed, within the maelstrom of city-regional growth we can witness postwar suburbs evolving into post-suburbs or new cities in their own right, while declining cities regress to dormitory suburbs for nearby urban centres (Phelps and Wood, 2011). While there is a degree of definitional ambiguity here, the central characteristic of post-suburbia is a balance between traditional suburban (residential) functions and emergent employment and economic activity. The term captures the sense that contemporary suburbanization processes represent a new mode of metropolitan development as well as a break from our traditional views of the relationship between the city and its core (Lucy and Phillips, 1997: 259). Post-suburbia thus indicates an incremental shift from previous suburban processes at a global scale, just as the postwar suburbs presented an evolution from pre-existing urban and industrial settlement patterns.

The nature of the shift toward post-suburbia can be witnessed in the evolving material and discursive production of suburban "downtowns" in the Greater Toronto Area (GTA) and the region's distinctly spiky metropolitan density-gradients (Filion, McSpurren, and Appleby, 2006). Through the 1970s, Metro Toronto attempted to foster development around mixed-use sub-centres in the inner suburbs. Suburban downtowns at Yonge-Eglinton, Etobicoke Centre, North York Centre, and Scarborough Centre were planned to act as distinct edge cities with integrated residential and business—following a planning framework based on the focused de-concentration of key functions from the urban core. Some success was realized in attracting development, investment, and integrating activities in a moderately pedestrian-friendly environment; however, despite increased **intensification** and diversification of land use, attempts to bring elements of "urban" development into suburban downtowns failed to live up to expectations (Charney, 2005). The auto-oriented nature of these mixed-use suburban centres, as well as their relatively inhospitable walking environments, infringed upon the potential benefits of concentrated, pedestrian-based urban synergy (Filion, McSpurren, and Huether, 2000). "Wasted density" (islands of high-density residential areas stranded in a sea of low-density single-family homes) must be seen as particularly problematic given that inner suburban areas poorly served by public transit and other social services are home to an increasing proportion of the city's marginalized residents.

Despite these challenges, suburban centres continue to hold a prime position within the structured coherence of the Toronto city-region, albeit on an expanded scale. Taking their cue from the Province of Ontario's landmark "Greenbelt" and "Places to Grow" growth management legislation (introduced over 2005–6), many of Toronto's neighbouring municipalities have actively embraced a reframed planning agenda centred on intensified, nodal urban development. For example, newly planned and competing suburban downtowns are rapidly rising up along Highway 7 and Highway 427 to challenge the primacy of the city of Toronto and radically reorient the centre-periphery dynamics of the region. Mississauga, Brampton, Vaughan, and Markham are *cities in waiting*, that is, emergent sites of urbanity at the cutting edge of suburban transformation. Not only are their built environments undergoing a profound reshaping in accordance with provincial mandates, but densification, mixed-use development, and multiple modes of mobility are attempting to restructure everyday suburbanism away from lifestyles traditionally understood and experienced through auto-mobility and the single family home. The City of Vaughan's 2020 strategic plan, for example, envisions the transition "from a growing suburban municipality to a fully urban space" (2011: 1).

The GTA's periphery is a place of multiple speeds and scales of movement that offer the potential to retrofit, reconfigure, and reimagine autocentric and atomized suburban space. Yet while emergent suburbanization processes and post-suburban landscapes produce new nodes within a polycentric urban region, they do not hold the same functional logics or spatial practices as the historical centre city or, even, postwar suburbia (Archer, 2011). The interactive patterns of contemporary suburbs "are less like its blocky spatial layout and more like the entwined overlay of paths and nodes in a rainforest, where clearings and connections for different uses are mixed together, connected by twisting links, lacking any easy visible order" (Kolb, 2008: 160). The typical "in-between" landscapes found in the periphery are in perpetual transition, structured both by the continuation of existing urban traditions and the implementation of new experiments and innovations (Young, Wood, and Keil, 2011).

Transformations in inner suburban Toronto reveal how landscapes that appear to be placeless (see Relph, 1976) can foster a sense of place as new users adapt what exists to meet changing needs. Postwar factories can be reborn as infill housing (or as big-box power centres) while strip malls—their retail equivalent—function as landing pads for immigrant entrepreneurs and "soft targets" for intensified development. In either case, old factories and strip malls have come to be seen by many as obsolete reminders of Toronto's postwar embrace of the car—spaces that might be rendered more "urban" and "productive" via compact, mixed-use redevelopment. In recent years, the spectre of suburban decline has pushed re-urbanization or intensified development to the forefront, where it has become Toronto's official pathway to inner suburban revitalization. The City's vision, expressed in its official plan, seeks the gradual redevelopment of low-rise commercial structures found along inner suburban Toronto's major avenues into mid-rise buildings with commercial units at grade and residences above.

The road to this more urban future is hardly unproblematic. In addition to skepticism about the scale of the transformation required and whether it can produce the more complete streets that urbanists rightly advocate, there is also the issue of what is lost. Far from being unused or abandoned, many old factories and strip malls are bustling hubs of activity. They function as a flexible and integrative infrastructure for new immigrants of limited means, who locate businesses, cultural centres, and places of worship in them. Shabby and often overlooked by experts, these modest buildings perform an important function in increasingly diverse, uneven, and socio-economically polarized Canadian metropolises. They provide low-cost spaces where newcomers and new ideas can take hold in an otherwise expensive and exclusionary city (Figure 24.3).

Suburban Politics

The neo-liberalization of suburban development has led to a reorientation of metropolitan politics that defies older political imaginaries and institutional as well as geographic boundaries. The political equation of regionalization and redistribution has been severed as aggressive suburban regimes have come to power regionally or even federally in Canada to use their political base to fundamentally shift the meaning of metropolitan politics. In general, we must recognize that the governance of suburbs is a process that combines the interplay of government, market, and private activities (Ekers, Hamel, and Keil, 2012). In Canada, historically, these activities have been mixed in a particular way:

There is now a truly Canadian story developing from coast to coast which is both internally differentiated (in a federalist

Figure 24.3   In suburban Scarborough, the former Lily Cup factory once produced disposable cups for fast food chains. Before it was demolished in 2010 to make way for the Lilly Factory Towns (a housing development now under construction), it was home to a South Asian banquet hall, and then a gathering place and Mandir (temple) for Bangladeshi Hindus. Part of a wider redevelopment boom in the area, factories that once provided middle-income employment for area residents have been replaced by townhouses, while little new retail or office space has been added to the area. Ironically, this actually reduces the mix of uses in the area. (Robert Fiedler)

context) and shows some remarkable similarities across the nation's (sub)urban reach. Cities, regions and their suburbs are now recognized as central to the governance of the vast territory of Canada, which is beginning to understand itself as a primarily urban country as the majority of its citizens now live in some form of urban or suburban area. (Keil et al., forthcoming)

The governance of these suburbanizing metropolitan regions is constituted through a new melange of politics that departs from the business as usual, in which central interests prevailed. An "in-between" type of politics has emerged that colonizes political spaces in the emergent post-suburban region:

The idea of post-suburbia includes the understanding that the traditional dichotomy in urban politics of taking either redeveloping inner cities or newly built suburbs as the natural arenas of urban action has to be challenged. Instead, post-suburbia now validates both the overlooked spaces in-between and the emerging metropolitan spaces of which they are part. (Young and Keil, forthcoming)

We have entered an era where urban and suburban politics are not easily separated, particularly in urban regions that aspire to be global. It is impossible now to imagine the suburbs neatly sequestered spatially and socially from a categorically different "inner city." While territorially bound political institutions, with their associated mechanisms of taxation and service provision, play a significant role in shaping urban growth and the socio-cultural identities of (sub)urban inhabitants, dynamic patterns of growth and the relational connectivity of global regionalization do not neatly align with such political jurisdictions (Harrison, 2010). We need to understand the phenomenon of the diverse suburb, therefore, in relation to the continued formation of the global city-region and the emergence of post-metropolitan forms of urbanization (Keil, 2011). This is an especially important consideration as strategic investments in infrastructure megaprojects integrate the peripheries of Canadian cities into global trade and logistics networks. This form of suburban globality is perhaps most evident in large-scale infrastructures—airports, intermodal yards, warehousing districts—that are conducive to the functioning of global economy and the internationalized movement of goods and capital.

Suburban and post-suburban communities are animated by a diverse collection of political contradictions that are emerging at different scales: between economic growth and the provision of collective consumption amenities, between continued development and environmental conservation, and between the forces of amalgamation and secession (Phelps, Wood, and Valler, 2010). Canadian city-regions have adapted to changes in the functional scale of urban areas and broad-scale economic imperatives in distinct ways and notably exhibit far higher levels of regional–governmental integration than do cities in the United States (Sancton, 2000). But significant variations in political cultures and economic development frameworks do exist between provinces and within regions (Andrew and Doloreux, 2012). For example, during the wave of municipal amalgamations that swept across Canada in the late 1990s,

Torontonians appeared more concerned with democratic accountability than direct participatory access within urban governance structures. On the other hand, debates in Montreal shifted attention to the inefficiency of government and to attempts to mediate the cultural and linguistic terrains of the city (Boudreau, 2003).

Suburban vs. City Politics: Municipal Amalgamation in Toronto

Canadian cities have a long history of regional governance experiments. Most notably, the innovative two-tier government structure of the Municipality of Metropolitan Toronto (Metro), formed in 1954, spurred the creation of regional governments across Canada during the 1970s, including for example the Regional Municipality of Ottawa-Carleton, Quebec's Outaouais and Montreal Urban Communities, and the Regional Municipalities of Durham, Halton, Peel, and York in the GTA (Frisken, 2007). However, whereas Metro was largely successful in integrating the City of Toronto's inner suburban municipalities, as the city grew beyond its territorial and political limits, new political configurations were required to produce institutional–political frameworks that conformed more closely to the prevailing conditions in city-regions. Restructuring followed Mike Harris's Progressive Conservative Party's victory in Ontario's 1995 provincial election. Harris's neo-liberal-populist "Common Sense Revolution" attempted to restore growth through a program of restructuring that placed Toronto at the forefront of urban neo-liberalization but that also further proposed the elimination of two-tier governance in Toronto by amalgamating the "old" city of Toronto with its adjacent suburban municipalities. Governmental actions taken "against" Toronto, including the rescaling of Toronto's local government, appeared to be intended to suburbanize the governance and political control of the City of Toronto (noted for its innovative social programs and "progressive" politics) (Keil, 2002).

In fact, city and suburban voters are diverging in terms of political attitudes and party preferences. Analysis of 1965, 1984, and 2000 Canadian federal election results has shown that inner cities have become more likely to vote for left-wing parties while suburban areas increasingly support right-wing parties and exhibit attitudes consistent with right-wing politics (Walks, 2005; 2006). On the one hand, supporters of leftist politics who often self-select into the inner-city areas consciously seek to construct those areas as an "oppositional space"—that is, a more environmentally and socially just place to live in. More suburban residents with right-political views and voting preferences, on the other hand, tend to voice an exclusionary discourse about immigrants and low-income housing being "out of place" in their suburban landscape (Walks, 2006).

The analysis above revealed that the inner suburbs practised a form of "suburban citizenship" that was dominated by strong normative understandings of suburban life. Principally, this meant that residents would use the private spaces of the home or subdivision for recreation and leisure activities, except where specific activities required dedicated facilities, for which user-fees would apply. Targeted programs were developed to provide "residual" access to less fortunate lower-income residents, which suggests that governance strategies, now identified as neo-liberal, may in fact have their roots in long established practices of suburban governance (Cowen, 2005).

Toward a New Suburban Politics

The suburbs re-emerged as a strategic battleground during Canada's 2011 federal election. Reminiscent, at first, of 1990s' campaigns, when white middle-class voters in conservative ridings north of Toronto formed the power base of a neo-liberal Tory government under Mike Harris, the suburban voters that were wooed in 2011 were new immigrants, visible minorities, and the elderly. These contentiously termed "ethnic voters" were audiences for stump speeches in suburbs like Surrey, British Columbia, and Brampton or Markham, Ontario, where politicians visited folkloristic and religious events. Issues such as social conservatism, immigration and settlement, and pension concerns took central stage as politicians assumed that these issues would resonate with the local, diverse electorate (Friesen, 2011). Some progressive candidates also made inroads into the electoral base of the ethnoburbs as a younger generation of visible-minority New Democrat politicians were elected in provincial and federal politics in Ontario (CBC News, 2011).

But official elections are not the only arena of new suburban politics in Canada. A new generation of activists has begun to change the style and substance of suburban political discourse. Ethnically diverse and multigenerational organizations, such as the citizens' environmental coalition "Sustainable Vaughan," have challenged the traditional development-driven political agenda in the suburbs (Citizens Environmental Coalition, 2012). A lively debate has started regarding culture and politics in the suburbs, in which young, often second-generation, immigrants are putting traditional notions of inner and outer cities to the test (Alang, 2011). The opening up of new understandings of ethno-racial relationships and the politics that accompany them are now on the agenda in Canadian suburbs. Long gone are the times where politics could safely be located along socio-demographic lines as was often assumed in the past. We will consequently need to pay attention to the "strategies of surveillance, dispersal, and consumption" that contextualize much of politics and governance in the post-suburban landscape of today (Quinby, 2011: 139). In contrast to the perception of the suburbs as a space ruled by rational choice, personal freedom, economic autonomy, and land ownership, politics in the urban periphery now deals with corporate power, lack of collective consumption services, the presence of a strong local state (social programs and police presence in marginalized communities), and poverty. In this reorientation, suburban politics may be less defined against the traditional imaginaries of the inner city and the landscape of power that those built. Suburban politics may now establish itself, municipality by municipality, community by community, in its own right, as a self-confident part of the post-suburban region.

If a closer examination of contemporary Canadian suburban political space indicates a disconnect between the predominant imaginaries and realities of the metropolis. Such a disconnect will have distinct ramifications for political practices engendered in negotiating diverse suburban spaces. As well, this disconnect will have an effect on integrating the political-economic realities between the urban core and its surrounding periphery within particular geographical contexts. The resistance to Metro Toronto's amalgamation and the resulting social cleavages revealed that a more suburb-sensitive exploration of metropolitan political spaces in Canada would be productive. Collective action in "the city" has received detailed coverage in recent years, particularly with regard to the gentrification of inner-city neighbourhoods (Blomley, 2004) or the restructuring/rescaling of urban politics (Boudreau, 2005). The self-conscious use of inner-city neighbourhood space as a marker of lifestyle and political distinctions (specifically as non-suburban or mass-society oriented) begs this question: Are the suburbs as conservative and reactionary as such inner-city perspectives indicate? More importantly, how prevalent is collective action in the suburbs that isn't related to property-oriented concerns, such as zoning/land use or taxation policies or actions? Finally, given the social diversity of many suburban areas, what new socio-political movements might be present (or emerging) within the changing dynamic?

Conclusion

The Canadian suburb has arrived in the global city. Suburbanization processes today cannot be understood, as they used to be, as outcomes mostly of national policy and Fordist-Keynesian economics. Suburban constellations are now in the crosshairs of international migration, flows of global capital and labour, locational decisions by transnational corporations, global networks of businesses and communities, and cultural diversities. Equally, suburbanisms as diverse ways of life are beginning to reshape the urban periphery in Canada. While the *Atlas of Suburbanisms* continues to show a sustained prevalence of the automobile-oriented suburban form in the outer reaches of small and

large urban regions in Canada (Moos and Kramer, 2012), the container-space of cul-de-sacs and shopping malls is filled with new social and cultural practices and even politics in the ever-changing geographies of the "arrival city" (Saunders, 2010). As the conclusion to a new collection of essays on global suburbanization suggests,

> to arrive in the global suburb is no longer an original experience. It is not *terra incognita*, empty unmarked space. The moving trucks taking the huddled masses to the air and light of the periphery have long disappeared. Arriving in the suburb is getting home to the metropolitan future that is most likely ours for some time to come. (Keil, 2013: 201)

Indeed, Canadian suburbs have ceased to be a derivative of the North American suburban phenomenon. They are also not mere extensions of European-influenced metropolitan landscapes of tower neighbourhoods and bungalow estates. Under the influence of changing immigration patterns and economic globalization, and under the severe stresses of neo-liberal urbanization, the Canadian periphery has entered a phase of suburbanization that is both universal in its appearance and unique in its outcomes and unprecedented in its myriad suburban ways of life. Therein lies the particular character of Canadian suburbanization and suburbanisms today.

Review Questions

1. Suburbs are sometimes portrayed as being homogeneous entities. Why is this depiction of Canadian suburbs no longer accurate? Was it ever accurate?
2. How has immigration changed Canadian suburbs?
3. In what ways do suburban high-rise apartment developments challenge traditional depictions of suburban ways of living?
4. How do you think the suburbs in your city will change over the coming years? What factors are contributing to these changes?

Notes

1. According to statistics published by Citizenship and Immigration Canada for the period 2003–12, the average number of new permanent residents (immigrants) each year was 249,455. Yearly intake during this period ranged from a low of 221,349 in 2003 to a high of 280,689 in 2010. See "Facts and Figures 2012—Immigration Overview: Permanent and Temporary Residents," at www.cic.gc.ca/english/resources/statistics/facts 2012/index.asp
2. Dissemination areas (DAs) are the smallest standard geographical unit for which Statistics Canada makes census data available for mapping and geographical analysis. They vary in geographic size, but typically contain a population of 400 to 700 persons.

References

Addie, J-P. D., and R.S. Fiedler. 2013. "On the (cutting) edge of the global city," *Satellite Magazine* 3: 34–43.

Alang, N. 2011. "Why white scenesters hate the 'burbs,'" *Toronto Standard*. At: www.torontostandard.com/the-sprawl/why-white-scenesters-hate-the-%E2%80%98burbs

Andrew, C., and D. Doloreux. 2012. "Economic development, social inclusion and urban governance: The case of the city-region of Ottawa in Canada," *International Journal of Urban and Regional Research*, 36: 1288–1305.

Archer, J. 2011. "Everyday suburbia: Lives and practices," *Public* 43(1): 10.

Atkinson, A. 2007. "Cities after oil: Sustainable development and energy futures," *City*, 11: 201–13.

Aulakh, R. 2011. "'Colony of wives thrives in Mississauga,' *Toronto Star,* May 29: A8. At: www.thestar.com/news/gta/article/998962---colony-of-wives-thrives-in-mississauga

Baluja, B. 2011. "Poverty hides in the suburbs: Will 'priority neighbourhoods' help?" *The Globe and Mail,* April 20: A11.

Black, S. 2011. "Life in 'Third City': Nasty, brutish and short," *Toronto Star,* June 8: A27.

Blomley, N. 2004. *Unsettling the City: Urban Land and the Politics of Property*. New York: Routeledge.

Boudreau, J-A. 2003. "Questioning the use of 'local democracy' as a discursive strategy for political mobilization in Los Angeles, Montreal and Toronto," *International Journal of Urban and Regional Research* 27: 793–810.

———. 2005. "Toronto's reformist regime, municipal amalgamation and participatory democracy," in P. Booth and B. Jouve, eds., *Metropolitan Democracies: Transformations of the State and Urban Policy in Canada, France and Great Britain*. Burlington, VT: Ashgate.

Bourne, L.S. 1996. "Reinventing the suburbs: Old myths and new realities," *Progress in Planning* 46: 163–84.

Bunting, T., R.A. Walks, and P. Filion. 2004. "The uneven geography of housing affordability stress in Canadian Metropolitan Areas," *Housing Studies* 19: 361–94.

CBC News. (2011) "Canada's first Tamil MP looks forward to challenge," *CBC News: Toronto*. At: www.cbc.ca/news/canada/toronto/story/2011/05/03/sitsabaiesan-ndp-election.html

Charney, I. 2005. "Canadian human landscape examples—two visions of suburbia: Mississauga City Centre and Heartland Business Community," *Canadian Geographer* 49: 214–20.

Citizens Environmental Coalition. 2012. *Sustainable Vaughan*. At: http://sustainablevaughan.com/

City of Vaughan. 2011. *Vaughan Vision 2020: The City of Vaughan Strategic Plan*. Vaughan, ON: City of Vaughan.

Cowen, D. 2005. "Suburban citizenship? The rise of targeting and the eclipse of social rights in Toronto," *Social & Cultural Geography* 6: 335–56.

Cowen, D., and V. Parlette. 2011. *Toronto's Inner Suburbs: Investing in Social Infrastructure in Scarborough*. Toronto, ON: Cities Centre, University of Toronto.

Donaldson, S. 1969. *The Suburban Myth*. New York: Columbia University Press.

Dowling, R. 1998. "Neotraditionalism in the suburban landscape: Cultural geographies of exclusion in Vancouver, Canada," *Urban Geography* 19: 105–22.

Ekers, M., P. Hamel, and R. Keil. 2012. "Governing suburbia: Modalities and mechanisms of suburban governance," *Regional Studies* 46: 405–22.

Fiedler, R.S., N. Schuurman, and J. Hyndman. 2006. "Hidden homelessness: An indicator-based approach for examining the geographies of recent immigrants at-risk of homelessness in Greater Vancouver," *Cities* 23: 205–16.

Filion, P., and G. Gad. 2006. "Urban and suburban downtowns: Trajectories of growth and decline," in T. Bunting and P. Filion, eds., *Canadian Cities in Transition: Local through Global Perspectives* (3rd edn.). Toronto: Oxford University Press.

———, K. McSpurren, and B. Appleby. 2006. "Wasted density? The impact of Toronto's residential-density-distribution policies on public transit use and walking," *Environment and Planning A* 38: 1367–92.

———, K. McSpurren, and N. Huether. 2000. "Synergy and movement within suburban mixed use centers: The Toronto experience," *Journal of Urban Affairs* 22: 419–38.

Fishman, R. 1987. *Bourgeois Utopias: The Rise and Fall of Suburbia*. New York: Basic Books.

Fong, E., C. Luk, and E. Ooka. 2005. "Spatial distribution of suburban ethnic businesses," *Social Science Research* 34: 215–35.

Friesen, J. 2011. "Brampton-Springdale: A suburban boom city grows, a political battlefield emerges," *The*

Globe and Mail, April 15: A1. At: http://m.theglobe andmail.com/news/politics/in-brampton-a-suburban-boom-city-grows-on-fertile-electoral-ground/article198 6393/?service=mobile

Frisken, F. 2007. *The Public Metropolis: The Political Dynamics of Urban Expansion in the Toronto Region, 1924–2003.* Toronto: Canadian Scholars Press Inc.

Garreau, J. 1991. *Edge City: Life on the New Frontier.* New York: Doubleday.

Hackworth, J., and K. Stein. 2012. "The collision of faith and economic development in Toronto's inner suburban industrial districts," *Urban Affairs Review* 48: 37–63.

Harris, R. 1996. *Unplanned Suburbs: Toronto's American Tragedy, 1900 to 1950.* Baltimore, MD: John Hopkins University Press.

———. 2004. *Creeping Conformity: How Canada Became Suburban, 1900–1960.* Toronto: University of Toronto Press.

———. 2010. "Meaningful types in a world of suburbs," in M. Clapson and R. Hutchinson, eds., *Suburbanization in Global Society.* Bingley: Emerald Group Publishing.

———, and R. Lewis. 1998a. "How the past matters: North American cities in the twentieth century," *Journal of Urban Affairs* 20: 159–74.

———, and R. Lewis. 1998b. "Constructing a fault(y) zone: Misrepresentations of American cities and suburbs, 1900–1950," *Annals of the Association of American Geographers* 88: 622–39.

———, and R. Lewis. 2001. "The geography of North American cities and suburbs, 1900–1950: A new synthesis," *Journal of Urban History* 27: 262–92.

Harrison, J. 2010. "Networks of connectivity, territorial fragmentation, uneven development: The new politics of city-regionalism," *Political Geography* 29: 17–27.

Hiebert, D. 2000. "Immigration and the changing Canadian city," *Canadian Geographer* 44: 25–43.

Hulchanski, D. 2010. *The Three Cities within Toronto: Income Polarization among Toronto's Neighborhoods, 1970–2005.* Toronto, ON: University of Toronto Centre for Urban and Community Studies.

Isin, E.F. 1998. "Governing Toronto without government: Liberalism and neoliberalism," *Studies in Political Economy* 56: 169–91.

Keil, R. 2002. "'Common Sense' neoliberalism: Progressive conservative urbanism in Toronto, Canada," *Antipode* 34: 578–601.

———. 2011. "Global suburbanization: The challenge of researching cities in the 21st century," *Public* 43: 54–61.

———. 2013. "Escape from the burbs?" in: R. Keil, ed., *Suburban Constellations: Governance, Land and Infrastructure in the 21st Century.* Berlin: Jovis Verlag.

———, and J.-P. D. Addie. Under review. "Social cleavages underlying the spatial imaginaries of new metropolitan identities in North America."

———, P. Hamel, E. Chou, and K. Williams. Forthcoming. "Modalities of suburban governance in Canada," in P. Hamel and R. Keil, eds., *Suburban Governance: A Global View.* Toronto: University of Toronto Press.

Kern, L. 2005. "In place at home in the city: Connecting privilege, safety and belonging for women in Toronto," *Gender Place and Culture* 12: 357–77.

Kolb, D. 2008. *Sprawling Places.* Athens, GA: University of Georgia Press.

Kruse, K.M., and T.J. Sugrue. 2006. *The New Suburban History.* Chicago, IL: University Of Chicago Press.

Lewis, R. 2000. *Manufacturing Montreal: The Making of an Industrial Landscape 1850 to 1930.* Baltimore, MD: John Hopkins University Press.

———. 2001. "A city transformed: Manufacturing districts and suburban growth in Montreal, 1850–1929," *Journal of Historical Geography* 27: 20–35.

Ley, D. 1999. "Myths and meanings of immigration and the metropolis," *Canadian Geographer,* 43: 2–19.

Li, W. 2009. *Ethnoburb: The New Ethnic Community in Urban America.* Honolulu, HI: University of Hawai Press.

Lo, L. 2011. "Immigrants and social services in the suburbs," in D. Young, P. Wood, and R. Keil, eds., *In-between Infrastructure: Urban Connectivity in an Age of Vulnerability.* Keolowna, BC: Praxis (e)Press.

Lucy, W.H., and D.L. Phillips. 1997. "The postsuburban era comes to Richmond: City decline, suburban transition and exurban growth," *Landscape and Urban Planning* 36: 259–75.

Markovich, J., and S. Hendler. 2006. "Beyond 'soccer moms,'" *Journal of Planning Education and Research* 25: 410–27.

McCann, L. 1999. "Suburbs of desire: The suburban landscape of Canadian cities, c.1900–1950," in R. Harris and P.J. Larkham, eds., *Changing Suburbs: Suburban Foundation, Form and Function.* London: E and FN Spon.

McCann, L. 2006. "A regional perspective on Canadian suburbanization: Reflections on Richard Harris's 'Creeping Conformity,'" *Urban History Review* 35: 32–45.

McManus, R., and P.J. Etherington. 2007. "Suburbs in transition: New approaches to suburban history," *Urban History* 34: 317–37. Miron, J.R. 1988. *Housing in Postwar Canada: Demographic Change, Household Formation, and Housing Demand.* Kingston and Montreal: McGill-Queen's University Press.

Moos, M., and P. Mendez. 2014. "Suburban ways of living and the geography of income: How homeownership, single-family dwellings and automobile use define the metropolitan social space," *Urban Studies,* OnlineFirst. At: http://usj.sagepub.com/content/early/2014/06/16/0 042098014538679.abstract

———, and A. Kramer. 2012. *Atlas of Suburbanisms.* At: http://env-blogs.uwaterloo.ca/atlas/

Murdie, R.A., and C. Teixeira. 2003. "Towards a comfortable neighbourhood and appropriate housing: Immigrant experiencess in Toronto," in P. Anisef and M. Lanphier, eds., *The World in a City*. Toronto, ON: University of Toronto Press.

Nicolaides, B.M. 2002. *My Blue Heaven: Life and Politics in the Working-class Suburbs of Los Angeles, 1920–1965*. Chicago: University of Chicago Press.

———. 2006. "How hell moved from the city to the suburbs: Urban scholars and changing perceptions of authentic community," in K.M. Kruse and T.J. Sugrue, eds., *The new Suburban History*. Chicago, IL: University of Chicago Press.

Phelps, N.A., and A. Wood. 2011. "The new post-suburban politics?" *Urban Studies* 48: 2591–2610.

———, A. Wood, and D. Valler. 2010. "A post-suburban world? An outline of a research agenda," *Environment & Planning A* 42: 366–83.

Pratt, G. 2003. "Valuing childcare: Troubles in suburbia," *Antipode* 35: 581–602.

Preston, V., and L. Lo. 2000. "Asian theme malls in suburban Toronto: Land use conflict in Richmond Hill," *Canadian Geographer* 44: 182–90.

Quinby, R. 2011. *Time and the Suburbs: The Politics of Built Environments and the Future of Dissent*. Winnipeg, MB: Arbeiter Ring Publishing.

Ransford, B. 2003. "Illegal secondary suites now a fact of life," *The Vancouver Sun* April 19: H1.

Ray, B., G. Halseth, and B. Johnson. 1997. "The changing 'face' of the suburbs: Issues of ethnicity and residential change in suburban Vancouver," *International Journal of Urban and Regional Research* 21: 75–99.

Relph, E. 1976. *Place and Placelessness*. London: Pion.

Rose, D. 2010. "Local state policy and 'new-build gentrification' in Montreal: The role of the 'population factor' in a fragmented governance context," *Population, Space and Place* 16: 413–28.

———, and P. Villeneuve. 1998. "Engendering class in the metropolitan city: Occupational pairings and income disparities among two-earner couples," *Urban Geography* 19: 123–59.

Rowe, P.G. 1991. *Making a Middle Landscape*. Cambridge, MA: The MIT Press.

Sancton, A. 2000. *Merger Mania: The Assault on Local Government*. Montreal and Kingston: McGill-Queen's University Press.

Saunders, D. 2010. *Arrival City: How the Largest Migration in History is Reshaping our World*. New York: Vintage Books.

Sieverts, T. 2003. *Cities without Cities: An Interpretation of the Zwischenstadt*. London: Spon Press.

Strong-Boag, V., I. Dyck, K. England, and L. Johnson. 1999. "What women's spaces? Women in Australian, British, Canadian and US suburbs," in R. Harris and P.J.

Larkham, eds., *Changing Suburbs: Suburban Foundation, Form and Function*. London: E & FN Spon.

Tanasescu, A. 2009. "Informal housing in the heart of the New West: An examination of state toleration of illegality in Calgary," *North American Dialogue* 12(2): 1–11.

Teaford, J. 1997. *Post-suburbia: Government and Polities in Edge Cities*. Baltimore, MD: Johns Hopkins University Press.

Teixeira, C. 2008. "Residential experiences and the culture of suburbanization: A case study of Portugese homebuyers in Mississauga," *Housing Studies* 22: 495–521.

United Way Toronto. 2004. *Poverty by Postal Code: The Geography of Neighbourhood Poverty, 1981–2001*. Toronto: United Way of Greater Toronto and Canadian Council on Social Development.

Walks, R.A. 2001. "The social ecology of the post-Fordist/global city? Economic restructuring and socio-spatial polarisation in the Toronto Urban Region," *Urban Studies* 38: 407–47.

———. 2005. "The City-Suburban cleavage in Canadian federal politics," *Canadian Journal of Political Science* 38: 383–414.

———. 2006. "The causes of city-suburban political polarization? A Canadian case study," *Annals of the Association of American Geographers* 96: 390–414.

———. 2009. "The urban in fragile, uncertain, neoliberal times: Towards new geographies of social justice," *Canadian Geographer* 53: 345–56.

———. 2013. "Suburbanism as a way of life, slight return," *Urban Studies* 50: 1471–88.

Wang, S.G. 1999. "Chinese commercial activity in the Toronto CMA: New development patterns and impacts," *Canadian Geographer* 43: 19–35.

Warner, S.B. 1962. *Streetcar Suburbs: The Process of Growth in Boston, 1870–1900*. Cambridge, MA: Harvard University Press and The MIT Press.

Wiese, A. 2004. *Places of their Own: African American Suburbanization in the Twentieth Century*. Chicago, IL: University of Chicago Press.

Wood, P.K., and L. Gilbert. 2005. "Multiculturalism in Canada: Accidental discourse, alternative vision, urban practice," *International Journal of Urban and Regional Research* 29: 679–91.

Wunsch, J. L. 1995. "The suburban cliché," *Journal of Social History* 28: 643–58.

Young, D., and R. Keil. Forthcoming. "Seeking the urban in-between: Tracking the urban politics of infrastructure in Toronto," *International Journal of Urban and Regional Research*.

Young, D., P. Wood, and R. Keil. Eds. 2011. *In-between Infrastructure: Urban Connectivity in an Age of Vulnerability*. Keolowna, BC: Praxis (e)Press.

Conclusion: In Search of New Urban Models

MARKUS MOOS AND TARA VINODRAI

25

Our current urban imaginary is filled with images of downtowns with vibrant public spaces, coffee shops, and busy streets. Many downtowns have experienced **revitalization** in recent years through **gentrification** that brought higher income earners to an inner city previously marked by economic activities, such as manufacturing in Montreal and Toronto or resource industries in Vancouver. But some Canadian downtowns are still struggling to recover from decline. As the chapters in this book reveal, there is as much that is generalizable about Canadian cities as there is context and place specificity. Not only should we be cautious about generalizations, but we should be especially guarded about generalizations from the past. For instance, central areas now host more high-income earners, who, according to traditional models of the urban social geography, should be found in the suburbs. Conversely, suburbs now contain more low-income earners and immigrants, who traditionally located in older inner-city neighbourhoods. New models will need to find an appropriate balance between necessary generalization and place specificity while accounting for emerging urban tendencies. These kinds of models have until now been largely elusive. We suggest that in searching for new urban models we ought to consider the dynamics of Canadian cities through at least three overarching themes: structure, state, and sustainability.

Changes to the physical structure of Canadian, and North American, metropolitan regions over the past 70 years can be characterized by the decentralization of housing, retailing, services, and workplaces, resulting in accelerated suburban expansion and the relative and sometimes absolute decline of inner-city neighbourhoods and of downtowns. The emergent urban structure is no longer focused on one historic downtown. Rather, many metropolitan areas have adopted a polycentric form, with multiple nodes serving key employment and commercial functions. And suburbs as a whole have become characterized by a growing diversity of housing types, uses, and populations. But urban transformations take place alongside traditional urban functions and forms. So, while higher order services have mostly supplanted the resource and manufacturing economies of previous eras, these activities are not to be forgotten. In places such as St. John's and Calgary, for example, the financial investments and skills requirements of the resource economy are shaping the trajectories of these cities. Other resources cities, however, such as Sudbury, continue to either stagnate or decline. Meanwhile many industrial cities in Quebec and Ontario are losing their economic base and face difficulties in finding new vocations.

A current shift, although not yet widespread, toward artisanal and micro-manufacturing is bringing production back to the city after decades of suburban or offshore relocation. Yet the spaces that could accommodate such activities are at a premium. As the downtowns of large metropolitan areas have registered escalating housing costs and, in some cases, such as Vancouver, are short of developable land, the next wave of restructuring will inevitably occur outside their historic cores. Demographic changes and fiscal and environmental pressures that constrain urban expansion will serve to cluster some of this development into nodes. At the same time, suburbanization will likely persist, especially at the urban fringe and in mid-sized cities near large metropolitan areas. New models will need to account for the diversity of both urban and suburban structures. The nodes that seem most likely to see new development will be those in the old suburbs, where land values have been suppressed, and in the downtowns of mid-sized cities that are connected by proximity and transportation networks to large metropolitan centres. Young adults unable to find or afford central city apartments are beginning to opt for higher-density suburban locations connected by transit to the central business district (CBD), such as Burnaby and New Westminster in Vancouver's old suburbs. Baby boomers looking to downsize are increasing in numbers in the downtowns of mid-sized cities, such as Kitchener-Waterloo, Victoria, or Quebec City. The next wave of restructuring, then, will present sharper generational demarcations.

Sustainability has become a key objective of policies and even of some business practices, although finding an agreed meaning for the term has proven difficult. Thus, different agents and organizations have at times used the term *sustainability* in a self-serving manner. In a general sense, sustainability is about considering the long-term implications of our actions and balancing the economic, environmental, and social dimensions of our decisions. As the chapters in this book discuss, sustainability is also about acknowledging ecological limits and adopting production and consumption patterns, lifestyles, and urban forms that respect these limits. Urban sustainability policies include a diversity of activities, such as

ecological restoration, environmental design, urban agriculture, the provision of parks, pollution and smog prevention, water conservation, and reliance on alternative sources of energy, among other activities.

In urban planning, sustainability has also become associated with a particular urban form characterized by higher density, walkability, reliance on public transit and cycling, and protection of environmentally significant and agricultural lands through growth boundaries. These policies can strain housing affordability as the re-centralization of development and the constraining of urban expansion limit the supply of developable land. However, lower land costs in a sprawling context come with higher greenhouse gas emissions and other pollutants as well as loss of land. Also, evidence points to higher household transportation expenses in low-density dispersed environments than in more compact urban environments; the relation between dispersed urban form and affordability is therefore less clear-cut than some opponents of sustainable urban policies suggest. The shape of the Canadian city of the future will be determined by whether and how we decide to implement the vision of a more sustainable city—low-density suburban expansion versus more walkable and central urban development—and whether and how we keep housing and transportation affordable in the context of centralization pressures.

Processes of urban evolution and development do not occur in an institutional vacuum. The state plays an important role in setting the rules of the game. The shift toward neo-liberal forms of government and governance are bringing about substantial changes in how we deal with urban policy. In the Canadian context, changes in policy directions at the federal and provincial levels are resulting in diverse interventions, leading to different urban trajectories. Local solutions and policy experiments are beginning to emerge, giving way to a diverse urban fabric. Future models need to account for the complexity of interactions among local actors and institutions organized at a variety of scales. Our current economic structure and contemporary neo-liberal governance are often blamed for fostering social and economic inequality. As a result, the very role of the state in society has come into question. And the restructuring of government roles and functions will produce winners and losers, requiring urban scholars to track new and exacerbated inequalities.

The diversity of changes occurring in Canadian cities will clearly challenge attempts at devising new template-like (sub)urban models. New models will need to be highly diversified. In addition to studying generalizable urban forms and population trends, new urban models could highlight contingencies under different place-based scenarios, and explore how defining themes, such as structure, state, and sustainability, interact and play out in different socio-political, institutional, and economic contexts.

Appendix A: Do We Still Have Quality Data to Study Canadian Cities?

TARA VINODRAI AND
MARKUS MOOS

Quality data of all sorts, whether qualitative or quantitative, are the foundation of research efforts and public-policy decisions. There have been non-trivial changes to the Canadian census in 2011 that alter the reliability and utility of this source of quantitative data. Why is the census particularly important to studying and learning about urban change in Canada? All but five of the chapters in this book use census data, or related surveys from Statistics Canada, to help us understand Canadian urbanism. Important questions about demographic change, household and family structure, immigration, migration, housing, income, affordability, inequality, gender, ethnicity, commuting patterns, industrial structure, and employment patterns are addressed using current and historical census data. On the ground in Canadian cities, urban planners, economic developers, activists, consultants, and policy-makers at all scales use these data to better understand and plan for societal, cultural, and economic change. Locational and business decisions by public, not-for-profit, and for-profit organizations are also often based on census data.

The act of collecting census data in Canada is not new and has been practised since Confederation (and even as early as 1644 in the colonies that eventually became Canada) (Sheikh, 2011). While there is some consistency to the census questions, the content of the questionnaire has reflected the concerns of the day (Dillon, 2010). As Dillon (2010: 390) notes, "the Canadian national census has served as an important tool of population measurement, at once flexible and enduring, providing consistent information on a core set of socio-economic, cultural, and demographic questions, while integrating new questions to respond to . . . changing [needs]."

A census enumerates a country's entire population and aspires to understand its basic socio-economic and demographic characteristics. To collect these data in Canada, a census form is sent to every household on the second Tuesday of May every five years (a quinquennial event). Under the Statistics Act it is mandatory (by law) to complete the census form; in other words, it is a responsibility of citizenship. Since 1971, four in five households have received the census 2A short form with a small number of questions (eight questions in 2006), while one in five households received the census 2B long form (61 questions in 2006, including the same eight questions as the short form). The responsibility to complete either the short or long form ensured the collection of extensive (and reliable) information on the Canadian population

However, unlike earlier censuses, the 2011 version marked a substantial departure from previous practices. In June 2010, the federal government under Prime Minister Stephen Harper announced that it was changing census procedures. Instead of continuing with long-established census data collections practices, now all households would receive a census questionnaire (eight questions, as in 2006, plus two additional questions related to language) that would still be mandatory under the Statistics Act. In addition, one in three households would receive a second questionnaire (64 questions): the *voluntary* National Household Survey (NHS). The important difference lies between the mandatory nature of the former long-form census and the voluntary NHS.

The federal government cited the privacy and cost concerns of Canadian citizens as reasons for the change. In regards to privacy, the government raised concerns about the mandatory nature of the long form and the extent to which it probed the details of Canadians' lives. Undoubtedly, there are legitimate concerns about surveillance of private citizens by both the state and other organizations. However, subsequent information accessed through the Freedom of Information Act revealed that concerns from constituents regarding the mandatory nature of the census were largely overstated. Indeed, the Federal Privacy Commissioner reported that there had only been 50 complaints in 20 years regarding the census (Thompson, 2010). The issue of cost is also debatable. On the one hand, cancelling a mandatory survey may eliminate some government expenses. On the other hand, a consistent and reliable source of national data is highly valuable for both the private and public sectors: it ensures that there is at least one consistent and reliable source of information on which to base decisions. Those decisions, on public spending and private investment, are likely worth a far higher value if based on reliable data than the money saved by cancelling the mandatory survey. Moreover, efficiencies are likely gained since data are collected only once in a systematic fashion rather than piecemeal by other government agencies or private sector companies.

The sudden shift in policy dictated by the federal government led to a widespread outcry from a diverse range of organizations and individuals. It is a rare day when marketing professionals, academics, religious organizations, health professionals,

Aboriginal and community development organizations, civil liberties groups, boards of trade, and chambers of commerce (among others) align on a single issue.[1] There were only six weeks left before the census forms were to be sent to the printer when the decision was made to cancel the long-form census (Veall, 2010). The controversial decision by the federal government prompted Munir Sheikh, the chief statistician of Statistics Canada, to resign. Heated debate and discussion abounded and has continued among academics and in the press about the long-term consequences and implications associated with the decision (Walton-Roberts et al., 2014).

The shift to a voluntary household survey greatly compromises our ability to carry out urban analysis, as Munir Sheikh noted in his resignation letter:

> I want to take this opportunity to comment on a technical statistical issue which has become the subject of media discussion. This relates to the question of whether a voluntary survey can become a substitute for a mandatory census. *It can not.* (O'Malley, 2010; emphasis added)

Indeed due to the voluntary nature of the NHS, there has been a great reduction in the response rate. But more problematic than lower response levels is the challenge of non-response bias. In other words, there may be systematic groups of individuals who do not respond to the survey but we will have no way of knowing who they are (Veall, 2010). Sending out more surveys does not solve the non-response bias—hence the utility of a census that surveys everyone (Green and Milligan, 2010).

Non-response and non-response bias introduce two substantial challenges: (1) comparability over time, and (2) conducting analysis using small-scale geographies. Statistics Canada (2013: 14) noted this:

> Any significant change in survey method or content can affect the comparability of the data over time, and that applies to the NHS as well. It is impossible to determine with

certainty whether, and to what extent, differences in a variable are attributable to an actual change or to non-response bias.

These comparability challenges may be even greater for urban scholars, who are often interested in conducting analysis at small-scale geographies (e.g., neighbourhoods) for small groups and/or over time. The challenges introduced by non-response bias are further compounded when focusing on a specific population in the city (e.g., understanding the location patterns of a particular social or ethnic group within the city). Statistics Canada (2013: 14) further notes this:

> Caution must be exercised when NHS estimates are compared with estimates produced from the 2006 Census long form, *especially when the analysis involves small geographies* [emphasis added]. Users are asked to use the NHS's main quality indicator, the global non-response rate, in assessing the quality of the NHS estimates and determining the extent to which the estimates can be compared with the estimates from the 2006 Census long form. Users are also asked to read any quality notes that may be included in dissemination products.

Indeed, the global non-response rate (GNR) is now reported by Statistics Canada for data in every table derived from the NHS; data where the GNR is greater than 50 per cent are suppressed. Notably, almost 12 per cent of Canada's municipalities are above this threshold, leading to speculation that the same will be true for specific groups or neighbourhoods within larger cities (Walton-Roberts et al., 2014). In other words, we will not have quality data to understand the social and spatial dynamics of neighbourhood change or other urban phenomena. Moreover, as Dillon (2010) notes, our ability to compare ourselves to other countries has been greatly compromised due to changes to the nature of data collection.

One might reasonably ask this question: Why can we not use other sources of information? The answer is we can, but we will not know whether our own surveys or other Statistics Canada surveys, such as the Labour Force Survey (LFS) or the Survey of Household Spending (used in calculating the Consumer Price Index) are representative of the population. For surveys, the census can be used to create what is called a stratified sample of Canadian households. We can sample a smaller number of people, and then use weights derived from the census to create total population estimates. However, if the data used to create the stratified sample for a survey such as the LFS are compromised due to the (unknown and unmeasurable) sampling bias introduced from the shift from mandatory to voluntary sampling, then the accuracy of such statistics will eventually be diminished as we cannot know if the sample truly represents the population it is trying to understand. Administrative data offer a possible solution, but again there are privacy, legal, and technical issues (for discussion, see Dillon, 2010; Thompson, 2010; Walton-Roberts et al., 2014).

Even surveys conducted by private organizations will be affected as they often rely on the information provided by the census to construct their samples. Furthermore, data-collection efforts undertaken by such organizations are not subject to the same levels of accountability, potentially raising new privacy concerns. Such surveys encounter issues related to very low response rates, representativeness, and the inability to understand change over time due to their often one-off nature. Surveys undertaken by private organizations are often purpose-specific, driven by consumer rather than citizen interests and by profit motives rather than the public good. And private organizations are under no obligation to share their data. In other words, due to the loss of the long-form census our knowledge of Canadian places, economy, and society will erode over time.

Counting is always political. Categories used in questionnaires construct and define social groups, with both positive and negative consequences to different political interests. However, the decision not to collect data in a systematic way, which allows for comparison over time and space, makes it difficult for all to gauge the country's evolution. But even more troubling is that the census decision made by the federal government parallels a number of other efforts to dismantle the infrastructure for collecting and maintaining data, which have included muzzling government scientists, destroying national data collections, closing scientific labs, and reducing or eliminating funding for social and scientific discovery. Such efforts, dubbed by some the "death of evidence," are extremely disconcerting as they have long-term consequences for the future of Canadian economy and society. In our view, the systematic collection of high-quality social-scientific data is necessary for guiding the formulation of urban policy, ensuring the long-term vitality of our economy and society, and understanding our urban age.

Note

1. A full list of organizations and individuals supporting or opposing the decision can be found at http://datalibre.ca/census-watch/

References

Dillon, L. 2010. "The value of the long form Canadian Census for long term national and international research," *Canadian Public Policy/Analyse de politiques* 36: 389–93.

Green, D.A., and K. Milligan. 2010. "The importance of the long form Census in Canada," *Canadian Public Policy/Analyse de politiques* 36: 383–8.

O'Malley, K. 2010. "CensusWatch: And that's all he wrote . . . Munir Sheikh resigns as Chief Statistician," *CBC News.* At: www.cbc.ca/newsblogs/politics/inside-politics-blog/2010/07/censuswatch-and-thats-all-he-wrote-munir-sheikh-resigns-as-chief-statistician.html

Sheikh, M.A. 2011. "Good data and intelligent government," in F. Gorbet and A. Sharpe, eds., *New Directions for Intelligent Government in Canada: Papers in Honour of Ian Stewart.* Ottawa: Centre for the Study of Living Standards.

Statistics Canada. 2013. *National Household Survey User Guide 2011.* Ottawa, ON: Statistics Canada, Catalogue no. 99-001-XWE2011001.

Thompson, D. 2010. "The politics of the Census: Lessons from abroad," *Canadian Public Policy/Analyse de politiques* 36: 377–82.

Veall, M.R. 2010. "2B or not 2B? What should have happened with the Canadian long form Census? What should happen now?" *Canadian Public Policy/Analyse de politiques* 36: 395–9.

Walton-Roberts, M., R. Beaujot, D. Hiebert, S. McDaniel, D. Rose, and R. Wright. 2014. "Why do we still need a census? Views from the age of 'truthiness' and the 'death of evidence,'" *The Canadian Geographer.* doi: 10.1111/j.1541-0064.2013.12065.x.

Appendix B: Select Data on Canada's Census Metropolitan Areas, 2011 (minimum and maximum values in bold)

Rank	CMA	Population (000s)[1]	Population Growth 1991–2011 (%)[1,2]	Foreign Born (% of Population)[3]	Recent Immigrants (% of Population)[3,4]	Single-Person Households (%)[3]	Population Aged 65 and over (%)[1]	Unemploy-ment Rate (%)[3]	Average Individual Income ($)[3,5]	Average Household Income ($)[3,5]	Prevalence of Low Income (%)[3]	University Degree (% of Population)[3,6]
1	Toronto	**5,583**	43.4	**45.4**	**14.1**	23.7	12.7	8.6	44,462	95,326	14.9	29.9
2	Montreal	3,824	22.3	22.1	8.4	32.6	14.6	7.7	38,281	70,286	17.9	23.5
3	Vancouver	2,313	44.4	39.5	12.7	28.2	13.5	7.1	41,031	83,666	17.4	27.7
4	Ottawa-Gatineau	1,236	34.3	19.0	6.0	28.2	12.7	6.6	47,727	91,780	11.7	31.5
5	Calgary	1,215	61.1	25.8	10.9	25.0	**9.8**	5.9	56,600	113,152	10.6	28.8
6	Edmonton	1,160	38.1	20.0	7.6	25.9	11.4	5.6	49,266	97,454	10.8	21.9
7	Quebec	766	18.6	4.3	2.3	34.6	16.5	**4.4**	39,124	69,504	12.3	22.4
8	Winnipeg	730	11.9	20.2	8.7	29.8	14.1	5.7	38,806	74,733	15.9	22.2
9	Hamilton	721	20.2	23.1	5.0	26.9	16.0	7.9	42,543	84,273	13.4	20.3
10	Kitchener	477	33.9	22.8	6.4	24.1	12.5	7.2	42,189	84,892	12.0	21.6
11	London	475	24.4	18.5	4.7	29.0	15.0	8.6	39,361	74,542	15.7	20.4
12	St. Catharines-Niagara	392	7.6	16.4	2.7	27.7	19.2	8.8	36,552	70,873	13.6	14.6
13	Halifax	390	21.8	8.0	3.0	28.6	13.1	7.2	40,453	76,193	15.1	27.0
14	Oshawa	356	48.3	15.8	2.5	**20.6**	12.5	8.9	43,652	90,516	10.7	15.7
15	Victoria	345	19.7	17.4	3.3	33.5	18.4	6.1	41,952	76,771	13.3	26.6
16	Windsor	319	21.8	22.0	5.7	28.0	14.9	**10.4**	37,971	72,720	18.3	19.2
17	Saskatoon	261	24.1	10.5	5.8	27.5	12.1	5.5	44,101	84,811	12.8	23.0

(continued)

Rank	CMA	Population (000s)[1]	Population Growth 1991-2011 (%)[1,2]	Foreign Born (% of Population)[3]	Recent Immigrants (% of Population)[3,4]	Single-Person Households (%)[3]	Population Aged 65 and over (%)[1]	Unemployment Rate (%)[3]	Average Individual Income ($)[3,5]	Average Household Income ($)[3,5]	Prevalence of Low Income (%)[3]	University Degree (% of Population)[3,6]
18	Regina	211	9.8	10.3	5.1	28.8	13.1	4.8	46,451	88,396	12.0	21.2
19	Sherbrooke	202	45.0	6.0	3.3	35.7	16.7	6.3	34,167	59,379	18.2	19.1
20	St. John's	197	14.6	3.0	1.1	23.9	12.7	7.6	41,515	82,184	13.8	22.0
21	Barrie	187	92.5[7]	12.0	2.4	20.7	12.6	8.4	40,537	83,533	11.4	14.2
22	Kelowna	180	60.8	13.6	2.8	26.7	19.2	8.1	38,851	74,998	14.2	15.4
23	Abbotsford-Mission	170	49.9[7]	22.9	7.0	23.1	14.1	8.2	35,602	76,451	13.8	13.6
24	Greater Sudbury	161	2.0	6.1	0.8	28.3	16.1	7.8	40,843	76,731	13.2	15.6
25	Kingston	160	17.0	11.3	2.2	28.5	16.3	8.1	41,118	77,872	13.1	23.5
26	Saguenay	158	-1.9[8]	1.1	0.6	31.0	17.5	7.0	35,498	64,158	14.9	13.8
27	Trois-Rivières	152	11.3	2.7	1.6	36.7	19.4	7.5	33,607	58,127	19.0	15.4
28	Guelph	141	45.1	19.5	4.7	24.9	13.4	6.6	43,648	87,452	11.1	26.1
29	Moncton	139	30.2	4.3	2.1	26.4	14.6	7.3	36,583	68,994	14.1	19.2
30	Brantford	136	39.5	11.1	1.6	25.1	15.2	7.6	37,402	73,082	13.0	12.1
31	Saint John	128	2.2	4.2	1.6	26.2	15.1	8.6	38,149	72,185	16.3	16.5
32	Thunder Bay	122	-2.3	9.0	1.2	31.4	17.2	8.4	39,097	72,822	14.1	17.4
33	Peterborough	119	21.3	8.0	1.1	26.4	19.5	8.5	37,786	73,086	13.1	17.8

Compiled by Michael Seasons, School of Planning, University of Waterloo.
Source: Custom tabulations using Census of Canada (1991, 1996, 2011) and 2011 National Household Survey.

1. Uses 2011 Census data; see Statistics Canada (n.d., b).
2. Population counts assume CMA boundaries unless otherwise noted.
3. Uses 2011 NHS data; see Statistics Canada (n.d., c).
4. Refers to immigrants who arrived between 2001 and 2011; see Statistics Canada (n.d., c).
5. Amounts denominated in 2010 dollars.
6. Refers to population aged 15 and over possessing a bachelor's degree or greater; see Statistics Canada (n.d., c).
7. Uses 1991 population counts based on Census Agglomeration (CA) boundaries; see Statistics Canada (n.d., d).
8. Uses 1991 population counts based on Chicoutimi-Jonquière CMA; see Statistics Canada (n.d., a).

Statistics Canada. (n.d., a). 1991 Census of Canada, Profile of Census Tracts. Custom tabulations using Canadian Census Analyser from CHASS (distributor).
Statistics Canada. (n.d., b). 2011 Census of Canada, Profile of Census Tracts. Custom tabulations using Canadian Census Analyser from CHASS (distributor).
Statistics Canada. (n.d., c). 2011 National Household Survey, Profile of Census Tracts. Custom tabulations using Canadian Census Analyser from CHASS (distributor).
Statistics Canada. (n.d., d). Population and Dwelling Counts, for Census Metropolitan Areas in Decreasing Order of 1996 Population, 1991 and 1996 Censuses–100% Data.
Retrieved 27 January 2014. At: www12.statcan.gc.ca/English/census96/data/popdwell/Table.cfm?T=205

Glossary

100-mile diet A local food concept, popularized by Canadian authors Alisa Smith and J.B. MacKinnon in a book by the same name, that encourages people to consume only food produced within 100 miles of their home.

age-friendly city/community A concept advanced by public agencies that asks local governments to take into account the particular needs of older people, who make up an increasing proportion of the population. This vision often draws on a three-part framework: (1) participation; (2) health; and (3) security and independence of the older population.

automobility Refers to the heavy reliance on the automobile as well as the influence of high levels of car use on urban form and lifestyle.

bid-rent curves A modelling concept in economic geography used to understand and depict the trade-offs made by economic agents (e.g., a household, a firm) between rent and distance. At any point along one bid-rent curve, the economic agent is equally satisfied with the combination of location and the rent cost to occupy that location. Any negative change in the desired distance from the urban centre, for example, along one bid-rent curve, is compensated for by an equally desirable change in rent cost, such that the economic agent remains indifferent.

biophilia A hypothesis that posits an instinctive bond between humans and other forms of life. It assumes that humans are naturally attracted to nature.

bioswales Provide a natural solution to the removal of pollution and silt from surface runoff water. They consist of slightly sloped channels filled with vegetation, compost, and stones.

brownfield sites Former industrial locations that can become the object of redevelopment efforts and may require decontamination; see *greyfield sites*.

business improvement areas (BIA) Districts within a city, composed primarily of retail and consumer-oriented establishments, where business owners have banded together, agreeing to pay costs (usually through an added municipal tax) to support renovations to make the area more attractive, functionally up-to-date, and competitive (e.g., street furniture and planting, parking, pedestrian amenities). BIA dues also serve to finance publicity campaigns and promotional events.

census metropolitan area (CMA) Statistics Canada defines CMA as follows: "Area consisting of one or more neighbouring municipalities situated around a core. A census metropolitan area must have a total population of at least 100,000 of which 50,000 or more live in the core." At: www12.statcan.gc.ca/census-recensement/2011/ref/dict/geo009-eng.cfm

central business district (CBD) District generally close to the historical centre of a metropolitan region hosting a concentration of employment, retailing, and institutions. CBDs represent a portion of downtowns. Downtowns cover a wider area, including high-density housing.

citizenship Formal legal rights and responsibilities conferred automatically upon the citizens of a state, as well as rights (e.g., voting) from which non-citizens are "excluded."

cognitive-cultural capitalism (or cognitive-cultural economy) A term used to describe the contemporary economy. It is associated with the increased use of digital technologies, alongside the increasing prevalence of cultural and knowledge-intensive (cognitive) work leading to the growth of technology-intensive, service, financial, craft, and cultural industries.

cohort Made up of people born in the same time period.

cohort approach A common research method used to compare people of the same age in different time periods, or to follow a given birth cohort over the members' lifetime.

commodification Making a commodity of some intangible attribute of urban space. Commodification of the core, for example, would entail the notion that one can purchase (or own) some of the ambience that is attributed to a core area; see *milieu effect*.

common interest development (CID) This housing formula entails common ownership and management of shared facilities such as swimming pools, recreation halls and security systems, which can include gates and guards. CIDs can be targeted at certain groups, mostly the elderly.

community gardens Land provided to individuals and/or groups who contract to actively use and maintain vegetation they have planted. Such gardens are believed to be a step toward municipal food self-sufficiency.

competitive city A city that competes, economically and culturally, with other cities on a national, continental, and especially global scale. Today, competition to gain *world city* status, or to strengthen a city's position in the global network, is believed to be a primary factor underlying a city's urban agenda, especially larger, fast-growing cities.

complete street design   An approach to designing and apportioning street right-of-way to prioritize safe use by all users, including pedestrians, bicyclists, transit riders, and private automobile users. This often involves some combination of cycling lanes, improved pedestrian crossings and sidewalks, transit lanes, and private vehicle lanes. Complete streets are also designed to account for users' different ages and abilities.

core housing need   A measure of the housing circum-stances of Canadians that combines three standards for housing: (1) adequacy, such that it does not require major repair; (2) suitability, as defined by the National Occupancy Standards for number and type of household members per room; and (3) affordability, as defined by the shelter cost-to-income ratio of 30 per cent of gross household income. A household that fails to meet any of the three standards and is unable to access alternative local housing is said to be in core housing need.

creative class   A term coined by Richard Florida to describe a segment of the labour force that he argues is responsible for driving economic growth and prosperity in the twenty-first century. The creative class is composed of professional and knowledge-intensive occupations (jobs) where people create new ideas, new technologies, and new creative content.

deindustrialization   The reversal of industrialization whereby former industrial facilities close down due to international outsourcing, competition from newer forms of production, or the obsolescence of the goods they produced.

dislocation   The exodus from a distinctive geographic zone within the city of major occupants or of a specific use, e.g., the dislocation of low-income residents from the centre of the city, in which case *gentrification* is most often identified as the dislocating force.

district energy systems (DES)   These systems centralize heating and cooling facilities servicing areas generally containing several buildings. The purpose of DES is to improve the energy efficiency of these facilities.

ecological footprint   The resource requirements of an urban area measured in terms of the surface of the earth needed to produce these resources. *Ecological footprint* can also refer to the surface of the planet needed to absorb (neutralize) the pollution generated by an urban area.

edge cities   Concentrations of employment and retail located at the fringe of large metropolitan areas in an otherwise traditionally lower-density suburban area.

ethnic enclaves   Spatial concentrations formed by residents' preference to live near others from the same ethnocultural group rather than by the processes of exclusion, as is the case in *ghettos*.

ethnoburb   A suburban area hosting a concentration of minority ethnic residents and businesses. Such areas have become points of entry for new immigrants.

exurban   Refers to portions of metropolitan regions located beyond the suburbs in environments that are still predominantly rural.

financialization   Refers to the situation in which the financial sector increases in importance in relation to other sectors of the economy. In this situation, some individuals are able to reap profits purely from their involvement in the financial sector instead of the production of goods and services.

food deserts   Areas of a city, usually low-income areas, without accessible outlets that provide healthy and affordable food for household consumption.

food systems   The areas and agents that constitute the supply end of the food chain along with all the components of food distribution and consumption in cities.

Fordism   A period of economic development that lasted roughly from the 1920s until the late 1970s, when growth rested on a correspondence between rising consumption and increasing mass production. Fordism required ongoing *Keynesian*-type government interven-tions to stimulate consumption.

Fordist-Keynesian   Economic development and economic and social policy-making that relied on government intervention in the form of various welfare-state and demand stimulation measures. The period lasted from the end of World War II until the late 1970s; see *Fordism*; *Keynesianism*.

Friendship Centres   Emerged in Canadian cities starting in the 1950s (but really took off in the 1960–70s) to provide a place for service referrals, advocacy, and social, cultural, and recreational programs for urban Aboriginal peoples.

gentrification   The process whereby high-income households purchase and upgrade central-city housing that once was occupied by residents of a significantly lower income. Today, some would consider other kinds of residential upgrading, such as condominium development, as gentrification.

ghettos   Spaces in cities that segregate low-income and/or minority households who lack the freedom, as a consequence of income and/or prejudice, to move into residential zones elsewhere in the city. Originally used in the eighteenth, nineteenth, and early twentieth centuries to refer to neighbourhoods that housed segregated Jewish populations.

globalization   The growing tendency for economic, political, and cultural exchanges to take place at a world scale.

governance   In contrast to *government*, which refers to formal state institutions, *governance* also involves non-governmental actors. Governmental and non-governmental actors work together to address complex problems or achieve collective projects through joint mobilization of their respective resources and knowledge. Governance thus provides a much broader perspective on the political process than the concept of government does.

green urbanism   The creation of transformation of cities in a fashion that respects the environment. Green urbanism concerns the form cities take along with the behaviour of organizations and people therein.

greenhouse gas emissions   A host of gases, such as carbon dioxide and methane, emitted when burning fossil fuels, such as coal, oil, and natural gas. There is concern among scientists that greenhouse gas emissions are contributing to global climate change.

greyfield sites   Abandoned retail locations; see *brownfield sites*.

gross domestic product (GDP)   The sum of all the value added by individuals and organizations engaged in the production of goods and services in a given country.

hinterland   Parts of Canada that depend on natural resources. The hinterland includes all the country with the exception of the *heartland* (see above).

induced demand   An increase in the supply of transportation infrastructure (e.g., adding an additional lane for traffic) that leads to an increase in use/consumption of that infrastructure (e.g., more drivers on roads). This is because when more roads are built, new demand for roads is cultivated because the cost of driving, for example as measured by time spent in congested traffic, is reduced. As the time-cost of driving goes down, people consume more of it, filling up the new road capacity and, in the medium to long run, reaching the prior level of congestion, though now with more vehicles on the road overall.

infrastructure deficit   Caused by long-term underinvestment by governments in the maintenance of municipal infrastructure. This produced a backlog estimated at well over $100 billion. Unable to overcome this backlog with available resources, municipal governments have demanded provincial and federal assistance.

intensification   An increase in the density of development on a given parcel of land or in a neighbourhood or sector of a city. Intensification leads to higher dwelling, and generally also population, densities.

intermediate goods   Products, finished or semi-finished, that represent an input into a final demand product—e.g., fenders or seat belts to auto-assembly lines—or to another good that will ultimately be input to a final demand good.

Keynesianism   An economic approach formulated by John Maynard Keynes, according to which the market economy benefits from countercyclical government spending. Keynesianism has been associated with public-sector economic development and social programs.

knowledge-based economy   Perspective by which economic development increasingly depends on the presence of an educated workforce. The importance of knowledge in the economy is related to *deindustrialization*, automation, and the growth of the high-order tertiary sector.

knowledge-intensive economic activity   That part of the economy based on ideas and higher-order services, as opposed to manufacturing and primary (resource) production.

land rent   A value derived within a land market for the use of land, affected by site characteristics such as location. An economic agent (e.g., firm or household) is willing to pay a certain rent to the landowner for the use of the owner's property for a period of time. For comparability of land values across an urban area, it is common to think of landowners who use that land themselves (e.g., for their private home), instead of renting it to others, as effectively paying "rent" to themselves for use of their property.

life course   A concept recognizing that individuals move through stages in life defined in part by their personal biographies but also converging around transitional events that are roughly in common throughout a population (e.g., leaving school, leaving the parental home, entering a conjugal relationship). Life course transitions can be examined schematically by grouping key transitional events into meaningful life stages.

livable cities   Cities generally considered "good" places to live. Often, livability is assessed using clearly defined indicators. Canadian cities have generally ranked high in published statistical reports that claim to measure urban quality of life or livability.

low income cutoffs (LICO)   Statistics Canada defines LICO as "income threshold below which a family will likely devote a larger share of its income on the necessities of food, shelter and clothing than the average family." (At: www.statcan.gc.ca/pub/75f0002m/2012002/lico-sfr-eng.htm, accessed July 2014)

massing   The combined effect of building height, distribution of bulk, and silhouette. The massing of a building or group of buildings is often considered in relationship to the surrounding streetscape and the overall urban design qualities being promoted for the street or precinct as a whole.

micro-spaces of the core   The concept that the urban core is comprised of specialized sub-areas, usually of a pedestrian or walkable scale, and most often identifiable by function—e.g., law courts, hospital/medical complexes, entertainment districts, retail areas—or by district affiliation—e.g., Gastown, Yorkville. In the twenty-first-century city, these spaces also might include distinctive residential areas, historic districts, and spaces with unique landscape features.

milieu effect   The positive and/or negative overall sense of place associated with a distinctive locale.

mixed-use development   Forms of urban development that comprise different types of activities. Mixed-use developments are often proposed as an instrument to reduce the dependence on the automobile.

multiculturalism   The official policy of the Canadian government that minority groups participate fully in Canadian society while also maintaining distinctively different cultural values, practices, and institutions, provided these adhere to the Canadian Charter of Rights and Freedoms and to provincial human rights legislation.

multi-level governance   Governance relationships that involve multiple levels of government in policy and planning.

new-build gentrification   Wherein the local state primes the redevelopment of former industrial sites, including large tracts adjacent to downtown cores, by inviting and offering incentives to private developers to create new residential zones comprised essentially of high-rise or low-rise condominium buildings.

New Deal for Cities and Communities   A policy initiative of the Liberal government led by Paul Martin (2003–6) that sought to directly involve the federal government in urban affairs. More generally, the "New Deal" refers to the federal and provincial response in the 1998–2006 period to local demands for more authority, autonomy, and resources.

neo-liberalism   Tendency for a withdrawal of governments from the economic and social scene, so as to increase reliance on the private sector and market processes. Neo-liberalism was meant to reverse *Keynesian* policies.

new economy   An economy that reflects recent economic changes stemming from deindustrialization, the rise of high-order tertiary activities, and globalization.

New Urbanism   An urban design movement proposing a return to pre–World War II urban development features and vernacular architecture. New urbanism designs emphasize the orientation of buildings toward the street, a grid street pattern, a diversity of housing types and uses, human-scale built form, garages in back lanes, and urban infrastructure facilitating a variety of transportation modes besides the car. Architect Andres Duany has been one of the most vocal and prolific champions of the New Urbanism movement.

NIMBY (not in my back yard)   Reactions against changes happening around one's residence. NIMBY movements are usually targeted at intensification of land use, infrastructure developments, and uses and activities that local residents do not want near them, such as strip clubs, halfway houses, group homes, and landfills. These movements can be locally based or consist of federations of local groups.

non-governmental organizations (NGOs)   Organizations that provide goods or services that might normally be delivered by a government agency—e.g., a homeless shelter. During neo-liberal times, Canadian cities have relied more heavily on NGOs to provide important municipal services that would have been provided by an arm of government during the era of the welfare state.

path dependence   A perspective by which certain patterns and behaviours are long-lasting and difficult to alter because they are supported by existing institutional arrangements and processes.

place-based public policy   Initiatives that address the distinctive contextual characteristics of local problems by merging the fiscal resources and technical knowledge of upper-level governments with the *tacit knowledge* of local stakeholders and municipalities.

place-making   Planning efforts to insert physical/architectural features and events into the urban environment to help make a city or a particular part of a city more appealing, and thus more competitive locally and globally.

polarization   A distribution that is skewed toward the extreme ends of the attribute that is being measured—akin to an hourglass. Under conditions of the new economy, income is said to be polarized because major segments in the population fall into either relatively high- or low-income groups.

post-Fordism   The period succeeding *Fordism,* characterized by a dismantling of Fordist mechanisms and their replacement by more market-oriented (*neo-liberal*) processes.

power centres   Clustering of specialized stores of different size along with discount department stores in an automobile-oriented environment. In contrast with shopping malls, there is little common space in power centres, notwithstanding large parking areas.

producer services   Services contracted out that cater to producers of final demand goods or services—e.g., contracted legal work, accounting, maintenance, and cleaning.

qualitative development   An approach to urban development that departs from a fixation on urban expansion and population growth (i.e., quantitative development), focusing instead on the existing built environment, infilling and redeveloping, and conserving or adapting existing buildings for reuse, with attention to preserving and accentuating a sense of place and urban quality, often at a pedestrian scale.

regenerative design   The expression refers to forms of design that rely on natural processes to minimize impact on the environment. Regenerative design typically makes use of closed loops to prevent the generation of waste.

revitalization/regeneration   Renewal or regrowth of an obsolete sector of the economy or area of the city, such as the reinvigoration of the core and inner city in Canadian metropolitan areas in the twenty-first century.

row plexes   Form of housing consisting of two (duplex) or three (triplex) units each occupying a full floor, one on top of another. In their Montreal variant, each unit in a plex tends to have its direct outdoor access.

second-wave feminism   Originated in the early 1960s and widened the concern of first-wave feminism for legal obstacles to gender equality (e.g., suffrage and property rights) to a much broader range of issues, including those relating to reproduction and daily-life gender relations as well as an end to all forms of discrimination or unequal treatment of women in employment based on marital or parental status.

shared street design   An approach to designing streets that prioritizes the most vulnerable user, the pedestrian. Other travel modes (e.g., bicycles, private automobiles) move through the street at a pace and priority that is respectful of the pedestrian pace, safety, and right of way. Curbs and lane markings are either absent or are very subtle. Paving materials are chosen to privilege the needs and urban quality considerations of pedestrians, not the rapid movement of vehicles.

shelter poverty   The expression refers to low-income households' difficulty in finding adequate housing. It also pertains to the consequences of these households' poor quality housing and the allocation of a high proportion of their income to housing.

slow food movement   A global grassroots movement that celebrates healthy and accessible food produced in local communities through sustainably and environmentally friendly production methods.

slow-growth cities   Cities where population growth over a 10-year period is less than 10 per cent. Given the high proportion of the Canadian urban system on slow-growth trajectories or in decline (losing population), urbanists are calling for more sophisticated and realistic approaches to urban development that are not centrally focused on unrealistic expectations of continuous growth; see *qualitative development*.

slums   Neighbourhoods in which poverty is concentrated, often due to the spatial concentration of poor-quality and under-maintained rental housing discrimination.

smart growth   A perspective on urban development that promotes forms of growth that respect the environment, show concern for quality of life, and attempt to reduce infrastructure expenses.

social housing   Government-funded housing provided to low-income households whose housing needs are not adequately met by the private real estate industry. Rent is subsidized such that the household does not pay more than 30 per cent of its gross income.

suburbanism   A diversity of ways of living, generally occurring at the urban periphery, distinct from the ways people generally live their lives in the city or in the countryside. In a North American context, suburban ways of living are often, but not always, associated with car use and single-family dwelling ownership. Suburban ways of living can also be found in some central locations.

suburbanization   Non-central population and economic growth occurring in tandem with the spatial expansion of an urban area.

survival curve   Depiction of the proportion of a population surviving at a particular age in life. Given the very low infant mortality rate and significantly reduced mortality at older ages, demographers and human health experts raise the possibility of nearly all humans living to a genetically fixed age limit as mortality at earlier ages becomes less common, creating a rectangular survival curve.

tacit knowledge   The experiential and practical lessons that come from front-line practitioners and the users or recipients of government intervention. As an input to policy-making, tacit knowledge is distinguished from the traditional technical knowledge of civil servants, think tanks, and university researchers.

technoburbs   Concentrations of high-tech industries in a suburban setting, the outcome of the movement of employment away from central cities permitted by advances in information and communications technology.

temporary foreign workers (TFWs)   Workers allowed into a country for a prescribed period in specified employment. As such, most rights of citizenship are not available to TFWs.

topophilia   Love of place; a term coined by geographer Y.-F. Tuan. The term pertains to the growing interest for place in planning and an awareness of the importance of place for many people. The opposite term, *topophobia*, denotes fear of place.

Tower in the Park   Model of urban development conceived by Le Corbusier, which consists of high-rise buildings set in a park-like environment. The model has been popular all over the world and has been criticized by Jane Jacobs.

transnational   Refers to people, activities, and organizations that are based in more than one country. The term can be used in reference to an immigrant who attains citizenship in one country but keeps up ties with his/her place of origin and/or former residence.

travel demand management (TDM)   A recent strategy used by transportation planners. In the past traffic was simply forecast and accommodated, but TDM attempts to change the demand itself rather than simply accommodate demand—e.g., shifting hours of work in one or more large employment sectors in order to reduce congestion during periods of rush hour or peak load.

urban dynamics   Human behaviour taking place in cities; also, journey patterns within urban areas.

urban ecosystem   How natural systems function within the built environments of cities.

urban form   The configuration of urban areas. Urban form can pertain to the distribution and density of activities within metropolitan regions or to design features of specific places within cities.

urban renewal   Strategic reuse of an area of the city that is underused and often run down due to forces of change and transition. Urban renewal schemes are usually planned comprehensively under the direction of professional planners and at least partially funded by one or more levels of government.

urban sprawl   Describes patterns of low-density development outward from the city centre, transforming often rural—*greenfield*—land into new suburban areas. New outward urban development does not necessarily constitute urban sprawl. *Sprawl* refers specifically to the features of the pattern of development, such as its low density of residents and jobs, and the separation of land uses across different zoning districts, at large distances from one another.

urban sustainability   Conditions required to ensure the long-term availability of the natural resources (including pure water and air) required for the existence of urban settlements. Urban sustainability is increasingly perceived in a global context, such as the contribution of cities to planetary environmental degradation, e.g., global warming. *Sustainability* can also be defined in more narrow economic terms.

vertical farms   The use of high-density urban space for purposes of food cultivation. The term spans a spectrum of practices, from roof gardens to "factory farms."

walkability   Configurations of urban space that are pedestrian-friendly and so promote walking from place to place within walkable sub-areas. A major goal of twenty-first-century land-use planning is to increase the walkability of Canadian cities.

weak-mayor system   A system of local government common in Canada in which the mayor has few formal powers in addition to those of councillors, and so can only further a policy agenda through persuasion and compromise. Weak-mayor systems are criticized for inhibiting innovative city-wide policy-making.

welfare state   Strong state/government involvement in the provision of basic needs, such as health care, housing, and old age security, as well as government intervention in matters more typically dealt with by the private sector, such as wage rates. In Canada the term is most often associated with the Fordist period of urban economic growth.

world city, global city   Very large cities that interact as much (if not more)—in terms of the flows of information, finances, goods, and people—with other places globally as with cities in their own country, and where growth is propelled by global rather than local factors. Various typologies rank different cities on a global hierarchy.

Index

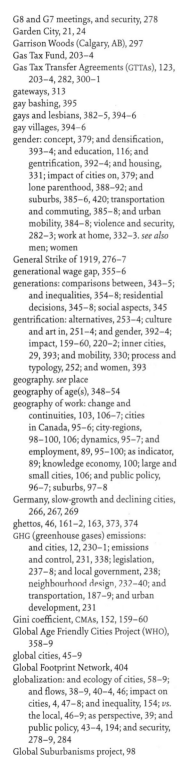